THE ISRAEL LOBBY AND

U.S. FOREIGN POLICY

ALSO BY JOHN J. MEARSHEIMER

Conventional Deterrence
Liddell Hart and the Weight of History
The Tragedy of Great Power Politics

ALSO BY STEPHEN M. WALT

The Origins of Alliances
Revolution and War
Taming American Power: The Global Response to U.S. Primacy

THE ISRAEL LOBBY AND

U.S. FOREIGN POLICY

—

JOHN J. MEARSHEIMER AND STEPHEN M. WALT

ALLEN LANE
an imprint of
PENGUIN BOOKS

ALLEN LANE

Published by the Penguin Group
Penguin Books Ltd, 80 Strand, London WC2R 0RL, England
Penguin Group (USA) Inc., 375 Hudson Street, New York, New York 10014, USA
Penguin Group (Canada), 90 Eglinton Avenue East, Suite 700, Toronto, Ontario, Canada M4P 2Y3
(a division of Pearson Penguin Canada Inc.)
Penguin Ireland, 25 St Stephen's Green, Dublin 2, Ireland (a division of Penguin Books Ltd)
Penguin Group (Australia), 250 Camberwell Road,
Camberwell, Victoria 3124, Australia (a division of Pearson Australia Group Pty Ltd)
Penguin Books India Pvt Ltd, 11 Community Centre,
Panchsheel Park, New Delhi – 110 017, India
Penguin Group (NZ), 67 Apollo Drive, Rosedale, North Shore 0632, New Zealand
(a division of Pearson New Zealand Ltd)
Penguin Books (South Africa) (Pty) Ltd, 24 Sturdee Avenue,
Rosebank, Johannesburg 2196, South Africa

Penguin Books Ltd, Registered Offices: 80 Strand, London WC2R 0RL, England

www.penguin.com

First published in the United States of America by Farrar, Straus and Giroux 2007
First published in Great Britain by Allen Lane 2007
1

Portions of this book were originally published, in different form,
in the *London Review of Books* in March 2006

Grateful acknowledgement is made to Amnesty International for permission to reprint excerpts from
"Israel/Lebanon: Deliberate Destruction or Collateral Damage? Israeli Attacks on Civilian Infrastructure",
AI Index MDE 18/007/2006, August 23, 2006; copyright © Amnesty International Publications,
1 Easton Street, London WC1X 0DW, United Kingdom, www.amnesty.org.

Printed in Great Britain by Clays Ltd, St Ives plc

A CIP catalogue record for this book is available from the British Library

978–1–846–14007–5

www.greenpenguin.co.uk

Penguin Books is committed to a sustainable future
for our business, our readers and our planet.
The book in your hands is made from paper
certified by the Forest Stewardship Council.

CONTENTS

PREFACE

In all affairs it's a healthy thing now and then to hang a question mark on the things you have long taken for granted.
                                                          —Bertrand Russell

In the fall of 2002, the *Atlantic Monthly* invited us to write a feature article on the Israel lobby and its effects on U.S. foreign policy. We accepted the commission with some reservations, because we knew this was a controversial subject and that any article that scrutinized the lobby, U.S. support for Israel, or Israeli policy itself was likely to provoke a harsh reaction. Nonetheless, we felt this was an issue that could no longer be ignored, especially in light of the September 11 terrorist attacks and the looming war with Iraq. If U.S. support for Israel was a significant source of anti-Americanism in the Middle East and a source of tension with key strategic allies, and if pro-Israel groups and individuals were a major influence on U.S. foreign policy in this vital region, then it was important to raise the issue openly and encourage public discussion of the lobby's actions and impact.

We worked on the article off and on over the next two years, in close collaboration with the *Atlantic's* editors, and we sent them a manuscript conforming to our prior agreements and incorporating virtually all of their suggestions in January 2005. A few weeks later, to our surprise, the editor informed us that the *Atlantic* had decided not to run the piece and that he was not interested in our attempting to revise it.

We considered submitting the article to several other journals but concluded that they would be unlikely to run the piece, either due to its content or its length. We also considered the possibility of turning the article into a book, but responses to our initial inquiries were not sufficiently enthusiastic to convince us to commit additional time and effort to it. So we put the manuscript aside and turned to other projects, although an abbreviated version of some of this material was included in Stephen M. Walt's *Taming American Power*, which was published by W. W. Norton in September 2005.

Then, in October 2005, a distinguished American academic contacted us and suggested that we consider publishing the article in the *London Review of Books*. Someone at the *Atlantic* had given him a copy of the rejected essay, and he told us he thought the editor of the *LRB*, Mary-Kay Wilmers, would be interested. We sent her the manuscript and she quickly expressed her desire to publish it. After another round of updating and revision, the article—now titled "The Israel Lobby"—was published in the March 23, 2006, issue. At the suggestion of one of the scholars who had read and commented on an earlier draft, we simultaneously posted a fully documented version of the article on the Faculty Working Papers website of Harvard's John F. Kennedy School of Government. We did this because the *LRB*'s format does not allow for extensive references or footnotes, and we wanted readers to see that our argument rested on a wide array of credible sources.

The case advanced in the article was straightforward. After describing the remarkable level of material and diplomatic support that the United States provides to Israel, we argued that this support could not be fully explained on either strategic or moral grounds. Instead, it was due largely to the political power of the Israel lobby, a loose coalition of individuals and groups that seeks to influence American foreign policy in ways that will benefit Israel. In addition to encouraging the United States to back Israel more or less unconditionally, groups and individuals in the lobby played key roles in shaping American policy toward the Israeli-Palestinian conflict, the ill-fated invasion of Iraq, and the ongoing confrontations with Syria and Iran. We suggested that these policies were not in the U.S. national interest and were in fact harmful to Israel's long-term interests as well.

The response to the essay was breathtaking. By July 2006, the Kennedy School's website had recorded more than 275,000 downloads of the working paper and we had received numerous requests to translate or reprint the *LRB* article. As expected, the essay initially generated a firestorm of criticism from prominent groups or individuals in the lobby, and we were denounced as anti-Semites by the Anti-Defamation League and by op-ed writers in the *Jerusalem Post, New York Sun, Wall Street Journal*, and *Washington Post*. The *New Republic* devoted four separate articles to attacking our article, and a number of critics accused us—erroneously—of having made numerous historical or factual mistakes. A few critics even predicted that the article (and its authors) would soon fade into what they thought would be a richly deserved obscurity.

They were wrong. A wide variety of readers—both Jewish and gentile—came out in support of the article. They did not agree with every point we had made, but almost all of them agreed that such an examination was long overdue. Predictably, reactions outside the United States were generally favorable, and there were even some positive responses in Israel itself. Respectful appraisals appeared in the *New York Times, Financial Times, New York Review of Books, Chicago Tribune, New York Observer, National Interest,* and *Nation,* and the controversy eventually received prominent coverage in a wide array of news outlets, from *Ha'aretz* in Israel to National Public Radio in the United States.

The distinguished journal *Foreign Policy* organized a symposium on the article in its July/August 2006 issue, and the *Washington Post Sunday Magazine* published a thoughtful cover story in July exploring the issues we had raised. Later that summer, a reviewer in *Foreign Affairs* described the article as a "hard-headed analysis . . . that might set in motion a useful paradigm shift in United States' Middle East policy."

Over the course of 2006, it became increasingly clear that the conversation about Israel and U.S. Middle East policy was indeed changing, and that it had become somewhat easier to discuss the lobby's role in shaping U.S. policy. This was not entirely our doing, of course, as awareness of the lobby's activities and impact was also increased by Israel's disastrous war in Lebanon in the summer of 2006, the continued debacle in Iraq, the personal attacks on Jimmy Carter following the publication of his book *Palestine: Peace Not Apartheid,* the simmering war of words between the United States and Iran, and the conspicuous but failed efforts to silence or smear other prominent critics of the lobby. A growing number of people seemed to realize that this subject needed airing, and more were willing to speak out.

Equally important, thoughtful individuals were beginning to recognize that the American Israel Public Affairs Committee and other hard-line groups in the lobby—including some vocal Christian Zionists—were not representative of mainstream opinion in the American Jewish community or the United States more broadly. There was a growing debate about whether the policies advocated by these groups were in America's or in Israel's interest. As a result, some pro-Israel groups began to talk openly about the need to shift the balance of power in more moderate directions, and prominent publications such as the *Economist* and the *New York Times* published commentaries suggesting that it was time for a new relationship between Israel and the United States, for the benefit of both.

We were gratified by these developments, because we wrote the original

article in order to foster a more clear-eyed and candid discussion of this subject. That conversation was now under way, although it still tended to be
shrill, confrontational, and overly personal. But should we write a book? Perhaps we had already said enough, and it was time to move on to other topics.
After some reflection, and despite some lingering misgivings, we concluded
that writing a book would help advance the dialogue in several ways.

First, although the original article was long by the standards of most
magazines, space limitations had forced us to omit a number of important issues and to deal with certain topics more briefly than we would have liked.
This unavoidable brevity may have contributed to some misunderstandings
of the original article, and writing a book would provide an opportunity to
present a more nuanced and detailed statement of our views.

Accordingly, this book contains a more complete definition of the lobby,
an extended discussion of the role of Christian Zionism, and a fuller account
of the lobby's evolution over time. We also provide a more detailed account
of Israel's past conduct and current behavior, especially toward the Palestinians. We do this not from any animus toward Israel or its supporters in the
United States, or because we are eager to highlight Israeli misconduct.
Rather, we address this topic because it is central to some of the moral arguments commonly used to justify an exceptional level of U.S. support for
the Jewish state. We focus on Israel's behavior, in other words, because the
United States focuses an extraordinary degree of support on Israel. We also
address the controversial issue of dual loyalty, which was not discussed in
the original article.

Second, writing this book enables us to respond to the central criticisms
that were lodged against our original article. We addressed some of them in
two subsequent letters to the *London Review of Books* and in the *Foreign Policy* symposium mentioned above, and we have also written a point-by-point
rebuttal of the various charges directed at the article (see "Setting the
Record Straight: A Response to Critics of 'The Israel Lobby,'" available
online at www.israellobbybook.com). Although the vast majority of charges
leveled against the original article were unfounded—as were the various
personal attacks leveled at us—there were a number of thoughtful critiques
that raised important issues of interpretation and emphasis. We have
learned from these criticisms even when not fully persuaded by them, and
we have tried to address them here.

Third, writing a book makes it possible to provide further empirical support for our core claims and to bring the analysis up to date. Not only has additional evidence come to light regarding important events such as the Iraq

war, but some other events—most notably the second Lebanon war of July/ August 2006—had not taken place when the original article appeared. America's response to that war proved to be a further illustration of the lobby's power, as well as its harmful influence on U.S. and Israeli interests. The lobby's activities could also be seen in the evolution of U.S. policy toward Iran and Syria, and in the harsh attacks on former President Jimmy Carter, the historian Tony Judt, and several other prominent critics of Israel's treatment of the Palestinians.

Finally, this book presents an opportunity to discuss how the United States should advance its interests in the Middle East, and how Americans, and indeed the rest of the world, should think about the influence of the pro-Israel lobby. The stakes are high—for Americans and non-Americans alike—because the Middle East is a volatile and strategically vital region and America's policies toward that region will inevitably have extensive repercussions. As the war in Iraq demonstrates, the United States can do great damage to itself and to others if its policies are misguided. This fact makes it all the more important to identify what is driving U.S. policy and to figure out what that policy ought to be. Our original article did not offer much in the way of positive prescriptions, but the concluding chapter of this book outlines a different approach to U.S. Middle East policy and identifies how the lobby's power might be mitigated or made more constructive.

Although we see encouraging signs of more open discussion on these vital issues, the lobby still has a profound influence on U.S. Middle East policy. The problems that the United States and Israel face in this region have not lessened since the original article appeared; indeed, they may well have grown worse. Iraq is a fiasco, Israelis and Palestinians remain locked in conflict, Hamas and Fatah are battling for dominance within the Palestinian community, and Hezbollah's role in Lebanon is deeply troubling. Iran is still seeking to acquire full control of the nuclear fuel cycle, groups like al Qaeda remain active and dangerous, and the industrial world is still dependent on Persian Gulf oil. These are all vexing problems, and the United States will not be able to address any or all of them effectively if Americans cannot have a civilized conversation about our interests in the region and the role of all the factors that shape U.S. foreign policy, including the Israel lobby. To encourage that continued conversation, we have written this book.

We acknowledge various personal debts at the end of the book, but we would like to register one of them here. For more than twenty-five years, we have been fortunate to enjoy the friendship and support of one of America's most accomplished social scientists, Samuel P. Huntington. We cannot

imagine a better role model. Sam has always tackled big and important questions, and he has answered these questions in ways that the rest of the world
could not ignore. Although each of us has disagreed with him on numerous
occasions over the years—and sometimes vehemently and publicly—he
never held those disagreements against us and was never anything but gracious and supportive of our own work. He understands that scholarship is
not a popularity contest, and that spirited but civil debate is essential both
to scholarly progress and to a healthy democracy. We are grateful to Sam for
his friendship and for the example he has set throughout his career, and we
are pleased to dedicate this book to him.

John J. Mearsheimer   *Stephen M. Walt*
University of Chicago   *Harvard University*

THE ISRAEL LOBBY AND

U.S. FOREIGN POLICY

INTRODUCTION

America is about to enter a presidential election year. Although the outcome is of course impossible to predict at this stage, certain features of the campaign are easy to foresee. The candidates will inevitably differ on various domestic issues—health care, abortion, gay marriage, taxes, education, immigration—and spirited debates are certain to erupt on a host of foreign policy questions as well. What course of action should the United States pursue in Iraq? What is the best response to the crisis in Darfur, Iran's nuclear ambitions, Russia's hostility to NATO, and China's rising power? How should the United States address global warming, combat terrorism, and reverse the erosion of its international image? On these and many other issues, we can confidently expect lively disagreements among the various candidates.

Yet on one subject, we can be equally confident that the candidates will speak with one voice. In 2008, as in previous election years, serious candidates for the highest office in the land will go to considerable lengths to express their deep personal commitment to one foreign country—Israel—as well as their determination to maintain unyielding U.S. support for the Jewish state. Each candidate will emphasize that he or she fully appreciates the multitude of threats facing Israel and make it clear that, if elected, the United States will remain firmly committed to defending Israel's interests under any and all circumstances. None of the candidates is likely to criticize Israel in any significant way or suggest that the United States ought to pursue a more evenhanded policy in the region. Any who do will probably fall by the wayside.

This observation is hardly a bold prediction, because presidential aspirants were already proclaiming their support for Israel in early 2007. The process began in January, when four potential candidates spoke to Israel's annual Herzliya Conference on security issues. As Joshua Mitnick reported in *Jewish Week*, they were "seemingly competing to see who can be most strident in defense of the Jewish State." Appearing via satellite link, John Edwards, the Democratic party's 2004 vice presidential candidate, told his Israeli listeners that "your future is our future" and said that the bond between the United States and Israel "will never be broken." Former Massachusetts governor Mitt Romney spoke of being "in a country I love with people I love" and, aware of Israel's deep concern about a possible nuclear Iran, proclaimed that "it is time for the world to speak three truths: (1) Iran must be stopped; (2) Iran can be stopped; (3) Iran will be stopped!" Senator John McCain (R-AZ) declared that "when it comes to the defense of Israel, we simply cannot compromise," while former House Speaker Newt Gingrich (R-GA) told the audience that "Israel is facing the greatest danger for [sic] its survival since the 1967 victory."[1]

Shortly thereafter, in early February, Senator Hillary Clinton (D-NY) spoke in New York before the local chapter of the powerful American Israel Public Affairs Committee (AIPAC), where she said that in this "moment of great difficulty for Israel and great peril for Israel . . . what is vital is that we stand by our friend and our ally and we stand by our own values. Israel is a beacon of what's right in a neighborhood overshadowed by the wrongs of radicalism, extremism, despotism and terrorism."[2] One of her rivals for the Democratic nomination, Senator Barack Obama (D-IL), spoke a month later before an AIPAC audience in Chicago. Obama, who has expressed some sympathy for the Palestinians' plight in the past and made a brief reference to Palestinian "suffering" at a campaign appearance in March 2007, was unequivocal in his praise for Israel and made it manifestly clear that he would do nothing to change the U.S.-Israeli relationship.[3] Other presidential hopefuls, including Senator Sam Brownback (R-KS) and New Mexico governor Bill Richardson, have expressed pro-Israel sentiments with equal or greater ardor.[4]

What explains this behavior? Why is there so little disagreement among these presidential hopefuls regarding Israel, when there are profound disagreements among them on almost every other important issue facing the United States and when it is apparent that America's Middle East policy has gone badly awry? Why does Israel get a free pass from presidential candidates, when its own citizens are often deeply critical of its present policies and when these same presidential candidates are all too willing to criticize many of the things that other countries do? Why does Israel, and no other country in the world, receive such consistent deference from America's leading politicians?

Some might say that it is because Israel is a vital strategic asset for the United States. Indeed, it is said to be an indispensable partner in the "war on terror." Others will answer that there is a powerful moral case for providing Israel with unqualified support, because it is the only country in the region that "shares our values." But neither of these arguments stands up to fair-minded scrutiny. Washington's close relationship with Jerusalem makes it harder, not easier, to defeat the terrorists who are now targeting the United States, and it simultaneously undermines America's standing with important allies around the world. Now that the Cold War is over, Israel has become a strategic liability for the United States. Yet no aspiring politician is going to say so in public, or even raise the possibility.

There is also no compelling moral rationale for America's uncritical and uncompromising relationship with Israel. There is a strong moral case for Israel's existence and there are good reasons for the United States to be committed to helping Israel if its survival is in jeopardy. But given Israel's brutal treatment of the Palestinians in the Occupied Territories, moral considerations might suggest that the United States pursue a more evenhanded policy toward the two sides, and maybe even lean toward the Palestinians. Yet we are unlikely to hear that sentiment expressed by anyone who wants to be president, or anyone who would like to occupy a position in Congress.

The real reason why American politicians are so deferential is the political power of the Israel lobby. The lobby is a loose coalition of individuals and organizations that actively works to move U.S. foreign policy in a pro-Israel direction. As we will describe in detail, it is not a single, unified movement with a central leadership, and it is certainly not a cabal or conspiracy that "controls" U.S. foreign policy. It is simply a powerful interest group, made up of both Jews and gentiles, whose acknowledged purpose is to press Israel's case within the United States and influence American foreign policy in ways that its members believe will benefit the Jewish state. The various groups that make up the lobby do not agree on every issue, although they share the desire to promote a special relationship between the United States and Israel. Like the efforts of other ethnic lobbies and interest groups, the activities of the Israel lobby's various elements are legitimate forms of democratic political participation, and they are for the most part consistent with America's long tradition of interest group activity.

Because the Israel lobby has gradually become one of the most powerful interest groups in the United States, candidates for high office pay close attention to its wishes. The individuals and groups in the United States that make up the lobby care deeply about Israel, and they do not want American politicians to criticize it, even when criticism might be warranted and might even be in Israel's own interest. Instead, these groups want U.S. leaders to treat Israel as if it were the fifty-first state. Democrats and Republicans alike fear the lobby's clout. They all know that any politician who challenges its policies stands little chance of becoming president.

THE LOBBY AND U.S. MIDDLE EAST POLICY

The lobby's political power is important not because it affects what presidential candidates say during a campaign, but because it has a significant influence on American foreign policy, especially in the Middle East. America's actions in that volatile region have enormous consequences for people all around the world, especially the people who live there. Just consider how the Bush administration's misbegotten war in Iraq has affected the long-suffering people of that shattered country: tens of thousands dead, hundreds of thousands forced to flee their homes, and a vicious sectarian war taking place with no end in sight. The war has also been a strategic disaster for the United States and has alarmed and endangered U.S. allies both inside and outside the region. One could hardly imagine a more vivid or tragic demonstration of the impact the United States can have—for good or ill—when it unleashes the power at its disposal.

The United States has been involved in the Middle East since the early days of the Republic, with much of the activity centered on educational programs or missionary work. For some, a biblically inspired fascination with the Holy Land and the role of Judaism in its history led to support for the idea of restoring the Jewish people to a homeland there, a view that was embraced by certain religious leaders and, in a general way, by a few U.S. politicians. But it is a mistake to see this history of modest and for the most part private engagement as the taproot of America's role in the region since World War II, and especially its extraordinary relationship with Israel today.[5] Between the routing of the Barbary pirates two hundred years ago and World War II, the United States played no significant security role anywhere in the region and U.S. leaders did not aspire to one.[6] Woodrow Wilson did endorse the 1917 Balfour Declaration (which expressed Britain's support for the creation of a Jewish homeland in Palestine), but Wilson did virtually nothing to advance this goal. Indeed, the most significant U.S. involvement during this period—a fact-finding mission dispatched to the region in 1919 by the Paris Peace Conference under the leadership of Americans Henry Churchill King and Charles Crane—concluded that the local population opposed continued Zionist inroads and recommended against the establishment of an independent Jewish homeland. Yet as the historian Margaret Macmillan notes, "Nobody paid the slightest attention." The possibility of a U.S. mandate over portions of the Middle East was briefly considered but never pursued, and Britain and France ended up dividing the relevant portions of the Ottoman Empire between themselves.[7]

The United States has played an important and steadily increasing role in Middle East security issues since World War II, driven initially by oil, then by anticommunism and, over time, by its growing relationship with Israel. America's first significant involvement in the security politics of the region was a nascent partnership with Saudi Arabia in the mid-1940s (intended by both parties as a check on British ambitions in the region), and its first formal alliance commitments were Turkey's inclusion in NATO in 1952 and the anti-Soviet Baghdad Pact in 1954.[8] After backing Israel's founding in 1948, U.S. leaders tried to strike a balanced position between Israel and the Arabs and carefully avoided making any formal commitment to the Jewish state for fear of jeopardizing more important strategic interests. This situation changed gradually over the ensuing decades, in response to events like the Six-Day War, Soviet arms sales to various Arab states, and the growing influence of pro-Israel groups in the United States. Given this dramatic transformation in America's role in the region, it makes little sense to try to explain current U.S. policy—and especially the lavish support that is now given to Israel—by referring to the religious beliefs of a bygone era or the radically different forms of past American engagement. There was nothing inevitable or predetermined about the current special relationship between the United States and Israel.

Since the Six-Day War of 1967, a salient feature—and arguably the central focus—of America's Middle East policy has been its relationship with Israel. For the past four decades, in fact, the United States has provided Israel with a level of material and diplomatic support that dwarfs what it provides to other countries. That aid is largely unconditional: no matter what Israel does, the level of support remains for the most part unchanged. In particular, the United States consistently favors Israel over the Palestinians and rarely puts pressure on the Jewish state to stop building settlements and roads in the West Bank. Although Presidents Bill Clinton and George W.

Bush openly favored the creation of a viable Palestinian state, neither was willing to use American leverage to make that outcome a reality.

The United States has also undertaken policies in the broader Middle East that reflected Israel's preferences. Since the early 1990s, for example, American policy toward Iran has been heavily influenced by the wishes of successive Israeli governments. Tehran has made several attempts in recent years to improve relations with Washington and settle outstanding differences, but Israel and its American supporters have been able to stymie any détente between Iran and the United States, and to keep the two countries far apart. Another example is the Bush administration's behavior during Israel's war against Lebanon in the summer of 2006. Almost every country in the world harshly criticized Israel's bombing campaign—a campaign that killed more than one thousand Lebanese, most of them civilians—but the United States did not. Instead, it helped Israel prosecute the war, with prominent members of both political parties openly defending Israel's behavior. This unequivocal support for Israel undermined the pro-American government in Beirut, strengthened Hezbollah, and drove Iran, Syria, and Hezbollah closer together, results that were hardly good for either Washington or Jerusalem.

Many policies pursued on Israel's behalf now jeopardize U.S. national security. The combination of unstinting U.S. support for Israel and Israel's prolonged occupation of Palestinian territory has fueled anti-Americanism throughout the Arab and Islamic world, thereby increasing the threat from international terrorism and making it harder for Washington to deal with other problems, such as shutting down Iran's nuclear program. Because the United States is now so unpopular within the broader region, Arab leaders who might otherwise share U.S. goals are reluctant to help us openly, a predicament that cripples U.S. efforts to deal with a host of regional challenges.

This situation, which has no equal in American history, is due primarily to the activities of the Israel lobby. While other special interest groups— including ethnic lobbies representing Cuban Americans, Irish Americans, Armenian Americans, and Indian Americans—have managed to skew U.S. foreign policy in directions that they favored, no ethnic lobby has diverted that policy as far from what the American national interest would otherwise suggest. The Israel lobby has successfully convinced many Americans that American and Israeli interests are essentially identical. In fact, they are not.

Although this book focuses primarily on the lobby's influence on U.S. foreign policy and its negative effect on American interests, the lobby's impact has been unintentionally harmful to Israel as well. Take Israel's settlements, which even a writer as sympathetic to Israel as Leon Wieseltier recently called a "moral and strategic blunder of historic proportions."[9] Israel's situation would be better today if the United States had long ago used its financial and diplomatic leverage to convince Israel to stop building settlements in the West Bank and Gaza, and instead helped Israel create a viable Palestinian state on those lands. Washington did not do so, however, largely because it would have been politically costly for any president to attempt it. As noted above, Israel would have been much better off if the United States had told it that its military strategy for fighting the 2006 Lebanon war was doomed to fail, rather than reflexively endorsing and facilitating it. By making it difficult to impossible for the U.S. government to criticize Israel's conduct and press it to change some of its counterproductive policies, the lobby may even be jeopardizing the long-term prospects of the Jewish state.

THE LOBBY'S MODUS OPERANDI

It is difficult to talk about the lobby's influence on American foreign policy, at least in the mainstream media in the United States, without being accused of anti-Semitism or labeled a self-hating Jew. It is just as difficult to criticize Israeli policies or question U.S. support for Israel in polite company. America's generous and unconditional support for Israel is rarely questioned, because groups in the lobby use their power to make sure that public discourse echoes its strategic and moral arguments for the special relationship.

The response to former President Jimmy Carter's *Palestine: Peace Not Apartheid* perfectly illustrates this phenomenon. Carter's book is a personal plea for renewed American engagement in the peace process, based largely on his considerable experience with these issues over the past three decades. Reasonable people may challenge his evidence or disagree with his conclusions, but his ultimate goal is peace between these two peoples, and Carter unambiguously defends Israel's right to live in peace and security. Yet because he suggests that Israel's policies in the Occupied Territories resemble South Africa's apartheid regime and said publicly that pro-Israel groups make it hard for U.S. leaders to pressure Israel to make peace, a number of these same groups launched a vicious smear campaign against him. Not only was Carter publicly accused of being an anti-Semite and a "Jew-hater," some critics even charged him with being sympathetic to Nazis.[10] Since the lobby seeks to keep the present relationship intact, and because in fact its strategic and moral arguments are so weak, it has little choice but to try to stifle or marginalize serious discussion.

Yet despite the lobby's efforts, a considerable number of Americans—almost 40 percent—recognize that U.S. support for Israel is one of the main causes of anti-Americanism around the world. Among elites, the number is substantially higher.[11] Furthermore, a surprising number of Americans understand that the lobby has a significant, not always positive influence on U.S. foreign policy. In a national poll taken in October 2006, 39 percent of the respondents said that they believe that the "work of the Israeli lobby on Congress and the Bush administration has been a key factor for going to war in Iraq and now confronting Iran."[12] In a 2006 survey of international relations scholars in the United States, 66 percent of the respondents said that they agreed with the statement "the Israel lobby has too much influence over U.S. foreign policy."[13] While the American people are generally sympathetic to Israel, many of them are critical of particular Israeli policies and would be willing to withhold American aid if Israel's actions are seen to be contrary to U.S. interests.

Of course, the American public would be even more aware of the lobby's influence and more tough-minded with regard to Israel and its special relationship with the United States if there were a more open discussion of these matters. Still, one might wonder why, given the public's views about the lobby and Israel, politicians and policy makers are so unwilling to criticize Israel and to make aid to Israel conditional on whether its actions benefit the United States. The American people are certainly not demanding that their politicians support Israel down the line. In essence, there is a distinct gulf between how the broader public thinks about Israel and its relationship with the United States and how governing elites in Washington conduct American policy.

The main reason for this gap is the lobby's formidable reputation inside the Beltway. Not only does it exert significant influence over the policy process in Democratic and Republican administrations alike, but it is even more powerful on Capitol Hill.[14] The journalist Michael Massing reports that a congressional staffer sympathetic to Israel told him, "We can count on well over half the House—250 to 300 members—to do reflexively whatever AIPAC wants." Similarly, Steven Rosen, the former AIPAC official who has been indicted for allegedly passing classified government documents to Israel, illustrated AIPAC's power for the *New Yorker*'s Jeffrey Goldberg by putting a napkin in front of him and saying, "In twenty-four hours, we could have the signatures of seventy senators on this napkin."[15] These are not idle boasts. As will become clear, when issues relating to Israel come to the fore, Congress almost always votes to endorse the lobby's positions, and usually in overwhelming numbers.

WHY IS IT SO HARD TO TALK ABOUT THE ISRAEL LOBBY?

Because the United States is a pluralist democracy where freedom of speech and association are guaranteed, it was inevitable that interest groups would come to dominate the political process. For a nation of immigrants, it was equally inevitable that some of these interest groups would form along ethnic lines and that they would try to influence U.S. foreign policy in various ways.[16] Cuban Americans have lobbied to maintain the embargo on Castro's regime, Armenian Americans have pushed Washington to acknowledge the 1915 genocide and, more recently, to limit U.S. relations with Azerbaijan, and Indian Americans have rallied to support the recent security treaty and nuclear cooperation agreements. Such activities have been a central feature of American political life since the founding of the country, and pointing them out is rarely controversial.[17]

Yet it is clearly more difficult for Americans to talk openly about the Israel lobby. Part of the reason is the lobby itself, which is both eager to advertise its clout and quick to challenge anyone who suggests that its influence is too great or might be detrimental to U.S. interests. There are, however, other reasons why it is harder to have a candid discussion about the impact of the Israel lobby.

To begin with, questioning the practices and ramifications of the Israel lobby may appear to some to be tantamount to questioning the legitimacy of Israel itself. Because some states still refuse to recognize Israel and some critics of Israel and the lobby do question its legitimacy, many of its supporters may see even well-intentioned criticism as an implicit challenge to Israel's existence. Given the strong feelings that many people have for Israel, and especially its important role as a safe haven for Jewish refugees from the Holocaust and as a central focus of contemporary Jewish identity, there is bound to be a hostile and defensive reaction when people think its legitimacy or its existence is under attack.

But in fact, an examination of Israel's policies and the efforts of its American supporters does not imply an anti-Israel bias, just as an examination of the political activities of the American Association of Retired Persons (AARP) does not imply bias against older citizens. We are not challenging

Israel's right to exist or questioning the legitimacy of the Jewish state. There are those who maintain that Israel should never have been created, or who want to see Israel transformed from a Jewish state into a binational democracy. We do not. On the contrary, we believe the history of the Jewish people and the norm of national self-determination provide ample justification for a Jewish state. We think the United States should stand willing to come to Israel's assistance if its survival were in jeopardy. And though our primary focus is on the Israel lobby's negative impact on U.S. foreign policy, we are also convinced that its influence has become harmful to Israel as well. In our view, both effects are regrettable.

In addition, the claim that an interest group whose ranks are mostly Jewish has a powerful, not to mention negative, influence on U.S. foreign policy is sure to make some Americans deeply uncomfortable—and possibly fearful and angry—because it sounds like a charge lifted from the notorious *Protocols of the Elders of Zion*, that well-known anti-Semitic forgery that purported to reveal an all-powerful Jewish cabal exercising secret control over the world.

Any discussion of Jewish political power takes place in the shadow of two thousand years of history, especially the centuries of very real anti-Semitism in Europe. Christians massacred thousands of Jews during the Crusades, expelled them en masse from Britain, France, Spain, Portugal, and other places between 1290 and 1497, and confined them to ghettos in other parts of Europe. Jews were violently oppressed during the Spanish Inquisition, murderous pogroms took place in Eastern Europe and Russia on numerous occasions, and other forms of anti-Semitic bigotry were widespread until recently. This shameful record culminated in the Nazi Holocaust, which killed nearly six million Jews. Jews were also oppressed in parts of the Arab world, though much less severely.[18]

Given this long history of persecution, American Jews are understandably sensitive to any argument that sounds like someone is blaming them for policies gone awry. This sensitivity is compounded by the memory of bizarre conspiracy theories of the sort laid out in the *Protocols*. Dire warnings of secretive "Jewish influence" remain a staple of neo-Nazis and other extremists, such as the hate-mongering former Ku Klux Klan leader David Duke, which reinforces Jewish concerns even more.

A key element of such anti-Semitic accusations is the claim that Jews exercise illegitimate influence by "controlling" banks, the media, and other key institutions. Thus, if someone says that press coverage in the United States tends to favor Israel over its opponents, this may sound to some like the old canard that "Jews control the media." Similarly, if someone points out that

American Jews have a rich tradition of giving money to both philanthropic and political causes, it sounds like they are suggesting that "Jewish money" is buying political influence in an underhanded or conspiratorial way. Of course, anyone who gives money to a political campaign does so in order to advance some political cause, and virtually all interest groups hope to mold public opinion and are interested in getting favorable media coverage. Evaluating the role of any interest group's campaign contributions, lobbying efforts, and other political activities ought to be a fairly uncontroversial exercise, but given past anti-Semitism, one can understand why it is easier to talk about these matters when discussing the impact of the pharmaceutical lobby, labor unions, arms manufacturers, Indian-American groups, etc., rather than the Israel lobby.

Making this discussion of pro-Israel groups and individuals in the United States even more difficult is the age-old charge of "dual loyalty." According to this old canard, Jews in the diaspora were perpetual aliens who could never assimilate and be good patriots, because they were more loyal to each other than to the country in which they lived. The fear today is that Jews who support Israel will be seen as disloyal Americans. As Hyman Bookbinder, the former Washington representative of the American Jewish Committee, once commented, "Jews react viscerally to the suggestion that there is something unpatriotic" about their support for Israel.[19]

Let us be clear: we categorically reject all of these anti-Semitic claims.

In our view, it is perfectly legitimate for any American to have a significant attachment to a foreign country. Indeed, Americans are permitted to hold dual citizenship and to serve in foreign armies, unless, of course, the other country is at war with the United States. As noted above, there are numerous examples of ethnic groups in America working hard to persuade the U.S. government, as well as their fellow citizens, to support the foreign country for which they feel a powerful bond. Foreign governments are usually aware of the activities of sympathetic ethnically based interest groups, and they have naturally sought to use them to influence the U.S. government and advance their own foreign policy goals. Jewish Americans are no different from their fellow citizens in this regard.[20]

The Israel lobby is not a cabal or conspiracy or anything of the sort. It is engaged in good old-fashioned interest group politics, which is as American as apple pie. Pro-Israel groups in the United States are engaged in the same enterprise as other interest groups like the National Rifle Association (NRA) and the AARP, or professional associations like the American Petroleum Institute, all of which also work hard to influence congressional legislation and presidential priorities, and which, for the most part, operate in the open.

With a few exceptions, to be discussed in subsequent chapters, the lobby's actions are thoroughly American and legitimate.

We do not believe the lobby is all-powerful, or that it controls important institutions in the United States. As we will discuss in several subsequent chapters, there are a number of cases where the lobby did not get its way. Nevertheless, there is an abundance of evidence that the lobby wields impressive influence. The American Israel Public Affairs Committee, one of the most important pro-Israel groups, used to brag about its own power on its website, not only by listing its impressive achievements but also by displaying quotations from prominent politicians that attested to its ability to influence events in ways that benefit Israel. For example, its website used to include a statement from former House Minority Leader Richard Gephardt telling an AIPAC gathering, "Without your constant support . . . and all your fighting on a daily basis to strengthen [the U.S.-Israeli relationship], it would not be."[21] Even the outspoken Harvard law professor Alan Dershowitz, who is often quick to brand Israel's critics as anti-Semites, wrote in a memoir that "my generation of Jews . . . became part of what is perhaps the most effective lobbying and fundraising effort in the history of democracy. We did a truly great job, as far as we allowed ourselves, and were allowed, to go."[22]

J. J. Goldberg, the editor of the Jewish weekly newspaper the *Forward* and the author of *Jewish Power: Inside the American Jewish Establishment*, nicely captures the difficulty of talking about the lobby: "It seems as though we're forced to choose between Jews holding vast and pernicious control or Jewish influence being non-existent." In fact, he notes, "somewhere in the middle is a reality that none wants to discuss, which is that there is an entity called the Jewish community made up of a group of organizations and public figures that's part of the political rough-and-tumble. There's nothing wrong with playing the game like everybody else."[23] We agree completely. But we think it is fair and indeed necessary to examine the consequences that this "rough-and-tumble" interest group politics can have on America and the world.

HOW WE MAKE OUR CASE

To make our case, we have to accomplish three tasks. Specifically, we have to convince readers that the United States provides Israel with extraordinary material aid and diplomatic support, the lobby is the principal reason for that support, and this uncritical and unconditional relationship is not in the American national interest. To do so, we proceed as follows.

Chapter 1 ("The Great Benefactor") addresses the first issue directly, by describing the economic and military aid that the United States gives to Israel, as well as the diplomatic backing that Washington has provided in peace and in war. Subsequent chapters also discuss the different elements of U.S. Middle East policy that have been designed in whole or in part to benefit Israel vis-à-vis its various rivals.

Chapters 2 and 3 assess the main arguments that are usually invoked to justify or explain the exceptional amount of support that Israel receives from the United States. This critical assessment is necessary for methodological reasons: in order to properly assess the impact of the Israel lobby, we have to examine other possible explanations that might account for the "special relationship" that now exists between the two countries.

In Chapter 2 ("Israel: Strategic Asset or Liability?"), we examine the familiar argument that Israel deserves lavish support because it is a valuable strategic asset. We show that although Israel may have been an asset during the Cold War, it is now increasingly a strategic liability. Backing Israel so strongly helps fuel America's terrorism problem and makes it harder for the United States to address the other problems it faces in the Middle East. Unconditional support for Israel also complicates U.S. relations with a number of other countries around the world, thereby imposing additional costs on the United States. Yet even though the costs of backing Israel have risen while the benefits have declined, American support continues to increase. This situation suggests that something other than strategic imperatives is at work.

Chapter 3 ("A Dwindling Moral Case") examines the different moral rationales that Israelis and their American supporters often use to explain U.S. support for the Jewish state. In particular, we consider the claim that the United States backs Israel because of shared "democratic values," because Israel is a weak and vulnerable David facing a powerful Arab Goliath, because its past and present conduct is more ethical than its adversaries' behavior, or because it has always sought peace while its neighbors always chose war. This assessment is necessary not because we have any animus toward Israel or because we think its conduct is worse than that of other states, but because these essentially moral claims are so frequently used to explain why the United States should give Israel exceptional levels of aid. We conclude that while there is a strong moral case for Israel's existence, the moral case for giving it such generous and largely unconditional support is not compelling. Once again, this juxtaposition of a dwindling moral case and ever-increasing U.S. backing suggests that something else must be at work.

Having established that neither strategic interests nor moral rationales can fully explain U.S. support for Israel, we turn our attention to that "something else." Chapter 4 ("What Is the 'Israel Lobby'?") identifies the lobby's different components and describes how this loose coalition has evolved. We stress that it is not a single unified movement, that its different elements sometimes disagree on certain issues, and that it includes both Jews and non-Jews, including the so-called Christian Zionists. We also show how some of the most important organizations in the lobby have drifted rightward over time and are increasingly unrepresentative of the larger populations on whose behalf they often claim to speak.

This chapter also considers whether Arab-American groups, the so-called oil lobby, or wealthy Arab oil producers are either a significant counterweight to the Israel lobby or even the real driving forces behind U.S. Middle East policy. Many people seem to believe, for example, that the invasion of Iraq was mostly about oil and that corporate oil interests were the primary movers behind the U.S. decision to attack that country. This is not the case: although access to oil is obviously an important U.S. interest, there are good reasons why Arab Americans, oil companies, and the Saudi royal family wield far less influence on U.S. foreign policy than the Israel lobby does.

In Chapter 5 ("Guiding the Policy Process") and Chapter 6 ("Dominating Public Discourse"), we describe the different strategies that groups in the lobby use in order to advance Israel's interests in the United States. In addition to direct lobbying on Capitol Hill, the lobby rewards or punishes politicians largely through an ability to guide the flow of campaign contributions. Organizations in the lobby also put pressure on the executive branch through a number of mechanisms, including working through government officials who are sympathetic to their views. Equally important, the lobby has gone to considerable lengths to shape public discourse about Israel by putting pressure on the media and academia and by establishing a tangible presence in influential foreign policy think tanks. Efforts to shape public perceptions often include charging critics of Israel with anti-Semitism, a tactic designed to discredit and marginalize anyone who challenges the current relationship.

These tasks accomplished, Part II traces the lobby's role in shaping recent U.S. Middle East policy. Our argument, it should be emphasized, is not that the lobby is the only factor that influences U.S. decision making in these issues. It is not omnipotent, so it does not get its way on every issue. But it is very effective in shaping U.S. policy toward Israel and the surrounding region in ways that are intended to benefit Israel—and believed also to benefit the United States. Unfortunately, the policies it has successfully encouraged have actually done considerable harm to U.S. interests and have been harmful to Israel as well.

Following a brief introduction to set the stage, Chapter 7 ("The Lobby Versus the Palestinians") shows how the United States has consistently backed Israel's efforts to quell or limit the Palestinians' national aspirations. Even when American presidents put pressure on Israel to make concessions or try to distance the United States from Israel's policies—as President George W. Bush has attempted to do on several occasions since September 11—the lobby intervenes and brings them back into line. The result has been a worsening image for the United States, continued suffering on both sides of the Israeli-Palestinian divide, and a growing radicalization among the Palestinians. None of these trends is in America's or Israel's interest.

In Chapter 8 ("Iraq and Dreams of Transforming the Middle East"), we show how the lobby—and especially the neoconservatives within it—was the principal driving force behind the Bush administration's decision to invade Iraq in 2003. We emphasize that the lobby did not cause the war by itself. The September 11 attacks had a profound impact on the Bush administration's foreign policy and the decision to topple Saddam Hussein. But absent the lobby's influence, there almost certainly would not have been a war. The lobby was a necessary but not sufficient condition for a war that is a strategic disaster for the United States and a boon for Iran, Israel's most serious regional adversary.

Chapter 9 ("Taking Aim at Syria") describes the evolution of America's difficult relationship with the Assad regime in Syria. We document how the lobby has pushed Washington to adopt confrontational policies toward Syria (including occasional threats of regime change) when doing so was what the Israeli government wanted. The United States and Syria would not be allies if key groups in the lobby were less influential, but the United States would have taken a much less confrontational approach and might even be cooperating with Syria in a number of limited but useful ways. Indeed, absent the lobby, there might already be a peace treaty between Israel and Syria, and Damascus might not be backing Hezbollah in Lebanon, which would be good for both Washington and Jerusalem.

In Chapter 10 ("Iran in the Crosshairs"), we trace the lobby's role in U.S. policy toward Iran. Washington and Tehran have had difficult relations since the 1979 revolution that overthrew the shah, and Israel has come to see Iran as its most serious adversary, in light of its nuclear ambitions and its support for groups like Hezbollah. Accordingly, Israel and the lobby have repeatedly pushed the United States to go after Iran and have acted to derail several earlier opportunities for détente. The result, unfortunately, is that Iran's nuclear ambitions have increased and more extreme elements (such as current President Mahmoud Ahmadinejad) have come to power, making a difficult situation worse.

Lebanon is the subject of Chapter 11 ("The Lobby and the Second Lebanon War"), and the pattern is much the same. We argue that Israel's response to Hezbollah's unjustified provocation in the summer of 2006 was both strategically foolish and morally wrong, yet the lobby's influence made it hard for U.S. officials to do anything except strongly back Israel. This case offers yet another classic illustration of the lobby's regrettable influence on American and Israeli interests: by making it hard for U.S. policy makers to step back and give their Israeli counterparts honest and critical advice, the lobby facilitated a policy that further tarnished America's image, weakened the democratically elected regime in Beirut, and strengthened Hezbollah.

The final chapter ("What Is to Be Done?") explores how this unfortunate situation might be improved. We begin by identifying America's core Middle East interests and then sketch the essential principles of a strategy—which we term offshore balancing—that could defend these interests more effectively. We do not call for abandoning the U.S. commitment to Israel—indeed, we explicitly endorse coming to Israel's aid if its survival were ever in jeopardy. But we argue that it is time to treat Israel like a normal country and to make U.S. aid conditional on an end to the occupation and on Israel's willingness to conform its policies to American interests. Accomplishing this shift requires addressing the political power of the lobby and its current policy agenda, and we offer several suggestions for how the power of the lobby might be modified to make its influence more beneficial for the United States and Israel alike.

THOSE WE LEARNED FROM

No author is an island, and we owe a considerable debt to other scholars and writers who examined these subjects before we did. To begin with, there is the extensive academic literature on interest groups that helped us understand how small but focused movements can exert influence far greater than their absolute numbers within the population might suggest.[24] There is also a robust literature on the impact of ethnic groups on U.S. foreign policy, which confirms that the Israel lobby is not unique in its basic activities, only in its unusual level of influence.[25]

A second body of literature addresses the lobby itself. A number of journalists, scholars, and former politicians have written about the lobby. Written from both critical and sympathetic perspectives, these works contain a considerable amount of useful information on the ways that the lobby has worked to influence U.S. foreign policy. We hope our account will extend the trail that these earlier writers blazed.[26]

We have also learned a great deal from other studies, too numerous to list in toto, that deal with particular aspects of U.S. Middle East policy, U.S.-Israeli relations, or specific policy issues. Although some of these works—such as Steven Spiegel's *The Other Arab-Israeli Conflict: Making America's Middle East Policy from Truman to Reagan* and Warren Bass's *Support Any Friend: Kennedy's Middle East and the Making of the U.S.-Israel Alliance*—tend to downplay the lobby's influence, serious works of scholarship such as these nonetheless contain considerable evidence of the lobby's impact and especially its growing clout.[27]

There is a final body of literature that has played an important role in helping us to think about Israel, the lobby, and America's relationship with the Jewish state. We refer to the so-called new history that has come out of Israel over the past twenty years. Using extensive archival research, Israeli scholars like Shlomo Ben-Ami, Simha Flapan, Baruch Kimmerling, Benny Morris, Ilan Pappe, Tom Segev, Avi Shlaim, and Zeev Sternhell have effectively overturned the conventional wisdom on Israel's founding and on its subsequent policies toward both the surrounding states and the Palestinians.[28] Scholars from other countries have also contributed to setting the historical record straight.[29] Together these individuals have undermined the original, highly romanticized version of the founding, in which the Jews are usually portrayed as the white hats and the Arabs as the black hats. Moreover, these works make clear that after Israel gained its independence, it behaved much more aggressively toward the Palestinians and other Arabs than is commonly recognized.

There are various disputes among these historians, of course, and we do not agree with every point they make. Nevertheless, the story they collectively tell is not just a matter of academic interest. In fact, it has profound implications for how one thinks about the moral rationale for supporting Israel over the Palestinians. It also helps one understand why so many people in the Arab and Islamic world are deeply angry at the United States for supporting Israel so generously and unconditionally.

A NOTE ON SOURCES

A brief word about sources is in order before we proceed. Much of this study—especially Part II—deals with recent history, or with events whose ultimate outcome remains uncertain. Because official documents regarding contemporary events are normally unavailable to scholars, we have been forced to rely on other sources: newspapers, magazines, scholarly articles, books, reports from human rights organizations, radio and television transcripts, and personal interviews that we conducted. In a few instances, we had to work with an admittedly spotty record of events. Although we think it is unlikely, some parts of our story may look different once official records become available.

In order to ensure that our various arguments are correct, we backed up virtually every significant point with multiple sources, which accounts for the extensive notes provided at the end of this book. We also relied heavily on Israeli sources like *Ha'aretz* and the *Jerusalem Post*, as well as the writings of Israeli scholars. Another indispensable source of information was American Jewish publications like the *Forward* and *Jewish Week*. Not only are these Israeli and Jewish-American sources filled with important information that is not found in the mainstream media in the United States, these newspapers were by and large not likely to be sympathetic to many of our arguments about the lobby. Our reliance on them should help make our conclusions even more reliable.

CONCLUSION

Our analysis begins by describing the material and diplomatic support that the United States provides to Israel. The fact that America gives considerable support to the Jewish state is hardly headline news, but readers may be surprised to learn just how extensive and varied this largesse actually is. Documenting that support is the subject of the next chapter.

PART I

THE UNITED STATES,

ISRAEL, AND THE LOBBY

1

THE GREAT BENEFACTOR

"We are more than thankful to you." Israeli Prime Minister Yitzhak Rabin was uncharacteristically effusive when he appeared before a joint session of Congress on July 26, 1994. Extending his remarks to the "wonderful people of America," Rabin emphasized that "no words can express our gratitude . . . for your generous support, understanding, and cooperation, which are beyond compare in modern history." Two years later, following Rabin's tragic assassination, one of his successors, Benjamin Netanyahu, stood in the same spot and offered similar words of appreciation: "The United States has given Israel—how can I tell it to this body? The United States has given Israel, apart from political and military support, munificent and magnificent assistance in the economic sphere. With America's help, Israel has grown to be a powerful, modern state." He told his audience, "I know that I speak for every Israeli and every Jew throughout the world when I say to you today, 'Thank you, people of America.'"[1]

These statements—and others like them—are not merely the gracious rhetoric that one typically hears from visiting foreign dignitaries. Rabin's and Netanyahu's words are an accurate description of the remarkable backing that the United States has long provided to the Jewish state. American taxpayers' money has subsidized Israel's economic development and rescued it during periods of financial crisis. American military assistance has strengthened Israel in wartime and helped preserve its military dominance in the Middle East. Washington has given Israel extensive diplomatic support in war and peace, and has helped insulate it from some of the adverse consequences of its own actions. U.S. aid has also been a key ingredient in the protracted Arab-Israeli peace process, with agreements such as the Camp

David Accords or the peace treaties with Egypt and Jordan resting on ex- plicit promises of increased American assistance. More than any other country, the United States has been Israel's great benefactor.

ECONOMIC AID

The most obvious indicator of Israel's favored position is the total amount of foreign aid it has received from America's taxpayers. As of 2005, direct U.S. economic and military assistance to Israel amounted to nearly $154 billion (in 2005 dollars), the bulk of it comprising direct grants rather than loans.[2] As discussed below, the actual total is significantly higher, because direct U.S. aid is given under unusually favorable terms and the United States pro- vides Israel with other forms of material assistance that are not included in the foreign assistance budget.

Because this level of support is rarely questioned today, it is easy to forget that the "special relationship" that now exists did not emerge until several decades after Israel's founding. Prior to World War II, American leaders occa- sionally offered rhetorical support for the Zionist goal of a Jewish homeland, but no president exerted much effort to advance that objective. President Harry S. Truman did play a key role in supporting the establishment of a Jew- ish homeland when he decided to back the UN partition plan in 1947 and to recognize Israel immediately after its declaration of independence in May 1948. But both the Truman and Eisenhower administrations also realized that embracing Israel too closely would jeopardize relations with the Arab world and provide the Soviet Union with enticing opportunities to gain influence in the Middle East. Accordingly, the United States sought to steer a middle course between Israel and its Arab neighbors during the 1950s; economic aid to Israel was modest and the United States provided hardly any direct military assistance.[3] Israeli requests to purchase American weaponry were politely re- jected, as were requests for a U.S. security guarantee.[4]

There were also several sharp diplomatic disagreements between Wash- ington and Jerusalem during this period. When Israel ignored UN demands that it halt work on a canal to divert water from the Jordan River in Septem- ber 1953, Secretary of State John Foster Dulles promptly announced that the United States was suspending foreign assistance. The threat worked: Is- rael agreed to stop the project on October 27 and U.S. aid was restored.[5] Similar threats to halt American aid played a key role in convincing Israel to withdraw from the territory it had seized from Egypt in the 1956 Suez War.

Israeli Prime Minister David Ben-Gurion saw the war as an opportunity for territorial expansion, and he began the prewar discussions with Britain and France (the primary instigators of the attack on Egypt) by suggesting that Jordan be divided between Israel and Iraq and that Israel be given portions of Lebanon and control over the Straits of Tiran.[6] Britain and France were preoccupied with Egypt and uninterested in this grand scheme. But Ben-Gurion made several statements following the conquest by the Israel Defense Forces (IDF) of the Sinai Peninsula (including a speech in the Knesset on November 7) suggesting that the 1949 armistice agreements were void and that Israel intended to keep the lands it had just seized. When Eisenhower threatened to block all public and private aid to Israel, Ben-Gurion quickly backtracked, agreeing "in principle" to withdraw in exchange for adequate assurances of Israel's security. Israel then worked to rally support in the United States, a campaign that reduced Eisenhower's congressional support and led him to make a nationally televised speech justifying his actions. Israel finally withdrew from all the territories it had conquered in the spring of 1957, in exchange for assurances regarding border security in Gaza and freedom of navigation in the Straits of Tiran.[7]

U.S.-Israeli relations had warmed by the late 1950s, but it was the Kennedy administration that made the first tangible U.S. commitment to Israel's military security.[8] In December 1962, in fact, Kennedy told Israeli Foreign Minister Golda Meir that the United States "has a special relationship with Israel in the Middle East really comparable only to that which it has with Britain over a wide range of world affairs," adding that "I think it is quite clear that in case of an invasion the United States would come to the support of Israel. We have that capacity and it is growing."[9] Kennedy soon thereafter authorized the first major sale of U.S. weaponry—Hawk antiaircraft missiles—to Israel in 1963. This shift reflected a number of strategic considerations—such as the desire to balance Soviet arms sales to Egypt, dampen Israel's nuclear ambitions, and encourage Israel's leaders to respond favorably to U.S. peace initiatives—but skillful Israeli diplomacy, the influence of several pro-Israel advisers, and Kennedy's understandable desire to maintain support from Jewish voters and donors played a role in his decision as well.[10] The Hawk sale opened the door to several additional weapons deals, most notably the sale of more than two hundred M48A battle tanks in 1964. In an attempt to disguise American involvement and thereby limit repercussions in the Arab world, the tanks were shipped to Israel by West Germany, which in turn received replacements from the United States.[11]

In terms of the absolute amount of U.S. aid, however, the real sea change took place following the Six-Day War in June 1967. After averaging roughly $63 million annually from 1949 to 1965 (more than 95 percent of which was economic assistance and food aid), average aid increased to $102 million per year from 1966 to 1970. Support soared to $634.5 million in 1971 (roughly 85 percent was military assistance) and more than quintupled after the Yom Kippur War in 1973. Israel became the largest annual recipient of U.S. foreign assistance in 1976, a position it has retained ever since. Support for Israel shifted from loans to direct grants during this period, with the bulk of U.S. aid consisting of military assistance rather than economic or technical support. According to Clyde Mark of the Congressional Research Service (CRS), the official research arm of the U.S. Congress, "Israel preferred that the aid be in the form of loans, rather than grants, to avoid having a U.S. military contingent in Israel to oversee a grant program. Since 1974, some or all of U.S. military aid to Israel has been in the form of loans for which repayment is waived. Technically, the assistance is called loans, but as a practical matter, the military aid is grant."[12]

Israel now receives on average about $3 billion in direct foreign assistance each year, an amount that is roughly one-sixth of America's direct foreign assistance budget and equal to about 2 percent of Israel's GDP. In recent years, about 75 percent of U.S. assistance has been military aid, with the remainder broken down into various forms of economic aid.[13] In per capita terms, this level of direct foreign assistance amounts to a direct subsidy of more than $500 per year for each Israeli. By comparison, the number two recipient of American foreign aid, Egypt, receives only $20 per person, and impoverished countries such as Pakistan and Haiti receive roughly $5 per person and $27 per person, respectively.[14] Jerusalem and Washington agreed to gradually phase out economic assistance beginning in 1997, and Congress has reduced economic aid to Israel by $120 million per year since FY1999. This step has been partly compensated for by a parallel U.S. commitment to increase its military aid by $60 million per year, and by congressional willingness to vote supplemental aid packages, such as the $1.2 billion provided to support implementation of the 1998 Wye Agreement (in which Israel agreed to withdraw forces from parts of the West Bank) and an additional $1 billion in foreign military financing (FMF) aid in 2003 to help Israel prepare for the war with Iraq.[15]

Three billion dollars per year is generous, but it is hardly the whole story. As noted above, the canonical $3 billion figure omits a substantial number of other benefits and thus significantly understates the actual level of U.S. support. Indeed, in 1991, Representative Lee Hamilton (D-IN) told reporters that Israel was one of three countries whose aid "substantially exceeds the popularly quoted figures" and said the annual figure was in fact more than $4.3 billion.[16]

The discrepancy arises in part because Israel gets its aid under more favorable terms than most other recipients of U.S. assistance.[17] Most recipients of American foreign aid get their money in quarterly installments, but since 1982, the annual foreign aid bill has included a special clause specifying that Israel is to receive its entire annual appropriation in the first thirty days of the fiscal year.[18] This is akin to receiving your entire annual salary on January 1 and thus being able to earn interest on the unspent portion until you used it.

Because the U.S. government normally runs budget deficits, transferring the aid all at once requires it to borrow the necessary amount of money up front, and the CRS estimates that it costs U.S. taxpayers "between $50 and $60 million per year to borrow funds for the early, lump-sum payment."[19] Moreover, the U.S. government ends up paying Israel additional interest when Israel reinvests the unspent portion in U.S. treasury bills. According to the U.S. embassy in Israel, early transfer of FMF funds has enabled Israel to earn some $660 million in extra interest as of 2004.[20] Israel has also received "excess defense articles" (surplus U.S. military equipment provided to friendly nations either free of charge or heavily discounted) beyond the normal limits imposed by the 1976 Arms Export Control Act. This limit was originally set at $250 million (excluding ships), but the appropriations bill of November 5, 1990, authorized a "one-time only" transfer to Israel of $700 million worth of surplus U.S. equipment in 1991.[21]

Likewise, the FMF program normally requires recipients of U.S. military assistance to spend all of the money here in the United States, to help keep American defense workers employed. Congress grants Israel a special exemption in the annual appropriations bill, however, authorizing it to use about one out of every four U.S. military aid dollars to subsidize its own defense industry. "No other recipient of U.S. military assistance has been granted this benefit," notes a recent CRS report, and "the proceeds to Israeli defense firms from purchases with U.S. funds have allowed the Israeli defense industry to achieve necessary economies of scale and become highly sophisticated." By 2004, in fact, Israel, a comparatively small country, had become the world's eighth largest arms supplier.[22]

Along with Egypt and Turkey, Israel is also permitted to apply its entire FMF funding to meet its current year obligations, rather than having to set aside portions to cover expected costs in subsequent years. According to the

U.S. General Accounting Office (GAO), this "cash flow" method of financing "permits a country to order more defense goods and services than it normally could because less money must be reserved when a contract is signed."[23] Israel can make its payments as long as the United States continues to provide similar amounts of aid, a situation that makes it harder for the United States to reduce its support in the future. And in a further manipulation of the methods of financing, recipients of U.S. aid are normally expected to draw down FMF loans and grants at an equal rate, but Israel is allowed to draw down the grant (or waived) portions of its FMF allocation before it uses any loaned portions. By delaying the date on which the loan is activated, this procedure reduces the amount of interest that Israel owes Uncle Sam.[24]

Remarkably, Israel is the only recipient of U.S. economic aid that does not have to account for how it is spent. Aid to other countries is allocated for specific development projects (HIV/AIDS prevention, counternarcotics programs, children's health, democracy promotion, improving education, etc.), but Israel receives a direct lump-sum cash transfer.[25] This exemption makes it virtually impossible for the United States to prevent its subsidies from being used for purposes that it opposes, such as building settlements on the West Bank. According to the CRS's Clyde Mark, "Because U.S. economic aid is given to Israel as direct government-to-government budgetary authority without any specific project accounting, and money is fungible, there is no way to tell how Israel uses U.S. aid."[26]

Another form of U.S. support is loan guarantees that permit Israel to borrow money from commercial banks at lower rates, thereby saving millions of dollars in interest payments. Israel requested and received approximately $10 billion in loan guarantees from the United States in the early 1990s in order to finance the costs of settling Soviet Jews immigrating to Israel. The U.S. government does not provide funds directly in a loan guarantee—it merely undertakes to reimburse private lenders in the event of a default—and advocates of these measures often claim that there is no real expenditure and thus no real cost to the U.S. taxpayer. Loan guarantees do have budgetary consequences, however, because Congress must appropriate funds to cover an estimate of what could be lost over the life of the loan based on its net present value. Estimates for the cost of the 1992 loan guarantee range from $100 million to $800 million.[27]

Washington authorized a second round of loan guarantees in 2003, totaling nearly $9 billion, to help Israel prepare for the war with Iraq, deal with a protracted economic crisis, and cover the costs imposed by the Second

Palestinian Intifada. Because Israel is legally barred from using U.S. economic aid in the Occupied Territories, the actual amount allocated was eventually reduced by an amount equivalent to Israel's estimated expenditures on settlement construction. This reduction is not as severe as it may sound, however, as it involved no decrease in direct U.S. aid and merely forced Israel to pay a slightly higher interest rate on a small portion of the borrowed funds.

In addition to government subsidized aid and loan guarantees, Israel receives an estimated $2 billion annually in private donations from American citizens, roughly half in direct payments and half via the purchase of State of Israel Bonds.[28] These bonds receive favorable treatment in U.S. law; although the interest paid on them is not tax-exempt, Congress specifically exempted them from the provisions of the 1984 Deficit Reduction Act, which imposed additional tax penalties on other bonds with yields below the federal rate.[29] Similarly, private donations to charities in most foreign countries are not tax deductible, but many private donations to Israel are, due to a special clause in the U.S.-Israel income tax treaty.[30]

This flow of money to Israel has been a crucial boon to the general economy, but private contributions from U.S. citizens have also played an important strategic role, going back to the preindependence era.[31] In his memoirs, Israeli Prime Minister Shimon Peres revealed that private contributions from wealthy diaspora Jews (including several Americans) had helped finance Israel's clandestine nuclear program in the 1950s and 1960s. According to the Israeli journalist Michael Karpin, a key coordinator of this fund-raising effort was Abraham Feinberg, a well-connected U.S. businessman, philanthropist, and political adviser, and contributors to the campaign reportedly included Canadian beverage magnate Samuel Bronfman and several members of the Rothschild family. Feinberg never divulged the names of the American donors, however, and his own role has never been officially confirmed.[32] Today, groups like the Friends of Israel Defense Forces raise funds in the United States to "support social, educational, cultural and recreational programs and facilities for the young men and women soldiers of Israel who defend the Jewish homeland." One recent dinner in New York reportedly raised some $18 million in contributions, which are tax deductible under U.S. law.[33]

Other private donations from U.S. citizens have also helped subsidize Israel's prolonged campaign to colonize the Occupied Territories. These contributions to settlements in the West Bank (including those made via U.S. charities or other "Friends of . . ." organizations) are not supposed to be tax-exempt in the United States, but such restrictions are inherently difficult to enforce and were loosely monitored in the past.[34] For example, in order to safeguard the tax-exempt status of U.S. donations to the Jewish Agency for Israel (a quasi-governmental organization that helps settle new arrivals in Israel), the task of aiding settlements in the Occupied Territories was taken out of the agency's Settlement Department and assigned to a new "Settlement Division" within the World Zionist Organization (WZO). But as Gershom Gorenberg points out, "The Division was a shell that contracted all services from the Jewish Agency . . . The change kept the U.S. Jewish philanthropies clear of the occupied territories. On the ground, the same people continued the same efforts."[35] This problem was underscored when an official Israeli government study directed by Talia Sasson, former chief criminal prosecutor, revealed that the Settlement Division of the WZO (which receives support from prominent Jewish organizations all over the world) was actively involved in the creation of unauthorized settlements in the Occupied Territories.[36] More broadly, because Israeli charities operate beyond the reach of U.S. tax authorities, donations from Jewish and Christian evangelical organizations are hard to monitor once they are transferred to Israel. In practice, therefore, the U.S. government cannot easily determine the extent to which tax-exempt private donations are being diverted for unauthorized purposes.[37]

All this largesse is especially striking when one realizes that Israel is not a poor or devastated country like Afghanistan, Niger, Burma, or Sierra Leone. On the contrary, Israel is now a modern industrial power. Its per capita income in 2006 was twenty-ninth in the world, according to the International Monetary Fund, and is nearly double that of Hungary and the Czech Republic, substantially higher than Portugal's, South Korea's, or Taiwan's, and far outstrips every country in Latin America and Africa.[38] It ranks twenty-third in the United Nations' 2006 Human Development Report and thirty-eighth in the Economist Intelligence Unit's 2005 "quality of life" rankings.[39] Yet this comparatively prosperous state is America's biggest aid recipient, each year receiving sums that dwarf U.S. support for impoverished states such as Bangladesh, Bolivia, and Liberia. This anomaly is even acknowledged by some of Israel's more fervent supporters in the United States. In 1997, for example, Mitchell Bard, the former editor of AIPAC's Near East Report, and Daniel Pipes, the hawkish founder of the pro-Israel Middle East Forum, wrote that "Israel has become an affluent country with a personal income rivaling Great Britain's, so the American willingness to provide aid to Israel is no longer based purely on need."[40]

The United States has taken on other economic burdens for Israel's benefit, often as part of efforts to persuade Israel to accept or implement peace agreements with its neighbors. As part of the 1975 disengagement agreement between Egypt and Israel, for example, Secretary of State Henry Kissinger signed a memorandum of understanding (MOU) that committed the United States to guarantee Israel's oil needs in the event of a crisis and to finance and stock "a supplementary strategic reserve" for Israel, at an estimated cost of several hundred million dollars.[41] The oil guarantee was reaffirmed during the final peace negotiations between Egypt and Israel in March 1979 and has been quietly renewed ever since.[42]

Finally, the aid that the United States provides to several of Israel's neighbors is at least partly intended to benefit Israel as well. Egypt and Jordan are the number two and three recipients of U.S. foreign aid, but most of this money should be seen as a reward for good behavior—specifically, their willingness to sign peace treaties with Israel. Egypt received $71.7 million in U.S. aid in 1974, but it got $1.127 billion in 1975 and $1.320 billion in 1976 (in constant 2005 dollars) following completion of the Sinai II disengagement agreement. U.S. aid to Egypt reached $2.3 billion in 1978 and soared to a whopping $5.9 billion in 1979, the year the Egypt-Israeli peace treaty was signed. Cairo still gets about $2 billion annually.[43] Similarly, Jordan received $76 million in direct aid in 1994 and only $57 million in 1995, but Congress rewarded King Hussein's decision to sign a peace treaty in 1994 by forgiving Jordan's $700 million debt to the United States and removing other restrictions on U.S. aid. Since 1997, U.S. aid to Jordan has averaged roughly $566 million annually.[44] U.S. willingness to reward Egypt and Jordan in this way is yet another manifestation of Washington's generosity toward the Jewish state.

MILITARY ASSISTANCE

These various forms of economic assistance have been and remain important to Israel, but the bulk of U.S. support is now committed to preserving Israel's military supremacy in the Middle East.[45] Not only does Israel receive access to top-drawer U.S. weaponry (F-15 and F-16 aircraft, Blackhawk helicopters, cluster munitions, "smart bombs," etc.), it has also become linked to the U.S. defense and intelligence establishments through a diverse array of formal agreements and informal links. According to the Congressional Research

Service, "U.S. military aid has helped transform Israel's armed forces into one of the most technologically sophisticated militaries in the world."[46]

Moreover, according to the *Wall Street Journal*, Israel "enjoys unusually wide latitude in spending the [military assistance] funds."[47] The Defense Security Cooperation Agency (DSCA) handles almost all the purchasing and monitors U.S. aid for all other military aid recipients, but Israel deals directly with military contractors for virtually all of its purchases and then gets reimbursed from its aid account.[48] Israel is also the only country where contracts for less than $500,000 are exempt from prior U.S. review.[49]

The potential risks inherent in these comparatively lax oversight arrangements were revealed in the early 1990s, when the head of Israeli Air Force procurement, Brigadier General Rami Dotan, was found to have embezzled and illegally diverted millions of dollars of U.S. aid. According to the *Wall Street Journal*, Dotan (who eventually pleaded guilty in Israel and received a lengthy jail sentence) reportedly "parceled out work orders to stay under the $500,000 threshold." Nonetheless, the head of DSCA's predecessor, the Defense Security Assistance Agency, Lieutenant General Teddy Allen, subsequently told a congressional subcommittee that the Department of Defense inspector general's recommendation that the aid program for Israel be "revamped" had been rejected because it might cause "turbulence in our relations" with Israel.[50]

In addition to the economic and military aid already described, the United States has provided Israel with nearly $3 billion to develop weapons like the Lavi aircraft, the Merkava tank, and the Arrow missile.[51] These projects were funded through the U.S. Department of Defense and often portrayed as joint research and development efforts, but the United States did not need these weapons and never intended to purchase them for its own use. The Lavi project was eventually canceled on cost-effectiveness grounds (with much of the cancellation cost being borne by the United States), but the other weapons went into Israel's arsenal at Uncle Sam's expense.[52] The FY2004 U.S. defense budget included a $136 million request for the Arrow, for example, with $66 million allocated for additional improvements to the system and $70 million authorized for the production of additional units. Thus, the money that Washington pays to help Israel's defense industry develop or produce these "joint weapons projects" is in reality another form of subsidy.[53] The United States sometimes benefits from the technology that Israeli firms develop, but America would benefit even more if these funds were used to support high-tech industries in the United States.

Military ties between the United States and Israel were upgraded in the

1980s, as part of the Reagan administration's effort to build an anti-Soviet "strategic consensus" in the Middle East. Secretary of Defense Caspar Weinberger and Israeli Minister of Defense Ariel Sharon signed a memorandum of understanding in 1981 establishing a "framework for continued consultation and cooperation to enhance their national security."[54] This agreement led to the creation of a Joint Security Assistance Planning Group (JSAP) and Joint Political Military Group, which meet regularly to review Israel's aid requests and to coordinate military plans, joint exercises, and logistical arrangements. Although Israeli leaders had hoped for a formal treaty of alliance and were disappointed by the limited nature of the framework agreement, it was a more formal expression of a U.S. commitment than earlier presidential statements, such as Kennedy's private remarks to Golda Meir in 1962.

Despite tensions over a wide array of issues—U.S. arms sales to Saudi Arabia, the 1981 bombing of Iraq's nuclear reactor, Israel's annexation of the Golan Heights in December 1981, its invasion of Lebanon in 1982, and its abrupt rejection of the "Reagan Plan" for peace in September 1982—security cooperation between Israel and the United States increased steadily in the Reagan years. Joint military exercises began in 1984, and in 1986 Israel became one of three foreign countries invited to participate in the U.S. Strategic Defense Initiative (aka "Star Wars"). Finally, in 1988, a new memorandum of agreement reaffirmed the "close partnership between Israel and the United States" and designated Israel a "Major Non-NATO Ally," along with Australia, Egypt, Japan, and South Korea. States enjoying this status are eligible to purchase a wider array of U.S. weapons at lower prices, get priority delivery on war surplus matériel, and participate in joint research and development projects and U.S. counterterrorism initiatives. Commercial firms from these states also get preferential treatment when bidding for U.S. defense contracts.[55]

Security links between the two countries have expanded ever since. The United States began prepositioning military supplies in Israel in 1989, and Congress voted in 2006 to increase the stockpile from roughly $100 million to $400 million by 2008.[56] This policy has been justified as a way to enhance the Pentagon's ability to respond quickly to a regional crisis, but prepositioning U.S. supplies in Israel is actually an inefficient way to prepare for this contingency and the Pentagon has never been enthusiastic about this policy. According to Shai Feldman, former head of Tel Aviv University's Jaffe Institute of Strategic Studies, "Present arrangements permit the storage only of materiel that could also be used in an emergency by Israeli forces. In the view of Pentagon planners, this implies that the United States cannot be absolutely certain that arms and ammunition stored in Israel would be available in a crisis situation. Moreover, this 'dual use' arrangement means that instead of storing weapons and ordnance for pre-designated U.S. units, weapons would have to be distributed from general stocks under crisis conditions and then integrated into different combat units, creating a logistical nightmare."[57] The real purpose of the stockpile program is to enhance Israel's matériel reserves, and it is hardly surprising that *Ynetnews*, a Web news service affiliated with the Israeli newspaper *Yedioth Ahronoth*, reported in December 2006 that "a great portion of the American equipment stored in Israel . . . was used for combat in the summer [2006] war in Lebanon."[58]

Building on the other working groups created during the 1980s, the United States and Israel established a Joint Anti-Terrorism Working Group in 1996 and set up an electronic "hotline" between the Pentagon and Israel's Ministry of Defense. Further cementing the links between the two states, Israel was given access to the U.S. satellite-based missile warning system in 1997. Then, in 2001, the two states established an annual "interagency strategic dialogue" to discuss "long-term issues." The latter forum was temporarily suspended during a dispute over Israeli sales of American military technology to China, but it reconvened in November 2005.[59]

As one would expect, U.S.-Israeli security cooperation also extends to the realm of intelligence. Cooperation between U.S. and Israeli intelligence services dates back to the late 1950s, and by 1985 the two countries had reportedly signed some two dozen intelligence-sharing arrangements. Israel gave the United States access to captured Soviet weaponry and to reports from émigrés from the Soviet bloc, while the United States provided Israel with satellite imagery during the 1973 October War and prior to the 1976 Entebbe hostage rescue, and reportedly helped finance several Israeli intelligence operations in Africa.[60] In the early 1980s, the United States even gave Israel access to certain forms of intelligence that it denied its closest NATO allies. In particular, Israel reportedly received almost unlimited access to intelligence from the sophisticated KH-11 reconnaissance satellite ("not only the information, but the photos themselves," according to the head of Israeli military intelligence), while British access to the same source was much more limited.[61] Access to this data was restricted following Israel's raid on Iraq's Osirak reactor in 1981, but the first President Bush is believed to have authorized the transfer of real-time satellite information about Iraq's Scud attacks during the 1991 Gulf War.[62]

In contrast to Washington's long-standing opposition to the spread of weapons of mass destruction, the United States has tacitly supported Israel's effort to maintain regional military superiority by turning a blind eye toward its various clandestine WMD programs, including its possession of upward of two hundred nuclear weapons.[63] The U.S. government has pressed dozens of states to sign the 1968 Non-Proliferation Treaty (NPT), but American leaders did little to pressure Israel to halt its nuclear program and sign the agreement. The Kennedy administration clearly wanted to restrain Israel's nuclear ambitions in the early 1960s, and it eventually persuaded Israel to permit U.S. scientists to tour Israel's nuclear research facility at Dimona to ascertain whether Israel was trying to produce a nuclear bomb. The Israeli government repeatedly denied that it had a weapons program, dragged its feet in scheduling visits, and imposed onerous restrictions on the inspectors' access when visits did occur. Thus, the first U.S. visit, on May 18, 1961, involved just two American scientists and lasted only four days, only one of them spent at the Dimona site. According to Warren Bass, "Israel's strategy was to permit a visit . . . but ensure that the inspectors did not find anything." Pressed to allow a follow-up visit a year later, the Israelis unexpectedly invited U.S. Atomic Energy Commission officials inspecting a different Israeli facility to make an impromptu tour of Dimona. As Bass notes, this visit "hardly merits the name 'inspection,'" but the Kennedy administration "did not seem eager to pick a fight."[64]

Kennedy stepped up the pressure the following year, however, sending both Ben-Gurion and his successor, Levi Eshkol, several stern letters demanding biannual inspections "in accord with international standards" and warning that "this Government's commitment to and support of Israel could be seriously jeopardized" if the United States were unable to resolve its concerns about Israel's nuclear ambitions.[65] Kennedy's threats convinced Israel's leaders to permit additional visits, but the concession did not lead to compliance. As Eshkol reportedly told his colleagues after receiving Kennedy's July 1963 démarche: "What am I frightened of? His man will come, and he will actually be told that he can visit [the Dimona site] and go anywhere he wishes, but when he wants a door opened at some place or another then [Emanuel] Prat [head of construction at Dimona] will tell him 'Not that.'"[66] On other visits, inspectors were not permitted to bring in outside instruments or take samples.

As the more recent cases of Iraq and North Korea remind us, such obfuscatory tactics are part of the standard playbook for all clandestine proliferators. U.S. officials remained suspicious about Jerusalem's nuclear plans, but Israel's deception worked because neither Kennedy nor his successor,

Lyndon Johnson, was willing to withhold U.S. support if Israel were not more forthcoming. As a result, notes Avner Cohen in his detailed history of Israel's nuclear program, "the Israelis were able to determine the rules of the [U.S.] visits and the Johnson administration chose not to confront Israel on the issue, fearing that Israel would end the arrangement . . . Kennedy threatened both Ben Gurion and [Levi] Eshkol that noncompliance . . . could 'jeopardize American commitment to Israel's security and well being,' but Johnson was unwilling to risk an American-Israeli crisis over the issue."[67] "Instead of inspections every six months," writes Bass, "in practice Johnson settled for a quick visit once a year or so."[68] And when CIA Director Richard Helms came to the White House in 1968 to inform Johnson that U.S. intelligence had concluded that Israel had in fact acquired a nuclear capability, Johnson told him to make sure that nobody else was shown the evidence, including Secretary of State Dean Rusk and Secretary of Defense Robert McNamara. According to the journalist Seymour Hersh, "Johnson's purpose in chasing Helms—and his intelligence—away was clear: he did not want to know what the CIA was trying to tell him, for once he accepted that information, he would have to act on it. By 1968, the President had no intention of doing anything to stop the Israeli bomb."[69]

In addition to its nuclear arsenal, Israel maintains active chemical and biological weapons programs and has yet to ratify either the Chemical or Biological Weapons Convention.[70] The irony is hard to miss: the United States has pressured many other states to join the NPT, imposed sanctions on countries that have defied U.S. wishes and acquired nuclear weapons anyway, gone to war in 2003 to prevent Iraq from pursuing WMD, and contemplated attacking Iran and North Korea for the same reason. Yet Washington has long subsidized an ally whose clandestine WMD activities are well-known and whose nuclear arsenal has given several of its neighbors a powerful incentive to seek WMD themselves.

With the partial exception of Soviet support for Cuba, it is hard to think of another instance where one country has provided another with a similar level of material aid over such an extended period.[71] America's willingness to provide some support to Israel is not surprising, of course, because U.S. leaders have long favored Israel's existence and understood that it faced a hostile threat environment. As discussed below and in Chapter 2, U.S. leaders also saw aid to Israel as a way to advance broader foreign policy goals. Nonetheless, the sheer magnitude of U.S. aid is remarkable. As we show in Chapter 3, Israel was stronger than its neighbors before significant American military aid commenced, and it is now a prosperous country. U.S. aid has undoubtedly been useful for Israel, but it may not have been essential to its survival.

The most singular feature of U.S. support for Israel is its increasingly unconditional nature. President Eisenhower could credibly threaten to withhold aid after the Suez War (though even he faced significant congressional opposition when he did), but those days are long past. Since the mid-1960s, Israel has continued receiving generous support even when it took actions American leaders thought were unwise and contrary to U.S. interests. Israel gets its aid despite its refusal to sign the Non-Proliferation Treaty and its various WMD programs. It gets its aid when it builds settlements in the Occupied Territories (losing only a small amount through reductions in loan guarantees), even though the U.S. government opposes this policy. It also gets its aid when it annexes territory it has conquered (as it did on the Golan Heights and in Jerusalem), sells U.S. military technology to potential enemies like China, conducts espionage operations on U.S. soil, or uses U.S. weapons in ways that violate U.S. law (such as the use of cluster munitions in civilian areas in Lebanon). It gets additional aid when it makes concessions for peace, but it rarely loses American support when it takes actions that make peace more elusive. And it gets its aid even when Israeli leaders renege on pledges made to U.S. presidents. Menachem Begin promised Ronald Reagan that he would not lobby against the proposed sale of AWACS aircraft to Saudi Arabia in 1981, for example, but Begin then went up to Capitol Hill and told a Senate panel that he opposed the deal.[72]

One might think that U.S. generosity would give Washington considerable leverage over Israel's conduct, but this has not been the case. When dealing with Israel, in fact, U.S. leaders can usually elicit cooperation only by offering additional carrots (increased assistance) rather than employing sticks (threats to withhold aid). For example, the Israeli Cabinet agreed to publicly endorse UN Resolution 242—which, originally passed in November 1967, called for Israel's withdrawal from territories seized in the Six-Day War—only after President Richard Nixon gave private assurances that Israel would receive additional U.S. aircraft.[73] Moreover, its acceptance of the cease-fire agreement that ended the so-called War of Attrition with Egypt (a protracted series of air, artillery, and infantry clashes that began along the Suez Canal in March 1969 and continued until July 1970) was bought by a U.S. pledge to accelerate aircraft deliveries to Israel, to provide advanced electronic countermeasures against Egypt's Soviet-supplied antiaircraft missiles, and, more generally, to "maintain the balance of power."[74] According to Shimon Peres (who served as Minister without Portfolio during this period), "As to the question of U.S. pressure on us to accept their programme, I would say they handled us more with a carrot than with a stick; in any event they never threatened us with sanctions."[75]

This pattern continued through the 1970s, with Presidents Nixon, Ford, and Carter pledging ever-larger sums of aid in the course of the disengagement talks with Egypt and during the negotiations that led to the 1978 Camp David Accords and the 1979 Egyptian-Israeli peace treaty. Specifically, U.S. aid to Israel increased from $1.9 billion in 1975 to $6.29 billion in 1976 (following completion of the Sinai II agreement) and from $4.4 billion in 1978 to $10.9 billion in 1979 (following the final peace treaty with Egypt).[76] As discussed below, the United States also made a number of other commitments to Israel in order to persuade it to sign. In much the same way, the Clinton administration gave Israel increased assistance as part of the peace treaty with Jordan in 1994, and Clinton's efforts to advance the Oslo peace process led him to pledge an additional $1.2 billion in military aid to Israel to win Israel's acceptance of the 1998 Wye Agreement. Prime Minister Netanyahu suspended the Wye Agreement shortly after it was signed, however, following a violent confrontation between a Palestinian crowd and two Israeli citizens.[77] According to U.S. negotiator Dennis Ross, "It was hard to escape the conclusion that Bibi [Netanyahu] . . . was seizing on this incident to avoid further implementation. This was unfortunate, because the Palestinians were working diligently to carry out most of their commitments under Wye, particularly in the area of making arrests and fighting terror."[78] Yet as the Israeli scholar Abraham Ben-Zvi observes, "The Clinton administration's frustration with Netanyahu's style was rarely translated into policy that harmed the American-Israeli special relationship."[79]

Indeed, attempts to use America's potential leverage face significant obstacles and are rarely attempted, even when U.S. officials are deeply upset by Israeli actions. When President Gerald Ford and Secretary of State Henry Kissinger grew impatient with Israeli intransigence during the disengagement negotiations with Egypt in 1975, a threat to curtail aid and conduct a far-reaching reassessment of U.S. policy was derailed when seventy-six senators signed a letter sponsored by AIPAC demanding that Ford remain "responsive" to Israel's economic and military needs. With their ability to reduce U.S. aid effectively blocked, Ford and Kissinger had little choice but to resume "step-by-step" diplomacy and try to gain Israeli concessions by offering additional inducements.[80]

President Jimmy Carter was similarly upset by Israeli Prime Minister Menachem Begin's failure to implement the full terms of the 1978 Camp David Accords (the breakthrough agreement that created the framework for the subsequent peace treaty between Egypt and Israel), but he never tried to link U.S. assistance to Israeli compliance.[81] Clinton administration officials were equally frustrated when Prime Ministers Netanyahu and Barak did not live up to all of Israel's commitments in the Oslo agreements, and Clinton was reportedly "furious" when Barak reneged on a commitment to transfer three Jerusalem villages to Palestinian control, declaring that Barak was making him a "false prophet" in the eyes of another foreign leader, Yasser Arafat. Clinton also erupted when Barak tried to shift ground during the 2000 Camp David Summit, telling him, "I can't go see Arafat with a retrenchment! You can sell it; there is no way I can. This is not real. This is not serious."[82] Yet Clinton did not react to these maneuvers by threatening to withhold support.

To be sure, America has occasionally withheld aid temporarily in order to express displeasure over particular Israeli actions, but such gestures are usually symbolic and short-lived, and have little lasting effect on Israeli conduct. In 1977, for example, Israel used U.S. armored personnel carriers to intervene in southern Lebanon (a step that violated both the Arms Export Control Act requirement that U.S. arms be used only for "legitimate self defense" and Prime Minister Menachem Begin's pledge to take no action in Lebanon without first consulting Washington) and then denied having done so. After sophisticated intelligence information exposed Israel's deception, the Carter administration threatened to terminate future military shipments and Begin ordered that the equipment be withdrawn.[83]

A similar example is the Reagan administration's decision to suspend the 1981 memorandum of understanding on strategic cooperation following Israel's de facto annexation of the Golan Heights, but Reagan later implemented the key provisions of the agreement even though Israel never reversed the annexation. The United States also halted shipments of cluster munitions after Israel violated prior agreements regarding their use during the 1982 invasion of Lebanon, but began supplying them again in 1988.[84] U.S. pressure also helped persuade Israel not to conduct a full-fledged assault on the PLO forces that had taken refuge in Beirut after Israel's 1982 invasion, but Israel's leaders were themselves reluctant to take this step and thus did not need much convincing.[85]

In 1991, the first Bush administration pressured the Shamir government to stop building settlements and to attend a planned peace conference by withholding the $10 billion loan guarantee, but the suspension lasted only a few months and the guarantees were approved once Yitzhak Rabin replaced Shamir as prime minister.[86] Israel agreed to halt construction of new settlements but continued to expand the existing blocs, and the number of settlers in the Occupied Territories increased by 8,000 (14.7 percent) in 1991, by 6,900 (10.3 percent) in 1993, by 6,900 (9.7 percent) in 1994, and by 7,300 (9.1 percent) in 1996, rates significantly higher than Israel's overall population growth during these years.[87]

A similar episode occurred in 2003, when the second Bush administration tried to signal its opposition to Israel's "security wall" in the West Bank by making a token reduction in U.S. loan guarantees to Israel. Withholding the entire guarantee or reducing direct foreign aid might have had an effect, but Bush merely withheld a portion of the loan guarantee equivalent to the estimated costs of those portions of the wall that were encroaching on Palestinian lands. Israel simply had to pay a higher interest rate on a small portion of its loan, a penalty amounting to a few million dollars. When compared to the billions of dollars of U.S. aid that Israel already gets (and expects to get in the future), this was barely a slap on the wrist. It had no discernible effect on Israel's behavior.

DIPLOMATIC PROTECTION AND WARTIME SUPPORT

In addition to these tangible forms of economic and military aid, the United States provides Israel with consistent diplomatic support. Between 1972 and 2006, Washington vetoed forty-two UN Security Council resolutions that were critical of Israel. That number is greater than the combined total of all the vetoes cast by all the other Security Council members for the same period and amounts to slightly more than half of all American vetoes during these years.[88] There were also numerous resolutions focusing on Israel that never reached a vote in the Security Council due to the threat of an American veto. In 2002, U.S. Ambassador to the UN John Negroponte reportedly told a closed meeting of the Security Council that the United States would henceforth veto any resolutions condemning Israel that did not simultaneously condemn terrorism in general and specifically mention Islamic Jihad, Hamas, and the al-Aqsa Martyrs Brigade by name.[89] The United States has voted to censure Israel on a few occasions, but only after particularly egregious Israeli actions, when the resolution in question offered only mild criticisms, or when Washington wanted to communicate a degree of displeasure with Israeli intransigence.[90]

Outside the Security Council, the United States routinely backs Israel whenever the UN General Assembly passes one of the many resolutions condemning Israeli behavior or calling for action on behalf of the Palestinians. Although these resolutions are nonbinding and largely symbolic, Washington's stance often puts it at odds with most of its allies and in the company of a tiny handful of other states. To take a typical example, UN General Assembly Resolution 59/124, on "Israeli Practices Affecting the Human Rights of the Palestinian People," passed by a vote of 149–7 (with 22 abstaining and 13 nonvoting) on December 10, 2004. Among the many nations supporting the resolution were Japan, Germany, France, China, and Great Britain. The six countries that joined with the United States to oppose the resolution were Israel, Australia, the Marshall Islands, Micronesia, Nauru, and Palau.[91]

Similarly, when Arab countries have tried to raise the issue of Israel's undeclared nuclear arsenal within the International Atomic Energy Agency, Washington has stepped in to prevent the organization from placing the matter on its agenda. As Israeli foreign ministry spokesman Jonathan Peled told the Jewish newspaper *Forward* in 2003, "The Arabs do this every year, but in order to have a comprehensive debate amid a consensus on a resolution against Israel, you need the okay of the board of governors [of the IAEA] and you don't have it" due to Washington's influence on the board.[92]

America's willingness to take Israel's side in diplomacy and war has increased significantly over time. During the 1950s, as previously noted, the Eisenhower administration forced Israel to withdraw from the territory it had seized during the Suez War, and they successfully halted unilateral Israeli attempts to divert key water resources. Since the early 1960s, however, the United States has become more committed to protecting Israel's interests during major confrontations and in the subsequent negotiations. Washington has not given Jerusalem everything it wanted, but U.S. support has been consistent and considerable.

When an escalating series of clashes between Israel and Syria in 1966–67 led Egyptian President Gamal Abdel Nasser to order troops back into the Sinai in May, alarming Israel's leaders and raising the danger of a wider war, the Johnson administration was nonetheless convinced that Israel was militarily superior to its Arab adversaries and exaggerating the danger of an Arab attack.[93] General Earle Wheeler, chairman of the Joint Chiefs of Staff, informed Johnson, "Our best estimate was that if there were a war, that the Israelis would win it in five to seven days," and Johnson himself told Israel Foreign Minister Abba Eban that if Egypt attacked, "you will whip hell out of them."[94] Key Israeli leaders privately agreed with this assessment but continued to send Washington alarming reports as part of a deliberate campaign to elicit sympathy and support.[95]

Based on its own appraisals, the United States tried to prevent the outbreak of war by convincing the Israeli government to refrain from using force and to pursue a diplomatic solution.[96] President Johnson called Egypt's decision to close the Straits of Tiran to Israeli shipping on May 26 "illegal" and was sympathetic to Israel's concerns, but he did not want to commit U.S. forces in light of American involvement in Vietnam and refused to make a blanket pledge to come to Israel's aid. His efforts to restrain Israel gradually softened, however, and by the first week of June, Johnson and several of his advisers were hinting to Israeli officials that the United States would not object if Israel acted, cautioning that they should not expect U.S. help if things went badly. Secretary of State Dean Rusk told a journalist that "I don't think it is our business to restrain anyone," and Michael Brecher reports that by June 3, "the perceived [Israeli] impression was that, if Israel took the initiative . . . the United States would not take an unfriendly view." In effect, Johnson gave the Israelis what one expert later called a "yellow light" for an attack.[97] The reasons for Johnson's shift remain obscure, although pressure from several pro-Israel friends and advisers, a letter-writing campaign organized by the Israeli embassy, and the growing sense that Israel was going to strike anyway may all have played a role.[98]

The United States did not put significant pressure on Israel to halt the fighting until it had emerged victorious and did not criticize Israel's action after the war. Indeed, when the Soviet Union threatened to intervene following Israel's occupation of the Golan Heights (which threatened Syria, the Soviets' ally), the president ordered the U.S. Sixth Fleet to move closer to Israel in order to deter Soviet interference. In sharp contrast with the 1956 Suez War, the Johnson administration made it clear there would be no American pressure for an Israeli withdrawal except in the context of a broader peace agreement.[99] Nor did the United States insist on a full and complete accounting of the tragic attack on the reconnaissance ship USS *Liberty* by Israeli naval and air forces on June 8, an event whose origins remain contested.[100] The United States may not have given Israel the diplomatic and military protection it originally sought at the onset of the crisis, but there was no doubt where America's sympathies lay.

The United States tilted even more strongly toward Israel during the 1969–70 War of Attrition. Aid to Israel increased during the fighting, consistent with Nixon and Kissinger's belief that steadfast support for Israel would reveal the limited value of Soviet aid and eventually convince Moscow's Arab clients to realign with the United States. Although the Nixon administration did not give Israel all the weapons it asked for, which occasionally led to sharp exchanges between the two governments, the United States did provide increased arms supplies while doing relatively little to encourage Israeli concessions in the various peace talks that occurred during this period. When the escalating violence raised new fears of a possible superpower confrontation, however, Washington took the lead in arranging a cease-fire and persuaded Israel to accept it by promising significant aid increases.[101] A memorandum of understanding in 1972 committed the United States to provide planes and tanks on a long-term basis, and Nixon and Kissinger pledged to consult Israel before offering any new peace proposals. By doing so, one of the world's two superpowers had in effect given a small country a quasi veto over subsequent diplomatic initiatives. By the early 1970s, writes William Quandt, "United States Middle East policy consisted of little more than open support for Israel," and Israeli Foreign Minister Abba Eban later termed this period the "golden age" in U.S. arms supplies.[102]

U.S. support was even more dramatic during the October War in 1973. Nixon and Kissinger were initially confident that Israel would win a quick victory and believed that America's postwar leverage would be maximized if its support for Israel was not too overt and Israel did not win too decisively. As Kissinger recounts in his memoirs, "If Israel won overwhelmingly—as we first expected—we had to avoid becoming the focal point of all Arab resentments. We had to keep the Soviet Union from emerging as the Arabs' savior . . . If the unexpected happened and Israel was in difficulty, we would have to do what was necessary to save it."[103] Given these expectations and strategic objectives, the United States responded slowly to Israel's initial requests for help. When Israel encountered unexpected difficulties and began running short of critical military supplies, however, Nixon and Kissinger ordered a full-scale airlift of vital military equipment, paid for with a $2.2 billion grant of supplemental military aid.[104] Although the tide of battle had already turned before significant U.S. aid arrived, the assistance boosted Israel's morale and helped seal its victory.[105] Unfortunately for the United States, the resupply effort also triggered an Arab oil embargo and production decrease that quickly sent world oil prices soaring and imposed significant economic costs on the United States and its allies.

Within certain limits, U.S. diplomacy during the war favored Israel: the United States helped convince King Hussein of Jordan to remain on the sidelines, and Kissinger handled the cease-fire negotiations (most notably his talks with Soviet leaders in Moscow on October 21) with an eye toward preserving Israel's freedom of action until the final stages of the war. Nixon had instructed Kissinger to tell Soviet General Secretary Leonid Brezhnev that the United States "wanted to use the war to impose a comprehensive peace in the Middle East," but in Moscow Kissinger successfully pressed for a simple cease-fire that would leave Israel with the upper hand and facilitate subsequent efforts to exclude the Soviet Union from the peace process. According to the historian Kenneth Stein, "The American-compiled minutes of the three meetings that Kissinger attended with Brezhnev unequivocally show that he accurately and repeatedly represented Israeli interests to Moscow, almost totally contrary to Nixon's preferences." Israel's leaders resented what they saw as Soviet-American collusion to author a cease-fire, but as Stein notes, "Kissinger, while not representing Israel to the Kremlin, certainly presented Israel's concerns."[106]

When the Security Council passed a cease-fire resolution on October 22, calling for an end to all fighting within twelve hours, Kissinger permitted Israel to violate it in order to consolidate its military position. He had previously told Israeli Ambassador Simcha Dinitz that Israel would be "well-advised" to use the time afforded by his trip to Moscow to complete its military operations, and according to the National Security Archive, a Washington-based research group that specializes in declassified U.S. sources, "Kissinger secretly gave Israeli authorities a green light to breach [the] ceasefire agreement" in order to "buy time for Israeli military advances despite the impending ceasefire deadline."[107] When the cease-fire broke down completely and the IDF surrounded Egypt's Third Army, prompting a blunt Soviet threat to intervene with its own troops, Nixon and Kissinger ordered a worldwide military alert, issued a sharp warning to Moscow to stay out, and told the Israelis it was now time to stop the fighting.

Although there was considerable hard bargaining during the subsequent "step-by-step" diplomacy leading to the 1975 Sinai II disengagement agreement, the United States still worked to protect Israel's interests. In addition to giving Israel increased military aid, the United States pledged to "concert action" with Israel when preparing for a subsequent peace conference and gave Israel a de facto veto over PLO participation in any future peace talks. Indeed, Kissinger promised that the United States would not "recognize or negotiate" with the PLO so long as it did not recognize Israel's right to exist or accept UN Resolutions 242 and 338 (the cease-fire resolutions that ended the 1967 and 1973 wars, respectively, and called for Israel's withdrawal from occupied territories along with acknowledgment of its sovereignty and independence), a pledge that Congress codified into law in 1984.[108] According to the Israeli historian Avi Shlaim, "[Israeli Prime Minister] Rabin made it clear to Kissinger that the cabinet would not ratify the Sinai II [disengagement] agreement unless it was accompanied by an American-Israeli agreement." Shlaim terms the result-ing arrangements "an alliance with America in all but name."[109]

The United States came to Israel's aid once again following its ill-conceived invasion of Lebanon in 1982. Amid escalating violence between Israel and PLO forces in southern Lebanon, Israeli Defense Minister Ariel Sharon sought American approval for a military response intended to drive the PLO from Lebanon, eliminate Syrian influence, and bring the leader of the Lebanese Christians, Bashir Gemayel, to power. U.S. Secretary of State Alexander Haig appeared to give conditional approval for the scheme in his talks with Israeli officials—saying at one point that a hypothetical Israeli re-sponse should be swift, "like a lobotomy"—though he probably did not know the full extent of Israel's ambitions and cautioned that Israel should act only if there were, as Haig put it, an "internationally recognized provocation."[110] Israel eventually invaded in June 1982 (even though Haig's criterion had not been met), but its ambitious plan to reorder Lebanese internal politics soon went awry. Although the IDF quickly routed the PLO and Syrian forces, the PLO remnants took refuge in Beirut and the IDF could not remove them without suffering extensive casualties and causing massive harm to Leba-nese civilians. U.S. Special Envoy Philip Habib eventually negotiated a deal to end the siege and permit the PLO to withdraw, and several thousand U.S. marines were subsequently dispatched to Lebanon as part of a multinational peacekeeping force.

Gemayel's assassination in September thwarted Israel's hope of creating a pro-Israel government in Lebanon, and the IDF then allowed Christian militias to enter the Sabra and Shatila refugee camps, where they proceeded to slaughter a large number of Palestinian and Lebanese civilians, with esti-mated death tolls ranging from roughly seven hundred to more than two thou-sand.[111] Repeated efforts to end Lebanon's internal struggles and foreign occupation failed, and U.S. personnel were gradually drawn into the inten-sifying Lebanese maelstrom. A suicide bomber struck the American em-bassy in April 1983, killing sixty-three people, and a truck bomb attack on the marine barracks in October left 241 marines dead and paved the way for a complete U.S. withdrawal the following year.

Even though U.S. officials—including President Reagan himself—were upset by Israel's conduct during the war, they did not try to punish Israel for its actions. Reagan did send Israeli Prime Minister Menachem Begin a sharply worded letter on June 9, calling on him to accept a proposed cease-fire with Syria, but the IDF's objectives vis-à-vis Syria had been accom-plished by that time and it involved no great sacrifice for Israel to agree.[112]

"Despite verbal protestations and other gestures and occasional genuine irritation," notes the historian and diplomat Itamar Rabinovich, the United
States "lent Israel the political support that enabled it to proceed with the
war for an unusually long time."[113]

Indeed, instead of sanctioning Israel for invading a neighboring country,
Congress voted to give Israel an additional $250 million in military assis-
tance in December 1982, over the strong objections of both President Reagan and his new secretary of state, George P. Shultz. As Shultz later recalled:

> In early December [1982] . . . I got word that a supplement was mov-
> ing through the lame-duck session of Congress to provide a $250 mil-
> lion increase in the amount of U.S. military assistance granted to
> Israel: this in the face of Israel's invasion of Lebanon, its use of clus-
> ter bombs, and its complicity in the Sabra and Shatila massacres! We
> fought the supplement and fought it hard. President Reagan and I
> weighed in personally, making numerous calls to senators and con-
> gressmen. On December 9, I added a formal letter of opposition say-
> ing that the supplement appeared "to endorse and reward Israel's
> policies." Foreign Minister Shamir called President Reagan's oppo-
> sition "an unfriendly act" and said that "it endangers the peace
> process." The supplement sailed right by us and was approved by
> Congress as though President Reagan and I had not even been there.
> I was astonished and disheartened. This brought home to me vividly
> Israel's leverage in our Congress. I saw that I must work carefully
> with the Israelis if I was to have any handle on congressional action
> that might affect Israel and if I was to maintain congressional support
> for my efforts to make progress in the Middle East.[114]

Yet Shultz and Reagan soon followed Congress's lead: the 1981 MOU on
strategic cooperation (suspended after Israel's annexation of the Golan
Heights) was reinstated in November 1983, because key U.S. officials believed that close cooperation with Israel was the only way to influence Israel's behavior.[115]

America's tendency to side with Israel extends to peace negotiations as
well. The United States played a key role in the abortive peace efforts that
followed the Six-Day War, as well as the talks that ended the War of Attrition in 1970. The United States agreed to consult with Israel before launching further peace initiatives in 1972, and Kissinger was never able to bring
much pressure to bear on Israel during his conduct of the "step-by-step"

diplomacy that followed the October War. Kissinger complained at one point during the negotiations, "I ask Rabin to make concessions, and he says he can't because Israel is weak. So I give him more arms, and then he says he doesn't need to make concessions because Israel is strong."[116] As discussed above, the disengagement agreements between Egypt and Israel were produced primarily through pledges of additional U.S. aid and by an American commitment to station civilian monitors in the Sinai.

The same pattern can be seen in the Clinton administration's handling of the negotiations that produced the 1993 Oslo Accords and the unsuccessful attempt to reach a final status agreement in 1999–2000. There was occasional friction between Clinton administration officials and their Israeli counterparts, but the United States coordinated its positions closely with Israel and generally backed Israel's approach to the peace process, even when U.S. representatives had serious reservations about Israel's strategy.[117] According to one Israeli negotiator, Ron Pundak, a key representative in the negotiations leading to Oslo and one of the architects of the subsequent framework agreement for the final status talks at Camp David in 2000, "The traditional approach of the [U.S.] State Department . . . was to adopt the position of the Israeli Prime Minister. This was demonstrated most extremely during the Netanyahu government, when the American government seemed sometimes to be working *for* the Israeli Prime Minister, as it tried to convince (and pressure) the Palestinian side to accept Israeli offers. This American tendency was also evident during Barak's tenure."[118]

U.S. participants in the peace process have offered similar judgments. According to Robert Malley, special assistant for Arab-Israeli affairs under President Clinton and another key Camp David participant, "The [Israeli] ideas put forward at Camp David were never stated in writing . . . They generally were presented as U.S. concepts, not Israeli ones." This practice underscores the degree to which the United States was providing Israel with diplomatic help even when supposedly acting as a neutral mediator. U.S. negotiators were also constrained by the "no-surprise rule," which Malley describes as "the American commitment, if not to clear, at least to share in advance, each of its ideas with Israel. Because Barak's strategy precluded early exposure of his bottom lines to anyone (the President included), he would invoke the 'no-surprise rule' to argue against US substantive proposals he felt went too far. The US ended up (often unwittingly) presenting Israeli negotiating positions and couching them as rock-bottom red lines beyond which Israel could not go."[119] As Aaron David Miller, an adviser to six different secretaries of state on Middle East and Arab-Israeli affairs and another key player in the Clinton administration's peace effort, put it during a 2005 postmortem on the failed negotiations: "Far too often, we functioned . . . as Israel's lawyer."[120]

CONCLUSION

Since Israel's founding in 1948, many important elements of America's Middle East policy have come to center around its commitment to the Jewish state. As we shall discuss in detail in Part II, this tendency has become even more pronounced with the passage of time. To note one final sign of Israel's privileged position among U.S. allies: since 1976, six Israeli leaders have addressed joint sessions of Congress, a higher total than for any other country.[121] A trivial indicator, perhaps, but it is still striking given that these six leaders represented a country whose 2007 population was less than that of New York City.

Yitzhak Rabin was right: America's generosity toward Israel *is* "beyond compare in modern history." It has grown from modest beginnings to a "special relationship" that has no equal. As Mitchell Bard and Daniel Pipes put it, "From a comparative perspective, the United States and Israel may well have the most extraordinary tie in international politics."[122]

This support has accomplished one positive end: it has helped Israel prosper. For many people, that fact alone might justify all of the support that the United States has provided over the years. Given this record, it is no surprise that a June 2003 Pew poll found that in twenty out of twenty-one countries surveyed—including close U.S. allies like Britain, France, Canada, and Australia—either a majority or plurality of the population believes that U.S. Middle East policy "favors Israel too much." What is more surprising, perhaps, is that a plurality of Israelis (47 percent) agreed.[123]

Although the United States has derived a number of benefits from its support for Israel and from Israel's undeniable achievements, it has given far more than it has gained. This generosity would be understandable if Israel were a vital strategic asset for the United States—that is, if Israel's existence and continued growth made the United States substantially safer. It would also be easy to explain if there were a compelling moral rationale for maintaining such high levels of material aid and diplomatic backing. But this is not the case. In the next two chapters, we show that neither strategic interests nor moral imperatives can explain why the United States continues to give Israel such generous and unconstrained support.

2

ISRAEL: STRATEGIC ASSET OR LIABILITY?

America's willingness to give Israel extensive economic, military, and diplomatic support would be easy to understand if it advanced America's overall strategic interests. Generous aid to Israel might be justified, for example, if it were a cost-effective way for the United States to deal with countries that Washington had previously identified as hostile. Steadfast U.S. support might also make sense if the United States received substantial benefits in return, and if the value of these benefits exceeded the economic and political costs of U.S. support. If Israel possessed vital natural resources (such as oil or natural gas), or if it occupied a critical geographic location, then the United States might want to provide support in order to maintain good relations and keep it out of unfriendly hands. In short, aid to Israel would be easy to explain if it helped make Americans more secure or more prosperous. Israel's strategic value to the United States would be further enhanced if backing it won America additional friends around the world and did not undermine U.S. relations with other strategically important countries.

Not surprisingly, those who favor generous U.S. support for Israel routinely make these sorts of arguments. In the 1980s, for example, scholars such as Steven Spiegel and A.F.K. Organski argued that Israel had become a major strategic asset in the Cold War and claimed that generous U.S. aid was a bargain given the benefits it produced for the United States.[1] As Hyman Bookbinder, Washington representative of the American Jewish Committee, put it in 1984, "We bend over backward to help people understand that help for Israel is also in America's strategic interests."[2] Today, the American Israel Public Affairs Committee, the most influential pro-Israel lobbying organization, declares that the United States and Israel have a "deep strategic partnership aimed at confronting the common threats to both nations" and says that United States–Israel cooperation in defense and homeland security "has proven to be of paramount and ever-increasing importance."[3] The neoconservative Project for the New American Century (PNAC) calls Israel "America's staunchest ally against international terrorism," and the Jewish Institute for National Security Affairs (JINSA) says, "U.S.-Israel strategic cooperation is a vital component in the global security equation for the United States."[4] According to Martin Kramer, a research fellow at Israel's Shalem Center and at the Washington Institute for Near East Policy (WINEP), the United States backs Israel not because of "Holocaust guilt or shared democratic values," but because aid to Israel "underpins the pax Americana in the Eastern Mediterranean" and provides a "low-cost way of keeping order in part of the Middle East."[5] The Israeli strategist Efraim Inbar agrees, declaring that "the case for the continued US support of Israel as an important strategic ally due to its strategic location and political stability, as well as its technological and military assets, is very strong."[6]

The *strategic rationale* for extensive U.S. support of the Jewish state portrays this policy not as an act of charity or as a moral obligation, and certainly not as a consequence of domestic lobbying.[7] Instead, steadfast support for Israel is said to be a reflection of America's overarching strategic interests: the United States backs Israel because doing so supposedly makes all Americans safer.

In this chapter, we show that this view is at best outdated and at worst simply wrong. Backing Israel may have yielded strategic benefits in the past, but the benefits have declined sharply in recent years while the economic and diplomatic costs have increased. Instead of being a strategic asset, in fact, Israel has become a strategic liability for the United States. Backing Israel so strongly is making Americans more vulnerable—not less—and making it harder for the United States to achieve important and urgent foreign policy goals. Although there are compelling reasons for the United States to support Israel's existence and to remain committed to its survival, the current level of U.S. support and its largely unconditional nature cannot be justified on strategic grounds.

We begin by evaluating Israel's role during the Cold War, because the claim that Israel was a strategic asset is most convincing during this period. We then consider the argument that was invoked after the Soviet Union disappeared—specifically, the claim that support for Israel is justified by a common threat from international terrorism and a set of hostile "rogue states"—and we show that this claim does not provide a credible strategic rationale for unconditional U.S. support either.

HELPING CONTAIN THE SOVIET BEAR

When Israel was founded in 1948, U.S. policy makers did not consider it a strategic asset. The new state was regarded as weak and potentially vulnerable, and American policy makers recognized that embracing Israel too closely would undermine the U.S. position elsewhere in the Middle East. President Truman's decision to support the UN partition plan and to recognize Israel was based not on strategic imperatives but on his genuine sympathy for Jewish suffering, a certain religious conviction that permitting Jews to return to their ancient homeland was desirable, and an awareness that recognition was strongly backed by many American Jews and would therefore yield domestic political benefits.[8] At the same time, several of Truman's key advisers—including Secretary of State George Marshall and policy-planning head George Kennan—opposed the decision because they believed it would jeopardize U.S. relations with the Arab world and facilitate Soviet penetration of the region. As Kennan noted in an internal memorandum in 1948, "Supporting the extreme objectives of political Zionism" would be "to the detriment of overall U.S. security objectives" in the Middle East. Specifically, he argued it would increase opportunities for the Soviet Union, endanger oil concessions, and jeopardize U.S. basing rights in the region.[9]

This view had eroded by the early 1960s, and the Kennedy administration concluded that Israel deserved more support in light of growing Soviet aid to Egypt, Syria, and Iraq.[10] Israeli leaders repeatedly emphasized their potential value as an ally, and their stunning victory in the Six-Day War in 1967 strengthened these claims by offering a vivid demonstration of Israel's military prowess. As discussed in the previous chapter, Nixon and Kissinger saw increased support for Israel as an effective way to counter Soviet influence throughout the region.[11] The image of Israel as a "strategic asset" took root in the 1970s and became an article of faith by the mid-1980s.

The case for Israel's strategic value from 1967 to 1989 is straightforward. By serving as America's proxy in the Middle East, Israel helped the United States contain Soviet expansion in that important region and occasionally helped the United States handle other regional crises.[12] By inflicting humiliating military defeats on Soviet clients like Egypt and Syria in the 1967 Six-

Day War and 1973 October War, Israel also damaged Moscow's reputation as an ally while enhancing U.S. prestige. This was a key element of Nixon and Kissinger's Cold War strategy: backing Israel to the hilt would make it impossible for Egypt or Syria to regain the territory lost in 1967 and thus demonstrate the limited value of Soviet support. This strategy bore fruit in the 1970s, when Egyptian President Anwar Sadat severed ties with Moscow and realigned with the United States, a breakthrough that paved the way to the Egyptian-Israeli peace treaty in 1979. Israel's repeated victories also forced the Soviets to expend precious resources rearming their clients after each defeat, a task that the overstretched Soviet economy could ill afford.

By providing the United States with intelligence about Soviet capabilities, Soviet client states, and the Middle East more generally, Israel also facilitated the broader American campaign against the Soviet Union. In 1956, for example, an Israeli spy obtained a copy of Soviet Premier Nikita S. Khrushchev's "secret speech" denouncing Stalin, which Israel promptly passed on to the United States. In the 1960s, Israel gave U.S. defense experts access to a Soviet MiG-21 aircraft obtained from an Iraqi defector and provided similar access to Soviet equipment captured in the 1967 and 1973 wars.[13] Finally, the United States benefited from access to Israeli training facilities, advanced technology developed by Israeli defense companies, and consultations with Israeli experts on counterterrorism and other security problems.

This justification for supporting Israel is factually correct, and Israel may well have been a net strategic asset during this period. Yet the case is not as open and shut as Israel's advocates maintain and was questioned by some U.S. experts at the time.[14] Why? Because in addition to the direct economic burden, the growing partnership with Israel imposed significant costs on the United States, and because Israel's capacity to help its vastly more powerful partner was inherently limited.

First, although Israel's military did help check Soviet client states like Egypt, Syria, and Iraq, America's commitment to Israel played a significant role in pushing those states into Moscow's arms in the first place. Egypt and Syria had been engaged in a bitter conflict with Israel since the late 1940s, and they were unable to get help from Washington despite several requests. American support for Israel was nowhere near as generous as it is today, but the United States was still committed to Israel's survival and was not going to do anything to undermine its security—in particular, the United States was unwilling to provide either Egypt or Syria with weapons that might be used against the Jewish state. As a result, when an Israeli attack on an Egyptian army base in Gaza in February 1955 killed thirty-seven Egyptian soldiers and wounded another thirty-one, Egyptian President Gamal Abdel Nasser was forced to turn to the Soviet Union for arms instead. Nasser repeatedly referred to the Gaza raid as a "turning point," precipitating the first major Arab arms deal with Moscow, which made the Soviet Union a major player in Middle East affairs virtually overnight. The raid also led Nasser to shut down a secret negotiating channel with the Israeli government and to shift from modest efforts to limit Arab infiltration to active support for it.[15] Given their continuing conflict with Israel and America's reluctance to provide them with arms, Israel's main Arab adversaries had little choice but to seek help from the Soviets, despite their own misgivings about moving closer to Moscow.[16]

Second, although U.S. support for Israel put more pressure on the Soviet Union, it also fueled the Arab-Israeli conflict and inhibited progress toward a settlement, a result that continues to haunt both Israel and the United States. The Nixon/Kissinger strategy eventually succeeded in pulling Egypt out of the Soviet orbit, but the tendency to view Middle East issues primarily through the prism of the Cold War (and thus to back Israel no matter what) also led the United States to overlook several promising opportunities for peace, most notably Egyptian President Anwar Sadat's repeated signals that he was prepared to cut a deal in 1971–72.[17] Speaking to a private group in 1975, Kissinger recalled that Secretary of State William Rogers's efforts to reach an interim agreement in 1971 had broken down "over whether or not 1,000 Egyptian soldiers would be permitted across the Canal. That agreement would have prevented the 1973 War. I must say now that I am sorry that I did not support the Rogers effort more than I did."[18]

Third, the expansion and deepening of U.S.-Israeli relations in the 1960s and 1970s also contributed to the rise of anti-Americanism across the Arab and Islamic world. "At the time of World War I," notes the Rice University historian Ussama Makdisi, "the image of the United States in the Arab provinces of the Ottoman Empire was generally positive; those Arabs who knew of the country saw it as a great power that was not imperialist as Britain, France, and Russia were."[19] Even after Israel was founded, Arab resentment was limited by U.S. efforts to play an evenhanded role in the Middle East and by the fact that France, not the United States, was Israel's main arms supplier until 1967. What conflicts there were with "progressive" Arab states such as Nasser's Egypt partly reflected disagreements about Israel but also stemmed from U.S. support for conservative Middle Eastern monarchies (the shah of Iran, King Hussein of Jordan, the House of Saud), who were all deeply hostile to Nasser as well. Unfortunately for the United States, its support for these regimes (which Washington saw as "moderate" and its opponents deemed "reactionary") and for Israel fueled a growing tendency for many Arabs to see it as the heir to Britain's former imperial role.[20]

Arab animosity increased as U.S. support for Israel grew and was compounded by Israel's occupation of the West Bank, Sinai, Gaza, and the Golan Heights in 1967 and by its subsequent repression of the Palestinian Arabs living in what came to be known as the Occupied Territories. During the Cold War, this situation made some Middle Eastern regimes more interested in close ties with the Soviet Union and further reduced U.S. influence. It also contributed to the rise of Arab and Islamic extremism, as some prescient analysts had predicted two decades ago. Writing in 1985–86, for example, Harry Shaw, former head of the Office of Management and Budget's Military Assistance Branch, warned that "Israel's settlement policy on the West Bank is at cross-purposes with U.S. interests and contrary to U.S. policy. The lack of progress toward a peace settlement—for which Israel and its Arab neighbors share responsibility—undercuts Arabs who are willing to live in peace and strengthens the influence of Islamic fundamentalists and other Arabs who have no interest in the kind of stable Middle East that would be compatible with U.S. interests and Israel's security."[21] America's relations with the Arab and Islamic world would hardly have been perfect were Israel not a U.S. ally, but a more evenhanded approach would have smoothed one important source of friction. This basic fact was not lost on the Israeli military leader and politician Moshe Dayan, whose memoirs contain a revealing account of a talk he had with Kissinger at the time of the 1973 October War. "Though I happened to remark that the United States was the only country that was ready to stand by us," wrote Dayan, "my silent reflection was that the United States would really rather support the Arabs."[22]

Support for Israel imposed additional costs on the United States, such as the Arab oil embargo and production decrease during the October War. The decision to use the "oil weapon" was a direct response to Nixon's decision to provide Israel with $2.2 billion of emergency military assistance during the war, and it ultimately did significant damage to the U.S. economy. The embargo and production decrease cost the United States some $48.5 billion in 1974 alone (equal to roughly $140 billion in 2000 dollars), due to higher petroleum costs and an estimated 2 percent reduction in GDP. The oil crisis also led to serious strains in America's relations with key allies in Europe and Asia.[23] Helping Israel defeat two Soviet clients may have been a positive development in terms of America's broader Cold War concerns, but the United States paid a high price for the victory.

Israel's other Cold War contributions were useful, but their strategic value should not be overstated. Israel did indeed provide the United States with helpful intelligence, for instance, but there is no evidence that Jerusalem gave Washington information that decisively altered the course of the superpower competition or enabled America to inflict a decisive blow against its Communist adversary. The primary benefit seems to have been access to captured Soviet weapons and to data regarding their battlefield performance, as well as debriefings from Soviet Jews who had immigrated to Israel. The United States used this information to help develop weapons and tactics that would have been valuable had the superpowers ever come to blows, and this information has undoubtedly helped the United States when it has fought former Soviet clients such as Iraq. But Iraq was a third-rate military power and the United States scarcely needed much help to defeat Saddam in 1991 or to oust him in 2003. Access to Israeli training facilities and consultations with Israeli experts were also useful and appreciated, but these arrangements were never essential to the development of American military power or to its ultimate triumph over the Soviet Union.

In fact, Israeli "assistance" was sometimes of dubious value. One former CIA official reports being "appalled at the lack of quality of the [Israeli] political intelligence on the Arab world . . . Their tactical military intelligence was first-rate. But they didn't know their enemy. I saw this political intelligence and it was lousy, laughably bad . . . It was gossip stuff mostly."[24] Israel also provided the United States with faulty or misleading intelligence on several occasions, probably in order to encourage the United States to take actions that Israel wanted. Prior to the Six-Day War, for example, Israeli intelligence assessments painted a grim and frightening picture of Egyptian capabilities and intentions, which American intelligence officials believed was both incorrect and politically motivated. As National Security Adviser W. W. Rostow told President Johnson, "We do not believe that the Israeli appreciation presented . . . was a serious estimate of the sort they would submit to their own high officials. We think it is probably a gambit intended to influence the US to do one or more of the following: (a) provide military supplies, (b) make more public commitments to Israel, (c) approve Israeli military initiatives, and (d) put more pressure on Nasser."[25] As we discuss in greater detail in Chapter 8, Israel also supplied the United States with alarmist reports about Iraq's weapons of mass destruction programs prior to the 2003 invasion, thereby contributing to U.S. miscalculations about the actual danger that Saddam Hussein presented.[26]

Nor has Israel been a reliable proxy safeguarding other U.S. interests in the region. When Martin Kramer claims that "American support for Israel . . . underpins the pax Americana in the Eastern Mediterranean" and has been a "low cost way of keeping order in part of the Middle East," he both exaggerates the benefits of this relationship and understates the costs.[27] Stability in the eastern Mediterranean is desirable, but the region is not a vital U.S. strategic interest, in sharp contrast to the oil-rich Persian Gulf. And if Israel's strategic value derives from its role enforcing the "pax Americana" in this region, then it has not been doing a particularly good job. Its invasion of Lebanon in 1982 made the region less stable and led directly to the formation of Hezbollah, the militant group that many believe is responsible for the devastating attacks on the U.S. embassy and marine barracks that cost more than 250 American lives. The suicide bombers are to blame for these deaths, but the loss of life was part of the price the United States had to pay in order to clean up the situation that Israel had created. Israel's prolonged campaign to colonize the West Bank and Gaza (indirectly subsidized by U.S. aid and undertaken in part with U.S.-made weapons) has also produced two major uprisings in which thousands of Palestinians and Israelis have been killed. Thus, Kramer seriously overstates Israel's value as a low-cost "regional stabilizer."

Israel's limited strategic value is further underscored by its inability to contribute to an undeniable U.S. interest: access to Persian Gulf oil. Despite Israel's vaunted military prowess, the United States could not count on its help during the Cold War to deter a direct Soviet assault on Western oil supplies or to protect them in the event of a regional war. As Harry Shaw noted in the mid-1980s, "Some Israeli officials explicitly reject Israeli engagement of Soviet ground forces beyond their country's immediate defense . . . These Israelis acknowledge as far-fetched the notion that Israeli divisions would advance beyond Israel's borders to meet a Soviet thrust toward the Persian Gulf."[28] According to a former Pentagon official, "Israel's strategic value to the United States was always grotesquely exaggerated. When we were drafting contingency plans for the Middle East in the 1980s, we found that the Israelis were of little value to us in 95 percent of the cases."[29]

As a result, when the shah of Iran fell in 1979, raising concerns about a possible Soviet invasion, the United States had to create its own Rapid Deployment Force (RDF) to counter that threat and arrange for basing rights and preposition war matériel in various Arab countries. The Pentagon could not count on Israel to deter the Soviet Union by itself and could not use Israel as a forward base—Israeli offers notwithstanding—because doing so would have caused political problems in the Arab world and made it even harder to keep the Soviets out of the region. As Shaw remarked in 1986, "The notion of using Israel as a platform for projecting U.S. forces into Arab states . . . is not widely supported outside Israel. Arab analysts argue that an Arab regime that accepted American help funneled through Israel would be discredited with its own people and therefore would be more likely to fall . . . U.S. officials also are skeptical of the feasibility of using Israeli bases. The Israeli offers may be designed primarily to entice the United States into closer relations and to enhance the rationale for more U.S. aid without requirements for specific Israeli commitments."[30] Israel's limited capacity to help in the Gulf was revealed in the late 1980s, when the Iran-Iraq War jeopardized the safety of oil shipments in the Persian Gulf. The United States and several of its European allies reinforced their naval forces in the region, began escorting oil tankers, and eventually attacked some Iranian patrol boats, but Israel had no part to play in these operations.[31]

Ultimately, although a limited case can be made for Israel's strategic value during the Cold War, it does not fully explain why the United States provided it with so much economic, military, and diplomatic support. It is easy to understand why the United States devoted billions to defending its NATO allies—Europe was a key center of industrial power that had to be kept out of Soviet hands—and equally easy to grasp the strategic motivation behind U.S. support for oil-rich countries like Saudi Arabia, despite sharply contrasting political values. In Israel's case, however, this sort of obvious strategic imperative was never as clear. Henry Kissinger may have used U.S. aid to Israel as a way to drive a wedge between Moscow and Cairo, but he admitted privately that "Israeli strength does not prevent the spread of communism in the Arab world . . . So it is difficult to claim that a strong Israel serves American interests because it prevents the spread of communism in the Arab world. It does not. It provides for the survival of Israel."[32] Ronald Reagan may have called Israel a "strategic asset" when he was campaigning for president in 1980, but he did not mention Israel's strategic value in his memoirs and referred instead to various moral considerations to explain his support for the Jewish state.[33]

Thoughtful Israeli analysts have long recognized this basic reality. As the Israeli strategic expert Shai Feldman, former head of Tel Aviv University's Jaffe Center for Strategic Studies, noted in his own study of U.S.-Israeli security cooperation, "The strategic dimension of America's motivation for supporting Israel never comprised the core of these relations. Rather, this dimension received growing emphasis in the 1980s as Israel's American supporters sought to base U.S.-Israel relations on grounds that would be more appealing to Republican administrations. Yet, the significance of U.S.-Israel strategic cooperation and the extent to which Israel is perceived as a strategic asset to the United States never approached that of the other elements in the U.S.-Israel relationship." Those "other elements," according to Feldman, were post-Holocaust sympathy, shared political values, Israel's underdog image, common cultural linkages, and "the role of the Jewish community in American politics."[34]

FROM THE COLD WAR TO 9/11

Even if Israel was a valuable ally during the Cold War, that justification ended when the Soviet Union collapsed. According to the Middle East historian Bernard Lewis (himself a prominent supporter of Israel), "Whatever value Israel might have had as a strategic asset during the Cold War, that value obviously ended when the Cold War itself came to a close." The political scientist Bernard Reich of George Washington University, the author of several books on U.S.-Israeli relations, drew a similar conclusion in 1995, noting that "Israel is of limited military or economic importance to the United States . . . It is not a strategically vital state." The Brandeis University defense expert Robert Art made the same point in 2003, noting that "Israel has little strategic value to the United States and is in many ways a strategic liability."[35] As the Cold War receded into history, Israel's declining strategic value became hard to miss.

In fact, the Gulf War in 1991 provided evidence that Israel was becoming a strategic burden. The United States and its allies eventually assembled more than four hundred thousand troops to liberate Kuwait, but they could not use Israeli bases or allow the IDF to participate without jeopardizing the fragile coalition against Iraq. And when Saddam fired Scud missiles into Israel in the hope of provoking an Israeli response that would fracture the coalition, Washington had to divert resources (such as Patriot missile batteries) to defend Israel and to keep it on the sidelines. Israel was not to blame for this situation, of course, but it illustrates the extent to which it was becoming a liability rather than an asset. As William Waldegrave, minister of state in the British Foreign Office, told the House of Commons, the United States might now be learning that a strategic alliance with Israel "was not particularly useful if it cannot be used in a crisis such as this." This point was not lost on Bernard Lewis, either, who wrote, "The change [in Israel's strategic value] was clearly manifested in the Gulf War . . . when what the United States most desired from Israel was to keep out of the conflict—to be silent, inactive, and, as far as possible, invisible . . . Israel was not an asset, but an irrelevance—some even said a nuisance."[36]

One might think that the shared threat from international terrorism provided a powerful rationale for United States–Israel cooperation in the immediate aftermath of the Cold War, but this is not the case. The Oslo peace process was under way during most of the 1990s, and Palestinian terrorist attacks against Israel were declining, from 67 killed and 167 injured in 1994 to only 1 dead and only 12 injured in 2000. (Israeli casualties rose again after Oslo collapsed, with 110 Israelis killed and 918 injured in 2001 and 320 killed and 1,498 injured in 2002.)[37] U.S. policy makers were becoming more concerned about Islamic terrorism—including al Qaeda—especially after the failed attempt to blow up the World Trade Center in 1993, the attacks on the Khobar Towers housing complex in Saudi Arabia in 1996, the bombing of American embassies in Kenya and Tanzania in 1998, and the attack on the USS *Cole* in Yemen in 1999. A number of new initiatives to deal with the problem were under way, but terrorism was still not widely perceived as a mortal threat and the U.S. "global war on terror" did not begin in earnest until after September 11, 2001.[38]

Similarly, although both Israel and the United States were worried about "rogue states" such as Iraq, Iran, Libya, and Syria during this period, these states were too weak to pose a serious threat to the United States itself. Consider that the *combined* population of these four states in 2000 was less than 40 percent of America's; their combined GDP was barely more than 5 percent of U.S. GDP, and their combined military spending equaled a scant 3 percent of the U.S. defense budget.[39] Iraq was subject to a punishing UN embargo, weapons inspectors were busy dismantling its WMD programs, and Iran's own WMD efforts were not far advanced. Syria, Iran, and Iraq were often at odds with each other, which made containing these states even easier and reduced the need to try to overthrow them.

Instead, the United States adopted a policy of "dual containment" toward Iran and Iraq and made a serious but unsuccessful attempt to broker a final peace treaty between Syria and Israel.[40] It also engaged in a protracted and ultimately successful effort to persuade Libya to give up its WMD programs and compensate the families of the victims of the Pan Am Flight 103 bombing, a campaign waged through economic sanctions and patient multilateral diplomacy.[41] Israel's capabilities were not needed to accomplish these objectives, because the United States could deal with these states by itself.

In other words, Israel was not seen as a prized ally because U.S. policy makers believed its help was essential for dealing with these so-called rogue states. Rather, Washington worried about these states in good part because it was already committed to protecting Israel. With respect to Iran, for example, the main points of contention between Tehran and Washington were Iran's opposition to the Camp David peace process, its support for Hezbollah, and its efforts to develop WMD. The importance of these issues was magnified substantially by the existing U.S. relationship with Israel.[42] Washington did have interests in the region that were unrelated to Israel, of course—such as its desire to prevent any single state from dominating the Gulf and thereby ensure access to oil—and its pursuit of these interests occasionally led to friction with some states in the region. In particular, the United States would have undoubtedly opposed Iran's WMD efforts even if Israel had never existed. But the U.S. commitment to Israel made these issues seem even more urgent, without making them easier to address.

Until September 11, 2001, the danger from terrorism and problems posed by these various rogue states did not provide a compelling strategic rationale for unconditional U.S. support of the Jewish state. These concerns explain why Israel wanted help from the United States but cannot account for America's willingness to provide that help as generously as it did.

"PARTNERS AGAINST TERROR": THE NEW RATIONALE

In the aftermath of the September 11 terrorist attacks, the main strategic justification behind U.S. support for Israel became the claim that the two states were now "partners against terror." This new rationale depicts the United States and Israel as threatened by the same terrorist groups and by a set of rogue states that back these groups and seek to acquire WMD. Their hostility to Israel and the United States is said to be due to a fundamental antipathy to the West's Judeo-Christian values, its culture, and its democratic institutions. In other words, they hate Americans for "what we are," not for "what we do." In the same way, they hate Israel because it is also Western, modern, and democratic, and not because it has occupied Arab land, including important Islamic holy sites, and oppressed an Arab population.

The implications of the new rationale are obvious: support for Israel plays no role in America's terrorism problem or the growing anti-Americanism in the Arab and Islamic world, and ending the Israeli-Palestinian conflict or making U.S. support for Israel more selective or conditional would not help. Washington should therefore give Israel a free hand in dealing with the Palestinians and groups like Hezbollah. In addition, Washington should not press Israel to make concessions (such as dismantling settlements in the

Occupied Territories) until all Palestinian terrorists are imprisoned, repentant, or dead. Instead, the United States should continue to provide Israel with extensive support and use its own power and resources to go after countries like the Islamic Republic of Iran, Saddam Hussein's Iraq, Bashar al-Assad's Syria, and other countries believed to be supporting terrorists.

Instead of seeing Israel as a major source of America's troubled relationship with the Arab and Islamic world, this new rationale portrays Israel as a key ally in the global "war on terror." Why? Because its enemies are said to be America's enemies. As Ariel Sharon put it during a visit to the United States in late 2001, after the horrific attacks on the World Trade Center and Pentagon: "You in America are in a war against terror. We in Israel are in a war against terror. It's the same war." According to a senior official in the first Bush administration, "Sharon played the president like a violin: 'I'm fighting your war, terrorism is terrorism' and so on."[43] Former Prime Minister Benjamin Netanyahu told the U.S. Senate in 2002, "If we do not immediately shut down the terror factories where Arafat is producing human bombs, it is only a matter of time before suicide bombers will terrorize your cities. If not destroyed, this madness will strike in your buses, in your supermarkets, in your pizza parlors, in your cafes." Netanyahu also published an op-ed in the *Chicago Sun-Times* declaring, "No grievance, real or imagined, can ever justify terror . . . American power topples the Taliban regime in Afghanistan, and the al-Qaida network there crumbles on its own. The United States must now act similarly against the other terror regimes—Iran, Iraq, Yasser Arafat's dictatorship, Syria, and a few others."[44] His successor, Ehud Barak, repeated this theme in an op-ed in the *Times* of London, declaring, "The world's governments know exactly who the terrorists are and exactly which rogue states support and promote their activity. Countries like Iran, Iraq, Libya, Sudan and North Korea have a proven track-record of sponsoring terrorism, while no one needs reminding of the carnage wrought by the terrorist thugs of Hamas, Hezbollah, Islamic Jihad, and even Yassir Arafat's own PLO."[45] Prime Minister Ehud Olmert struck the same note in his own address to Congress in 2006, declaring, "Our countries do not just share the experience and pain of terrorism. We share the commitment and resolve to confront the brutal terrorists that took these innocent people from us."[46]

Israel's American supporters offer essentially the same justification. In October 2001, WINEP's executive director, Robert Satloff, explained why the United States should continue to back Israel after September 11: "The answer should be clear, given the democratic values we share and the common enemies we face . . . No country has suffered more from the same sort of terrorism that hit the World Trade Center and the Pentagon than Israel."[47] Senator Charles Schumer (D-NY) declared in December 2001 that "the PLO is the same as the Taliban, which aids, abets and provides safe haven for terrorists. And Israel is like America, simply trying to protect its homefront . . . Arafat is to Israel as Mullah Mohammed [Omar] is to America."[48] In April and May 2002, Congress passed by overwhelming margins (352–21 in the House, 94–2 in the Senate) two nearly identical resolutions declaring that "the United States and Israel are now engaged in a common struggle against terrorism."[49] The official theme of the 2002 AIPAC annual conference was "America and Israel Standing Against Terror," and the conference presentations emphasized the shared threat from Yasser Arafat, Osama bin Laden, Saddam Hussein, the Taliban, Hamas, Hezbollah, Iran, and Syria.[50] PNAC made the same point in an open letter to President Bush in April 2002, signed by William Kristol, Richard Perle, William Bennett, Daniel Pipes, James Woolsey, Eliot Cohen, Norman Podhoretz, and twenty-eight others, most of them prominent neoconservatives. It declared, "No one should doubt that the United States and Israel share a common enemy. We are both targets of what you [Bush] have correctly called an 'Axis of Evil' . . . As Secretary of Defense Rumsfeld has pointed out, Iran, Iraq, and Syria are all engaged in 'inspiring and financing a culture of political murder and suicide bombing' against Israel, just as they have aided campaigns of terrorism against the United States . . . You have declared war on international terrorism, Mr. President. Israel is fighting the same war."[51]

This new justification has a certain prima facie plausibility, and it is not surprising that many Americans equate what happened on September 11 with attacks on Israelis. Upon further inspection, however, the "partners against terror" rationale unravels almost completely, especially as a justification for unconditional U.S. support. Viewed objectively, Israel is a liability in both the "war on terror" and in the broader effort to deal with so-called rogue states.

To begin with, the new strategic rationale depicts "terrorism" as a single, unified phenomenon, thereby suggesting that Palestinian suicide bombers are as much a threat to the United States as they are to Israel itself, and that the terrorists who attacked America on September 11 are part of a well-organized global movement that is also targeting Israel. But this claim rests on a fundamental misconception of what terrorism is. Terrorism is not an organization or a movement or even an "enemy" that one can declare war on; terrorism is simply the tactic of indiscriminately attacking enemy targets— especially civilians—in order to sow fear, undermine morale, and provoke counterproductive reactions from one's adversary. It is a tactic that many different groups sometimes employ, usually when they are much weaker than their adversaries and have no other good option for fighting against superior military forces. Zionists used terrorism when they were trying to drive the British out of Palestine and establish their own state—for example, by bombing the King David Hotel in Jerusalem in 1946 and assassinating UN mediator Folke Bernadotte in 1948, among other acts—and the United States has backed a number of "terrorist" organizations in the past (including the Nicaraguan contras and the UNITA guerrillas in Angola). American presidents have also welcomed a number of former terrorists to the White House (including PLO chairman Yasser Arafat, and Israeli Prime Ministers Menachem Begin and Yitzhak Shamir, who played key roles in the main Zionist terror organizations), which merely underscores the fact that terrorism is a tactic and not a unified movement. Clarifying this issue in no way justifies attacks on innocent people—which is always morally reprehensible—but it reminds us that groups that employ this method of struggle do not always threaten vital U.S. interests and that the United States has sometimes actively supported such groups.

In contrast to al Qaeda, in fact, the terrorist organizations that threaten Israel (such as Hamas, Islamic Jihad, and Hezbollah) do not attack the United States and do not pose a mortal threat to America's core security interests. With respect to Hezbollah, for example, the Hebrew University historian Moshe Maoz observes that it "is mostly a threat against Israel. They did attack U.S. targets when there were American troops in Lebanon, but they killed to oust foreign forces from Lebanon. I doubt very much whether Hezbollah will go out of its way to attack America." The Middle East expert Patrick Seale agrees: "Hezbollah is a purely local phenomenon directed purely at the Israelis," and the terrorism experts Daniel Benjamin and Steven Simon echo this view with respect to Hamas, noting, "Thus far, Hamas has not targeted Americans."[52] We may believe that all terrorist acts are morally wrong, but from the perspective of U.S. strategic interests, not all terrorists are alike.

There is no convincing evidence linking Osama bin Laden and his inner circle to the various Palestinian terrorist groups, and most Palestinian terrorists do not share al Qaeda's desire to launch a global Islamic restoration or restore the caliphate. In fact, the PLO was secular and nationalist—not Islamist—and it is only in the last decade or so, as the occupation has ground on, that many Palestinians have become more attracted to Islamist ideas. Nor are their activities—however heinous and deplorable—simply random violence directed against Israel or the West. Instead, Palestinian terrorism has always been directed solely at their perceived grievances against Israel, beginning with resistance to the original Zionist influx and continuing after the expulsion of much of the Palestinian population in the 1948 war. Today, these actions are largely a response to Israel's prolonged campaign to colonize the West Bank and Gaza Strip and a reflection of the Palestinians' own weakness. These territories contained few Jews when Israel captured them in 1967, but Israel spent the next forty years colonizing them with settlements, road networks, and military bases, while brutally suppressing Palestinian attempts to resist these encroachments.[53] Not surprisingly, Palestinian resistance has frequently employed terrorism, which is usually how subject populations strike back at powerful occupiers.[54] And while groups like Hamas have yet to publicly accept Israel's existence, we should not forget that Yasser Arafat and the rest of the PLO did, and that Palestinian President Mahmoud Abbas has reiterated that commitment on numerous occasions.

More important, claiming that Israel and the United States are united by a shared terrorist threat has the causal relationship backward. The United States did not form an alliance with Israel because it suddenly realized that it faced a serious danger from "global terrorism" and urgently needed Israel's help to defeat it. In fact, the United States has a terrorism problem in good part because it has long been so supportive of Israel. It is hardly headline news to observe that U.S. backing for Israel is unpopular elsewhere in the Middle East—that has been true for several decades—but many people may not realize how much America's one-sided policies have cost it over the years. Not only have these policies helped inspire al Qaeda, but they have also facilitated its recruitment efforts and contributed to growing anti-Americanism throughout the region.

Of course, those who believe that Israel is still a valuable strategic asset often deny that there was any connection between U.S. support for Israel and the terrorism problem, and especially not the September 11 attacks. They claim that Osama bin Laden seized on the plight of the Palestinians only recently, and only because he realized it was good for recruiting purposes. Thus, WINEP's Robert Satloff claims that bin Laden's identification with Palestine is "a recent—and almost surely opportunistic—phenomenon," and Alan Dershowitz declares, "Prior to September 11, Israel was barely on bin Laden's radar screen." Dennis Ross suggests that bin Laden was merely "trying to gain legitimacy by implying that his attack on America was about the plight of the Palestinians," and Martin Kramer says he knows of no "unbiased terrorism expert" who believes that "American support for Israel is the source of popular resentment, propelling recruits to al Qaeda." The former *Commentary* editor

Norman Podhoretz likewise argues that "if Israel had never come into existence, or if it were magically to disappear, the United States would still stand
as an embodiment of everything that most of these Arabs consider evil."[55]

It is not surprising that some of Israel's defenders offer such claims, because acknowledging that U.S. support for Israel has fueled anti-American
terrorism and encouraged growing anti-Americanism would require them to
admit that unconditional support for Israel does in fact impose significant
costs on the United States. Such an admission would cast doubt on Israel's
net strategic value and imply that Washington should make its support conditional on Israel adopting a different approach toward the Palestinians.

Contrary to these claims, there is in fact abundant evidence that U.S.
support for Israel encourages anti-Americanism throughout the Arab and Islamic world and has fueled the rage of anti-American terrorists. It is not
their only grievance, of course, but it is a central one.[56] While some Islamic
radicals are genuinely upset by what they regard as the West's materialism
and venality, its alleged "theft" of Arab oil, its support for corrupt Arab
monarchies, its repeated military interventions in the region, etc., they are
also angered by U.S. support for Israel and Israel's harsh treatment of the
Palestinians. Thus, Sayyid Qutb, the Egyptian dissident whose writings have
been an important inspiration for contemporary Islamic fundamentalists,
was hostile to the United States both because he saw it as a corrupt and li-
centious society and also because of U.S. support for Israel.[57] Or as Sayyid
Muhammed Husayn Fadlallah, spiritual leader of Hezbollah, put it in 2002,
"I believe that America bears responsibility for all of Israel, both in its occupation of the lands of [19]48 or in all its settlement policies [in the lands occupied since 1967], despite the occasional utterance of a few timid and
embarrassed words which disapprove of the settlements . . . America is a
hypocritical nation . . . for it gives solid support and lethal weapons to the
Israelis, but gives the Arabs and the Palestinians [only] words."[58] One need
not agree with such sentiments to recognize the potency of these arguments
in the minds of many Arabs and to realize how unquestioned support for Israel has fueled anger and resentment against the United States.

An even clearer demonstration of the connection between U.S. support for
Israel and anti-American terrorism is the case of Ramzi Yousef, who master-
minded the first attack on the World Trade Center in 1993 and is now serving
a life sentence in a U.S. prison. Not only did Yousef mail letters to several New
York newspapers, taking credit for the attack and demanding that the United
States terminate aid to Israel, he also told the agents who flew him back to the
United States following his arrest in Pakistan in 1995 that he felt guilty about

causing U.S. deaths. But as Steve Coll recounts in his prizewinning book *Ghost Wars*, Yousef's remorse was "overridden by the strength of his desire to stop the killing of Arabs by Israeli troops" and by his belief that "bombing American targets was the 'only way to cause change.'" Yousef reportedly also said that "he truly believed his actions had been rational and logical in pursuit of a change in U.S. policy toward Israel." According to Coll, Yousef "mentioned no other motivation during the flight and no other issue in American foreign policy that concerned him." Further corroboration comes from Yousef's associate Abdul Rahman Yasin, who told the CBS news correspondent Lesley Stahl that Yousef had recruited him by telling him that acts of terrorism would be "revenge for my Palestinian brothers and my brothers in Saudi Arabia," adding that Yousef "talked to me a lot about this."[59]

Or consider the most obvious case: Osama bin Laden and al Qaeda. Contrary to the declarations of Satloff, Dershowitz, Kramer, and others, considerable evidence confirms that bin Laden has been deeply sympathetic to the Palestinian cause ever since he was a young man and that he has long been angry at the United States for backing Israel so strongly. According to Michael Scheuer, who directed the CIA's intelligence unit on al Qaeda and its founder, the young bin Laden was for the most part gentle and well behaved, but "an exception to Osama's well-mannered, nonconfrontational demeanor was his support for the Palestinians and negative attitude towards the United States and Israel."[60] After September 11, bin Laden's mother told an interviewer that "in his teenage years he was the same nice kid . . . but he was more concerned, sad, and frustrated about the situation in Palestine in particular, and the Arab and Muslim world in general."[61]

Moreover, bin Laden's first public statement intended for a wider audience—released December 29, 1994—directly addressed the Palestinian issue. As Bruce Lawrence, compiler of bin Laden's public statements, explains, "The letter makes it plain that Palestine, far from being a late addition to bin Laden's agenda, was at the centre of it from the start."[62]

Bin Laden also condemned the United States on several occasions prior to September 11 for its support of Israel against the Palestinians and called for jihad against America on this basis. According to Benjamin and Simon, the "most prominent grievance" in bin Laden's 1996 fatwa (titled "Declaration of War Against the Americans Occupying the Land of the Two Holy Places") is "bin Laden's hallmark: the 'Zionist-Crusader alliance.'" Bin Laden refers explicitly to Muslim blood being spilled "in Palestine and Iraq" and blames it all on the "American-Israeli conspiracy."[63] When the CNN reporter Peter Arnett asked him in March 1997 why he had declared jihad against the United States, bin Laden replied, "We declared jihad against the US government, because the US government is unjust, criminal, and tyrannical. It has committed acts that are extremely unjust, hideous, and criminal, whether directly or through its support of the Israeli occupation of the Land of the Prophet's Night Journey [Palestine]. And we believe the US is directly responsible for those who were killed in Palestine, Lebanon, and Iraq."[64] These comments are hardly anomalous. As Max Rodenbeck, Mideast correspondent for the *Economist*, writes in a prominent review of two important books about bin Laden, "Of all these themes, the notion of payback for injustices suffered by the Palestinians is perhaps the most powerfully recurrent in bin Laden's speeches."[65]

The 9/11 Commission confirmed that bin Laden and other key al Qaeda members were motivated both by Israel's behavior toward the Palestinians and by U.S. support for Israel. A background study by the commission's staff notes that bin Laden tried to accelerate the date of the attack in the fall of 2000, after Israeli opposition party leader Ariel Sharon's provocative visit (accompanied by hundreds of Israeli riot police) to the Temple Mount in Jerusalem, the site of al-Aqsa Mosque, one of the three holiest sites in Islam. According to the staff statement, "although bin Laden recognized that [Mohamed] Atta and the other pilots had only just arrived in the United States to begin their flight training, the al Qaeda leader wanted to punish the United States for supporting Israel."[66] The following year, "when bin Laden learned from the media that Sharon would be visiting the White House in June or July 2001, he attempted once more to accelerate the operation."[67] In addition to informing the timing of the 9/11 attacks, bin Laden's anger at the United States for backing Israel had implications for his preferred choice of targets. In the first meeting between Atta, the mission leader, and bin Laden in late 1999, the initial plans called for hitting the U.S. Capitol because it was "the perceived source of U.S. policy in support of Israel."[68] In short, bin Laden and his deputies clearly see the issue of Palestine as central to their agenda.

The 9/11 Commission also notes that Khalid Sheikh Mohammed—whom it described as "the principal architect of the 9/11 attacks"—was primarily motivated by the Palestinian issue. In the commission's words, "By his own account, KSM's animus toward the United States stemmed not from his experiences there as a student, but rather from his violent disagreement with U.S. foreign policy favoring Israel."[69] It is hard to imagine more compelling evidence of the role that U.S. support for Israel played in inspiring the 9/11 attacks.

Even if bin Laden himself were not personally engaged by the Palestinian issue, it still provides him with an effective recruiting tool. Arab and Islamic anger has grown markedly since the end of the Cold War, and especially since the outbreak of the Second Intifada in 2000, in part because the level of violence directed against the Palestinians has been both significantly greater and more visible.[70] The First Intifada (1987–92) was much less violent, and there was relative calm in the Occupied Territories during the Oslo years (1993–2000). The development of the Internet and the emergence of alternative media outlets such as Al Jazeerah now provide round-the-clock coverage of the carnage. Not only is Israel inflicting more violence upon its Palestinian subjects, but Arabs and Muslims around the world can see it with their own eyes. And they can also see that it is being done with American-made weapons and with tacit U.S. consent. This situation provides potent ammunition for America's critics, which is why the deputy leader of Hezbollah, Sheik Naim Qassem, told a Lebanese crowd in December 2006, "There is no longer a political place for America in Lebanon. Do you not recall that the weapons fired on Lebanon were American weapons?"[71]

These policies help explain why many Arabs and Muslims are so angry with the United States that they regard al Qaeda with sympathy, and some are even willing to support it, either directly or tacitly. A 2004 survey of Moroccans reported that 8 percent had a "favorable" or "very favorable" image of President Bush, but the comparable figure for bin Laden was 45 percent. In Jordan, a key U.S. ally, the numbers were 3 percent for Bush and 55 percent for bin Laden, who beat Bush by a margin of 58 percent in Pakistan, whose government is also closely allied with the United States.[72] The Pew Global Attitudes Survey reported in 2002—before the invasion of Iraq—that "public opinion about the United States in the Middle East/Conflict Area is overwhelmingly negative," and much of this unpopularity stems from the Palestinian issue.[73] According to the Middle East expert Shibley Telhami, "No other issue resonates with the public in the Arab world, and many other parts of the Muslim world, more deeply than Palestine. No other issue shapes the regional perceptions of America more fundamentally than the issue of Palestine."[74] Ussama Makdisi agrees, writing that "on no issue is Arab anger at the United States more widely and acutely felt than that of Palestine . . . For it is over Palestine that otherwise antithetical Arab secularist and Islamist interpretations of history converge in their common perception of an immense gulf separating official American avowals of support for freedom from actual American policies."[75] U.S. support for Israel is not the only source of anti-Americanism, of course, but it is an important one, and it makes winning the war on terror and advancing other U.S. interests more difficult.

Other government studies and numerous public opinion polls offer the same conclusion: Arab populations are deeply angered by America's support for Israel, which they regard as insensitive to Arab concerns and inconsistent with professed U.S. values. Although many Arabs have somewhat favorable views of U.S. science and technology, U.S. products, American movies and TV, and even surprisingly positive views of the American people and U.S. democracy, their views of American foreign policy—and especially U.S. support for Israel—are strongly negative.[76] As a visiting Yemeni physicist remarked in 2001, "When you go there, you really love the United States . . . but when you go back home, you find the US applies justice and fairness to its own people, but not abroad."[77] A 2004 report by the Pentagon's Defense Science Board concluded that "Muslims do not 'hate our freedom,' but rather they hate our policies," and the 9/11 Commission acknowledged that "it is simply a fact that American policy regarding the Israeli-Palestinian conflict and American policy in Iraq are dominant staples of popular commentary across the Arab and Muslim world."[78]

Similarly, when the respected polling firm Zogby International asked citizens of six Arab countries if their attitude toward America was shaped by their feelings about American values or by U.S. policies, "an overwhelming percentage of respondents indicated that policy played a more important role." When asked open-ended questions about their "first thought" when they think of America, the most common answer is "unfair foreign policy." And when asked what the United States could do to improve its image, the most frequent answers are "change Middle East policy" and "stop supporting Israel."[79] Not surprisingly, after Congress directed the State Department to establish an "advisory group on public diplomacy for the Arab and Muslim World" in June 2003, the group's report found that "citizens in these countries are genuinely distressed at the plight of the Palestinians and at the role they perceive the United States to be playing."[80]

Prominent Arab leaders and well-informed public commentators confirm that unconditional U.S. support for Israel has made the United States increasingly unpopular throughout the Middle East. UN Special Envoy Lakhdar Brahimi, whom the Bush administration enlisted to help form an interim Iraqi government in June 2004, said that "the great poison in the region is the Israeli policy of domination and the suffering imposed on the Palestinians," adding that people throughout the Middle East recognized the "injustice of this policy and the equally unjust support of the United States for this policy." In 2004, Egyptian President Hosni Mubarak warned, "There exists a hatred [of America] never equaled in the region," in part because Arabs "see [Israeli Prime Minister] Sharon act as he wants, without the Americans saying anything."[81] King Abdullah II of Jordan offered a similar view in March 2007, telling a joint session of Congress that "the denial of justice and peace in Palestine . . . is the core issue. And this core issue is not only producing severe consequences for our region, it is producing severe consequences for our world."[82] Not surprisingly, these pro-American regimes want the United States to change a policy that reinforces popular discontent over their own ties to the United States.

U.S. support for Israel is hardly the only source of anti-Americanism in the Arab and Islamic world, and making it more conditional would not remove all sources of friction between these countries and the United States. Examining the consequences of Israel's treatment of the Palestinians and tacit U.S. support of these policies is not to deny the presence of genuine anti-Semitism in various Arab countries or the fact that groups and governments in these societies sometimes fan these attitudes and use the Israel-Palestine conflict to divert attention from their own mistakes. Rather, our point is simply that the United States pays a substantial price for supporting Israel so consistently. This posture fuels hostility toward the United States in the Middle East, motivates anti-American extremists and aids their recruiting, gives authoritarian governments in the region an all-too-convenient scapegoat for their own failings, and makes it harder for Washington to convince potential supporters to confront extremists in their own countries.

When it comes to fighting terrorism, in short, U.S. and Israeli interests are not identical. Backing Israel against the Palestinians makes winning the war on terror harder, not easier, and the "partner against terror" rationale does not provide a compelling justification for unconditional U.S. support.

CONFRONTING ROGUE STATES

The new strategic rationale also portrays Israel as an essential ally in the campaign against authoritarian rogue states that support terrorism and that seek to acquire WMD. Like the "partners against terror" argument, this familiar justification sounds convincing at first hearing. Isn't it obvious that dictatorships like Syria, Iran, or Saddam Hussein's Iraq are hostile both to Israel and the United States? Aren't such regimes likely to use WMD to blackmail the United States, or give WMD to terrorists? Given these dangers, doesn't it make sense to continue generous aid to Israel, both to protect it from these dangerous neighbors and to keep the pressure on them, thereby hastening the day when these brutal regimes either collapse or change their ways?

In fact, this rationale does not stand up to careful scrutiny either. Although the United States does have important disagreements with each of these regimes—most notably their support for certain terrorist organizations and their apparent interest in acquiring WMD—they are not a dire threat to vital American interests, apart from the U.S. commitment to Israel itself. America's main strategic interest in the Middle East is oil, and protecting access to this commodity mainly depends on preventing any single country from controlling the entire region. This concern could justify going after one of these states if it grew too strong or too aggressive—as the United States did when it expelled Iraq from Kuwait in 1990–91—but it does not justify going after Iran, Iraq, and Syria at the same time.

The other features that are frequently invoked to explain why the United States should back Israel against these rogue states are even less compelling on strategic grounds. Does the fact that they are dictatorships justify relentless U.S. hostility? No, because the United States has allied itself with other dictatorships when doing so advanced its interests, and it still does so today. Is their support for terrorist groups a sufficient rationale? Not really, because these states and these terrorist groups have refrained from attacking the United States and because the United States has often turned a blind eye toward the promotion of terrorism in the past, including terrorism supported by these same states. Like most countries, the United States has been willing to cooperate with regimes it did not necessarily like when doing so advanced U.S. interests. Washington backed Saddam Hussein and Iraq during its war with Iran in the 1980s, for example, and it still backs Pakistan's military dictatorship despite that government's well-documented support for Islamic terrorism in Kashmir and elsewhere. U.S. leaders were also happy to accept Iran's help when dealing with the Taliban and pleased to get intelligence information about al Qaeda from Syria. These admittedly are limited instances of cooperation, but they do suggest that neither state is a mortal threat to vital U.S. interests.

What about Syrian meddling in Lebanon or a potential Iranian challenge to U.S. allies in the Persian Gulf? These issues are not trivial, but they do not justify backing Israel as strongly as the United States does. Israel's own meddling in Lebanon has repeatedly complicated U.S. efforts there, and its own WMD arsenal and frequent willingness to use force have encouraged other Middle Eastern states to desire WMD of their own. As previously noted, Israel is not much of an asset when it comes to maintaining stability in Lebanon or preserving a balance of power in the Gulf. As we discuss at length in Part II, Israel and the lobby have repeatedly frustrated U.S. efforts to deal more effectively with these admittedly problematic regimes.

As a justification for helping Israel, in fact, this particular strategic argument is essentially circular. Israel is portrayed as a vital ally for dealing with its dangerous neighbors, but the commitment to Israel is an important reason why the United States sees these states as threats in the first place. Indeed, Washington might find it easier to address the various conflicts that it does have with these states were its policies not constrained by the prior commitment to Israel. In any case, these states are at present too weak to harm the United States significantly (though they can certainly make life much more difficult for certain U.S. actions, most notably in Iraq), and Israel has not been much of an asset when America has been forced to take steps against them.

Even the threat posed by WMD does not provide a compelling reason to support Israel as strongly as the United States currently does. The United States has its own reasons to oppose the spread of WMD in the Middle East (and elsewhere), but it would not be a strategic disaster for the United States if some of these states in this region were eventually to acquire WMD despite our best efforts. Instead, U.S. concerns about Saddam's WMD programs or Iran's current nuclear ambitions derive largely from the threat they are said to pose to Israel. President Bush admitted as much in March 2006, saying, "The threat from Iran is, of course, their stated objective to destroy our strong ally Israel."[83]

Yet given that both Israel and the United States have powerful nuclear forces of their own, this danger is overstated. Attacking the United States or Israel directly is out of the question, because Israel has several hundred weapons of its own and the United States has thousands. If either country were ever attacked, the perpetrator would immediately face a devastating retaliation. Neither country could be blackmailed by a nuclear-armed rogue state, because the blackmailer could not carry out the threat without facing the same fate. The Soviet Union had thousands of nuclear weapons during the Cold War, was committed to and guided by a revolutionary ideology, and was governed by ruthless men who placed little value on human life. Yet Moscow could not use its vast arsenal to "blackmail" the United States, and Stalin, Khrushchev, and Brezhnev never even tried. The reason is obvious: the United States had its own weapons and could (and would) retaliate in kind.

The danger that a rogue state might decide to give one of its nuclear weapons to a terrorist group is equally remote, because the country's leaders could never be sure the transfer would remain undetected or that they would not be blamed and punished afterward. Indeed, giving away the nuclear weapons that they had run grave risks to obtain is probably the last thing such regimes would ever do. They would no longer control how the weapons might be used and they could never be certain that the United States (or Israel) would not incinerate them if either country merely *suspected* that a particular "rogue state" had provided terrorists with the ability to carry out a WMD attack. If the United States could live with a nuclear Soviet Union or a nuclear China (whose former leaders were among the greatest mass murderers the world has ever known), and if it can tolerate a nuclear Pakistan and embrace a nuclear India, then it could live (however reluctantly) with a nuclear Iran as well.

It is sometimes said that deterrence cannot work against these regimes, because their leaders (such as Iranian President Mahmoud Ahmadinejad) are irrational religious fanatics who would welcome martyrdom and thus could not be effectively deterred. In the words of the *Washington Post's* Charles Krauthammer, "Against millenarian fanaticism glorying in a cult of death, deterrence is a mere wish."[84] Disproving such an assertion is impossible, of course, because one can never be 100 percent certain that some world leader might not succumb to suicidal madness. There are nonetheless good reasons to be skeptical of such frightening claims. None of these allegedly irrational leaders could launch a WMD attack by himself; mounting an actual strike would require the active assistance and assent of many other people, all of whom would have to willingly embrace martyrdom themselves. (In Iran, for instance, authority over the military is not even in President Ahmadinejad's hands.) Moreover, there is no evidence suggesting that any of these leaders has ever sought martyrdom (Saddam Hussein certainly didn't, until the noose was nearly around his neck).

Finally, it is worth noting that such claims have been heard before and turned out to be wrong. U.S. hard-liners once argued that Soviet leaders were ideologically driven and contemptuous of human life and thus might not be deterrable, and other U.S. leaders feared China's acquisition of nuclear weapons because they thought Mao Zedong was an irrational leader who might be willing to risk tens of millions of people in a nuclear exchange. Secretary of State Dean Rusk once warned that "a country whose behavior is as violent, irascible, unyielding, and hostile as that of Communist China is led by leaders whose view of the world and of life itself is unreal," but Chinese nuclear conduct turned out to be quite prudent.[85] U.S. leaders should not be complacent about the spread of WMD in the Middle East, but this problem is not a sufficient strategic justification for backing Israel as strongly as the United States currently does.

Even if Syria or Iran does present challenges for the United States in places like Lebanon or Iraq, or if they either have or want WMD, the U.S. relationship with Israel actually makes it harder to deal effectively with them. Israel's nuclear arsenal is one reason why some of its neighbors want nuclear weapons, and threatening them with regime change has merely reinforced that desire. America's willingness to back Israel in spite of Israel's own nuclear arsenal and its refusal to sign the NPT also makes the United States look hypocritical when it tries to confront would-be proliferators about their own weapons programs. Yet Israel is not much of an asset when Washington contemplates using force against these regimes—as it has done twice in Iraq—because Israel cannot participate in the fight.

Moreover, the combination of U.S. support for Israel and Israel's continued oppression of the Palestinians has also eroded America's standing in many other quarters and made it more difficult to obtain meaningful cooperation on important strategic issues like the war on terrorism or the related effort to democratize the Middle East. As noted in Chapter 1, foreign populations generally see the United States as "too supportive" of Israel, and many foreign elites think its tacit support for Israel's policies in the Occupied Territories is morally obtuse. In April 2004, for example, fifty-two former British diplomats sent Prime Minister Tony Blair a letter saying that the conflict between Israel and the Palestinians had "poisoned relations between the West and the Islamic and Arab worlds," and warning that the policies of Bush and Sharon were "one-sided and illegal" and will "cost yet more Israeli and Palestinian blood." Blair did not really need to be told, however, as he tried repeatedly (though unsuccessfully) to get the Bush administration to engage this issue more seriously. Not to be outdone, a group of eighty-eight former U.S. diplomats quickly followed suit with a similar letter to President Bush.[86] Even prominent Israelis such as the veteran military correspondent Ze'ev Schiff understood that "the continuation of this conflict, including the Israeli occupation, will most certainly lead to new waves of terror; international terrorism, which the Americans fear so much, will spread."[87]

The consequences of all this became clear in 2006, when U.S. efforts to forge a Sunni coalition to help deal with the deteriorating situation in Iraq and to balance a rising Iran were undermined by Sunni concerns that the United States had consistently taken Israel's side in its conflict with the Palestinians, and their awareness that it would be politically dangerous to get too close to the Americans. According to the *Wall Street Journal*, "Arab diplomats say countries such as Saudi Arabia, Egypt, Qatar, Kuwait and the United Arab Emirates will find it difficult to publicly stand with the U.S. on

Iran and on broad regional stability unless Washington pressures Israel on a peace initiative." Or as one Arab diplomat put it, "The road to Baghdad runs through Jerusalem, and not the other way around."[88] And that is why the bipartisan Iraq Study Group concluded in December 2006 that "the United States will not be able to achieve its goals in the Middle East unless the United States deals directly with the Arab-Israeli conflict."[89]

In short, treating Israel as America's most important ally in the campaign against terrorism and against assorted Middle East dictatorships exaggerates Israel's ability to help on these issues, overlooks how the relationship contributes to these problems, and ignores the ways that Israel's policies make U.S. efforts to address them more difficult. Israel's strategic value has declined steadily since the end of the Cold War. Steadfast support for Israel can no longer be justified by the argument that it is helping us defeat a great power rival; instead, backing Israel unconditionally helps make the United States a target for radical extremists and makes America look callous and hypocritical in the eyes of many third parties, including European and Arab allies. The United States still benefits from various acts of strategic cooperation with Israel, but on balance, it is more of a liability than an asset.

A DUBIOUS ALLY

A final reason to question Israel's strategic value is that it sometimes does not act like a loyal ally. Like most states, Israel looks first and foremost to its own interests, and it has been willing to do things contrary to American interests when it believed (rightly or wrongly) that doing so would advance its own national goals. In the notorious "Lavon affair" in 1954, for example, Israeli agents tried to bomb several U.S. government offices in Egypt, in a bungled attempt to sow discord between Washington and Cairo. Israel sold military supplies to Iran while U.S. diplomats were being held hostage there in 1979–80, and it was one of Iran's main military suppliers during the Iran-Iraq War, even though the United States was worried about Iran and tacitly backing Iraq. Israel later purchased $36 million worth of Iranian oil in 1989 in an attempt to obtain the release of Israeli hostages in Lebanon. All of these acts made sense from Israel's point of view, but they were contrary to American policy and harmful to overall U.S. interests.[90]

In addition to selling weapons to America's enemies, Israel has transferred American technology to third countries, including potential U.S. adversaries like China, actions that violated U.S. laws and threatened American interests. In 1992, the State Department's inspector general reported that starting in 1983 there was evidence of a "systematic and growing pattern of unauthorized transfers" by Israel.[91] At about the same time, the General Accounting Office officials looking into the "Dotan affair" (the embezzlement and illegal diversion of millions of dollars of U.S. military aid by the former head of Israeli Air Force procurement) made repeated efforts to meet with Israeli officials to discuss the matter. According to the GAO, "The Government of Israel declined to discuss the issues or allow [U.S.] investigators to question Israeli personnel."[92]

Little has changed in recent years. Indeed, even Douglas Feith, the former undersecretary of defense and a consistent supporter of Israel, was reportedly angry when Israel agreed in 2004 to upgrade a killer drone it had sold to China in 1994.[93] "Something is going badly wrong in the [U.S.-Israeli] military relationship," said another senior Bush administration official.[94]

Amplifying these tensions is the extensive espionage that Israel engages in against the United States. According to the GAO, the Jewish state "conducts the most aggressive espionage operations against the United States of any ally."[95] Stealing economic secrets gives Israeli firms important advantages over American businesses in the global marketplace and thus imposes additional costs on U.S. citizens.

More worrying, however, are Israel's continued efforts to steal America's military secrets. This problem is highlighted by the infamous case of Jonathan Pollard, an American intelligence analyst who gave Israel large quantities of highly classified material between 1981 and 1985. After Pollard was caught, the Israelis refused to tell the United States what Pollard gave them.[96] The Pollard case is but the most visible tip of a larger iceberg. Israeli agents tried to steal spy-camera technology from a U.S. firm in 1986, and an arbitration panel later accused Israel of "perfidious," "unlawful," and "surreptitious" conduct and ordered it to pay the firm, Recon/Optical Inc., some $3 million in damages. Israeli spies also gained access to confidential U.S. information about a Pentagon electronic intelligence program and tried unsuccessfully to recruit Noel Koch, a senior counterterrorism official in the Defense Department. The *Wall Street Journal* quoted John Davitt, former head of the Justice Department's internal security section, saying that "those of us who worked in the espionage area regarded Israel as being the second most active foreign intelligence service in the United States."[97]

A new controversy erupted in 2004 when a key Pentagon official, Larry Franklin, was arrested on charges of passing classified information regarding U.S. policy toward Iran to an Israeli diplomat, allegedly with the assistance of two senior AIPAC officials, Steven Rosen and Keith Weissman. Franklin eventually accepted a plea bargain and was sentenced to twelve years in prison for his role in the affair, and Rosen and Weissman are scheduled to go on trial in the fall of 2007.[98]

Israel is of course not the only country that spies on the United States, and Washington conducts extensive espionage against both allies and adversaries as well. Such behavior is neither surprising nor particularly reprehensible, because international politics is a rough business and states often do unscrupulous things in their efforts to gain an edge over other countries. Nonetheless, the close relationship between Washington and Jerusalem has made it easier for Israel to steal American secrets, and it has not hesitated to do just that. At the very least, Israel's willingness to spy on its principal patron casts further doubt on its overall strategic value, especially now that the Cold War is over.

CONCLUSION

There is no question that Israel has derived substantial benefits from U.S. support, although one might also argue that this support has been used to pursue policies—such as settlement construction—that were not in Israel's long-term interest. It is also clear that the United States derived some strategic value from its aid to Israel, especially during the Cold War. Yet these benefits cannot fully justify or explain why the United States has been willing to give Israel such consistent support over such an extended period. Subsidizing and protecting Israel may have been a net plus for the United States at the height of the Cold War—though even this claim is not open and shut—but that rationale evaporated when the Soviet Union collapsed and the superpower competition in the Middle East ended. Today, America's intimate embrace of Israel—and especially its willingness to subsidize it no matter what its policies are—is not making Americans safer or more prosperous. To the contrary: unconditional support for Israel is undermining relations with other U.S. allies, casting doubt on America's wisdom and moral vision, helping inspire a generation of anti-American extremists, and complicating U.S. efforts to deal with a volatile but vital region. In short, the largely unconditional "special relationship" between the United States and Israel is no longer defensible on strategic grounds. If a convincing rationale is to be found, we must look elsewhere. In the next chapter, we examine the moral case for American support.

3

A DWINDLING MORAL CASE

When George W. Bush spoke at the annual policy conference of the American Israel Public Affairs Committee in May 2004, he invoked a set of moral themes to help explain U.S. support for Israel. The president began his speech by applauding AIPAC's efforts "to strengthen the ties that bind our nations—our shared values, our strong commitment to freedom." He went on to emphasize that Israel and the United States "have much in common. We're both . . . born of struggle and sacrifice. We're both founded by immigrants escaping religious persecution in other lands. We have both built vibrant democracies, built on the rule of law and market economies. And we're both countries founded on certain basic beliefs: that God watches over the affairs of men, and values every life. These ties have made us natural allies, and these ties will never be broken."

Bush also noted one important difference and drew a moral conclusion from it. Whereas the United States was relatively safe in the past because of its geographical location, "Israel has faced a different situation as a small country in a tough neighborhood. The Israeli people have always had enemies at their borders and terrorists close at hand. Again and again, Israel has defended itself with skill and heroism. And as a result of the courage of the Israeli people, Israel has earned the respect of the American people."[1]

Bush's remarks underscore the degree to which U.S. support for Israel is often justified not on strategic grounds but on the basis of essentially moral claims. The *moral rationale* for American support rests on several distinct lines of argument, and Israel's supporters often invoke one or more of these claims in order to justify the "special relationship." Specifically, Israel is said to deserve generous and nearly unconditional U.S. support because it is weak and surrounded by enemies dedicated to destroying it; it is a democracy, which is a morally preferable form of government; the Jewish people have suffered greatly from past crimes; Israel's conduct has been morally superior to its adversaries' behavior, especially compared to the Palestinians; the Palestinians rejected the generous peace offer that Israel made at Camp David in July 2000 and opted for violence instead; and it is clear from the Bible that Israel's creation is God's will. Taken together, these arguments underpin the more general claim that Israel is the one country in the Middle East that shares American values and therefore enjoys broad support among the American people. Many U.S. policy makers accept these various arguments, but even if they did not, the American people supposedly want them to back Israel and certainly do not want them to put any pressure on the Jewish state.

Upon close inspection, the moral rationale for unqualified U.S. support is not compelling. There is a strong moral case for supporting Israel's existence, but that fortunately is not in danger at present. Viewed objectively, Israel's past and present conduct offers little moral basis for privileging it over the Palestinians or for undertaking policies in the region that are not in America's strategic interest.

The moral rationale relies heavily on a particular understanding of Israel's history that is widely held by many Americans (both Jews and gentiles). In that story, Jews in the Middle East have long been victims, just as they were in Europe. "The Jew," Elie Wiesel tells us, "has never been an executioner; he is almost always the victim."[2] The Arabs, and especially the Palestinians, are the victimizers, bearing a marked similarity to the anti-Semites who persecuted Jews in Europe. This perspective is clearly evident in Leon Uris's famous novel *Exodus* (1958), which portrays the Jews as both victims and heroes and the Palestinians as villains and cowards. This book sold twenty million copies between 1958 and 1980 and was turned into a popular movie (1960). Scholars have shown that the *Exodus* narrative has had an enduring influence on how Americans think about the Arab-Israeli conflict.[3]

The conventional wisdom about how Israel was created and how it has subsequently behaved toward the Palestinians as well as neighboring states is wrong. It is based on a set of myths about past events that Israeli scholars have systematically demolished over the past twenty years.[4] While there is no question that Jews were frequently victims in Europe, in the past century they have often been the victimizers in the Middle East, and their main victims were and continue to be the Palestinians. Not only is the basic point backed up by an abundance of evidence, but it is also intuitively plausible. After all, how could Jews coming to Palestine from Europe create a state of their own without taking harsh measures against the Arab population that already dwelt in the land they wanted for their new state? Just as the Europeans who created the United States and Canada could not do so without committing significant crimes against the native inhabitants, it was virtually impossible for the Zionists to carve out a Jewish state in Palestine without committing similar crimes against the local residents, who were bound to resent their encroachments and attempt to resist them. Unfortunately, this "new history," as it is called in Israel, has not been adequately acknowledged in the United States, which is one reason why the moral rationale still carries significant weight for many Americans.[5]

Israel's more recent conduct is a different matter, however. With the global reach of the Internet and twenty-four-hour cable news networks, many Americans have seen considerable evidence of Israel's brutal treatment of its Palestinian subjects in the Occupied Territories. They have also seen the consequences of Israel's actions in the second Lebanon war (2006), in which the Israel Defense Forces pummeled civilian targets across Lebanon and then dumped several million deadly cluster bomblets in the towns and villages of southern Lebanon.[6]

Although these actions have tarnished Israel's public image in the United States, its supporters remain undaunted and continue to make the moral case for sustaining the present relationship between those two countries. In fact, a good case can be made that current U.S. policy conflicts with basic American values and that if the United States were to choose sides on the basis of moral considerations alone, it would back the Palestinians, not Israel. After all, Israel is prosperous and has the most powerful military in the Middle East. No state would deliberately start a war with it today. Israel does have a serious terrorism problem, but that is mainly the consequence of colonizing the Occupied Territories. By contrast, the Palestinians are stateless, impoverished, and facing a deeply uncertain future. Even allowing for the Palestinians' various shortcomings, which group now has the stronger moral claim to U.S. sympathy?

Getting to the bottom of this issue requires that we look in more detail at the particular arguments that make up the moral rationale. Our focus will be primarily on Israeli behavior, and no attempt will be made to compare it with the actions of other states in the region or in other parts of the world. We are not focusing on Israel's conduct because we have an animus toward the Jewish state, or because we believe that its behavior is particularly worthy of censure. On the contrary, we recognize that virtually all states have committed serious crimes at one time or another in their history, and we are cognizant of the fact that state building is often a violent enterprise. We are also aware that some of Israel's Arab neighbors have at times acted with great brutality. We focus on Israel's actions because the United States provides it with a level of material and diplomatic support that is substantially greater than what it gives to other states, and it does so at the expense of its own interests. Our aim is to determine whether Israel deserves special treatment because it acts in an exceptionally virtuous manner, as many of its supporters claim. Does Israel behave significantly better than other states do? The historical record suggests that it does not.

BACKING THE UNDERDOG

Israel is often portrayed as weak and besieged, a Jewish David surrounded by a hostile Arab Goliath. This image has been carefully nurtured by Israeli leaders and sympathetic writers, but the opposite is closer to the truth. Israel has always been militarily stronger than its Arab adversaries. Consider Israel's 1948 War of Independence, where the popular belief is that the Zionists—who fought against five Arab armies as well as the Palestinians— were badly outnumbered and outgunned. Benny Morris, a prominent Israeli historian, refers to this description of the balance of power as "one of the most tenacious myths relating to 1948."[7]

One might think that Israeli forces were at a significant quantitative and qualitative disadvantage in 1948, because it was a small new country surrounded by Arab states that had far more people and far greater material resources. In fact, comparing the population size and the resources of Israel and the Arab world tells you little about the balance of military power between them. As Morris notes, "The atlas map showing a minuscule Israel and a giant surrounding Arab sea did not, and, indeed, for the time being, still does not, accurately reflect the true balance of military power in the region. Nor do the comparative population figures; in 1948, the Yishuv [the Jewish settlement in Palestine before Israel was created] numbered some 650,000 souls—as opposed to 1.2 million Palestinian Arabs and some 30 million Arabs in the surrounding states (including Iraq)."[8] The reason is simple: the Arab states have been remarkably ineffective at translating those latent resources into actual military power, while Israel, by contrast, has been especially good at doing so.

The War of Independence was actually two separate conflicts. The first was a civil war between the Jews and the Palestinians, which started on November 29, 1947 (the day of the UN decision to partition Mandate Palestine) and ran until May 14, 1948 (the day Israel declared its independence). The second was an international war between Israel and five Arab armies, which began on May 15, 1948, and ended on January 7, 1949.

The Zionists won a lopsided victory over the Palestinians in their civil war because they enjoyed a decisive advantage in numbers and quality of both soldiers and weapons.[9] Jewish fighting units were far better organized and trained than the Palestinian forces, which had been decimated by the British during the 1936–39 revolt and had not recovered by 1948. As the Israeli historian Ilan Pappe notes, "A few thousand irregular Palestinians and Arabs were facing tens of thousands of well-trained Jewish troops."[10] Not surprisingly, Israeli leaders were fully aware of this power imbalance and sought to take advantage of it. In fact, Yigal Yadin, a senior military commander in the 1948 war and the IDF's second chief of staff, maintained that if it had not been for the British presence in Palestine until May 1948, "we could have quelled the Arab riot in one month."[11]

The Israelis also had a clear advantage in manpower throughout their war with the five Arab armies. Morris notes that when the fighting started in mid-May, Israel "fielded some 35,000 armed troops as compared with the 25–30,000 of the Arab invading armies. By the time of Operation Dani, in July, the IDF had 65,000 men under arms and by December, close to 90,000 men under arms—at each stage significantly outnumbering the combined strength of the Arab armies ranged against them in Palestine."[12] Israel also enjoyed an advantage in weaponry, save for a brief twenty-five days at the start of that conflict (May 15–June 10, 1948). Moreover, with the possible exception of Transjordan's small Arab Legion, the quality of the Israeli fighting forces was far superior to their Arab adversaries and they were much better organized as well. In short, the Zionists won the civil war against the Palestinians and the international war against the invading Arab armies because they were more powerful than their adversaries, despite the absolute advantage in population that their Arab foes enjoyed. As Morris notes, "It was superior Jewish firepower, manpower, organization, and command and control that determined the outcome of battle."[13]

The IDF won quick and decisive victories against Egypt in 1956 and against Egypt, Jordan, and Syria in 1967—*before* large-scale U.S. aid began flowing to Israel. In October 1973, Israel was a victim of a stunning surprise attack by the Egyptian and Syrian armies. Although an outnumbered IDF suffered serious setbacks in the first days of fighting, it quickly recovered and was on the verge of destroying the Egyptian and Syrian armies when the United States and the Soviet Union intervened to halt the fighting. The remarkable turnaround, according to Morris, was due to the fact that "the IDF's machines, both in the air and on the ground, were simply superior. So was its manpower: Israeli pilots, maintenance and ground control staffs, tank officers, and men were far better trained and led than their Arab counterparts."[14] These victories offer eloquent evidence of Israeli patriotism, organizational ability, and military prowess, but they also reveal that Israel was far from helpless even in its earliest years.[15]

Today, Israel is the strongest military power in the Middle East. Its conventional forces are far superior to those of its neighbors, and it is the only state in the region with nuclear weapons. Egypt and Jordan have signed peace treaties with Israel, and Saudi Arabia has offered to do so as well. Syria has lost its Soviet patron, Iraq has been decimated by three disastrous wars, and Iran is hundreds of miles away and has never directly attacked Israel. The Palestinians barely have effective police, let alone a military that could threaten Israel's existence, and they are further weakened by profound internal divisions. The deaths caused by Palestinian suicide bombers are tragic and strike fear in the hearts of all Israelis, but they do relatively little damage to Israel's economy, much less threaten its territorial integrity.[16] Groups like Hezbollah can launch low-yield missiles and rockets at Israel and might be able to kill a few hundred Israelis over the course of months or years, but these attacks do not represent an existential threat to Israel. According to a 2005 assessment by Tel Aviv University's prestigious Jaffee Center for Strategic Studies, "The strategic balance decidedly favors Israel, which has continued to widen the qualitative gap between its own military capability and deterrence powers and those of its neighbors."[17] If backing the underdog were a compelling rationale, the United States would be supporting Israel's opponents.

Of course, there is another dimension to the argument that Israel has long been under siege and is always the victim: the claim that despite Israel's military superiority, its Arab neighbors are determined to destroy it. Indeed, some argue that the Arabs precipitated wars in 1948, 1967, and 1973 in order "to drive the Jews into the Sea."[18]

While there is no question that Israel faced serious threats in its early years, the Arabs were not attempting to destroy Israel in any of those three wars. This is not because the Arabs were happy about the presence of a Jewish state in their midst—they clearly were not—but rather because they have never had the capability to win a war against Israel, much less defeat it decisively. There is no question that some Arab leaders talked about "driving the Jews into the Sea" during the 1948 war, but this was largely rhetoric designed to appease their publics. In fact, the Arab leaders were mainly concerned with gaining territory for themselves at the expense of the Palestinians, one of the many occasions when Arab governments put their own interests ahead of the Palestinians' welfare. Morris, for example, writes:

> What ensued, once Israel declared its independence on 14 May 1948 and the Arab states invaded on 15 May, was "a general land grab," with everyone—Israel, Transjordan, Syria, Egypt, and even Lebanon—bent on preventing the birth of a Palestinian Arab state and carving out chunks of Palestine for themselves. Contrary to the old historiography, Abdullah's [king of Transjordan] invasion of eastern Palestine was clearly designed to conquer territory for his kingdom—at the expense of the Palestinian Arabs—rather than to destroy the Jewish state. Indeed, the Arab Legion stuck meticulously, throughout the war, to its non-aggressive stance vis-à-vis the Yishuv and the Jewish state's territory . . . It is not at all clear that Abdullah and Glubb [the British general who commanded Transjordan's Arab Legion] would have been happy to see the collapse in May 1948 of the fledgling Jewish republic. Certainly Abdullah was far more troubled by the prospects of the emergence of a Palestinian Arab state and of an expanded Syria and an expanded Egypt on his frontiers than by the emergence of a small Jewish state.[19]

And Abdullah, as Morris notes, was the only Arab leader who "committed the full weight" of his military power to attacking Israel, "indicating either inefficiency or, perhaps, a less than wholehearted seriousness about the declared aim of driving the Jews into the sea." Shlomo Ben-Ami, a noted historian and a former Israeli foreign minister, has a similar view of Arab goals in the 1948 war: "Ill prepared and poorly co-ordinated, the Arab armies were dragged into the war by popular pressure in their home states, and because their leaders each had his own agenda of territorial expansion. Securing the establishment of a Palestinian state . . . was less of a motive for the Arab leaders who sent their armies to Palestine than establishing their own territorial claims or thwarting those of their rivals in the Arab coalition."[20]

The myth of Israel as a victim is also reflected in the conventional wisdom about the 1967 war, which claims that Egypt and Syria are principally re-

sponsible for starting it. In particular, the Arabs are said to have been preparing to attack Israel when the IDF beat them to the punch and scored a stunning victory.[21] It is clear from the release of new documents about the war,
however, that the Arabs did not intend to initiate a war against Israel in the
late spring of 1967, much less try to destroy the Jewish state.[22] Avi Shlaim,
a distinguished Israeli "new historian," writes, "There is general agreement
among commentators that [Egyptian President] Nasser neither wanted nor
planned to go to war with Israel."[23] In fact, Israel bears considerable responsibility for the outbreak of the war. Shlaim writes that "Israel's strategy of escalation on the Syrian front was probably the single most important factor in
dragging the Middle East to war in June 1967, despite the conventional wisdom on the subject that singles out Syrian aggression as the principal cause
of war."[24] Ben-Ami goes even farther, writing that Yitzhak Rabin, the IDF
chief of staff, "intentionally led Israel into a war with Syria. Rabin was determined to provoke a war with Syria . . . because he thought this was the only
way to stop the Syrians from supporting Fatah attacks against Israel."[25]

None of this is to deny that Egypt's decision in May 1967 to close the
Straits of Tiran was a legitimate cause of concern to Israel. But it was not a
harbinger of an imminent Egyptian attack, and that point was recognized by
American policy makers and many Israeli leaders. Serious diplomatic efforts
were also under way to solve the crisis peacefully. Yet Israel chose to attack
anyway, because its leaders ultimately preferred war to a peaceful resolution
of the crisis. In particular, Israel's military commanders wanted to inflict significant military defeats on their two main adversaries—Egypt and Syria—
in order to strengthen Israeli deterrence over the long term.[26] Some also had
territorial ambitions. General Ezer Weizman, the IDF's chief of operations,
reflected this sentiment when he said on the eve of the war, "We are on the
brink of a second War of Independence, with all its accomplishments."[27] In
short, Israel was not preempting an impending attack when it struck the first
blow on June 5, 1967. Instead, it was launching a preventive war—a war
aimed at affecting the balance of power over time—or, as Menachem Begin
put it, a "war of choice." In his words, "We must be honest with ourselves.
We decided to attack him [Egyptian President Nasser]."[28]

The Egyptians and the Syrians certainly did attack Israel in October
1973, but it is a well-established fact that both Arab armies were pursuing a
limited aims strategy. The Egyptians hoped to conquer a slice of territory
in the Sinai Peninsula and then bargain with Israel for the return of the rest
of the Sinai, while the Syrians hoped to recapture the Golan Heights. Neither the Egyptians nor the Syrians intended to invade Israel, much less

threaten its existence. Not only did Israel have the most formidable army in the region, but it also had nuclear weapons, which would have made any attempt to conquer it suicidal. Benny Morris puts the point well: "Presidents Anwar Sadat of Egypt and Hafez Assad of Syria sought to regain the territories lost in 1967. Neither aimed to destroy Israel."[29] In fact, key decision makers in both Cairo and Damascus recognized that they were pursuing an especially risky strategy by picking a fight with the mighty IDF. General Hassan el Badri, who helped plan the Egyptian attack, remarked that "it almost seemed that success would be impossible."[30] And these doubters were correct, because the IDF, after recovering from the initial attack, routed both Arab armies.

With the possible exception of Iran, it is hard to make the case today that Israel's neighbors are bent on destroying it. As noted, Israel has signed peace treaties with Egypt and Jordan, and, as will be discussed in Chapter 9, Israel walked away from a possible peace treaty with Syria in 2000. At an Arab summit in March 2002, the crown prince of Saudi Arabia attempted to defuse the Israeli-Palestinian conflict by putting forward a proposal calling for full recognition of Israel by virtually every Arab government and normalization of relations with the Jewish state. In return, Israel would have to withdraw from the Occupied Territories and work toward a fair solution to the Palestinian refugee problem. The initiative was unanimously endorsed by the Arab League. Even Saddam Hussein backed it.[31] The proposal went nowhere at the time, but the Saudis resurrected it in early 2007. There is certainly no evidence that post-Saddam Iraq is interested in destroying Israel. While Hamas and Hezbollah may reject Israel's existence and inflict suffering, they do not, as noted, have the capability to pose a mortal danger. Iran would obviously be a serious threat to Israel if it acquired nuclear weapons, but as long as Israel has its own nuclear arsenal, Iran cannot attack it without being destroyed itself.

AIDING A FELLOW DEMOCRACY

American backing is often justified by the claim that Israel is a fellow democracy. Indeed, its defenders frequently remind Americans that Israel is the only democracy in the Middle East and that it is surrounded by hostile dictatorships. This rationale sounds convincing, but it cannot account for the current level of U.S. support. After all, there are many democracies around the world, but none receives the level of unconditional aid that Israel does.

In fact, whether a country is democratic is not a reliable indicator of how Washington will relate to it. The United States has overthrown a few democratic governments in the past and has supported numerous dictators when doing so was thought to advance U.S. interests. The Eisenhower administration overthrew a democratically elected government in Iran in 1953, while the Reagan administration supported Saddam Hussein in the 1980s. Today, the Bush administration has good relations with dictators like Hosni Mubarak in Egypt and Pervez Musharraf in Pakistan, and at the same time it has worked to undermine the democratically elected Hamas government in the Occupied Territories. It also has an acrimonious relationship with Hugo Chávez, the elected leader of Venezuela. Being democratic neither justifies nor fully explains the extent of American support for Israel.

The "shared democracy" rationale is also weakened by aspects of Israeli democracy that are at odds with core American values. The United States is a liberal democracy where people of any race, religion, or ethnicity are supposed to enjoy equal rights. While Israel's citizens are of many backgrounds, including Arab, Muslim, and Christian, among others, it was explicitly founded as a Jewish state, and whether a citizen is regarded as Jewish ordinarily depends on kinship (verifiable Jewish ancestry).[32] Israel's Jewish character is clearly reflected in the Declaration of the Establishment of the State of Israel, which was officially proclaimed on May 14, 1948. It explicitly refers to the United Nations' recognition "of the right of the Jewish people to establish their state," openly proclaims "the establishment of a Jewish state in Eretz-Israel," and later describes the new state as "the sovereign Jewish people settled in its own land."[33]

Given Israel's Jewish character, its leaders have long emphasized the importance of maintaining an unchallenged Jewish majority within its borders. Israelis worry a great deal about the flow of Jews and Palestinians into and out of Israel, the relative birthrates of Palestinians and Jews, and the possibility that expanding Israel's borders beyond the pre-1967 lines might result in many more Arabs living in their midst. David Ben-Gurion, for example, proclaimed that "any Jewish woman who, as far as it depends on her, does not bring into the world at least four healthy children is shirking her duty to the nation, like a soldier who evades military service."[34] There are now about 5.3 million Jews and 1.36 million Arabs living in Israel, including the disputed area of East Jerusalem. There are another 3.8 million Palestinians in Gaza and the West Bank, which means that there are only about 140,000 more Jews than Palestinians living in what used to be called Mandate Palestine, and by almost all accounts the Palestinians have a higher birthrate than the Jews.[35] It is not surprising, in light of these numbers, that it is commonplace these days for Israeli Jews to talk about their fellow Arab citizens and Palestinian subjects as a potential "demographic threat."[36]

One might think that although Israel is a Jewish state at its core, its Basic Laws (there are eleven) still guarantee equal rights for all its citizens, Arabs or Jews. But that is not the case. The initial draft of the Basic Law on Human Dignity and Liberty, which approximates the U.S. Bill of Rights, contained language that promised equality for all Israelis: "All are equal before the law, and there shall be no discrimination on the grounds of gender, religion, nationality, race, ethnic group, country of origin or any other irrelevant factor."[37] Ultimately, however, a Knesset committee removed that clause from the final version that became law in 1992. Since then, Arab members of Israel's Knesset have made numerous attempts to amend that Basic Law by adding language that provides for equality before the law. But their Jewish colleagues have refused to go along, a situation that stands in marked contrast to the United States, where the equality principle is enshrined in law.[38]

In addition to Israel's commitment to maintaining its Jewish identity and its refusal to grant de jure equality for non-Jews, Israel's 1.36 million Arabs are de facto treated as second-class citizens. An Israeli government commission found in 2003, for example, that Israel behaves in a "neglectful and discriminatory" manner toward them.[39] Indeed, there is widespread support among Israeli Jews for this unequal treatment of Israeli Arabs. A poll released in March 2007 found that 55 percent of Israeli Jews wanted segregated entertainment facilities, while more than 75 percent said they would not live in the same building as an Israeli Arab. More than half of the respondents said that for a Jewish woman to marry an Arab is equal to national treason, and 50 percent said that they would refuse employment if their immediate supervisor was an Arab.[40] The Israel Democracy Institute reported in May 2003 that 53 percent of Israeli Jews "are against full equality for the Arabs," while 77 percent of Israeli Jews believe that "there should be a Jewish majority on crucial political decisions." Only 31 percent "support having Arab political parties in the government."[41] That sentiment squares with the fact that Israel did not appoint its first Muslim Arab cabinet minister until January 2007, almost six decades after the founding of the state. And even that one appointment, which was to the minor portfolio of science, sports, and culture, was highly controversial.[42]

Israel's treatment of its Arab citizens is more than just discriminatory. For example, to limit the number of Arabs in its midst, Israel does not permit

Palestinians who marry Israeli citizens to become citizens themselves and does not give these spouses the right to live in Israel. The Israeli human rights organization B'Tselem called this restriction "a racist law that determines who can live here according to racist criteria."[43] Also, the Olmert government is pushing—and the Knesset's ministerial committee on legislation approved on January 10, 2007—a law that would allow the courts to revoke the citizenship of "unpatriotic" citizens. This legislation, which is clearly aimed at Israeli Arabs, was labeled "a drastic and extreme move that harms civil liberties" by Israel's attorney general.[44] Such laws may be understandable in light of Israel's founding principles—the explicit aim of creating a Jewish state—but they are not consistent with America's image of a multiethnic democracy in which all citizens are supposed to be treated equally regardless of their ancestry.

In early 2007, Benjamin Netanyahu apologized to ultra-Orthodox Israelis with large families for the hardships that were caused by welfare cuts that he had made in 2002 when he was finance minister. He noted, however, that there was at least one important and unexpected benefit of these cuts: "there was a dramatic drop in the birth rate" within the "non-Jewish public."[45] For Netanyahu, like many Israelis who are deeply worried about the so-called Arab demographic threat, the fewer Israeli Arab births, the better.

Netanyahu's comments would almost certainly be condemned if made in the United States. Imagine the outcry that would arise here if a U.S. cabinet official spoke of the benefits of a policy that had reduced the birthrates of African Americans and Hispanics, thereby preserving a white majority. But such statements are not unusual in Israel, where important leaders have a history of making derogatory comments about Palestinians and are rarely sanctioned for them. Menachem Begin once said that "Palestinians are beasts walking on two legs," while former IDF Chief of Staff Rafael Eitan referred to them as "drugged roaches in a bottle" and also said that "a good Arab is a dead Arab." Another former chief of staff, Moshe Ya'alon, referred to the Palestinian threat as like a "cancer" on which he was performing "chemotherapy."[46]

Such discriminatory views are not restricted to Israeli leaders. In a recent survey of Jewish high school students in Israel, 75 percent of the respondents said that Arabs are "uneducated." The same percentage said that they are "uncivilized," while 74 percent of those polled said that Arabs are "unclean." Commenting on this last finding, Larry Derfner wrote in the *Jerusalem Post*: "To say Arabs are unclean is not a hard-line political statement. It's not an unduly harsh comment on Arab behavior. To say Arabs are unclean is to evince an irrational, hysterical, impenetrable, absolute hatred for an entire ethnic group—which, in fact, happens not to be unclean, no more than Jews are. To say Arabs are unclean is an expression of racism in about its purest, most virulent form." The person who oversaw the survey said, "We were not surprised by the outcome of the research. Anyone who is familiar with the field knows that these warped perceptions exist, but these findings are at the most severe extreme of a disturbing phenomenon." It is noteworthy that the same survey polled Israeli Arab youth as well, and Derfner reports that "while their attitudes toward Jews are awful, they're considerably less awful than the Jewish students' attitudes toward them."[47]

These hostile attitudes toward Israeli Arabs, coupled with fears about a "demographic threat" and the desire to maintain a Jewish majority, have led to considerable support among Israeli Jews for expelling or "transferring" much of the Arab population from Israel. Indeed, Avigdor Lieberman, who was appointed deputy prime minister for strategic threats in 2006, has made it clear that he favors expulsion, so as to make Israel "as much as possible" a homogeneous Jewish state. Specifically, he advocates trading portions of Israel that are densely packed with Arabs for areas of the West Bank that contain Jewish settlers. He is not the first Israeli cabinet minister to advocate expulsion.[48]

Although he is a controversial figure, Lieberman is not an outlier in Israel on this issue. The Israel Democracy Institute reported in May 2003 that 57 percent of Israel's Jews "think that the Arabs should be encouraged to emigrate." A 2004 survey conducted by Haifa University's Center for the Study of National Security found that the number had increased to 63.7 percent. One year later, in 2005, the Palestinian Center for Israel Studies found that 42 percent of Israeli Jews believed that their government should encourage Israeli Arabs to leave, while another 17 percent tended to agree with the idea. The following year, the Center for Combating Racism found that 40 percent of Israel's Jews wanted their leaders to encourage the Arab population to emigrate, while the Israel Democracy Institute found the number to be 62 percent.[49] If 40 percent or more of white Americans declared that blacks, Hispanics, and Asians "should be encouraged" to leave the United States, it would surely prompt vehement criticism.

These attitudes are perhaps to be expected, given the long conflict between Israelis and Palestinians and the considerable suffering it has produced on both sides. They are also no worse than the attitudes that many Americans had for different minority groups (especially African Americans) throughout much of American history. Yet whatever their origins, they are clearly attitudes that would now earn widespread condemnation here in the United States, if their existence were more widely known, and they pose a serious challenge to clichés about "our shared values, our strong commitment to freedom."

Finally, Israel's democratic status is undermined by its refusal to grant the Palestinians a viable state of their own and by its continued imposition of a legal, administrative, and military regime in the Occupied Territories that denies them basic human rights. Israel at present controls the lives of about 3.8 million Palestinians in Gaza and the West Bank, while colonizing lands on which they have long dwelt. Israel formally withdrew from Gaza in the summer of 2005 but continues to maintain substantial control over its residents.[50] Specifically, Israel controls air, sea, and land access, which means that the Palestinians are effectively prisoners within Gaza, able to enter or leave only with Israeli approval. Jan Egeland, a senior UN figure, and Jan Eliasson, the Swedish foreign minister, wrote in September 2006 that the Palestinians are "living in a cage," which naturally has had devastating effects on their economy, as well as their mental and physical well-being.[51]

On the West Bank, Israel continues to expropriate Palestinian land and build settlements. The situation was succinctly described in a *Ha'aretz* editorial in late December 2006: "Virtually not a week goes by without a new revelation, each more sensational and revolting than the previous one, about the building spree in West Bank settlements, in blatant violation of the law and in complete contradiction to official government policy."[52] Indeed, the Israeli organization Peace Now recently released a study based on Israeli government records, which shows that more than 32 percent of the land that Israel holds for the purpose of building settlements is privately owned by Palestinians. Israel intends to keep almost all of this land forever. This seizure of Palestinian property violates not only Israeli law but also a fundamental principle of democracy: the protection of private property.[53]

In sum, Israel has a vibrant democratic order for its Jewish citizens, who can and do criticize their government and choose their leaders in open and free elections. Freedom of the press is also alive and well in Israel, where, paradoxically, it is much easier to criticize Israeli policy than it is in the United States. This is why so much of the evidence in this study is drawn from the Israeli press. Despite these positive features, Arab Israelis are systematically marginalized, the millions of Palestinians in the Occupied Territories are denied full political rights, and the "shared democracy" rationale is correspondingly weakened.

COMPENSATION FOR PAST CRIMES

A third moral justification is the history of Jewish suffering in the Christian West, especially the tragic experience of the Holocaust. Because Jews were persecuted for centuries and many believe they can be safe only in a Jewish homeland, Israel is said to deserve special treatment. This view formed the basis for the original Zionist program, played an important role in convincing the United States and other countries to back Israel's founding, and continues to resonate today.

There is no question that Jews suffered greatly from the despicable legacy of anti-Semitism and that Israel's creation was an appropriate response to a long record of crimes. This history provides a strong moral case for supporting Israel's founding and continued existence. This backing is also consistent with America's general commitment to national self-determination. But one cannot ignore the fact that the creation of Israel involved additional crimes against a largely innocent third party: the Palestinians. Crimes against Jews justify backing Israel's existence, but its crimes against Palestinians undermine its claim to special treatment.

The history of these events is well documented. When political Zionism began in earnest in the late nineteenth century, there were only about fifteen thousand to seventeen thousand Jews living in Palestine.[54] In 1893, for example, the Arabs comprised roughly 95 percent of the population, and though under Ottoman control, they had been in continuous possession of this territory for thirteen hundred years.[55] The old Zionist adage that Palestine was "a land without people for a people without a land" was dead wrong regarding the land; it was occupied by another people.[56]

The early Zionists hoped that the waves of Jews who began leaving Europe in the last decades of the nineteenth century would come to Palestine, allowing the Jews to gain a decisive numerical advantage over the Arabs there. But that did not happen, mainly because most of these Jews preferred to go to the United States. Only one hundred thousand of the four million Jews who left Europe between 1880 and 1920 went to Palestine.[57] In fact, until Hitler came to power, the Jews in Palestine could not fill "the generous immigration quotas allowed by the British."[58] In 1948, when Israel was founded, its 650,000 Jews were only about 35 percent of Palestine's population and they owned only 7 percent of its land.[59]

From the start, the leading Zionists were determined to create a Jewish state that covered virtually all of Palestine, and even parts of Lebanon and Syria.[60] Of course, there were differences among them on where they thought the borders should be drawn in an ideal world, and almost all recognized that it might not be possible to realize all of their territorial ambitions. The mainstream Zionist leadership, it should be emphasized, was never interested in establishing a binational state where Arabs and Jews lived side by side in a country that had no religious identity and might even have more Arabs than Jews. The goal from the beginning was to create instead a Jewish state in which Jews comprised at least 85 percent of the population.[61]

The Zionists' ambitions also went beyond a permanent partition of Palestine. It is widely believed in the United States, especially among Israel's supporters, that the Zionists were willing to agree to a permanently partitioned Palestine, and indeed they did agree to the partition plans put forward by Britain's Peel Commission in 1937 and the UN in 1947. But their acceptance of these plans did not mean that they intended to accept only part of Palestine in perpetuity, or that they were willing to support the creation of a Palestinian state. As recent scholarship makes abundantly clear, the Zionist leadership was sometimes willing to accept partition as a first step, but this was a tactical maneuver and not their real objective. They had no intention of coexisting alongside a viable Palestinian state over the long run, as that outcome was in direct conflict with their dream of creating a Jewish state in all of Palestine.

There was fierce opposition among the Zionists to the Peel Commission's partition plan, and their leader, David Ben-Gurion, was barely able to get his fellow Zionists to accept it. They eventually agreed to the proposal, however, because they recognized that Ben-Gurion intended eventually to take all of the land of Palestine. The Zionist leader made this point clearly in the summer of 1937 when he told the Zionist Executive, "After the formation of a large army in the wake of the establishment of the state, we will abolish partition and expand to the whole of Palestine." Similarly, he told his son Amos that same year, "Erect a Jewish State at once, even if it is not in the whole land. The rest will come in the course of time. It must come."[62]

The Peel Commission's plan went nowhere in 1937, and over the course of the ensuing decade the Zionists remained committed to incorporating all of Mandate Palestine into a future Jewish state. Ben-Gurion made a number of comments in the first half of 1947 that show he still wanted all of Palestine. For example, the Israeli scholar Uri Ben-Eliezer reports:

On May 13, 1947, Ben-Gurion told a meeting of the Jewish Agency Executive which was held in the United States: "We want the Land of Israel in its entirety. That was the original intention." A week later, speaking to the Elected Assembly in Jerusalem, the leader of the Yishuv wondered: "Does anyone among us disagree that the original intention of the Balfour Declaration and the Mandate, and the original intention of the hopes harbored by generations of the Jewish people, was finally to establish a Jewish state in the whole Land of Israel?" Speaking to the Mapai Secretariat in June, Ben-Gurion stated that it would be a mistake to forgo any part of the land. We have no right to do that, he said, and there is no need for it.[63]

Later that year, in November, the UN devised a new plan to partition Palestine between the Zionists and the Palestinian Arabs. The Zionists publicly accepted this plan as well. But in fact Ben-Gurion had already negotiated a deal with King Abdullah of Transjordan to divide up Palestine between Israel and Transjordan and deny the Palestinians a state.[64] This secret arrangement, which Britain endorsed, allowed Transjordan to acquire the West Bank and Israel to take what it could of the rest of Palestine. The deal was ultimately implemented during the 1948 war, although in a somewhat disjointed fashion. Israeli leaders, not surprisingly, gave serious thought during the war to conquering the West Bank and taking all of Mandate Palestine for their new state, but they decided that the likely costs outweighed the potential benefits. Transjordan, which later became Jordan, controlled the West Bank until the 1967 Six-Day War, when the IDF conquered it. In short, Israel's founding fathers were determined from the beginning to create a "greater Israel," which left no room for a Palestinian state and little room for Palestinians inside the Jewish state.

Given that Arabs heavily outnumbered Jews in Palestine and that the Zionists were bent on conquering as much territory as feasible, they had little choice but to expel large numbers of Arabs from the territory that would eventually become Israel. There was no other way to accomplish their objective, as the Arabs were hardly likely to give up their land voluntarily. This is why the Peel Commission's plan to partition Palestine called explicitly for population transfer. It is also why the UN partition plan, which called for establishing an Israel that was 55 percent Jewish and 45 percent Arab, was unworkable.[65] There was certainly no way that a Jewish state could be created in all of Palestine without convincing large numbers of Arabs to leave.

In light of these realities, expulsion was a frequent topic of conversation among Zionists since the earliest days of the movement, and it was widely recognized as the only realistic way to solve the demographic problem that stood in the way of creating a Jewish state.[66] Ben-Gurion saw the problem clearly, writing in 1941 that "it is impossible to imagine general evacuation [of the Arab population] without compulsion, and brutal compulsion."[67] Or as he wrote his son in October 1937, "We shall organize a modern defense force . . . and then I am certain that we will not be prevented from settling in other parts of the country, either by mutual agreement with our Arab neighbors or by some other means."[68] No doubt he would have preferred to do so via "mutual agreement," but Ben-Gurion understood that this was a remote possibility and that the Zionists would need a strong army to accomplish their aims. Morris puts the point succinctly: "Of course, Ben-Gurion was a transferist. He understood that there could be no Jewish state with a large and hostile Arab minority in its midst . . . Ben-Gurion was right. If he had not done what he did, a state would not have come into being. That has to be clear. It is impossible to evade it. Without the uprooting of the Palestinians, a Jewish state would not have arisen here."[69]

Expulsion is a horrible and controversial strategy and it makes no sense for any group contemplating the transfer of a rival population to announce its intentions to the world. Thus, after commenting in 1941 that he could not imagine how transfer could be accomplished without "brutal compulsion," Ben-Gurion went on to say that the Zionists should not "discourage other people, British or American, who favour transfer from advocating this course, but we should in no way make it part of our programme."[70] He was not rejecting this policy, however; he was simply noting that the Zionists should not openly proclaim it. Further reflecting how "highly sensitive" the subject of transfer was to Israel's founding fathers, Benny Morris notes that "it was common practice in Zionist bodies to order stenographers to 'take a break' and thus to exclude from the record discussion on such matters." Moreover, he notes that "Jewish press reports" describing how Ben-Gurion and other Zionist leaders reacted to the Peel Commission's plan for partitioning Palestine "generally failed to mention that Ben-Gurion, or anyone else, had come out strongly in favor of transfer or indeed had even raised the subject."[71]

The opportunity to expel the Palestinians and create a Jewish state came in 1948, when Jewish forces drove up to seven hundred thousand Palestinians into exile.[72] Israelis and their supporters in the United States long claimed that the Arabs fled because their leaders told them to, but scholars have demolished this myth. In fact, most Arab leaders urged the Palestinian population to stay home, but fear of violent death at the hands of Zionist forces led most of them to flee.[73] After the war, Israel barred the return of the Palestinian exiles. As Ben-Gurion put it in June 1948, "We must prevent at all costs their return."[74] By 1962, Israel owned almost 93 percent of the land inside its borders.[75] To achieve this outcome, 531 Arab villages were destroyed "and eleven urban neighborhoods emptied of their inhabitants."[76] Former Israeli Defense Minister Moshe Dayan captures the catastrophe that the Zionists inflicted on the Palestinians to create the state of Israel: "Jewish villages were built in the place of Arab villages. You do not even know the names of these Arab villages, and I do not blame you because geography books no longer exist, not only do the books not exist, the Arab villages are not there either . . . There is not a single place built in this country that did not have a former Arab population."[77]

The fact that the creation of Israel entailed a grave injustice against the Palestinian people was well understood by Israel's leaders. As Ben-Gurion told Nahum Goldmann, president of the World Jewish Congress, in 1956, "If I was an Arab leader I would never make terms with Israel. That is natural: we have taken their country. Sure, God promised it to us, but what does that matter to them? Our God is not theirs. We come from Israel, it's true, but two thousand years ago, and what is that to them? There has been anti-semitism, the Nazis, Hitler, Auschwitz, but was that their fault? They only see one thing: we have come here and stolen their country. Why should they accept that?"[78]

Ze'ev Jabotinsky, the founding father of the Israeli right, made essentially the same point when he wrote in 1923, "Colonization is self-explanatory and what it implies is fully understood by every sensible Jew and Arab. There can only be one purpose in colonization. For the country's Arabs that purpose is essentially unacceptable. This is a natural reaction and nothing will change it."[79] Berl Katznelson, a close ally of Ben-Gurion and a leading intellectual force among the early Zionists, put the point bluntly: "The Zionist enterprise is an enterprise of conquest."[80]

In the six decades since Israel was created, its leaders have repeatedly sought to deny the Palestinians' national ambitions.[81] Prime Minister Golda Meir, for example, famously remarked that "there was no such thing as a Palestinian."[82] Many Israeli leaders also maintained a deep interest in incorporating the West Bank and Gaza into Israel. In 1949, for example, Moshe Dayan proclaimed that Israel's boundaries were "ridiculous from all points of view." Israel's eastern border, he felt, should be the Jordan River. Dayan was no exception in this regard; many of his fellow generals as well as Ben-Gurion himself were keen on acquiring the West Bank for Israel.[83] Benny Morris is certainly correct when he notes that "the vision of 'Greater Israel' as Zionism's ultimate objective did not end with the 1948 war."[84]

After the start of the First Intifada in December 1987, some Israeli leaders began to countenance giving the Palestinians limited autonomy in particular areas of the West Bank and Gaza. Prime Minister Yitzhak Rabin, who signed the 1993 Oslo Accords, is often said to have been willing to allow the Palestinians to have a viable state in almost all of the Occupied Territories. But this view is not correct; Rabin in fact opposed creating a full-fledged Palestinian state. Speaking in 1995, the year that he was murdered, Rabin said, "I seek peaceful coexistence between Israel as a Jewish state, not all over the land of Israel, or most of it; its capital, the united Jerusalem; its security border with Jordan rebuilt; next to it, a Palestinian entity, less than a state, that runs the life of Palestinians . . . This is my goal, not to return to the pre–Six-Day War lines but to create two entities, a separation between Israel and the Palestinians who reside in the West Bank and the Gaza Strip."[85]

The depth of Israel's opposition to creating a Palestinian state—even in the late 1990s—is reflected in an incident involving First Lady Hillary Clinton. In the spring of 1998, Israelis and their American supporters sharply criticized her for saying that "it would be in the long-term interests of peace in the Middle East for there to be a state of Palestine, a functioning modern state that is on the same footing as other states." White House officials, according to the New York Times, immediately "disowned" her comments and "insisted that she was speaking only for herself." Her view, the White House press secretary said, "is not the view of the President."[86]

By 2000, however, it was finally acceptable for American politicians to speak openly about the desirability of a Palestinian state. At the same time, pressure from extremist violence and the growing Palestinian population has forced recent Israeli leaders to dismantle the settlements in the Gaza Strip and to explore territorial compromises involving the West Bank. Still, no Israeli government has been willing to offer the Palestinians a viable state of their own. As discussed below, even Prime Minister Ehud Barak's purportedly generous offer at Camp David in July 2000 would have given the Palestinians only a disarmed and dismembered state under de facto Israeli control. In 2002, former Prime Minister Yitzhak Shamir reiterated his opposition to giving the Palestinians any kind of state, while former Prime Minister Benjamin Netanyahu made it clear the following year that he favored only a semisovereign Palestinian state.[87]

Europe's crimes against the Jews provide a strong moral justification for Israel's right to exist. No new settler state can hope to come into existence without some degree of violence, but Israel has continued to impose terrible violence and discrimination on the Palestinians for decades. These policies can no longer be justified on the grounds that the existence of Israel is at stake. Israel's survival is not in doubt, even if some Islamic extremists harbor unrealistic hopes or Iranian President Mahmoud Ahmadinejad says that Israel "should vanish from the page of time."[88] More important, the past suffering of the Jewish people does not obligate the United States to help Israel no matter what it does today.

"VIRTUOUS ISRAELIS" VERSUS "EVIL ARABS"

Another moral argument portrays Israel as a country that has sought peace at every turn and showed great and noble restraint even when provoked. The Arabs, by contrast, are said to have acted with deep wickedness and indiscriminate violence. This narrative is endlessly repeated by Israeli leaders and by American apologists for Israel such as Alan Dershowitz and the *New Republic* editor in chief Martin Peretz. Israel, according to Peretz, adheres closely to a doctrine called "purity of arms," which means that "everything reasonable must be done to avoid harming civilians, even if that entails additional risks to Israeli soldiers." Moreover, he maintains that "Israel has for years vacillated between responding to terror with exquisitely calibrated force and pacifying terrorists by giving them some of what they want," while its Arab enemies are part "of the very same terror that was launched on us on Sept. 11."[89] The IDF, according to Ariel Sharon and Ehud Olmert, among others, "is the most moral army in the world."[90] This description of Israeli behavior is yet another myth, another element in what Meron Benvenisti, the former deputy mayor of Jerusalem, calls Israel's "sacred narrative."[91]

Israeli scholarship shows that the early Zionists were far from benevolent toward the Palestinian Arabs.[92] The Arab inhabitants did resist the Zionists' encroachments, sometimes killing Jews and destroying their homes. But this resistance would be expected given that the Zionists were trying to create their own state on Arab lands. "Were I an Arab," Ben-Gurion candidly remarked in June 1937, "I would rebel even more vigorously, bitterly, and desperately against the immigration that will one day turn Palestine and all its Arab residents over to Jewish rule."[93] The Zionists responded vigorously and often ruthlessly, and thus neither side owns the moral high ground during this period.

This same scholarship also reveals that the creation of Israel in 1948 involved explicit acts of ethnic cleansing, including executions, massacres, and rapes by Jews.[94] Of course, Zionist leaders did not tell their troops to murder and rape Palestinians, but they did advocate using brutal methods to remove huge numbers of Palestinians from the land that would soon be the new Jewish state. Consider what Ben-Gurion wrote in his diary on January 1, 1948, at a time when he was involved in a series of important meetings with other Zionist leaders about how to deal with the Palestinians in their midst: "There is a need now for strong and brutal reaction. We need to be accurate about timing, place and those we hit. If we accuse a family—we need to harm them without mercy, women and children included. Otherwise, this is not an effective reaction . . . There is no need to distinguish between guilty and not guilty."[95] It is hardly surprising that this sort of guidance from the Zionist leadership—Ben-Gurion was summarizing the emerging policy—led Jewish soldiers to commit atrocities. After all, we have seen this pattern of behavior in many wars, fought by many different peoples. Regardless, the occurrence of atrocities in this period undercuts Israel's claim to a special moral status.

Israel's subsequent conduct toward its Arab adversaries and its Palestinian subjects has often been severe, belying any claim to morally superior conduct. Between 1949 and 1956, for example, Morris estimates that "Israeli security forces and civilian guards, and their mines and booby-traps, killed somewhere between 2,700 and 5,000 Arab infiltrators." Some of them were undoubtedly bent on killing Israelis, but according to the available evidence, "the vast majority of those killed were unarmed; the overwhelming majority had infiltrated for economic or social reasons." Morris notes that this "free-fire" policy led to "a series of atrocities" against the infiltrators.[96]

These kinds of acts were not anomalous. The IDF murdered hundreds of Egyptian prisoners of war in both the 1956 and 1967 wars.[97] In 1967, it expelled between 100,000 and 260,000 Palestinians from the newly conquered West Bank and drove 80,000 Syrians from the Golan Heights.[98] When the victims of these ethnic cleansings tried to sneak back to their homes, often unarmed, Israelis sometimes shot them on sight.[99] Amnesty International estimates that between 1967 and 2003, Israel destroyed more than ten thousand homes in the West Bank and the Gaza Strip.[100] Israel was also complicit in the massacre of innocent Palestinians by a Christian militia at the Sabra and Shatila refugee camps following its invasion of Lebanon in 1982. An Israeli investigatory commission found Defense Minister Ariel Sharon to bear "personal responsibility" for these atrocities by allowing the Phalangists to enter the camps.[101] While the commission's willingness to hold a top official like Sharon accountable is admirable, we should not forget that Israeli voters subsequently elected him prime minister.

Israel has now controlled the West Bank and Gaza for forty years, making it, as the historian Perry Anderson notes, "the longest official military occupation of modern history."[102] When the occupation began, Benny Morris explains, Israelis "liked to believe, and tell the world, that they were running an 'enlightened' and 'benign' occupation, qualitatively different from other military occupations the world had seen. The truth was radically different. Like all occupations, Israel's was founded on brute force, repression and fear, collaboration and treachery, beatings and torture chambers, and daily intimidation, humiliation, and manipulation."[103] During the First Intifada (1987–91), for example, the IDF distributed truncheons to its troops and encouraged them to break the bones of Palestinian protestors. The Swedish branch of the Save the Children organization released a thousand-page report in May 1990 that detailed the effects of that conflict on the children in the Occupied Territories. It estimated that "23,600 to 29,900 children required medical treatment for their beating injuries in the first two years of the [first] intifada." Moreover, it estimated that almost one-third of the children were ten years or under; one-fifth were five and under; more than four-fifths "had been beaten on their heads and upper bodies and at multiple locations"; and almost one-third of the children "sustained broken bones, including multiple fractures."[104]

Ehud Barak, the IDF's deputy chief of staff during the First Intifada, said at the time, "We do not want children to be shot under any circumstances . . . When you see a child you don't shoot." Nevertheless, Save the Children estimated that sixty-five hundred to eighty-five hundred children were wounded by gunfire during the first two years of the Intifada. Regarding the 106 recorded cases of "child gunshot deaths," the report concluded that almost all of them "were hit by directed—not random or ricochet—gunfire"; almost 20 percent suffered multiple gunshot wounds; about 12 percent were shot from behind; 15 percent of the children were ten years or younger; "most children were not participating in a stone-throwing demonstration when shot"; and "nearly one-fifth of the children were shot dead while at home or within ten meters of their homes."

Israel's response to the Second Intifada (2000–05) was even more violent, leading the Israeli newspaper *Ha'aretz* to declare that "the IDF . . . is turning into a killing machine whose efficiency is awe-inspiring, yet shocking."[105] The IDF fired one million bullets in the first days of the uprising, which is hardly a measured response.[106] Over the course of that uprising, Israel killed 3,386 Palestinians, while 992 Israelis were killed by the Palestinians, which means that Israel killed 3.4 Palestinians for every Israeli lost.

Among those killed were 676 Palestinian children and 118 Israeli children; thus, the ratio of Palestinian to Israeli children killed was 5.7 to 1. Of the 3,386 Palestinian deaths, 1,815 were believed to be bystanders, 1,008 were killed while fighting the Israelis, and the circumstances of 563 deaths are unknown. In other words, well over half of the Palestinian fatalities appear to have been noncombatants. A similar pattern holds on the Israeli side, where 683 of its 992 deaths were civilians; the remaining 309 were military.[107] Israeli forces have also killed several foreign peace activists, including a twenty-three-year-old American woman crushed by an Israeli bulldozer in March 2003.[108] Yet the Israeli government rarely investigates these civilian deaths, much less punishes the perpetrators.[109]

These facts about Israel's conduct have been amply documented by numerous human rights organizations—including prominent Israeli groups—and are not disputed by fair-minded observers.[110] And that is why four former officials of Shin Bet (the Israeli domestic security organization) condemned Israel's conduct during the Second Intifada in November 2003. One of them declared, "We are behaving disgracefully," and another termed Israel's conduct "patently immoral."[111]

A similar pattern can be seen in Israel's response to the escalation in violence in Gaza and Lebanon in 2006. The killing of two Israeli soldiers and the capture of a third by Hamas in June 2006 led Israel to reoccupy Gaza and launch air strikes and artillery fire that destroyed critical infrastructure, including the electric power station that provided residents of Gaza with half of their electricity. The IDF has also killed hundreds of Palestinians since moving back into Gaza, many of them children.[112] This dire situation led the UN high commissioner for human rights, Louise Arbour, to proclaim in November 2006 that "the violation of human rights in this territory . . . is massive."[113] Likewise, when Hezbollah units crossed the Israeli-Lebanese border in July 2006 and captured two IDF soldiers and killed several more, Israel unleashed a bombing campaign that was designed to inflict massive punishment on Lebanon's civilian population by destroying critical infrastructure like roads, bridges, gas stations, and buildings. More than one thousand Lebanese died, most of them innocent civilians. As discussed in Chapter 11, this response was both strategically foolish and a violation of the laws of war. In short, there is little basis for the often-heard claim that Israel has consistently shown great restraint in dealing with its adversaries.

An obvious challenge to this point is the claim that Israel has faced a mortal threat throughout its history, both from "rejectionist" Arab governments and from Palestinian terrorists. Isn't Israel entitled to do whatever it takes to protect its citizens? And doesn't the unique evil of terrorism justify continued U.S. support, even if Israel often responds harshly?

In fact, this argument is not a compelling moral justification either. Palestinians have used terrorism against their Israeli occupiers as well as innocent third parties; their willingness to attack civilians is wrong and should be roundly condemned. This behavior is not surprising, however, because the Palestinians have long been denied basic political rights and believe they have no other way to force Israeli concessions. As former Prime Minister Barak once admitted, had he been born a Palestinian, he "would have joined a terrorist organization."[114] If the situation were reversed and the Israelis were under Arab occupation, they would almost certainly be using similar tactics against their oppressors, just as other resistance movements around the world have done.[115]

Indeed, terrorism was one of the key tactics that the Zionists used when they were in a similarly weak position and trying to obtain their own state. It was Jewish terrorists from the infamous Irgun, a militant Zionist group, who in late 1937 introduced into Palestine the now-familiar practice of placing bombs in buses and large crowds. Benny Morris speculates that "the Arabs may well have learned the value of terrorist bombings from the Jews."[116] Between 1944 and 1947, several Zionist organizations used terrorist attacks to drive the British from Palestine and took the lives of many innocent civilians along the way.[117] Israeli terrorists also murdered the UN mediator Count Folke Bernadotte in 1948, because they opposed his proposal to internationalize Jerusalem.[118] The perpetrators of these acts were not isolated extremists: the leaders of the murder plot were eventually granted amnesty by the Israeli government and one of them was later elected to the Knesset. Another terrorist leader, who approved of Bernadotte's murder but was not tried, was future Prime Minister Yitzhak Shamir. He openly argued that "neither Jewish ethics nor Jewish tradition can disqualify terrorism as a means of combat." Rather, terrorism had "a great part to play . . . in our war against the occupier [Britain]." Nor did Shamir express regrets about his terrorist past, telling an interviewer in 1998 that "had I not acted as I did, it is doubtful that we would have been able to create an independent Jewish state of our own."[119]

Of course, Menachem Begin, who headed the Irgun and later became prime minister, was one of the most prominent Jewish terrorists in the years before Israeli independence. When speaking of Begin, Prime Minister Levi Eshkol often referred to him simply as "the terrorist."[120] The Palestinians' use of terrorism is morally reprehensible today, but so was the Zionists' reliance on it in the past. Thus, one cannot justify American support for Israel on the grounds that its past or present conduct was morally superior.

Another possible line of defense is that Israel does not purposely target noncombatants, while Hezbollah and the Palestinians do aim to kill Israeli civilians. Moreover, the terrorists who strike at Israel use civilians as human shields, which regrettably leaves the IDF no choice but to kill innocent civilians when it strikes at its deadly foes. These rationales are not convincing either. As discussed in Chapter 11, the IDF targeted civilian areas in Lebanon, and there is little evidence that Hezbollah was using civilians as human shields. While there is also no evidence that it has been official Israeli policy to kill Palestinian civilians, the IDF has often failed to take care to avoid civilian casualties when fighting against groups like Hamas and Islamic Jihad. The fact that Hezbollah and the Palestinians target civilians does not entitle Israel to jeopardize civilian lives by using disproportionate force.

There is no question that Israel is justified in responding with force to violent acts by groups like Hamas and Hezbollah, but its willingness to use its superior military power to inflict massive suffering on innocent civilians casts doubt on its repeated claims to a special moral status. Israel may not have acted worse than many other countries, but it has not acted any better.

CAMP DAVID MYTHS

The portrayal of Israel as primed for peace and the Palestinians as bent on war is reinforced by the standard interpretation of the Clinton administration's failed effort to complete the Oslo peace process. According to this story, Prime Minister Barak offered the Palestinians "almost everything" they wanted at Camp David in July 2000.[121] But Arafat, still determined to derail the peace process and eventually destroy Israel, rejected this generous offer and instead launched the Second Intifada in late September 2000. Israel accepted and Arafat rejected an even more generous proposal—the so-called Clinton parameters—put forth by President Clinton on December 23, 2000, providing further evidence that he had no interest in peace.

In this story, the failure of the peace process was almost entirely Arafat's fault. Israel was eager to make peace but could not find a reliable partner, confirming Abba Eban's famous quip that "the Arabs never miss an opportunity to miss an opportunity." This account also implies that neither Israel nor the United States bears responsibility for the continued conflict and bolsters the argument that Israel was correct in refusing to make concessions to the Palestinians as long as Arafat was in charge.

There is only one problem with this widely held version of events: it is not correct.[122] Although Barak deserves credit for being the first—indeed, the only—Israeli leader to offer the Palestinians their own state, the terms he offered them at Camp David were far from generous. To start, it seems clear that Barak's best offer at Camp David promised the Palestinians immediate control of Gaza and eventual control of 91 percent of the West Bank.[123] Even so, there were major problems with this offer from the Palestinians' perspective. Israel planned to keep control of the Jordan River Valley (roughly 10 percent of the West Bank) for between six and twenty-one years (different accounts of the negotiations vary on this point), which meant that the Palestinians would be given immediate control over no more than 81 percent of the West Bank, not 91 percent. The Palestinians, of course, could not be sure that Israel would ever relinquish control of the Jordan River Valley.

In addition, the Palestinians had a slightly more expansive definition of what constituted the West Bank than the Israelis did. This difference, which amounted to roughly 5 percent of the territory in question, meant that the Palestinians saw themselves immediately getting 76 percent of the West Bank and, if the Israelis were willing to surrender the Jordan River Valley at some future date, maybe 86 percent. What made this deal especially difficult for the Palestinians to accept was the fact that they had already agreed in the 1993 Oslo Accords to recognize Israeli sovereignty over 78 percent of the original British Mandate.[124] From their perspective, they were now being asked to make another major concession and accept at best 86 percent of the remaining 22 percent.

To make matters worse, the final Israeli proposal at Camp David in the summer of 2000 would not have given the Palestinians a continuous piece of sovereign territory in the West Bank. The Palestinians maintain that the West Bank would have been divided into three cantons separated by Israeli territory. Israelis dispute this claim, but Barak himself acknowledges that Israel would have maintained control of a "razor-thin" wedge of territory running from Jerusalem to the Jordan River Valley.[125] This wedge, which would completely bisect the West Bank, was essential to Israel's plan to retain control of the Jordan River Valley. Thus, the Palestinian state proposed at Camp David would have been composed of either two or three distinct cantons in the West Bank, and Gaza, which is itself separated from the West Bank by Israeli territory. Barak later said that the Palestinian areas on the West Bank could have been connected by "a tunnel or bridge," while Gaza and the West Bank would have been connected by a travel corridor.[126]

With regard to the thorny issue of Jerusalem, Barak's proposal to divide the city was a major step in the right direction. Nonetheless, the Palestinians were not offered full sovereignty in a number of Arab neighborhoods in East Jerusalem, which made the proposal significantly less attractive to them. Israel would also have kept control over the new Palestinian state's borders, its airspace, and its water resources, and the Palestinians would be permanently barred from building an army to defend themselves.[127] It is hard to imagine any leader accepting these terms. Certainly no other state in the world has such curtailed sovereignty, or faces so many obstacles to building a workable economy and society. Given all this, it is not surprising that Barak's former foreign minister, Shlomo Ben-Ami, who was a key participant at Camp David, later told an interviewer, "If I were a Palestinian I would have rejected Camp David, as well."[128]

The common claim that Arafat launched the Second Intifada in late September 2000—either to enhance his leverage in the negotiations or to destroy the peace process itself—does not stand up against the evidence either.[129] He continued negotiating with the Israelis and the Americans after Camp David, and he even visited Prime Minister Ehud Barak's home a few nights before the violence broke out. According to Charles Enderlin, a French journalist who has written an important book on the failure of these negotiations, the two leaders were uncharacteristically friendly and optimistic about the negotiations that evening.[130] Moreover, the former head of Shin Bet, Ami Ayalon, has stated that "Arafat neither prepared nor triggered the Intifada."[131] The so-called Mitchell Commission, headed by former U.S. Senator George Mitchell and charged with restarting the peace process, reached the same conclusion.[132]

The Second Intifada broke out shortly after Ariel Sharon visited the Temple Mount, Judaism's most holy site, on September 28, 2000. He had to be accompanied by more than a thousand Israeli police, because Muslims consider that same site, the location of the al-Aqsa Mosque, to be the third holiest site in Islam. But Sharon's provocative move was only the precipitating cause, not the root cause, of the violence. Trouble had been brewing among the Palestinians well before Sharon's visit, and key individuals on both sides recognized the danger. In fact, Palestinian leaders asked American and Israeli officials to bar Sharon's visit precisely because they anticipated a violent reaction and wanted to prevent it.[133]

Part of the problem was the Palestinians' growing dissatisfaction with

Arafat, whose corrupt leadership had done little to improve their lives, much less deliver a state. But the main cause was Israel's provocative policies in the Occupied Territories, compounded by its harsh response to the demonstrations that immediately followed Sharon's visit.[134] Ben-Ami is exactly right that the Second Intifada "did not start merely as a tactical move. It erupted out of the accumulated rage and frustration of the Palestinian masses at the colossal failure of the peace process since the early days of Oslo to offer them a life of dignity and well-being, and at the incompetence and corruption of their own leaders in the Palestinian Authority."[135]

The Palestinians' frustrations are not hard to fathom. Between the start of the Oslo peace process in September 1993 and the outbreak of the Second Intifada seven years later, Israel confiscated more than forty thousand acres of Palestinian land, built 250 miles of bypass and security roads, established thirty new settlements, and increased the settler population in the West Bank and Gaza by almost one hundred thousand, which effectively doubled that population.[136] The Israelis also reneged on promises to transfer territory back to the Palestinians and created a system of checkpoints that sharply reduced the Palestinians' freedom of movement and badly damaged their economy. The Palestinians were primed to explode by 2000, and when they did, the Israelis unleashed their superior firepower with scant restraint.[137] The IDF, as noted, fired more than a million bullets in the first few days of the uprising.

Although Arafat did not launch the Second Intifada, he exploited the resulting violence in a foolish attempt to enhance his bargaining position. Not only did this move make Barak less willing to cut a deal, but it also damaged Barak's standing with the Israeli electorate and paved the way for Sharon's election in February 2001. Arafat's attempt to leverage the uprising also delayed the negotiations, which meant that the lame-duck Clinton administration had even less time in which to complete the process.

Some argue that Arafat's ultimate goal in manipulating the violence was to erase Israel from the map. That was certainly his goal when he first emerged on the world stage in the 1960s, but he recognized by the late 1980s that there was no way that the Palestinians could make Israel go away. Arafat went to some lengths in the 1990s—certainly by participating in the Oslo peace process—to make clear that he accepted Israel's existence and that his struggle with Israel was over control of the Occupied Territories, not all of historic Palestine.[138] When Camp David failed and the Second Intifada began, almost all of Israel's key intelligence figures believed that Arafat accepted Israel's existence and merely sought a Palestinian state in the West Bank and Gaza.[139] Furthermore, as the Middle East specialist Jeremy

Pressman points out, if Arafat and the Palestinians were determined to eliminate Israel, they would have accepted Barak's offer and used the new state
as "a launching pad for the elimination of Israel." But instead they negotiated "as if they expected to abide by any agreements and live for the long
term within the framework of a two-state solution."[140]

Finally, the oft-repeated claim that Arafat rejected the December 2000
Clinton parameters, which did improve on Barak's last offer at Camp David,
is also wrong. The official Palestinian response thanked Clinton for his con-
tinued efforts, declared that considerable progress had been made, asked for
clarification on some points, and expressed reservations about others.[141] The
Israeli government also had its own reservations about the proposal, which
Barak outlined in a twenty-page single-spaced document. Thus, both the
Palestinians and the Israelis accepted the Clinton parameters and saw them
as the basis for continued negotiation, but neither side accepted them in toto.
The White House spokesman Jake Siewert made just this point on January 3,
2001, when he said that "both sides have now accepted the President's ideas
with some reservations," and Clinton confirmed this point in a speech to the
Israel Policy Forum four days later.[142] Negotiations between Israelis and
Palestinians continued at Taba, Egypt, until late January 2001, when Ehud
Barak, not Arafat, broke off the talks. With elections in Israel imminent and
public opinion there running strongly against the talks, Barak felt that the
clock had run out on him.[143] His successor, Ariel Sharon, who was adamantly opposed to the Oslo peace process as well as the Clinton parameters, refused to resume negotiations despite repeated Palestinian requests.
We will never know if peace was within sight by early 2001, but the charge
that Arafat and the Palestinians rejected a last chance for peace and chose
violence over reconciliation is false.

SUPPORTING ISRAEL IS GOD'S WILL

There is a final moral claim that some say justifies the close embrace between the United States and Israel. As discussed in more detail in Chapter 4,
some evangelical Christians—especially so-called Christian Zionists—view
the establishment of the Jewish state as the fulfillment of biblical prophecy.
Genesis says that God gave Abraham and his descendants the land of Israel;
by colonizing the West Bank, Jews are merely taking back what God gave
them. Some Christians also see the creation of a greater Israel as a key event
leading to the end-time "final battle" depicted in the New Testament's Book

of Revelation. Both perspectives imply that Israel deserves U.S. support not because it is a democracy, an underdog, or a morally superior society, but because backing Israel is God's will.

This line of argument undoubtedly appeals to some fervently religious individuals, but anticipating Armageddon is not a sound basis for making American foreign policy. Church and state are separate in the United States, and the religious opinions of any group are not supposed to determine the country's foreign policy. It is also an odd reading of Christian ethics to support the powerful Israeli state in its mistreatment of dispossessed Palestinians and its suppression of their rights.

WHAT DO THE AMERICAN PEOPLE WANT?

The six moral arguments that we have just examined underpin the broader claim that the real basis of U.S. support for Israel is the American people's enduring identification with the Jewish state. The columnist Jeff Jacoby of the *Boston Globe* writes that "solidarity with Israel is an abiding feature of American public opinion. Because the American people are pro-Israel, the American government is pro-Israel. And because Americans so strongly support Israel in its conflict with the Arabs, American policy in the Middle East is committed to Israel's defense." As the AIPAC spokesman Josh Block said on the eve of its 2007 Policy Conference, "There's one issue—that is, support for the U.S. relationship with Israel—that brings everyone together." In fact, he argued that "all trends indicate that Americans . . . understand quite clearly that the basic values we celebrate are reflected in only one country in the Middle East—our ally Israel."[144]

This claim, however widely believed, does not stand up to close inspection. There is a degree of cultural affinity between the United States and Israel, based in part on the shared Judeo-Christian tradition. There is also no question that many Americans look favorably on Israel because it is a democracy, because of the history of anti-Semitism, and because they sympathize with Israel in its fight against Palestinian terrorism. But the common roots of Judaism and Christianity have hardly been a reliable source of amity between Jews and Christians in the past.[145] Not only have Christians waged brutal wars against each other, but they have also been the primary perpetrators of violent anti-Semitism in previous centuries. And some fundamentalists—including Christian Zionists—still regard the conversion of Jews as an important evangelical objective. By itself, therefore, this "cultural affinity" cannot account for the consistent level of U.S. support, or even the generally favorable attitudes that many Americans express toward the Jewish state.

As will become clear in later chapters, the American people are inclined to support Israel in part because its supporters in the United States cultivate sympathy by stifling criticism of Israel while simultaneously portraying it in a favorable light. Indeed, there is much more criticism of Israel's actions in Israel itself than there is in America. If there were a more open and candid discussion about what the Israelis are doing in the Occupied Territories, and about the real strategic value of Israel as a U.S. ally, there would be much less sympathy for Israel in the American public.

Nonetheless, the degree of public support for Israel—and for specific Israeli policies—should not be overstated. Although the American people have favorable perceptions of Israel and clearly support the existence of a Jewish state, support for Israel is not especially deep. Most Americans also recognize that the United States pays a price for its unyielding support of Israel. For example, the Pew Research Center for the People and the Press has been asking Americans for many years whether they sympathize more with Israel or the Palestinians. There has always been much more sympathy for Israel, but from 1993 through 2006, the number went above 50 percent only once—it was 52 percent during the second Lebanon war in 2006—and was as low as 37 percent in July 2005.[146]

Regarding the consequences of U.S. support for Israel, a Pew survey conducted in November 2005 found that 39 percent of the American public said that it was "a major cause of global discontent." Among opinion leaders, the numbers were substantially higher. Indeed, 78 percent of members of the news media, 72 percent of military leaders, 72 percent of security experts, and 69 percent of foreign affairs specialists believe that backing Israel seriously damages America's image around the world.[147] A *Newsweek* poll released a few weeks after the September 11 attacks found that 58 percent of the respondents believed that U.S. support for Israel was a factor in Osama bin Laden's decision to attack America.[148]

The American people are considerably more critical of some Israeli actions than U.S. politicians are, and the public clearly supports taking a hard-nosed approach to dealing with Israel when they think it is in the national interest to do so. As we explain in Chapter 7, a survey in the spring of 2003 showed that 60 percent of Americans were willing to withhold aid to Israel if it resisted U.S. pressure to settle its conflict with the Palestinians. In fact, 73 percent said the United States should not favor either side in the conflict.[149] Two years later, the Anti-Defamation League found that 78 percent of Americans believed that Washington should favor neither Israel nor the Palestinians.[150] Andrew Kohut, the director of the Pew Research Center for the People and the Press, points out that "average Americans see shades of gray in the Middle East conflict, and their sympathies notwithstanding, they favor a neutral role for the United States."[151]

Unlike their leaders, the American people displayed a tough-minded approach to dealing with Israel during the Lebanon war in 2006. As discussed in Chapter 11, polls showed that slightly more than half of the public thought that Israel was either equally responsible or mainly responsible for the war, and in at least two polls more than half of the respondents said that the United States should not take sides.[152] But the United States emphatically took Israel's side in Lebanon, as it has in every recent conflict involving Israel. This enthusiastic and unconditional support cannot be explained by the generally favorable opinion of Israel held by most Americans.

CONCLUSION

The moral or strategic arguments commonly invoked by Israel's backers cannot account for America's remarkable relationship with the Jewish state over the past three decades. This is especially true for the post–Cold War period, when the strategic rationale largely evaporated and the moral rationale was badly undermined by Israeli behavior in the Occupied Territories. Yet the relationship continued to grow and deepen.

Some Americans surely do not find this situation anomalous, as they sincerely believe that there are powerful moral and strategic reasons behind U.S. support for Israel. Because the essential facts in this story are so at odds with this perspective, it is hard to imagine that the number of true believers is large enough to account for America's exceptional relationship with the Jewish state. We are left with a puzzle: either a relatively small number of true believers are exerting a disproportionate influence on U.S. foreign policy, or they have managed to persuade lots of other people—especially key politicians and policy makers—that these flawed rationales are in fact correct. Because the strategic and moral case is increasingly weak, something else must be behind the striking pattern of ever-increasing U.S. support. We address that issue in the next chapter.

4

WHAT IS THE "ISRAEL LOBBY"?

In the United States, interest groups routinely contend to shape perceptions of the national interest and to convince legislators and presidents to adopt their preferred policies. The interplay of competing factions was famously extolled by James Madison in the *Federalist No. 10*, and the influence of different interest groups has long shaped various aspects of American foreign policy, including decisions for war.

When a particular interest group is especially powerful or politically adept, it may influence policy in ways that are not good for the country as a whole. A tariff that shields a particular industry from foreign competition will benefit certain companies but not the many consumers who have to pay more for that industry's goods. The National Rifle Association's success in thwarting gun control legislation undoubtedly benefits gun manufacturers and dealers, but it leaves the rest of society more vulnerable to gun-related violence. When a former lobbyist for the American Petroleum Institute becomes chief of staff at the White House's Council on Environmental Quality, and uses this position to water down reports on the connection between greenhouse gas emissions and global warming (before resigning to take a job at ExxonMobil), one may reasonably worry that the oil industry is protecting its interests in ways that may harm all of us.[1]

The influence of the Israel lobby on U.S. foreign policy merits the same scrutiny as the impact of energy interests on environmental regulations or the role of pharmaceutical companies in shaping policy on prescription drugs. We believe the activities of the groups and individuals who make up the lobby are the main reason why the United States pursues policies in the Middle East that make little sense on either strategic or moral grounds.

Were it not for the lobby's efforts, the strategic and moral arguments that are commonly invoked to justify unconditional American support would be called into question more frequently and U.S. policy in the Middle East would be significantly different than it is today. Pro-Israel forces surely believe that they are promoting policies that serve the American as well as the Israeli national interest. We disagree. Most of the policies they advocate are not in America's or Israel's interest, and both countries would be better off if the United States adopted a different approach.

As we have already noted, we are not questioning American support for Israel's right to exist, because that right is clearly justified and is now endorsed by more than 160 countries around the world. What we are questioning—and what needs to be explained—is the magnitude of U.S. support for Israel and its largely unconditional nature (as described in Chapter 1), as well as the degree to which U.S. Middle East policy is conducted with Israel's welfare in mind (as explored in detail in Part II). To begin that task, this chapter identifies the central components of the Israel lobby and describes how it has evolved over time. We also discuss why it has become so influential, especially when compared to potential competitors like the "Arab lobby" and the "oil lobby." The following chapters describe the different strategies that have made it such a powerful interest group and a remarkably effective player in the making of U.S. Middle East policy.

DEFINING THE LOBBY

We use "Israel lobby" as a convenient shorthand term for the loose coalition of individuals and organizations that actively work to shape U.S. foreign policy in a pro-Israel direction. The lobby is not a single, unified movement with a central leadership, however, and the individuals and groups that make up this broad coalition sometimes disagree on specific policy issues. Nor is it some sort of cabal or conspiracy. On the contrary, the organizations and individuals who make up the lobby operate out in the open and in the same way that other interest groups do.

Using the term "Israel lobby" is itself somewhat misleading, insofar as many of the individuals and some of the groups in this loose coalition do not engage in formal lobbying activities (direct efforts to persuade elected officials). Rather, the various parts of the lobby work to influence U.S. policy in a variety of ways, much as other interest groups do. One might more accurately dub this the "pro-Israel community" or even the "help Israel movement," because the range of activities that different groups undertake goes beyond simple lobbying. Nonetheless, because many of the key groups do lobby, and because the term "Israel lobby" is used in common parlance (along with labels such as the "farm lobby," "insurance lobby," "gun lobby," or other ethnic lobbies), we have chosen to employ it here.[2]

As with other special interest groups, the boundaries of the Israel lobby cannot be identified precisely, and there will always be some borderline individuals or organizations whose position is hard to classify.[3] It is easy to identify groups that are clearly part of the lobby—such as the Zionist Organization of America (ZOA)—as well as individuals who are key members— such as Malcolm Hoenlein, executive vice chairman of the Conference of Presidents of Major American Jewish Organizations. There are also many groups that are obviously not part of the lobby—such as the National Association of Arab-Americans—and individuals who should clearly be excluded as well—such as Columbia University scholar Rashid Khalidi. Nevertheless, there will always be some groups and individuals whose position is more ambiguous. Like other social and political movements, the Israel lobby's boundaries are somewhat fuzzy.

This situation highlights that the lobby is not a centralized, hierarchical organization with a defined membership. There are no membership cards or initiation rites. It has a core consisting of organizations whose declared purpose is to encourage the U.S. government and the American public to provide material aid to Israel and to support its government's policies, as well as influential individuals for whom these goals are also a top priority. The lobby, however, also draws support from a penumbra of groups and individuals who are committed to Israel and want the United States to continue supporting it, but who are not as energetically or consistently active as the groups and individuals that form the core. Thus, a lobbyist for the American Israel Public Affairs Committee (AIPAC), a research fellow at the Washington Institute for Near East Policy (WINEP), or the leadership of organizations like the Anti-Defamation League (ADL) and Christians United for Israel (CUFI) are part of the core, while individuals who occasionally write letters supporting Israel to their local newspaper or send checks to a pro-Israel political action committee should be seen as part of the broader network of supporters.

This definition does not mean that every American with favorable attitudes toward Israel is a member of the lobby. To offer a personal illustration, the authors of this book are "pro-Israel," in the sense that we support its right to exist, admire its many achievements, want its citizens to enjoy secure and prosperous lives, and believe that the United States should come to Israel's aid if its survival is in danger. But we are obviously not part of the Israel lobby. Nor does it imply that every American official who supports Israel is part of the lobby either. A senator who consistently votes in favor of aid to Israel is not necessarily part of the lobby, because he or she may simply be responding to political pressure from pro-Israel interest groups.

To be part of the lobby, in other words, one has to actively work to move American foreign policy in a pro-Israel direction. For an organization, this pursuit must be an important part of its mission and consume a substantial percentage of its resources and agenda. For an individual, this means devoting some portion of one's professional or personal life (or in some cases, substantial amounts of money) to influencing U.S. Middle East policy. A journalist or academic who sometimes covers Middle East issues and occasionally reports events that portray Israel favorably—such as the *New York Times* reporter David Sanger or the Duke University professor Bruce Jentleson— should not be seen as part of the lobby. But a journalist or scholar who predictably takes Israel's side and devotes a significant amount of his or her writing to defending steadfast U.S. support for Israel—such as the *Washington Post* columnist Charles Krauthammer or the former Princeton University historian Bernard Lewis—clearly is.

Of course, the level of effort and the specific activities will vary in each case, and these various groups and individuals will not agree on every issue that affects Israel. Some individuals—such as Morton Klein of ZOA, John Hagee of CUFI, and Rael Jean Isaac of Americans for a Safe Israel—oppose a two-state solution between Israel and the Palestinians and believe instead that Israel should retain all or most of the Occupied Territories. Others, such as Dennis Ross of WINEP and Martin Indyk of the Brookings Institution, favor a negotiated settlement and have occasionally criticized specific Israeli actions. Despite these differences, however, each of these individuals believes that the United States should give Israel substantial diplomatic, economic, and military support even when Israel takes actions the United States opposes, and each has devoted a significant amount of his or her professional life to encouraging this sort of support. Thus, although it would clearly be wrong to think of the lobby as a single-minded monolith, much less portray it as a cabal or conspiracy, it would be equally mistaken to exclude anyone who works actively to preserve America's special relationship with the Jewish state.

THE ROLE OF AMERICAN JEWRY

The bulk of the lobby is comprised of Jewish Americans who are deeply committed to making sure that U.S. foreign policy advances what they believe to be Israel's interests. According to the historian Melvin I. Urofsky, "No other ethnic group in American history has so extensive an involvement with a foreign nation." Steven T. Rosenthal agrees, writing that "since 1967 . . . there has been no other country whose citizens have been as committed to the success of another country as American Jews have been to Israel."[4] In 1981, the political scientist Robert H. Trice described the pro-Israel lobby as "comprised of at least 75 separate organizations—mostly Jewish—that actively support most of the actions and policy positions of the Israeli government."[5] The activities of these groups and individuals go beyond merely voting for pro-Israel candidates to include writing letters to politicians or news organizations, making financial contributions to pro-Israel political candidates, and giving active support to one or more pro-Israel organizations, whose leaders often contact them directly to convey their agenda.

Yet the Israel lobby is not synonymous with American Jewry, and "Jewish lobby" is not an appropriate term for describing the various individuals and groups that work to foster U.S. support for Israel. For one thing, there is significant variation among American Jews in their depth of commitment to Israel. Roughly a third of them, in fact, do not identify Israel as a particularly salient issue. In 2004, for example, a well-regarded survey found that 36 percent of Jewish Americans were either "not very" or "not at all" emotionally attached to Israel.[6] Furthermore, many American Jews who care a lot about Israel do not support the policies endorsed by the dominant organizations in the lobby, just as many gun owners do not support every policy that the NRA advocates and not all retirees favor every position endorsed by the AARP. For example, American Jews were less enthusiastic about going to war in Iraq than the population as a whole, even though key organizations in the lobby supported the war, and they are more opposed to the war today. Finally, some of the individuals and groups that are especially vocal on Israel's behalf, such as the Christian Zionists, are not Jewish. So while American Jews are the lobby's predominant constituency, it is more accurate to refer to this loose coalition as the Israel lobby. It is the specific political agenda that defines the lobby, not the religious or ethnic identity of those pushing it.

The attachment that many American Jews feel for Israel is not difficult to understand, and as noted in the Introduction, it resembles the attitudes of other ethnic groups that retain an affinity for other countries or peoples with similar backgrounds in foreign lands.[7] Although many Jews in the United States were ambivalent about Zionism during the movement's early years, support grew significantly after Hitler came to power in 1933 and especially after the horrors inflicted on the Jews during World War II became widely known.[8]

Relatively few Jews chose to leave the United States and move to Israel after its founding in 1948, a pattern that Prime Minister David Ben-Gurion and other Israeli leaders initially criticized. Nevertheless, a strong commitment to Israel soon became an important element of identity for many American Jews.[9] The establishment of a Jewish state in historic Palestine seemed miraculous in itself, especially in the aftermath of the Nazi Holocaust. Israel's achievements in "making the desert bloom" were an obvious source of pride, and a close identification with Israel provided a new basis for community for a population that was rapidly assimilating into American society and becoming increasingly secular at the same time. As Rosenthal notes:

> To equate Israel with Judaism was a comforting way to avoid the encumbrances of religion by focusing one's Jewishness on a secular state 8,000 miles from home . . . Synagogues, the new mainstay of American Jewish life in the postwar era, became Israel-centered. A new class of Jewish professionals . . . arose in the suburbs. They soon discovered that Israel was the most effective means to counter the growing religious indifference of their constituencies. Primarily in response to Israel's overwhelming need for financial and political support, new institutions . . . arose, and fundraising and lobbying increasingly defined American Jews' relationship to Israel.[10]

American Jews have formed an impressive array of civic organizations whose agendas include working to benefit Israel, in many cases by influencing U.S. foreign policy. Key organizations include AIPAC, the American Jewish Congress, ZOA, the Israel Policy Forum (IPF), the American Jewish Committee, the ADL, the Religious Action Center of Reform Judaism, Americans for a Safe Israel, American Friends of Likud, Mercaz-USA, Hadassah, and many others. Indeed, the sociologist Chaim I. Waxman reported in 1992 that the *American Jewish Yearbook* listed more than eighty national Jewish organizations "specifically devoted to Zionist and pro-Israel activities . . . and for many others, objectives and activities such as 'promotes

Israel's welfare,' 'support for the State of Israel' and 'promotes understanding of Israel' appear with impressive frequency."[11] Fifty-one of the largest and most important organizations come together in the Conference of Presidents of Major American Jewish Organizations, whose self-described mission includes "forging diverse groups into a unified force for Israel's well-being" and working to "strengthen and foster the special U.S.-Israel relationship."[12]

The lobby also includes think tanks such as the Jewish Institute for National Security Affairs (JINSA), the Middle East Forum (MEF), and WINEP, as well as individuals who work in universities and other research organizations. There are also dozens of pro-Israel PACs ready to funnel money to pro-Israel political candidates or to candidates whose opponents are deemed either insufficiently supportive of or hostile to Israel. The Center for Responsive Politics, a nonpartisan research group that tracks campaign contributions, has identified roughly three dozen such "pro-Israel" PACs (many of them "stealth PACs" whose names do not reveal a pro-Israel orientation) and reports that these organizations contributed approximately $3 million to congressional candidates in the 2006 midterm election.[13]

Of the various Jewish organizations that include foreign policy as a central part of their agenda, AIPAC is clearly the most important and best known. In 1997, when *Fortune* magazine asked members of Congress and their staffs to list the most powerful lobbies in Washington, AIPAC came in second behind AARP but ahead of heavyweight lobbies like the AFL-CIO and the NRA.[14] A *National Journal* study in March 2005 reached a similar conclusion, placing AIPAC in second place (tied with AARP) in Washington's "muscle rankings."[15] Former Congressman Mervyn Dymally (D-CA) once called AIPAC "without question the most effective lobby in Congress," and the former chairman of the House Foreign Affairs Committee, Lee Hamilton, who served in Congress for thirty-four years, said in 1991, "There's no lobby group that matches it . . . They're in a class by themselves."[16]

The influence that groups like AIPAC now enjoy did not emerge overnight. During Zionism's early years, and even after Israel's founding, lobbying on Israel's behalf tended to occur quietly behind the scenes and usually depended on personal contacts between influential government officials, especially the president, and a small number of Jewish leaders, pro-Zionist advisers, or Jewish friends. For example, Woodrow Wilson's support for the Balfour Declaration in 1917 was due in part to the influence of his Jewish friends Supreme Court Justice Louis D. Brandeis and Rabbi Stephen Wise.

Similarly, Harry S. Truman's decision to back Israel's creation and to recognize the new state was influenced (though not determined) by intercessions from Jewish friends and advisers.[17]

The tendency for Israel's supporters to keep a low profile reflected concerns about lingering anti-Semitism in the United States, as well as the fear that overt lobbying on Israel's behalf would expose American Jews to the charge of dual loyalty. AIPAC itself had explicitly Zionist roots: its founder, I. L. "Si" Kenen, was head of the American Zionist Council in 1951, which was a registered foreign lobbying group. Kenen reorganized it as a U.S. lobbying organization—the American Zionist Committee for Public Affairs—in 1953–54, and the new organization was renamed AIPAC in 1959. Kenen relied on personal contacts with key legislators rather than public campaigns or mass mobilization, and AIPAC generally followed "Kenen's Rules" to advance Israel's cause. Rule No. 1 was: "Get behind legislation; don't step out in front of it (that is, keep a low profile)."[18]

According to J. J. Goldberg, the editor of the Jewish newspaper *Forward*, Zionist influence "increased exponentially during the Kennedy and Johnson administrations, because the affluence and influence of Jews in American society had increased," and also because Kennedy and Johnson "counted numerous Jews among their close advisers, donors and personal friends."[19] AIPAC was still a small operation with a modest staff and budget, and as Stuart Eizenstat points out, "Not until the mid-1960s did overt organized Jewish political activity on behalf of the state of Israel come into its own."[20]

The lobby's size, wealth, and influence grew substantially after the Six-Day War in June 1967. According to Eizenstat, that conflict "galvanized the American Jewish public like no event since Israel's War of Independence . . . The sense of pride in 'new Jews,' proud, strong, capable of defending themselves, had an incalculable effect on American Jewry." The successful campaign against anti-Semitism, aided by the widespread awareness of the horrors of the Holocaust, helped remove lingering discriminatory barriers, and Jewish Americans "lost the sense of fear that had stunted their political will" in earlier years. And because Israel was becoming a central focus of Jewish identity in a world where assimilation was increasingly viable and widespread, there were few reasons not to express that attachment in politics.[21]

The heightened concern with Israel's well-being within Jewish organizations continued during the War of Attrition (1969–70) and the October War (1973). These conflicts reinforced pride in Israel's military prowess, but they also raised fears about Israel's security, thereby reinforcing the Israelcentric focus of many Jewish community-relations groups.[22] Albert Chernin, the executive director of the National Jewish Community Relations Advisory Council (NJCRAC, later renamed the Jewish Council for Public Affairs), expressed this perspective in 1978 when he said that our "first priority is Israel, of course, reflecting the complete identity of views of the American Jewish leadership with the concerns of the rank and file." The historian Jack Wertheimer terms this comment a "stunning admission that political efforts to shore up Israel superseded all other concerns of Jewish community relations organizations in the United States."[23]

As American foreign aid to Israel began to exceed private contributions, pro-Israel organizations increasingly focused on political activities intended to preserve or increase U.S. governmental support. According to Wertheimer, "The overall responsibility for lobbying for Israel was assumed by the Conference of Presidents . . . and AIPAC. Both had been founded in the 1950s and had played a modest role prior to 1967. The needs of Israel for political support catapulted these two organizations to prominence in the 1970s and 1980s."[24]

This increased effort reflected awareness that backing Israel was costly for the United States and therefore had to be justified and defended in the political sphere. As Morris Amitay, who replaced Kenen as AIPAC's executive director in 1975, put it, "The name of the game, if you want to help Israel, is political action."[25] Under Amitay and his successor, Tom Dine, AIPAC was transformed from an intimate, low-budget operation into a large, mass-based organization with a staff of more than 150 employees and an annual budget (derived solely from private contributions) that went from some $300,000 in 1973 to an estimated $40–60 million today.[26] Instead of shunning the limelight, as it had done under Kenen, AIPAC increasingly sought to advertise its power. According to one former staffer, "The theory was, no one is scared of you if they don't know about you."[27] In contrast to the earlier patterns of intimate lobbying on behalf of Jews by Jewish advisers and sympathetic gentiles, AIPAC and other groups in the lobby did not define their public agenda as humanitarian support for Jews in Israel. Rather, the evolution of the lobby increasingly involved the formulation and promotion of sophisticated arguments about the alignment of America's and Israel's strategic interests and moral values.

Flush with cash and well positioned in the Cold War political landscape, AIPAC found its political muscle enhanced by new federal rules on campaign financing, which triggered the creation of independent PACs and made it easier to channel money toward pro-Israel candidates. AIPAC may not have been all that formidable in the early 1960s, but by the 1980s, notes Warren Bass, it was a "Washington powerhouse."[28]

UNITY IN DIVERSITY AND THE NORM AGAINST DISSENT

As noted above, the lobby is not a centralized, hierarchical movement. Even among the Jewish elements of the lobby, there are important differences on specific policy issues. In recent years, AIPAC and the Conference of Presidents have tilted toward Likud and other hard-line parties in Israel and were skeptical about the Oslo peace process (a phenomenon we discuss at greater length below), while a number of other, smaller groups—such as Ameinu, Americans for Peace Now, Brit Tzedek v'Shalom (Jewish Alliance for Justice and Peace), Israel Policy Forum, Jewish Voice for Peace, Meretz-USA, and the Tikkun Community—strongly favor a two-state solution and believe Israel needs to make significant concessions in order to bring it about.[29]

These differences have occasionally led to rifts within or among these different organizations. In 2006, for example, the Israel Policy Forum, Americans for Peace Now, Jewish Voice for Peace, and Brit Tzedek v'Shalom openly opposed an AIPAC-sponsored congressional resolution (HR 4681) that would have imposed even more draconian restrictions on aid to the Palestinians than the Israeli government sought.[30] A watered-down version of the resolution passed by a comfortable margin, but the episode reminds us that pro-Israel groups do not form a monolith with a single party line.

These divisions notwithstanding, the majority of organized groups in the American Jewish community—especially the largest and wealthiest among them—continue to favor steadfast U.S. support for Israel no matter what policies the Jewish state pursues. As an AIPAC spokesman explained in June 2000, when concerns about Israel's arms sales to China led to calls for a reduction in U.S. support, "We are opposed to linking Israel's aid under any circumstances because once it starts it never stops."[31] Even the dovish Americans for Peace Now supports "robust U.S. economic and military assistance to Israel," opposes calls to "cut or condition" U.S. aid, and seeks only to prevent U.S. aid from being used to support settlement activities in the Occupied Territories.[32] Similarly, the moderate Israel Policy Forum does not advocate making American aid more conditional but rather focuses its efforts on persuading the U.S. government to work more actively and effectively for a two-state solution.[33] Despite differences on the peace process and related issues, in short, almost every pro-Israel group wants to keep the "special relationship" intact. A notable exception is Jewish Voice for Peace (JVP), which has called for the U.S. government to suspend military aid to Israel until it ends the occupation of the West Bank, Gaza, and East Jerusalem.[34] Indeed, given this position, one might argue that JVP is not part of the lobby at all.

Given their desire to maximize U.S. backing, Israeli officials frequently engage American Jewish leaders and ask them to help mobilize support in the United States for particular Israeli policies. As Rabbi Alexander Schindler, former chair of the Conference of Presidents, told an Israeli magazine in 1976, "The Presidents' Conference and its members have been instruments of official governmental Israeli policy. It was seen as our task to receive directions from government circles and to do our best no matter what to affect the Jewish community." (Schindler thought this situation was "not acceptable," telling the interviewer that "American Jewry is in no mood to be used by anyone.")[35] Yet Albert Chernin of NJCRAC offered a similar appraisal in the 1970s, saying that "in domestic areas we made policy, but in Israel affairs the policy was a given . . . In reality, [the Conference of Presidents] was the vehicle through which Israel communicated its policy to the community."[36] Ori Nir of the *Forward* quotes an unnamed activist with a major Jewish organization claiming in 2005 that "it is routine for us to say: 'This is our policy on a certain issue, but we must check what the Israelis think.' We as a community do it all the time." Or as Hyman Bookbinder, a high-ranking official of the American Jewish Committee, once admitted, "Unless something is terribly pressing, really critical or fundamental, you parrot Israel's line in order to retain American support. As American Jews, we don't go around saying Israel is wrong about its policies."[37]

Israel's ability to galvanize support within the United States has been demonstrated on numerous occasions. Zionist (and later, Israeli) officials encouraged American Jewish leaders to campaign for the UN partition plan in 1947 and for U.S. recognition in 1948, and to lobby against the abortive peace plan formulated by the UN mediator Folke Bernadotte in 1948. Coordinated efforts such as these also helped convince the Truman administration to significantly increase economic aid to Israel in 1952 and to abandon a Pentagon and State Department proposal for a $10 million grant of military assistance to Egypt.[38] During the crisis preceding the 1967 Six-Day War, the Israeli government instructed its ambassador in Washington to "create a public atmosphere that will constitute pressure on the [Johnson] administration . . . without it being explicitly clear that we are behind this public campaign." The effort involved getting sympathetic Americans to write letters, editorials, telegrams, and public statements, etc.—"in a variety of styles"—whose purpose, according to the Israeli Foreign Ministry, was "to create a public atmosphere . . . that will strengthen our friends within the administration." White House officials eventually asked their Israeli counterparts to shut down the letter-writing campaign, but the Israeli ambassador reported back to Jerusalem that "of course we are continuing it." According to the historian Tom Segev, the White House was "inundated with letters from citizens calling on the president to stand by Israel."[39]

This tendency to support Israel's actions reflexively may be less prevalent today, but major organizations in the lobby still defer to the preferences of Israel's leaders on many occasions. Following the release of the Bush administration's "road map" for Middle East peace in March 2003, for example, Malcolm Hoenlein of the Conference of Presidents reportedly told *Ha'aretz* that if the Israeli government expressed reservations about the road map, it would have the support of America's Jewish community. And, Hoenlein emphasized, "We will not hesitate to make our voice heard."[40]

Despite the fissures that have emerged between the Israeli government and some groups within American Jewry, this community "has generally accepted the principle that on matters of fundamental security there ought to be no public criticism of Israel."[41] According to Steven Rosenthal, "For millions of American Jews, criticism of Israel was a worse sin than marrying out of the faith." Or as Bookbinder once acknowledged, "There is a feeling of guilt as to whether Jews should double-check the Israeli government . . . They automatically fall into line for that very reason."[42] Recent surveys of American Jewish opinion reveal that roughly two-thirds of the respondents agree that "regardless of their individual views on the peace negotiations with the Arabs, American Jews should support the policies of the duly-elected government of Israel."[43] Thus, even when both leaders and rank and file of important Jewish-American organizations have serious reservations about Israeli policy, they rarely call for the U.S. government to put significant pressure on the Israeli government.

The norm against public criticism has been vividly illustrated on a number of occasions over the past several decades. In 1973, for example, a group of progressive American Jews formed a new organization, Breira (Alternative), which called for more open discussion between Israel and the diaspora and sought to mobilize support for withdrawal from the Occupied Territories and a peace settlement with the Palestinians. In addition to making their views publicly known through advertisements in major American newspapers, several Breira leaders were part of a delegation of American

Jews who met in a private capacity with a group of Palestinian representatives, under the auspices of the American Friends Service Committee.

Although a few Jewish leaders defended Breira, a powerful backlash soon emerged from the major Jewish organizations. AIPAC's *Near East Report* accused Breira of undermining support for Israel, and the president of the Reform rabbinate, Arthur Lelyveld, said that groups like Breira "gave aid and comfort . . . to those who would cut aid to Israel and leave it defenseless before murderers and terrorists." A Hadassah newsletter labeled Breira members "cheerleaders for defeatism" and warned its own members to "reject the advances of these organizations with their dogmas that run counter to Israeli security and Jewish survival." The president of the conservative Rabbinical Assembly declared that Breira was "fronting for the PLO," and forty-seven rabbis issued a statement terming Breira's positions "practically identical with the Arab point of view." The prosettlement group Americans for a Safe Israel distributed a thirty-page pamphlet smearing Breira's leaders for their involvement with other left-wing causes and referring to them as "Jews for *Fatah*." Not to be outdone, the ZOA magazine *American Zionist* accused Breira of abusing the right of free speech, warning that "the Jews who cry 'Foul!' in public must realize the treacherous consequences of their efforts . . . Ramifications are felt not by them, but by fellow Jews thousands of miles away."

In the face of this assault, Breira stood little chance of building a following or establishing a more open climate for discussion. Local community groups excluded Breira representatives, and the Jewish Community Council of New Haven agreed to admit the local Breira chapter only on the condition that it confine its criticism within the community. An internal memorandum prepared by the American Jewish Committee recommended co-opting the group, but only if it agreed to "direct the exposition of their different views on sensitive Israel-Diaspora issues to the Jewish community itself and refrain from appealing to the general public." Unable to attract sustained funding and weakened by leadership defections, Breira disbanded after five years.[44]

In response to the Breira controversy, organizations like the Conference of Presidents, the Synagogue Council of America, the American Jewish Committee, and NJCRAC conducted internal studies or public inquiries on the proper place of dissent. According to J. J. Goldberg, "All these organizations reached the same conclusion: American Jews had the right to discuss issues freely, but only within discreet forums outside public view." In 1976, the Israeli ambassador to the United States, Simcha Dinitz, working with representatives from NJCRAC and the Conference of Presidents, developed a set of principles to guide behavior within the Jewish community. The first principle, Goldberg notes, was that "Israelis were the only ones entitled to decide Israeli policy" and the second was that "American Jews should stand publicly united with Israel and air disputes only in private."[45] By the 1970s, writes Edward Tivnan, "Total support of Israel had become a requirement of leadership in local Jewish communities throughout America."[46]

The norm against public criticism of Israeli policy remains for the most part intact.[47] In October 1996, for example, the president of ZOA, Morton Klein, sent a letter to ADL head Abraham Foxman protesting an invitation to New York Times columnist Thomas L. Friedman to speak at an ADL dinner, charging that Friedman "regularly defames Israel and its Prime Minister Benjamin Netanyahu." Klein then circulated the letter to an array of officials at the Conference of Presidents, leading Foxman to denounce him as a "thought policeman." The dispute intensified when David Bar-Illan, Netanyahu's director of communications, weighed in and declared that Friedman should not be given a platform by "any organization that purports to be Zionist." Though sometimes critical of certain Israeli policies, Friedman is hardly anti-Israel, and Foxman himself is one of Israel's most ardent defenders. But Klein's response shows how deep the opposition to open discussion runs.[48]

A few years later, Edgar Bronfman Sr., then president of the World Jewish Congress, was accused of "perfidy" when he wrote a letter to President Bush urging him to pressure Israel to curb construction of its controversial "security fence." The executive vice president of the congress, Isi Liebler, declared that "it would be obscene at any time for the president of the World Jewish Congress to lobby the president of the United States to resist policies being promoted by the government of Israel."[49] Liebler and others were similarly incensed two years later, when the president of the moderate Israel Policy Forum, Seymour Reich, advised Secretary of State Condoleezza Rice to pressure Israel to reopen a critical border crossing in the Gaza Strip in November 2005. Reich's advice to Rice was reasonable and well intentioned, but Liebler denounced his action as "irresponsible behavior," and the president of the Orthodox Union, Stephen Savitzky, said it was "not only disrespectful to Israel's government but offensive to millions of American Jews who categorically reject such an approach." Liebler also warned, "There is obviously something sick in the state of World Jewry when purportedly mainstream leaders feel that they can lobby freely against the security policies of the democratically elected government of Israel. If this sort of behavior is to be tolerated we may as well write off our one remaining ally—Diaspora Jewry." Recoiling from these attacks, Reich announced that "the word pressure is not in my vocabulary when it comes to Israel."[50]

The reluctance to criticize Israel's policies openly is not difficult to fathom. In addition to the obvious desire not to say anything that might aid Israel's enemies, groups or individuals who criticize Israeli policy or the U.S.-Israel relationship are likely to find it harder to retain support and raise funds within the Jewish community. They also run the risk of being ostracized by the larger mainstream organizations. Although groups like Americans for Peace Now, the Tikkun Community, the Israel Policy Forum, and the New Israel Fund have endured and thrived where Breira did not, other progressive Jewish groups, such as New Jewish Agenda, encountered the same opposition that Breira had faced and lasted little more than a decade.[51] Similarly, although Americans for Peace Now was eventually admitted to the Conference of Presidents in 1993 after a contentious struggle, the progressive Meretz USA and the liberal Reconstructionist Rabbinical Association were denied membership in 2002 despite support from moderate groups within the Conference. On a smaller scale, Jewish Voice for Peace was denied a booth at a major Jewish community event in the San Francisco area on the grounds that it was insufficiently supportive of Israel, and the Hillel chapter at the University of Texas refused to give an organization called Jewish Students for Palestinian Rights space to conduct a study group.[52]

Efforts to marginalize dissenting Jewish voices continue to this day. When the Union of Progressive Zionists (UPZ) sponsored campus appearances in 2006 by Breaking the Silence, an organization of former Israeli soldiers that is critical of IDF operations in the Occupied Territories, ZOA denounced UPZ and demanded that it be expelled from the Israel on Campus Coalition (ICC), a network of pro-Israel groups that includes AIPAC and the ADL. According to ZOA's Klein, sponsoring groups that are critical of Israel "is not the mission of the ICC." UPZ's director emphasized the group's "love for Israel," other groups rallied to its defense, and the ICC steering committee unanimously rejected ZOA's demand. Undeterred, Klein denounced the members of the steering committee and said, "Their mission includes fighting incitement, and yet we are astonished that they would ignore this incitement by Israelis against Israel." ZOA also issued a press release urging member organizations in the ICC to change their votes. The press release quoted an Israeli Foreign Ministry report saying, "The willingness of Jewish communities to host these organizations and even sponsor them is unfortunate . . . Their negative effect on Israel's image must be stopped." At least one Orthodox group on the ICC steering committee subsequently announced it was now in favor of removing the UPZ.[53]

THE LOBBY MOVES RIGHT

Most American Jews have long supported liberal causes and the Democratic party, and a majority of them favor a two-state solution to the Israeli-Palestinian conflict.[54] Nonetheless, some of the most important groups in the lobby—including AIPAC and the Conference of Presidents—have become increasingly conservative over time and are now led by hard-liners who support the positions of their hawkish counterparts in Israel. As J. J. Goldberg chronicles in his important book, *Jewish Power*, the Six-Day War and its aftermath brought into prominence a group of "New Jews" drawn disproportionately from hard-line Zionist, Orthodox, and neoconservative circles. "Their defiance was so strident, and their anger so intense," he writes, "that the rest of the Jewish community respectfully stood back and let the New Jews take the lead. The minority was permitted to speak for the mass and become the dominant voice of Jewish politics."[55]

This trend was reinforced by the campaign on behalf of the 1974 Jackson-Vanik amendment (which linked most-favored-nation trading status for the Soviet Union to Moscow's willingness to permit greater Jewish emigration), by the emergence and growth of the so-called neoconservative movement (see below), and by the Likud party's successful effort to cultivate and strengthen hard-line support in key pro-Israel organizations during the years when Likud was sharing power with Israel's Labor party. According to Goldberg, "The genius of Shamir's strategy . . . was to manipulate the central bodies of Jewish representation so that, without taking sides, they became voices for the Likud half of the government." Likud party officials (including Prime Minister Shamir's chief of staff Yossi Ben-Aharon) worked to ensure that the Conference of Presidents was chaired by more conservative officials and also helped engineer the selection of Malcolm Hoenlein as executive vice chairman of the conference in 1986. More hard-line groups were given greater access and attention by Israeli leaders, which reinforced the perception that they were the authoritative voices of the Jewish community. As an adviser to Labor party leader Shimon Peres later admitted, "Ignoring American Jewry was one of the biggest mistakes we made . . . We let Shamir's people do whatever they wanted."[56]

This rightward shift also reflects the way decisions are made in some key organizations in the lobby, as well as the growing influence of a small number of wealthy conservatives who increasingly dominate organizations like AIPAC. There are more than fifty organizations represented in the Conference of Presidents, for example, and each has a single vote regardless of size. But as Michael Massing points out, "Smaller conservative groups in the conference decisively outnumber the larger liberal ones and so can neutralize their influence. And that leaves considerable discretion in the hands of [executive vice chairman] Malcolm Hoenlein," who is a longtime supporter of Israel's settler movement and was deeply skeptical about the Oslo peace process.[57]

Similarly, membership on AIPAC's board of directors is based on each director's financial contributions, not, observes Massing, on "how well they represent AIPAC's members."[58] The individuals willing to give the largest amounts to AIPAC (and to sympathetic politicians) tend to be the most zealous defenders of Israel, and AIPAC's top leadership (consisting primarily of former presidents of the organization) is considerably more hawkish on Middle East issues than are most Jewish Americans. Although AIPAC formally endorsed the Oslo peace process in 1993, it did little to make it work and dropped its opposition to a Palestinian state—without endorsing the idea— only after Ehud Barak became prime minister in 1999.[59]

Indeed, AIPAC and other hard-line groups have occasionally backed more extreme positions than those favored by the Israeli government. In 1994, for example, the hawkish ZOA successfully lobbied for an amendment to the foreign aid bill that placed additional restrictions on U.S. aid to the Palestinian Authority, even though both the Clinton administration and the Rabin government in Israel opposed the measure.[60] The Conference of Presidents never endorsed the Oslo peace process, and AIPAC helped sponsor the 1995 Jerusalem Embassy Act, a transparent attempt to disrupt the peace process by requiring the United States to move its embassy from Tel Aviv to Jerusalem.[61] Indeed, the key donors that form AIPAC's inner circle reportedly ousted executive director Tom Dine because his views were insufficiently hawkish.[62]

In addition to this tendency for those with more extreme views to back and dominate key organizations in the lobby, there is another reason that many pro-Israel groups have moved rightward: to keep contributions flowing in. As Waxman notes, "Many American Jewish organizations now need Israel to legitimate their own existence. Although these organizations may have been established for the purpose of enhancing and strengthening Israel, today Israel is vital for their continued viability."[63] Portraying Israel as beleaguered and vulnerable and issuing dire warnings about continued or growing anti-Semitism helps maintain a high level of concern among potential supporters and thus helps ensure these organizations' continued existence. Writing in 1992, Jonathan Woocher of the Jewish Education Service of North America made precisely this point: "We have seen the emergence of a whole new industry in America, of organizations monitoring and purporting to fight anti-Semitism everywhere in the world . . . The success of the Simon Wiesenthal Center has been particularly striking. It has become a major direct mail fundraising enterprise by outflanking even the ADL in the hunt for anti-Semitic threats to Jewish security. It is (sadly) not uncommon today to see organizations jockeying for position in a context to determine who among them is 'toughest' in fighting anti-Semitism that is waged in the Jewish press and barrages of direct mail appeals."[64] Or as Thomas L. Friedman of the *New York Times* remarked three years later, "Ever since Mr. Rabin and Mr. Arafat shook hands they have received only the most tepid support from mainstream American Jewish groups, like the Conference of Presidents, and outright hostility from the orthodox and fringe Jewish groupings. It is as if these organizations can only thrive if they have an enemy, someone to fight."[65]

It bears repeating that a number of groups in the American Jewish community are critical of certain Israeli policies, and especially its continued presence in the Occupied Territories. Some of these organizations, such as the Israel Policy Forum or Brit Tzedek v'Shalom, actively promote U.S. engagement in the peace process and have been able to win some minor legislative victories in recent years. Yet such groups lack the financial resources and the influence of AIPAC, the ADL, ZOA, or the Conference of Presidents, whose right-of-center views are unfortunately taken by politicians, policy makers, and the media to be the representative voice of American Jewry.[66] For the moment, therefore, the major organizations in the lobby will continue to advocate policy positions at odds with many of the people in whose name they claim to speak.

THE ROLE OF THE NEOCONSERVATIVES

The lobby's drift to the right has been reinforced by the emergence of the neoconservatives. The neoconservative movement has been an important part of American intellectual and political life since the 1970s, but it has drawn particular attention since September 11. This group has been prominent in shaping the Bush administration's unilateralist foreign policy, and especially the ill-fated decision to invade Iraq in March 2003.

Neoconservatism is a political ideology with distinct views on both domestic and foreign policy, although only the latter is relevant here.[67] Most neoconservatives extol the virtues of American hegemony—and sometimes even the idea of an American empire—and they believe U.S. power should be used to encourage the spread of democracy and discourage potential rivals from even trying to compete with the United States.[68] In their view, spreading democracy and preserving U.S. dominance is the best route to long-term peace. Neoconservatives also believe that America's democratic system ensures that it will be seen as a benign hegemon by most other countries, and that U.S. leadership will be welcomed provided it is exercised decisively. They tend to be skeptical of international institutions (especially the UN, which they regard as both anti-Israel and as a constraint on America's freedom of action) and wary of many allies (especially the Europeans, whom they see as idealistic pacifists free-riding on the Pax Americana).[69] Viewing U.S. leadership as "good both for America and for the world," to quote the website of the neoconservative Project for New American Century, neoconservatives generally favor the unilateral exercise of American power instead.

Very importantly, neoconservatives believe that military force is an extremely useful tool for shaping the world in ways that will benefit America. If the United States demonstrates its military prowess and shows that it is willing to use the power at its disposal, then allies will follow our lead and potential adversaries will realize it is futile to resist and will decide to "bandwagon" with the United States.[70] Neoconservatism, in short, is an especially hawkish political ideology.

Neoconservatives occupy influential positions at a variety of organizations and institutions. Prominent neoconservatives include former and present policy makers like Elliott Abrams, Kenneth Adelman, William Bennett, John Bolton, Douglas Feith, the late Jeane Kirkpatrick, I. Lewis "Scooter" Libby, Richard Perle, Paul Wolfowitz, James Woolsey, and David Wurmser; journalists like the late Robert Bartley, David Brooks, Charles Krauthammer, William Kristol, Bret Stephens, and Norman Podhoretz; academics like Fouad Ajami, Eliot Cohen, Aaron Friedberg, Bernard Lewis, and Ruth Wedgwood; and think-tank pundits like Max Boot, David Frum, Reuel Marc Gerecht, Robert Kagan, Michael Ledeen, Joshua Muravchik, Daniel Pipes, Danielle Pletka, Michael Rubin, and Meyrav Wurmser. The leading neoconservative magazines and newspapers are *Commentary*, the *New York Sun*, the *Wall Street Journal* op-ed page, and the *Weekly Standard*. The think tanks and advocacy groups most closely associated with these neoconserva- tives are the American Enterprise Institute (AEI), the Center for Security Policy (CSP), the Hudson Institute, the Foundation for Defense of Democ- racies (FDD), the Jewish Institute for National Security Affairs (JINSA), the Middle East Forum (MEF), the Project for a New American Century (PNAC), and the Washington Institute for Near East Policy (WINEP).

Virtually all neoconservatives are strongly committed to Israel, a point they emphasize openly and unapologetically. According to Max Boot, a lead- ing neoconservative pundit, supporting Israel is "a key tenet of neoconser- vatism," a position he attributes to "shared liberal democratic values."[71] Benjamin Ginsberg, a political scientist who has written extensively about American politics as well as anti-Semitism, convincingly argues that one of the main reasons that the neoconservatives moved to the right was "their at- tachment to Israel and their growing frustration during the 1960s with a Democratic party that was becoming increasingly opposed to American mil- itary preparedness and increasingly enamored of Third World causes." In particular, writes Ginsberg, they embraced Ronald Reagan's "hardline anti- communism" because they saw it as a "political movement that would guar- antee Israel's security."[72]

Given their hawkish orientation, it is not surprising that the neoconser- vatives tend to align with right-wing elements in Israel itself. For example, it was a group of eight neoconservatives (led by Richard Perle and including Douglas Feith and David Wurmser) that drafted the 1996 "Clean Break" study for incoming Likud Prime Minister Benjamin Netanyahu. That study advo- cated that Israel abandon the Oslo peace process and use bold measures— including military force—to topple unfriendly Middle Eastern regimes and thereby "transcend" the Arab-Israeli conflict.[73]

Many neoconservatives are connected to an overlapping set of Washington- based think tanks, committees, and publications whose agenda includes promoting the special relationship between the United States and Israel. Consider Richard Perle, one of the most prominent neoconservatives, who is a fellow at AEI and also affiliated with the right-wing CSP, the Hudson Insti- tute, JINSA, PNAC, MEF, and FDD, and also serves on WINEP's board of advisers. His fellow neoconservatives are similarly well connected: William Kristol is the editor of the *Weekly Standard*, cofounder of PNAC, and previ- ously associated with FDD, MEF, and AEI. The *Washington Post* columnist Charles Krauthammer is a past recipient of AEI's Irving Kristol Award (named for William's father, one of neoconservatism's founding figures), a signatory of several PNAC open letters, a contributing editor at the *Weekly Standard*, and is also affiliated with FDD. The list of past and present connections would delight a network theorist: Elliott Abrams (CSP, Hudson, PNAC); William Bennett (AEI, CSP, PNAC); John Bolton (AEI, JINSA, PNAC); Douglas Feith (CSP, JINSA); David Frum (AEI, *Weekly Standard*); Reuel Marc Gerecht (AEI, PNAC, *Weekly Standard*); Michael Ledeen (AEI, JINSA); Jeane Kirkpatrick (AEI, FDD, JINSA, PNAC, WINEP); Joshua Muravchik (AEI, JINSA, PNAC, WINEP); Daniel Pipes (PNAC, MEF, WINEP); Norman Podhoretz (Hudson, *Commentary*, PNAC); Michael Rubin (AEI, CSP, MEF); Paul Wolfowitz (AEI, PNAC, WINEP); David Wurmser (AEI, MEF, FDD); and James Woolsey (CSP, JINSA, PNAC, FDD).

This summary by no means exhausts the interrelated affiliations within the neoconservative movement, but what may seem to some like a shadowy conspiracy (or even a "right-wing cabal") is anything but. On the contrary, the various think tanks, committees, foundations, and publications that have nurtured the neoconservative movement operate much as other policy networks do. Far from shunning publicity or engaging in hidden plots, these groups actively court publicity for the explicit purpose of shaping public and elite opinion and thereby moving U.S. foreign policy in the directions they favor. The neoconservative network is both undeniably impressive and similar to networks that have arisen in other policy areas, such as tax reform, the environment, or immigration.

Of course, the neoconservatives care about America's security as well as Israel's, and they believe that their policy prescriptions will benefit both countries. In the 1980s, however, some more traditional conservatives—sometimes referred to as "paleoconservatives"—claimed that the neoconservatives were more concerned about Israel than the United States. For example, Russell Kirk, the well-known conservative political theorist, maintained that "what really animates the neoconservatives . . . is the preservation of Israel. That lies in back of everything."[74] The neoconservatives vehemently denied these charges, which led to several bitter exchanges between these contending conservative factions. That conflict eventually subsided, but tension still remains between these two strands of the conservative movement.[75]

A number of commentators have emphasized the Jewish roots of neoconservatism, even though many of the movement's key tenets run counter to the liberal attitudes that still predominate in the American Jewish community. In *The Neoconservative Revolution: Jewish Intellectuals and the Shap-*

ing of Public Policy, a book that paints a sympathetic portrait of its subject, Murray Friedman goes so far as to describe neoconservatism as "American Jewish conservatism."[76] But not all neoconservatives are Jewish, which reminds us that the lobby is defined not by ethnicity or religion but by a political agenda. There are a number of prominent gentiles who have adopted most if not all of the basic tenets of neoconservatism, to include vigorous support for Israel and a tendency to favor its more hard-line elements. Their ranks include the *Wall Street Journal* editor Robert Bartley, former Secretary of Education William Bennett, former UN Ambassadors John Bolton and Jeane Kirkpatrick, and former CIA director James Woolsey. Although these non-Jews have played an important role in pushing forward the neoconservative agenda, Jews nonetheless comprise the core of the neoconservative movement. In this sense, neoconservativism is a microcosm of the larger pro-Israel movement. Jewish Americans are central to the neoconservative movement, just as they form the bulk of the lobby, but non-Jews are active in both. Neoconservatives are also emblematic insofar as much of their political agenda is at odds with the traditional political views of most American Jews.

THE CHRISTIAN ZIONISTS

The lobby includes another important group of gentiles—the Christian Zionists, a subset of the broader politically oriented Christian Right. Prominent members of this constituency include religious figures such as the late Jerry Falwell, Gary Bauer, Pat Robertson, and John Hagee, as well as politicians like former House Majority Leaders Tom DeLay (R-TX) and Richard Armey (R-TX), and Senator James Inhofe (R-OK). Although support for Israel is not their only concern, a number of Christian evangelicals have become increasingly visible and vocal in their support for the Jewish state, and they have recently formed an array of organizations to advance that commitment within the political system.[77] In a sense, the Christian Zionists can be thought of as an important "junior partner" to the various pro-Israel groups in the American Jewish community.

The origins of Christian Zionism lie in the theology of dispensationalism, an approach to biblical interpretation that emerged in nineteenth-century England, largely through the efforts of Anglican ministers Louis Way and John Nelson Darby. Dispensationalism is a form of premillennialism, which asserts that the world will experience a period of worsening tribulations until Christ returns. Like many other Christians, dispensationalists believe that Christ's return is foretold in Old and New Testament prophecy, and that the return of the Jews to Palestine is a key event in the preordained process that will lead to the Second Coming. The theology of Darby, Way, and their followers influenced a number of prominent English politicians and may have made British Foreign Secretary Arthur Balfour more receptive to the idea of creating a Jewish national home in Palestine.[78]

Dispensationalist theology was popularized in the United States in the nineteenth and early twentieth centuries by a number of Protestant theologians, including the evangelist Dwight Moody (founder of Chicago's Moody Bible Institute), C. I. Schofield, and William E. Blackstone. Recent popular expressions include Hal Lindsey's best-selling *Late Great Planet Earth* and Timothy LaHaye's *Left Behind* series, a fictional account of Armageddon whose combined sales reportedly total more than fifty million copies.[79]

The founding of the state of Israel in 1948 gave new life to the dispensationalist movement, but the Six-Day War in 1967, which its leaders saw as a "miracle of God," was even more important for its emergence as a political force.[80] Dispensationalists interpreted Israel's seizure of all of Jerusalem and the West Bank (which, like Israel's Likud party, they refer to as Judea and Samaria) as the fulfillment of Old and New Testament prophecy, and these "signs" encouraged them and other Christian evangelicals to begin working to ensure that the United States was on the "right side" as the Bible's blueprint for the end-times unfolded.[81] According to Timothy Weber, former president of the Memphis Theological Seminary, "Before the Six Day War, dispensationalists were content to sit in the bleachers of history, explaining the End-Time game on the field below . . . But after [the] expansion of Israel into the West Bank and Gaza, they began to get down on the field and be sure the teams lined up right, becoming involved in political, financial, and religious ways they never had before."[82] Their efforts were part of the broader rise of the so-called Christian Right (not all of whom are strongly committed to Israel) and were clearly aided by the growing political prominence of the evangelical movement.

Given these beliefs, it is not surprising that Daniel Pipes believes that "other than the Israel Defense Forces, America's Christian Zionists may be the Jewish state's ultimate strategic asset." Or as Michael Freund, former director of communications for Benjamin Netanyahu, wrote in 2006, "Thank God for Christian Zionists. Like it or not, the future of the relationship between Israel and the U.S. may very well hinge far less on America's Jews than on its Christians."[83]

Christian Zionists have formed a number of organizations whose avowed purpose is to encourage support for Israel. These groups include Christians United for Israel (CUFI, described by founder John Hagee as "a Christian version of the American Israel Public Affairs Committee"), the National Christian Leadership Conference for Israel, the Unity Coalition for Israel, Christian Friends of Israeli Communities (CFIC), the Christians' Israel Public Action Committee, the International Christian Embassy Jerusalem (ICEJ), and a host of smaller groups.[84] Christian Zionists are also key players in the International Fellowship of Christians and Jews (IFCJ), a Chicago-based organization run by Rabbi Yechiel Eckstein, whose mission is "to promote understanding and cooperation between Jews and Christians and to build broad support for Israel." In 2002, IFCJ allied with the former Christian Coalition director and GOP strategist Ralph Reed to form a new group, Stand for Israel, that seeks "to engage people both spiritually and politically on behalf of Israel" and sponsors an annual "international day of prayer and solidarity" on Israel's behalf.[85]

In this modern, activist phase, Christian Zionist beliefs naturally align with groups in the American Jewish community and in Israel·that support the settler movement and oppose a two-state solution. According to CUFI founder Hagee, "We support Israel because all other nations were created by an act of men, but Israel was created by an act of God!" Hagee has also told followers that "God opposes giving away the land" and claims his movement has raised more than $12 million to help settle new immigrants in Israel, including in settlements in the Occupied Territories.[86]

Hagee's views are typical of Christian Zionism. The late Ed McAteer, founder of the evangelical Religious Roundtable and a major organizing force in the Christian Right, once declared that "every grain of sand between the Dead Sea, the Jordan River, and the Mediterranean Sea belongs to the Jews. This includes the West Bank and Gaza."[87] According to ICEJ director Malcolm Hedding, "We stand for the right that all the land that God gave under the Abrahamic covenant 4000 years ago is Israel's . . . There is no such thing as a Palestinian."[88] Similarly, Ted Beckett, founder of CFIC, describes the mission of CFIC as providing "solidarity, comfort and aid" to settlers in "Judea, Samaria, and Gaza"; the organization pairs U.S. churches with individual Israeli settlements so that the former can support the latter. In one celebrated example, Faith Bible Chapel in Arvada, Colorado, "adopted" the West Bank settlement of Ariel, reportedly providing funds for a library, health clinic, and other needs.[89]

As noted above, Christian Zionists oppose a two-state solution or any other form of territorial concession to the Palestinians. On the eve of Egyptian President Anwar Sadat's breakthrough visit to Jerusalem in 1977, evangelical groups published advertisements in major American newspapers saying that they viewed "with grave concern any effort to carve out of the Jewish homeland another nation or political entity."[90] In 1996, the Third International Christian Zionist Congress resolved that "the Land which He promised to His People is not to be partitioned . . . It would be further error for the nations to recognize a Palestinian state in any part of Eretz Israel."[91] Such ardent beliefs led the Christian Right leader (and former GOP presidential hopeful) Pat Robertson to suggest that the stroke suffered by Israeli Prime Minister Ariel Sharon in January 2006 was divine retribution for Sharon's decision to withdraw from the Gaza Strip. In Robertson's words, "He was dividing God's land and I would say woe unto any prime minister of Israel who takes a similar course to appease the [European Union], the United Nations, or the United States of America . . . God says, 'this land belongs to me. You better leave it alone.'" Robertson later apologized for his "inappropriate and insensitive" remarks, but they offer a revealing insight into how some Christian evangelicals justify a greater Israel.[92]

These same beliefs appear to have influenced several prominent U.S. politicians. In 2002, House Majority Whip (and later Majority Leader) Tom DeLay told AIPAC's annual policy conference that he opposed giving land to the Palestinians, saying, "I've toured Judea and Samaria, and I've stood on the Golan Heights. I didn't see occupied territory. I saw Israel."[93] DeLay's predecessor as Majority Leader, Richard Armey, told *Hardball's* Chris Matthews in May 2002 that he was "content to have Israel grab the entire West Bank" and that he "happened to believe that the Palestinians should leave."[94] Or as Senator James Inhofe told his colleagues in a floor speech explaining why Israel had the right to all of Palestine: "This is the most important reason: Because God said so . . . It is at this place [Hebron] where God appeared to Abraham and said, 'I am giving you this land,' the West Bank."[95]

Given the Christian Zionists' support for an expansionist Israel, it is not surprising that Israeli hard-liners have been eager to make common cause with them, especially given the growing opposition to the occupation within mainline Christian churches. As Colin Shindler observes, "A symbiotic relationship thus came into existence after 1977 that served both the ideologies of the Israeli Right and the Christian Right."[96] Menachem Begin's Likud government actively courted evangelicals in this period, giving Falwell a private jet in 1979 and making him in 1980 the only gentile ever to receive the coveted Jabotinsky Medal for "outstanding achievement" (other recipients include authors Leon Uris and Elie Wiesel). When Israel bombed Iraq's Osirak reactor in 1981, Begin reportedly called Falwell before calling President Reagan, asking Falwell to "get to work for me" and explain Israel's action to the American public.[97] Prime Minister Benjamin Netanyahu brought a group of evangelical leaders to Israel in 1996 under the auspices of the Israel Christian Advocacy Council, and Pat Robertson and Ehud Olmert (mayor of Jerusalem at the time) served as cochairs of the Praying for Jerusalem campaign in 2002.[98]

The Israeli government has encouraged Christian tour groups to visit Israel, both as a source of tourism income and to solidify evangelical support back in the United States. Thus, in 2002, Prime Minister Ariel Sharon told ICEJ's annual Feast of Tabernacles meeting (reportedly the largest foreign religious gathering in Israel) that "we need you and we need your support . . . I also have a message I would like you to take home: send more people like you to visit Israel."[99] Sharon's successor, Ehud Olmert, offered a similar message when he was mayor of Jerusalem, telling the gathering, "You are part of our army, of our power, of our defense."[100]

Christian Zionist organizations have become increasingly visible on other Middle East issues as well. CUFI organized a pro-Israel meeting in Washington during the second Lebanon war in the summer of 2006, and Jerry Falwell chose that moment to warn, "We are on the verge of a war without borders," which "will serve as a prelude or forerunner to the future Battle of Armageddon and the glorious return of Jesus Christ."[101] The best-selling millenarian author Hal Lindsey wrote in January 2007 that a preemptive nuclear strike on Iran was "the only logical choice available to Israel," and John Hagee warned in his 2006 book, *Jerusalem Countdown*, "The coming nuclear showdown with Iran is a certainty. The war of Ezekiel 38–39 could begin before this book gets published."[102] Hagee also condemned the bipartisan Iraq Study Group report in December 2006, saying that James Baker "is once again sticking the knife in Israel's back" and declaring that "my father's generation . . . would have bombed Iran by this time."[103]

Some Jewish-American organizations have welcomed this alliance with the Christian Zionists, despite lingering concerns that these groups seek to advance a Christian agenda in the United States and to convert Jews to Christianity. AIPAC established its own liaison office to work with the evangelical movement, pro-Likud organizations such as the Zionist Organization of America forged close links with Falwell, and cooperation with Christian evangelicals even received a blessing in the pages of *Commentary* from Irving Kristol, one of neoconservatism's founding fathers.[104] According to

Nathan Perlmutter, former director of the ADL, "Jews can live with all the domestic priorities of the Christian Right, on which liberal Jews differ so radically, because none of these concerns is as important as Israel." Perlmutter's successor, Abraham Foxman, who has regularly criticized the domestic political agenda of the Christian Right, echoed this view in early 2007, saying that the ADL welcomed evangelical support "at a time when there are serious threats to the Jewish state."[105] According to David Harris, executive director of the American Jewish Committee, willingness to align with the Christian Right was essentially pragmatic: "the end of time may come tomorrow, but Israel hangs in the balance today."[106]

The strong ties between the two main branches of the lobby were on display at the 2007 AIPAC Policy Conference, where John Hagee's address to the opening dinner received an overwhelmingly enthusiastic reception from those in attendance. The response to Hagee is somewhat surprising, given that he has recently written that Jews "have everything but spiritual life," that anti-Semitism was the result of the Jews' "rebellion [against God]," and that God was going to drag "anti-Semitic nations to the nations of Israel to crush them so that the Jews of Israel as a whole will confess that He is the Lord."[107] Despite Hagee's worrisome statements, ADL's Foxman declared, "There is a role for him . . . because of his support for Israel."[108]

Awareness of the Christian Zionists' agenda has made more moderate Israelis and Jewish Americans deeply wary of their embrace. "But for the needs of Israel," observes the historian Naomi Cohen, "most American Jews would have rejected out of hand any dealings with the New Christian Right."[109] They fear that converting Jews to Christianity is still a long-term goal of many evangelical groups, and they worry that the Christian Zionists' uncompromising views will make it more difficult to reach a lasting peace with the Palestinians. Jo-Ann Mort of Americans for Peace Now terms the collaboration between American Jews and the Christian Right an "unholy alliance," and the Israeli moderate Yossi Alpher warns that Christian support for continued settlement expansion is "leading us into a scenario of out-and-out disaster." As he told CBS News, "God save us from these people." Similarly, the Israeli-American scholar Gershom Gorenberg notes that dispensationalist theology does not foresee a happy fate for Jews: in the end-times "the Jews die or convert." In particular, he warns, the Christian Zionists "don't love real Jewish people. They love us as characters in their story, in their play . . . [and] it's a five act play in which the Jews disappear in the fourth act."[110]

How important is the Christian Zionist branch of the Israel lobby? By providing financial support to the settler movement and by publicly inveighing against territorial concessions, the Christian Zionists have reinforced hard-line attitudes in Israel and the United States and have made it more difficult for American leaders to put pressure on Israel. Absent their support, settlers would be less numerous in Israel, and the U.S. and Israeli governments would be less constrained by their presence in the Occupied Territories as well as their political activities. Plus, Christian tourism (a substantial portion occurring under evangelical auspices) has become a lucrative source of income for Israel, reportedly generating revenues in the neighborhood of $1 billion each year.[111]

The presence of a vocal but non-Jewish voice in support of Israel also makes U.S. backing more than just a response to special pleading by American Jewry and probably exerts some effect on the political calculations of politicians who do not have large Jewish constituencies. Irvine Anderson suggests that dispensationalist thinking reinforces "an American cultural predisposition to support the State of Israel, based in part on the influence of the Christian Bible." In particular, "having grown up hearing Bible stories . . . or having read about . . . the ingathering of Jews to Palestine as a prelude to the Second Coming, it is not surprising that many, though certainly not all, Americans simply assume that it is right and proper for Jews to return to Palestine and create their own state there."[112]

Yet the influence of the Christian Zionists should not be overstated. Their strong commitment to a "greater Israel" and resulting opposition to a two-state solution did not prevent the Clinton administration from pursuing the latter at Camp David in 2000, did not halt the 1998 Wye Agreement mandating an Israeli redeployment from parts of the West Bank, and, perhaps most revealingly, did not stop President George W. Bush, who has close ties to the Christian Right, from declaring his own support for a Palestinian state in 2001.

There are several reasons why Christian Zionists exert less impact on U.S. Middle East policy than the other parts of the Israel lobby do. Although the Christian Right has been a key part of President Bush's political base (which has to some degree magnified the visibility of the Christian Zionist elements within this broader movement), the alliance goes well beyond the issue of Israel to include a broad array of social issues. Supporting Israel is only one of the many issues that evangelicals like Robertson, Bauer, and Falwell have been concerned with, and it may not even be the most important. Leaders of the Christian Right often claim to speak on behalf of forty million or more professed evangelical Christians, but the number of followers who care deeply about Israel is undoubtedly smaller. In addition, and in sharp contrast to groups like AIPAC, Christian Zionists lack the organizational capacity to analyze national security topics or to offer specific legislative guidance on concrete foreign policy issues. Surveys of congressional aides by Ruth Mouly in the 1980s and Irvine Anderson in 1999 found "little evidence of extensive direct lobbying of Congress by Falwell or other prominent members of the Religious Right on the subject of Israel."[113] Similarly, Rabbi Yechiel Eckstein, founder of IFCJ, told the Israeli writer Zev Chafets that a delegation of evangelicals he had taken to visit then National Security Adviser Condoleezza Rice in 2003 "was the only Christian group ever to lobby the White House specifically on behalf of Israel."[114] Even if Eckstein overstated the case somewhat, it is clear that Israel is only one of many items on the evangelicals' list of concerns. By contrast, groups like AIPAC, the Anti-Defamation League, ZOA, and the Conference of Presidents put U.S. support for Israel at the top of their agenda, and their efforts to influence foreign policy are reinforced by think tanks like JINSA and WINEP.

Furthermore, Christianity contains a complex set of moral and religious teachings, and many of its most important precepts neither justify nor encourage unconditional support for Israel. Christian Zionists may believe that biblical prophecy justifies Jewish control of all of Palestine, but other Christian principles—such as Christ's command to "love thy neighbor as thyself"—are sharply at odds with Israel's treatment of its Palestinian subjects. Familiarity with Old Testament stories and other aspects of the Judeo-Christian tradition has not prevented many mainline Christian churches from openly backing a two-state solution and criticizing various aspects of Israeli policy, based on their own commitment to Christian principles of peace and justice.[115] Just as many American Jews do not support everything that Israel is doing, neither do many Christians, including evangelicals.

Christian Zionists also lack the financial power of the major pro-Israel Jewish groups, and they do not have the same media presence when it comes to Middle East issues.[116] Leaders like Robertson or Bauer may get lots of media attention when they speak on moral or religious questions, but media organizations are more likely to turn to the Brookings Institution or WINEP when discussing current events in Israel or the Middle East. For all these reasons, the Christian Zionists are best seen as a significant adjunct to the Jewish elements of the lobby, but not its most important part.

THE LOBBY'S SOURCES OF POWER

Why is the Israel lobby so effective? One reason is the wide-open nature of the American political system. The United States has a divided form of government, a well-established tradition of free speech, and a system in which elections are very expensive to run and where campaign contributions are weakly regulated. This environment gives different groups many different ways to gain access or influence policy. Interest groups can direct campaign contributions to favored candidates and try to defeat candidates whose views are suspect. They can also lobby elected representatives and members of the executive branch, and they can try to get their own supporters appointed to key policy-making positions. Moreover, there are numerous ways for interest groups to mold public opinion: by cultivating sympathetic journalists; writing books, articles, and op-eds; and working to discredit or marginalize anyone with different views. For a group that is highly motivated and has sufficient resources, there is no shortage of ways to influence public policy.[117]

The lobby's effectiveness also reflects the basic dynamics of interest group politics in a pluralistic society. In a democracy, even relatively small groups can exercise considerable influence if they are strongly committed to a particular issue and the rest of the population is largely indifferent. Even if the group's absolute numbers are small, policy makers—and especially members of Congress—will tend to accommodate them, because they can be confident that the rest of the population will not penalize them for doing so. As one U.S. senator put it, when asked why he and his colleagues signed a piece of controversial legislation pushed by the lobby, "There is no political advantage in not signing. If you do sign you don't offend anyone. If you don't you might offend some Jews in your state."[118]

The disproportionate influence of small but focused interest groups increases even more when opposing groups are weak or nonexistent, because politicians have to accommodate only one set of interests and the public is likely to hear only one side of the story. Whether the issue is farm subsidies or foreign policy, special interest groups often wield political power that far exceeds their absolute numbers in the population.

As will become clear in the next chapter, the Israel lobby enjoys a number of advantages in the competition for influence in the United States. American Jews are relatively prosperous and well educated, and have an admirable philanthropic tradition. They give generously to political parties and have very high rates of political participation. A sizable minority of American Jews is not strongly committed to Israel, but a clear majority is at least somewhat engaged and a significant minority is strongly energized by this issue. When married to the support Israel gets from Christian Zionists, it is a potent base.

Equally important is the impressive level of resources and expertise within the major Jewish organizations in the lobby. According to the political scientist Robert Trice, "Most major Jewish groups are characterized by large memberships, well-trained professional staffs, adequately financed social, welfare and political programs, specialized working groups for particular problems and elaborate internal communications networks." Moreover, the existence of numerous organizations at the local and national level explains "the ability of the pro-Israel movement to mobilize rapidly and in a coordinated fashion on a national scale when important foreign policy issues arise."[119]

These efforts are facilitated by Israel's generally favorable image in the United States. As former Senator Warren Rudman (R-NH) once commented, "They have a pretty good product to sell."[120] As we shall see, that favorable image is due in good part to the lobby's own efforts to make sure that Israel is portrayed favorably, as well as the broad sense that the United States and Israel are part of a common Judeo-Christian culture and are linked by various informal connections.[121]

Finally, the lobby benefits from the absence of effective opposition. As one senator explained, "There's no countervailing sentiment . . . If you vote contrary to the tremendous pressure of AIPAC, nobody says to you, 'That's great.'"[122] Although Arab Americans are a significant minority, they are neither as wealthy, well organized, numerous, or politically active as Jewish Americans. As a group, Arab Americans have not been as successful in reaching prominent positions in academia, business, and the media, and they are also less visible in politics. This is partly because the main waves of Arab immigration to the United States occurred relatively recently, and first-generation immigrants are less affluent, less represented in important professions, less familiar with American mores and institutions, less active in politics, and therefore less influential than subsequent generations tend to be.

Pro-Arab organizations are also no match for the major groups that make up the Israel lobby. There are a handful of pro-Arab and pro-Palestinian interest groups in the United States, but they are smaller than AIPAC and other pro-Israel organizations, not nearly as well funded, and nowhere near as effective. According to Mitchell Bard, the former editor of AIPAC's *Near East Report*, "From the beginning, the Arab lobby has faced not only a disadvantage in electoral politics but also in organization. There are several politically oriented groups, but many of these are one-man operations with little financial or popular support." U.S. politicians rarely, if ever, complain about pressure from an "Arab-American lobby" and have little reason to adjust their behavior to accommodate it. As Harry Truman famously remarked, "In all of my political experience I don't ever recall the Arab vote swinging a close election."[123]

Moreover, because Arab Americans come from a variety of countries and backgrounds, and include Christians as well as Muslims, they are unlikely to speak with a unified voice on Middle East issues. Indeed, they sometimes hold sharply opposing views. And whereas many Americans sense a degree of cultural proximity between Israel and the United States and believe Israelis are "like us," Arabs are often seen as part of an alien (or even hostile) civilization. As a result, winning hearts and minds in the United States is an uphill battle for its Arab-American citizens in ways that it has not been for American Jews or their Christian allies. Robert Trice's 1981 assessment of Arab-American groups remains true today: "Their impact on most aspects of U.S. Middle East policy remains negligible."[124]

THE (MODEST) IMPACT OF OIL

Neither Arab governments nor the vaunted "oil lobby" pose a significant counterweight to the Israel lobby. The belief that oil companies and/or wealthy oil sheikhdoms exert a powerful influence on U.S. Middle East policy is widespread and is reflected in the frequent claim that the war in Iraq in 2003 was a "war for oil" and for related corporate interests such as Halliburton.[125] Interestingly, this view is advanced by some of Israel's most persistent critics—such as Noam Chomsky and Stephen Zunes—as well as by fervent defenders like Martin Peretz.[126] More conspiratorial versions of this perspective suggest that personal and financial connections between the Bush family and the House of Saud have shaped U.S. Middle East policy to America's detriment.[127] These various interpretations portray the Israel lobby as just one player among many, and probably not the most important one.

There is no question that the United States has a major strategic interest in the energy resources located in the Persian Gulf. Although the United States currently imports more of its energy from Canada, Mexico, and Venezuela than from states in the Middle East, oil and natural gas are bought and sold in a tightly integrated world market and thus anything that reduces the overall supply is going to push prices up and hurt the American economy.[128] As discussed in Chapter 2, this is why U.S. leaders see the Persian Gulf as a vital interest and why they have taken steps to preserve a local balance of power there and prevent any hostile state from interfering with the flow of oil from that region. This basic fact also explains why the United States has sought to preserve good relations with a number of different countries in the Gulf, despite differing with them on various domestic and foreign policy issues. The importance of Middle East oil led the United States to become a close ally of Saudi Arabia after World War II and is one reason why Washington backed the shah of Iran for many years. After his regime fell in 1979, this same desire to maintain a local balance of power and to keep the oil flowing convinced the Reagan administration to tilt toward Saddam Hussein's Iraq during the Iran-Iraq War (1980–88). The United States then intervened to evict Iraq from Kuwait after it seized the sheikhdom in 1990, a policy consistent with the long-standing U.S. policy of preventing any single power from establishing hegemony in the region. A powerful lobby was not needed to encourage these policies, because few questioned the need to keep Persian Gulf oil out of unfriendly hands.

Beyond this obvious interest in preserving access to Middle East oil, however, there is little evidence that either wealthy Arab states or a powerful "oil lobby" has had much impact on the broad thrust of U.S. Middle East policy. After all, if Arab petrodollars or energy companies were driving American policy, one would expect to see the United States distancing itself from Israel and working overtime to get the Palestinians a state of their own. Countries like Saudi Arabia have repeatedly pressed Washington to adopt a more evenhanded position toward the Israeli-Palestinian conflict, but to little avail, and even wielding the "oil weapon" during the 1973 October War had little effect on U.S. support for Israel or on overall American policy in the region. Similarly, if oil companies were driving U.S. policy, one would also have expected Washington to curry favor with big oil producers like Saddam Hussein's Iraq, Muammar Gaddafi's Libya, or the Islamic Republic of Iran, so that U.S. companies could make money helping them develop their energy resources and bringing them to market. Instead, the United States imposed sanctions on all three of these countries, in sharp opposition to what the oil industry wanted. Indeed, as we will show in Part II, in some cases the U.S. government deliberately intervened to thwart business deals that would have benefited U.S. companies. If the oil lobby were as powerful as some critics believe, such actions would not have occurred.

Wealthy oil producers such as Saudi Arabia have hired public relations firms and professional lobbyists to enhance their image in the United States and to lobby for specific arms deals, and their efforts have occasionally borne fruit. Their most notable achievement was convincing Congress to approve the sale of AWACS aircraft to Saudi Arabia in 1982, despite AIPAC's strong opposition. This episode is sometimes invoked to demonstrate the Israel lobby's limited influence and the power of the "Arab lobby," but the latter's victory in this case was mostly due to a set of unusually favorable conditions. The strategic importance of Saudi oil was obvious, the Soviet Union was seen as a serious military threat to the Gulf at that time, Ronald Reagan was a popular president, and his administration pulled out all the stops to win congressional approval. Even so, the sale barely squeaked through (the final Senate vote was 52–48 in favor), and Reagan was forced to withdraw several subsequent arms packages to Saudi Arabia and Jordan in the face of renewed opposition from the lobby and from Congress.[129]

One reason why Arab oil producers have only limited influence is their lack of an indigenous base of support in the United States. Because they are forced to rely on professional lobbyists and public relations firms, it is easier for critics to denigrate their representatives as mere agents of a foreign power. AIPAC's Tom Dine once dismissed Saudi lobbying efforts by saying, "They hire foreign agents like Fred Dutton to do their bidding. Their support is not rooted in American soil."[130] The Israel lobby, by contrast, is a manifestation of the political engagement of a subset of American citizens, and so its activities are widely and correctly seen as a legitimate form of political activity.

Furthermore, because most oil-exporting governments depend on large revenues to keep themselves in power, threatening to cut off the supply is not credible and their leverage is thus reduced. Many of these governments also have sizable investments in Western economies and would suffer considerable losses in the event of a sustained economic downturn. Reducing production would drive prices up and make alternative energy sources more attractive, and give the United States and other countries a big incentive to wean themselves from oil dependence once and for all. Because major oil exporters like Saudi Arabia want to keep the industrial powers hooked on oil and gas, they have an obvious disincentive to using what little leverage may be at their disposal. As a result, U.S. dependence on imported energy supplies has not given these countries much influence over U.S. policy.

What about energy companies? These corporations do engage in plenty of lobbying activities, but their efforts in recent decades have focused almost entirely on their commercial interests rather than on broader aspects of foreign policy. Specifically, energy companies concentrate on tax policy, government regulation, environmental concerns, access to potential drilling sites, and other practical dimensions of energy policy. For them, foreign policy is normally a secondary concern, and according to Robert Trice, their "primary goal . . . is to create a political and economic environment in the Middle East that will allow them to maximize profits. As such, the political interests of corporate actors are generally much narrower than those of the pro-Arab groups."[131]

This relatively narrow focus is apparent when one examines the website of the American Petroleum Institute, the flagship trade association of the oil industry. Five topics appear under the general heading of "policy issues": climate change, exploration/production, fuels, taxes and trade, and homeland security. There is no reference to "Israel" or the "Arab-Israeli conflict" anywhere on the site, and few references to foreign policy at all. By contrast, Israel and U.S. foreign policy are front and center on the websites of AIPAC, the ADL, and the Conference of Presidents.[132] As AIPAC's Morris Amitay noted in the early 1980s, "When oil interests and other corporate interests lobby, 99 percent of the time they are acting in what they perceive to be their own self-interest—they lobby on tax bills . . . We very rarely see them lobbying on foreign policy issues . . . In a sense, we have the field to ourselves."[133]

In addition, American corporations appear to be discouraged from trying to influence U.S. Middle East policy by the fear of retaliation from well-organized pro-Israel groups. In 1975, for example, the revelation that Gulf Oil had underwritten a number of pro-Arab activities in the United States led to public condemnations by the Conference of Presidents and the Anti-Defamation League. In response, Gulf bought a half-page ad in the *New York Times* in which it apologized for its action and told readers, "You may be certain it will not happen again." As Trice notes, "A vigilant, sensitive, and reactive pro-Israel lobby is one reason why U.S. corporations have tended to avoid direct participation in domestic political debates on Middle East questions."[134]

Some commentators believe that oil and gas companies are driving U.S. policy either to gain lucrative concessions in places like Iraq, or to foment instability that will drive up oil prices and enable them to reap windfall profits.[135] Not only is there little direct evidence of such behavior, but it runs counter to the long-term interests of major energy companies. Energy companies do not like wars in oil-rich regions, sanctions, or regime change—the staples of U.S. Middle East policy in recent years—because each of them threatens access to oil and gas reserves and thus their ability to make money, and such events also encourage Americans to think more seriously about reducing demand for the oil companies' main product. Thus, when Vice President Dick Cheney was the president of Halliburton, Inc., a major oil services firm, in the 1990s, he opposed U.S. sanctions on Iran (a policy, as discussed in Chapter 10, driven largely by the lobby) and complained that

U.S. firms were being "cut out of the action" by America's "sanctions happy" policy.[136] Cheney's earlier position suggests that if oil companies controlled Middle East policy, the United States would have pursued a very different agenda in recent years.

None of this denies that oil companies, good capitalists that they are, will seek to profit from foreign policy initiatives that they did not encourage. It is not surprising that oil companies want to obtain lucrative concessions in post-Saddam Iraq, just as they would have been happy to do business with Saddam himself. On balance, however, wealthy Arab governments and the oil lobby exert much less influence on U.S. foreign policy than the Israel lobby does, because oil interests have less need to skew foreign policy in the directions they favor and they do not have the same leverage.[137] Writing in the early 1970s, the Columbia University professor and former Assistant Secretary of State Roger Hilsman observed, "It is obvious to even the most casual observer . . . that United States foreign policy in the Middle East, where oil reigns supreme, has been more responsive to the pressures of the American Jewish community and their natural desire to support Israel than it has to American oil interests." In his comparison of the Israel and Arab lobbies, Mitchell Bard acknowledges that although oil companies like Aramco have conducted lobbying campaigns in the past, the effort "has had no observable impact on U.S. policy." Or as AIPAC's former legislative director, Douglas Bloomfield, told *BBC News* in 2003, "AIPAC has one enormous advantage. It really doesn't have any opposition."[138]

THE QUESTION OF "DUAL LOYALTY"

This picture of a powerful special interest group, comprised mainly of American Jews and working to move U.S. policy in a pro-Israel direction, is bound to make some people uncomfortable, because it seems to invoke the specter of "dual loyalty," which was once a common anti-Semitic canard in old Europe. The charge, in its original incarnation, was that Jews in the diaspora were perpetual aliens who could not assimilate and become good patriots. According to this now-discredited argument, Jews were thought to be loyal only to each other. The infamous *Protocols of the Elders of Zion*, a tsarist forgery that was exposed and discredited long ago, claimed that Jews operate as a fifth column in the countries where they live, working for a committee of Jewish elders who are secretly plotting to dominate the world.

In this earlier, anti-Semitic incarnation, dual loyalty was in fact a misnomer, as the charge implied that Jews were loyal only to each other and felt no genuine loyalty to their home countries. Today, however, both scholars and commentators use the term in a neutral and nonpejorative fashion to describe the widespread circumstance where individuals feel genuine attachments (or loyalties) to more than one country. Thus, in his recent comparison of different ethnic diasporas, the Israeli political scientist Gabriel Sheffer distinguishes among "total," "dual," and "divided" loyalty, and notes that all three responses occur when members of a particular ethnic, national, or religious group are scattered across different states.[139] As discussed below, other thoughtful Jewish Americans have used "dual loyalty" to describe their own attitudes and experiences, but their use of the term is very different from its past employment as an anti-Semitic slander.

Any notion that Jewish Americans are disloyal citizens is wrong. We fully agree with Malcolm Hoenlein, who directs the Conference of Presidents, that "it is safe to say that American Jews are among the most patriotic and loyal of American citizens."[140] As we have made clear, those who lobby on Israel's behalf are acting in ways that are consistent with long-standing political traditions. Indeed, political life in the United States has long proceeded from the assumption that all individuals have a variety of attachments and loyalties—to country, religion, family, employer, just to name a few—and that American citizens will create formal and informal associations that reflect those loyalties and interests. Consider, for example, a 2006 Pew Global Attitudes survey of Christians in thirteen countries in which 42 percent of the U.S. respondents saw themselves as Christians first and Americans second.[141] These different attachments, which sometimes include an affinity for a foreign country, may reflect ancestry, religious affiliation, personal experience (such as overseas study or a Peace Corps assignment), or any number of other sources. It is legitimate for U.S. citizens to express such attachments and affinities in political life; this is in fact what democratic theory implies that they should do. As we have noted, it is even permissible for Americans to hold dual citizenship and to serve in foreign armies— including the IDF—and some have done so.

Americans who work to influence U.S. foreign policy in ways that benefit Israel almost always believe that the policies they favor will benefit the United States as well. As former AIPAC executive director Tom Dine told one interviewer, "I came to this job thinking American foreign policy and how to strengthen America's position in the world. At the same time, I thought a lot about Israel because I am Jewish."[142] More to the point, Theodore Mann, a former head of the Conference of Presidents, said in

2001 that "leading American Jews really feel very deeply that American interests and Israeli interests are one and the same."[143]

While there is no question that this perspective is widely and deeply held, there is a problem with it: no two countries will always have the same interests. It is just not the way international politics works. There have been instances in the past, and there will be more in the future, where U.S. and Israeli interests were at odds. For example, it made good strategic sense for Israel to acquire nuclear weapons in the 1960s, but it was not in America's interest to have Israel go nuclear. Nor is it in the U.S. national interest when Israel kills or wounds innocent Palestinian civilians (even if only unintentionally) and especially not when it uses American-made weapons to do it. One sees a similar divergence of interests in Israel's decision to invade Lebanon in 1982, and in its recent opposition to U.S. plans to sell advanced weaponry to Saudi Arabia and other Persian Gulf states.[144]

Nonetheless, many of Israel's supporters find it hard to acknowledge that Jerusalem and Washington could have fundamentally different interests. In other words, they fully accept the strategic and moral rationales that we laid out and refuted in Chapters 2 and 3, and they work hard to convince policy makers of their continued validity. They may also hold to these views because humans are usually uncomfortable when important values conflict. Even when U.S. and Israeli interests are clearly at odds, some of Israel's American backers will find it difficult to acknowledge that a significant tradeoff exists.

There are, however, thoughtful Jewish Americans—including some prominent policy makers—who openly acknowledge that conflicts can and do arise among their Jewish identities, their understandable interest in Israel's well-being, and their genuine loyalty to the United States. To his credit, Henry Kissinger dealt forthrightly with this issue in his memoirs, writing that "though not practicing my religion, I could never forget that thirteen members of my family had died in Nazi concentration camps . . . Most Israeli leaders were personal friends. And yet . . . I had to subordinate my emotional preferences to my perception of the national interest . . . It was not always easy; occasionally it proved painful."[145]

Kissinger acknowledges what many would deny: tensions are bound to arise whenever Americans have strong affinities for other countries, no matter what the origins of those attachments and no matter how consistently they resolve them on behalf of their homeland. Or as one of Bill Clinton's Middle East advisers admitted anonymously, "We act in America's interest, but through a prism." Another veteran Jewish-American diplomat expressed a similar feeling by saying, "I thank God that I'm not working in Middle East affairs or at the U.N., where you might have to vote to condemn the Israelis."[146]

These statements are in no sense confessions of disloyalty; on the contrary, they are admirably honest reflections on the multiple loyalties that all human beings feel and that sometimes come into conflict. The journalist Eric Alterman offered an equally candid acknowledgment in 2003, noting that his own "dual loyalties" were "drilled into me by my parents, my grandparents, my Hebrew school teachers and my rabbis, not to mention Israeli teen-tour leaders and AIPAC college representatives." But instead of pretending that potential tradeoffs will never arise, Alterman recognizes that "we ought to be honest enough to at least imagine a hypothetical clash between American and Israeli interests. Here, I feel pretty lonely admitting that, every once in a while, I'm going to go with what's best for Israel."[147]

Yet Alterman is not in fact alone. Consider the remarks of Stephen Steinlight, former director of national affairs at the American Jewish Committee. After recounting his own upbringing in America as a "Jewish nationalist, even a quasi-separatist," Steinlight remarks,

> The process of my nationalist training was to inculcate the belief that the primary division of the world was between "us" and "them." Of course we saluted the American and Canadian flags and sang those anthems, usually with real feeling, but it was clear where our primary loyalty was meant to reside. I am also familiar with the classic, well-honed answer to this tension anytime this is cited: Israel and America are democracies; they share values; they have common strategic interests; loyalty to one cannot conceivably involve disloyalty to the other, etc., etc. All of which begs huge questions . . . and while it may be true in practice most of the time, it is by no means an absolute construct, devoid of all sort of potential exceptions . . . We have no less difficult a balancing act between group loyalty and a wider sense of belonging to America. That America has largely tolerated this dual loyalty—we get a free pass, I suspect, largely over Christian guilt about the Holocaust—makes it no less a reality.[148]

It is important to emphasize that this phenomenon is not confined to Jewish Americans; rather, such tensions are an inevitable feature of a melting pot society that has drawn its citizens from all over the world.[149] It is equally important to note that most American Jews would surely reject any suggestion that they would place Israel's interests ahead of America's if an obvious conflict arose between them.

Jews and non-Jews who believe that the United States should continue to give Israel strong and unconditional support have every right to advocate their positions, and it is wrong to question their loyalty when they do. Yet it is equally legitimate for critics to point out that organizations like AIPAC are not neutral, or that the individuals who run AIPAC, the ADL, the Conference of Presidents, and similar organizations are motivated by an attachment to Israel that is bound to shape their thinking about many foreign policy issues. Why else would Malcolm Hoenlein describe his job as follows: "I devote myself to the security of the Jewish state"?[150] Or why does John Hagee of CUFI address the potential conflict between his support for Israeli settlements and official U.S. opposition to them by saying that "the law of God transcends the laws of the United States government and the U.S. State Department"?[151] If he were not inspired by a strong attachment to Israel, why would Lenny Ben-David, the former director of information and research at AIPAC, agree to serve as Israel's deputy chief of mission in Washington from 1997 to 2000?[152]

It is equally legitimate to question whether the policies advocated by these individuals and the organizations they represent are in the U.S. national interest, just as it is legitimate to question the impact of other special interest lobbies on other elements of U.S. domestic or foreign policy. Their patriotism can be above reproach, but their advice might be fostering policies that are wreaking havoc in a region of considerable strategic importance to the United States and indeed to the rest of the world. To question the soundness of that advice has nothing to do with the older, discredited use of "dual loyalty" to imply that Jews were unpatriotic.

CONCLUSION

The Israel lobby is the antithesis of a cabal or conspiracy; it operates out in the open and proudly advertises its own clout. In its basic operations, the Israel lobby is no different from interest groups like the farm lobby, steel and textile workers, and a host of ethnic lobbies, although the groups and individuals who comprise the Israel lobby are in an unusually favorable position to influence U.S. foreign policy. What sets it apart, in short, is its extraordinary effectiveness. In the next two chapters, we examine the strategies it employs to achieve its goals.

5

GUIDING THE POLICY PROCESS

The groups and individuals who make up the lobby pursue two broad strategies to encourage steadfast U.S. support for Israel. First, they exert significant influence on the policy-making process in Washington. Second, these organizations go to considerable lengths to ensure that public discourse about Israel is favorable and that it echoes the strategic and moral rationales discussed in Chapters 2 and 3. We examine the first of these strategies in this chapter and explore the lobby's efforts to shape public discourse in Chapter 6.

Because political power in the United States is divided between the legislative and executive branches, the lobby's tactics sometimes vary depending on which branch of government is involved. In addition to helping get sympathetic individuals elected or appointed to key positions, groups in the lobby strive to shape the political calculations of officials who might be tempted to chart a more independent course. Whatever a legislator's or policy maker's personal views might be, the lobby wants uncritical support for Israel to be the "smart" political choice. Like other powerful interest groups, in short, the Israel lobby achieves its aims by constraining the policies key officials are willing to consider, pressing them to take steps they would rather avoid (but will pretend to favor), making it hard for U.S. leaders to sustain initiatives that groups in the lobby oppose, and shaping perceptions and framing options so that many key leaders willingly favor the policies that these groups endorse.[1]

HOLDING SWAY ON CAPITOL HILL

A key pillar of the lobby's effectiveness is its influence in the U.S. Congress. Unlike virtually every other country, Israel is largely immune from criticism on Capitol Hill. This situation is remarkable by itself, because Congress frequently deals with contentious issues and competing viewpoints are usually easy to find. Whether the issue is abortion, arms control, affirmative action, gay rights, the environment, trade policy, health care, immigration, or welfare, there is almost always a lively debate on Capitol Hill. But where Israel is concerned, potential critics fall silent and there is hardly any debate at all.

The absence of serious deliberation when Israel is involved was revealed in a hearing on the Israeli-Palestinian peace process held on February 14, 2007, by the Subcommittee on the Middle East and South Asia in the House of Representatives. With Secretary of State Condoleezza Rice trying to restart the moribund peace process, the subcommittee sought testimony from three witnesses. Despite some differences on certain policy issues, all three are central players in the lobby: Martin Indyk, the former AIPAC official and former U.S. ambassador to Israel who now heads the Saban Center for Middle East Policy at the Brookings Institution; David Makovsky of the pro-Israel Washington Institute for Near East Policy; and the neoconservative pundit Daniel Pipes, who directs the right-wing Middle East Forum. No critic of Israel, much less a Palestinian or Arab American, was brought in to offer alternative views or suggest the United States take a different approach. M. J. Rosenberg, who once worked for AIPAC and is now a key figure with the Israel Policy Forum, a moderate pro-Israel group that actively supports a two-state solution, nicely summed up the situation: "This was a hearing about two sides of a conflict where only one side was allowed to speak," adding that "everyone who saw an official Congressional hearing that banned the Arab point of view was either hurt by the spectacle or angered by it. And that damages the interests of America, and of Israel."[2]

One reason for the lobby's success in Congress is that some key members have been Christian Zionists, such as former House Speaker Richard Armey, who said in September 2002 that "my No. 1 priority in foreign policy is to protect Israel." One would think that the top priority for any U.S. representative would be to "protect America," but that is not what Armey said. Regarding Tom DeLay, Armey's successor as speaker, Morton Klein, the president of ZOA, said that "he cared about Israel in every fiber of his being." DeLay himself said that he was "an Israeli at heart."[3]

There are also Jewish senators and representatives who work to make

U.S. foreign policy support Israel's interests. In 2006, in fact, a record number of Jewish Americans were elected to the House and Senate, a fact that underscores their impressive achievements in American society and their traditionally high level of civic engagement and political participation.[4] Some of these legislators—such as Senators Joseph Lieberman (D-CT) and Charles Schumer, and Representatives Jerrold Nadler (D-NY), Henry Waxman (D-CA), and Robert Wexler (D-FL)—are ardent defenders of Israel.[5] Indeed, Waxman said in the wake of the 2006 election that "there will be some Democratic chairmen who may not share all my views . . . on Israel." He made it clear, however, that "they will not be chairing committees dealing with Israel and the Middle East."[6] He was right, of course: the chair of the House subcommittee that held the hearing described above was Gary Ackerman (D-NY), another avid backer of Israel, while the chair of the larger Committee on Foreign Affairs is Tom Lantos (D-CA), who has no rival on Capitol Hill in his devotion to Israel. As one former AIPAC leader put it, Lantos "is true blue and white."[7]

But it isn't only the representatives themselves who can tilt legislation in a pro-Israel direction. Congressional staffers are at the center of the legislative process, registering the positions of outside interest groups and parsing different policy options for their bosses. As Morris Amitay, a former head of AIPAC, once noted, "There are a lot of guys at the working level up here [on Capitol Hill] . . . who happen to be Jewish, who are willing . . . to look at certain issues in terms of their Jewishness . . . These are all guys who are in a position to make the decision in these areas for those senators . . . You can get an awful lot done just at the staff level."[8] As discussed below, representatives from groups in the lobby sometimes participate directly in this process, helping Hill staffers draft legislation, providing them with talking points that legislators can use in public, helping write the "Dear Colleague" letters that legislators send one another to position themselves on key issues, and drafting and circulating open letters designed to put congressional pressure on the executive branch.

Of all the groups that make up the lobby, it is AIPAC that holds the key to influence in Congress, a fact that is widely acknowledged by politicians from both parties.[9] Bill Clinton once described AIPAC as "stunningly effective" and "better than anyone else lobbying in this town," while former House Speaker Newt Gingrich called it "the most effective general-interest group . . . across the entire planet." Senate Majority Leader Harry Reid (D-NV) agrees, saying, "I can't think of a policy organization in the country as well-organized and respected [as AIPAC]." The *New Yorker*'s Jeffrey Goldberg calls it "a leviathan among lobbies," and AIPAC's own website proudly quotes the *New York Times's* assessment that it is "the most important organization affecting America's relationship with Israel."[10]

AIPAC's success is due in large part to its ability to reward legislators and congressional candidates who support its agenda and to punish those who do not, based mainly on its capacity to influence campaign contributions. Money is critical to U.S. elections, which have become increasingly expensive to win, and AIPAC makes sure that its friends get financial support so long as they do not stray from AIPAC's line.

This process works in several ways. To begin with, many of the same individuals who bankroll AIPAC are often important political contributors in their own right. Using data from the Federal Election Commission (FEC), the journalist Michael Massing found that "between 1997 and 2001, the 46 members of AIPAC's board of directors gave well in excess of $3 million in campaign contributions," and many of them remain generous donors to pro-Israel PACs and candidates today.[11] "Since 2000," the *Washington Post* reported in 2004, "[AIPAC] board members have contributed an average of $72,000 each to campaigns and political committees."[12]

Second, AIPAC helps connect political candidates to other donors and sources of funds. Despite its name, AIPAC is not a political action committee and does not officially endorse candidates or give money directly to their campaigns. Instead, AIPAC screens potential candidates and arranges meetings with potential donors and fund-raisers, and provides information to the growing number of pro-Israel PACs. According to the historian David Biale, "The American Jewish 'Israel lobby' has developed since the Six Day War into one of the most sophisticated and effective lobbying organizations in the United States Congress. It has done so in part by developing a national network of Jewish Political Action Committees for contributing funds to congressional candidates based on the criterion of support for Israel."[13] As AIPAC President Howard Friedman told the organization's members in August 2006, "AIPAC meets with every candidate running for Congress. These candidates receive in-depth briefings to help them completely understand the complexities of Israel's predicament and that of the Middle East as a whole. We even ask each candidate to author a 'position paper' on their views of the U.S.-Israel relationship—so it's clear where they stand on the subject."[14]

Friedman's description of AIPAC's modus operandi is consistent with testimony from other political figures. Tom Hayden, the antiwar figure who was running for a seat in the California Assembly in the early 1980s, explains how he won support from the local power broker Michael Berman (brother of longtime California Congressman Howard Berman) on the condition that he would always be a "good friend to Israel." Hayden, who won the election, notes that he "had to be certified 'kosher,' not once but over and over again. The certifiers were the elites, beginning with rabbis and heads of the multiple mainstream Jewish organizations . . . An important vetting role was held as well by . . . [AIPAC], a group closely associated with official parties in Israel. When necessary, Israeli ambassadors, counsels general and other officials would intervene with statements declaring someone a 'friend of Israel.'" Hayden, one may note, merely held state-level offices in his political career, although he was unusually visible in that role.[15]

In the same vein, Harry Lonsdale, the Democratic candidate who ran unsuccessfully against Senator Mark Hatfield (R-OR) in 1990, has described his own visit to AIPAC headquarters during that campaign. "The word that I was pro-Israel got around," he writes. "I found myself invited to AIPAC in Washington, D.C., fairly early in the campaign, for 'discussions.' It was an experience I will never forget. It wasn't enough that I was pro-Israel. I was given a list of vital topics and quizzed (read grilled) for my specific opinion on each. Actually, I was told what my opinion *must* be, and exactly what words I was to use to express those opinions in public . . . Shortly after that encounter at AIPAC, I was sent a list of American supporters of Israel . . . that I was free to call for campaign contributions. I called; they gave, from Florida to Alaska."[16]

Former Idaho governor John V. Evans tells a similar story about his 1986 campaign against incumbent Idaho Senator Steven Symms. He visited AIPAC headquarters, where, according to Evans, they "emphasized constantly that they were not a PAC (political action committee) . . . But they noted that there were Jewish organizations all over the country that had their own PACs and that if we could contact them, they would be able to help us." According to the *Wall Street Journal*, AIPAC "steered Mr. Evans to a series of supposedly independent organizations—many of them run by people with ties to AIPAC—that gave him $204,950 for his losing race against Republican Sen. Steve Symms."[17]

AIPAC also keeps track of congressional voting records and makes these records available to its members, so that they can decide which candidates or PACs to support.[18] Candidates or incumbents who are seen as hostile to Israel, on the other hand, can expect AIPAC to guide campaign contributions toward their opponents. Internal AIPAC documents acquired by the *Washington Post* in 1988 revealed that its deputy political director was actively "trying to help raise money for several candidates in the 1986 Senate race," and the *Wall Street Journal* reported in 1987 that "despite AIPAC's claims of non-involvement in political spending, no fewer than 51 pro-Israel PACs—most of which draw money from Jewish donors and operate under obscure-sounding names—are operated by AIPAC officials or people who hold seats on AIPAC's two major policymaking bodies."[19] Although the Federal Election Commission later ruled that there was "insufficient evidence" to conclude that AIPAC controlled the network of pro-Israel PACs, the belief that AIPAC helps guide contributions remains widespread.[20] The veteran diplomat David Newsom, who served as assistant secretary of state in the Nixon administration and as undersecretary of state under Jimmy Carter, reports that "when a prominent member of Congress was once asked the reason for the power of AIPAC in the legislature, he replied, 'Money. It's as simple as that.'"[21]

The Center for Responsive Politics (CRP), a nonpartisan research group that tracks campaign contributions, has identified roughly three dozen pro-Israel PACs active in recent elections. In the 2006 midterms, these groups gave more than $3 million to candidates from both parties.[22] Between 1990 and 2004, reports the *Economist*, pro-Israel groups contributed nearly $57 million to candidates and parties, while Arab-American and Muslim PACs contributed slightly less than $800,000.[23] When combined with individual contributions to particular candidates and donations given to the national party organizations themselves, pro-Israel forces wield considerable electoral clout. According to CRP's Steven Weiss, "If you are a candidate and you get the pro-Israel label from AIPAC, the money will start coming in from contributors all over the country."[24]

There is little doubt about the potency of these tactics. In 2006, for example, money from pro-Israel groups and individuals helped Senator Joseph Lieberman retain his seat by running independently following his defeat by Ned Lamont in the Democratic primary. Lieberman received a total of more than $145,000 from two dozen different pro-Israel PACs, and none of these groups helped Lamont. In the same year, $76,000 worth of pro-Israel PAC contributions helped Sheldon Whitehouse defeat incumbent Senator Lincoln Chaffee (R-RI), who had long been regarded as lukewarm on Israel.[25] Other beneficiaries of pro-Israel PAC support include successful candidates such as Robert Menendez (D-NJ) and Brad Ellsworth (D-IN). According to Ron Kampeas of the *Jewish Telegraph Agency*, the money for these (and other candidates) was "raised by a loose network of donors, many of whom have strong ties to [AIPAC], the pro-Israel lobby."[26]

AIPAC and its related network cannot influence every election, of course, and even large donations from pro-Israel groups could not get Lonsdale or Evans elected or prevent former Senate Minority Leader Tom Daschle (D-SD) or incumbent Senator Rick Santorum (R-PA) from being defeated in their respective bids for reelection in 2004 and 2006.[27] But over the past three decades it has helped many successful candidates win their races, while driving from office a number of individuals it considered unfriendly to Israel. In 2002, for example, it helped defeat Congresswoman Cynthia McKinney (D-GA) by funneling campaign money to her opponents. McKinney returned to office in 2004 but was again defeated for reelection in 2006. Hank Johnson, her victorious opponent in the 2006 Democratic primary, received at least $34,000 from seven pro-Israel PACs.[28] In another well-known case, wealthy Chicago businessman and former AIPAC President Robert Asher helped recruit and vet an Illinois attorney, Richard Durbin, to run against incumbent Congressman Paul Findley (R-IL) in 1982. Durbin had never held elected office, and as Asher later recalled, "I probed [Durbin's] views . . . I wanted to make sure we were supporting someone who was not only against Paul Findley but also a friend of Israel. He beat Findley with a lot of help from Jews, in-state and out-of-state. Now, how did the Jewish money find him? I traveled around the country talking about how we had the opportunity to defeat someone unfriendly to Israel. And the gates opened."[29] Asher solicited funds with a letter to potential donors declaring that the election was the "best chance" to remove a "dangerous enemy of Israel" from Congress, and Durbin eventually received a total of $104,325 in campaign funds from thirty-one different pro-Israel PACs. By way of comparison, in the 1982 election, other Illinois congressional candidates received an average of about $3,700 from the same groups.[30] Durbin went on to narrowly beat Findley, who had served eleven previous terms, and he later won election to the Senate, where he currently serves as majority whip.

In 2002, Mayer "Bubba" Mitchell, another member of the "Gang of Four" (the group of wealthy donors that guides AIPAC's policy making), used similar tactics to oust Congressman Earl Hilliard (D-AL). Like Durbin, Hilliard's opponent got financial help from AIPAC supporters across the country. According to the *New Yorker*'s Jeffrey Goldberg, Asher later said that he had "asked Bubba how he felt after [Hilliard's opponent] won, and he said 'Just like you did when Durbin got elected.'"[31] AIPAC has also played an important role in defeating a number of other politicians who took positions it disagreed with, including Representative Pete McCloskey (R-CA) and Senators J. William Fulbright (D-AR) and Roger Jepson (R-IA), to name

a few. Jepson's fate is particularly revealing: he was targeted after he suc-
cumbed to a personal plea from President Ronald Reagan and agreed to support the 1981 sale of AWACS aircraft to Saudi Arabia. His opponent in the
1984 Senate race, Democrat Tom Harkin, received more than $100,000 in
pro-Israel PAC money and Jepson lost his seat. Senator Alan Cranston
(D-CA) later commented that Jepson's fate "has sort of struck terror into the
hearts of senators about switching" on Middle East votes.[32]

Another example of the lobby's ability to influence elections concerns
former Senator Adlai Stevenson (D-IL), who ran for governor of Illinois in
1982. He first ran afoul of pro-Israel groups in 1980, when he introduced an
amendment to a Senate bill that called for reducing foreign aid to Israel if it
did not stop building settlements. Stevenson knew the amendment would
never pass, but he wanted to show that his colleagues would support Israel
even if it was acting in ways that were contrary to official U.S. policy. The
measure was easily defeated, gaining only seven votes. One reluctant opponent of the amendment, Senator Quentin Burdick (D-ND), told the Illinois
senator, "Sorry, Adlai, but I am up for reelection." When Stevenson ran for
governor two years later, he quickly discovered that campaign contributions
began to dry up, and indeed, went to his opponent. According to the former
senator, he and his wife "were reviled as anti-Semitic. Some in the press
turned hostile. Jewish Democratic Committeemen wilted under pressure.
Jewish friends and supporters were also reviled." Stevenson was narrowly
defeated, and as he later said, "the lobby made the difference in that election many times over."[33]

Perhaps the most renowned example of the costs that can befall a politician who crosses AIPAC is the defeat of Senator Charles Percy (R-IL) in
1984. Despite a generally pro-Israel voting record, Percy incurred AIPAC's
wrath by declining to sign the AIPAC-sponsored "Letter of 76" protesting
President Ford's threatened "reassessment" of U.S. Middle East policy in
1975. He also made the mistake of calling PLO leader Yasser Arafat more
"moderate" than some other Palestinian terrorists. Percy's opponents in both
the primary and general election in 1984 received large sums from pro-Israel
PACs, and a businessman from another state (California), Michael Goland,
who was also a major contributor to AIPAC, spent $1.1 million on anti-Percy
advertising in Illinois. (Goland was later convicted of making illegal campaign contributions in the 1986 California Senate race.)[34] As Tom Dine
boasted after Percy's narrow defeat, "All the Jews in America, from coast to
coast, gathered to oust Percy. And the American politicians—those who hold
public positions now, and those who aspire—got the message."[35] Dine's hy-

perbole notwithstanding, the basic lesson of these cases is hard to miss. As J. J. Goldberg, the editor of the *Forward*, said in 2002, "There is this image in Congress that you don't cross these people or they take you down."[36]

AIPAC and pro-Israel PACs focus on more than getting Israel-friendly candidates elected. They have also had notable success turning politicians who have been critical of Israel into steadfast supporters. Former Senator Jesse Helms (R-NC) was an outspoken critic of the U.S. foreign aid program for much of his career, which also meant that he opposed giving substantial aid to Israel. In 1984, however, Helms was in a hard-fought (and expensive) race for reelection against James Hunt, the popular governor of North Carolina. Sensing an opportunity to put a formidable enemy out of business, AIPAC channeled large amounts of campaign money to Hunt, who came within a hair of winning. Helms got the message: he traveled to Israel the following year and had his picture taken with a yarmulke on his head kissing the Western Wall. The same trip also produced a picture of the senator with Ariel Sharon for his office wall. More important, Helms became a vocal supporter of Israel and remained one until his retirement in 2002.[37]

One sees a similar evolution on the part of Senator Hillary Clinton, whose support for Palestinian statehood in 1998 and public embrace of Suha Arafat (wife of Yasser Arafat) in 1999 provoked strong criticism from groups in the lobby. Clinton became an ardent defender of Israel once she began running for office herself, and she now gets strong backing, including financial support, from pro-Israel organizations and individuals. After Clinton appeared at a pro-Israel rally in July 2006 and expressed strong support for Israel's highly destructive war against Lebanon, Helen Freedman, executive director of the hard-line Americans for a Safe Israel, declared, "I thought her remarks were very good, especially in light of her history, and we can't forget her kiss to Suha."[38] Pro-Israel PACs contributed more than $30,000 to Clinton's 2006 reelection campaign, and the *Forward* reported in January 2007 that Clinton was "expected to snare the lion's share of the Jewish community's substantial political donations in the race for the 2008 Democratic Presidential nomination."[39]

If electoral pressure and persuasion don't work, AIPAC has been known to threaten politicians who appear reluctant to follow its lead.[40] In 2006, for example, Congresswoman Betty McCollum (D-MN), a liberal with a solid pro-Israel voting record, nonetheless opposed the AIPAC-backed Palestinian Anti-Terrorism Act. The measure, which sought to impose draconian measures on the Palestinian Authority in the aftermath of the election of Hamas, was also opposed by the State Department, the Catholic Bishops, and other pro-Israel groups like Americans for Peace Now and the Israel Policy Forum. Nonetheless, an AIPAC lobbyist told McCollum's chief of staff that the representative's "support for terrorists will not be tolerated," a threat that led McCollum to demand an apology from AIPAC chief Howard Kohr and to bar AIPAC representatives from her offices.[41]

The basic message is clear: any senator or representative who crosses AIPAC is playing with fire. Although the lobby's efforts are hardly the only reason that these defeated candidates faced electoral challenges and eventually lost (for example, Cynthia McKinney's prospects were also damaged by a much-publicized confrontation with a Capitol Hill security guard, and Lincoln Chafee faced an uphill battle given anti-Republican sentiment in 2006), its ability to affect a politician's electoral prospects is well known. As one congressional source put it in 1991, "Voting against Israel has become like voting against lumber in Washington state, except AIPAC does it all over the country."[42] And that is why Morris Amitay, the former AIPAC director who later served as the organization's treasurer, could say in 2002 that "everyone seems to be very good nowadays," and why Jimmy Carter said in February 2007 that "I don't see any present prospect that any member of the US Congress, the House or Senate, would say, 'Let's take a balanced position between Israel and the Palestinians and negotiate a peace agreement.'" He added, "It's almost politically suicidal . . . for a member of the Congress who wants to seek reelection to take any stand that might be interpreted as anti-policy of the conservative Israeli government."[43]

AIPAC's clout also explains why attendance at its annual Policy Conference has become a command performance for prominent members of both parties as well as leading officials from the executive branch. Speakers at the 2007 Policy Conference included Vice President Dick Cheney, Speaker of the House Nancy Pelosi (D-CA), Senate Majority Leader Harry Reid and Minority Leader Mitch McConnell (R-KY), and House Minority Leader John Boehner (R-OH). The previous year's speakers included Cheney, Boehner, UN Ambassador John Bolton, Senators Susan Collins (R-ME) and Evan Bayh (D-IN), and Representatives Roy Blunt (R-MO), Shelley Berkley (D-NV), Artur Davis (D-AL), Bill Pascrell (D-NJ), and Robert Wexler, as well as former senator and presidential hopeful John Edwards. Speakers in other years have included President George W. Bush, Secretaries of State Colin Powell and Condoleezza Rice, former House Speakers Dennis Hastert (R-IL), Richard Armey, and Newt Gingrich, and a bevy of prominent pro-Israel pundits. It is hard to think of any other lobbying organization that is wooed as strenuously by politicians in both parties.

AIPAC's ability to influence elections helps ensure that Israel gets generous aid each year and makes it dangerous for senators or representatives to utter even mild criticisms of Israel's conduct. But its influence on Capitol Hill goes even farther. Lobbying groups of all types exercise influence not merely by direct persuasion and by using campaign contributions to gain access, but also by providing a "legislative subsidy" to sympathetic lawmakers and supplying overworked staffs with direct assistance in analyzing issues, framing legislation, and offering talking points and speeches to give to constituents.[44] Not only does every member of Congress receive AIPAC's biweekly newsletter *Near East Report*, its personnel are also available to help staffers when issues affecting Israel arise. According to Douglas Bloomfield, a former AIPAC staff member, "It is common for members of Congress and their staffs to turn to AIPAC first when they need information, before calling the Library of Congress, the Congressional Research Service, committee staff or administration experts." More important, he notes that AIPAC is "often called upon to draft speeches, work on legislation, advise on tactics, perform research, collect co-sponsors and marshal votes."[45] In other words, AIPAC inserts itself directly into the legislative and policy-making process with considerable frequency, as we explore in more detail in Part II.

To seal the deal, an AIPAC sister organization, the American Israel Education Foundation (AIEF), funds free congressional trips to Israel itself. These junkets burnish a legislator's pro-Israel credentials and facilitate fund-raising, and also expose him or her to the policy preferences and basic worldview of Israel's leaders. This situation helps explain why about 10 percent of all congressional trips overseas are to Israel, even though it is but one of the nearly two hundred countries in the world. The Center for Public Integrity reports that AIEF spent nearly $1 million on these visits from January 2000 to mid-2005. Not surprisingly, AIPAC and other Jewish groups lobbied hard—and successfully—to make sure that the new ethics rules enacted following the Jack Abramoff and Tom DeLay scandals did not interfere with these visits.[46]

It is important to emphasize again that AIPAC's activities are similar to the behavior of other influential lobbies and consistent with the interest group tradition of the U.S. political system. In his study *Jews and American Politics*, Stephen Isaacs described AIPAC's Morris Amitay as saying, "What is important . . . is that none of this is untoward . . . You use the traditional tactics of the democracy . . . letters, calls."[47]

These "traditional tactics" to influence Congress also enable the lobby to put pressure on the executive branch when it takes actions that are considered to be not in Israel's interest. When that happens, the president or cabinet official is likely to get a hard-hitting letter from one or both houses of Congress, signed by most of its members, as President Gerald Ford did when he threatened a reassessment of U.S.-Israeli relations in 1975. President Bush got a similar letter in April 2002, when he briefly sought to pressure Israel to end a large-scale military incursion in the Occupied Territories. The lopsided percentage of signatories for each of these letters is eloquent testimony to AIPAC's ability to twist arms. As Senator Daniel Inouye (D-HI) commented after signing the letter to Ford in 1975, "It's easier to sign one letter than to answer 5000." Or as Senator John Culver (D-IA) later admitted, "The pressure was just too great. I caved."[48] Secretary of State Condoleezza Rice felt the same pressure as she sought to restart the peace process by visiting the Middle East in March 2007. Just before her departure, Rice received an AIPAC-sponsored letter signed by seventy-nine senators, urging her to avoid contact with the new Palestinian "unity government" until it recognized Israel, renounced terror, and agreed to abide by Israeli-Palestinian agreements.[49] No wonder former Secretary of State Lawrence Eagleburger once told AIPAC's Tom Dine, "Dine, I deal with you because you could hurt me."[50]

The bottom line is that AIPAC, which bills itself as "America's Pro-Israel Lobby," has an almost unchallenged hold on Congress.[51] One of the three main branches of the American government is firmly committed to supporting Israel. Open debate about U.S. policy toward Israel does not occur there, even though that policy has important consequences for the entire world. As Senator Ernest Hollings (D-SC) noted as he was leaving office in 2004, "You can't have an Israeli policy other than what AIPAC gives you around here."[52] Another senator, speaking on condition of anonymity, told a *Washington Post* reporter in 1991, "My colleagues think AIPAC is a very, very powerful organization that is ruthless, and very, very alert. Eighty percent of the senators here roll their eyes on some of the votes. They know that what they're doing isn't what they really believe is right, but why fight on a situation where they're liable to get beat up on?"[53]

Small wonder, then, that former Israeli Prime Minister Ariel Sharon once told an American audience, "When people ask me how they can help Israel, I tell them—Help AIPAC." His successor, Ehud Olmert, agrees, remarking, "Thank God we have AIPAC, the greatest supporter and friend we have in the whole world."[54]

THE MAKING OF PRO-ISRAEL PRESIDENTS

Whether through influence on Congress or in more direct ways, groups in the lobby also exert significant leverage over the executive branch. American presidents are not as sensitive to pressure as Congress is, and most of them have taken positions that Israel or the lobby opposed at one time or another. But such instances are becoming increasingly rare, even though Israel's strategic value has declined and some of its actions (such as the continued effort to colonize the Occupied Territories) are at odds with stated U.S. policy.

Influence over the executive branch derives in part from the impact Jewish voters have on presidential elections. Despite their small numbers in the population (less than 3 percent), American Jews make large campaign donations to candidates from both parties. As presidential adviser and former White House Chief of Staff Hamilton Jordan wrote in a confidential memorandum to President Jimmy Carter, "Wherever there is major political fundraising in this country, you will find American Jews playing a significant role."[55] Indeed, the *Washington Post* once estimated that Democratic presidential candidates "depend on Jewish supporters to supply as much as 60 percent of the money raised from private sources."[56] Other estimates are lower, but contributions from Jewish Americans form a substantial share— between 20 and 50 percent—of the contributions made to the Democratic party and its presidential candidates.[57] Israel is not the only issue that inspires these contributions, of course, but candidates who are perceived as hostile (or even indifferent) to Israel run the risk of seeing some of these funds go to their opponents.

Furthermore, Jewish voters have high turnout rates and are concentrated in key states like California, Florida, Illinois, New Jersey, New York, and Pennsylvania, which increases their weight in determining who becomes president. Although they still favor the Democratic party, their support for Democratic candidates can no longer be taken for granted. John F. Kennedy received 82 percent of the Jewish vote in 1960, for example, but George McGovern received only 64 percent in 1972, and Jimmy Carter got a mere 45 percent in 1980. In close races, therefore, the so-called Jewish vote can tip the balance in key states. Jeffrey Helmreich of the Jerusalem Center for Public Affairs exaggerates only slightly when he writes that "American Jewish voters maintain the potential to be *the* decisive factor in national election results . . . American Jews wield power through their high concentration in key states and their tendency to behave as a swing vote in ways that set them apart from virtually all other groups in American politics."[58] Because Jewish voters matter in close elections, presidential candidates go to considerable lengths to cultivate their support. Indeed, a 2007 story in the *Jerusalem Post* referred to this effort to court Jewish support as "a Washington ritual as reliable as the cherry blossoms."[59] Candidates are especially eager to appeal to AIPAC and other organizations in the lobby—and not just to Jewish voters as a bloc—because they know that the seal of approval from these prominent organizations will facilitate fund-raising and encourage higher turnout on their behalf.

Gaining and retaining that support means backing Israel down the line, which is why presidential candidates John Edwards, Mitt Romney, and John McCain all made emphatic pro-Israel speeches to the 2007 Herzliya conference (an annual meeting on Israeli national security organized by the hawkish Institute for Policy and Strategy). They wanted to avoid the fate that befell Howard Dean in the 2004 presidential campaign, when he made the mistake of recommending that the United States take a more "even-handed role" in the Arab-Israeli conflict. In response, one of Dean's rivals for the nomination, Joseph Lieberman, accused him of selling Israel down the river and labeled his statement "irresponsible."[60] Even more remarkably, virtually all of the top Democrats in the House of Representatives signed a hard-hitting letter to Dean criticizing his comments, and the *Chicago Jewish Star* reported that "anonymous attackers . . . are clogging the e-mail inboxes of Jewish leaders around the country, warning—without much evidence—that Dean would somehow be bad for Israel."[61]

This worry was absurd, because Dean is in fact an unabashed supporter of Israel.[62] His campaign cochair was former AIPAC president Steven Grossman, and Dean said his own views on the Middle East more closely reflected those of AIPAC than the more moderate Americans for Peace Now. Moreover, Dean's wife is Jewish and his children were raised Jewish as well. Dean wasn't questioning U.S. support for Israel; he had merely suggested that to "bring the sides together," Washington should act as an honest broker. This is not a radical idea, but key groups in the lobby do not welcome the idea of evenhandedness when it comes to the Arab-Israeli conflict. Dean's failure to win the Democratic nomination has many causes, of course, but the incident underscored the potential cost of being anything less than ardently pro-Israel during a presidential campaign.

KEEPING THE ADMINISTRATION IN LINE

Key organizations in the lobby also directly target the administration in power. The principal mission of the Conference of Presidents is to pressure the White House when it acts in ways that the Conference opposes, as it did when Gerald Ford threatened to reassess U.S. support for Israel, when George H. W. Bush briefly withheld loan guarantees in 1992, or, as discussed in Chapter 7, when George W. Bush called for the creation of a Palestinian state in the immediate aftermath of September 11.

But there is an even more obvious way to shape an administration's policy: the lobby's goals are served when individuals who share its perspective occupy important positions in the executive branch. In a notorious incident in 1992, for example, the New York businessman Haim Katz, calling as a potential donor to pro-Israel candidates, secretly taped a phone call with AIPAC President David Steiner. In addition to describing how AIPAC had helped direct campaign contributions to friendly politicians, Steiner told Katz that he had met personally to "cut a deal" with Secretary of State James Baker for $3 billion in foreign aid to Israel, plus "a billion dollars in other goodies that people don't even know about." More to the point, he told Katz that "we have a dozen people in [Clinton's] campaign, in the headquarters . . . and they're all going to get big jobs." Steiner was forced to resign after Katz went public, and he later said his statements to Katz were not true, but there is little reason to doubt the thrust of his remarks.[63] After all, wouldn't any powerful interest group want individuals who shared its views to get key appointments in each administration? In fact, plenty of other lobbies have done exactly that. Former Secretary of the Interior Gale Norton and Deputy Secretary J. Steven Griles both worked as lobbyists for oil or mining industries prior to their appointments in the Bush administration, for example, and Daniel A. Troy was a lawyer who frequently represented tobacco and pharmaceutical companies before being appointed chief counsel to the Food and Drug Administration in 2001.[64]

The Israel lobby is no different. As we have noted, the Clinton administration's Middle East policy was heavily shaped by officials with close ties to Israel or to prominent pro-Israel organizations. The two most notable individuals in this regard were Martin Indyk, the former deputy director of research at AIPAC and cofounder of the pro-Israel Washington Institute for Near East Policy, who served on Clinton's National Security Council, as ambassador to Israel (1995–97, 2000–01), and as assistant secretary of state (1997–2000); and Dennis Ross, who served as Clinton's special envoy to the

Middle East and joined WINEP after leaving government in 2001.[65] They were among President Clinton's closest advisers at the Camp David summit in July 2000.

Although both Indyk and Ross supported the Oslo peace process and favored the creation of a Palestinian state—which led hard-liners to denounce them unfairly for betraying Israel—they did so only within the limits of what would be acceptable to Israeli leaders.[66] As discussed in Chapter 1, the American delegation at Camp David took most of its cues from Israeli Prime Minister Ehud Barak, coordinated negotiating positions with Israel in advance, and did not offer its own independent proposals for settling the conflict. Even the "Clinton parameters" presented in December 2000 were less an independent American proposal than Clinton's summary of where the negotiations stood and his assessment of the bargaining space within which a solution might be found. Palestinian negotiators complained that the Israelis would sometimes present them with a specific proposal, and then later the Americans would offer the same idea, only the Americans would label it a "bridging proposal." As another member of the U.S. team later admitted, Israeli proposals were often "presented [to the Palestinians] as U.S. concepts, not Israeli ones," a subterfuge that fooled no one and reinforced Palestinian suspicions. Not surprisingly, Palestinian representatives protested that they were "negotiating with two Israeli teams—one displaying an Israeli flag, and one an American flag."[67]

The issue is not whether individuals like Indyk or Ross were dedicated public servants acting in what they thought to be the best interest of the United States—they surely were. The issue, rather, is whether their well-known sympathies for Israel made it more difficult for the administration to operate effectively during the negotiations and made it less inclined to bring U.S. leverage to bear on the Israeli government, thus reducing the chances of securing a peace deal. We believe that this situation hampered the entire Oslo process, including the abortive Camp David summit.

The problem is even more pronounced in the second Bush administration, whose ranks have included staunchly pro-Israel neoconservatives like Elliott Abrams, John Bolton, Douglas Feith, Aaron Friedberg, John Hannah, I. Lewis Libby, William Luti, Richard Perle, Paul Wolfowitz, and David Wurmser. As we shall see in Part II, these officials consistently pushed for policies favored by Israel and backed by key organizations in the lobby.

By the same token, groups in the lobby also try to make sure that people who are seen as critical of Israel do not get important foreign policy jobs. In 1987, former AIPAC head Tom Dine told an interviewer that AIPAC was helping vet presidential advisers, saying, "This is an actual example . . . One of the [1988] presidential candidates called us and said 'I will be publicly declaring soon, and I am interested in hiring so and so for a top campaign position. Tell me what you think about him.'" Dine said his answer was "thumbs up" in that case, but others are less fortunate.[68] Jimmy Carter wanted to make George Ball his first secretary of state, but he knew that Ball was perceived as critical of Israel and that the lobby would oppose the appointment.[69] Similarly, Richard Marius, a Harvard lecturer hired in 1995 as Vice President Al Gore's chief speechwriter, has said that he was fired before he began work after the *New Republic* publisher Martin Peretz (who was Gore's undergraduate tutor and a close confidant) falsely claimed that Marius was an anti-Semite, based on a book review Marius had published in *Harvard Magazine* in 1992.[70]

A few years later, in 2001, when Bruce Riedel left his position handling Middle East issues on the National Security Council, the *New Republic* reported that the Pentagon had "held up the appointment of Riedel's designated successor, the Middle East expert Alina Romanowski, whom Pentagon officials suspect of being insufficiently supportive of the Jewish state."[71] The person appointed instead was Elliott Abrams, who had previously pleaded guilty to withholding information from Congress during the Iran-contra affair. Abrams is hardly objective about Israel, having previously written in a 1997 book that "there can be no doubt that Jews, faithful to the covenant between God and Abraham, are to stand apart from the nation in which they live. It is the very nature of being Jewish to be apart—except in Israel—from the rest of the population."[72] This is a remarkable comment coming from an individual who holds a critically important position on Middle East policy in the U.S. government. "For the government of Israel," wrote Nathan Guttman in *Ha'aretz*, his appointment was "a gift from heaven."[73]

CONCLUSION

Like other foreign policy interest groups, the Israel lobby seeks to influence the U.S. government through a variety of different channels. It is in a better position to do so than most other groups, which is one reason its efforts are so effective. But its efforts are not limited to building influence inside the Beltway. The lobby also strives to shape public discourse about Israel and the Middle East, so that the American public generally supports a pro-Israel orientation and does not question the merits of unconditional U.S. backing. This second strategy is the subject of the next chapter.

6

DOMINATING PUBLIC DISCOURSE

One of the lobby's central concerns is to ensure that public discourse about Israel echoes the strategic and moral rationales dissected in Chapters 2 and 3. Its various elements do this by constantly reaffirming Israel's strategic value, by repeating one-sided accounts about Israel and its founding, and by defending Israel's actions in policy debates. The goal is to convince the public that America's and Israel's interests and values are one and the same.

At the same time, groups in the lobby try to marginalize anyone who criticizes Israeli policy or challenges the "special relationship," and try to prevent that person's views from getting a fair hearing in the public arena. To do this, the lobby sometimes employs heavy-handed tactics to silence critics, accusing them of being anti-Israel or anti-Semitic. Channeling public discourse in a pro-Israel direction is critically important, because an open and candid discussion of Israeli policy in the Occupied Territories, Israeli history, and the lobby's role in shaping America's Middle East policy might easily lead more Americans to question existing policy toward Israel and to call for a relationship with Israel that more effectively serves the U.S. national interest.

Accordingly, key elements in the lobby strive to influence discourse about Israel in the media, think tanks, and academia, because these institutions are critical to shaping popular opinion. They promote efforts to portray Israel in a positive light and they go to considerable lengths to marginalize anyone who questions Israel's past or present conduct or seeks to cast doubt on the merits of unconditional U.S. backing. Pro-Israel forces are well aware that dominating discussions about the Jewish state is essential to their agenda. These efforts do not always succeed, of course, but are still remarkably effective.

THE MEDIA IS THE MESSAGE

A key part of preserving positive public attitudes toward Israel is to ensure that the mainstream media's coverage of Israel and the Middle East consistently favors Israel and does not call U.S. support into question in any way. While serious criticism of Israel occasionally reaches a large audience across the United States, the American media's coverage of Israel tends to be strongly biased in Israel's favor, especially when compared with news coverage in other democracies.

This claim might sound to some like the old anti-Semitic accusation that "Jews control the media." It is anything but. There is no question that some Jewish Americans, such as Martin Peretz and Mortimer Zuckerman, use their positions in the media to advance their views on Israel and the Middle East. This behavior is legitimate and unsurprising, as all elites tend to use their privileged positions to advance their various interests. More to the point, however, there are certainly owners, publishers, editors, columnists, and reporters in the mainstream media who have no special feelings for Israel and would feel comfortable criticizing its policies as well as the United States–Israel relationship. There are surely even influential individuals who may be strongly pro-Israel but would nevertheless welcome a more open discourse about that country.

It is therefore wrong—and objectionable—to argue that Jews or pro-Israel forces "control" the media and what they say about Israel. In fact, the reason that the lobby works so hard to monitor and influence what the mainstream media says about Israel is precisely that the lobby does not control them. If the media were left to their own devices, they would not serve up as consistent a diet of pro-Israel coverage and commentary. Instead, there would be a more open and lively discussion about the Jewish state and U.S. policy toward it, as there is in virtually every other democracy in the world. Indeed, that debate is especially lively in Israel itself, the one state where Jews clearly *do* "control the media."

The lobby's perspective on Israel is widely reflected in the mainstream media in part because a substantial number of American commentators who write about Israel are themselves pro-Israel. In a 1976 comparison of domestic interest groups and U.S. Middle East policy, Robert H. Trice found that "one of the most serious political handicaps of pro-Arab groups during the 1966–1974 period was their inability to gain support from any of the best-known and nationally-syndicated columnists." Trice also found that "pro-Israel groups could count on media support not only from national columnists but also from the editors of some of the country's most widely read newspapers." Pro-Israel groups were more active shaping media coverage than pro-Arab groups were; in 1970, for example, the Conference of Presidents distributed press kits (complete with photos and feature stories) to more than seventeen hundred newspapers and to major wire services. In Trice's words, "At virtually every level of media organization—from local communities, syndicated columnists, and major national papers, to the international news services that supply the country with information—pro-Israel groups were more successful than pro-Arab groups at getting their side of the story transmitted to both the articulate and mass publics."[1]

Matters have not changed much since then. The debate among Middle East pundits, wrote the media critic Eric Alterman in 2002, is "dominated by people who cannot imagine criticizing Israel." He listed fifty-six "columnists and commentators who can be counted upon to support Israel reflexively and without qualification." Conversely, Alterman identified only five pundits who consistently criticize Israeli behavior or endorse pro-Arab positions.[2] Although some readers subsequently challenged Alterman's coding of a handful of cases and a few of those he listed are now deceased, the disparity remains overwhelming and the challenges did not undermine his core claim.[3]

Consider the columnists who have covered the Middle East for the *New York Times* and the *Washington Post* in recent years. William Safire and the late A. M. Rosenthal were passionate defenders of Israel (and in Safire's case, especially favorable toward Ariel Sharon); today, David Brooks consistently defends Israel's position. Thomas L. Friedman is more moderate; he has been critical of some of Israel's policies (and occasionally the lobby itself), but he almost never takes the Palestinians' side or advocates that the United States distance itself from Israel. Nicholas D. Kristof is frequently critical of various aspects of American foreign policy and wrote one controversial column in March 2007 decrying the lack of serious public discussion of U.S. relations with Israel. But the Middle East is not a frequent theme in his commentary and he certainly did not take a pro-Palestinian position.[4] Maureen Dowd has been sharply critical of pro-Israel neoconservatives, but like Kristof, she rarely writes about the Jewish state or U.S. policy toward it. No one in the *Times*'s stable of regular columnists is a consistent defender of the Palestinians, or even as evenhanded as former columnist Anthony Lewis, who retired in 2001.

As for the *Washington Post*, it has had several columnists in recent years who consistently supported Israel: Jim Hoagland, Robert Kagan, Charles

Krauthammer, and George Will. It used to feature two others: the late Michael Kelly and William Kristol, who runs the *Weekly Standard* and has a column in *Time*. Not only were these individuals staunchly pro-Israel, they tended to favor the ideas and policies of the hawkish Likud party rather than Israeli moderates. Richard Cohen also writes about the Middle East for the *Post*, but he has the same profile as the *Times*'s Friedman: attached to Israel but willing to offer qualified and intelligent criticism. Neither of these papers—which are arguably the two most influential daily newspapers in the United States—employs any full-time commentator who consistently favors the Arab or Palestinian side.

In recent years, the only prominent columnist who has frequently criticized Israel is Robert Novak, whose column is syndicated by the *Chicago Sun-Times* and regularly appears in the *Post*. Still, Novak is hardly a champion of the Palestinian cause. The fact is that the "other side" has no equivalent of Safire and Krauthammer, or even Friedman and Cohen, at either the *Times* or the *Post*, or any other major American newspaper, for that matter. The *Los Angeles Times*, for example, regularly publishes three opinion columnists who are staunch defenders of Israel: Max Boot, Jonathan Chait, and Jonah Goldberg. It employs no columnist who is critical of Israel, much less anyone who routinely defends the Palestinians against the Israelis.

Although these papers occasionally publish guest op-eds that challenge Israeli policy, the balance of opinion clearly favors Israel. There is no American commentator comparable to a Robert Fisk or a Patrick Seale, who are often sharply critical of Israel and who publish regularly in British newspapers, and no one remotely like Israeli commentators Amira Hass, Akiva Eldar, Gideon Levy, and Bradley Burston, all of whom are openly critical of particular policies that their country pursues. The point here is not that these individuals are always right and pro-Israel commentators are wrong; the point is that voices like theirs are almost entirely absent from major American newspapers.

Not surprisingly, this pro-Israel bias is also reflected in newspaper editorials. Robert Bartley, the late editor of the *Wall Street Journal*, once remarked, "Shamir, Sharon, Bibi—whatever those guys want is pretty much fine by me."[5] The *Journal*, along with other prominent newspapers like the *Chicago Sun-Times*, the *New York Sun*, and the *Washington Times*, regularly runs editorials that read as if they were written by the Israeli prime minister's press office. To its credit, the *New York Times*'s editorials sometimes criticize Israeli policies, and in recent years, the criticism has occasionally been strongly worded. The *Times* recognizes that the Palestinians have legitimate grievances and a right to have their own state. Still, its treatment of the two sides over the years has not been evenhanded.[6] In his memoirs, former *Times* executive editor Max Frankel recounted the impact his own pro-Israel attitudes had on his editorial choices: "I was much more deeply devoted to Israel than I dared to assert . . . Fortified by my knowledge of Israel and my friendships there, I myself wrote most of our Middle East commentaries. As more Arab than Jewish readers recognized, I wrote them from a pro-Israel perspective."[7]

Magazines like *Commentary*, the *New Republic*, and the *Weekly Standard* also zealously defend Israel at every turn. Indeed, *Commentary's* former editor, Norman Podhoretz, once told a gathering of journalists in Jerusalem that "the role of Jews who write in both the Jewish and general press is to defend Israel, and not join in the attacks on Israel."[8] Martin Peretz, the longtime editor of the *New Republic*, once proclaimed, "I am in love with the state of Israel," and admitted that "there's a sort of party line on Israel" at his journal.[9]

The media's reporting of news events involving Israel is less slanted than their editorial commentary, in part because most reporters strive to be objective, but also because it is difficult to cover events in the Occupied Territories or in southern Lebanon without acknowledging Israel's actual behavior. But still, to discourage unfavorable reporting on Israel, groups in the lobby organize letter-writing campaigns, demonstrations, and boycotts against news outlets whose content they consider anti-Israel. As the *Forward* reported in April 2002, "Rooting out perceived anti-Israel bias in the media has become for many American Jews the most direct and emotional outlet for connecting with the conflict 6,000 miles away."[10] One CNN executive has said that he sometimes gets six thousand e-mail messages in a single day complaining that a story is anti-Israel, and papers such as the *Chicago Tribune*, the *Los Angeles Times*, the *Miami Herald*, the *New York Times*, the *Philadelphia Inquirer*, and the *Washington Post* have faced consumer boycotts over their Middle East reporting.[11] One correspondent told the journalist Michael Massing that newspapers were "afraid" of AIPAC and other pro-Israel groups, saying that "the pressure from these groups is relentless. Editors would just as soon not touch them."[12] As the former spokesman for the Israeli consulate in New York, Menachem Shalev, once put it, "Of course, a lot of self-censorship goes on. Journalists, editors, and politicians are going to think twice about criticizing Israel if they know they are going to get thousands of angry calls in a matter of hours. The Jewish lobby is good at orchestrating pressure."[13]

America's Jewish press is not exempt from pressure, either. In 1989, for example, AIPAC's media director, Toby Dershowitz, asked Andrew Carroll, the editor of *Washington Jewish Week*, not to assign the reporter Larry Cohler to an ongoing story about AIPAC, because his earlier reports—which had been somewhat critical of AIPAC—were supposedly "inaccurate." When Cohler received the assignment anyway, Dershowitz and AIPAC legal counsel David Ifshin called Carroll. Ifshin said that if Cohler remained on the assignment, AIPAC would reexamine his earlier stories "with an eye toward litigation." This not-too-subtle attempt to pressure Carroll did not succeed, but in 1991, AIPAC's foreign policy director, Steven Rosen, sent several board members of *Washington Jewish Week* an internal AIPAC memorandum arguing that Carroll was too sympathetic to the political left and "sought to bring down the organized Jewish community." In April 1992, a new editor with no professional newspaper experience was hired over Carroll, who resigned three months later and was replaced by the former editor of the AIPAC newsletter *Near East Report*.[14]

One of the lobby's most energetic media watchdog groups—though not the only one—is the Committee for Accuracy in Middle East Reporting in America (CAMERA). It has been especially critical of National Public Radio, which it sometimes refers to as "National Palestine Radio."[15] In addition to maintaining a website to publicize alleged examples of media bias, CAMERA organized demonstrations outside National Public Radio stations in thirty-three cities in May 2003, and it tried to convince contributors to withhold support from NPR until its Middle East coverage became more sympathetic to Israel. One of Boston's public radio stations, WBUR, reportedly lost more than $1 million in contributions as a result of these efforts. In 2006, CAMERA ran expensive full-page advertisements in the *New York Times* and *New York Sun* criticizing Jimmy Carter's book *Palestine: Peace Not Apartheid*, ads that included the publisher's phone number and encouraged readers to call and complain.[16]

Additional pressure on NPR comes from Israel's friends in Congress. In March 2003, for example, a group of congressmen—whose ranks included staunch defenders of Israel such as California Democrats Tom Lantos, Brad Sherman, and Henry Waxman—wrote a letter to NPR President Kevin Klose, asking for an internal audit of its Middle East coverage. Klose refused, but he also began reaching out to various Jewish groups in an effort to deflect the pressure.[17]

The lobby's efforts to gain favorable coverage take other forms as well. In August 2003, for example, the writer Ian Buruma wrote an article in the

New York Times Magazine titled "How to Talk About Israel." He made the obvious point that it is sometimes difficult to talk "critically and dispassionately" about Israel in the United States and pointed out that "even legitimate criticism of Israel, or of Zionism, is often quickly denounced as anti-Semitism by various watchdogs." In response, Bret Stephens, then the editor of the *Jerusalem Post* and now a columnist and editorial board member at the *Wall Street Journal*, published a vitriolic open letter in the *Post* that began by asking Buruma, "Are you a Jew?" Two paragraphs later, Stephens declared, "What matters to me is that *you* say, 'I am a Jew.'" Why did this matter? Because in Stephens's view, "One must be at least a Jew to tell the goyim how they may or may not talk about Israel." The message of this remarkable letter was, in short, that non-Jews should talk about this subject only in ways that Jews deem acceptable.[18] Sensitivity on this point may also explain why an editor at the *New York Times* asked the historian Tony Judt to identify himself as Jewish in an op-ed he had written defending our original *London Review of Books* article.[19]

Stephens's views are undoubtedly anathema to many people—including most American Jews—but the fact remains that some leading figures in the lobby are uncomfortable with a free and open discussion of issues related to Israel. ADL head Abraham Foxman told *New York Times Magazine* writer James Traub that it is "naïve" to think that the "free market of ideas ultimately sifts falsehood to produce truth." As Traub recounts, "Experience . . . has taught [Foxman] that the truth does not win on its own merits; the market for falsehood is too powerful." Falsehood, in this view, is what would follow from a serious interrogation of the United States–Israel relationship and Israel's strategic and moral standing. Groups like the ADL want to make sure that critics of Israel and unconditional U.S. support for the Jewish state remain on the margins of public discourse, and that their views about Israel be regarded as illegitimate.[20]

The final way to encourage favorable coverage of Israel is to co-opt prominent commentators so that they disseminate a pro-Israel perspective. Toward this end, the Conference of Presidents helped establish America's Voices in Israel, a nonprofit group whose purpose, according to the Conference's website, is "to strengthen American understanding of and support for Israel by inviting U.S.-based radio talk show hosts to see Israel and broadcast their programs live from Jerusalem." The America's Voices website describes the organization as being "on the forefront of Israel's hasbara (public relations) efforts," and Conference of Presidents head Malcolm Hoenlein (who is also president of the America's Voices board) calls it "one of the most important, exciting, and effective hasbara initiatives." Participants have included radio personalities such as Oliver North, Glenn Beck, Monica Crowley, Michael Medved, Armstrong Williams, and many others. The campaign helps ensure that a growing array of talk show hosts will purvey a pro-Israel message to their listeners.[21]

These diverse efforts share a common purpose: to make it less likely that mainstream media organizations will report information or events that portray Israel negatively, and to promote public commentary that reinforces the strategic and moral rationales that are used to justify strong U.S. support. These efforts are not 100 percent successful, of course, but they are still quite effective.

THINK TANKS THAT THINK ONE WAY

Pro-Israel forces wield significant influence in think tanks, which play an increasingly important role in shaping public debate as well as actual policy on key issues. Instead of relying on government officials or academics to provide analysis and commentary, news media increasingly depend on experts from Washington-based think tanks, most of which have energetic public relations and media relations offices designed to promote their experts' views in the public arena. Many think tanks also distribute brief and easily digested policy memorandums to legislators and other government officials; organize seminars, working breakfasts; and briefings for officials and their staffs; and encourage their own analysts to publish op-eds and other visible forms of commentary, all with the goal of shaping the prevailing climate of ideas. Think tanks like the American Enterprise Institute or Brookings supply advisers to presidential campaigns and officials to new administrations, offer the same people a safe haven when they are out of power, and provide them with platforms from which they can continue to influence debate inside and outside the Beltway. They serve as incubators for new policy ideas and are a critical part of the web of power in Washington.[22]

Recognizing the need for a prominent but seemingly "objective" voice in the policy arena surrounding Israel, former AIPAC president Larry Weinberg; his wife, Barbi Weinberg; AIPAC's vice president; and AIPAC deputy director for research Martin Indyk founded the Washington Institute for Near East Policy in 1985.[23] Although WINEP plays down its links to Israel and claims that it provides a "balanced and realistic" perspective on Middle East issues, this is not the case.[24] In fact, WINEP is funded and run by individuals who are deeply committed to advancing Israel's agenda. Its board of advisers includes prominent pro-Israel figures such as Edward Luttwak, Martin Peretz, Richard Perle, James Woolsey, and Mortimer Zuckerman, but includes no one who might be thought of as favoring the perspective of any other country or group in the "Near East." Many of its personnel are genuine scholars or experienced former officials, but they are hardly neutral observers on most Middle East issues and there is little diversity of views within WINEP's ranks.

The lobby's influence in the think tank world extends well beyond WINEP. As discussed in Chapter 4, over the past twenty-five years, pro-Israel individuals have established a commanding presence at the American Enterprise Institute, the Center for Security Policy, the Foreign Policy Research Institute, the Heritage Foundation, the Hudson Institute, the Institute for Foreign Policy Analysis, and the Jewish Institute for National Security Affairs. These think tanks are all decidedly pro-Israel and include few, if any, critics of U.S. support for the Jewish state.

Another indication of the lobby's influence in the think tank world is the evolution of the Brookings Institution. For many years, its senior expert on Middle East issues was William B. Quandt, a distinguished academic and former NSC official with a well-deserved reputation for evenhandedness regarding the Arab-Israeli conflict. In the mid-1970s, in fact, Brookings released an influential report on the Middle East that emphasized the need for Israeli withdrawals, Palestinian self-determination (including the possibility of an independent state), open access to religious sites in Jerusalem, and security guarantees for Israel. The Brookings study was produced by a diverse group of experts and is widely seen as the blueprint behind the Carter administration's successful efforts to negotiate an Egyptian-Israeli peace treaty.[25]

Today, however, Brookings's work on these issues is conducted through its Saban Center for Middle East Policy, which was established in 2002 with a $13 million grant, primarily financed by Haim Saban, an ardent Zionist. The *New York Times* described him as "perhaps the most politically connected mogul in Hollywood, throwing his weight and money around Washington and, increasingly, the world, trying to influence all things Israeli." This "tireless cheerleader for Israel" told the *Times*, "I'm a one-issue guy, and my issue is Israel." His efforts led Ariel Sharon to describe him as "a great American citizen and a man who always stood by Israel and the Jewish people in times of need."[26] The man chosen to run the Saban Center was Martin Indyk, the former Clinton administration official who had previously served as AIPAC's deputy director of research and helped found WINEP.

It is hard to imagine that a research institute funded by Saban and directed by Indyk is going to be anything but pro-Israel. To be sure, the Saban Center occasionally hosts Arab scholars and exhibits some diversity of opinion. Saban Center fellows—like Indyk himself—often endorse the idea of a two-state settlement between Israel and the Palestinians. But Saban Center publications never question U.S. support for Israel and rarely, if ever, offer significant criticism of key Israeli policies. Moreover, individuals who stray from the Center's line do not remain for long, as former NSC official Flynt Leverett's brief tenure there illustrates.[27]

The Center's pro-Israel proclivities are on display at its annual Saban Forum, which brings together prominent U.S. and Israeli leaders for a two-day conference, held in either Washington or Jerusalem. The 2006 Forum, titled "America and Israel: Confronting a Middle East in Turmoil," featured appearances by Israeli Foreign Minister Tzipi Livni, Bill Clinton, Senator Hillary Clinton, Shimon Peres, William Kristol, Representatives Tom Lantos and Jane Harman, and Israel Minister of Strategic Affairs Avigdor Lieberman, among others. Pro-Arab voices, or voices who might articulate a different view of U.S.-Israeli relations, were conspicuously absent.[28]

Given the important role that these institutions play in shaping ideas and policy, the balance of power inside the Beltway strongly favors Israel. There are a few smaller think tanks that are not reflexively pro-Israel—like the New America Foundation, the Cato Institute, and the Middle East Institute—but the largest and most visible foreign policy research institutions in Washington usually take Israel's side and do not question the merits of unconditional U.S. support.

Finally, a word is in order about the prestigious Council on Foreign Relations, which is based in New York City. Its impressive staff of experts has a more diverse range of views than the leading think tanks in Washington, for many years hosting both visible critics of Israeli policy such as Henry Siegman, former head of the American Jewish Congress, along with ardent pro-Israel figures like Max Boot. But the Council is not exempt from pressure, as the reaction to its invitation to Iranian President Mahmoud Ahmadinejad in September 2006 illustrates. Prominent Jewish organizations angrily protested the invitation and an effort to organize a set of high-profile resignations was headed off only when Council president Richard Haass agreed to downgrade the session from a dinner to a "working meeting." As the ADL's Abe Foxman told the *New York Times Magazine*, "To break bread with the guy . . . was crossing the line." Given Ahmadinejad's offensive remarks about Israel and the Holocaust, this reaction is understandable.[29] Yet it illustrates once again the lobby's efforts to ensure that the various institutions that shape public discourse remain sensitive to its concerns.

POLICING ACADEMIA

The lobby's campaign to mold debate about Israel has faced the greatest difficulty in academia. Not only do many professors have tenure (which insulates them from many forms of pressure), but they also work in a realm where intellectual freedom is a core value and where challenging the prevailing wisdom is common and often prized. There is also a deep-seated commitment to freedom of speech on college and university campuses. The internationalization of American universities over the past thirty years has brought large numbers of foreign-born students and professors to the United States, and these people are often more critical of Israel's conduct than Americans tend to be.

Even so, groups in the lobby did not devote significant efforts to shaping discussion on campus during the 1990s, mainly because the Oslo peace process was under way. There was relatively little violence between Israel and the Palestinians during this period, and many believed the conflict was on the verge of being solved. As a result, there was only mild criticism of Israel in the 1990s and little need for the lobby to intervene.

Criticism at colleges and universities rose sharply after the Oslo process collapsed and Ariel Sharon came to power in February 2001, and it became especially intense in the spring of 2002 when the IDF reoccupied Palestinian-controlled areas in the West Bank and employed massive force against the Second Intifada. As one would expect, the lobby moved aggressively to "take back the campuses." New groups sprang up, like the Caravan for Democracy, which brought "speakers from Israel to discuss the challenges Israel faces as the only democracy in the Middle East."[30] The Jewish Council for Public Affairs (JCPA) initiated a series of advocacy training sessions for college students who wanted to defend Israel on their campuses, and a new organization—the Israel on Campus Coalition—was formed to coordinate the twenty-six different groups that now sought to make Israel's case on campus.

Not to be outdone, Christians United for Israel recently formed a partnership with the David Project, a Boston-based pro-Israel group focused on campus issues. Their goal is to establish college chapters and training programs (the first being at California State University, Bakersfield) designed to help Christian students "make the case for Israel." CUFI executive director David

Brog said the purpose of the program was to "build the next generation," and David Project director Charles Jacobs said it "will teach them how to respond so that they can say more than just God gave Israel the land. We will teach them how to understand the conflict, not as a border war, but as a regional conflict between Arabs and Jews, as the centerpiece of a global war."[31]

Predictably, the most important organization in the effort to win back the campuses was AIPAC, which had been monitoring campus activity and training young advocates for Israel since at least the late 1970s. AIPAC more than tripled its spending on college programs as Israel came under fire. The aim of this effort, according to Jonathan Kessler, the director of leadership development at AIPAC, was "to vastly expand the number of students involved on campus, their competence, and their involvement in the national pro-Israel effort." In the summer of 2003, AIPAC brought 240 college students on all-expenses-paid trips to Washington, D.C., for four days of intensive advocacy training. Students were instructed that when they returned to school they should concentrate on networking with campus leaders of all kinds and winning them over to Israel's cause.[32] In 2007, more than 1,200 students from nearly 400 colleges and universities attended AIPAC's annual Policy Conference, including 150 student body presidents.[33]

This campaign to cultivate students has been accompanied by efforts to influence university faculty and hiring practices. In the early 1980s, for example, AIPAC recruited students to help it identify professors and campus organizations that might be considered anti-Israel. The findings were published in 1984 in *The AIPAC College Guide: Exposing the Anti-Israel Campaign on Campus*. At the same time, the ADL, which was compiling files on individuals and organizations it considered suspect regarding Israel, surreptitiously distributed a small booklet containing "background information on pro-Arab sympathizers active on college campuses" who "use their anti-Zionism as merely a guise for their deeply felt anti-Semitism."[34]

This effort intensified in September 2002, when Daniel Pipes established Campus Watch, a website that posted dossiers on suspect academics and, stealing a page from AIPAC's playbook, encouraged students to report comments or behavior that might be considered hostile to Israel.[35] This transparent attempt to blacklist and intimidate scholars prompted a harsh reaction and Pipes later removed the dossiers, but the website still invites students to report alleged anti-Israel behavior at U.S. colleges.[36]

Pipes's campaign to stamp out criticism of Israel on campuses did not stop there. Together with Martin Kramer, an Israeli-American scholar who has appointments at both WINEP and Israel's Shalem Center, and Stanley

Kurtz, a contributing editor at the *National Review* and research fellow at the conservative Hoover Institution, Pipes began encouraging Congress to curtail or at least closely monitor the Title VI funding that the federal government gives to Middle East and other area studies programs at major universities. The aim is to silence or at least inhibit critics of Israel and as a result force universities to hire scholars whose views are more in line with those of Pipes, Kramer, and Kurtz. The International Studies in Higher Education Act (HR 3077), which they supported, would have set up a government-appointed board to watch over international studies centers receiving federal monies. The board's mandate would include making recommendations to the Secretary of Education and Congress that would help ensure that the activities of centers receiving funding "reflect diverse perspectives and the full range of views on world regions, foreign languages and international affairs."[37] Though seemingly innocuous, this aspect of the proposed legislation was in fact a response to Kramer and Kurtz's claims that existing Middle East studies programs were biased and fostering anti-American and anti-Israel attitudes.[38]

Had the legislation passed as written, universities that wanted government support would have faced a clear incentive to hire individuals for their area studies programs who supported existing U.S. policy and were not critical of Israel. Key groups in the lobby backed the initiative, with AIPAC, the ADL, the American Jewish Congress, and five other organizations dispatching a letter to Congress that accused existing Title VI centers of "uncritically promoting a positive image of Palestinians, Arabs, and the Islamic World, while ignoring or denigrating Israel."[39] HR 3077 was approved by the House but was never formally considered by the full Senate.[40] Similar legislation was reintroduced in 2005 and passed the House by a narrow margin (221 to 199) in March 2006, but the Senate again declined to act and the legislation expired at the end of the 109th Congress.[41]

Kramer and Kurtz claimed victory in 2007, however, when a congressionally mandated National Research Council study of the Title VI programs recommended the creation of an executive-level presidential appointee to oversee international studies and language programs.[42] The NRC study defended the integrity of existing area studies programs and did not endorse Kramer and Kurtz's accusations of bias. In fact, one member of the study group, former Census Bureau director Kenneth Prewitt, told reporters that bias would have been visible if it were rampant, but in his words, "it's not out there."[43] Some supporters of existing Title VI centers suggested that assigning these programs to a high-level presidential appointee would enhance their status and help them obtain greater resources. However, giving a single individual such extensive oversight also raises the worrisome possibility that a future presidential appointee might one day be in a position to implement the Pipes/Kramer/Kurtz program of ideological conformity.

Moreover, the April 2007 version of the Title VI legislation on international education programs, now under consideration in the Senate, would create a complaint procedure for individuals who felt that an existing Title VI program did not contain sufficiently diverse views. If complainants were not satisfied by the university's response, their grievance could be "filed with the Department [of Education] and reviewed by the Secretary." The draft legislation also directs the secretary to "take the review of such complaints into account when determining the renewal of grants."[44] If this clause becomes law, one can easily imagine groups in the lobby leveling repeated complaints against any Middle East studies program that employs someone who has criticized Israeli policies, in order to convince the Department of Education to cut off Title VI support or to encourage the university in question to safeguard its funding by tilting in a pro-Israel direction.

To further counter a perceived anti-Israel bias in academia, a number of philanthropists have established Israel studies programs at U.S. universities (in addition to the roughly 130 Jewish studies programs that already exist), so as to increase the number of "Israel-friendly" scholars on campus.[45] NYU announced the establishment of the Taub Center for Israel Studies on May 1, 2003, and similar programs have been established at other schools, including Berkeley, Brandeis, and Emory. Academic administrators emphasize the pedagogical value of these programs, but they are also intended to promote Israel's image on campus. Fred Lafer, the head of the Taub Foundation, makes clear that his foundation funded the NYU center to help counter the "Arabic [sic] point of view" that he thinks is prevalent in NYU's Middle East programs.[46]

Similar motives reportedly lay behind gambling mogul Sheldon Adelson's proposed multimillion-dollar gift to expand the existing Program for Jewish Civilization at Georgetown University so as to create a center focusing on the "Jewish theme as a paradigm of international relations." Ha'aretz reported in August 2006 that "one of the key goals of Adelson and other advocates of the Jewish center is to moderate the Arab presence at the university." The program's first director, Yossi Shain (who also heads the Hartog School of Government at Tel Aviv University), said it was important to set up such a program at Georgetown "because it's a Jesuit school, because it's in Washington, because it's in the foreign service school." Similarly, university rabbi Harold White said that establishing the new center would balance Georgetown's existing Arab center, and this was particularly important because "many Georgetown graduates end up at the State Department."[47]

The lobby's desire to police academia has led to several noteworthy efforts to pressure administrators or influence personnel decisions. In the summer of 2002, for example, pro-Israel groups at the University of Chicago claimed that there was "an atmosphere of intimidation and hate for Jewish students on campus" and charged that the faculty and administration were doing nothing about the problem. Indeed, it was said that faculty and administrators "sanction and even encourage such outbursts." Stung by the allegations, the administration collected all the students' claims and investigated them. Only two charges were found to be valid: an instance of anti-Semitic graffiti in a dormitory, which the resident staff failed to deal with promptly, and an e-mail sent out by a graduate student on a department mailing list that told a joke about Auschwitz. Although regrettable, this hardly constituted evidence of an "atmosphere of persecution and estrangement," which is how one Jewish student described Chicago in 2002. Nevertheless, the Israeli consul general in Chicago and then the Israeli ambassador to the United States visited the university shortly thereafter. Their aim was to force the president and the provost to find ways to improve Israel's profile on campus. During this same period, the prominent Palestinian-American historian Rashid Khalidi, who was then on Chicago's faculty, had his e-mail system bombarded with spam.[48]

When Columbia recruited Khalidi away from the University of Chicago, reports Jonathan Cole, the former provost at Columbia, "The complaints started flowing in from people who disagreed with the content of his political views." Princeton faced much the same problem a few years later when it tried to woo Khalidi away from Columbia.[49] The late Palestinian-American scholar Edward Said, who taught at Columbia for many years, was the target of similar denunciations, and Cole later said that "any public statement in support of the Palestinian people by the preeminent literary critic Edward Said will elicit hundreds of e-mails, letters, and journalistic accounts that call on us to denounce Said and to either sanction or fire him."[50] Columbia's travails did not end there: in 2004, the David Project produced a propaganda film alleging that faculty in Columbia University's Middle East Studies program were anti-Semitic and were intimidating Jewish students who defended Israel.[51] Columbia was raked over the coals in neoconservative publications like the New York Sun, but a faculty committee assigned to investigate the charges found no evidence of anti-Semitism and the only incident worth noting was the possibility that one professor had "responded heatedly" to a student's question. The committee also found that the accused professors had been the target of an overt intimidation campaign.[52]

One would like to think that these were just isolated incidents, but much the same thing happened again in 2006, when the Departments of History and Sociology at Yale University voted an appointment for Professor Juan Cole, a distinguished historian at the University of Michigan. Cole is also the author of a prizewinning weblog ("Informed Comment"), and he has been critical of a number of Israeli policies in recent years. Pro-Israel columnists in the *Wall Street Journal* and the *Washington Times* attacked Cole's appointment, and the newspaper *Jewish Week* reported that several prominent Jewish donors had called Yale officials to protest the decision, which was subsequently overturned by Yale's appointments committee. The actual impact of donor pressure is unknown, but the incident underscores the importance that some of Israel's supporters have placed on shaping discourse on campus.[53]

Efforts to protect Israel from criticism have also targeted individual speakers, visiting professors, and guest lecturers, in order to create an atmosphere where free expression and open debate are curtailed. In 1984, a student group at Stanford University invited alumnus and former Congressman Pete McCloskey to teach as a visiting lecturer. McCloskey was a prominent critic of unconditional U.S. support for Israel, having proposed an amendment in 1980 that would have reduced American aid by the amount that Israel was spending annually on its West Bank settlements. His actions led to charges that he was an anti-Semite and helped ensure his defeat in his 1982 Senate campaign. But the controversy did not stop there: the director of Stanford's Hillel chapter said his appointment was "a slap in the face of the Jewish community," and members of the student governing council threatened to reduce his compensation or terminate his appointment if he did not remove an article by former Assistant Secretary of State George Ball from his course syllabus and add materials reflecting pro-AIPAC views. In sharp contrast with normal academic practice, they also insisted that he schedule additional class sessions with guests representing alternative perspectives. A faculty review found the student group guilty of "serious abridgments" of academic freedom and McCloskey eventually received a formal apology from the Stanford provost.[54]

We have some experience with this tactic ourselves. In early 2006, we were each independently invited to appear on a panel at the U.S. Naval War College's annual Current Strategy Forum. The topic of the panel was "The

Nature of Power," which, it is worth noting, had little to do with Middle East politics or U.S. foreign policy in that region. Following the publication of our original article, "The Israel Lobby," in March 2006, the president of the War College received phone calls from several members of Congress who questioned whether it was appropriate to have us speak at the conference.[55] To his credit, the president took no action in response to these calls and we appeared without incident. A subsequent invitation to Walt to speak in a lecture series at the University of Montana also provoked heated denunciations by several faculty members, who began a protracted but unsuccessful campaign to have the faculty coordinator of the lecture series removed from his post.[56]

In addition to targeting faculty and hiring on campus, a number of pro-Israel academics and groups have tried to suppress publication of scholarly works that challenged their particular views. In 1998, for example, the ADL called on the publisher of Norman Finkelstein and Ruth Bettina Birn's *A Nation on Trial* (Metropolitan Books) to halt its release. *A Nation on Trial* is a sharply worded critique of Daniel Goldhagen's controversial best seller *Hitler's Willing Executioners*, which argues that the Holocaust was not simply the product of Nazi beliefs and Hitler's own madness but also was rooted in a pervasive "eliminationist ideology" in German society that predated the Nazi period. Like the Goldhagen book, *A Nation on Trial* elicited both praise and criticism from respected scholars. Yet ADL head Abraham Foxman said *A Nation on Trial* should not have been published, insisting that the issue was not "whether Goldhagen's thesis is right or wrong but what is 'legitimate criticism' and what goes beyond the pale."[57]

A similar episode took place in 2003, when lawyers representing the Harvard law professor Alan Dershowitz sent threatening letters to the University of California Press in an attempt to halt publication of Finkelstein's book *Beyond Chutzpah*, an extended critique of Dershowitz's own *The Case for Israel*. Dershowitz also wrote to California governor Arnold Schwarzenegger (who has nominal authority of public institutions like the university) as part of his campaign against Finkelstein. Dershowitz subsequently claimed that he was not trying to suppress publication, but that is certainly how officials at UC Press interpreted his actions. They resisted these pressures and issued Finkelstein's book anyway.[58]

The campaign to keep Americans from reading or hearing critical views about Israel even occurs at the high school level. In February 2005, for example, the *New York Sun* reported that Columbia's Khalidi was involved in a lecture program for high school teachers sponsored by New York City's Department of Education. The *Sun* and some local politicians immediately went to work to get him fired. The *Sun* accused him of calling Israel a "racist state" (a charge Khalidi vehemently denied), and his participation was labeled "outrageous" by Congressman Anthony Weiner (D-NY), at that time a candidate for mayor, and "an abomination" by Brooklyn City Council member Simcha Felder. Joel Klein, the chancellor of the Department of Education, dropped him from the program the next day and issued a public statement saying, "Rashid Khalidi should not have been included in a program that provided professional development for [Department of Education] teachers and he won't be participating in the future."[59] The following year, New York's City Council approved a study program on Israel "initiated by the public relations department of the Israeli Consulate in New York."[60] Meanwhile, a coalition of thirty-plus Jewish groups had already organized a new nationwide program to train high school students to be more effective advocates for Israel.[61]

Pro-Israel groups and individuals have fought a multifront battle—against students, professors, administrators, and the curriculum itself—to shape discourse on campus. Their efforts have not been as successful in academia as they have been on Capitol Hill or even in the media, but their work has not been in vain. Despite the continued turmoil in the region and Israel's continued expansion in the Occupied Territories, there is less criticism of Israel on college campuses today than there was five years ago.[62]

OBJECTIONABLE TACTICS

As we have repeatedly emphasized, lobbying on Israel's behalf is wholly legitimate, as are overt efforts to shape public perceptions by participating in public discourse about matters relating to Israel. We do not think the lobby's current influence serves the interest of either the United States or Israel, but most of its tactics are reasonable and simply part of the normal rough-and-tumble that is the essence of democratic politics. Unfortunately, some pro-Israel individuals and groups have occasionally taken their defense of Israel to illegitimate extremes, attempting to silence individuals who hold views they dislike. This endeavor can involve intimidating and smearing critics of Israel, or even attempting to damage or wreck their careers. The previous discussion of the lobby's actions in academia provides a number of examples of this kind of behavior, which has no place in a democratic society. The lobby, however, does not confine its strong-arm tactics to the academic world.

Consider what happened in October 2006 to Tony Judt, a New York University historian who is Jewish but frequently critical of Israel's actions. He was scheduled to give a lecture at the Polish consulate in New York City, "The Israel Lobby and U.S. Foreign Policy." The Polish government was not sponsoring the event; the consulate had merely rented its facilities to Network 20/20, an independent group that sponsors lectures on a wide range of topics. David Harris, the executive director of the American Jewish Committee, got wind of the event and contacted the Polish consul general. Harris later explained that he had called as a "friend of Poland" and said that the lecture "was going to be entirely contrary to the entire spirit of Polish foreign policy." The consul general also received two inquiries from the ADL, and he later described the calls as "exercising a delicate pressure . . . We are adults and our IQs are high enough to understand that." The consulate canceled Judt's lecture at the last minute, which led a group of prominent American intellectuals to issue an open letter denouncing this obvious effort to stifle free discussion.[63] Judt has also reported receiving death threats against him and his family on other occasions, inspired by his previous criticisms of Israeli policy.[64]

A similar incident occurred later that same month, when the French embassy in the United States scheduled a reception to celebrate the publication of Carmen Callil's *Bad Faith*, a widely hailed examination of the role that a scurrilous French official (Louis Darquier) had played in the deportation of French Jews to Auschwitz. Although the book is a passionate and moving indictment of French complicity in the Holocaust, the embassy reportedly received complaints about a brief passage in Callil's postscript: "What caused me anguish, as I tracked down Louis Darquier, was to live so closely to the helpless terror of the Jews of France, and to see what the Jews of Israel were passing on to the Palestinian people." Bowing to the pressure, the French embassy said that "it could not endorse a personal opinion of the author expressed in the postscript of the book" and canceled the reception.[65]

An even more prominent case involved *My Name Is Rachel Corrie*, a play about the young woman who was killed in March 2003 by an Israeli bulldozer when she was attempting to prevent the IDF from demolishing a Palestinian home in the Gaza Strip. The play, which was based on Corrie's diaries and e-mails, opened in April 2005 at the Royal Court Theatre in London and was widely acclaimed. It was scheduled to open in March 2006 at the New York Theater Workshop, which has a well-established reputation for staging controversial productions, only to be postponed about a month before its scheduled opening. The *New York Times* reported that the workshop's artistic director had decided to postpone the play "after polling local Jewish religious and community leaders as to their feelings about the work," and the *Los Angeles Times* quoted him saying that "what we heard was that after Ariel Sharon's illness and the election of Hamas in the recent Palestinian elections, we had a very edgy situation."[66] (The original Royal Court production of the play was eventually brought to New York in the fall of 2006 for a limited run of eighty performances.) A similar occurrence took place in Canada in December 2006 when that country's largest not-for-profit theater canceled a scheduled production of the play, due to fears that it would anger Toronto's Jewish community.[67] And the same thing happened again in April 2007, when Miami's Mosaic Theatre canceled plans to mount the play after protests from what the *Miami Herald* called an "impassioned, vocal minority" of subscribers and outside individuals.[68]

The overzealous pursuit of supposedly "dangerous critics" has even landed one prominent group in the lobby in a courtroom. In the 1980s and early 1990s, the ADL enlisted the services of a private investigator named Roy Bullock who also did intelligence gathering for the apartheid government in South Africa. Bullock, in turn, obtained information from a Los Angeles police intelligence officer who allegedly removed confidential documents from the police department and the Department of Motor Vehicles. In all, the two reportedly maintained files on some twelve thousand individuals and six hundred organizations in California, some of which were provided to the ADL. In addition to white supremacists and neo-Nazi groups, the targets of this surveillance included a number of Jewish dissidents, Arab-American groups, and other critics of Israeli government policies. The San Francisco district attorney launched a criminal investigation, and the police officer ultimately pleaded no contest to the unauthorized use of a police computer. But the district attorney was reluctant to prosecute the ADL because he thought it was a force for good. Instead, the district attorney accepted an offer by the ADL to pay $75,000 to fight bigotry in the local area, and no criminal charges were filed against the organization or Bullock.

There was, however, a civil suit brought by three of the targets, two of them Jewish. The ADL eventually agreed to settle out of court and to pay each $50,000 plus court costs. ADL head Abraham Foxman denied that the ADL spied on anyone, but defended its practice of investigating groups critical of Israel by saying "a viable, safe, secure haven" in Israel is "part and parcel of the safety and security and survival of the Jewish people." The ADL was not protecting the community from anti-Semitism or bigotry, which is its stated mission; it was simply targeting individuals thought to be critical of Israel or of U.S. support.[69]

THE "NEW ANTI-SEMITISM"

No discussion of how the lobby operates would be complete without examining one of its most powerful weapons: the charge of anti-Semitism. Anyone who criticizes Israeli actions or says that pro-Israel groups have significant influence over U.S. Middle East policy stands a good chance of getting labeled an anti-Semite. In fact, anyone who says that there is an Israel lobby runs the risk of being charged with anti-Semitism, even though AIPAC and the Conference of Presidents are hardly bashful about describing their influence and the Israeli media themselves refer to America's "Jewish lobby."[70] In effect, the lobby both boasts of its own power and frequently attacks those who call attention to it.

This accusation is now being made in the context of alarmist claims about a resurgence of virulent anti-Semitism, especially in Europe. In October 2002, Conference of Presidents chairman Mortimer B. Zuckerman wrote in *U.S. News & World Report* of a "shameful contagion of anti-Semitism," warning that "Europe is sick again," and the *Boston Globe* columnist Jeff Jacoby devoted a March 2004 column to the resurgent "cancer of anti-Semitism in Europe."[71] We are "getting to a point," the U.S. ambassador to the European Union said in early 2004, "where it is as bad as it was in the 1930s."[72]

Measuring anti-Semitism is a complicated matter, but the weight of evidence points in the opposite direction. Indeed, in the spring of 2004, when accusations of European anti-Semitism were prevalent in America, separate surveys of European public opinion conducted by the ADL and the Pew Research Center for the People and the Press showed that it was actually declining.[73]

Consider France, which pro-Israel groups often portray as the most anti-Semitic state in Europe, and whose capital, according to the *New Republic*'s Martin Peretz, is "the headquarters of anti-Semitic Europe today, just as during the Third Republic."[74] Yet a poll of French citizens in 2002 found that 89 percent could envisage living with a Jew; 97 percent believed making anti-Semitic graffiti is a serious crime; 87 percent thought attacks on French synagogues are scandalous; and 85 percent of practicing French Catholics rejected the charge that Jews have too much influence in business and finance.[75] The head of the French Jewish community declared in the summer of 2003 that "France is not more anti-Semitic than America."[76] According to *Ha'aretz*, the French police reported that anti-Semitic incidents in France had declined by almost 50 percent in 2005, and this despite the fact that France has the largest Muslim population of any country in Europe.[77]

When a French Jew was brutally murdered by a Muslim gang in February 2006, tens of thousands of French demonstrators poured into the streets to condemn anti-Semitism. President Jacques Chirac and Prime Minister Dominique de Villepin both attended the victim's memorial service in a public show of solidarity with French Jewry.[78] It is also worth noting that in 2002, more Jews from the former Soviet empire immigrated to Germany than to Israel, making it "the fastest growing Jewish community in the world," according to an article in the Jewish newspaper *Forward*.[79] If Europe were really "as bad as it was in the 1930s," it is hard to imagine that Jews would be moving there in large numbers.

We recognize that Europe is not free of the scourge of anti-Semitism. No one would deny that there are still some virulent autochthonous anti-Semites in Europe (as there are in the United States), but their numbers are small and their extreme views are rejected by the vast majority of Europeans. Nor would we deny that there is anti-Semitism among European Muslims, some of it provoked by Israel's behavior toward the Palestinians and some of it straightforwardly racist.[80] In Great Britain, for example, the Community Security Trust (CST), a watchdog group that monitors anti-Semitism, reported a 31 percent rise in such incidents in 2006. Although such deplorable events should never be taken lightly, the total number of incidents reported was 594 (in a country of more than sixty million people), and nearly a quarter of them coincided with the 2006 war in Lebanon. As CST's Mark Gardner acknowledged, "This is certainly not comparable with the 1930s or anything remotely like that."[81] Several other groups—including the Israel-based Global Forum Against Anti-Semitism—reported that anti-Semitic incidents had actually declined during this same period. Given potential coding and underreporting issues, these conflicting results suggest that claims of a substantial rise or fall in actual anti-Semitism should be made and interpreted with some caution.[82]

When pressed to go beyond vague assertions, pro-Israel groups now claim that there is a "new anti-Semitism," which they equate with criticism of Israel.[83] When the synod of the Church of England voted in early 2006 to divest from Caterpillar Inc. on the grounds that Caterpillar manufactures the bulldozers used to demolish Palestinian homes, the chief rabbi of the U.K. complained that it would "have the most adverse repercussions on . . . Jewish-Christian relations in Britain," while Rabbi Tony Bayfield, the head of the Reform movement, said, "There is a clear problem of anti-Zionist—verging on anti-Semitic—attitudes emerging in the grass roots, and even in the middle ranks of the Church."[84] The church was guilty of neither anti-Zionism nor anti-Semitism; it was merely protesting Israeli policy.[85]

Supporters of Israel, in fact, have a history of using fears of a "new anti-Semitism" to shield Israel from criticism. In 1974, when Israel was under increasing pressure to withdraw from the lands it had conquered in 1967, Arnold Forster and Benjamin Epstein of the ADL published *The New Anti-Semitism*, which argued that anti-Semitism was on the rise and exemplified by the growing unwillingness of other societies to support Israel's actions.[86] In the early 1980s, when the invasion of Lebanon and Israel's expanding settlements triggered additional criticisms, and when U.S. arms sales to its Arab allies were hotly contested, then ADL head Nathan Perlmutter and his wife, Ruth Ann Perlmutter, released *The Real Anti-Semitism in America*, which argued that anti-Semitism was on its way back, as shown by the pressure on Israel to make peace with the Arabs and by events like the sale of AWACS aircraft to Saudi Arabia.[87] The Perlmutters also suggested that many "a-Semitic" actions, which they define as acts not motivated by hostility to Jews, may nonetheless harm Jewish interests (and especially Israel's well-being), and could easily bring back genuine anti-Semitism.[88]

The troubling logic of this argument is revealed by the fact that there was little mention of anti-Semitism during the 1990s, when Israel was involved in the Oslo peace process. Indeed, one Israeli scholar wrote in 1995 that "never before, at least since the time Christianity seized power over the Roman Empire, has anti-Semitism been less significant than at present."[89] Charges of anti-Semitism became widespread only in the spring of 2002, when Israel came under severe criticism around the world for its brutal behavior in the Occupied Territories.

Critics are also accused of holding Israel to an unfair standard or questioning its right to exist. Thus, Natan Sharansky, the former Soviet dissident who is now a prominent Israeli author and politician, declares, "The new anti-Semitism appears in the guise of 'political criticism of Israel,' consisting of a discriminating approach and double standard towards the state of the Jews, while questioning its right to exist."[90] The implication is that anyone who criticizes Israel's actions (or the actions of its supporters) is opposed to its existence and is therefore hostile to Jews. But this is a bogus charge, because it conflates criticism of Israel's actions with the rejection of Israel's legitimacy. In fact, Western critics of Israel hardly ever question its right to exist. Instead, they question its behavior toward the Palestinians, which is a legitimate criticism; many Israelis question it themselves.

Israel is not being judged by a double standard when Western critics offer such charges. Although a few critics may single Israel out for undue criticism, Israel is for the most part being judged by the same standard that people in the West apply to all democracies. This criterion is entirely appropriate, especially since Israel and its American supporters constantly emphasize that it deserves special treatment because it is the "only democracy in the Middle East." Israel, in other words, is expected to behave like contemporary Britain, Canada, Denmark, the United States, and so forth, and not like the military junta in Burma, Pervez Musharraf's Pakistan, or Fidel Castro's Cuba. Israel's treatment of the Palestinians elicits criticism because it is contrary to widely accepted human rights norms and international law, as well as the principle of national self-determination. And it is hardly the only state that has faced sharp criticism on these grounds. The United States was widely condemned for the abuses that occurred at Abu Ghraib prison and also for the way it has treated detainees at Guantánamo. But America is not being held to a double standard either; it is merely being expected to live up to its own stated values and to widely accepted human rights principles. And so is Israel.

THE GREAT SILENCER

These fine points notwithstanding, the charge of anti-Semitism remains a widely used weapon for dealing with critics of Israel, especially in the United States. This tactic has been effective for a number of reasons. First, anti-Semitism is a set of beliefs that led to great evils in the past, including the monstrous crimes of the Holocaust, and it is now utterly discredited in most segments of society. The charge of anti-Semitism is one of the most powerful epithets one can level at someone in America, and no respectable person wants to be tarred with that brush. Undoubtedly, the fear of being called an anti-Semite discourages many individuals from voicing reservations about Israel's conduct or the merits of U.S. support.

Second, smearing critics of Israel or the lobby with the charge of anti-Semitism works to marginalize them in the public arena. If the accusation sticks, the critic's arguments will not be taken seriously by the media, government officials, and other influential elites, and groups that might otherwise pay attention to that person's views will be discouraged from soliciting them. Politicians will be especially reluctant to associate themselves with anyone who has been charged as anti-Semitic, because doing so could have a chilling effect on their own careers.

Third, this tactic works because it is difficult for anyone to prove beyond all doubt that he or she is not anti-Semitic, especially when criticizing Israel or the lobby. Proving a negative is hard to do under any circumstances, especially when it comes to something like intentions and motivations that cannot be observed directly, and pointing to other behavior that is inconsistent with anti-Semitism is not likely to carry much weight. Until recently, therefore, the charge of anti-Semitism has been a potent way to make sure that criticisms of Israel or the lobby were rarely spoken and were either ignored or disparaged when they were.

The accusation is likely to resonate among American Jews, many of whom still believe that anti-Semitism is rife. Not only does the history of Jews in the diaspora provide plenty of cause to worry, that tendency is magnified by the role that the Holocaust plays in the attitudes of a significant number of Jewish Americans. As Peter Novick makes clear in his seminal book, *The Holocaust in American Life*, that cataclysmic event has become a key element of American Jewish consciousness. It defines how many American Jews think about the world around them, and not surprisingly, it has fostered a powerful sense of victimization for some of them. Despite the great success Jews have achieved in America, many Jewish Americans still worry that virulent anti-Semitism could return at any time. As Jack Wertheimer notes, "By virtually any measure, domestic anti-Semitism has declined sharply; however, many American Jews continue to believe that *other* Jews in the United States are targets of bigotry." Frank Rich, the *New York Times* columnist, acknowledges this thinking when he writes, "Like many other Jews, I am perhaps all too willing to believe that the entire world is anti-Semitic."[91]

This profound sense of fear among American Jews was clearly evident when Israel was harshly criticized around the world in the spring of 2002. Nat Hentoff, who writes for the *Village Voice*, remarked at the time that "if a loudspeaker goes off and a voice says, 'all Jews gather in Times Square,' it could never surprise me," and Ron Rosenbaum wrote in the *New York Observer*, "There is likely to be a second Holocaust." These concerns grew so loud that Leon Wieseltier of the *New Republic*, himself a deeply committed defender of Israel, felt compelled to write a cover story titled "Hitler Is Dead: The Case Against Jewish Ethnic Panic." Describing Jews in the United States, he wrote, "The community is sunk in excitability, in the imagination of disaster. There is a loss of intellectual control. Death is at every Jewish door. Fear is wild. Reason is derailed. Anxiety is the supreme proof of authenticity. Imprecise and inflammatory analogies abound. Holocaust imagery is everywhere."[92] In short, many American Jews find it easy to believe that a person (and especially a gentile) who criticizes either Israel's actions or the influence of groups like AIPAC is probably an anti-Semite at heart.

For all these reasons, when faced with criticism of Israel's policies, some of its defenders are quick to invoke the charge of anti-Semitism. The first and most visible case is the heated reaction to Jimmy Carter's recent book, *Palestine: Peace Not Apartheid*. Despite its provocative title, the book is neither polemical nor unsympathetic to Israel's strategic situation. Carter is certainly critical of Israel's occupation of the West Bank and what that means for the Palestinians living there, and he correctly observes that it is difficult to have a candid discussion of these issues in the United States. But as Yossi Beilin, a prominent Israeli politician, noted, "There is nothing in the criticism that Carter has for Israel that has not been said by Israelis themselves."[93] Even Carter's use of the term "apartheid"—which seems to have provoked much of the ire directed at him—echoes the use of the term by Israeli critics of the occupation and by prominent South Africans such as Nobel Peace Prize winner Bishop Desmond Tutu and current Minister of Intelligence Ronnie Kasrils.[94]

As noted, the ADL and CAMERA attacked Carter's book in prominent ads in major newspapers, and though a number of critics addressed the substance of Carter's claims, others immediately launched personal attacks on the former president.[95] Abraham Foxman said, "I believe he is engaging in anti-Semitism," while Martin Peretz wrote that Carter "will go down in history as a Jew-hater."[96] Deborah Lipstadt, the historian who won a landmark suit against notorious Holocaust denier David Irving, wrote in the *Washington Post* that "Carter has repeatedly fallen back—possibly unconsciously—on traditional anti-Semitic canards" and suggested that there was a strong similarity between some of Carter's views and those of former Ku Klux Klan leader David Duke.[97] As Carter himself said, "I have been called an anti-Semite. I have been called a bigot. I have been called a plagiarist. I have been called a coward."[98] It was a remarkable reaction to the man who in his stewardship of the Egyptian-Israeli peace process had done as much as any human being to enhance Israel's overall security.

A similar reaction—albeit on a smaller scale—occurred when former neoconservative Francis Fukuyama published an article critiquing Charles Krauthammer's 2004 Irving Kristol Lecture at the American Enterprise Institute. Fukuyama's analysis was pointed but respectful (among other things, he called Krauthammer a "gifted thinker" whose ideas were "worth taking seriously"), but his suggestion that Krauthammer's views on how to deal with the Islamic world derived too much from Israel's experience led Krauthammer to charge Fukuyama with anti-Semitism.[99]

We are not unacquainted with this line of attack. When our original article, "The Israel Lobby," was published in the *London Review of Books* in

March 2006, we were widely and falsely accused of being anti-Semites. Eliot Cohen published an op-ed about our piece in the *Washington Post* titled "Yes, It's Anti-Semitic," and the *New York Sun* immediately linked us with David Duke.[100] The ADL termed our article "a classical conspiratorial anti-Semitic analysis invoking the canards of Jewish power and Jewish control"—ignoring our explicit statement that the lobby was just another interest group engaged in legitimate political activities—while the *New Republic* published four separate attacks on our paper, all describing it as anti-Semitic.[101] In separate op-eds in the *Wall Street Journal*, William Kristol accused us of "anti-Judaism," and Ruth Wisse, a Harvard professor of Yiddish literature, likened our piece to the writings of a notorious nineteenth-century German anti-Semite. And in his own critique of Carter's book, Shmuel Rosner of *Ha'aretz* generously opined that the ex-president and Nobel Peace Prize winner was "not as anti-Semitic as Walt-Mearsheimer."[102]

The tendency to accuse critics of Israel of being anti-Semitic reached new heights (or perhaps a new low) in early 2007, when the American Jewish Committee released a paper by the Indiana University English professor Alvin H. Rosenfeld titled "'Progressive' Jewish Thought and the New Anti-Semitism." Rosenfeld identified a group of liberal American Jews (including the playwright Tony Kushner, the historian Tony Judt, the poet Adrienne Rich, and the *Washington Post* columnist Richard Cohen) who have been critical of Israel and charged them with participating "alongside" a new anti-Semitism that denies Israel's right to exist. In his introduction to the paper, the committee's executive director, David Harris, wrote, "The most surprising—and distressing—feature of this new trend is the very public participation of some Jews in the verbal onslaught against Zionism and the Jewish state."[103]

The targets of Rosenfeld's critique vehemently denied his various charges, and Rabbi Michael Lerner of *Tikkun* pointed out the consequences of such unwarranted accusations. "When we talk to Congressional representatives who are liberal or even extremely progressive on every other issue," he wrote, "they tell us privately that they are afraid to speak out about the way Israeli policies are destructive to the best interests of the United States or the best interests of world peace—lest they too be labeled anti-Semitic and anti-Israel. If it can happen to Jimmy Carter, some of them told me recently, a man with impeccable moral credentials, then no one is really politically safe."[104]

In all of these cases, there was no evidence of actual anti-Semitism. True anti-Semitism conceives of Jews as being different from other people, in various invidious ways, which gives those others license to single them out and persecute them in both large and small ways. Anti-Semites maintain that Jews who are engaged in what seem like legitimate political activities—running for office, contributing to political campaigns, writing articles and books, or organizing lobbying groups—are actually engaged in dark and secret conspiracies. Real anti-Semites sometimes favor harsh measures to deny Jews full political rights and at times advocate even more violent persecution of Jews. Even in its milder forms, anti-Semitism indulges in various forms of stereotyping and implies that Jews should be viewed with suspicion or contempt, while seeking to deny them the ability to participate fully and freely in all realms of society. In its essential features, true anti-Semitism resembles other forms of racist or religious discrimination, all of which have been roundly condemned in Europe and the United States since the end of World War II.

By contrast, almost all of the many gentiles and Jews who now criticize Israeli policy or worry about the lobby's impact on U.S. foreign policy find such views deeply disturbing and categorically reject them. Rather, they believe that Jews are like other human beings, which means that they are capable of both good and bad deeds, and that they are entitled to the same status as other members of society. They also believe that Israel acts like other states, which is to say that it vigorously defends its own interests and sometimes pursues policies that are wise and just and sometimes does things that are strategically foolish and even immoral. This perspective is the opposite of anti-Semitism. It calls for treating Jews like everyone else and treating Israel as a normal and legitimate country. Israel, in this view, should be praised when it acts well and criticized when it does not. Americans are also entitled to be upset and critical when Israel does things that harm U.S. interests, and Americans who care about Israel should be free to criticize it when its government takes actions that they believe are not in Israel's interest either. There is neither special treatment nor a double standard here. Similarly, most critics of the lobby do not see it as a cabal or conspiracy; rather, they argue—as we have—that pro-Israel organizations act as other interest groups do. While the charge of anti-Semitism can be an effective smear tactic, it is usually groundless.

Indeed, there are signs that the reflexive charge of anti-Semitism is beginning to lose its power to stifle debate. The attacks on Jimmy Carter's book did not deter the former president from publicizing it widely (including a visible and successful appearance at Brandeis University), and a number of other public figures and mainstream publications have recently offered intelligent criticisms of Israeli policy and the lobby's influence.[105] Even William Kristol seems to have recognized that calling critics of Israel or the lobby anti-Semites is losing its capacity to silence others, writing in the *Wall Street Journal* that "the mainstream Jewish organizations have played the 'anti-Semitism' card so often that it has been devalued."[106] The obvious reason is that increasing numbers of people recognize that this serious charge keeps getting leveled at individuals who are not anti-Semites but who are merely questioning Israeli policies or pointing out that the lobby promotes policies that are not always in the U.S. national interest.

Let us be clear: anti-Semitism is a despicable phenomenon with a long and tragic history, and all people should remain vigilant against its resurgence and condemn it when it arises. Furthermore, we should all be disturbed by the presence of genuine anti-Semitism in parts of the Arab and Islamic world (and in other societies—e.g., Russia), as well as its lingering presence in some segments of American and European society. But it is essential that we distinguish between true anti-Semitism and legitimate criticism of Israeli policy, because blurring them makes it harder to fight true bigotry and makes it more difficult to intelligently discuss U.S. foreign policy. Americans should be free to discuss the activities of groups that are pushing the United States to support Israel generously and unconditionally, in the same way that we examine the political activities of other interest groups without having to worry about being smeared or marginalized.

CONCLUSION

The various strategies that groups in the lobby employ—as discussed in this chapter and the previous one—are mutually reinforcing. If politicians know that it is risky to question Israeli policy or the United States' unyielding support for Israel, then it will be harder for the mainstream media to locate authoritative voices that are willing to disagree with the lobby's views. If public discourse about Israel can be shaped so that most Americans have generally positive impressions of the Jewish state, then politicians will have even more reason to follow the lobby's lead. Playing the anti-Semitism card stifles discussion even more and allows myths about Israel to survive unchallenged. Although other interest groups employ similar strategies in varying form, most of them can only dream of having the political muscle that pro-Israel organizations have amassed. The question, therefore, is what effect does the Israel lobby have on U.S. foreign policy? Is its influence in the American national interest, or has it encouraged policies that are bad for the United States and even for Israel itself? It is to that question that we now turn.

PART II

THE LOBBY IN ACTION

INTRODUCTION TO PART II

The Israel lobby's influence would not be especially worrisome if its agenda were limited to making sure that Congress continued to provide foreign aid for the Jewish state. Although there might be better uses for this money, the United States is a wealthy country and can afford the $3 billion–plus that it annually provides to Israel. But the lobby's efforts have not been limited to foreign aid. Like a number of other special interest groups, it also works to influence various aspects of U.S. foreign policy, in its case focusing primarily on the Middle East. These efforts to shape policy in the region are understandable: although material aid is valuable, it is even more helpful to have the world's only superpower bring its vast capabilities to bear on Israel's behalf.

Even so, this aspect of the lobby's agenda would be of little concern if it encouraged policies that were obviously in America's best interest. In the next five chapters, we show that this is not the case. The United States has three main interests in the Middle East today: keeping Persian Gulf oil flowing to world markets, discouraging the spread of weapons of mass destruction, and reducing anti-American terrorism originating in the region. There are instances where the lobby has supported policies that advanced these interests, but many of the policies that organizations in the lobby have promoted over time have ultimately left the United States worse off. That was not their intention, of course, and the groups and individuals who pushed for these policies undoubtedly believed that the actions they favored would be good for the United States. They were wrong. Indeed, although these policies were intended to benefit Israel, many of them have damaged Israel's interests as well.

THE LOBBY'S AGENDA

In addition to preserving U.S. aid to Israel, groups in the lobby have sought to ensure that American power is used to shape the Middle East environment in ways they believed would advance Israel's interests, especially in security. In practical terms, this meant backing Israel in its long struggle with the Palestinians and directing American power against other movements or states that might be at odds with Israel.

As noted in Chapter 4, there are differences within the pro-Israel community about the virtues of creating a viable Palestinian state, with the leaders of the lobby tending to be more hostile to that idea than the rank and file. Nevertheless, few supporters of Israel advocate an evenhanded policy toward the two sides, and fewer still have called for the United States to pressure Israel to produce a settlement.

Most pro-Israel groups—and especially the central organizations in the lobby—also want the United States to help Israel remain the dominant military power in the Middle East. In addition to maintaining generous aid to Israel's military establishment, these groups favor using American power to deal with Israel's main regional adversaries: Iran, Iraq under Saddam, and Syria. At the very least, the lobby wants America to contain these so-called rogue states and to make sure that they do not acquire nuclear weapons. Some of these groups have gone farther, advocating that the United States use its power to topple the regimes in Iran, Iraq, and Syria and replace them with leaders willing to live peacefully with Israel. In the best of all possible worlds, Washington would transform the entire region by spreading democracy and drying up support for terrorism against both the United States and Israel.

Finally, the lobby has pushed American leaders to disarm Hezbollah and help create a Lebanon that is friendly to Israel. But these goals cannot be accomplished without radically changing the behavior of Iran and Syria, since those states support and arm Hezbollah, and Syria has a long history of involvement in Lebanese politics. Given these and other links among Israel's adversaries, the lobby tends to see all of them as part of a seamless web of evil that the United States must at least keep at bay if not destroy.

To deal with these different threats to Israel, key groups within the lobby have encouraged the United States to deploy substantial military forces in the Middle East. As we will show, the lobby played an important role in making the case for war with Iraq, which was the first step in a broader campaign of regional transformation. Even today, many of Israel's most vocifer-

ous supporters oppose withdrawing American forces from Iraq and rede-
ploying them outside of the region, because keeping U.S. forces in the
neighborhood leaves them well positioned to threaten Israel's adversaries or
to take action against them should the need or the opportunity arise.

THE UNITED STATES AND ISRAEL AFTER 9/11

The lobby made considerable progress pushing its agenda during the 1990s,
even though it was more difficult to make the case that Israel was a strategic asset for the United States once the Cold War was over. Then came the
attacks of September 11, 2001, which forced Americans to focus considerable attention on the Arab and Islamic world, and especially the Middle
East. This was a critical moment for Israel and the lobby.

Would the Bush administration conclude that close ties between the
United States and Israel were fueling anti-American terrorism, and would it
therefore try to improve its image in the Arab and Islamic world by distanc-
ing itself—even if only slightly—from Israel? Specifically, would President
Bush put pressure on the Sharon government to end its efforts to colonize
the West Bank and instead create a viable Palestinian state? Might the
United States also begin to reduce its military presence in the wider Middle
East, which had grown considerably since 1990 and which had worked to
Israel's advantage?

These were not idle fears. As we describe in Chapter 2, there was compelling evidence showing that Osama bin Laden was committed to the Palestinian cause and was angry at the United States for backing Israel so strongly.
It was also clear that he deeply resented the presence of American troops on
Arab soil, especially in Saudi Arabia, and that the combination of these two
policies was fueling Arab and Islamic anger at the United States and facilitating al Qaeda's efforts. Might the United States respond to this situation by returning to its earlier position as an "offshore balancer" in the Middle East and
pressing more vigorously for an end to the Israeli-Palestinian conflict? There
were precedents for precisely this sort of response: the Reagan administration had briefly deployed U.S. troops in Lebanon in the early 1980s but had
removed them after a suicide bomber killed 241 marines in Beirut. Presidents Jimmy Carter and George H. W. Bush had also made genuine progress
toward peace in the region, but only by putting pressure on Israel and by paying less attention to the lobby.

Yet despite these concerns, the post–September 11 focus on Middle

East threats was also an opportunity for Israel and its American advocates. If the Bush administration could be convinced that Israel was a critical ally in the war on terror and that Israel's enemies were America's enemies as well, then perhaps the United States could be induced to back Sharon's hard-line approach toward the Palestinians and to take aim at Israel's regional adversaries: Hezbollah, Iran, Iraq, and Syria. In essence, American policy makers had to be shown that it made good strategic sense for the United States to try to rid the Middle East of Israel's foes, which were also said to be America's foes. As one would expect, Israel and key groups in the lobby began working together to turn this opportunity into a reality.

Their efforts succeeded. The Bush administration eventually embraced the lobby's views about the new threat environment and rejected the alternative paradigm. Not only did the United States gradually adopt Israel's policy preferences toward the Palestinians, Iran, and the rest of the region, it also adopted many of Israel's justifications for these policies. American and Israeli leaders began to sound as if they were speaking from the same page.

The conventional wisdom is that this outcome was overdetermined. In this version of events, Bush and Sharon (and now Ehud Olmert) saw the world in essentially the same way. The president and his advisers needed little encouragement from the lobby, because they had accepted Israel's views on how to deal with the Arab Islamic world from the very beginning, and even more so after 9/11.[1]

This interpretation of how U.S. Middle East policy evolved after 9/11 is not accurate, because it overlooks the very real disagreements that occasionally emerged between the Bush administration and the Israeli government. In the first year after September 11, Bush and Sharon clashed on a number of occasions over the Palestinian issue. Even after those disputes were resolved, there were still important differences between them regarding the Palestinians. In fact, Bush's efforts to deal with the Israeli-Palestinian conflict sometimes reflected the alternative paradigm, which called for greater effort to promote Israeli-Palestinian peace and defuse Arab hostility. This view enjoyed considerable support within the State Department and the U.S. intelligence community, as well as among the uniformed military. Bush also had important differences with Israel and the lobby over U.S. policy toward Syria. On both the Palestinian and Syrian issues, however, the lobby successfully pressured Bush to change course and to adopt its policy preferences instead.

Furthermore, the lobby played a critical role in shaping U.S. policy toward Iraq and Iran, as well as the Bush administration's grand scheme for transforming the Middle East into a sea of democracies. And the lobby worked overtime to convince Americans that Israel was in the right during its war in Lebanon in the summer of 2006 and to ensure that politicians from both parties supported Israel unreservedly.

These are controversial claims and should not be made lightly. Both before and during the war in Iraq, a number of public figures suggested that President Bush's Middle East policy—especially his decision to invade Iraq—was at least partly intended to benefit Israel. Not surprisingly, both Israelis and prominent pro-Israel Americans challenged this view, in some cases invoking the familiar charge that such individuals were anti-Semites. But controversial or not, the issue here is a factual one: Did the lobby exert a significant influence on U.S. Middle East policy? And if so, were the results beneficial for the United States or for Israel? The answer to the first question is clearly yes, and we believe the answer to the second question is emphatically no.

Let us look more closely at the Bush administration's policies in the Middle East, starting with its support for Israel's policies in the Occupied Territories, followed by an examination of its decision to invade Iraq. We will then consider Washington's broader policy of regional transformation, paying special attention to its policy toward Syria and Iran. Finally, we will examine America's handling of the 2006 Lebanon war. We argue that in each case, U.S. policy would have been different if the lobby were not as powerful, or if the main groups within it had favored a different approach. America's actions would have also have been more in line with its national interest, and better for Israel as well.

7

THE LOBBY VERSUS
THE PALESTINIANS

It is now largely forgotten, but in the fall of 2001, and again in the spring of 2002, the Bush administration sought to reduce anti-American sentiment in the Arab and Islamic world by pressing Israel to halt its expansionist policies in the Occupied Territories and by advocating the creation of a Palestinian state. Following the September 11 attacks, American policy makers believed that shutting down the Israeli-Palestinian conflict, or at least making a serious attempt to do so, would undermine support for terrorist groups like al Qaeda and facilitate the building of an international coalition against terrorism— which might even include states like Iran and Syria.[1]

Yet the Bush administration was unable to persuade Jerusalem to change its policies, and Washington instead ended up backing Israel's hard-line approach toward the Palestinians. Over time, Bush and his lieutenants also adopted Israel's justifications for this approach, and U.S. and Israeli rhetoric became similar. A *Washington Post* headline in February 2003 summarized the situation: "Bush and Sharon Nearly Identical on Mideast Policy."[2] The lobby's influence was one of the central reasons for this shift.

The story begins in late September 2001. President Bush began pushing Israeli Prime Minister Ariel Sharon to show restraint in the Occupied Territories and to do everything possible to contain the violence of the Second Intifada. The administration put what the *New York Times* described as "enormous pressure" on Sharon to allow Israeli foreign minister Shimon Peres to meet with Palestinian leader Yasser Arafat, even though Bush was highly critical of Arafat's leadership.[3] In early October, the new American president said publicly for the first time that he supported a Palestinian state. This event was itself a surprising development, since even President

Clinton, who had worked assiduously for a two-state solution, did not dare utter the words "Palestinian state" in public until his last month in office.[4] Bush had emphasized before 9/11 that he intended to take a hands-off approach toward the Arab-Israeli conflict, which makes his sudden interest in this issue especially revealing.

Israeli leaders were alarmed by these developments, fearing that Washington might "sell out" the Jewish state to win favor with the Arabs. The *Washington Post* reported that "sources close to Sharon say he is furious at U.S. attempts to enlist Iran, Syria and other states that have sponsored attacks on Israel into the U.S.-led coalition."[5] In early October, Sharon erupted, accusing Bush of trying "to appease the Arabs at our expense." Israel, he warned, "will not be Czechoslovakia."[6] Hours after making these comments, the Israel Defense Forces invaded several Palestinian areas in Hebron.[7]

Bush was reportedly angry at Sharon's likening his actions to Neville Chamberlain's capitulation at Munich, and White House press secretary Ari Fleischer called Sharon's remarks "unacceptable."[8] The Israeli prime minister offered a pro forma apology, but the basic problem remained unresolved.[9] Later in October, following the assassination of Israeli Minister of Tourism Rehavam Zeevi by a renegade Palestinian splinter group, the IDF launched another large-scale incursion into Palestinian-controlled territory in the West Bank. Bush met personally with Israeli Foreign Minister Shimon Peres and demanded a quick withdrawal, saying that he hoped "the Israelis would move their troops as quickly as possible."[10] The Israeli government rejected that demand and said it would leave when it was satisfied that Arafat had cracked down on Palestinian terrorists. The *Guardian* wrote that Ariel Sharon had "provoked the most bruising confrontation with Washington since George Bush came to power, flatly rejecting a demand to end an occupation of Palestinian lands that threatens the survival of Yasser Arafat."[11]

Sharon and the pro-Israel lobby moved quickly to resolve this growing dispute by convincing the Bush administration and the American people that the United States and Israel faced a common threat from terrorism. Israeli officials and key groups in the lobby would repeatedly emphasize over the next few years that there was no real difference between Arafat and Osama bin Laden and that therefore the United States and Israel should isolate the Palestinians' elected leader and not politically engage with him. As Sharon told his self-described "longtime supporter," the columnist William Safire of the *New York Times*, in December 2001, "You in America are in a war against terror. We in Israel are in a war against terror. It's the same war."[12]

Sharon's concerns about U.S. Middle East policy actually began imme-diately after 9/11, several weeks before Bush first expressed his support for a Palestinian state. He had a telephone conversation with American Jewish leaders on September 14, in which he made it clear that he was worried that the Bush administration would treat Arafat differently from bin Laden and that Bush would try to be tough on Israel as a way of winning Arab support for the war on terrorism. Sharon asked those leaders for their help.[13] But lit-tle happened in the wake of that conversation, in part because almost everyone in the United States was still reeling from the events of 9/11, but also because it was not clear at that point where American policy was headed. In that uncertain moment, the Project for the New American Cen-tury released an open letter to Bush on September 20, signed by many neoconservatives, including William J. Bennett, Eliot Cohen, Aaron Fried-berg, Reuel Marc Gerecht, Robert Kagan, Charles Krauthammer, Jeane Kirk-patrick, William Kristol, Richard Perle, and Norman Podhoretz. The letter described Israel as "America's staunchest ally against international terror-ism" and called for the president to "fully support our fellow democracy." It also recommended that the United States cut off all support for the Pales-tinian Authority.[14]

The broad outlines of Bush's policy to defeat terrorism became much clearer after he backed a two-state solution, and neither Sharon nor the lobby was happy with the new agenda. The American Israel Public Affairs Committee immediately responded to Bush's comments about a Palestinian state by issuing a statement declaring that the advisers who were pushing this idea on Bush were "undermining America's war against terrorism. They are encouraging the president to reward, rather than punish those that har-bor and support terrorism."[15] At the same time, Mortimer Zuckerman, the chairman of the Conference of Presidents of Major American Jewish Orga-nizations, said that Bush was pursuing "a very short-sighted and erroneous policy."[16] Pro-Israel forces began repeating this basic message at every opportunity.

Influential figures in the lobby began to put pressure on the Bush admin-istration to allow the IDF to remain in the Palestinian areas it had recently reoccupied for as long as Sharon saw fit. Abraham Foxman, the head of the Anti-Defamation League, wrote a letter to Secretary of State Colin Powell on October 23, in which he said that he was "extremely troubled" by the State Department's demand that Israel withdraw its forces from the recently seized areas. "We consider such comments to be inappropriate," he wrote, "and contrary to the long-standing American policy that Israel has the right to defend itself. The world is uniting to fight terrorism and unfortunately, the Palestinian Authority has refused to take steps to stem violence and terrorism."[17] Zuckerman echoed this view, saying Bush's effort to press Israel was "inappropriate, intemperate and defies logic in the face of U.S. efforts in the war on terrorism."[18]

The lobby also worked the halls of Congress. On November 16, eighty-nine senators sent Bush a letter praising him for refusing to meet with Arafat until the Palestinian leader took the necessary steps to end the violence against Israel. They also demanded that the United States not restrain Israel from retaliating against the Palestinians and insisted that the administration state publicly that it stood steadfastly behind Israel. According to the *New York Times,* the letter "stemmed from a meeting two weeks ago between leaders of the American Jewish community and key senators," adding that AIPAC was "particularly active in providing advice on the letter."[19]

By late November, relations between Jerusalem and Washington had improved considerably. This was due in part to the lobby's efforts, but also to America's initial victory in Afghanistan, which reduced the perceived need for Arab support in dealing with al Qaeda. Sharon visited the White House in early December and had a friendly meeting with Bush. In fact, just before the meeting began, the IDF attacked targets in Gaza in response to three suicide bombings in Israel. Bush neither criticized the Israelis nor asked them for restraint in the future. The White House spokesman emphasized instead that "Israel is a sovereign government" and that it "has a right to live in security." At the same time, Bush demanded that Arafat do more to stop terrorism against Israel.[20]

Sharon visited the White House again in February 2002 and had another amicable visit with Bush. The Israeli prime minister reiterated the accusation that Arafat was supporting terrorism and identified him as the principal obstacle to settling the Israeli-Palestinian conflict. Bush was now clearly receptive to this line of argument. He believed reports that Arafat was behind the controversial *Karine A* incident that had occurred a month earlier, in January 2002. The *Karine A* was a freighter loaded with fifty tons of weapons and explosives that was apparently sailing from Iran when it was captured by the Israeli navy in the Red Sea. Its final destination appeared to be Gaza, although the evidence at the time was not clear. In fact, some argued that the arms were bound for Hezbollah in Lebanon.[21]

While there was no definitive evidence that directly implicated Arafat, the Israeli government and the lobby worked hard to make the case that Arafat had procured the weapons and explosives to abet his terrorism campaign against Israel.[22] The Palestinian leader denied responsibility for the *Karine A*, and Secretary of State Colin Powell and others said that they had not seen evidence that contradicted Arafat's claim of innocence.[23] In the end, however, Bush agreed with Israel and its supporters. With Sharon at his side at the White House, Bush said, "Mr. Arafat has heard from us. I can't be any more clear . . . He must do everything in his power to fight terror. Obviously, we were, at first, surprised, and then extremely disappointed when the *Karine A* showed up loaded with weapons, weapons that could have only been intended for one thing, which was to terrorize."[24]

THE LOBBY HUMILIATES BUSH

Although the American and Israeli positions were now converging, trouble between the two states erupted again in late March 2002, when a Hamas suicide bomber killed thirty Israelis at a Passover seder. The Palestinian Authority immediately denounced the attack and pledged to prosecute those responsible. But its dismal record of punishing militants left the Israelis cold; they had had enough. Sharon launched Operation Defensive Shield in which the IDF resumed control of virtually all of the major Palestinian areas on the West Bank.[25] Bush knew right away that Israel's action would damage America's image in the Arab and Islamic world and undermine the war on terrorism, so he demanded on April 4 that Sharon "halt the incursions and begin withdrawal." He underscored this message two days later, saying this meant "withdrawal without delay." On April 7, Bush's national security adviser, Condoleezza Rice, told reporters that "'without delay' means without delay. It means now." That same day Secretary of State Powell set out for the Middle East to pressure all sides to stop fighting and start negotiating.

The administration soon came under fire to adopt a different approach. A key target was Powell, who was not only considered unsympathetic, if not hostile, to Israel, but was also planning to meet with Arafat during his Middle East trip. The secretary of state immediately began feeling the heat from staunch supporters of Israel in the vice president's office and the Pentagon, who pushed Bush and Rice to abandon the effort to restrain Israel. Rice was constantly on the phone to Powell, sometimes sounding like she was giving him a "dressing-down." He believed that her concerns reflected "the views of somebody in the White House."[26]

Neoconservatives in the media piled on Powell as well. Robert Kagan and William Kristol wrote in the *Weekly Standard* on April 11 that Powell had "virtually obliterated the distinction between terrorists and those fighting terrorists."[27] The following day, David Brooks, then working for the *Weekly Standard*, described Powell's trip on the *NewsHour with Jim Lehrer* as "a disaster as opposed to an unmitigated disaster." He went on to say that Powell "hurt U.S. prestige . . . shredded U.S. policy in the Middle East . . . and most importantly, he hurt our moral clarity."[28] Former Israeli Prime Minister Benjamin Netanyahu, who was making Israel's case in the United States at the time, said even before Powell arrived in Israel that his trip "won't amount to anything."[29] He was right: the balance of power inside the administration shifted against Powell so quickly and completely that his deputy in Washington called the secretary in Israel and told him, "I'm holding back the fucking gates here. They're eating cheese on you."[30] Powell later said that his trip to the Middle East was "ten of the most miserable days imaginable."[31]

Powell got the message, as reflected in his behavior at a joint press conference he held with Ariel Sharon before leaving Israel. "The Secretary of State's language, body and verbal," John Simpson of the *Sunday Telegraph* wrote, "certainly were not that of the paymaster coming to call a client to account. Far from it. Mr. Powell seemed ingratiating, deferential; no doubt he realizes how much support Mr. Sharon has back in Washington and how much influence his friends have there with the President."[32] Netanyahu's prediction proved correct. Powell's trip did not "amount to anything."

A second target was Bush himself, who was being pressed by Jewish leaders and Christian evangelicals. Tom DeLay and Dick Armey were especially outspoken about the need to support Israel, and DeLay and Senate Minority Leader Trent Lott visited the White House on April 10 and personally warned Bush to back off.[33] On the following day, according to *Time* magazine, "a group of Evangelical leaders led by the Reverend Jerry Falwell and former presidential candidate Gary Bauer sent Bush a letter demanding that the Administration 'end pressure' on Sharon to withdraw from the West Bank. After Falwell adjured his followers to do the same, the White House was flooded with calls and e-mails. The next day, sources say, senior presidential aides phoned Falwell to reassure him that Bush stood behind Sharon."[34]

The first external sign that Bush was caving came that same day (April 11)—only one week after he insisted that Sharon withdraw his forces—when Ari Fleischer said the president believed that Sharon was "a man of peace."[35] Bush publicly repeated this statement on April 18 on Powell's return from his abortive mission, and the president also told reporters that Sharon had responded satisfactorily to his call for a full and immediate withdrawal.[36] Sharon had done no such thing, but Bush was no longer willing to make an issue of it. Israel announced the formal end of Defensive Shield on April 21, but IDF forces remained in many Palestinian areas, and significant elements of the Israeli control regime are still in force today.

Other groups in the lobby kept up the pressure. The Conference of Presidents and the United Jewish Communities sponsored a major rally in Washington in mid-April, with appearances by Armey, Netanyahu, Zuckerman, House Minority Leader Richard Gephardt, and other prominent officials. The crowd even booed Deputy Secretary of Defense Paul Wolfowitz (shouting "Down with Arafat") when he briefly referred to Palestinian suffering and the possibility of a Palestinian state. Morton Klein, the head of the Zionist Organization of America, said that "if Bush doesn't get the message to stop pressuring Israel, we will have lost a great opportunity with this rally." Responding to the gathering, an unnamed administration official remarked that "policy is not based on what's popular." But the same official also admitted that "we hear so much from Jewish leaders, to see that many Jews turn out for this [rally] will just speak volumes."[37]

Meanwhile, Congress was also moving to back Sharon. Netanyahu visited Capitol Hill in mid-April, where he met forty senators, accompanied by a "security cordon fit for a head of state."[38] On May 2, it overrode the administration's objections and passed two resolutions reaffirming support for Israel (the Senate vote was 94 to 2; the House version passed 352 to 21). Both resolutions emphasized that the United States "stands in solidarity with Israel," and that the two countries are, to quote the House resolution, "now engaged in a common struggle against terrorism." The House version also condemned "the ongoing support of terror by Yasir Arafat," who was portrayed as a central element of the terrorism problem.[39]

A few days later, a bipartisan congressional delegation on a fact-finding mission in Israel publicly proclaimed that Sharon (who was then in Washington meeting with Bush) should resist the administration's pressure to negotiate with Arafat.[40] Then, on May 9, a House appropriations subcommittee met to consider giving Israel an extra $200 million to fight terrorism. The White House was opposed to the package and Secretary of State Powell took the lead and met with congressional leaders in an attempt to stop it. But the lobby backed it, just as it had helped author the two congressional resolutions. Powell lost and Bush reluctantly signed the legislation, giving Israel the money.[41]

Sharon and the lobby had taken on the president of the United States and his secretary of state and triumphed. Chemi Shalev, a journalist for the Israel newspaper *Ma'ariv*, reported that Sharon's aides "could not hide their satisfaction in view of Powell's failure. Sharon saw the white in President Bush's eyes, they bragged, and the President blinked first." Indeed, Bush's humiliation was not lost on commentators around the world. Spain's leading daily, *El País*, expressed the views of many outside observers when it commented, "If a country's weight is measured by its degree of influence on events, the superpower is not the USA but Israel."[42] But it was pro-Israel forces in the United States, not Sharon or Israel, that played the key role in thwarting Bush's efforts to pursue a more evenhanded policy.

"THE MORE THINGS CHANGE . . ."

Despite these setbacks, Bush continued looking for a way to end the Second Intifada and create a viable Palestinian state living in peace next door to Israel. He understood that it is in America's national interest to settle the Arab-Israeli conflict as soon as possible. Bush has not come close to achieving that goal, however, mainly because there has been little change in the balance of power between Bush and the lobby since the spring of 2002. This situation has given Israeli leaders considerable leverage over Bush's Middle East policies and enables them to ignore or neutralize policies they dislike.

Seeking to move beyond his troubles in the spring of 2002, Bush gave a major speech on the Middle East on June 24.[43] It was a noteworthy address for two reasons. First, Bush maintained that Arafat had to give up power before the peace process could move forward. "Peace," he said, "requires a new and different political Palestinian leadership." In effect, as David Landau pointed out in *Ha'aretz*, "Yasser Arafat, the seemingly immortal leader of the Palestinian national movement, was politically assassinated . . . by President George W. Bush."[44] The Israelis, who had been calling for Arafat's isolation for months, were ecstatic. In fact, at least two prominent conservative Israelis, Natan Sharansky and Benjamin Netanyahu, claimed that they had played a major role in convincing Bush to insert that demand in his speech.[45] *Ha'aretz* ran a story on the speech with the headline, "Analysis: Ariel Sharon Agrees to His Own Ideas."[46]

Second, Bush called for creating a Palestinian state by 2005. In pursuit of that goal, he emphasized that "Israeli settlement activity in the occupied territories must stop" and, as the security situation improved, "Israel forces need to withdraw fully to positions they held prior to September 28, 2000 [the start of the Second Intifada]." Bush was widely criticized for not saying more about what the final settlement would look like and how he planned to get from here to there.[47] While the speech was certainly vague about the particulars of a future agreement, Bush's comments were nevertheless important. At the time, the Bush administration was working closely with the European Union, Russia, and the UN to fashion a "Road Map" leading to a negotiated peace between Israel and the Palestinians. The plan of the so-called Quartet was specifically designed to build on the main points laid out in Bush's speech.

In essence, the Bush administration decided in the summer of 2002 that the Road Map was the best way to resolve the Israeli-Palestinian conflict. But little progress was made in implementing it until the spring of 2003. The delay was due to the fact that it took time to convince Arafat to step aside and for the Quartet to work out the details of the Road Map. Furthermore, the Bush administration was busy preparing for war with Iraq, which it invaded on March 19, 2003. Serious movement on the Road Map finally began on March 7, when Arafat signaled that he was reducing his own political power by nominating Mahmoud Abbas to be the prime minister of the Palestinian Authority.[48] A week later, on March 14, Bush proclaimed that he was ready to promote the Road Map. On April 30, the Quartet released the details of that peace plan.[49]

Then in early June, the president traveled to the Middle East to push the Road Map and try to strengthen Abbas's hand vis-à-vis Arafat. Bush's prestige was sky-high in the wake of the successful ouster of Saddam. His triumphant "Mission Accomplished" photo op on the USS *Abraham Lincoln* had occurred the previous month, the problems of postwar reconstruction in Iraq were barely apparent, and Bush's popularity at home was at near-record levels. He was in an ideal position to press all sides to get serious about peace. He met first with Arab leaders in Egypt on June 3 and then the following day with Abbas and Sharon in Aqaba, Jordan. Before the trip, reporters were skeptical about whether Bush could put pressure on Israel to achieve his goals, especially with his reelection campaign looming in 2004. "Of course I can," he told them. "Listen, if I were afraid of making the decisions necessary—for political reasons—to move the process forward, I wouldn't be going."[50]

The meetings were cordial and Bush's efforts to get directly involved in the peace process appeared to be off to a good start. But the Road Map went nowhere. Despite occasionally paying lip service to the Quartet's plan, Sharon was opposed to creating a viable Palestinian state, and thus he had no interest in negotiating with the Palestinians, since the aim of such negotiations was to create just such a state in the Occupied Territories. His opposition to the Road Map was clear well before March 2003. The *Washington Post* opined in an editorial on December 16, 2002, that although Sharon "has been telling voters about his readiness to support the Bush scheme," the fact is that his "envoys have been harshly criticizing the draft 'road map' in meetings with U.S. officials. According to Israeli press reports, Mr. Sharon himself dismissed the administration's plan as 'irrelevant' in a recent cabinet meeting."[51]

Sharon did not say much publicly in mid-March 2003, when Bush announced that he was pushing the Road Map forward, mainly because he did not want to criticize Bush when the United States was getting ready to invade Iraq.[52] Nevertheless, Sharon's views on the plan had not changed, as Chemi Shalev made clear in an article in the *Forward*: "The strategic goal of Sharon and his advisors is ultimately to undermine the road map and to exclude the three remaining members [the EU, UN, and Russia] of the so-called Madrid Quartet . . . from active involvement in the peace process."[53] In mid-April, *Ha'aretz* declared in an editorial that Sharon "has not internalized the conceptual change necessary to achieve a peace arrangement based on compromise. Apparently . . . the prime minister has yet to give up the vision of the settlements and the creeping annexation of the West Bank."[54]

Given Sharon's opposition to the Road Map, it is hardly surprising that the heads of the key organizations in the lobby viewed Bush's plan as the "road map to nowhere," to quote Conference of Presidents chairman Zuckerman.[55] Within hours after Bush said on March 14 that he was getting behind the Road Map, National Security Adviser Condoleezza Rice met at the White House with a delegation of Jewish leaders. The aim of the meeting, according to an article in *Ha'aretz*, was "to neutralize American Jewish reservations about the plan."[56] But according to the same article, "Rice was unable to allay the concerns of many of the participants at the meeting." Abraham Foxman, the head of the ADL, and Malcolm Hoenlein, the executive vice chairman of the Conference of Presidents, were especially critical. Although Hoenlein said it was necessary to wait for Israel's reaction to the plan, he emphasized that the American Jewish community would support Israel if it expressed reservations.

AIPAC also sponsored a letter to President Bush on Capitol Hill, urging him not to put pressure on Israel regarding the Road Map and demanding that the Palestinians be required to comply fully with the plan's security requirements before Israel had to make any concessions. By early May, 85 senators and 283 representatives had signed the letter.[57] While AIPAC ultimately endorsed the Road Map—with qualifications—it did not campaign to win it support in Congress, which "effectively left the lobbying front open to groups that openly oppose the plan."[58] Many pro-Israel commentators lambasted the administration's decision to push the Road Map forward. For example, Charles Krauthammer, writing in the *Washington Post,* maintained that "proceeding along the road map" as long as Arafat retained any power was "diplomatic suicide."[59] Thomas L. Friedman of the *New York Times,* however, was critical of the major Jewish organizations for not supporting the peace plan.[60] Apart from more dovish groups such as the Tikkun Community and the Israel Policy Forum, there were few pro-Israel groups enthusiastically backing the Road Map. That meant it had no future.

Consequently, Israeli hard-liners were not worried much about the Road Map when its details were spelled out on April 30. In an article in *Ha'aretz* the following day, Bradley Burston asked, "So why are these people smiling?"[61] The answer is that the Bush administration had privately reached a series of understandings with Sharon and his lieutenants that greatly allayed their fears about the Quartet's peace plan.[62] In fact, the *Financial Times* reported that Elliott Abrams and Stephen Hadley, two key players on the National Security Council, secretly assured Sharon "that he would not face US pressure over the road map."[63]

Still, Sharon must have been worried after Bush's trip to the Middle East in early June 2003, which was widely seen as an important step in promoting the president's peace effort. Shortly after the president returned to the United States, Israel tried but failed to kill Abdel Aziz Rantisi, a key Hamas leader. It was the first of seven targeted assassinations in five days.[64] Sharon had promised Secretary of State Powell in May that Israel would stop targeted assassinations unless they involved a "ticking bomb," which was clearly not the case in this instance.[65] Indeed, Hamas had announced the day *before* the attack that it was willing to renew talks about a cease-fire.[66] Moreover, the *Forward* reported that at the Aqaba summit meeting Sharon had "agreed to avoid actions that might 'inflame' the situation and weaken the rookie Palestinian prime minister."[67] Israeli commentators understood that the Israeli prime minister was now attempting to sink the Road Map. "The curious timing of the assassination campaign," a *Ha'aretz* correspondent wrote, "was not lost on Israelis."[68]

Bush was not pleased. Yet he only mildly rebuked Sharon, saying on June 10, "I am troubled by the recent Israeli helicopter gunship attacks." His aides' remarks, according to the *Washington Post,* were only "slightly stronger." But even the slightest criticism of Israel was unacceptable to the hard-liners in the lobby, who soon mobilized to check Bush's brief show of independence. DeLay had a private meeting with the president's aides and told them that he would push forward a congressional resolution supporting Israel if Bush continued to criticize it. On the evening of June 11, Bush hosted a dinner at the White House with one hundred Jewish leaders to celebrate a new exhibit at the Holocaust Memorial Museum. Malcolm Hoenlein, who met privately with Bush that evening, said that the president "and others at the White House recognized that their reaction could be counterproductive." Hoenlein went on to say that "people were taken a little aback by the comments and, from what everyone could tell, the White House was well aware of it."[69]

By the next day, June 12, the White House had done another U-turn and was firmly supporting Israel. The *Washington Post* reported that "in coordinated statements, White House and State Department officials tried to shift the diplomatic focus from Israeli actions to the commitments made by Arab leaders at a summit last week in Egypt to cut off funding and support for terrorist attacks against Israelis. Secretary of State Colin Powell made that point in a round of phone calls to Arab foreign ministers."[70] Ari Fleischer, the White House press secretary, said, "The issue is not Israel," it is "terrorists who are killing in an attempt to stop a hopeful process from moving forward."[71] Later that month, the House passed a resolution—by a vote of 399 to 5—expressing "solidarity with the Israeli people" and saying that Israel was fully justified in using force to deal with terrorism.[72]

Bush had once again tried to curb Israeli actions that strengthened anti-Americanism in the Arab and Islamic world and undermined the administration's war on terrorism, but he ended up suffering another humiliating defeat.[73]

UNILATERALISM IN, ROAD MAP OUT

Much the same pattern was evident in late July 2003, when the Bush administration began to voice its objections to Israel's so-called security fence, which was widely seen as an Israeli attempt to create "facts on the ground" that would be a major obstacle to a negotiated settlement. The issue was not construction of the fence itself but rather its intended route, which in effect would incorporate additional parts of the Occupied Territories and impose significant additional hardships on thousands of Palestinians.[74] Bush expressed his displeasure at a joint White House press conference with Palestinian Prime Minister Mahmoud Abbas on July 25: "I think the wall is a problem, and I discussed this with Ariel Sharon. It is very difficult to develop confidence between the Palestinians and Israel with a wall snaking through the West Bank."[75] But four days later at the White House, with Bush standing at his side, Sharon made it clear that he intended to continue building the fence, although he said he would try to minimize the hardships it inflicted on the Palestinians. Bush did not challenge Sharon but instead accepted the prime minister's view that Palestinian terrorism was "the fundamental obstacle to peace."[76]

Nevertheless, the Bush administration continued to express its unhappiness with the security barrier. Secretary of State Powell suggested in an interview that the fence was an Israeli attempt to appropriate Palestinian land, and Condoleezza Rice hinted that the administration might deduct the cost of the fence from $9 billion in loan guarantees that the United States had approved in April.[77] Israel's supporters in Congress mobilized and emphasized to the White House, as Senator Charles Schumer put it, that if the president "flouts the will of Congress and tries to penalize Israel for defending itself, Congress will do everything in its power to ensure that these loan guarantees are not held up."[78] The Israelis themselves were not seriously concerned. As one senior Israeli official put it, "We are not under any pressure . . . The United States is a very vibrant democracy, and this is a very politically oriented administration. Reality is made sometimes by political constraints."[79]

The issue of loan guarantees would not go away, however, and in late November the Bush administration said that it would cut $289.5 million from the $3 billion in loan guarantees allocated to Israel earlier that year. The lobby did not protest strongly, mainly because the punishment was effectively a weak slap on the wrist. The United States was not cutting direct foreign aid, the real meat and potatoes of its material support to Israel. Reducing the loan guarantees by roughly 10 percent simply meant that Israel had to pay a higher interest rate on a small portion of the overall amount it intended to borrow. The former director general of Israel's Finance Ministry estimated that it would cost Israel about $4 million a year in higher interest costs, which is not a lot of money for a prosperous state like Israel.[80]

The Bush administration won another small victory in the fall of 2003. Sharon was threatening to expel Arafat from the West Bank and send him into exile. Powell and Rice told the Israelis that expelling the Palestinian leader was unacceptable to the United States. They got the message and Arafat remained in the West Bank.[81]

But these small victories were not indications of a changing tide. On the contrary, in the fall of 2003, Sharon began moving to wreck George Bush's Road Map once and for all by pushing forward his own plan for unilateral disengagement.[82] In November, Sharon invited Elliott Abrams, the senior director for Near East and North African Affairs on the National Security Council (NSC) and a well-known neoconservative, to a secret meeting in Rome. At the meeting, Sharon informed the American official that instead of pursuing a negotiated settlement, as called for in the Road Map, he intended to impose his own settlement on the Palestinians.[83] As the policy evolved in the next few months, it became clear that Israel would first withdraw all of its settlements from Gaza and turn that territory over to the Palestinians. Israel would then turn some areas of the West Bank over to the Palestinians but keep large parts of that contested land for Israel.

Sharon's decision to leave these parts of the Occupied Territories to the Palestinians was based not on sympathy for their plight but on the fear that if Israel retained Gaza and all of the West Bank, Arabs would soon outnumber Jews in "greater Israel." The demographic issue, in other words, was driving the prime minister's policy.[84]

The Palestinians would have virtually no say in the process. Israel would dictate the terms of the settlement, and in the end, the Palestinians would not get a state of their own. Dov Weisglass, Sharon's closest adviser, made this clear when he said that "the significance of what we did . . . is the freezing of the political process. And when you freeze that process you prevent the establishment of a Palestinian state and you prevent a discussion about the refugees, the borders and Jerusalem. Effectively, this whole package that is called the Palestinian state, with all that it entails, has been removed from our agenda indefinitely." Weisglass also said that Sharon's plan "is actually formaldehyde. It supplies the amount of formaldehyde that's necessary so that there will not be a political process with the Palestinians."[85]

One might have expected Bush to be angry with Sharon and to try to keep the Road Map alive, especially since the president, according to his national security adviser, believed that "it is the only course that will bring durable peace and security."[86] But that is not what happened. In the spring of 2004, Bush publicly embraced Sharon's unilateral approach, saying that it was a "bold courageous step" and that the world owed Sharon a "thank you" for pursuing it.[87] Then in a dramatic shift, on April 14, Bush reversed the stated policy of every president since Lyndon Johnson by proclaiming that Israel would not have to return virtually all of the territories that it occupied in 1967, and that Palestinian refugees would not be allowed to return to their former homes in Israel but would have to settle in a new Palestinian state.[88] Previously, American policy was that the Israelis and the Palestinians would negotiate these issues. These moves sparked outrage in the Middle East but were widely seen in the United States as smart politics in a year when George Bush was up for reelection.[89]

Writing in early 2004, Thomas L. Friedman of the *New York Times* captured the essence of Bush's predicament regarding the Israeli-Palestinian conflict: "Mr. Sharon has the Palestinian leader Yasir Arafat under house arrest in his office in Ramallah, and he's had George Bush under house arrest in the Oval Office. Mr. Sharon has Mr. Arafat surrounded by tanks, and Mr. Bush surrounded by Jewish and Christian pro-Israel lobbyists, by a vice president, Dick Cheney, who's ready to do whatever Mr. Sharon dictates, and by political handlers telling the president not to put any pressure on Israel in an election year—all conspiring to make sure the president does nothing."[90]

During this entire period, the Israelis continued building settlements in the West Bank, despite American protests and despite the fact that the Road Map explicitly calls upon Israel to "freeze all settlement activity (including natural growth of settlements)."[91] They also continued assassinating Palestinian leaders, sometimes at the most unhelpful moments—at least from a U.S. perspective. For example, the IDF scuttled a proposed Palestinian cease-fire on July 22, 2002, when it killed Sheik Salah Shehada, a prominent Hamas leader, and fourteen others (including nine children). The White House denounced the attack as "heavy handed" but did not force Israel to end its targeted assassinations policy.[92] As noted previously, the IDF undermined another emerging cease-fire in June 2003, when it tried but failed to kill Rantisi, another Hamas leader.

On March 22, 2004, Israel assassinated Hamas leader Sheik Ahmed Yassin with American-made Hellfire missiles. This move was generally perceived as a serious blow to America's position in the Middle East, not only because U.S. weapons were used but also because many in the Arab world believed that the Bush administration had given Israel the green light to kill a paraplegic in a wheelchair. The *Washington Post* columnist Jim Hoagland wrote in the wake of that killing, "With the possible exception of Charles de Gaulle, no friendly foreign leader has complicated modern American diplomacy and strategy more consistently or gravely than Ariel Sharon. He pursues Israel's interests with a warrior's tenacity and directness that take away the breath, and the options, of everyone else."[93] Less than a month later, on April 17, 2004, the IDF finally killed Rantisi.[94]

ARAFAT DIES AND NOTHING CHANGES

Arafat died in November 2004 and Abbas emerged as the Palestinian's new leader, eventually winning office in January 2005 in a peaceful democratic election that was hailed by outside observers as free and fair. One would think that this event would have been an ideal opportunity to push the peace process forward, as Abbas recognized Israel, renounced terrorism, and was eager to work out a negotiated settlement to the conflict.[95] Furthermore, Bush had just won reelection to a second term and thus was in about as good a position as any president could be to help bolster the moderate Abbas. The Bush administration embraced the new Palestinian leader from the start, but it did virtually nothing to help him negotiate a viable state, and so ultimately undermined his power base.

The main reason Bush did little to help Abbas was that he had already committed himself to supporting Sharon's plan (and that of his successor, Ehud Olmert) to disengage unilaterally from the Palestinians. Contrary to his own pronouncements about the necessity of the Road Map, Bush was backing a strategy that held no promise of the Palestinians getting a viable state of their own, which doomed the plan from the start.

Some pro-Israel groups like the Zionist Organization of America and the Orthodox organizations were opposed to giving up any territory to the Palestinians. But the major organizations like the Anti-Defamation League, the American Jewish Congress, and the American Jewish Committee backed disengagement. Senior officials in the Conference of Presidents estimated that somewhere between 60 and 75 percent of the leaders favored the pullout, which was more than enough to ensure that the lobby ultimately backed Sharon and Bush's shift in policy, although not with great enthusiasm.[96]

By refusing to negotiate with Abbas and making it impossible for him to deliver tangible benefits to the Palestinian people, Sharon contributed directly to Hamas's electoral victory in January 2006. The *Ha'aretz* columnist Bradley Burston wrote just before that election, "If it appears to you . . . that Israel is Hamas' campaign manager in next week's elections for the Palestinian parliament, few would argue—especially in Hamas."[97] With Hamas in power, Israel had another reason not to negotiate and the Bush administration was even less likely to push them to talk with the Palestinians.

To make matters worse, Israel's policy of unilateral disengagement collapsed in the summer of 2006, about two months after Bush had hailed the policy during Ehud Olmert's first visit to the White House as the new prime minister.[98] After pulling out of Gaza in August 2005, the Israelis effectively cordoned off that small piece of real estate, making it impossible for the Palestinians living there to lead a decent life, much less have a state of their own. The Palestinians in Gaza continued launching rockets into Israel, and then they captured an Israeli soldier on June 25, 2006. The Israelis felt that the situation had become intolerable, so three days later they reentered Gaza.[99] It quickly became apparent to most Israelis, and certainly to Olmert, that Israel would face a similar situation if it unilaterally withdrew from some parts of the West Bank and effectively locked up the Palestinians left behind.

A few weeks later, on July 12, Hezbollah captured two Israeli soldiers along the Israel-Lebanon border, precipitating a war in which Hezbollah fired rockets and missiles into northern Israel. Given that Israel had unilaterally withdrawn from southern Lebanon in 2000, this crisis reinforced the point that simply pulling back from parts of the West Bank would not by itself end Israel's conflict with the Palestinians. Consequently, with the Israeli public behind him, Olmert abandoned unilateral disengagement in the late summer of 2006. In a candid interview with the Chinese news agency Xinhua in January 2007, Olmert said that when he took over from the incapacitated Sharon in January 2006, he was confident that a unilateral strategy, or what he called his "convergence plan," could solve the Palestinian problem. But he was wrong, and now, "under the existing circumstances, it would be more practical to achieve a two-state solution through negotiations rather than [unilateral] withdrawal."[100]

RICE GETS "POWELLIZED"[101]

The Bush administration had also figured out that unilateralism was a losing strategy, and it began pushing again for a negotiated settlement along the lines of the Road Map. In late 2006, Secretary of State Condoleezza Rice took the lead in trying to get the Palestinian and Israeli leaders talking to each other.[102] Her goal was to start a discussion about what the broad outlines of a comprehensive settlement—which she termed the "political horizon"—should look like.

While Rice was pushing the Israelis and the Palestinians to negotiate seriously, the Saudis convinced the Arab League in March 2007 to reissue its 2002 peace plan. The new proposal, like the original one, offered Israel peace and normal relations not just with the Palestinians but with all twenty-two members of the Arab League. In return, Israel would have to withdraw from all of the Occupied Territories and the Golan Heights, accept the establishment of a sovereign Palestinian state in the Occupied Territories with East Jerusalem as its capital, and negotiate a "just solution" to the Palestinian refugee problem that was "agreed upon" by the relevant parties.[103] The Saudis made it clear that the proposal was a basis for negotiation, not a take-it-or-leave-it deal.

Both the Americans and the Saudis had powerful incentives to put an end to the conflict between Israel and the Palestinians.[104] Continuing U.S. support for Israeli policies in the Occupied Territories was not only helping fuel America's terrorism problem, but it was making it difficult for the Bush administration to get Arab states to help it deal with the war in Iraq and Iran's nuclear program. The Saudis, for their part, wanted to work closely with the Americans to contain Iran, but they were limited in what they could do because there was so much anger among the Saudi people over U.S. support for Israel's treatment of the Palestinians. The Saudis also wanted to end the conflict, because Iran was gaining influence with radical Palestinian forces in the Occupied Territories.

Given these circumstances, conditions would seem ripe for serious movement forward in the peace process. But that did not happen. Olmert showed little interest in the Arab League initiative, which appeared destined to share the same fate as the 2002 peace proposal. The Israeli prime minister was unhappy with some parts of the proposal, such as the stipulation that Israel would have to withdraw from all of the Occupied Territories. He also rejected any compromise on the issue of a Palestinian "right of return," telling the *Jerusalem Post* in March 2007, "I will not agree to any kind of Israeli responsibility for this problem. Full stop." He went on to say that the return of even one Palestinian refugee to Israel was "out of the question."[105]

But that point of dispute and any others could have been dealt with in the negotiations that would have ensued if Israel had agreed to talks on the basis of the proposal. *Ha'aretz* put the point well in a late March editorial: "A realistic government would have rushed to embrace this willingness for recognition and reconciliation, expressing reservations for what it does not accept and seeking dialogue on the regional level."[106] In mid-May, Olmert was widely criticized for failing to seriously pursue peace with the Arabs, including by two staunch supporters of Israel: Abraham Foxman of the ADL and the Nobel laureate Elie Wiesel. In the face of this mounting criticism, the prime minister responded by saying that Israel was willing to discuss the Arab League initiative, but he has taken little action beyond his rhetoric. Instead, Israel has launched a diplomatic campaign to blame the Arabs for the failure of the peace initiative.[107]

The Bush administration did nothing substantive to push Olmert to embrace the Arab League's proposal, although it did urge Arab leaders to alter the proposal to Israel's liking.[108] So far, Rice's own efforts to push the peace process forward have come to naught. For starters, Rice made it clear in an early February 2007 meeting with leaders from fifteen major Jewish organizations that not only would the administration refrain from putting pressure on Israel, but it would not offer its own suggestions on what the "political horizon" might look like.[109] Those concessions greatly limited the secretary's effectiveness. Rice then traveled to Jerusalem where, on February 19, she brought Olmert and Abbas together for talks. But Rice's efforts to revive the peace talks were a bust, as the Israeli prime minister refused to discuss the outlines of a possible settlement. In fact, both Olmert and Abbas refused to appear with her at the press conference afterward. Shortly thereafter, the New York Times ran an editorial on the meeting titled "Charade in Jerusalem," which pointed out that Rice could not even get the two leaders to stand at her side while she read a "content-free joint statement to which they have grudgingly agreed."[110]

In late March 2007, Rice returned to Israel to meet with Olmert and raise the possibility that she might serve as a mediator between Israel and the Palestinians. It was her seventh visit to Israel in eight months. Olmert flatly rejected the idea of Rice acting as a diplomatic broker, forcing her to cancel the press conference planned for after the meeting. The Daily Telegraph (London) headline the day after the Olmert-Rice meeting said it all: "Israel Snubs Condoleezza Rice."[111] The secretary of state returned to Washington empty-handed and with little prospect that the Bush administration would make meaningful progress toward Arab-Israeli peace before leaving office.

This outcome, which is not only humiliating for the secretary of state but is contrary to America's national interest as well, is the result of at least two factors. First, Olmert, like his predecessor Sharon, has no interest in negotiating a peace settlement with the Palestinians, because it would require Israel to give up almost all of the West Bank and create a viable Palestinian state on that territory. Olmert has made it clear that he would be willing to give up some parts of the West Bank, but he intends to keep large parts of it for Israel. Indeed, his government announced in late December 2006 that it was constructing its first new settlement in the West Bank in ten years, and the following month Israel announced that it planned to build new houses in Ma'aleh Adumim, Israel's largest existing settlement.[112] Israel would prefer the occupation to peace, if the latter means giving 95 percent or so of the West Bank to the Palestinians.[113]

One might argue that the real obstacle to peace is not Israel but Hamas, which came to power in January 2006 and remains formally committed to Israel's destruction. There is no question that Hamas's growing stature within the Palestinian community complicated any efforts to achieve peace. Nevertheless, this problem is not insurmountable. If the Israelis were genuinely interested in reaching a peace agreement with the Palestinians, they could work with the Arab League, Abbas, and the more moderate elements within Hamas to push the peace process forward and isolate—or maybe even convert—the rejectionists in Hamas and other radical groups like Islamic Jihad.[114] But instead, the Israelis have shown little enthusiasm for working with the growing number of Arabs who are genuinely interested in making peace with the Jewish state. By undermining moderates who want to negotiate peace, this policy merely strengthens those factions that claim that violence is the only effective tactic.

Second, pro-Israel forces in the United States have made it impossible for the United States, especially Secretary of State Rice, to push the Olmert government toward peace. Inside the White House, the main obstacle to putting any kind of meaningful pressure on Israel is Elliott Abrams. He has help, however, from two powerful neoconservatives who work for the vice president, John Hannah and David Wurmser. The journalist Jim Lobe reports that various sources have told him that "Abrams has been working systematically to undermine any prospect for serious negotiations designed to give substance to Rice's hopes—and increasingly impatient demands by Saudi King Abdullah—of offering the Palestinians a 'political horizon' for a final settlement."[115]

Abrams has a close relationship with Yoram Turbowitz, Olmert's chief of staff, and Shalom Turgeman, Olmert's diplomatic adviser, who all work together to make sure that the Bush administration does not push Israel to pursue policies that Olmert dislikes. Daniel Levy, a former adviser in the Israeli prime minister's office, notes that "if Rice is getting too active with her peace-making quest, then T+T (Yoram Turbowitz and Shalom Turgeman) can always be dispatched to Elliott Abrams at the White House, who in turn will enlist Cheney to keep the president in tow."[116] Correspondingly, Henry Siegman, who long worked on Middle East issues at the Council on Foreign Relations, maintains that "every time there emerged the slightest hint that the United States may finally engage seriously in a political process, Elliott Abrams would meet secretly with Olmert's envoys in Europe or elsewhere to reassure them that there exists no such danger."[117] Right before Rice arrived in Israel for her February 19 meeting with Abbas and Olmert, the Israeli prime minister put the secretary of state in her place by letting the media know that he had talked to Bush the day before and that "the prime minister and president see eye-to-eye." As Aluf Benn and Shmuel Rosner wrote in Ha'aretz, "The message was unmistakable: What Rice had to say barely mattered."[118]

The extent to which the balance of power inside the Bush administration is stacked against Rice is further illustrated by Philip Zelikow's resignation as the State Department's counselor at the end of 2006. He was Rice's longtime friend and coauthor and one of her closest advisers. By the late summer of 2006, he was encouraging Rice to make a serious effort to negotiate a peace agreement between Israel and the Palestinians. He felt that was essential if Washington hoped to get the Arab states and the Europeans to form an effective coalition against Iran. He made this very point on September 15, 2006, in a speech at the Washington Institute for Near East Policy.[119]

Following the speech, there was an immediate outcry from pro-Israel groups, and, according to the New York Times, "The State Department quickly distanced itself from the speech, issuing a statement denying any linkage, and Israeli officials, flustered by Mr. Zelikow's remarks, said Ms. Rice later assured the Israeli foreign minister, Tzipi Livni, that the United States saw the Iranian and Palestinian issues as two separate matters."[120] Zelikow announced he was leaving the State Department the following month. He gave anodyne reasons for his departure in his resignation letter, although one unnamed White House source said that his departure was due in part to his unhappiness with U.S. Middle East policy. In early March 2007, Rice named Eliot Cohen, a neoconservative who had signed all the earlier PNAC letters, as Zelikow's successor.[121]

Despite the restrictions on her room to maneuver, Rice has tried to help strengthen Abbas at the expense of Hamas. But the lobby has limited her effectiveness on that front as well. Specifically, President Bush decided in late

January 2007 to give Abbas $86 million to beef up his security forces. But Congresswoman Nita Lowey (D-NY), a stalwart defender of Israel and the chair of an important appropriations subcommittee, held up the request.[122] Another pro-Israel lawmaker, Anthony Weiner, wrote to Rice and asked her to withdraw the requested money.[123] Morton Klein, the president of the Zionist Organization of America, weighed in, saying that Bush "should be as tough on Abbas as he is on Hamas and al Qaeda."[124]

Klein's uncompromising views on Abbas were shared by many Jewish leaders.[125] They were especially upset with Abbas for agreeing in February 2007 to join a unity government with Hamas, even though the Palestinian president made it clear that he remained committed to negotiating a two-state settlement and living in peace with Israel. AIPAC tried to push Congress to make it impossible for the U.S. government to deal with anyone in the unity government, Abbas included; but that effort failed.[126] To mollify Lowey, the administration reduced the requested amount to $59 million and stipulated that it would be used only for training, purchasing nonlethal equipment, and improving security at a critical crossing point between Israel and Gaza. Lowey consented to this arrangement and the money was authorized.[127]

Nevertheless, the Bush administration's efforts to isolate and marginalize Hamas backfired in June 2007, when Hamas preempted the American attempt to strengthen Fatah's security forces by driving them from Gaza and seizing power there. In a belated effort to bolster Abbas, Israel has promised to release Palestinian prisoners as well as frozen Palestinian tax revenues, and Jerusalem and Washington have lifted some economic restrictions. But there is no sign that Israel will give the Palestinian leader the one thing he needs to establish his authority and trump the rejectionists: the realistic prospect of a viable state. Thus, the conflict will continue to fester, doing further damage to America's position in the Arab and Islamic world.

CONCLUSION

Absent the lobby, the Bush administration almost certainly would have been much more self-interested and hard-nosed in pushing for peace between Israel and the Palestinians. After all, the United States has a rich history, especially in recent years, of using various tools to force other states to change their behavior to suit America's interests. Washington extracted repeated concessions from Soviet leaders as the Soviet Union broke up, and it later pressed Ukraine, Kazakhstan, and Belarus to give up their nuclear arsenals. A similar effort eventually persuaded Libya to give up its own weapons of mass destruction programs in exchange for a lifting of extensive economic sanctions. The Clinton administration fought an intense air war to force Serbia to withdraw from Kosovo in 1999, and the Bush administration has pressured numerous countries to reject the convention establishing an International Criminal Court. And as we discuss at length in Chapter 10, the United States has gone to considerable lengths to convince Iran to give up its own nuclear ambitions. Putting pressure on Israel, the Palestinians, and the relevant Arab states in order to reach a final peace arrangement would hardly be inconsistent with America's conduct on other issues.

The United States has enormous potential leverage at its disposal for dealing with Israel and the Palestinians. It could threaten to cut off all economic and diplomatic support for Israel. If that were not enough, it would have little difficulty lining up international support to isolate Israel, much the way South Africa was singled out and shunned at the end of the last century. Regarding the Palestinians, the United States could hold out the promise of fulfilling their dream of a viable state in the Occupied Territories coupled with massive long-term economic aid. In return, the Palestinians would have to end all terrorism against Israel. Given the political divisions within Israel and the often dysfunctional Palestinian leadership, as well as the presence of violent rejectionists on both sides, achieving a final settlement would not be easy. But doing nothing, or backing Israel so consistently, has not made things better. On the contrary, this policy has almost certainly made things worse for Palestinians and Israelis alike and continues to erode America's reputation in the world and make it more difficult to deal with urgent issues like Iran and Iraq.

It might be argued that this analysis is unrealistic given Israel's generally favorable image in the eyes of many Americans. In this view, the real reason Bush has backed Israel against the Palestinians is that U.S. public opinion strongly favors Israel. The president, in short, is just responding to the will of the people. We have seen this claim before—it is the heart of the moral rationale for the special relationship between the United States and Israel. Yet this interpretation ignores the evidence that the American people would be willing to put pressure on Israel if it were part of a larger peace deal. Although U.S. surveys show greater sympathy for Israel than for the Palestinians, they also reveal considerable support for a more evenhanded policy. For example, most Americans were generally supportive of Bush's efforts to be tough on Israel in the spring of 2002. A *Time*/CNN poll taken on April

10–11 found that 60 percent of Americans felt that U.S. aid to Israel should be cut off or reduced if Sharon refused to withdraw from the Palestinian areas he had recently occupied. Moreover, 75 percent of those surveyed thought that Powell should meet with Arafat when he visited Israel. Regarding Sharon, only 35 percent found him trustworthy, while 35 percent thought he was a warmonger, 20 percent saw him as a terrorist, and 25 percent considered him an enemy of the United States.[128]

One year later, a May 2003 poll conducted by the University of Maryland reported that over 60 percent of Americans would be willing to withhold aid to Israel if it resisted U.S. pressure to settle the conflict. That number rose to 70 percent among "politically active" Americans. Indeed, 73 percent said that the United States should not favor either side in the conflict. It is also worth noting that only 17 percent of respondents agreed with the claim made by Bush and Sharon that the Israeli-Palestinian conflict is "part of the war on terrorism." Instead, 54 percent viewed it "as a conflict between two national groups fighting over the same piece of land." The same survey showed that although most Americans did not know much about the Road Map, 55 percent had a "positive view" of it. When informed of its key elements, support rose to 74 percent.[129] Even a 2005 survey conducted by the ADL found that 78 percent of Americans believe that their government should favor neither Israel nor the Palestinians.[130]

Since September 11, the American people have been receptive to pressuring Israel when they believed that doing so would be in the U.S. national interest. President Bush has also recognized that getting the Palestinians a viable state of their own was the only way to end the Israeli-Palestinian conflict, and his administration has tried to advance that goal on several occasions. But neither public opinion nor presidential initiatives mattered very much, because the lobby has made it nearly impossible for the United States to put pressure on Israel to negotiate a settlement.

As we have seen, Bush formally endorsed the idea of a Palestinian state in the fall of 2001. In the spring of 2002, he called for Israel to withdraw its forces from several Palestinian areas in the West Bank and sent Secretary of State Colin Powell to the region to jump-start the peace process. That same summer, Bush launched the Road Map initiative, which was supposed to provide a clear timetable leading to an independent and democratic Palestinian state. The following year, Bush traveled to the Middle East to promote the Road Map. After the collapse in 2006 of the Israeli plan to impose a unilateral settlement on the Palestinians, the administration—with Secretary of State Condoleezza Rice in the lead—made a renewed effort to end the conflict.

In each case, the lobby moved quickly and effectively to neutralize the Bush administration's efforts. Groups in the lobby employed a variety of tactics: open letters, congressional resolutions, op-eds and press releases, and direct meetings between administration officials and the leaders of influential Jewish and evangelical groups. Sympathetic government officials, such as the NSC's Elliott Abrams, helped in these efforts, at times meeting with Israeli officials to thwart ongoing initiatives. Instead of using U.S. leverage to move toward peace (for example, by linking U.S. support to Israel's cooperation on the Road Map), Bush ended up instead backing Sharon's (and now Olmert's) chosen policy at every turn. As former national security adviser Brent Scowcroft declared in October 2004, Sharon had President Bush "wrapped around his little finger."[131]

Israel's ability to defy the United States—and even to get Washington to follow its preferred approach to dealing with the Palestinians—offers a classic illustration of interest group politics at work. Although public opinion polls show that the American people would support compelling Israel to offer the Palestinians a fair settlement, groups in the lobby—and especially its more hard-line elements—care more about this issue than the average American does. As a result, groups like AIPAC and the leaders of organizations like the Conference of Presidents can put disproportionate pressure on elected officials and their policy preferences are more likely to win out, even if they are bad for the United States as a whole and unintentionally harmful for Israel as well.

Maintaining U.S. support for Israel's policies against the Palestinians is a core goal of many groups in the lobby, but their objectives are not limited to that goal. They also want America to help Israel remain the dominant regional power. The Israeli government and pro-Israel groups in the United States have worked together to shape the Bush administration's policy toward Iraq, Syria, and Iran, as well as its grand scheme for reordering the Middle East. Let us now consider how the lobby and Israel influenced America's decision to invade Iraq in March 2003 in the hope that this bold stroke would lead to the democratization of the entire region.

8

IRAQ AND DREAMS OF TRANSFORMING THE MIDDLE EAST

Why did the United States invade Iraq? In *The Assassins' Gate: America in Iraq*, George Packer declares that "it still isn't possible to be sure, and this remains the most remarkable thing about the Iraq war." He quotes Richard Haass, the director of policy planning in the State Department during Bush's first term and now president of the Council on Foreign Relations, saying that he would "go to his grave not knowing the answer."[1]

In one sense, their uncertainty is understandable, because the decision to overthrow Saddam Hussein even now seems difficult to fathom. He was clearly a brutal tyrant with worrisome ambitions—including a desire to obtain WMD—but his own incompetence had put these dangerous objectives out of reach. His army had been routed in the 1991 Gulf War and further weakened by a decade of UN sanctions. As a result, Iraq's military power, never impressive except on paper, was a pushover by 2003. Intrusive UN inspections had eliminated Iraq's nuclear program and eventually led Saddam to destroy his biological and chemical weapons stockpiles as well. There were no convincing links between Saddam and Osama bin Laden (who were in fact hostile to each other), and bin Laden and his associates were in Afghanistan or Pakistan, not Iraq. Yet in the aftermath of 9/11, when one would have expected the United States to be focusing laserlike on al Qaeda, the Bush administration chose to invade a deteriorating country that had nothing to do with the attacks on the World Trade Center and the Pentagon and was already effectively contained. From this perspective, it *is* a deeply puzzling decision.

From another angle, however, the decision is not that hard to understand. The United States was the world's most powerful country, and there was never any doubt about its ability to oust Saddam if it so chose. The United States had not only won the long Cold War, it had also enjoyed a remarkable run of military successes after 1989: defeating Iraq handily in 1991, halting the Balkan bloodletting in 1995, and beating Serbia in 1999. The rapid ouster of the Taliban in the immediate aftermath of 9/11 reinforced an image of military invincibility and made it harder for skeptics on Iraq to convince others that going to war was unnecessary and unwise. Americans were also shocked and alarmed by 9/11, and many of their leaders were convinced that the United States could not allow even remote dangers to grow in an era when terrorists might acquire WMD. Those who favored war believed that toppling Saddam would convince other rogue states that America was simply too powerful to oppose and compel these regimes to conform to U.S. wishes instead. In the period before the war, in short, the United States was simultaneously powerful, confident of its military prowess, and deeply worried about its own security—a dangerous combination.[2]

These various elements form the strategic context in which the decision for war was made and help us understand some of the underlying forces that facilitated that choice. But there was another variable in the equation, and the war would almost certainly not have occurred had it been absent. That element was the Israel lobby, and especially a group of neoconservative policy makers and pundits who had been pushing the United States to attack Iraq since well before 9/11. The prowar faction believed that removing Saddam would improve America's and Israel's strategic position and launch a process of regional transformation that would benefit the United States and Israel alike. Israeli officials and former Israeli leaders supported these efforts, because they were eager to see the United States topple one of their main regional adversaries—and the man who had launched Scud missiles at Israel in 1991.

Pressure from Israel and the lobby was not the only factor behind the Bush administration's decision to attack Iraq in March 2003, but it was a critical element. Many Americans believe that this was a "war for oil" (or for corporations like Halliburton), but there is little direct evidence to support this claim and considerable evidence that casts doubt on it. Other observers blame political advisers such as the Republican strategist Karl Rove and suggest that the war was part of a Machiavellian scheme to keep the country on a war footing and thus ensure a lengthy period of Republican control. This view has a certain partisan appeal, but it too lacks supporting evidence and cannot explain why so many prominent Democrats supported going to war. Another interpretation views the war as the first step in a bold effort to transform the Middle East by spreading democracy. This view is correct, but as we will see, this remarkably ambitious scheme was inextricably linked to concerns about Israel's security.

In contrast to these alternative explanations, we argue that the war was motivated at least in good part by a desire to make Israel more secure. This was a controversial claim before the war started, but it is even more controversial now that Iraq has turned into a strategic disaster. To be clear, the individuals and groups that pushed for war believed it would benefit both Israel and the United States, and they certainly did not anticipate the debacle that ultimately occurred. Regardless, a proper account of the lobby's role in encouraging the war is ultimately a question of evidence, and there is considerable evidence that Israel and pro-Israel groups—especially the neoconservatives—played important roles in the decision to invade.

Before examining the evidence, however, it is worth noting that a number of knowledgeable and well-respected individuals have said openly that the war was linked with Israel's security. Philip Zelikow, a member of the president's Foreign Intelligence Advisory Board (2001–03), executive director of the 9/11 Commission, and counselor to Secretary of State Condoleezza Rice (2005–06), told a University of Virginia audience on September 10, 2002, that Saddam was not a direct threat to the United States. "The real threat," he argued, is "the threat against Israel." He went on to say, "And this is the threat that dare not speak its name, because the Europeans don't care deeply about that threat . . . And the American government doesn't want to lean too hard on it rhetorically, because it is not a popular sell."[3]

General Wesley Clark, the retired NATO commander and former presidential candidate, said in August 2002 that "those who favor this attack now will tell you candidly, and privately, that it is probably true that Saddam Hussein is no threat to the United States. But they are afraid that at some point he might decide if he had a nuclear weapon to use it against Israel."[4] In January 2003, a German journalist asked Ruth Wedgwood, a prominent neoconservative academic and a member of the influential Defense Policy Board (chaired by Richard Perle), why the journalist should support the war. I could "be impolite," Wedgwood said, "and remind Germany of its special relationship with Israel. Saddam presents an existential threat to Israel. That is simply true." Wedgwood did not justify the war by saying that Iraq posed a direct threat to Germany or the United States.[5]

A few weeks before the United States invaded Iraq, the journalist Joe Klein wrote in *Time* magazine, "A stronger Israel is very much embedded in the rationale for war with Iraq. It is a part of the argument that dare not speak its name, a fantasy quietly cherished by the neo-conservative faction in the Bush Administration and by many leaders of the American Jewish community."[6] Former Senator Ernest Hollings made a similar argument in May 2004. After noting that Iraq was not a direct threat to the United States, he asked why we invaded that country.[7] "The answer," which he said "everyone knows," is "because we want to secure our friend Israel." A number of Jewish groups promptly labeled Hollings an anti-Semite, with the ADL calling his comments "reminiscent of age-old, anti-Semitic canards about a Jewish conspiracy to control and manipulate government."[8] Hollings adamantly rejected the charge, noting that he had long been a staunch supporter of Israel and that he was simply stating the obvious, not making an untruthful claim. He demanded that his critics "apologize to me for talking about anti-Semitism."[9]

A handful of other public figures—Patrick Buchanan, Arnaud de Borch-grave, Maureen Dowd, Georgie Anne Geyer, Gary Hart, Chris Matthews, Congressman James P. Moran (D-VA), Robert Novak, Tim Russert, and General Anthony Zinni—either said or strongly hinted that pro-Israel hard-liners in the United States were the principal movers behind the Iraq war.[10] In Novak's case, he referred to the war well before it happened as "Sharon's war" and continues to do so today. "I am convinced," he said in April 2007, "that Israel made a large contribution to the decision to embark on this war. I know that on the eve of the war, Sharon said, in a closed conversation with senators, that if they could succeed in getting rid of Saddam Hussein, it would solve Israel's security problems."[11]

The connection between Israel and the Iraq war was widely recognized long before the fighting started. When the prospect of an American invasion was beginning to dominate the headlines in the fall of 2002, the journalist Michael Kinsley wrote that "the lack of public discussion about the role of Israel . . . is the proverbial elephant in the room: Everybody sees it, no one mentions it."[12] The reason for this reluctance, he observed, was fear of being labeled an anti-Semite. Two weeks before the war started, Nathan Guttman reported in *Ha'aretz* that "the voices linking Israel to the war are getting louder and louder. It is claimed the desire to help Israel is the major reason for President George Bush sending American soldiers to a superfluous war in the Gulf. And the voices come from all directions."[13]

A few days later, Bill Keller, who is now the executive editor of the *New York Times*, wrote, "The idea that this war is about Israel is persistent and more widely held than you may think."[14] Finally, in May 2005, two years after the war began, Barry Jacobs of the American Jewish Committee acknowledged that the belief that Israel and the neoconservatives were responsible for getting the United States to invade Iraq was "pervasive" in the U.S. intelligence community.[15]

Some will surely argue that anyone who suggests that concerns about Israel's security had a significant influence on the Bush administration's decision to invade Iraq is either an anti-Semite or a self-hating Jew. Such charges are both predictable and false. As we will now show, there is abundant evidence that Israel and the lobby played crucial roles in making that war happen. This is not to assert that either Israel or the lobby "controls" U.S. foreign policy; it is simply to say that they successfully pressed for a particular set of policies and were able, in a particular context, to achieve their objective. Had the circumstances been different, they would not have been able to get the United States to go to war. But without their efforts, America would probably not be in Iraq today.

ISRAEL AND THE IRAQ WAR

Israel has always considered Iraq an enemy, but it became especially concerned about Iraq in the mid-1970s, when France agreed to provide Saddam with a nuclear reactor. For good reason, Israel worried that Iraq might use the reactor as a stepping-stone to building nuclear weapons. Responding to the threat, in 1981, the Israelis bombed the Osirak reactor before it became operational.[16] Despite this setback, Iraq continued working on its nuclear program in dispersed and secret locations. This situation helps explain Israel's enthusiastic support for the first Gulf War in 1991; its main concern was not to push Iraqi troops out of Kuwait but to topple Saddam and especially to make sure that Iraq's nuclear program was dismantled.[17] Although the United States did not remove Saddam from power, the UN inspections regime imposed on Baghdad after the war reduced—but did not eliminate—Israel's concerns. In fact, *Ha'aretz* reported on February 26, 2001, that "Sharon believes that Iraq poses more of a threat to regional stability than Iran, due to the errant, irresponsible behavior of Saddam Hussein's regime."[18]

Sharon's comments notwithstanding, by early 2002, when it was becoming increasingly apparent that the Bush administration was thinking seriously about another war against Iraq, some Israeli leaders told U.S. officials that they thought Iran was a greater threat.[19] They were not opposed to toppling Saddam, however, and Israel's leaders, who are rarely reticent when it comes to giving their American counterparts advice, never tried to convince the Bush administration not to go to war against Iraq. Nor did the Israeli government ever try to mobilize its supporters in the United States to lobby against the invasion. On the contrary, Israeli leaders were worried only that the United States might lose sight of the Iranian threat in its pursuit of Saddam. Once they realized that the Bush administration was countenancing a bolder scheme, one that called for winning quickly in Iraq and then dealing with Iran and Syria, they began to push vigorously for an American invasion.

In short, Israel did not initiate the campaign for war against Iraq. As will become clear, it was the neoconservatives in the United States who conceived that idea and were principally responsible for pushing it forward in the wake of September 11. But Israel did join forces with the neoconservatives to help sell the war to the Bush administration and the American people, well before the president had made the final decision to invade. Indeed, Israeli leaders worried constantly in the months before the war that President Bush might decide not to go to war after all, and they did what they could to ensure Bush did not get cold feet.

The Israelis began their efforts in the spring of 2002, a few months before the Bush administration launched its own campaign to sell the Iraq war to the American public. Former Israeli Prime Minister Benjamin Netanyahu came to Washington in mid-April and met with U.S. senators and the editors of the *Washington Post*, among others, to warn them that Saddam was developing nuclear weapons that could be delivered against the American homeland in suitcases or satchels.[20] A few weeks later, Ra'anan Gissen, Sharon's spokesman, told a Cleveland reporter that "if Saddam Hussein is not stopped now, five years from now, six years from now, we will have to deal with an Iraq that is armed with nuclear weapons, with an Iraq that has delivery systems for weapons of mass destruction."[21]

In mid-May, Shimon Peres, the former Israeli prime minister now serving as foreign minister, appeared on CNN, where he said that "Saddam Hussein is as dangerous as bin Laden," and the United States "cannot sit and wait" while he builds a nuclear arsenal. Instead, Peres insisted, it was time to topple the Iraqi leader.[22] A month later, Ehud Barak, another former Israeli prime minister, wrote an op-ed in the *Washington Post* recommending that the Bush administration "should, first of all, focus on Iraq and the removal of Saddam Hussein. Once he is gone there will be a different Arab world."[23]

On August 12, 2002, Sharon told the Foreign Affairs and Defense Committee of the Knesset that Iraq "is the greatest danger facing Israel."[24] Then, on August 16, ten days before Vice President Cheney kicked off the campaign for war with a speech to the Veterans of Foreign Wars convention in Nashville, Tennessee, several newspapers and television and radio networks (including *Ha'aretz*, the *Washington Post*, CNN, and CBS News) reported that Israel was urging the United States not to delay an attack on Iraq. Sharon told the Bush administration that postponing the operation "will not create a more convenient environment for action in the future." Putting off an attack, Ra'anan Gissen said, would "only give him (Saddam) more of an opportunity to accelerate his program of weapons of mass destruction." Foreign Minister Peres told CNN that "the problem today is not if, but when." Postponing an attack would be a grave mistake, he said, because Saddam would be better armed down the road. Deputy Defense Minister Weizman Shiry offered a similar view, warning, "If the Americans do not do this now, it will be harder to do it in the future. In a year or two, Saddam Hussein will be further along in developing weapons of mass destruction." Perhaps CBS best captured what was going on in the headline for its story: "Israel to US: Don't Delay Iraq Attack."[25]

Peres and Sharon both made sure to emphasize that they "did not want to be seen as urging the United States to act and that America should act according to its own judgment."[26] Israeli leaders—and many of their supporters in the United States—were well aware that some American commentators, most notably Patrick Buchanan, had argued that the driving force behind the 1991 Gulf War was "the Israeli Defense Ministry and its amen corner in the United States."[27] Denying any responsibility made good political sense, but there is no question—based on their own public comments—that by August 2002 Israel's leaders saw Saddam as a threat to the Jewish state and were encouraging the Bush administration to launch a war to remove him from power.

News stories around the same time also reported that "Israeli intelligence officials have gathered evidence that Iraq is speeding up efforts to produce biological and chemical weapons."[28] Peres told CNN that "we think and know that he [Saddam] is on his way to acquiring a nuclear option."[29] *Ha'aretz* reported that Saddam had given an "order . . . to Iraq's Atomic Energy Commission last week to speed up its work."[30] Israel was feeding these alarming reports about Iraq's WMD programs to Washington at a time when, by Sharon's own reckoning, "strategic coordination between Israel and the U.S. has reached unprecedented dimensions."[31] Following the invasion and the revelation that there were no WMD in Iraq, the Senate Intelligence Committee and the Israeli Knesset released separate reports revealing that much of the intelligence Israel gave to the Bush administration was false. As one retired Israeli general put it, "Israeli intelligence was a full partner to the picture presented by American and British intelligence regarding Iraq's non-conventional capabilities."[32]

Of course, Israel is hardly the first state to push another country to take a costly or risky action on its behalf. States facing external dangers often try to pass the buck to others, and the United States has a rich tradition of similar behavior itself.[33] It backed Saddam Hussein in the 1980s in order to help contain the threat from revolutionary Iran, and it armed and backed the Afghan mujahideen following the Soviet invasion of that country in 1979. The United States did not send its own troops to fight these wars; it merely did what it could to help others—who had their own reasons for fighting—do the heavy lifting.

Given their understandable desire to have the United States eliminate a regional rival, it is not surprising that Israeli leaders were distressed when President Bush decided to seek UN Security Council authorization for war in September 2002, and even more worried when Saddam agreed to let UN inspectors back into Iraq. These developments troubled Israel's leaders because they seemed to reduce the likelihood of war. Foreign Minister Peres told reporters, "The campaign against Saddam Hussein is a must. Inspections and inspectors are good for decent people, but dishonest people can overcome easily inspections and inspectors."[34] On a visit to Moscow in late September, Sharon made it clear to Russian President Vladimir Putin, who was leading the charge for new inspections, that it was too late for them to be effective.[35] Peres became so frustrated with the UN process in the following months that in mid-February 2003 he lashed out at France by questioning its status as a permanent member of the Security Council.[36]

Israel's adamant opposition to inspections put it in a lonely and awkward position, as Marc Perelman made clear in an article in the *Forward* in mid-September 2002: "Saddam Hussein's surprise acceptance of 'unconditional' United Nations weapons inspections put Israel on the hot seat this week, forcing it into the open as the only nation actively supporting the Bush administration's goal of Iraqi regime change."[37]

Pressing ahead in the face of UN diplomacy, Israelis portrayed Saddam in the direst terms, often comparing him to Adolf Hitler. If the West did not stand up to Iraq, they claimed, it would be making the same mistake it made with Nazi Germany in the 1930s. Shlomo Avineri, a prominent Israeli scholar, wrote in the *Los Angeles Times* that "all who condemn the 1930s appeasement of Germany should reflect long and hard on whether a failure to act today against Iraq will one day be viewed the same way."[38] The implication was unmistakable: anyone who opposed invading Iraq—or, as we have seen, pushed Israel to negotiate with the Palestinians—was an appeaser, just like Neville Chamberlain, and bound to be regarded as such by future generations. The *Jerusalem Post* was especially hawkish, frequently running editorials and op-eds favoring the war and rarely running pieces arguing against it.[39] Indeed, it went so far as to editorialize that "ousting Saddam is the linchpin of the war on terrorism, without which it is impossible to begin in earnest, let alone win."[40]

Other Israeli public figures echoed Peres and Sharon's advocacy for war instead of diplomatic wrangling. Former Prime Minister Ehud Barak wrote a *New York Times* op-ed in early September 2002 claiming that "Saddam Hussein's nuclear-weapons program provides the urgent need for his removal." He went on to warn that "the greatest risk now lies in inaction."[41] His predecessor, Benjamin Netanyahu, published a similar piece a few weeks later in the *Wall Street Journal* titled "The Case for Toppling Saddam." Netanyahu declared, "Today nothing less than dismantling his regime will do," adding that "I believe I speak for the overwhelming majority of Israelis in supporting a pre-emptive strike against Saddam's regime," which he claimed was "feverishly trying to acquire nuclear weapons."[42]

Netanyahu's influence, of course, extended well beyond writing op-eds and appearing on television. Having gone to high school, college, and graduate school in the United States, he speaks fluent English and is not only familiar with how the American political system works but operates skillfully in it. He has close ties with neoconservatives inside and outside of the Bush administration, and he has extensive contacts on Capitol Hill, where he has either spoken or testified on numerous occasions.[43] Barak is also well connected with American policy makers, politicians, security experts, and pundits.

The Israeli government's war fervor did not diminish in the months before the fighting started. *Ha'aretz*, for example, ran a story on February 17, 2003, titled "Enthusiastic IDF Awaits War in Iraq," which said that Israel's "military and political leadership yearns for war in Iraq." Ten days later James Bennet wrote a story in the *New York Times* with the headline "Israel Says War on Iraq Would Benefit the Region." The *Forward* published a piece on March 7, 2003, titled "Jerusalem Frets as U.S. Battles Iraq War Delays," which made it clear that Israel's leaders were hoping for war sooner rather than later.[44]

Given all this activity, it is unsurprising that Bill Clinton recounted in 2006 that "every Israeli politician I knew" believed that Saddam Hussein was so great a threat that he should be removed even if he did not have WMD.[45] Nor was the desire for war confined to Israel's leaders. Apart from

Kuwait, which Saddam conquered in 1990, Israel was the only country out-side of the United States where a majority of politicians and the public en-thusiastically favored war. A poll taken in early 2002 found that 58 percent of Israeli Jews believed that "Israel should encourage the United States to attack Iraq."[46] Another poll taken a year later in February 2003 found that 77.5 percent of Israeli Jews wanted the United States to invade Iraq.[47] Even in Tony Blair's Britain, a poll taken just before the war revealed that 51 per-cent of the respondents opposed it, while only 39 percent supported it.[48]

This rather unusual situation prompted Gideon Levy of Ha'aretz to ask, "Why is it that in England 50,000 people have demonstrated against the war in Iraq, whereas in Israel no one has? Why is it that in Israel there is no pub-lic debate about whether the war is necessary?" He went on to say, "Israel is the only country in the West whose leaders support the war unreservedly and where no alternative opinion is voiced."[49]

Israel's enthusiasm for war eventually led some of its allies in America to tell Israeli officials to damp down their hawkish rhetoric, lest the war look like it was being fought for Israel.[50] In the fall of 2002, for example, a group of American political consultants known as the Israel Project circulated a six-page memorandum to key Israelis and pro-Israel leaders in the United States. The memo was titled "Talking about Iraq" and was intended as a guide for public statements about the war. "If your goal is regime change, you must be much more careful with your language because of the potential backlash. You do not want Americans to believe that the war on Iraq is being waged to protect Israel rather than to protect America."[51]

Reflecting that same concern on the eve of the war, Sharon, according to several reports, told Israeli diplomats and politicians to keep quiet about a possible war in Iraq and certainly not to say anything that made it appear that Israel was pushing the Bush administration to topple Saddam. The Is-raeli leader was worried by the growing perception that Israel was advocat-ing a U.S. invasion of Iraq. In fact, Israel was; it just did not want its position to be widely known.[52]

THE LOBBY AND THE IRAQ WAR

The driving force behind the Iraq war was a small band of neoconservatives who had long favored the energetic use of American power to reshape criti-cal areas of the world. They had advocated toppling Saddam since the mid-1990s and believed this step would benefit the United States and Israel alike.[53] This group included prominent officials in the Bush administration such as Paul Wolfowitz and Douglas Feith, the number two and three civilians in the Pentagon; Richard Perle, Kenneth Adelman, and James Woolsey, members of the influential Defense Policy Board; Scooter Libby, the vice president's chief of staff; John Bolton, undersecretary of state for arms control and international security, and his special assistant, David Wurmser; and Elliott Abrams, who is in charge of Middle East policy at the National Security Council. It also included a handful of well-known journalists like Robert Kagan, Charles Krauthammer, William Kristol, and William Safire.

The appointment of a number of neoconservatives to top policy positions was seen by Israelis and their American allies as a very positive development. When Wolfowitz was selected to be deputy defense secretary in January 2001, the *Jerusalem Post* reported that "the Jewish and pro-Israel communities are jumping with joy."[54] In the spring of 2002, the *Forward* pointed out that Wolfowitz is "known as the most hawkishly pro-Israel voice in the Administration," and it selected him later in 2002 as the first among fifty notables who "have consciously pursued Jewish activism."[55] At about the same time, JINSA gave him its Henry M. Jackson Distinguished Service Award for promoting a strong partnership between Israel and the United States, and the *Jerusalem Post*, describing Wolfowitz as "devoutly pro-Israel," named him its "Man of the Year" in 2003.[56]

Feith's role in shaping the case for war should also be understood in the context of his long-standing commitment to Israel and his prior association with hard-line groups there. Feith has close ties with key organizations in the lobby like the Jewish Institute for National Security Affairs and the Zionist Organization of America. He wrote articles in the 1990s supporting the settlements and arguing that Israel should retain the Occupied Territories.[57] More important, as we noted in Chapter 4, Feith was a coauthor, along with Perle and Wurmser, of the famous "Clean Break" report in June 1996.[58] Written under the auspices of a right-wing Israeli think tank for incoming Israeli Prime Minister Benjamin Netanyahu, the report recommended, among other things, that Netanyahu "focus on removing Saddam Hussein from power in Iraq—an important Israeli strategic objective in its own right." It also called for Israel to take steps to reorder the entire Middle East. Netanyahu did not implement their advice, but Feith, Perle, and Wurmser were soon advocating that the Bush administration pursue those same goals. This situation prompted the *Ha'aretz* columnist Akiva Eldar to warn that Feith and Perle "are walking a fine line between their loyalty to American governments . . . and Israeli interests."[59] As George Packer notes in *The Assassins' Gate*, "For Feith and Wurmser, the security of Israel was probably the prime mover" behind their support for the war.[60]

John Bolton and Scooter Libby were staunch supporters of Israel as well. As America's ambassador to the UN, Bolton consistently and enthusiastically defended Israel's interests. So much so, in fact, that in May 2006, the Israeli ambassador to the UN jokingly described Bolton as "a secret member of Israel's own team at the United Nations." He went on to say that "the secret is out. We really are not just five diplomats. We are at least six including John Bolton."[61] When Bolton's controversial reappointment to that position became an issue later in 2006, pro-Israel groups weighed in on Bolton's side.[62] Regarding Libby, the *Forward* reported when he left the White House in the fall of 2005 that "Israeli officials liked Libby. They described him as an important contact who was accessible, genuinely interested in Israel-related issues and very sympathetic to their cause."[63]

Neoconservatives outside the Bush administration are every bit as devoted to Israel as are their compatriots in the government. Consider the comments that the columnist Charles Krauthammer made in Jerusalem on June 10, 2002, after receiving the Guardian of Zion Award from Bar-Ilan University.[64] The theme of his talk was characterizing Israel's participation in the Oslo peace process as an example of misguided Jewish messianism. In his remarks, Krauthammer explicitly identified himself with Israel—indeed, as Israeli. At one point he observed that "thirty-five years ago today the Six-Day war ended. It seemed like a new era . . . Jerusalem had been re-united, the Temple Mount was ours, Israel." He went on to say, "My thesis tonight is that many of our troubles today, as a people and as a Jewish state, are rooted precisely in this new Messianic enthusiasm." Krauthammer, like virtually all other neoconservative pundits, was a relentless advocate for war right up until the invasion.

Although many of the prominent neoconservatives were Jewish Americans with strong attachments to Israel, some of the leading members of the prowar party were not. In addition to John Bolton, the signatories of the open letters to Presidents Bush and Clinton sponsored by the Project for the New American Century included gentiles such as former CIA director James Woolsey and former Secretary of Education William Bennett. Woolsey was particularly obsessed with proving that Saddam was responsible for 9/11, and he devoted considerable effort trying to confirm an early report that Mohammed Atta, one of the 9/11 hijackers, had met with an Iraqi intelligence agent in Prague. The story was implausible and is widely believed to be false, but Woolsey and Vice President Dick Cheney both invoked it to bolster the case for war.[65]

The neoconservatives were not the only part of the lobby pushing for war with Iraq. Key leaders of the major pro-Israel organizations lent their voices to the campaign for war. Of course, many of the neoconservatives themselves had close ties to these organizations. In mid-September 2002, when the selling of the war was just getting under way, Michelle Goldberg wrote in *Salon* that "mainstream Jewish groups and leaders are now among the strongest supporters of an American invasion of Baghdad."[66] This same point was made in a *Forward* editorial written well after the fall of Baghdad: "As President Bush attempted to sell the . . . war in Iraq, America's most important Jewish organizations rallied as one to his defense. In statement after statement community leaders stressed the need to rid the world of Saddam Hussein and his weapons of mass destruction. Some groups went even further, arguing that the removal of the Iraqi leader would represent a significant step toward bringing peace to the Middle East and winning America's war on terrorism." The editorial goes on to say that "concern for Israel's safety rightfully factored into the deliberations of the main Jewish groups."[67]

Although there was hardly any opposition to the war among the major Jewish organizations, there was disagreement about how vocal they should be in backing it. The main concern was the fear that too open support for an invasion would make it look like the war was being fought for Israel's sake.[68] Nonetheless, the Jewish Council for Public Affairs and the Conference of Presidents of Major American Jewish Organizations voted to support the use of force against Iraq ("as a last resort") in the fall of 2002, and some prominent figures in the lobby went further.[69] Among the most outspoken proponents of the invasion was Mortimer Zuckerman, the chairman of the Conference of Presidents, who made frequent public statements promoting the war. In late August 2002, he wrote in *U.S. News & World Report*, where he is editor in chief, "Those who predict dire results if we try to unseat Saddam simply refuse to understand—as President Bush manifestly does—that if we opt to live with a nightmare, it will only get worse. Much worse. The best medicine here, in other words, is preventive medicine."[70]

Jack Rosen, the president of the American Jewish Congress, and Rabbi David Saperstein, the head of the Religious Action Center of Reform Judaism, were also enthusiastic war hawks. Saperstein, who is known for his liberal political views and whom the *Washington Post* called "the quintessential religious lobbyist on Capitol Hill," said in September 2002 that "the Jewish Community would want to see a forceful resolution to the threat that Saddam Hussein poses."[71] *Jewish Week*, an influential newspaper in the greater New York area, backed the war as well. Gary Rosenblatt, its editor and publisher, wrote an editorial in mid-December 2002 in which he emphasized that "Washington's imminent war on Saddam Hussein is not only an opportunity to rid the world of a dangerous tyrant who presents a particularly horrific threat to Israel." He went on to say that "when a despot announces his evil intentions, believe him. That's one of the lessons we should have learned from Hitler and the Holocaust. What's more, the Torah instructs that when your enemy seeks to kill you, kill him first. Self-defense is not permitted; it is commanded."[72] Organizations like AIPAC and the ADL also supported the war, but they did so with minimum fanfare.

Now that the war has turned into a disaster, supporters of Israel sometimes argue that AIPAC, which is the most visible group in the lobby, did not back the invasion.[73] But this claim fails the common sense test, as AIPAC usually supports what Israel wants, and Israel certainly wanted the United States to invade Iraq. Nathan Guttman made this very connection in his reporting on AIPAC's annual conference in the spring of 2003, shortly after the war started: "AIPAC is wont to support whatever is good for Israel, and so long as Israel supports the war, so too do the thousands of AIPAC lobbyists who convened in the American capital."[74] AIPAC executive director Howard Kohr's statement to the *New York Sun* in January 2003 is even more revealing, as he acknowledged that "'quietly' lobbying Congress to approve the use of force in Iraq" was one of "AIPAC's successes over the past year."[75] And in a lengthy *New Yorker* profile of Steven J. Rosen, who was AIPAC's policy director during the run-up to the Iraq war, Jeffrey Goldberg reported that "AIPAC lobbied Congress in favor of the Iraq war."[76]

AIPAC has remained a firm supporter of the U.S. presence in Iraq. In the fall of 2003, when the Bush administration was having difficulty convincing Senate Democrats to allocate more money for the war, Senate Republicans asked AIPAC to lobby their Democratic colleagues to support the funding request. AIPAC representatives talked to some Democratic senators and the money was approved.[77] When Bush gave a speech at AIPAC in May 2004 in which he defended his Iraq policy, he received twenty-three standing ovations.[78] At AIPAC's 2007 conference, by which time American public opinion on the war had soured, Vice President Cheney made the case for staying the course in Iraq. According to David Horovitz of the *Jerusalem Post*, he received "considerable applause."[79] And John Boehner, the House minority leader, received a standing ovation when he said, "Who does not believe that failure in Iraq is not a direct threat to the state of Israel? The consequences of failure in Iraq are so ominous for the United States that you can't even begin to think about it." By contrast, when Speaker of the House Nancy Pelosi criticized the Bush administration's "surge" strategy, many in the audience booed.[80]

AIPAC is not the only major group in the lobby to stick with Bush on Iraq, or at least not come out against the war. As the *Forward* reported in March 2007, "Most Jewish organizations have refused to speak out against the war, and at times they displayed support for the administration."[81] This behavior is especially striking given the attitudes of most American Jews toward the war itself. According to a 2007 Gallup Organization study based on the results of thirteen polls taken since 2005, American Jews are significantly more opposed to the Iraq war (77 percent) than the general American public (52 percent).[82] With respect to Iraq, the larger and wealthier pro-Israel organizations are clearly out of step with the broader population of American Jews. A few Jewish organizations, such as the Tikkun Community and Jewish Voice for Peace, opposed the war before it started and continue to do so today. But as noted in Chapter 4, these groups are neither as well funded nor as influential as organizations like AIPAC.

This gap between the political positions taken by key groups in the lobby and the public attitudes of American Jews underscores an essential point that deserves special emphasis. Although prominent Israeli leaders, the neoconservatives, and many of the lobby's leaders were eager for the United States to invade Iraq, the broader American Jewish community was not.[83] In fact, Samuel Freedman, a journalism professor at Columbia University, reported just after the war started that "a compilation of nationwide opinion polls by the Pew Research Center shows that Jews are less supportive of the Iraq war than the population at large, 52% to 62%."[84] It would therefore be a cardinal error to attribute the war in Iraq to "Jewish influence," or to "blame the Jews" for the war. Rather, the war was due in large part to the *lobby's* influence, and especially its neoconservative wing. And the lobby, as we have emphasized before, is not always representative of the larger community for which it often claims to speak.

SELLING THE WAR TO A SKEPTICAL AMERICA

The neoconservatives began their campaign to use military force to topple Saddam well before Bush became president. They caused a stir in early 1998 by organizing two letters to President Clinton calling for Saddam's removal from power. The first letter (January 26, 1998) was written under the auspices of the Project for the New American Century and was signed by Elliott Abrams, John Bolton, Robert Kagan, William Kristol, Richard Perle, Donald Rumsfeld, and Paul Wolfowitz, among others. The second letter (February 19, 1998) was written under the auspices of the Committee for Peace and Security in the Gulf, the organization set up in 1990 by Perle, Ann Lewis (the former political director of the Democratic National Committee), and former Congressman Stephen J. Solarz (D-NY), to lobby for the first Gulf War. It was signed by the individuals mentioned above who signed the first letter as well as Douglas Feith, Michael Ledeen, Bernard Lewis, Martin Peretz, and David Wurmser, just to name a few.[85]

In addition to these two high-profile letters, the neoconservatives and their allies in the lobby worked assiduously in 1998 to get Congress to pass the Iraq Liberation Act, which mandated that "it should be the policy of the United States to support efforts to remove the regime headed by Saddam Hussein from power in Iraq and to promote the emergence of a democratic government to replace that regime." The neoconservatives were especially enthusiastic about this legislation not only because it sanctioned regime change in Iraq, but also because it provided $97 million to fund groups committed to overthrowing Saddam.[86] The main group they had in mind was the Iraqi National Congress (INC), which was headed by their close associate, Ahmed Chalabi. Perle, Wolfowitz, and Woolsey all lobbied hard on behalf of the legislation, as did JINSA.[87] The act passed in the House by a vote of 360–38 and by unanimous consent in the Senate. President Clinton then signed it on October 31, 1998.

Clinton had little use for the Iraq Liberation Act, but he could not afford to veto it because he was facing midterm elections and impeachment.[88] Both he and his key advisers held Chalabi in low regard, and they did little to implement the law. In fact, by the time Clinton left office, he had spent hardly any of the allotted money for opposition groups like the INC. The president did pay lip service to the goal of ousting Saddam but did little to make it happen, and he was certainly not considering using the U.S. military to drive the Iraqi dictator from power.[89] In short, the neoconservatives were unable to sell the idea of war against Iraq during the Clinton years, although they did succeed in making regime change in Baghdad an official goal of the U.S. government.

Nor were they able to generate much enthusiasm for invading Iraq in the early months of the Bush administration, even though a number of prominent neoconservatives held important positions in the new government and had lost none of their enthusiasm for the enterprise. Richard Perle later said that the advocates for toppling Saddam were losing the arguments inside the administration during this early period.[90] In fact, in March 2001, the *New York Times* reported that "some Republicans" were complaining that Rumsfeld and Wolfowitz "are failing to live up to their pre-election advocacy of stepping up efforts to overthrow President Hussein." At the same time, the *Washington Times* ran an editorial titled "Have Hawks Become Doves?" The text of that editorial was the January 26, 1998, PNAC letter to President Clinton.[91]

Given the publicity and the controversy surrounding two books published in 2004—Richard Clarke's *Against All Enemies* and Ron Suskind's *The Price of Loyalty*—one might think Bush and Cheney were bent on invading Iraq from the moment they assumed office in late January 2001.[92] This interpretation, however, is wrong. They were certainly interested in toppling Saddam, but there is no evidence in the public record showing that Bush and Cheney were seriously contemplating war against Iraq before 9/11. Bush did not advocate using force against Saddam during the 2000 campaign, and he made it clear to Bob Woodward that he was not thinking about going to war against Saddam before 9/11.[93] Interestingly, his main foreign policy adviser in the campaign, Condoleezza Rice, wrote a prominent article in *Foreign Affairs* in early 2000 saying that the United States could live with a nuclear-armed Iraq. Rice declared that Saddam's "conventional military power" had been "severely weakened" and said "there need be no sense of panic" about his regime.[94]

Vice President Cheney maintained throughout the 1990s that conquering Iraq would be a major strategic blunder and he did not sign either of the letters calling for military action against Saddam that the neoconservatives sent to President Clinton in early 1998.[95] In the closing stages of the 2000 campaign, he defended the 1991 decision not to go to Baghdad—in which he played a major role as secretary of defense—and said that "we want to maintain our current posture vis-à-vis Iraq."[96] There is no evidence to suggest that either his thinking or that of the president had changed significantly by early 2001.[97] Secretary of Defense Rumsfeld, who had signed both of the 1998 letters to President Clinton, appears to have been the only top-tier Bush administration official who may have favored war with Iraq upon taking office. None of the other groups that are sometimes blamed for the war—such as oil companies, weapons manufacturers, Christian Zionists, or defense contractors like Kellogg Brown & Root—were making noise about invading Iraq at this time. In the beginning, the neoconservatives were largely alone.

Yet as important as the neoconservatives were as the chief architects of the war, they had been unable to persuade either Clinton or Bush to support an invasion. They needed help to achieve their aim, and that help arrived on 9/11. Specifically, the events of that tragic day led Bush and Cheney to reverse course and become strong proponents of a preventive war to topple Saddam. Robert Kagan put the point well in an interview with George Packer: "September 11 is the turning point. Not anything else. This is not what Bush was on September 10." The neoconservatives—most notably Scooter Libby, Paul Wolfowitz, and the Princeton historian Bernard Lewis—played a critical role in persuading the president and vice president to favor war. For them, 9/11 was the new context to sell their old view of American foreign policy. Possibly their greatest advantage was that they had, in Kagan's words, "a ready-made approach to the world" at a time when both the president and the vice president were trying to make sense of an unprecedented disaster that seemed to call for radically new ways of thinking about international politics.[98]

Wolfowitz's behavior is especially revealing. At a key meeting with Bush at Camp David on September 15, 2001, Wolfowitz advocated attacking Iraq before Afghanistan, even though there was no evidence that Saddam was involved in the attacks on the United States and bin Laden was known to be in Afghanistan.[99] Wolfowitz was so insistent on conquering Iraq that five days later Cheney had to tell him to "stop agitating for targeting Saddam."[100] According to one Republican lawmaker, he "was like a parrot bringing [Iraq] up all the time. It was getting on the President's nerves."[101] Bush rejected Wolfowitz's advice and chose to go after Afghanistan instead, but war with Iraq was now regarded as a serious possibility and the president tasked U.S. military planners on November 21, 2001, with developing concrete plans for an invasion.[102]

Other neoconservatives were also hard at work within the corridors of power. Although we do not have the full story yet, there is considerable evidence that scholars like Bernard Lewis and Fouad Ajami of Johns Hopkins University played an important role in convincing Vice President Cheney to favor war against Iraq.[103] Indeed, Jacob Weisberg, the editor of Slate, describes Lewis as "perhaps the most significant intellectual influence behind the invasion of Iraq."[104] Cheney's views were also heavily influenced by neoconservatives on his staff like Eric Edelman and John Hannah. But surely the most important influence on the vice president was his chief of staff, Scooter Libby, who was one of the most powerful individuals in the administration and whose views on Iraq were similar to those of his close friend and longtime mentor, Paul Wolfowitz.[105] Shortly after 9/11, the New

York Times reported that "some senior administration officials, led by Paul D. Wolfowitz . . . and I. Lewis Libby . . . are pressing for the earliest and broadest military campaign against not only the Osama bin Laden network in Afghanistan, but also against other suspected terrorist bases in Iraq and in Lebanon's Bekka region."[106] Of course, the vice president's position helped convince President Bush by early 2002 that the United States would probably have to take Saddam out.[107]

Two other considerations show how profoundly important the neoconservatives inside the administration were for making the Iraq war happen. First, it is no exaggeration to say that they were not just determined; they were obsessed with removing Saddam from power. As one senior administration figure put it in January 2003, "I do believe certain people have grown theological about this. It's almost a religion—that it will be the end of our society if we don't take action now." A *Washington Post* journalist described Colin Powell returning from White House meetings during the run-up to the Iraq war, "rolling his eyes" and saying, "Jeez, what a fixation about Iraq." Bob Woodward reports that Kenneth Adelman, a member of the Defense Policy Board, "said he had worried to death as time went on and support seemed to wane that there would be no war."[108]

Second, there was little enthusiasm for going to war against Iraq inside the State Department, the intelligence community, or the uniformed military. Although Secretary of State Powell ultimately supported the president's decision for war, he believed that it was a bad idea. The rank and file in his department shared his skepticism. There were two key outliers in the State Department, however—John Bolton and David Wurmser, both prominent neoconservatives who had close ties to the White House. George Tenet, the head of the CIA, also supported the White House on Iraq, but he was not a forceful advocate for war. Indeed, few individuals within the intelligence community found the case for war convincing, which is why, as discussed below, the neoconservatives established their own intelligence units. The military, especially the army, was filled with Iraq skeptics. General Eric Shinseki, the army chief of staff, was severely criticized by Wolfowitz (who dismissed Shinseki's estimate of the necessary troop levels required for the occupation as "wildly off the mark") and later Rumsfeld for expressing doubts about the war plan.[109] The war hawks within the administration were mainly high-level civilians in the White House and the Pentagon, almost all of whom were neoconservatives.

They lost no time making the case that invading Iraq was essential to winning the war on terrorism. Their efforts were partly aimed at keeping pressure on Bush and partly intended to overcome opposition to the war inside and outside of the government. On September 13, 2001, JINSA put out a press release titled "This Goes Beyond Bin Laden," which maintained that "a long investigation to prove Osama Bin Laden's guilt with prosecutorial certainty is entirely unnecessary. He is guilty in word and deed. His history is the source of his culpability. The same holds true for Saddam Hussein. Our actions in the past certainly were not forceful enough, and now we must seize the opportunity to alter this pattern of passivity."[110] One week later, on September 20, a group of prominent neoconservatives and their allies published an open letter to Bush, telling him that "even if evidence does not link Iraq directly to the [9/11] attack, any strategy aiming at the eradication of terrorism and its sponsors must include a determined effort to remove Saddam Hussein from power in Iraq."[111] The letter also reminded Bush that "Israel has been and remains America's staunchest ally against international terrorism."

Little more than a week later, on September 28, Charles Krauthammer argued in the *Washington Post* that after we were done with Afghanistan, Syria should be next, followed by Iran and Iraq. "The war on terrorism," he argued, "will conclude in Baghdad," when we finish off "the most dangerous terrorist regime in the world." Shortly thereafter, in the October 1 issue of the *Weekly Standard*, Robert Kagan and William Kristol called for regime change in Iraq immediately after the Taliban was defeated.[112] Other pundits, like Michael Barone in *U.S. News & World Report*, were arguing even before the dust had settled at the World Trade Center that "evidence is accumulating that Iraq aided or perhaps planned the attack."[113]

Over the next eighteen months, the neoconservatives waged an unrelenting public relations campaign to win support for invading Iraq. On April 3, 2002, they released yet another open letter to Bush, which clearly linked Israel's security with a war to topple Saddam.[114] The letter starts by commending the president for his "strong stance in support of the Israeli government as it engages in the present campaign to fight terrorism." It then argues that "the United States and Israel share a common enemy" and are "fighting the same war." It urges Bush "to accelerate plans for removing Saddam Hussein from power," because otherwise "the damage our Israeli friends and we have suffered until now may someday appear but a prelude to much greater horrors." The letter concludes with the following message: "Israel's fight against terrorism is our fight. Israel's victory is an important part of our victory. For reasons both moral and strategic, we need to stand with Israel in its fight against terrorism."

The basic aim of the letter was to portray Arafat, bin Laden, and Saddam as critical parts of a looming menace that threatened both Israel and the United States. Not only did this depiction of a shared and growing danger justify close relations between America and Israel, it also justified the United States treating these three individuals as mortal enemies and backing Israel's hard-line response to the Second Intifada. As noted in the previous chapter, relations between the Bush administration and the Sharon government were especially contentious in early April 2002, when the letter was written. The signatories included Kenneth Adelman, William Bennett, Linda Chavez, Eliot Cohen, Midge Decter, Frank Gaffney, Reuel Marc Gerecht, Donald Kagan, Robert Kagan, William Kristol, Joshua Muravchik, Martin Peretz, Richard Perle, Daniel Pipes, Norman Podhoretz, and James Woolsey, among others.

Other pro-Israel pundits, who are not normally thought of as neoconservatives, offered a steady drumbeat of prowar advocacy as well. The case for war got a major boost with the publication in 2002 of Kenneth Pollack's ominously titled *The Threatening Storm,* which argued that Saddam was too risk acceptant and irrational to be deterred and concluded that preventive war was the only realistic option. Because Pollack was a former Clinton administration official who had previously called ousting Saddam the "rollback fantasy," his conversion to a prowar position seemed especially telling despite the book's tendentious treatment of evidence.[115] Pollack moved from the Council on Foreign Relations to Brookings's Saban Center for Middle East Policy during this period, where he and Saban Center director Martin Indyk produced a number of op-eds and commentary in the months before the war, warning that Saddam was undeterrable, that UN inspections were no solution, and that however regrettable, force would almost certainly be necessary.[116]

The neoconservatives and their allies deployed the same arguments and almost the same language that the Israelis used to promote the war. The neoconservatives made frequent reference to the 1930s and Munich, comparing Saddam with Hitler and opponents of the war (like Brent Scowcroft and Senator Chuck Hagel) with appeasers like Neville Chamberlain.[117] Israel and the United States, they maintained, were facing a nebulous common enemy, "international terrorism," and Iraq, to quote the *New York Times* columnist William Safire, was "the center of world terror."[118] The war hawks portrayed Saddam as an especially aggressive and reckless leader who would not only use weapons of mass destruction against the United States and Israel but would also pass them on to terrorists.[119] Identifying diplomacy and multilateralism with weakness, neoconservative commentators had nothing but contempt for the UN and its inspectors in Iraq, not to mention

France.[120] Indeed, they repeated the old Israeli adage that force has great utility in the Middle East, because it is a region where, to quote Krautham-mer, "power, above all, commands respect."[121]

One might argue that this analysis exaggerates the impact that open let-ters to presidents, newspaper columns, books, and op-eds can have on the policy-making process. After all, relatively few people actually read the vari-ous open letters and there were plenty of other articles, editorials, and op-eds written in U.S. newspapers that had nothing to do with Iraq. This perspective would be wrong, however. The signatories of the various letters written to Presidents Bush and Clinton are powerful individuals who have connections and influence with important policy makers and lawmakers on Capitol Hill, some of whom they had worked closely with in the course of their careers. In fact, a number of the individuals who signed the earlier let-ters to Clinton—including Rumsfeld, Wolfowitz, and Feith—became key policy makers in the Bush administration. Thus, the signatories of the letters written to Bush in the period between 9/11 and the invasion of Iraq were not shouting into a void. The same was true for journalists like Charles Krauthammer and William Safire, who wrote frequently about Iraq for two of the country's leading newspapers, the *Washington Post* and the *New York Times*, respectively. Their views were taken seriously by influential people inside and outside of the U.S. government, as were the articles that ap-peared in neoconservative magazines like the *Weekly Standard*. Indeed, these writings by outsiders worked to reinforce the arguments made by Bush administration insiders, who shared their views on the need to invade Iraq. The underlying purpose of all these efforts was to define the terms of debate in a way that would facilitate an affirmative decision for war. By making war seem both necessary and beneficial, by portraying potential opponents as "soft" on terror, and by linking America's fate to Israel's through the repeti-tion of familiar moral and strategic arguments, these efforts helped stifle se-rious discussion about the pros and cons of an invasion and were an important part of the broader campaign for war.[122]

FIXING THE INTELLIGENCE ON IRAQ

A key part of the public relations campaign to win support for invading Iraq was the manipulation of intelligence information in order to make Saddam look like an imminent threat. Scooter Libby was an important player in this endeavor, visiting the CIA several times to pressure analysts to find evidence that would make the case for war. He also helped prepare a detailed briefing on the Iraq threat in early 2003 that was pushed on Colin Powell, who was then preparing his infamous presentation to the UN Security Council.[123] According to Bob Woodward, Powell's deputy, Richard Armitage, "was appalled at what he considered overreaching and hyperbole. Libby was drawing only the worst conclusions from fragments and silky threads."[124] Although Powell discarded Libby's most outlandish claims, his UN presentation was still riddled with errors, as Powell now acknowledges.[125]

The effort to manipulate intelligence, which was then leaked to an alarmist prowar press, also involved two organizations that were created after 9/11 and reported directly to Undersecretary of Defense Douglas Feith.[126] The Policy Counterterrorism Evaluation Group was tasked to find links between al Qaeda and Iraq that the intelligence community supposedly missed. Its two key members were David Wurmser and Michael Maloof, a Lebanese American who had close ties with Richard Perle. The *New York Times* reporter James Risen writes that "Israeli intelligence played a hidden role in convincing Wolfowitz that he couldn't trust the CIA," and this dissatisfaction helped cause him to rely on Ahmed Chalabi for intelligence and to create the Policy Counterterrorism Evaluation Group.[127]

The Office of Special Plans (OSP) was directed to find evidence that could be used to sell the war against Iraq. It was headed by Abram Shulsky, a neoconservative long associated with Wolfowitz, and its ranks included several recruits from pro-Israel think tanks like Michael Rubin from the American Enterprise Institute, David Schenker from the Washington Institute for Near East Policy, and Michael Makovsky, who had worked for then Prime Minister Shimon Peres after graduating from college.[128] OSP relied heavily on information from Chalabi and other Iraqi exiles and it had close connections to various Israeli sources. Indeed, the *Guardian* reported that it "forged close ties to a parallel, ad hoc intelligence operation inside Ariel Sharon's office in Israel specifically to bypass Mossad and provide the Bush administration with more alarmist reports on Saddam's Iraq than Mossad was prepared to authorize."[129] The Pentagon's inspector general released a report in February 2007 that was critical of OSP for disseminating "alternative intelligence assessments" that "were, in our opinion, inappropriate given that the intelligence assessments were intelligence products and did not clearly show the variance with the consensus of the Intelligence Community."[130]

The neoconservatives in the Pentagon and the White House not only relied heavily on Chalabi and his fellow exiles for intelligence about Iraq, they also championed him as Iraq's future leader after Saddam was gone. The

CIA and the State Department, on the other hand, considered Chalabi dishonest and unreliable and kept him at arm's length. That severe judgment has now been vindicated, as we know that Chalabi and the INC fed the United States false information, and his relations with the U.S. occupation forces soon deteriorated, with Chalabi later being accused of providing classified information to Iran (a charge that he has denied). The neoconservatives' hopes that he would be the "George Washington of Iraq" fared no better than their other prewar forecasts.[131]

So why did neoconservatives embrace Chalabi? The INC leader had gone to considerable lengths to establish close ties with individuals and groups in the lobby, and he had especially close links with JINSA, where he had been "a frequent guest at board meetings, symposia and other events since 1997."[132] He also cultivated close ties with pro-Israel organizations like AIPAC, AEI, the Hudson Institute, and WINEP. Max Singer, who helped found the Hudson Institute, described Chalabi as a "rare find. He's deep in the Arab world and at the same time he is fundamentally a man of the West."[133] When an embattled Chalabi returned to give his eighth address to the AEI in early November 2005, that think tank's president introduced him as a "very great and very brave Iraqi patriot, liberal and liberator."[134] Another big supporter of Chalabi was Bernard Lewis, who argued that the INC leader should be put in charge of Iraq after Baghdad fell.[135]

In return for the lobby's support, Chalabi pledged to foster good relations with Israel once he gained power. According to Feith's former law partner, L. Marc Zell, Chalabi also promised to rebuild the pipeline that once ran from Haifa in Israel to Mosul in Iraq.[136] This was precisely what pro-Israel proponents of regime change wanted to hear, so they backed Chalabi in return. The journalist Matthew Berger laid out the essence of the bargain in the *Jewish Journal*: "The INC saw improved relations as a way to tap Jewish influence in Washington and Jerusalem and to drum up increased support for its cause. For their part, the Jewish groups saw an opportunity to pave the way for better relations between Israel and Iraq, if and when the INC is involved in replacing Saddam Hussein's regime."[137] Not surprisingly, Nathan Guttman reports that "the American Jewish community and the Iraqi opposition" had for years "taken pains to conceal" the links between them.[138]

The neoconservatives and their allies did not operate in a vacuum, of course, and they did not lead the United States to war by themselves. As emphasized earlier, the war would probably not have occurred absent the September 11 attacks, which forced President Bush and Vice President Cheney to consider adopting a radically new foreign policy. Neoconservatives like

Deputy Defense Secretary Paul Wolfowitz, who had been urging regime change in Iraq since early 1998, were quick to link Saddam Hussein with 9/11—even though there was no evidence that Saddam was involved—and to portray his overthrow as critical to winning the war on terror. The lobby's actions were a necessary but not sufficient condition for war.

Indeed, Richard Perle made precisely this point to George Packer in a discussion about the role that the neoconservatives played in making the Iraq war happen. "If Bush had staffed his administration with a group of people selected by Brent Scowcroft and Jim Baker," Perle noted, "which might well have happened, then it could have been different, because they would not have carried into it the ideas that the people who wound up in important positions brought to it."[139] The New York Times columnist Thomas L. Friedman offered a similar appraisal in May 2003, telling Ari Shavit of Ha'aretz that Iraq was "the war the neoconservatives wanted . . . the war the neoconservatives marketed . . . I could give you the names of 25 people (all of whom are at the moment within a five-block radius of this office [in Washington, D.C.]), who, if you exiled them to a desert island a year and a half ago, the Iraq war would not have happened." We agree completely with Perle's and Friedman's observations, while recognizing that it was a combination of individuals, ideas, and circumstances that came together to produce the ultimate decision for war.[140]

WAS IRAQ A WAR FOR OIL?

Some readers might concede that the Israel lobby had some influence over the decision to invade Iraq but argue that its overall weight in the decision-making process was minimal. Instead, many American and foreign observers appear to think that oil—not Israel—was the real motivation behind the invasion of Iraq in 2003. In one variant of this story, the Bush administration was determined to control the vast reserves of oil in the Middle East, because that would give the United States enormous geopolitical leverage over potential adversaries. Conquering Iraq, according to this scenario, was seen by the administration as a giant step toward achieving that goal. An alternative version sees the oil-producing states and especially the oil companies as the real culprits behind the Iraq war, driven primarily by a desire for higher prices and greater profits. Even scholars who are often critical of Israel and of the lobby, such as Noam Chomsky, apparently subscribe to this idea, which was popularized in filmmaker Michael Moore's 2004 documentary Fahrenheit 9/11.[141]

The claim that the conquest of Iraq was mainly about oil has a certain prima facie plausibility, given the importance of oil to the world economy.[142] But this explanation faces both logical and empirical difficulties. As emphasized in Chapter 2, U.S. policy makers have long been concerned about who controls Persian Gulf oil; they have been especially concerned about the danger that one state might control all of it. The United States has been involved with various oil-producing countries in the Gulf, but no American government, including the Bush administration, has seriously considered conquering the major oil-producing countries in that region to gain coercive leverage over other countries around the world. The United States might consider invading a major oil-producing state if a revolution or an embargo caused its oil to stop flowing into world markets. But that was not the case with Iraq; Saddam was eager to sell his oil to any customer willing to pay for it. Moreover, if the United States wanted to conquer another country in order to gain control of its oil, Saudi Arabia—with larger reserves and a smaller population—would have been a much more attractive target. Plus, bin Laden was born and raised in Saudi Arabia, and fifteen of the nineteen terrorists who struck the United States on September 11 were Saudis (none were from Iraq). If control of oil were Bush's real objective, 9/11 would have been an ideal pretext to act. Occupying Saudi Arabia would not have been a simple task, but it would almost certainly have been easier than trying to pacify the large, restive, and well-armed population of Iraq.

There is also hardly any evidence that oil interests were actively pushing the Bush administration to invade Iraq in 2002–03. In 1990–91, by contrast, Saudi Arabia's leaders clearly pressed the first Bush administration to use force to drive Iraq out of Kuwait. They feared, like many American policy makers at the time, that Saddam might next invade Saudi Arabia, which would place much of the region's oil under his control. Prince Bandar, the Saudi ambassador to the United States, worked closely with pro-Israel groups here to build support for ousting Saddam from Kuwait.[143] But the story was very different in the run-up to the second Gulf War: this time Saudi Arabia publicly opposed using American force against Iraq.[144] Saudi leaders feared that a war would lead to the breakup of Iraq and destabilize the Middle East. And even if Iraq remained intact, the Shia were likely to ascend to power, which worried the Sunnis who ran Saudi Arabia not only for religious reasons but also because it would increase Iran's influence in the region. In addition, the Saudis faced growing anti-Americanism at home, which was likely to get worse if the United States launched a preventive war against Iraq.

Nor were the oil companies, which generally seek to curry favor with big oil producers like Saddam's Iraq or the Islamic Republic of Iran, major players in the decision to conquer Iraq. They did not lobby for the 2003 war, which most of them thought was a foolish idea. As Peter Beinart noted in the *New Republic* in September 2002, "It isn't war that the American oil industry has been lobbying for all these years; it's the end of sanctions."[145] The oil companies, as is almost always the case, wanted to make money, not war.

DREAMS OF REGIONAL TRANSFORMATION

The Iraq war was not supposed to be a costly quagmire. Rather, it was intended as the first step in a larger plan to reorder the Middle East in ways that would benefit long-term American and Israeli interests. Specifically, the United States was not just going to remove Saddam Hussein from power and go home; the invasion and occupation would, in this dream, quickly turn Iraq into a democracy, which would then serve as an attractive model for people living in the various authoritarian states in the region. The results from Iraq would trigger a cascade of democratic dominoes, although it still might be necessary to use the sword to spread democracy to some countries in the Middle East besides Iraq. But once democracy took hold across the region, regimes friendly to Israel and the United States would be the norm, the conflict between Israel and the Palestinians would, in the words of the "Clean Break" study, be "transcended," other regional rivalries would be muted, and the twin problems of terrorism and nuclear proliferation would largely disappear.

Vice President Cheney laid out this ambitious rationale for regional transformation in the speech to the VFW convention on August 26, 2002, opening the administration's campaign to sell the Iraq war. "When the gravest of threats are eliminated," he said, "the freedom-loving peoples of the region will have a chance to promote the values that can bring lasting peace . . . Extremists in the region would have to rethink their strategy of jihad. Moderates throughout the region would take heart. And our ability to advance the Israeli-Palestinian peace process would be enhanced."[146] Cheney would repeat these arguments on several occasions over the next six months.

President Bush spoke with similar enthusiasm about regional transformation as he made the case for war against Iraq. On February 26, 2003, he told an audience at AEI that the United States aims to "cultivate liberty and

peace in the Middle East." He emphasized that "the world has a clear interest in the spread of democratic values, because stable and free nations do
not breed the ideologies of murder. They encourage the peaceful pursuit of
a better life. And there are hopeful signs of a desire for freedom in the Middle East." Furthermore, he claimed, "Success in Iraq could also begin a new
stage for Middle Eastern peace, and set in motion progress towards a truly
democratic Palestinian peace."[147]

This ambitious strategy, grounded in an almost theological belief in the
transformative power of freedom, was a dramatic departure from previous
U.S. policy, and there was certainly no indication before 9/11 that either
Bush or Cheney would embrace it. Indeed, both men—as well as National
Security Adviser Rice—were on record as being opposed to the ambitious
kind of nation building that was at the heart of regional transformation, and
Bush had sharply criticized the Clinton administration for its emphasis on
nation building during the 2000 campaign. So what had produced this shift?
According to a March 2003 story in the *Wall Street Journal*, the critical driv-
ing forces behind this major change in U.S. Middle East policy were Israel
and the neoconservatives in the lobby. The headline says it all: "President's
Dream: Changing Not Just Regime but a Region: A Pro-U.S., Democratic
Area Is a Goal That Has Israeli and Neoconservative Roots."[148]

Charles Krauthammer says this grand scheme to spread democracy across
the Middle East was the brainchild of Natan Sharansky, the Israeli politician
whose writings are said to have impressed President Bush.[149] But Sharansky
was hardly a lone voice in Israel. In fact, Israelis across the political spectrum
maintained that toppling Saddam would alter the Middle East to Israel's advantage. Writing in the *New York Times* in early September 2002, former
Prime Minister Ehud Barak argued that "putting an end to Saddam Hussein's
regime will change the geopolitical landscape of the Arab world." He claimed
that "an Arab world without Saddam Hussein would enable many from this
generation [leaders about to come into power] to embrace the gradual democratic opening that some of the Persian Gulf states and Jordan have begun to
enjoy." Barak also maintained that toppling Saddam would "create an opening
for forward movement on the Israeli-Palestinian conflict."[150]

In August 2002, Yuval Steinitz, a Likud party member of the Knesset's
Foreign Affairs and Defense Committee, told the *Christian Science Monitor*,
"After Iraq is taken by U.S. troops and we see a new regime installed as in
Afghanistan, and Iraqi bases become American bases, it will be very easy to
pressure Syria to stop supporting terrorist organizations like Hizbullah and

Islamic Jihad, to allow the Lebanese army to dismantle Hizbullah, and maybe to put an end to the Syrian occupation in Lebanon. If this happens we will really see a new Middle East."[151] Similarly, Aluf Benn reported in *Ha'aretz* in February 2003 that "senior IDF officers and those close to Prime Minister Ariel Sharon, such as National Security Advisor Ephraim Halevy, paint a rosy picture of the wonderful future Israel can expect after the war. They envision a domino effect, with the fall of Saddam Hussein followed by that of Israel's other enemies: Arafat, Hassan Nasrallah, Bashar Assad, the ayatollah in Iran and maybe even Muhammar Gadaffi. Along with these leaders will disappear terror and weapons of mass destruction."[152]

The *New York Times* also reported that Halevy gave a speech in Munich in February 2003 where he said, "The shock waves emerging from post-Saddam Baghdad could have wide-ranging effects in Tehran, Damascus, and in Ramallah."[153] The author of the article noted that Israel "is hoping that once Saddam Hussein is dispensed with, the dominoes will start to tumble. According to this hope . . . moderates and reformers throughout the region would be encouraged to put new pressure on their own governments, not excepting the Palestinian Authority of Yasir Arafat." The *Forward* summed up Israeli thinking about regional transformation in an article published just before the war: "Israel's top political, military and economic echelons have come to regard the looming Iraq war as a virtual *deus ex machina* that will turn the political and economic tables and extricate Israel from its current morass."[154]

Some might argue that Israel's leaders are too sophisticated and experienced to believe in a deus ex machina and countenance such an ambitious scheme, and too familiar with the complexities of their region to believe it could succeed. But in fact, Israel's leaders have a long history of favoring remarkably ambitious plans to remake the local map. The original Zionist dream of reestablishing a Jewish state where none had existed for nearly two millennia was nothing if not ambitious, and as discussed in Chapter 1, David Ben-Gurion had hoped to seize all of the West Bank, part of Lebanon, and portions of Egypt in the 1956 Suez War. Similarly, Ariel Sharon believed the invasion of Lebanon in 1982 would lead to the creation of a pro-Israel Christian state there and vanquish the PLO once and for all, thereby cementing Israel's control of the Occupied Territories. Given that history, it is perhaps not so surprising that many Israeli leaders held out the hope that the United States might be able to succeed where their earlier plans had failed.

THE LOBBY'S ROLE IN REMAKING THE MIDDLE EAST

By 2002, many neoconservatives were also heavily invested in the idea that the United States could democratize the Middle East and make it a more friendly environment for America and Israel. They had reached that position over the course of the 1990s as they became increasingly disenchanted with U.S. foreign policy after the Cold War.

Pro-Israel groups—and not only neoconservatives—have long been interested in having the U.S. military directly involved in the Middle East so that it can help protect Israel. They are especially interested in seeing large numbers of American troops permanently stationed there.[155] But they had limited success on this front during the Cold War, because America acted as an offshore balancer in the region. Most U.S. forces designated for the Middle East, like the Rapid Deployment Force, were kept "over the horizon" and out of harm's way. Washington maintained a favorable balance of power by playing local powers against each other, which is why the Reagan administration supported Saddam against revolutionary Iran during the Iran-Iraq War (1980–88).

This policy changed after the first Gulf War, when the Clinton administration adopted a strategy of "dual containment." Instead of using Iran and Iraq to balance each other—with the United States shifting sides as needed—the new strategy called for stationing substantial American forces in the region to contain both of them at once. The father of dual containment was Martin Indyk, who first articulated the strategy in May 1993 at WINEP and then implemented it as director for Near East and South Asian Affairs at the National Security Council.[156] As Indyk's Brookings colleague Kenneth Pollack observes, dual containment was a policy adopted largely in response to "Israel's security concerns." Specifically, Israel made it clear to the Clinton administration that it "was willing to move ahead in the peace process only if it felt reasonably secure" from Iran.[157]

There was considerable dissatisfaction with dual containment by the mid-1990s, because it made the United States the mortal enemy of two countries that hated each other, and it forced Washington to bear the burden of containing both of them. As discussed in Chapter 10, AIPAC and other groups in the lobby not only saved the policy, they persuaded Congress and Clinton to toughen it up. The neoconservatives went even further, however; they were increasingly convinced that dual containment was not working and that Saddam Hussein had to be removed from power and replaced by a democratic government. Their thinking was reflected in the two open letters that they sent to President Clinton in early 1998 as well as their support for the Iraq Liberation Act.

At about the same time, the belief that spreading democracy across the Middle East would pacify the entire area was beginning to take root within neoconservative circles. A few neoconservatives had flirted with this idea in the wake of the Cold War, but it was not widely embraced until the latter part of the 1990s.[158] This line of thinking, of course, was evident in the 1996 "Clean Break" study that a group of neoconservatives had written for Netanyahu. By 2002, when invading Iraq had become a front-burner issue, regional transformation had become an article of faith among neoconservatives, who, in turn, helped make it the centerpiece of U.S. foreign policy.[159] Thus, Israeli leaders, neoconservatives, and the Bush administration all saw war with Iraq as the first step in an ambitious campaign to remake the Middle East.

CONCLUSION

The Bush administration's plans for Iraq and the wider region have been a stunning failure. Not only is the American military stuck in a losing war, but there is little prospect of exporting democracy across the Middle East anytime soon. Iran has been the main beneficiary of this ill-conceived adventure and it seems as determined as ever to acquire a nuclear capability. Syria, like Iran, remains at odds with Washington, and both states have a powerful interest in having the U.S. military bogged down in Iraq. Hamas now dominates Gaza and the Palestinian Authority is badly split—making peace with Israel even more elusive—and Hezbollah is more powerful than ever in Lebanon, after having stood up to Israel in the 2006 war. We may be witnessing the "birth pangs of a new Middle East," to use Secretary of State Rice's regrettable phrase, but it will almost certainly be more unstable and dangerous than the one that existed before the United States invaded Iraq.[160]

The war in Iraq has not been good for Israel either, especially since it has strengthened Iran's hand in the region. Indeed, the *Forward* reported in early 2007 that there is a "growing chorus" of voices in Israel who are saying that the Jewish state "could find itself in more danger" now that Saddam has been removed from power.[161] Amatzia Baram, an Israeli expert on Iraq who argued for Saddam's ouster in prewar interviews in the AIPAC newsletter *Near East Report*, now says, "If I knew then what I know today [January

2007], I would not have recommended going to war, because Saddam was far less dangerous than I thought." Moreover, he admitted that the invasion had produced "much, much more [terrorism] than I expected." Yuval Diskin, the head of Shin Bet, Israel's domestic security service, said in February 2006, "I'm not sure we won't miss Saddam."[162]

As the United States looks for ways to extricate itself from this disastrous situation, pressure has been growing on the Bush administration to talk with Iran and Syria, and to make a concerted effort to settle the Israeli-Palestinian conflict. The neoconservatives and the Israelis, of course, believed that the road to Jerusalem ran through Baghdad. Once the United States won in Iraq, they believed, the Palestinians would make peace on Israel's terms. But the bipartisan Iraq Study Group, British Prime Minister Tony Blair, and many others believe the opposite is true: the road to Baghdad runs through Jerusalem.[163] In other words, creating a viable Palestinian state will help the United States deal with Iraq and other regional problems. Israel and the lobby have vigorously challenged this line of argument, insisting that America's troubles in Iraq have nothing to do with the Palestinians. Indeed, *Ha'aretz* reported in late November 2006, just before the release of the Iraq Study Group report, that Prime Minister Ehud Olmert "hopes the Jewish lobby can rally a Democratic majority in the new Congress to counter any diversion from the status quo on the Palestinians."[164] Similarly, a number of pro-Israel groups still maintain that the United States should refuse to talk with Iran and Syria until these states agree to all of Washington's demands.[165]

The Bush administration faces growing pressure to pull out of Iraq, but Israeli leaders have encouraged it to stay and finish the job. Why? Because these leaders believe that a U.S. withdrawal would jeopardize Israel's security. Both Foreign Minister Tzipi Livni and Prime Minister Olmert made this point to AIPAC's annual conference in March 2007. Livni said that "in a region where impressions are important, countries must be careful not to demonstrate weakness and surrender to extremists."[166] Olmert was even blunter: "Those who are concerned for Israel's security . . . for the stability of the entire Middle East should recognize the need for American success in Iraq and responsible exit." He ended his remarks by saying that "when America succeeds in Iraq, Israel is safer. The friends of Israel know it. The friends who care about Israel know it."[167] Critics castigated Olmert for making these remarks, mainly because his comments provided additional evidence that Israel had backed the U.S. invasion of Iraq. Bradley Burston, who writes for *Ha'aretz*, was especially angry with Olmert for venturing into the American debate on Iraq. He had a simple message for the prime minister: "Stay the hell out of it."[168]

Olmert had actually expressed his support for America's continued presence in Iraq during a visit to the White House in November 2006, saying, "We are very much impressed and encouraged by the stability which the great operation of America in Iraq brought to the Middle East."[169] Even some of Israel's consistent backers were put off by Olmert's prowar remarks, with Congressman Gary Ackerman saying, "I'm shocked. It's a very unrealistic observation. Most of us here understand that our policy has been a thorough and total disaster for the United States."[170]

Given that many Americans now share Ackerman's sentiments about the war, we should not be surprised that some Israelis and their American allies have tried to rewrite the historical record to absolve Israel of any responsibility for the Iraq disaster. In March 2007, the editor of the *Jerusalem Post*, David Horovitz, wrote about "the false notion that Israel encouraged the US to fight the Iraq War."[171] Similarly, Shai Feldman, former head of the Jaffee Center for Strategic Studies and now head of the Crown Center for Middle East Studies at Brandeis, told Glenn Frankel of the *Washington Post* in the summer of 2006, "Look, Israel didn't mobilize anybody over Iraq, and associating Israel with the neocons on this issue is preposterous. Israel didn't see Iraq as a danger, and what's more, it had no interest in pushing the Bush administration's democracy agenda."[172] This view undoubtedly reflects Feldman's beliefs about Israel's interests and the hierarchy of threats it faced, but as we have shown, it is contrary to what Israel's leaders were actually saying and doing in the run-up to the war.

Not to be outdone, Martin Kramer, a research fellow at WINEP, claims that any attempt to link Israel and the lobby with the war in Iraq is "simply a falsehood," arguing that "in the year preceding the Iraq War, Israel time and again disagreed with the United States, arguing that Iran posed the greater threat."[173] But as shown above, Israel's concerns about Iran never led it to undertake a significant effort to halt the march to war. To the contrary, top Israeli officials were doing everything in their power to make sure that the United States went after Saddam and did not get cold feet at the last moment. They considered Iraq a serious threat and were convinced that Bush would deal with Iran after he finished with Iraq. They might have preferred that America focus on Iran before Iraq, but as Kramer admits, Israelis "shed no tears over Saddam's demise." Instead, their leaders took to the American airwaves, wrote op-eds, testified before Congress, and worked closely with the neoconservatives in the Pentagon and the vice president's office to shape the intelligence about Iraq and coordinate the drive to war.

Yossi Alpher, an Israeli strategist at the Jaffe Center, now maintains that former Prime Minister Sharon had serious reservations about invading Iraq and he privately warned Bush against it. Alpher even hints that Sharon might have been able to prevent the war had he spoken out about his concerns. He writes, "Had Sharon made his criticism public, citing the dangers posed to vital Israeli interests, might he have made a difference in the pre-war debate in the United States and the world?"[174] This is a convenient alibi now that the occupation of Iraq has gone south, but there is no evidence in the public record that Sharon ever advised Bush not to attack Iraq. In fact, there is considerable evidence that the Israeli leader and his key advisers strongly endorsed the war and encouraged Bush to begin it sooner rather than later. If Sharon believed the war to be a mistake, why did his own spokesman repeatedly stress the danger of Iraq's WMD and why did Sharon himself warn the Bush administration that putting off the attack "will not create a more convenient environment for action in the future"?[175]

It is possible that Sharon made different arguments behind closed doors than he made in public. This is not likely, however, as word of Sharon's opposition to the war would surely have leaked out before it began, if not in the first year or two after Baghdad fell. Sharon was rarely reticent about expressing his views—even when doing so involved disagreements with the United States—and it is hard to believe that he would have kept silent in public if he thought that the decision to invade Iraq would be harmful to Israel. In short, neither facts nor logic support Alpher's claim.

"Victory has a thousand fathers, but defeat is an orphan." As the various progenitors of the Iraq disaster now seek to deny their paternity, President John F. Kennedy's rueful remark is more appropriate than ever. But Iraq did not always look like the blunder it has turned out to be. For a few short months in the spring of 2003, the United States appeared to have won a stunning victory and there was little need for Israel's defenders to deny responsibility for the war. During this brief window of opportunity, in fact, key Israelis and their American allies began to pressure the Bush administration to bring U.S. power to bear on Syria and Iran, in the hope that these two rogue states would suffer the same fate as Saddam Hussein's regime. Let us now consider how Israel and the lobby influenced U.S. policy on Syria, and then turn to Iran.

9

TAKING AIM AT SYRIA

America has had a problematic relationship with Syria for nearly fifty years. The Ba'th regime was a key Soviet client during the Cold War, and its authoritarian government has committed serious human rights abuses in the past and still denies basic freedoms to its population. President Bush did not include Syria in his infamous "axis of evil," but it is often depicted as a "rogue state" that threatens important American interests. U.S. policy toward Syria became more hostile after September 11, 2001, and the fall of Baghdad in April 2003 fueled speculation that the United States was going to go after Damascus as well. The deteriorating situation in Iraq has ended such talk for the moment, but relations with Damascus have not improved and confrontation remains the order of the day.

Yet if one looks at Syria with a more detached eye, it is not obvious why it would be in the U.S. national interest to have a strictly adversarial relationship with that Arab country. Washington and Damascus have never been especially friendly, but they have cooperated to their mutual benefit on a number of occasions, and Syria's modest military capabilities pose no serious threat to vital U.S. interests. It is difficult to see—given present circumstances—why Syria should be considered an ideal candidate for regime change while equally odious dictatorships in the Middle East and elsewhere enjoy American patronage.

In fact, the Bush administration's unremitting hostility toward Syria has been strategically unwise. Specifically, it has damaged America's position in the Arab and Islamic world, hindered U.S. efforts to thwart nuclear proliferation, made it more difficult to stabilize Iraq, and made America's terrorism problem worse, not better. Thus, it is not surprising that many voices inside the United States have recently called for President Bush to reverse course and seek a modus vivendi with Damascus. The Iraq Study Group, for example, called in December 2006 for the Bush administration to "actively engage" with Syria in "diplomatic dialogue, without preconditions."[1] That same month, four U.S. senators visited Damascus to talk with Syria's president, Bashar al-Assad, and in April 2007, Speaker of the House Nancy Pelosi led a bipartisan delegation of six House members—including Tom Lantos and Henry Waxman, whose pro-Israel credentials are well established—to Syria to speak with Assad about pushing the peace process forward.[2]

Israel and the lobby have played a central role in pushing the Bush administration to pursue an increasingly confrontational policy toward Syria, albeit with some reluctance. The lobby has worked hard to get the United States to isolate and pressure Damascus, even when doing so jeopardized valuable forms of collaboration. In the absence of this pressure, Washington's relationship with Syria would be markedly different and would probably be more consistent with the American national interest. The United States and Syria would hardly be allies if the lobby was less influential, but a pragmatic and mutually beneficial relationship would be much more likely.

THE SYRIAN THREAT

Syria is not a serious military threat to the United States or to Israel. Its defense budget is less than one-fifth the size of Israel's, and it has an unimpressive army and air force that the Israel Defense Forces would easily defeat if serious fighting ever occurred.[3] The IDF had little difficulty routing Syria's forces during its 1982 invasion of Lebanon, and that war occurred when Syria was still getting a great deal of help from its Soviet patron. Damascus has been on its own since the Soviet Union collapsed, however, while Israel has continued to receive significant U.S. aid every year. A war between Israel and Syria would be a gross mismatch, which is why Syria's leaders go to considerable lengths to avoid provoking Israel.

The American military would have even less trouble defeating the Syrians in a war. Syria's military is much weaker than Iran's or Iraq's under Saddam, and it has not engaged a serious adversary since Israel trounced it in 1982. Unlike Iran today or Iraq under Saddam, Syria lacks the population size and wealth to be a regional hegemon. It can make life more difficult for the United States and for Israel, but it lacks the wherewithal to be a serious threat to either country.

Furthermore, Syria does not have a nuclear weapons program, and there is no reason to think that it will pursue one anytime soon. It does have chemical weapons, which were first acquired from Egypt in 1973, and it may have a biological weapons program.[4] It also has a large inventory of ballistic missiles and thus the capability to deliver its chemical weapons against Israel and other countries in the region, although not the United States. But Israel has never worried much about this threat, because it has its own chemical, biological, and nuclear weapons, and it could inflict far greater damage on Syria than Syria could inflict on Israel. In other words, Israel has an effective deterrent against Syria's chemical weapons.[5]

Syria's ability to create trouble rests mostly in its support for a number of terrorist organizations, notably Hezbollah, but also Hamas and Islamic Jihad. Indeed, Hamas leader Khaled Meshal lives in Damascus. All of these groups threaten Israel, but unlike al Qaeda, none of them—including Hezbollah—directly threatens the United States. As Moshe Maoz, an expert on Syria at Hebrew University, notes, "Syria is not a saint—everybody knows that—but Hezbollah is mostly a threat against Israel."[6] Moreover, Syria and al Qaeda are bitter enemies, mainly because bin Laden is a Sunni and an Islamic fundamentalist, while Assad is the Shia leader of a secular state. In fact, al Qaeda is believed to have links to the Syrian Muslim Brotherhood, an Islamic terrorist group that has battled the secular Ba'thist government in Syria for more than twenty years.[7] Given that Damascus and Washington share a common enemy in al Qaeda, it is hardly surprising that in the wake of 9/11 Syria began providing the Bush administration with important intelligence about bin Laden's organization. Contrary to the rhetoric about the global war on terror, it would be wrong to argue that Syria supports "international terrorism"—a global network of terrorist groups and states that target America and Israel alike. Rather, Syria supports a particular set of terrorist organizations whose agenda is focused primarily on Israel alone.

One might argue that Syria is a serious threat to the United States, because it supports the insurgency in Iraq. But there is little hard evidence that Damascus is providing support to the Iraqi insurgents, which is surely why the Bush administration has mainly made that charge against Iran, not Syria. It is probably the case that Syria is turning a blind eye to some of the fighters and weapons that flow across its borders into Iraq. But Washington has pursued a confrontational policy toward Damascus since September 11, which gives the Syrians powerful incentives to keep the U.S. military busy in Iraq. Ultimately, however, Syria is not the source of America's troubles in Iraq, and Damascus would have little interest in undermining the U.S. occupation if President Bush and his lieutenants were not threatening the Assad regime. The bottom line is that Syria is not a serious danger to the United States, and it has little reason to pick a quarrel with the world's most powerful state.

In fact, Damascus has had reasonably good relations with Washington at a number of points in the recent past. Syria fought alongside the United States in the 1991 war against Iraq, and the two countries had cordial if guarded relations during the 1990s, when the United States was attempting to broker a peace deal between Damascus and Jerusalem.[8] President Clinton even visited Damascus in October 1994 to meet with President Hafez al-Assad, the first visit to Syria by an American president in twenty years. Afterward, Clinton remarked, "I went there because I was convinced that we needed to add new energy to the talks, and I came away convinced that we have."[9] Later, in the fall of 2002, when Syria was a nonpermanent member of the Security Council, it voted for UN Resolution 1441, which called for the return of UN weapons inspectors to Saddam Hussein's Iraq. And although the Bush administration played a key role in forcing Syria out of Lebanon in 2005, for many years the United States had counted on Syria to shut down Lebanon's civil war (1976–89) and to keep the peace there.[10]

Syrian President Assad is certainly not interested in being America's enemy. Flynt Leverett, a former Bush administration official and one of the West's foremost experts on Syria, notes that "Bashar has repeatedly stated his interest in a better relationship with the United States. Such interest is fully in keeping with father Hafez's script and in line with any realistic assessment of Syria's strategic needs." Leverett also believes improved relations are "critical to his [Assad's] long-term ambitions for internal reform."[11] Seymour Hersh, who visited Assad in his Damascus office in 2003, found him eager to talk because "he wanted to change his image, and the image of his country."[12]

Syria has also been trying to negotiate a peace agreement with Israel since the early 1990s. They came close to reaching a deal in early 2000, but Ehud Barak, the Israeli prime minister at the time, got cold feet at the last moment. Since then, the Syrians have made numerous offers to restart the negotiations and try to settle their differences. But Barak's successors— Ariel Sharon and Ehud Olmert—have refused and instead have pursued confrontational policies toward Syria. Those same Israeli leaders have also pushed the United States to treat Damascus as a dangerous adversary.

ISRAEL AND THE GOLAN HEIGHTS

To grasp the essence of the complex dance between Washington, Jerusalem, and Damascus, and the role that the lobby has played, one must first understand why Israel came tantalizingly close to signing a peace agreement with Syria in 2000 but has been unwilling to talk with Assad since then.[13]

The taproot of the present conflict between Israel and Syria involves the Golan Heights. Israel took that territory from Syria in the 1967 war and drove eighty thousand Syrians from their homes. Israeli law was extended over the Golan Heights in 1981, in what was essentially a de facto annexation.[14] There are now about eighteen thousand Jewish settlers living there in thirty-two settlements and one city.[15] Syria is deeply committed to getting this territory back, and toward this end it supports terrorist groups like Hamas and Hezbollah; the Syrian military is too weak to threaten Israel and these groups are its only means of putting pressure on Israel. In 1994, Prime Minister Yitzhak Rabin agreed in principle to return all of the Golan Heights to Syria in return for full normalization of relations between the two countries. It was widely understood that the "Rabin deposit," as it came to be known, meant that Israel would withdraw to the border that existed on June 4, 1967, and that Syria would then end all support for Hezbollah, Hamas, and Islamic Jihad.[16]

Rabin was assassinated a year later, but his successors—Shimon Peres and Benjamin Netanyahu—remained committed in principle to withdrawing to the June 4, 1967, borders. Peres's tenure in office was too short to craft a deal, however, and Netanyahu, for various reasons, did not place a sufficiently high priority on it. Netanyahu's successor, Ehud Barak, was also willing to give back virtually all of the Golan Heights to Syria, although he would not commit himself to a full withdrawal to the 1967 border.[17]

Relations between Israel and Syria were not that bad in the latter half of the 1990s, as the two sides maneuvered to reach an agreement. The Clinton administration was deeply involved in the negotiating process, devoted to brokering the final deal, much the way Jimmy Carter pushed forward a deal between Egypt and Israel at Camp David in 1979. And this meant that Syria and the United States had a reasonably good relationship during this period, even though Syria was a one-party dictatorship and the Clinton administration was publicly committed to "expanding democracy." Israel actually welcomed this cordial relationship between Damascus and Washington at the time, because it wanted the United States to help resolve its long-standing feud with Syria. A headline in the *New York Times* after President Clinton visited Damascus in October 1994 makes this point clear: "Israelis Look to Clinton Trip for Progress with Syrians."[18]

In the fall of 1999, Clinton thought he finally had the makings of a deal between Israel and Syria. At the strong urging of Barak, he gathered the two sides together in Shepherdstown, West Virginia, in early January 2000. But Barak, suddenly aware that Israeli public opinion was cool to giving the Golan Heights back to Syria, became inflexible and tried to show that he was being a tough negotiator by slowing the process. The talks collapsed, with Dennis Ross, Clinton's chief Middle East negotiator, later remarking, "If not for Barak's cold feet, there might have been a deal in January 2000."[19] A subsequent meeting two months later in Geneva between Assad and Clinton went nowhere, mainly because the Syrian leader no longer trusted Barak. Clinton clearly blamed Israel, not Syria, for the collapse of the negotiations.[20]

Sharon replaced Barak as prime minister in February 2001. This development changed Israeli-Syrian relations for the worse, which in turn undermined Syrian-American relations as well. Unlike his four predecessors, Sharon had no intention of giving back the Golan Heights. "What was offered back then," he said, "in my wildest imagination, I would not have considered."[21] Sharon's successor, Ehud Olmert, has also made it clear that "the Golan Heights will remain in our hands forever."[22]

This insistence on keeping that disputed territory as part of Israel enjoys widespread support on the Israeli right. When Javier Solana, the secretary general of the Council of the European Union, said in March 2007 that he would like to help Syria get back the territory it lost in 1967, Yisrael Katz, a Knesset member from Likud, responded, "Israel will never retreat from the Golan Heights; the region is an integral part of Israel and vital for its security and protection."[23] Moreover, Benjamin Netanyahu apparently now believes that Israel must remain in the Golan Heights.[24] Israeli public opinion is clearly in favor of hanging on to the territory as well; a December 2006 survey indicated that 64 percent of the respondents opposed withdrawing from the Golan even if it led to full peace with Syria. By contrast, only 19 percent favored the deal. A previous poll in early October 2006 produced similar results: 70 percent opposed full withdrawal in exchange for peace while 16 percent favored it.[25]

Despite this entrenched resistance to withdrawal, there is substantial support within Israel's governing circles for trying to negotiate a deal with Syria, especially within the military. The IDF chief of staff said in 2004 that Israel was capable of defending itself without the Golan Heights and would be more secure if it signed a peace treaty with Syria.[26] Not only would Israel then have normal relations with a long-standing enemy, but Hezbollah, Hamas, and Islamic Jihad would no longer receive support from Syria, and in the case of Hezbollah, loss of Syrian backing would make it much more difficult for Iran to supply it with weapons. Even more important, Syria could use its considerable influence in Lebanon to rein in Hezbollah. This line of argument took on greater urgency after the 2006 Lebanon war, in which Hezbollah was able to fight the IDF to a standstill. In response, a number of influential Israelis, including a former chief of staff and a former head of Shin Bet, created an organization called the Forum of the Peace Initiative with Syria. Its goal is to persuade the Israeli government to respond to Syrian peace overtures and hopefully reach a peace agreement between Damascus and Jerusalem.[27] *Ha'aretz* has also been a strong supporter of negotiations with Damascus, as has Olmert's defense minister, Amir Peretz.[28] This approach, however, was firmly rejected by both Sharon and Olmert.

Given that Israel's current leaders do not intend to return the Golan Heights to Syria, they have no interest in reopening peace talks with Damascus.[29] What is there to talk about? To justify their intransigence, they seek to portray Syria as a rogue state that cannot be trusted and that understands only the mailed fist. It is no wonder that the Syrian ambassador to Washington said in early 2004 that "the more we talk about peace, the more we are attacked."[30] Confrontation, not cooperation, is the best policy for dealing with Syria, according to Israel's current leaders, who have an obvious interest in getting the Bush administration to see Syria in a similar light. Thus, in contrast to the late 1990s, when Israel favored cooperation with Syria, since 2001 both Israel and a number of its American backers have worked hard to convince the U.S. government to treat Syria as a hostile and dangerous enemy.

Syria still hopes to get the Golan Heights back, and it has made repeated attempts to reopen talks with Israel and negotiate a peace agreement along the lines of the "Rabin deposit."[31] But Israel's leaders have refused even to countenance a dialogue with Syria. After a Syrian peace offer in early December 2003, the veteran military correspondent Ze'ev Schiff observed in *Ha'aretz* that "the most astonishing thing about the Syrian president's proposal to resume talks with Israel is the response of official Israel . . . Prime Minister Ariel Sharon has remained silent. Not a word has been heard from him . . . In the past we always hoped for such proposals."[32]

In a mid-December 2006 interview with the Italian newspaper *La Repubblica*, President Assad called on Olmert to negotiate with him: "Talk to

Syria, and like many Israelis are saying, 'even if you think it's a bluff you have nothing to lose.'"[33] At the same time, the Syrian foreign minister told the *Washington Post* that Syria would be willing to begin talks with Israel without any preconditions, which appeared to be a significant change in Syria's bargaining position.[34] Olmert rejected the opportunity to start talks and blamed it on President Bush, who, according to the prime minister, had forbidden him to negotiate with Syria.[35] The implication of the prime minister's comments—which have been repeated by many other Israelis—is that he would talk with Assad were it not for his loyalty to Bush.

This argument is unconvincing. Not only did the U.S. ambassador to Israel deny that Washington was preventing Israel from talking with Syria, but Israel is not in the habit of taking orders from any U.S. leader when its vital interests are at stake.[36] Most important, there is hardly any evidence that Olmert is genuinely interested in meaningful peace talks with Syria. A senior Israeli government official told Aluf Benn of *Ha'aretz* that Israel, in Benn's words, "never requested American permission to talk with Syria, as it has not yet decided whether it wishes to do so."[37] The prime minister's refusal to negotiate is unsurprising, because an agreement "comes with a price tag," to quote Defense Minister Peretz, which is giving up the Golan Heights, and Olmert is opposed to making that concession. Olmert grasped "the pretext" provided by Bush, the *Ha'aretz* reporter Gideon Samet writes, "because he will not admit the real reason: He does not want to come down from the Golan Heights."[38]

Further evidence of Syria's interest in making peace with Israel and Israel's unwillingness to seize the opportunity was revealed in January 2007, when the Israeli press reported that Israelis and Syrians had met secretly in Europe between September 2004 and July 2006 for the purpose of coming up with a proposal for an agreement between the two states. The meetings were unofficial and did not involve policy makers in either government. However, both governments were kept informed of the talks and, according to *Ha'aretz*, "The European mediator and the Syrian representative in the discussions held eight separate meetings with senior Syrian officials, including Vice President Farouk Shara, Foreign Minister Walid Muallem, and a Syrian intelligence officer with the rank of 'general.'"[39] The two sides reached an agreement calling for Israel to return to the June 4, 1967, border between the two countries. In return, Syria would stop supporting Hamas and Hezbollah, and even "distance itself from Iran." The talks ended when the Syrians proposed that they be moved from an "academic level" to an "official level," and the Olmert government refused.

Then, in April 2007, Speaker of the House Pelosi visited President Assad in Damascus and told him that Olmert, with whom she had previously met in Israel, "is ready to restart negotiations as well as to talk peace."[40] Pelosi had misunderstood Olmert's position, however, and the Israeli government let her know in no uncertain terms that he had no interest in talking with Syria, which the official statement denounced as "part of the axis of evil and a force that encourages terror in the entire Middle East."[41]

Olmert's position on the Golan Heights could always change, of course. Indeed, there were press reports in early June 2007 that he might be willing to open negotiations with the Syrians, although Shimon Peres, then vice premier, immediately threw cold water on the idea by claiming that Syria was not ready for serious talks.[42] It is also possible that some future Israeli leader might be willing, as Yitzhak Rabin was, to return the disputed territory in exchange for peace. Our argument is not that Israel will forever refuse to give up the Golan Heights, but instead that Israeli policy toward Damascus, whatever it might be, largely determines U.S. policy toward Syria, not the other way around.

Given Israel's strong opposition to negotiating with Syria since Ariel Sharon came to power in February 2001, it is hardly surprising that the Bush administration, which came to power a month earlier, has gone to considerable lengths during this same time period to isolate and put pressure on the Assad government. Some might say that this analysis misses the crucial point that Syria continues to support terrorist organizations like Hamas and Hezbollah, and thus fully merits being treated as a rogue state by President Bush. But remember: none of those terrorist groups threatens vital U.S. interests, and Damascus backs them mainly because they are the only levers it has to pressure Israel into returning the Golan Heights. Israel could end Syria's ties to Hamas and Hezbollah by agreeing to make peace with Syria, which is why Israeli leaders negotiated with Syria during the 1990s, even though Damascus supported terrorism then as it does now.

As noted, there has been significant resistance inside the U.S. government to treating Syria as an implacable foe. The CIA and the State Department have been especially vocal in making the case that confrontation with Damascus is strategically unwise. Israel and the lobby have taken the opposite position, however, and they have ultimately carried the day with President Bush. Let us look in more detail at the evolution of U.S. policy toward Syria since 9/11.

JERUSALEM AND DAMASCUS AFTER SEPTEMBER 11

From the outset, Prime Minister Sharon and his lieutenants made it clear to the Bush administration that they viewed Syria as a dangerous threat to the United States as well as Israel.[43] They did not push Washington to focus on Syria before March 2003, however, mainly because they were more concerned about Iran, and they were pushing for war against Iraq and did not want Washington to get distracted by other problems. As soon as Baghdad fell in mid-April 2003, Israeli leaders began urging the United States to concentrate on Damascus and to use its unmatched power to change the regime's behavior, or perhaps the regime itself.[44]

Sharon laid out his demands in a high-profile interview on April 15, 2003. In *Yedioth Ahronoth*, the prime minister said that Syrian President Assad "is dangerous. His judgment is impaired," and he claimed that Assad had allowed Saddam to move military equipment into Syria just before the Iraq war began. Sharon called for the United States to put "very heavy" pressure on Syria, in order to force Assad to end its support for Hamas and Islamic Jihad, push Iran's Revolutionary Guards out of the Bekka valley in Lebanon, cease cooperating with Iran, remove Hezbollah from the Israeli-Lebanese border and replace it with the Lebanese army, and eliminate Hezbollah's missiles aimed at Israel.[45] On seeing this remarkably bold request, one high-ranking Israeli diplomat warned that Sharon should adopt a lower profile with regard to offering his advice about relations between Damascus and Washington.[46]

But Sharon was not the only high-level Israeli official asking the Bush administration to get tough with Syria. Defense Minister Shaul Mofaz told *Ma'ariv* on April 14, "We have a long list of issues that we are thinking of demanding of the Syrians and it is appropriate that it should be done through the Americans."[47] Specifically, he wanted Syria to stop all assistance to Hamas and Islamic Jihad and to dismantle Hezbollah. Two weeks later, Sharon's national security adviser, Ephraim Halevy, came to Washington and encouraged U.S. officials to take what the *Forward* reporter Ori Nir termed "decisive action" against Syria. In addition to warning about Syria's weapons of mass destruction, Halevy reportedly described Assad as "irresponsible" and "brash."[48] Addressing a WINEP conference on May 3, he said Assad was "prone to bad influence" and warned that he "cannot be left to his old tricks." Instead, Halevy emphasized, "There are many measures short of war that can be employed to draw the fangs of the young, arrogant, and inexperienced president of Syria."[49]

With Saddam gone, Israel was trying to convince the Bush administration that Syria was at least as dangerous as Iraq, maybe even more so. The claim is absurd if one looks even briefly at Syria's capabilities—it is, after all, a country with fewer than nineteen million people and a defense budget that is 1/300th that of the United States. Yet the Israeli strategist Yossi Alpher now warned that, from Israel's perspective, "Syria could do a lot of damage, a lot more than Iraq." The *Washington Post* reported in mid-April 2003 that Sharon and Mofaz were fueling the campaign against Syria by feeding the United States intelligence reports about the actions of Syrian President Assad.[50]

In their efforts to demonize Syria and bait the United States into ratcheting up the pressure, Israel accused Damascus of harboring high-level Iraqis from Saddam's regime and, even worse, of hiding Iraq's weapons of mass destruction.[51] In August 2003, when a suicide truck bomber blew up UN headquarters in Baghdad, Israel's ambassador to the UN caused a diplomatic spat by suggesting that Syria had provided the truck, in effect implying that Syria was partly responsible.[52] In much the same vein, Itamar Rabinovich, the former Israeli ambassador to the United States, told Seymour Hersh that he "wondered . . . whether, given the quality of their sources, the Syrians had had advance information about the September 11th plot—and failed to warn the United States."[53] There was little or no evidence to support these alarming charges, but Israel's willingness to make them shows how eager it was to get the United States embroiled with another Arab regime.

THE LOBBY AND DAMASCUS AFTER 9/11

It is worth recalling that some important figures in the lobby had their sights on Syria well before the Twin Towers fell. Damascus was a prominent target in the 1996 "Clean Break" study written by a handful of neoconservatives for incoming Prime Minister Netanyahu. In addition, Daniel Pipes and Ziad Abdelnour, the head of the U.S. Committee for a Free Lebanon (USCFL), had coauthored a report in May 2000 calling for the United States to use military threats to force Syria to remove its troops from Lebanon, get rid of its WMD, and stop supporting terrorism.[54] The USCFL is a close cousin to the lobby; numerous neoconservatives are among its major activists and supporters, including Elliott Abrams, Douglas Feith, Richard Perle, and David Wurmser. In fact, all of them signed the 2000 report, as did pro-Israel Congressman Eliot Engel (D-NY), another core USCFL supporter.[55]

This proposal, and others like it, did not gain much traction in Washington during the Clinton years, mainly because Israel was committed to achieving peace with Syria during that period. Apart from these hard-liners, most groups in the lobby had little incentive to challenge Clinton's policy toward Syria, because the president's approach tended to mirror Israel's. But when Sharon came to power in 2001, Israel's thinking about Syria changed dramatically. Reacting to this shift, a number of groups in the lobby began to press for a more aggressive policy toward Damascus.

In the spring of 2002, when Iraq was becoming the main issue, the American Israel Public Affairs Committee was also promoting legislation to formally place Syria on the "axis of evil" and Congressman Engel introduced the Syria Accountability Act in Congress.[56] It threatened sanctions against Syria if it did not withdraw from Lebanon, give up its WMD, and stop supporting terrorism.[57] The proposed act also called for Syria and Lebanon to take concrete steps to make peace with Israel. This legislation was strongly endorsed by a number of groups in the lobby—especially AIPAC—and "framed," according to the Jewish Telegraphic Agency, "by some of Israel's best friends in Congress." JTA also reported that its "most avid proponent in the administration" was Elliott Abrams, who, as we have seen, is in frequent contact with Olmert's office.[58]

The Bush administration opposed the Syria Accountability Act in the spring of 2002, in part because it feared that the legislation might undermine efforts to sell the Iraq war, and in part because it might lead Damascus to stop providing Washington with useful intelligence about al Qaeda. Congress agreed to put the legislation on the back burner until matters were settled with Saddam.

But as soon as Baghdad fell in April 2003, the lobby renewed its campaign against Syria. Encouraged by what then looked like a decisive victory in Iraq, some of Israel's backers were no longer interested in simply getting Syria to change its behavior. Instead, they now wanted to topple the regime itself. Paul Wolfowitz declared that "there has got to be regime change in Syria," and Richard Perle told a journalist that "we could deliver a short message, a two-worded message [to other hostile regimes in the Middle East]: 'You're next.'"[59] The hawkish Defense Policy Board, which was headed by Perle and whose members included Kenneth Adelman, Eliot Cohen, and James Woolsey, was also advocating a hard line against Syria.[60]

In addition to Abrams, Perle, and Wolfowitz, the other key insider pushing for regime change in Syria was Assistant Secretary of State (and later UN Ambassador) John Bolton. He had told Israeli leaders a month before the

Iraq war that President Bush would deal with Syria, as well as Iran and North Korea, right after Saddam fell from power.[61] Toward that end, Bolton reportedly prepared to tell Congress in mid-July that Syria's WMD programs had reached the point where they were a serious threat to stability in the Middle East and had to be dealt with sooner rather than later. The CIA and other government agencies objected, however, and claimed that Bolton was inflating the danger. Consequently, the administration did not allow Bolton to give his testimony on Syria at that time.[62] Yet Bolton was not put off for long. He appeared before Congress in September 2003 and described Syria as a growing threat to U.S. interests in the Middle East.[63]

In early April, WINEP released a bipartisan report stating that Syria "should not miss the message that countries that pursue Saddam's reckless, irresponsible and defiant behavior could end up sharing his fate."[64] On April 15, the Israeli-American journalist Yossi Klein Halevi wrote a piece in the *Los Angeles Times* titled "Next, Turn the Screws on Syria," while that same day neoconservative Frank Gaffney, the head of the Center for Security Policy, wrote in the *Washington Times* that the Bush administration should use "whatever techniques are necessary—including military force—to effect behavior modification and/or regime change in Damascus."[65] The next day Zev Chafets, an Israeli-American journalist and former head of the Israeli government press office, wrote an article for the *New York Daily News* titled "Terror-Friendly Syria Needs a Change, Too." Not to be outdone, Lawrence Kaplan wrote in the *New Republic* on April 21 that Syrian leader Assad was a serious threat to America.[66]

The charges leveled against Syria were remarkably similar to those previously made against Saddam. Writing in *National Review Online*, conservative commentator Jed Babbin maintained that even though Assad's army was a paper tiger, he is still "an exceedingly dangerous man." The basis for that claim was an "Israeli source" who had told Babbin that "Israel's military and intelligence arms are convinced that Assad will take risks a prudent leader wouldn't" and, therefore, "Assad's unpredictability is itself a great danger."[67] Marc Ginsberg, former U.S. ambassador to Morocco, warned of "Syria's secret production of weapons of mass destruction and its weaponization of missile batteries and rockets."[68] And like their Israeli counterparts, American supporters of Israel suggested that Syria was hiding Saddam's WMD. "It wouldn't surprise me," Congressman Engel remarked, "if those weapons of mass destruction that we cannot find in Iraq wound up and are today in Syria."[69]

Back on Capitol Hill, Engel reintroduced the Syria Accountability Act on

April 12.[70] Three days later, Richard Perle called for Congress to pass it.[71] But the Bush administration still had little enthusiasm for the legislation and was able to stall it again. In mid-August, Engel and a group of politicians and Jewish leaders from New York traveled to Israel and met for ninety minutes with Ariel Sharon in his Jerusalem office. The Israeli leader complained to his visitors that the United States was not putting enough pressure on Syria, although he specifically thanked Engel for sponsoring the Syria Accountability Act and made it clear that he strongly favored continued efforts to push the legislation on Capitol Hill.[72] The following month, Engel, who announced he was "fed up with the . . . administration's maneuvering on Syria," began pushing the bill again. With AIPAC's full support, Engel began rounding up votes on Capitol Hill.[73] Bush could no longer hold Congress back in the face of this full-court press from the lobby, and the anti-Syrian act passed by overwhelming margins (398–4 in the House; 89–4 in the Senate). Bush signed it into law on December 12, 2003.[74]

WHY DID BUSH WAVER?

Although Congress had voted overwhelmingly to turn the screws on Syria, the Bush administration was deeply divided about the wisdom of this policy. While neoconservatives like Perle, Bolton, and Wolfowitz were eager to pick a fight with Damascus, there was widespread opposition to that approach inside the State Department and the CIA.[75] Even the president had little enthusiasm for directly confronting Syria, as reflected in the Jewish Telegraphic Agency's description of his signing of the Syria Accountability Act: "Bush signed the act on a Friday night, the time the administration reserves for activities it would rather not share with the public, and the White House statement on the subject was about as 'I've gotta do this but I don't wanna' as it gets."[76] Even after signing the law, Bush emphasized that he would go slowly in implementing it.[77]

Bush had good reasons to be ambivalent. As noted, the Syrian government had provided the United States with important intelligence about al Qaeda since 9/11, and it had also warned Washington about a planned terrorist attack in the Gulf.[78] Moreover, Syria gave CIA interrogators access to Mohammed Zammar, the alleged recruiter of some of the 9/11 hijackers. Flynt Leverett, who worked for Bush in the White House at the time, writes that the president, "in his communications with Bashar, whether by letter or phone, always acknowledged Syria's cooperation with the United States against al-Qaeda."[79] Targeting the Assad regime would jeopardize these valuable connections and undermine the campaign against international terrorism in general and al Qaeda in particular. The president recognized that a confrontational policy toward Syria could put America at risk.

Bush also understood that Syria was not a threat to the United States, even taking into account its possible role in helping the Iraqi insurgency. Assad was actually eager to cooperate with Washington; according to Seymour Hersh, his chief of military intelligence told the administration that Syria would even be willing to work through back channels to discuss ways of restricting the military and political activities of Hezbollah.[80] Playing hardball with Assad would make the United States look like a bully with an insatiable appetite for beating up Arab states. And putting Syria on the American hit list would give Damascus compelling reasons to cause trouble in Iraq and keep the U.S. military pinned down there, so that it could not strike Syria. Even if the president wanted to pressure Syria, it made good sense to finish the job in Iraq first.

The neoconservatives in the administration were naturally opposed to cooperating with Syria. They were even unhappy with the intelligence channel that was providing Washington with important information about al Qaeda. "Neoconservatives in the Office of the Secretary of Defense and the Office of the Vice President," Leverett writes, "opposed accepting Syrian help, arguing that it might create a sense of indebtedness to Damascus and inhibit an appropriate American response to a state sponsor of terrorism."[81] President Bush, however, has shown little interest in this kind of "appropriate response." Indeed, he instructed the Pentagon not to plan for war against Syria in mid-April 2003, when the United States appeared to have just won a dramatic victory in Iraq and when talk about striking Syria was beginning to fill the air.[82] He certainly has not changed his mind on this matter in light of what has happened in Iraq since those heady days. The president has also been slow to implement the Syria Accountability Act, as he promised when he signed it, much to the irritation of pro-Israel hard-liners in the United States. By the spring of 2004, Congressman Engel and some of his colleagues were so frustrated with Bush over his foot dragging that they threatened to introduce a new and tougher version of the legislation.[83]

Contrary to Olmert's claims, there have even been scattered reports in the media over the past few years that the Bush administration might react positively if Israel accepted Assad's offer to reopen peace talks. Ze'ev Schiff, for example, wrote in December 2003 that "in the opinion of American sources familiar with the thinking in the administration, it would have responded positively to an Israeli acceptance of Assad's proposal. The United States is not looking in principle for a military confrontation with Damascus and is ready to let Assad get onto a positive track."[84] A month later, Aluf Benn wrote in Ha'aretz that "senior American officials" had told the Israelis that the United States "will not object, should Israel choose to take up Syrian President Bashar Assad's offer to resume negotiations." Benn noted, however, that "Israel has received contradictory advice from lower-level administration officials."[85] There have also been other reports saying that Washington was opposed to Israel talking with Syria.[86] The Bush administration's bottom line is difficult to discern, due to the continuing tug-of-war among policy makers over how best to deal with Damascus and a recognition of competing interests.

Although Bush has not taken serious measures to topple Assad, the lobby has pushed him to take a more confrontational line toward Syria than he would probably have adopted on his own.[87] The president and his key advisers have consistently used harsh rhetoric or made veiled threats when talking about Damascus, and they have repeatedly charged Syria with supporting the insurgents in Iraq. They have also been quick to blame Syria anytime there is trouble in Lebanon, and Bush has made no attempt to forge a pragmatic relationship with Syria or to mend fences with it. Neoconservatives inside and outside the administration have continued to call for using military force against Assad's regime. Such calls were especially evident during the Lebanon war in the summer of 2006.[88] Meyrav Wurmser, who runs the Center for Middle East Policy at the Hudson Institute, commented after the war that there was much anger toward Israel among her neoconservative colleagues "over the fact that Israel did not fight against the Syrians. Instead of Israel fighting against Hizbullah, many parts of the American administration believe that Israel should have fought against the real enemy, which is Syria and not Hizbullah."[89]

CONCLUSION

Unfortunately, Washington's confrontational approach toward Damascus has produced nothing but negative consequences for the United States and undermined Israel's long-term interests too. To begin with, Syria has stopped providing Washington with intelligence about al Qaeda.[90] Assad has done little to help the United States shut down the insurgency in Iraq and may be trying to protect his own position by helping to keep it going.[91] After all, keeping the United States bogged down in Baghdad makes it less likely that the United States will be free to go after Syria. Damascus also has continued to support

Hezbollah in Lebanon and has formed a tacit alliance with Iran, which makes it harder to maintain peace in Lebanon and to discourage Iran from pursuing nuclear weapons. Although these developments are not good for the United States, hard-liners in the lobby remain committed to a policy of confrontation and are quick to criticize anyone who suggests a different course.

Yet in the wake of Israel's debacle in Lebanon last summer, and especially given the disastrous situation facing the United States in Iraq, significant pressure is now being put on President Bush to extend an olive branch to Syria.[92] The hope is that Damascus might help stabilize the situation in Iraq, allow American troops to be withdrawn, and establish some semblance of order there. It also might be possible to peel Syria away from its alliance with Iran and weaken Hezbollah in the process. As noted, a number of senators and representatives—including Speaker of the House Nancy Pelosi—have defied the Bush administration and traveled to Damascus to meet with President Assad. Their aim is to improve relations between Syria and the United States, as recommended by the bipartisan Iraq Study Group, which would make it easier to address a number of regional security issues.

But Israeli leaders—who appear determined to hold on to the Golan Heights—have no interest in seeing the United States establish cooperative relations with Syria.[93] The most powerful groups in the lobby share Israel's perspective, and they have worked hard—and thus far successfully—to keep the Bush administration from pursuing a more cooperative relationship with the Assad regime. The result is that the United States continues to pursue a strategically foolish policy toward Syria and will in all likelihood continue to do so until Israel gets a prime minister like Yitzhak Rabin, who understood that exchanging the Golan Heights for peace with Syria would leave Israel in a substantially better strategic position.

The story here is a simple one: without the lobby's influence, there would have been no Syria Accountability Act and U.S. policy toward Damascus would have been more in line with the American national interest. One could add that a different U.S. policy might well have produced a Syrian-Israeli peace treaty by now, a treaty that would have further enshrined Israel's legitimacy and regional supremacy and reduced international support for its most determined, recalcitrant, and violent foes: Hamas, Hezbollah, and Islamic Jihad.

America's misguided approach to Syria is not the only case where the lobby has insisted on a counterproductive policy of confrontation, to the detriment of the United States and Israel alike. One sees much the same story in recent U.S. policy toward Iran, which is the subject of the next chapter.

10

IRAN IN THE CROSSHAIRS

The United States and Iran have had an adversarial relationship ever since the 1979 revolution established the Islamic Republic. Given past U.S. interference in Iran—most notably the 1953 coup that restored Mohammad Reza Shah Pahlavi to power—and the new regime's support for various radical groups, it is hardly surprising that the two states have remained suspicious of one another and only occasionally engaged in limited acts of cooperation.

Iran is a more serious strategic challenge for the United States and Israel than is Syria. Both Damascus and Tehran support Hezbollah, Hamas, and Islamic Jihad, and both are enemies of al Qaeda. Each has chemical weapons and might have biological weapons, although the evidence for the latter is not conclusive. But there are three fundamental differences between Iran and Syria.

First, Iran is seeking to master the full nuclear fuel cycle, which would allow it to build nuclear weapons if it so chose. It is also developing missiles that could deliver nuclear warheads against its neighbors, including Israel.[1] This is why Israelis often refer to Iran as an "existential" threat. Iran will not be able to strike the American homeland with nuclear missiles anytime soon, but any weapons it might develop could be used against U.S. forces stationed in the Middle East, or against European countries.

Second, some Iranian leaders—and especially current President Mahmoud Ahmadinejad—have made deeply disturbing remarks questioning both the occurrence of the Holocaust and Israel's right to exist. Although Ahmadinejad's call for Israel to "vanish from the page of time" (or to be "erased from the pages of history") is often mistranslated as a call for Israel's physical destruction (i.e., to "wipe Israel off the map"), it was still an outrageous assertion that was bound to be profoundly troubling to Israelis and many others.[2] Iran's sponsorship of a conference on the Holocaust in December 2006, which featured prominent Holocaust deniers and other discredited extremists, merely reinforced global concerns about Iran's intentions.

Third, Iran is the most powerful Islamic state in the Persian Gulf and has the potential to dominate that oil-rich area.[3] This is especially true in light of what has happened to Iraq since America invaded in March 2003. Iraq had been Iran's principal rival in the region, but it is now a divided and wartorn society and is in no position to check Iran. Iran has links to several of the dominant Shia factions in Iraq, giving it far more influence over Iraq's evolution than it possessed when Saddam Hussein ruled in Baghdad. This dramatic shift in the regional balance of power explains why some believe that "Iran looks like the winner of the Iraq War."[4] Of course, Iran's power advantage over its neighbors would be even more pronounced if it acquired a nuclear arsenal.

Iran's growing power is not good for the United States, which has long sought to prevent any one country from establishing hegemony in the Persian Gulf. This basic principle explains why the Reagan administration backed Saddam in the 1980s, when it looked like Iran might defeat Iraq in their bloody war. The United States also has strong incentives to prevent Iran from getting nuclear weapons. Israel is equally averse to seeing Iran dominate the Gulf, because a regional powerhouse of that sort could be a long-term strategic threat. The prospect of a nuclear Iran is even more worrisome for Israeli leaders, who tend to view it as the ultimate nightmare scenario.

But Israel is not the only Middle East country that is now worried about Iran. Many of Iran's Arab neighbors are also concerned about its nuclear ambitions as well as its growing influence in the region. They fear that an especially powerful Iran might someday try to coerce them or even invade their country, as Saddam invaded Kuwait in August 1990. They are also somewhat suspicious of Iran because it is a Persian rather than an Arab state, and because they care about the balance of power within Islam between Shia and Sunnis. Iran is governed by deeply committed Shia, which alarms the leaders of Sunni-dominated states like Saudi Arabia, Kuwait, and the United Arab Emirates, who see Shia influence growing in the Arab world. For the first time, Shia govern Iraq, and Hezbollah, a Shia organization, has gained greater influence in Lebanon in the wake of its 2006 war with Israel. To make matters worse, Tehran has close ties with some Iraqi leaders and is a longtime supporter of Hezbollah.

The United States, Israel, and Iran's Arab neighbors, including many of America's Gulf allies, have an independent interest in keeping Iran non-nuclear and preventing it from becoming a regional hegemon. Washington would be committed to keeping Iran in check even if Israel did not exist, so as to prevent the other Gulf states from being conquered or cowed by Tehran. Unqualified support from the Arab world would make it easier for the United States to preserve the balance of power in the Gulf, and obtaining that support requires an effective strategy.

Over the past fifteen years, Israel and the lobby have pushed the United States to pursue a strategically unwise policy toward Iran. In particular, they are the central forces today behind all the talk in the Bush administration and on Capitol Hill about using military force to destroy Iran's nuclear facilities. Unfortunately, such rhetoric makes it harder, not easier, to stop Iran from going nuclear. During the 1990s, Israel and its American supporters encouraged the Clinton administration to pursue a confrontational policy toward Iran, even though Iran was interested in improving relations between the two countries. That same pattern was at play again in the early years of the Bush administration, as well as in December 2006, when Israel and the lobby made a concerted effort to undermine the Iraq Study Group's recommendation that President Bush negotiate with Iran. Were it not for the lobby, the United States would almost certainly have a different and more effective Iran policy.

U.S. efforts to deal with Iran are further undermined by Israel's repressive policies in the Occupied Territories, which make it harder for the United States to gain the cooperation of Arab countries. Indeed, one of the main reasons that Secretary of State Condoleezza Rice finally began pushing forward the Arab-Israeli peace process in late 2006 was Saudi Arabia's insistence that it could not fashion an effective Iran policy with Washington as long as there was so much anger toward the United States in the Arab world over the Palestinian issue. As discussed in Chapter 7, Rice's efforts are likely to fail, because Israel's current leaders do not want to create a viable Palestinian state and the lobby will make it very difficult for President Bush or any other president to get Israel to change its approach to this issue. In short, thanks in good part to Israel and its American backers, the United States has pursued a counterproductive policy toward Iran since the early 1990s and is having difficulty getting support from states that have their own reasons to help Washington deal with Iran and would otherwise be inclined to do so.

CONFRONTATION OR CONCILIATION?

The United States had excellent relations with Iran from 1953 until 1979, when the American-backed shah was toppled and Ayatollah Khomeini and his Islamic theocracy came to power. Since then, relations between the two countries have been almost entirely adversarial. Israel has also had hostile relations with Tehran since the shah's overthrow. During the 1980s, however, neither the United States nor Israel was seriously threatened by Iran, mainly because it was involved in a lengthy war with Iraq, which pinned it down and sapped its strength. To preserve the regional balance of power, the United States simply had to make sure that the war ended in a stalemate. It accomplished this objective by helping Saddam Hussein's forces stymie Iran's army on the battlefield. Iran was exhausted when the war ended in 1988, and it was in no position to cause trouble in the region for at least a few years. Furthermore, Iran's nuclear program was put on the back burner during the 1980s, possibly because of the war.

Israel's perception of the Iranian threat underwent a fundamental change in the early 1990s, as evidence of Tehran's nuclear ambitions began to accumulate. Israeli leaders began warning Washington in 1993 that Iran was a grave threat not only to Israel but to the United States as well. There has been no letup in that alarmist and aggressive rhetoric since then, largely because Iran has continued to move ahead on the nuclear front. Today, many experts believe the Iranians will eventually build nuclear weapons unless something is done to topple the clerical regime, alter its ambitions, or deny it the capacity. The lobby has followed Israel's lead and echoed its warnings about the dangers of allowing Iran to become a nuclear power.

Israel and the lobby are also troubled by Iran's support for Hezbollah, by its endorsement of the Palestinian cause, and by its refusal to accept Israel's right to exist. Needless to say, statements like President Ahmadinejad's reinforce these concerns. Israel and its supporters tend to see Iran's policies as a reflection of deep ideological antipathy to the Jewish state, but they are more accurately seen as tactical measures intended to improve Iran's overall position in the region. In particular, endorsing the Palestinian cause (and helping groups like Hezbollah) wins sympathy in the Arab world and helps discourage an Arab alliance against Persian Iran. As the Iran expert Trita Parsi convincingly shows, Iran's commitment to Hezbollah and to the Palestinians has varied considerably over time, usually in response to the overall threat environment. Relations between the clerical regime in Iran and the largely secular PLO were not warm during the 1980s, and Iran began backing hard-line Palestinian groups like Islamic Jihad only after its exclusion from the 1991 Madrid Conference and the onset of the Oslo peace process. These events led Tehran to resist what it correctly saw as a broad U.S. effort to isolate it and deny it a significant regional role, and it did so by backing extremist groups that also opposed Oslo. As Martin Indyk, who played a key role in formulating U.S. policy at the time, later recalled, Iran "had an incentive to do us in on the peace process in order to defeat our policy of containment and isolation. And therefore, they took aim at the peace process."[5]

There are two broad alternatives for dealing with Iran's nuclear program and its regional ambitions. One approach, which is favored by the Israeli government and its key American supporters, proceeds from the belief that Iran cannot be contained once it acquires nuclear weapons. This view assumes that Tehran is likely to use its nuclear weapons against Israel, because Iranian leaders, with their apocalyptic vision of history, would not fear Israeli retaliation.[6] They might give nuclear weapons to terrorists or use them against the United States themselves, even if doing so invited automatic and massive retaliation. Therefore, Iran cannot be allowed to acquire a nuclear arsenal. Israel would like Washington to solve this problem, but Israeli leaders do not rule out the possibility that the Israel Defense Forces might try to do the job if the Americans get cold feet.

This approach also assumes that conciliatory diplomacy and positive incentives will not convince Iran to abandon its nuclear program. In concrete terms, this means that the United States has to impose sanctions on Iran—and maybe even conduct a preventive war—if it continues down the nuclear road. To facilitate putting serious pressure on Iran, Israelis and the lobby want the United States to maintain a substantial American military presence in the Middle East, in contrast to America's pre-1990 strategy of acting as an offshore balancer and keeping its military forces over the horizon.

For the past fifteen years, this confrontational formula for dealing with Iran's nuclear program has vied with a second strategy, one more consistent with the American national interest. This alternative approach asserts that while it would be better for the United States if Iran did not acquire nuclear weapons, there is good reason to think a nuclear Iran could be contained and deterred, just as the Soviet Union was contained during the Cold War.[7] It also argues that the best way to stop Iran from building nuclear weapons is to engage it diplomatically and attempt to normalize its relationship with the United States. This strategy requires taking the threat of preventive war off the table, because threatening Iran with regime change simply gives its leaders even more reason to want a nuclear deterrent of their own. The Iranians, like the Americans and the Israelis, recognize that nuclear weapons are the best protection available for a state that is on another state's hit list. As the Iran expert Ray Takeyh of the Council on Foreign Relations has written, "Iran's nuclear calculations are not derived from an irrational ideology, but rather from a judicious attempt to craft a viable deterrent capability against an evolving range of threats . . . Iran's leadership clearly sees itself as being in Washington's cross hairs, and it is precisely this perception that is driving its accelerated nuclear program."[8]

The case for engagement is buttressed by the fact that preventive war looks like a very unattractive alternative. Even if the United States could eliminate Iran's nuclear facilities, Tehran would almost certainly rebuild them, and this time the Iranians would go to even greater lengths to disperse, hide, and harden them against an attack.[9] Also, if Washington launched a preventive strike against Iran, Tehran would be bound to retaliate wherever and whenever it could, including going after oil shipments in the Persian Gulf and using its considerable influence to make matters worse for the United States in Iraq. Additionally, Iran would be likely to establish closer ties with China and Russia, which is not in America's interest. By contrast, if the United States were to remove the threat of war and engage Iran, then Tehran would be more inclined to help Washington deal with al Qaeda, tamp down the war inside Iraq, and stabilize Afghanistan. It would also be less likely to align with China and Russia.[10]

Given the history of poisonous relations between America and Iran, there is no guarantee that engagement would produce a "grand bargain" that would halt Iran's nuclear program. After all, there is little chance that Israel will give up its own nuclear weapons, and Iranian leaders might believe that if Israel has a nuclear deterrent, then so must Iran. Nonetheless, this approach is more likely to work than threatening preventive war, and if it does fail, the United States can always fall back on deterrence.

One might have expected the United States to have adopted some variation on the engagement strategy by this time, especially given that a decade and a half of confrontation has not borne fruit. Engagement enjoys substantial support in the CIA, the State Department, and even the U.S. military, which has shown little enthusiasm for bombing Iran's nuclear facilities. London's *Sunday Times* reported in late February 2007 that "some of America's most senior military commanders are prepared to resign if the White House orders a military strike against Iran, according to highly placed defense and intelligence sources."[11] In fact, Iran has repeatedly signaled an interest in engagement: its leaders have reached out to the United States on a number of occasions over the past fifteen years, hoping to improve relations between the two countries. Remarkably, Iran has even offered to put its nuclear program up for negotiation and offered to work out a modus vivendi with Israel.

Yet despite these promising opportunities, Israel and the lobby have worked overtime to prevent both the Clinton and Bush administrations from engaging Iran, and they have prevailed at almost every turn. Unfortunately, but predictably, this hard-line approach has not worked as advertised and has left the United States worse off than if it had pursued a strategy of engagement. In response to this failed strategy, there is a growing chorus of voices inside and outside of Washington calling for a new opening toward Iran. Equally unsurprising, Israel and the lobby are fighting to prevent the United States from reversing course and seeking a rapprochement with Tehran. They continue to promote an increasingly confrontational and counterproductive policy instead.

THE CLINTON ADMINISTRATION AND DUAL CONTAINMENT

In early 1993, just as the Clinton administration was coming to power, Israeli Prime Minister Yitzhak Rabin and his foreign minister, Shimon Peres, started claiming that Iran was a growing threat to both Israel and the United States. Israeli leaders portrayed Iran as a dangerous adversary in part because they saw it as a way of fostering closer relations between Jerusalem and Washington now that the Soviet threat had disappeared. The hope was that the United States would see Israel as a bulwark against Iranian expansionism, much the way Israel had been treated as a bulwark against Soviet influence in the Middle East. Israel was also justifiably concerned about Iran's renewed interest in developing a sophisticated nuclear program.[12] The *Washington Post* reported in mid-March 1993 that "across the Israeli political spectrum, there is a conviction that American public opinion and political leaders need to be further convinced of the urgency of restraining Iran, and that the United States is the only global power capable of doing so."[13]

The Clinton administration responded to Israel's entreaties by adopting the policy of dual containment, as we have discussed. Not only was the policy first enunciated at the Washington Institute for Near East Policy by Martin Indyk, but Robert Pelletreau, the assistant secretary of state for Near Eastern affairs at the time, told Trita Parsi that the policy was essentially a copy of an

Israeli proposal.[14] Kenneth Pollack of Brookings's Saban Center also notes that "Jerusalem was one of the few places on Earth where dual containment was not regularly misunderstood."[15] The new policy called for the United States to abandon its traditional strategy of acting as an offshore balancer in the Persian Gulf and instead station a substantial number of troops in Kuwait and Saudi Arabia for the purpose of containing both Iran and Iraq. In fact, the policy was designed to do more than just contain Iran; it also aimed to cause "dramatic changes in Iran's behavior." Among its goals was forcing Iran to stop supporting terrorists and to abandon its nuclear program.[16]

Israel's concerns notwithstanding, there was no good reason for the United States to adopt a hard-line policy toward Iran in the early 1990s. If anything, just the opposite was the case. Akbar Hashemi Rafsanjani, who became Iran's president in 1989, was committed to improving relations with Washington, and Iran, which had recently suffered through a devastating war with Iraq, was hardly a military threat to the United States. In the early 1990s, in fact, American leaders were much more concerned about Saddam Hussein, against whom the United States had just fought a war.[17] Plus, Iran's nuclear program had barely gotten off the ground in 1993. Few voices in Washington were calling for tougher policies against Iran before Israel began clamoring for a more confrontational policy, and dual containment was widely criticized when it was first announced.[18]

By the mid-1990s, there was growing dissatisfaction with dual containment, because it forced the United States to maintain hostile relations with two countries that disliked each other intensely, and it left Washington pretty much alone to handle the demanding task of keeping them in line. Consequently, pressure began to build in the United States to think about engaging Iran rather than confronting it.[19] At the same time, however, Rabin was under pressure in Israel to get the Clinton administration to toughen up the policy.[20] Rabin's critics felt that dual containment had no real teeth because it had done little to stop the substantial economic intercourse between Iran and the United States. Israel and the lobby, especially the American Israel Public Affairs Committee, mobilized to save dual containment and to close the loopholes that allowed American companies to trade and invest in Iran. In mid-1994, Parsi reports, "At the behest of the Israeli government, AIPAC drafted and circulated a 74-page paper in Washington arguing that Iran was not only a threat to Israel, but also to the United States and the West."[21] According to Pollack, "The right, AIPAC, the Israelis were all screaming for new sanctions [on Iran]."[22] The Clinton administration was willing to go along, largely because it was focusing on the Oslo peace process and wanted to make sure that Israel felt secure and that Iran, a potential spoiler, did not derail the process.

AIPAC laid out its basic game plan in April 1995, when it issued a report titled "Comprehensive U.S. Sanctions Against Iran: A Plan for Action."[23] By that point, however, steps were already being taken to tighten the economic noose around Iran's neck. Senator Alfonse D'Amato (R-NY)—with, according to Pollack, "some help from the Israelis"—introduced legislation in January 1995 to end all economic links between the United States and Iran.[24] The Clinton administration opposed the legislation at first and it stalled in Congress.

But two months later, groups in the lobby achieved their first success after Iran chose Conoco, an American oil company, to develop the Sirri oil fields.[25] Iran deliberately selected Conoco over several other foreign bidders in order to signal its interest in improving relations with the United States. But this friendly overture went nowhere, because Clinton killed the deal on March 14. One day later, he issued an executive order banning American companies from helping Iran develop its oil fields. Clinton later said that "one of the most effective opponents" of the Conoco deal was Edgar Bronfman Sr., the powerful former head of the World Jewish Congress.[26] AIPAC also played a key role in scuttling that deal.[27]

On May 6, the president issued a second executive order banning all trade and financial investments with Iran, which he labeled an "unusual and extraordinary threat to the national security, foreign policy, and economy of the United States."[28] Clinton had actually announced that he was going to take that step one week earlier in a speech to the World Jewish Congress.[29] His decision to nix the Conoco deal and issue those two executive orders was, notes Pollack, "a major demonstration of our support for Israel."[30] Ironically, although Israel lay behind the American decision to cut economic ties to Iran, Israel did not pass any laws barring Israeli-Iranian trade and Israelis continued to purchase Iranian goods through third parties.[31]

But those executive orders were not enough for the lobby, because executive orders could be quickly reversed if Clinton ever changed his mind. A. M. Rosenthal, a strong defender of Israel, made this point in a *New York Times* column in which he criticized the Conoco deal: "The only problem [with executive orders] is that what the President giveth he can canceleth."[32] In response to this potential problem, Trita Parsi reports that "on its own initiative, AIPAC revised" the bill that Senator D'Amato had introduced in January 1995 "and convinced the New York Senator to reintroduce it in 1996—with AIPAC's proposed changes."[33] The new bill, which eventually became the Iran-Libya Sanctions Act, imposed sanctions on any foreign companies investing more than $40 million to develop petroleum resources in Iran or Libya. Although the proposed legislation infuriated America's European allies, the House passed it by a vote of 415–0 on June 19, 1996, and the Senate passed it by unanimous consent one month later. Clinton signed the bill on August 5, even though there was significant opposition to the new legislation throughout the administration. Indeed, Kenneth Pollack writes that "much of the executive branch hated the D'Amato bill. In fact, for many, 'hated' was too mild a word." However, "many of President Clinton's domestic policy advisors thought it would be sheer stupidity for the White House not to endorse the bill."[34]

Since Clinton was up for reelection in three months, they were probably right. As Ze'ev Schiff, the military correspondent for *Ha'aretz*, noted at the time, "Israel is but a tiny element in the big scheme, but one should not conclude that it cannot influence those within the beltway."[35] Similarly, James Schlesinger, who has held a number of cabinet-level positions in different administrations, remarked in the wake of these sanctions, "It is scarcely possible to overstate the influence of Israel's supporters on our policies in the Middle East."[36]

The Conoco episode casts further doubt on the oft-repeated claim that the "oil lobby" is the real hidden hand behind U.S. Middle East policy. In this case, an American oil company wanted to deal with Iran, and Iran wanted to do business with it. The oil industry was opposed to overturning the Conoco deal, and it also opposed the legislation to impose sanctions on Iran.[37] As noted in Chapter 4, Dick Cheney, a prominent advocate of confronting Iran today, publicly opposed the U.S. sanctions program when he was president of the oil-services company Halliburton in the 1990s. But oil interests were steamrolled by AIPAC on every decision. These outcomes provide more evidence of how little influence the oil companies have on U.S. Middle East policy, when compared with Israel and the lobby.

The American posture continued to harden even as new opportunities for engagement became apparent. On May 23, 1997, Mohammad Khatami was elected president of Iran. He was even more enthusiastic than his predecessor about improving relations with the West, and the United States in particular. He made conciliatory remarks in his inaugural speech on August 4 and in his first press conference on December 14. Most important, he went out of his way in a lengthy CNN interview on January 7, 1998, to express his respect for "the great American people" and "their great civilization." He also made it clear that Iran did not "aim . . . to destroy or undermine the American government" and that he regretted the infamous takeover of the U.S. embassy in 1979. Recognizing the existing hostility between Tehran and Washington, he called for "a crack in this wall of mistrust to prepare for a change and create an opportunity to study a new situation."[38]

Furthermore, Khatami did not rule out the possibility of an Israeli state in historic Palestine and declared that "terrorism should be condemned in all its forms and manifestations." He also denounced terrorism against Israelis, while noting that "supporting peoples who fight for the liberation of their land is not, in my opinion, supporting terrorism." This caveat notwithstanding, Khatami's remarks were still a marked shift in Iran's position, and other Iranian spokesmen soon echoed Iran's willingness to accept Israel if it reached an agreement with the Palestinians.[39]

In the wake of Khatami's conciliatory comments, the Clinton administration—after checking with Israel and key figures in Congress—made a number of small gestures to improve relations between Iran and the United States.[40] Clinton and Secretary of State Madeleine Albright made contrite remarks about past Western conduct, and the United States eased visa restrictions on travel between the two countries. Even Martin Indyk, the architect of dual containment who was then serving as U.S. ambassador to Israel, told reporters that "the United States has made it clear repeatedly that we have nothing against an Islamic government in Iran . . . We are ready for a dialogue."[41] But the commercial restrictions remained in force and dual containment continued for the rest of Clinton's second term. This failure to alter course was partly due to hard-liners inside Iran, who were strongly opposed to Khatami's plans to engage with the "great Satan."[42] But Israel and its supporters in the United States also played an important role in discouraging an American-Iranian rapprochement.

For starters, the lobby had been largely responsible for developing and sustaining dual containment in the years before Khatami came to power in 1997. That policy, of course, helped poison relations between Tehran and Washington, which, in turn, increased the political power of the Iranian politicians who opposed Iran's new and more moderate leader. Furthermore, as soon as it became clear in mid-December 1997 that Khatami was calling for better relations with America, Israeli officials moved to thwart his initiative. *Ha'aretz* reported that "Israel has expressed its concern to Washington at reports of an impending change of policy by the United States towards Iran," adding that Prime Minister Netanyahu "has asked AIPAC . . . to act vigorously in Congress to prevent such a policy shift."[43]

AIPAC did as Netanyahu asked. According to Gary Sick, one of America's leading experts on Iran, "The gradual improvement of U.S.-Iran relations after the election of Khatami was not reflected in AIPAC's positions. In fact, by early 1999 only AIPAC, the Iranian monarchists in exile and the terrorist Mojahedin-e Khalq persisted in their relentless insistence that little or nothing had changed in Iran."[44] Even after the Israeli ambassador to the United States had said in the spring of 2000 that it would be acceptable for Clinton to allow certain food and medical supplies to be exported to Iran, AIPAC still campaigned against the legislation. AIPAC did not oppose Clinton's decision to lift the ban on caviar, Persian rugs, and pistachios imported from Iran, but the Anti-Defamation League and the Conference of Presidents of Major American Jewish Organizations did.[45] Clinton ultimately got his way in both cases, mainly because each involved small amounts of trade and little controversy. But the United States did not make a serious effort to grasp the hand that Khatami had tentatively extended.

It made good sense for the United States to engage Iran during the 1990s and attempt to improve relations between the two countries. Dual containment, as Brent Scowcroft observed, "was a nutty idea."[46] Israeli leaders, however, believed that it was in Israel's interest to prevent President Clinton from pursuing engagement, even if that more aggressive policy was not in America's national interest. Ephraim Sneh, one of Israel's leading hawks on Iran, put the point succinctly: "We were against it [United States–Iran dialogue] . . . because the interest of the US did not coincide with ours."[47] The lobby followed Israel's lead.

THE BUSH ADMINISTRATION AND REGIME CHANGE

As discussed in Chapter 8, the attacks on September 11, 2001, led President Bush to abandon dual containment and pursue the even more ambitious strategy of regional transformation. The American military would now be used to topple hostile regimes across the Middle East. From Israel's perspective, Iran was ideally suited to be the first target on the Bush administration's hit list. Since the early 1990s, Israeli leaders have tended to portray Iran as their most dangerous enemy because it is the adversary most likely to acquire nuclear weapons. As Israeli Defense Minister Binyamin Ben-Eliezer remarked one year before the Iraq war, "Iraq is a problem . . . But you should understand, if you ask me, today Iran is more dangerous than Iraq."[48]

Nevertheless, Sharon and his lieutenants recognized by early 2002 that the United States was determined to confront Iraq first and deal with Iran after Saddam had been removed from power. They raised no serious objections to this ordering of the agenda, although they kept reminding the Bush administration that it had to deal with Iran as soon as it finished the job in Baghdad. Sharon began publicly pushing the United States to confront Iran in November 2002, in an interview with the *Times* of London.[49] Describing Iran as the "center of world terror" and bent on acquiring nuclear weapons, he declared that the Bush administration should put the strong arm on Iran "the day after" it conquered Iraq.

In late April 2003, after the fall of Baghdad, *Ha'aretz* reported that the Israeli ambassador in Washington was now calling for regime change in Iran. The overthrow of Saddam, he noted, was "not enough." In his words, America "has to follow through. We still have great threats of that magnitude coming from Syria, coming from Iran."[50] Ten days later, the *New York Times* reported that Washington was growing increasingly concerned about Iran's nuclear ambitions and that there is "a lot of hammering from the Israelis for us to take this problem seriously."[51] Shimon Peres then published an op-ed in the *Wall Street Journal* on June 25 titled "We Must Unite to Prevent an Ayatollah Nuke." His description of the Iranian threat sounded just like his earlier description of the threat from Saddam, even including a ritual reference to the lessons of appeasement in the 1930s. Iran, he emphasized, must be told in no uncertain terms that the United States and Israel will not tolerate it going nuclear.[52]

The neoconservatives also lost no time in making the case for regime change in Tehran. In late May 2003, Inter Press Service reported that "the neo-cons' efforts to now focus US attention on 'regime change' in Iran have become much more intense since early May and [have] already borne substantial fruit."[53] In early June, according to the *Forward*, "Neoconservatives inside and outside the administration have been urging an active effort to promote regime change in Tehran. Reports of possible covert actions have surfaced in recent weeks."[54]

As usual, there was a bevy of articles by prominent neoconservatives—essentially the same people who had helped push the war in Iraq—making the case for going after Iran. William Kristol wrote in the *Weekly Standard* on May 12 that "the liberation of Iraq was the first great battle for the future of the Middle East . . . But the next great battle—not, we hope, a military battle—will be for Iran."[55] Michael Ledeen, one of the leading hawks on Iran, wrote in the *National Review Online* on April 4, "There is no more time for diplomatic 'solutions.' We will have to deal with the terror masters, here and now. Iran, at least, offers us the possibility of a memorable victory, because the Iranian people openly loath the regime, and will enthusiastically combat it, if only the United States supports them in their just struggle."[56]

Other pundits offering similar views at this time include Daniel Pipes of the Middle East Forum and WINEP's Patrick Clawson, who published a piece in the *Jerusalem Post* on May 20 titled "Turn Up the Pressure on Iran." They called for the Bush administration to support the Mojahedin-e Khalq, a group based in Iraq that is bent on overthrowing the regime in Tehran but that the U.S. government has designated a terrorist organization. Lawrence Kaplan argued in the *New Republic* on June 9 that the United States needed to get tougher with Iran over its nuclear programs, which he feared were further along than most American policy makers recognized.[57]

On May 6, the American Enterprise Institute cosponsored an all-day conference on the future of Iran with two other pro-Israel organizations, the Foundation for the Defense of Democracies and the Hudson Institute.[58] The speakers were all strong supporters of Israel like Bernard Lewis, Senator Sam Brownback, Uri Lubrani (senior adviser to the IDF and former Israeli government coordinator for southern Lebanon), Morris Amitay from the Jewish Institute for National Security Affairs (and former executive director of AIPAC), Michael Ledeen, Reuel Marc Gerecht from the AEI, and Meyrav Wurmser from the Hudson Institute. The main question on the table was the obvious one: "What steps can the United States take to promote democratization and regime change in Iran?" The answer was predictable: each of the speakers called for the United States to do much more to bring down the Islamic Republic and replace it with a democratic state.

Toward this end, the lobby has struck up a close relationship with Reza Pahlavi, the son of the late shah of Iran. He is believed to have had personal meetings with both Sharon and Netanyahu, and he has extensive contacts with pro-Israel groups and individuals in the United States. The evolving relationship is much like the one that influential groups in the lobby had previously cultivated with Iraqi exile Ahmed Chalabi. Seemingly unaware that Pahlavi (like Chalabi) has little legitimacy in his homeland, pro-Israel groups have promoted his cause. In return, he makes it clear that if he were to come to power in Iran, he would make sure that his country has friendly relations with Israel.[59]

On May 19, 2003, Senator Sam Brownback announced that he planned to introduce legislation to fund opposition groups and promote democracy in Iran. The so-called Iran Democracy Act was backed not only by Iranian exiles but also by AIPAC, JINSA, and the Coalition for Democracy in Iran, whose founders included Morris Amitay of JINSA and Michael Ledeen of

AEI. The bill was introduced in the House by Brad Sherman (D-CA), another dedicated supporter of Israel, and by late July it had been passed by both houses of Congress, although the funding was removed from the final legislation.[60]

The groups backing this legislation have emphasized that Iran is a major menace because it supports terrorism and is close to becoming a nuclear power. But they also have tried to blame Iran for some of the other problems that the United States has faced since the fall of Baghdad. Neoconservatives in the Pentagon suggested that Iran was harboring some of the al Qaeda operatives who had attacked U.S. and other targets in Riyadh, Saudi Arabia, on May 12, 2003. The Iranians denied this charge, and both the CIA and the State Department viewed the neoconservatives' accusations with considerable skepticism.[61] The neoconservatives have also been among the most forceful proponents of the claim that Iran has been supporting attacks against American troops in Iraq. As Michael Ledeen wrote in April 2004, "Iraq cannot be peaceful and secure so long as Tehran sends its terrorist cadres across the border."[62]

If Iran is contributing to militias in Iraq, it hardly proves that U.S. and Iranian interests are irreconcilable. Iran is not the main source of America's problems in Iraq, and the United States would be in deep trouble there even if Iran were doing nothing. Nor would it be surprising if Iran were acting in this way. After all, the world's most powerful country has invaded two of Iran's neighbors while simultaneously declaring that Tehran is part of the "axis of evil." The U.S. Congress has passed a law calling for regime change in Iran, and the Bush administration has funded Iranian exile groups and hinted on several occasions that it might strike Iran with military force. Wouldn't any country facing this sort of threat do whatever it could to protect itself, including using its influence with different Iraqi factions and possibly sending them various forms of aid? If a hostile power conquered Canada or Mexico and tried to set up a sympathetic government there, wouldn't the United States try to complicate that hostile power's efforts and ensure an outcome more favorable to U.S. interests? Americans have good reason to resent Iran's influence in Iraq, but they should hardly be surprised by it or see it as evidence of unremitting Iranian hostility. It is also worth noting that deep antipathy did not prevent the U.S. government from engaging Soviet leaders throughout the Cold War, even when Moscow was providing millions of dollars' worth of military aid to North Vietnam, which used this assistance to kill thousands of American soldiers.

RISING TO ISRAEL'S DEFENSE

Israel and the lobby have been remarkably successful at convincing Bush and other leading American politicians that a nuclear-armed Iran is an unacceptable threat to Israel and that it is the responsibility of the United States to prevent that threat from increasing. In fact, there is some evidence that some individuals in the lobby think they have been too successful for Israel's own good.

The president's current rhetoric clearly reflects Israel's preferred approach toward Iran, as is apparent from a speech he gave in Cleveland on March 20, 2006. "The threat from Iran," he said, "is, of course, their stated objective to destroy our strong ally Israel. That's a threat, a serious threat . . . I made it clear, I'll make it clear again, that we will use military might to protect our ally, Israel."[63] Bush's comments were consistent with his previous statements. He said a month earlier in an interview with Reuters that "we will rise to Israel's defense, if need be."[64] Moreover, most of the 2008 presidential candidates, Democrats and Republicans alike, appear to agree with the president. In April 2007, for example, Senator John McCain said explicitly that he agreed with Bush that the United States had a responsibility to protect Israel from Iran and to make sure that Iran did not get nuclear weapons that might threaten Israel.[65] He reiterated that claim in a May 2007 interview with the *Jerusalem Post,* and fellow candidates Barack Obama, Mitt Romney, Bill Richardson, and Sam Brownback offered similar comments as well.[66]

Bush's enthusiasm for defining Iran as a mortal threat to Israel but not the United States, coupled with his stated commitment to go to war against Iran for Israel's benefit, has set off alarm bells in various parts of the lobby. In the spring of 2006, the *Forward* reported, "Jewish community leaders have urged the White House to refrain from publicly pledging to defend Israel against possible Iranian hostilities." The point is not that these leaders oppose the use of American power to protect Israel, but rather that they fear that Bush's public statements "create an impression that the United States is considering a military option against Iran for the sake of Israel—and could lead to American Jews being blamed for any negative consequences of an American strike against Iran."[67] As Malcolm Hoenlein, executive vice chairman of the Conference of Presidents, put it in April 2006, "As much as we appreciate it, the question is whether it's beneficial to tie this to Israel."[68]

Israeli leaders share the same concern, as reflected in Prime Minister Olmert's comment later that spring that he hoped pro-Israel groups would maintain a low profile regarding Iran. "We don't want it to be about Israel," he said, which was just the opposite of what the president was saying.[69]

Rhetoric aside, the Bush administration has worked assiduously to shut down Iran's nuclear program and has in general taken a more aggressive posture. It has imposed economic sanctions and threatened military strikes if Iran continues down the nuclear road. "No option," American leaders are fond of saying, "is off the table."[70] James Bamford and Seymour Hersh have separately described how many of the same individuals who planned the Iraq war have devised the Pentagon's plans for a military campaign against Iran. For example, Douglas Feith, the undersecretary of defense for policy until August 2005, played a central role in developing the plans for striking the Islamic Republic. "There has also been close, and largely unacknowledged, cooperation with Israel," noted Hersh in early 2005. "Defense Department civilians, under the leadership of Douglas Feith, have been working with Israeli planners and consultants to develop and refine potential nuclear, chemical-weapons, and missile targets inside Iran." The Pentagon has also been conducting intelligence-gathering operations inside of Iran and it has updated its "contingency plans for a broader invasion of Iran."[71]

In January 2007, the Bush administration ratcheted up the military pressure on Iran in a number of ways. It arrested five Iranian officials in the Iraqi city of Erbil, who were in a building that the local Kurds and the Iranians considered a consular facility. The president then announced that he was sending an additional carrier battle group to the Persian Gulf as well as Patriot antimissile defense systems to defend the states in the Gulf Cooperation Council. At the same time, U.S. military officials in Baghdad were claiming that Iran was shipping key components of especially deadly roadside bombs into Iraq to be used against American troops. Both Stephen Hadley, the president's national security adviser, and Secretary of State Condoleezza Rice made it clear that the administration had not ruled out the possibility that U.S. forces might cross into Iran in pursuit of Iranians trafficking in roadside bombs and other weapons.[72]

These confrontational moves notwithstanding, David Wurmser, who advises Vice President Cheney on Middle East affairs, apparently felt that Rice and Hadley were too interested in negotiating with Iran—even if the diplomacy was backed up by threats—and not sufficiently committed to the military option. In spring 2007, Wurmser gave a series of talks at the American Enterprise Institute and other conservative Washington think tanks in which he said that the vice president was unhappy with the secretary of state—as well as with President Bush—for pursuing diplomacy at all, and that Cheney was interested in working with Israel to come up with a military strategy to eliminate Iran's nuclear program that he could sell to the president. When Wurmser's activities became public knowledge, Rice denied that there were differences within the administration on Iran, and emphasized that the vice president fully supported the president's policy.[73]

While Washington has relied primarily on threats rather than negotiations in its dealings with Iran, the European Union has worked in the opposite direction and has attempted to find a diplomatic solution to the crisis. The EU-3 (Britain, France, and Germany) initiated negotiations with Tehran in early August 2003, and on October 21, Iran agreed to suspend its enrichment and reprocessing programs and to allow the International Atomic Energy Agency to conduct especially intrusive inspections. A year later, on November 15, 2004, Iran agreed "to continue and extend its suspension to include all enrichment related and reprocessing activities" and "to begin negotiations, with a view to reaching a mutually acceptable agreement on long term arrangements."[74] Efforts to reach a satisfactory deal failed, however, and Iran announced in August 2005 that it would resume enriching its uranium. The EU-3 has continued talking with Iran, but to little avail.

Although the United States was willing to allow the EU-3 to try to halt Iran's nuclear program through negotiations, it had little enthusiasm for that bargaining process and was never strongly committed to making it work.[75] In fact, by constantly threatening Iran and pushing the European negotiators to be as tough as possible with their Iranian counterparts, the Bush administration virtually guaranteed that the negotiations would lead nowhere. If there was any hope that diplomacy would succeed, the military threat had to be taken off the table.

After diplomacy backed by threats failed to resolve the problem, the Bush administration began pushing hard in the fall of 2005 to get the UN Security Council to impose sanctions on Iran. It finally succeeded in late December 2006, when China and Russia agreed, after much foot dragging, to a package of limited sanctions.[76] In late March 2007, the Security Council approved a second set of sanctions on Iran over its refusal to shut down its nuclear enrichment facilities. These new sanctions, which were also limited in scope, included a ban on Iranian arms exports, travel restrictions on individuals associated with Iran's nuclear program, and freezing the assets of some individuals and organizations untouched by the first set of UN sanctions.[77] Few experts believe that these measures will cause Iran to abandon its nuclear program, and few believe that the United States will be able to convince the Security Council to go along with the kind of tough sanctions that might work. But if UN sanctions are not the answer, what is?

THE ALTERNATIVES

The Bush administration has three options left for halting Iran's nuclear program: it can try to coerce Tehran by markedly increasing the pressure on it with military measures short of war, tougher U.S. sanctions, and an anti-Iran coalition that includes Israel and the Arab states; it can try to eliminate it with military force; or it can make a serious attempt to strike a grand bargain that keeps Iran from developing nuclear weapons. Israel and most of the key organizations in the lobby, especially the neoconservatives, favor the second option. But Israeli leaders and their American supporters are well aware that there is widespread opposition to attacking Iran inside and outside of the U.S. government, as well as in the international community, especially given the dire situation in Iraq. Moreover, it is clear that despite the rhetoric, President Bush has shown little enthusiasm for the military option, which is not to say he would never strike Iran.

Bush's plan for 2007 appears to call for ramping up the pressure on Iran in the hopes that it will cave in to U.S. demands to stop enriching uranium.[78] As noted, the administration made a number of confrontational military moves in January that were aimed directly at Iran. And the president and Secretary of State Rice have also begun making a concerted effort to get the Arab states in the Middle East to line up with the United States and Israel against Iran. Against this backdrop, key groups in the lobby, which have been going along with Bush's policy for now, are mobilizing. The *Forward* reported on the eve of the March 2007 AIPAC conference that "the pro-Israel lobby is backing new congressional legislation that would toughen sanctions against Iran and target foreign entities doing business with the Islamic Republic."[79]

So far this strategy has failed to produce results. The United States was heavily criticized by many Iraqis and even by the Kurds for arresting the five Iranians. And then in March, the Iranians proved that two can play the game when they detained fifteen British naval troops in the Persian Gulf, accusing them of trespassing in Iranian territorial waters.[80] Meanwhile, Iran continues to develop its nuclear program and support Shia groups in Iraq. There is no evidence that sending additional carrier battle groups to the Gulf has had any effect on Tehran's behavior. Congress may enact much tougher sanctions, but the fact is that the administration is only mildly enthusiastic about taking that route, because this policy ends up imposing sanctions on allies that do business with Iran. It is a policy certain to strain U.S. relations with those allies, possibly undermining their willingness to help Washington put additional pressure on Iran.[81]

The administration's attempt to work closely with Arab states has made little progress, in good part because of America's continuing support of Israel over the Palestinians. In March, King Abdullah of Saudi Arabia not only invited Iranian President Ahmadinejad to visit Riyadh but also canceled a visit to the White House and condemned the U.S. occupation of Iraq as "illegal." The director of the Center for Strategic Studies at the University of Jordan said that Abdullah was "telling the U.S. they need to listen to their allies rather than imposing decisions on them and always taking Israel's side." As discussed in Chapter 7, Saudi Arabia was then pushing the Arab League to reissue its 2002 peace initiative for ending the Israeli-Palestinian conflict; the United States, however, was pressuring the Saudis to change the proposal because Israel was unhappy with it. Secretary Rice condescendingly asked Arab countries to "begin reaching out to Israel." This admonition angered the Saudis, especially Abdullah, who responded by lashing out at the American presence in Iraq.[82]

Coercion is unlikely to alter Tehran's calculations. This point is not lost on Israeli leaders and their allies in the United States, most of whom see a nuclear Iran as a mortal threat to Israel. For that reason, many have lobbied relentlessly not only to keep the military option on the table but also to make the case that Iran is so dangerous that if it does not capitulate to Washington's demands, it will be necessary to use force. Consider what Prime Minister Ehud Olmert told a joint session of Congress on May 24, 2006. He likened Iran with nuclear weapons to "the savagery of slavery, to the horrors of World War II, to the gulags of the communist bloc." He emphasized that a nuclear-armed Iran was not just a threat to Israel but would put "the security of the entire world . . . in jeopardy." He made it clear that he expected the United States to play the key role in preventing this "dark and gathering storm [from] casting its shadow over the world."[83]

A few months later, in November 2006, Olmert told a *Newsweek* interviewer that he did not believe that Iran would accept a "compromise unless they have good reason to fear the consequences of not reaching a compromise. In other words, Iran must start to fear."[84] By the spring of 2007, Olmert was intensifying the campaign to sell the military option. He told Germany's *Focus* magazine in late April, "It is impossible perhaps to destroy the entire nuclear program but it would be possible to damage it in such a way that it would be set back years." Olmert estimated that "it would take 10 days and would involve the firing of 1,000 Tomahawk cruise missiles."[85] One Israeli general, however, questioned whether Bush had sufficient "political power to attack Iran" and suggested instead that Israel "help him pave the way by lobbying the Democratic Party . . . and US newspaper editors . . . to turn the Iranian issue into a bipartisan one."[86]

Israeli officials also warn they may take preemptive action themselves should Iran continue down the nuclear road. Besides sending a signal to Iran, these threats keep the pressure on Washington to solve the problem, because the United States does not want Israel to act on its own. Prime Minister Ariel Sharon warned in late 2005 that "Israel—and not only Israel—cannot accept a nuclear Iran. We have the ability to deal with this and we're making all the necessary preparations to be ready for such a situation." London's *Sunday Times* reported in January 2007 that Israeli pilots were rehearsing a tactical nuclear strike against Iran's facilities; although Israel officially denied the report, it did serve as a powerful reminder of the importance Israel attaches to this issue. As one Israeli defense analyst told the Associated Press, "It is possible that this was a leak done on purpose, as deterrence, to say 'someone better hold us back, before we do something crazy.'"[87] Just in case this message was not getting through, Avigdor Lieberman, the deputy prime minister, told *Der Spiegel* in February 2007 that if the international community does not solve the problem, "Israel may have to act alone."[88]

Some in the lobby have moved beyond vague calls for "regime change" and begun to make the case that a nuclear-armed Iran is intolerable and the United States must be prepared to use force to deal with the problem.[89] Neoconservative pundits have been especially outspoken about the threat from Iran and the need to use force, or at least threaten it, to bring Iran to heel. The essence of their perspective is captured in the headline of an op-ed that Michael Rubin of the American Enterprise Institute published in the *New York Daily News* on October 3, 2006: "To End Iran Standoff, Plan for War." Joshua Muravchik, who is also at the AEI, declared a month later that "President Bush will need to bomb Iran's nuclear facilities before leaving office. It is all but inconceivable that Iran will accept any peaceful inducements to abandon its drive for the bomb."[90] Similarly, Richard Perle said approvingly in January 2007 that "I have no doubt that if it becomes apparent to President Bush that during his term Iran will achieve nuclear weapons, he will not hesitate to order a strike."[91] Finally, Norman Podhoretz published a widely discussed article on May 30, 2007, in the online version of the *Wall Street Journal* titled "The Case for Bombing Iran: I Hope and Pray That Bush Will Do It."

AIPAC has also played a central role in publicizing the threat from Iran and pushing forward the military option. Its annual conference for the past two years has put the Iran issue up in bright lights and emphasized the imperative of ending its nuclear program.[92] Indeed, John Hagee, who heads Christians United for Israel, was invited to address the 2007 conference. Hagee had told the *Jerusalem Post* in 2006 that "I would hope the United States would join Israel in a military pre-emptive strike to take out the nuclear capability of Iran for the salvation of Western civilization."[93] He did not disappoint the attendees at the March 2007 conference, telling them, "It is 1938; Iran is Germany, and Ahmadinejad is the new Hitler. We must stop Iran's nuclear threat and stand boldly with Israel." He received multiple standing ovations.[94] By contrast, the *New York Post* reports that Senator Hillary Clinton "drew grumbles" the previous month when she suggested to an AIPAC audience that it might make sense to engage with Iran before employing stronger measures.[95]

Perhaps the best evidence of AIPAC's influence on U.S. policy toward Iran was revealed in mid-March 2007, when Congress was attempting to attach a provision to a Pentagon spending bill that would have required President Bush to get its approval before attacking Iran. In light of what has happened in the Iraq war, this was a popular measure on Capitol Hill and appeared likely to gain approval. It was also consistent with Congress's constitutional authority. But AIPAC was firmly opposed, because it saw the legislation as effectively taking the military option against Iran off the table. It went to work in the halls of Congress, and with the help of a handful of pro-Israel representatives— Gary Ackerman, Eliot Engel, and Shelley Berkley (D-NV)—the provision was removed from the spending bill.[96] One month later, when Congressman Michael Capuano (D-MA) was asked why the language on Iran was stripped out of the bill, he answered with one word: "AIPAC." Congressman Dennis Kucinich (D-OH) offered the same assessment.[97]

Despite the commitment that Israel and some in the lobby have to pushing the military option against Iran, it is widely recognized that threatening to use force against Iran is counterproductive and actually attacking that country's nuclear facilities would have disastrous consequences.[98] It would further destabilize the Middle East and cause Iran to lash out at the United States and its allies. The last thing that Washington needs at this point is another war against an Islamic country. The American military is already bogged down in Baghdad, and Iran has substantially more territory and people than

Iraq. Furthermore, Iran would almost certainly not give up its nuclear program but would redouble its efforts to rebuild it, as Iraq did after Israel destroyed its incipient nuclear capability in 1981. It is unsurprising that Charles Kupchan, an expert on European security issues, says, "I have yet to find a European policymaker who thinks war is preferable to a nuclear Iran."[99]

In fact, Israel is the only country in the world where a substantial number of people advocate the military option against Iran if it does not end its nuclear program—perhaps as much as 71 percent of the Israeli population, according to a May 2007 poll.[100] Similarly, the core organizations in the lobby are the only significant groups in the United States that favor going to war against the Islamic Republic. In early 2007, when retired General Wesley Clark was asked why the Bush administration seemed headed for war with Iran, he answered, "You just have to read what's in the Israeli press. The Jewish community is divided but there is so much pressure being channeled from the New York money people to the office seekers." Clark was immediately smeared as an anti-Semite for suggesting that Israel and some American Jews were pushing the United States toward war with Iran, but as the journalist Matthew Yglesias pointed out, "Everything Clark said is true. What's more, everybody *knows* it's true."[101] Even more pointedly, former UN weapons inspector turned author Scott Ritter said in his 2006 book *Target Iran*, "Let there be no doubt: If there is an American war with Iran, it is a war that was made in Israel and nowhere else."[102] In short, if Israel and the lobby were not pressing this case, there would be little serious discussion inside or outside the Beltway about attacking Iran.

THE LEAST BAD OPTION

As noted earlier, the best option available to the Bush administration is to remove the threat of force and attempt to reach a comprehensive agreement with Iran.[103] It is difficult to say whether this strategy would work, but there is good reason to think that it might have worked in the past and might even work in the future. Iran signaled on two separate occasions since 9/11 that it was seriously interested in reaching a negotiated settlement with the United States.[104] Iran helped the United States topple the Taliban in the fall of 2001 by providing advice on targets to strike in Afghanistan, facilitating U.S. cooperation with the Northern Alliance, and helping with search-and-rescue missions. After the war, Tehran helped Washington put a friendly government in place in Kabul. At the same time, Iran's President Khatami made it clear once again that he wanted to improve relations with the United States and saw events in Afghanistan as a major step in that direction.

As was the case in the 1990s, there was substantial support within the CIA and the State Department for taking Khatami at his word and attempting to normalize relations with Tehran. The neoconservatives inside and outside of the administration, however, vehemently opposed that idea; they favored getting tough with Iran, and they carried the day with Bush and Cheney. In his State of the Union address in late January 2002, the president rewarded Iran for its cooperation in Afghanistan by including it in the infamous "axis of evil." Moreover, Bush made it clear in the following months that although he was preoccupied with regime change in Iraq, he would eventually turn to Iran and try to topple that government as well.

Despite America's hostility, Iran tried again in the spring of 2003, as it had in 1997 during the Clinton administration, to reach out to the United States. Khatami said he was willing to negotiate on Iran's nuclear program, so that it would be readily transparent that "there are no Iranian endeavors to develop or possess WMD." Regarding terrorism, he said that Iran would end "any material support to Palestinian opposition groups (Hamas, Jihad, etc.)" and put "pressure on these organizations to stop violent action against civilians" within Israel's 1967 borders. On Hezbollah, Iran's goal would be to make it "a mere political organization within Lebanon." Khatami also indicated "acceptance" of the 2002 Saudi peace initiative, which he made clear meant acceptance of a two-state solution. Plus, Iran would help stabilize Iraq. In return, Khatami wanted the United States to remove Iran from the axis of evil and take away the threat to use military force against his country. Sanctions also had to go, and Iran wanted "full access to peaceful nuclear technology." In essence, Khatami was pushing forward a solution that had all the ingredients of a grand bargain.[105]

Iran's offer was presented in May 2003, just after the United States appeared to have scored a stunning victory in Iraq, on the heels of what seemed to be a stunning victory in Afghanistan. At that point, many people believed that the United States might actually be able to reorder the entire Middle East. It was, in fact, an ideal time to push Tehran to cut a deal, because U.S. prestige and leverage were at their peak and Iran's sense of vulnerability was acute. Unfortunately, America's favorable position made Bush more inclined to dictate rather than deal. Not only was Israel pressing the Bush administration hard at that point to take aim at Iran, but so were the neoconservatives and others in the lobby. Bush paid hardly any attention to Khatami's offer to negotiate a comprehensive settlement between Iran and the United States, and U.S. officials were ordered not to pursue it.

One cannot know whether a grand bargain would have been struck had the Bush administration pursued these opportunities. There were still plenty of Iranian hard-liners who would have resisted making any kind of deal with the "great Satan." Nevertheless, Bush was foolish not to try to reach an agreement with Khatami, if only because that approach was the least bad option. Trying to cut a deal might well have prevented the election of President Ahmadinejad, whose irresponsible statements and bellicose attitude have made a difficult situation worse. And if engagement had failed and Iran ultimately acquired nuclear weapons, the United States could still fall back on a strategy of deterrence.

It may not be too late to strike a deal with Iran, although the chances of achieving success are less likely now than in either 2001 or 2003. Not only has America's bargaining position been eroded by events in Iraq, but Iranian leaders have more reason than ever not to trust Bush. Furthermore, Mahmoud Ahmadinejad has replaced Khatami as Iran's president, and he has shown little interest in reaching out to the Bush administration. Nonetheless, there are still compelling reasons to pursue a grand bargain. Not only is it still the best strategy for stopping Iran from acquiring a nuclear arsenal, but the United States needs Iran's help to rescue the situation in Afghanistan as well as Iraq. This is why the Iraq Study Group recommended in December 2006 that President Bush negotiate with Iran rather than confront it.[106] Its members understood that confronting Iran—as the Bush administration has done in the past—gives it powerful incentives to meddle in Afghanistan and Iraq, which is definitely not in America's interest.[107]

There is actually substantial support within the United States for engaging Iran in serious negotiations.[108] As noted, many in the CIA, the State Department, and the military would back the idea. A poll taken in late November 2006, just before the Iraq Study Group released its report, found that 75 percent of Americans believe that the United States "should deal with the government of Iran primarily by trying to build better relations." Only 22 percent favor "pressuring it with implied threats that the US may use military force."[109] The recommendation to engage Iran from the Iraq Study Group—a bipartisan committee of prominent individuals—is another indicator of the breadth of support for negotiations. Even Thomas L. Friedman of the New York Times, who is usually attuned to Israel's concerns, remarked in early 2007 that Iran is a "natural ally" of the United States.[110]

Although it makes good strategic sense for the United States to pursue a grand bargain with Iran, and although there is plenty of support for that policy inside and outside of America, it is unlikely to happen anytime soon. Israel and the lobby will almost certainly try to thwart any efforts to seriously engage Iran before they get started, as they have consistently done since 1993. Indeed, the lobby has gone out of its way to undermine the Iraq Study Group's recommendation that the Bush administration negotiate with Iran. The release of the report, according to the *Forward*, "has produced an outpouring of protest from Jewish groups opposing its call for talks with Iran, Syria and the Palestinians." Nevertheless, "insiders say that the real target of Israel's anxiety is neither Syria nor the Palestinians, but Iran and its nuclear program."[111]

The lobby is also likely to try to make sure that the United States continues to threaten Iran with military strikes unless it abandons its nuclear enrichment program. Given that this threat has not worked in the past and is unlikely to work in the future, some of Israel's American backers, especially the neoconservatives, will continue to call for the United States to carry out the threat. Although there is still some chance that President Bush will decide to attack Iran before he leaves office, it is impossible to know for sure. There is also some possibility, given the inflexible rhetoric of the presidential candidates, that his successor will do so, particularly if Iran gets closer to developing weapons and if hard-liners there continue to predominate. If the United States does launch such an attack, it will be doing so in part on Israel's behalf, and the lobby would bear significant responsibility for having pushed this dangerous policy. And it would not be in America's national interest.

CONCLUSION

As with U.S. policy toward the Palestinians, the tragic decision to invade Iraq, and the confrontational approach to Syria, the Israel lobby's influence on American policy toward Iran has been harmful to the national interest. By opposing any détente between Iran and the United States, much less cooperation, the lobby has also strengthened Iran's hard-liners, thereby making Israel's security problems worse. But its negative impact does not stop there. The lobby's influence during the 2006 war in Lebanon also did considerable harm to both the United States and to Israel, as the next chapter will show.

11

THE LOBBY AND
THE SECOND LEBANON WAR

In the summer of 2006, Israel fought a thirty-four-day war against Lebanon. On July 12, Hezbollah, the Shia organization that controls the southern part of Lebanon, made a cross-border raid that killed and captured several Israeli soldiers. In response, the Israel Defense Forces launched a major air campaign in Lebanon, which killed more than eleven hundred Lebanese, most of whom were civilians and roughly a third of whom were children. It also did extensive damage to Lebanon's infrastructure, including roads, bridges, office buildings, apartment buildings, gas stations, factories, water-pumping stations, airport runways, homes, and supermarkets.[1] Although virtually no one challenged Israel's right to respond to the raid, or to defend itself, its excessive response was widely condemned around the globe.

Despite strong support from the United States, Israel failed to achieve its military or political objectives and Hezbollah emerged from the war with its popularity and prestige significantly enhanced. The IDF's chief of staff, Lieutenant General Dan Halutz, resigned a few months later, and an official Israeli government investigation chaired by former Supreme Court Justice Eliyahu Winograd subsequently issued a scathing assessment of Israel's planning and handling of the war. In particular, the Winograd Commission found that Israel's leaders had failed to "consider the whole range of options," "failed to adapt the military way of operations and its goals to the reality on the ground," and pursued goals that were "not clear and could not be achieved."[2]

The war was also a major setback for the United States. It weakened the Siniora government in Beirut, whose election after the "Cedar Revolution" of 2005 had been one of the few successes in the Bush administration's Middle East policy. The war also solidified the informal alliance among Hezbollah, Syria, and Iran, and intensified anti-American attitudes throughout the region, thereby undermining the war on terror and complicating U.S. efforts to forge a regional consensus on Iraq and Iran.

How did this happen? Although primary responsibility for mishandling the war lies with Israel's leaders, the United States encouraged their mistakes by offering them unconditional support before and during the war. Israel had briefed the Bush administration on its plans to go after Hezbollah well before the war began on July 12 and was given a tacit green light by Washington. Unlike the rest of the world, including virtually all the major democracies, the United States did not criticize Israel's actions during the war and gave it valuable diplomatic and military backing instead. The Israel lobby worked throughout the war to keep the United States in Israel's corner.

It did not make strategic sense for the Bush administration to back Israel's disproportionate response to Hezbollah's provocations, and there was also no compelling moral case for supporting Israel's conduct. America's uncritical backing was not in Israel's interest either. As the Winograd report suggests, Israel would have been much better off if its leaders had examined "the whole range of options." In other words, the United States would have been a better ally if it had urged a different course of action when Israel first outlined its plan to attack Lebanon. Had the United States done so, Israel would have been forced to come up with a smarter response and might have avoided the debacle that subsequently befell it in Lebanon.

Israelis and many of their American supporters do not want to admit that the lobby heavily influenced U.S. policy both before and during the second Lebanon war, and they offer several alternative explanations designed to counter this charge. As is the case in other contexts, some defenders argue that the U.S. government's unflinching support for Israel's assault reflects the American public's deep commitment to the Jewish state. The American people, in this view, wanted U.S. leaders to back Israel to the hilt, and so President Bush and the Congress were simply bowing to the will of the people. Others claim that Israel was acting as America's client state in its war with Hezbollah. According to this version of events, the Bush administration was the driving force behind the war and it got its loyal Israeli client to do its bidding. These alternative explanations might seem intuitively plausible to some observers, but neither is consistent with the available evidence.

PREWAR PLANNING

Israel has launched a number of major military strikes against Lebanon over the past forty years, but it previously had fought only one genuine war on Lebanese territory. Under the leadership of Prime Minister Menachem Begin and Defense Minister Ariel Sharon, Israel invaded Lebanon in June 1982. It was eighteen years before the IDF finally left Lebanon, and it was Hezbollah that drove them out. Israel and Hezbollah remained bitter enemies even after Israel withdrew, and occasional skirmishes continued to take place along the Israeli-Lebanese border. It was just such a skirmish on July 12, 2006, that erupted into Israel's second war in Lebanon.

Concerned about the huge stockpile of missiles and rockets that Hezbollah had acquired from Syria and especially Iran, Israel had been planning to strike at Hezbollah for months before the July 12 abductions. Gerald Steinberg, a well-connected Israeli strategist, made these points during the war: "Of all of Israel's wars since 1948, this was the one for which Israel was most prepared. In a sense, the preparation began in May 2000, immediately after the Israeli withdrawal, when it became clear the international community was not going to prevent Hezbollah from stockpiling missiles and attacking Israel. By 2004, the military campaign scheduled to last about three weeks that we're seeing now had already been blocked out and, in the last year or two, it's been simulated and rehearsed across the board."[3]

Similarly, Seymour Hersh reported, "Several current and former officials involved in the Middle East told me that Israel viewed the soldiers' kidnapping as the opportune moment to begin its planned military campaign against Hezbollah. 'Hezbollah, like clockwork, was instigating something small every month or two,' the U.S. government consultant with ties to Israel said."[4] Indeed, Israeli Prime Minister Ehud Olmert told the Winograd Commission that "his decision to respond to the abduction of soldiers with a broad military operation was made as early as March 2006," which was four months before the conflict started. At that time, he asked to see the existing "operational plans" for war with Lebanon, because "he did not want to make a snap decision in the case of an abduction." Olmert also said that in November 2005, his predecessor, Ariel Sharon, "ordered the army to prepare a 'list of targets' for a military response in Lebanon" after a failed Hezbollah attempt to capture IDF troops in a border village. Olmert held his first meeting on Lebanon in early January 2006, four days after he was appointed to replace the incapacitated Sharon, and he subsequently "held more meetings on the situation in Lebanon than any of his recent predecessors."[5]

Israeli officials reportedly briefed key individuals inside and outside of the Bush administration about their intentions well before July 12. Hersh writes, "According to a Middle East expert with knowledge of the current thinking of both the Israeli and the U.S. governments, Israel had devised a plan for attacking Hezbollah—and shared it with Bush Administration officials—well before the July 12th kidnappings." Likewise, Matthew Kalman reports in the *San Francisco Chronicle* that "more than a year ago, a senior Israeli army officer began giving PowerPoint presentations, on an off-the-record basis, to U.S. and other diplomats, journalists and think tanks, setting out the plan for the current operation in revealing detail. Under the ground rules of the briefings, the officer could not be identified."[6]

The available evidence indicates that the Bush administration endorsed Israel's plans for war in Lebanon. According to Hersh, "Earlier this summer, before the Hezbollah kidnappings, the U.S. government consultant said, several Israeli officials visited Washington, separately, 'to get a green light for the bombing operation and to find out how much the United States would bear.' The consultant added, 'Israel began with Cheney. It wanted to be sure that it had his support and the support of his office and the Middle East desk of the National Security Council.' After that, 'persuading Bush was never a problem, and Condi Rice was on board,' the consultant said."[7]

There is not much information in the public record about the decision-making process that led President Bush to back Olmert's plan to attack Lebanon at an opportune moment. Nevertheless, there is reason to think that the neoconservatives played a key role in that process. Not only had the neoconservatives been angling to smash Hezbollah since September 11, but the two most influential advisers on Middle East affairs in the White House in the months before and during the Lebanon war were dedicated supporters of Israel and its hard-line policies toward its adversaries, including Hezbollah.[8] Elliott Abrams was the key person on the National Security Council dealing with Middle East policy. The *New York Times* reported during the war that he "has pushed the administration to throw its support behind Israel."[9]

The other key figure was David Wurmser, Vice President Cheney's adviser on Middle East affairs.[10] He was one of the authors of the 1996 "Clean Break" study, which advocated that Israeli Prime Minister Benjamin Netanyahu end the Oslo peace process and use military force to change the political landscape in the Middle East. In particular, it called for "securing" Israel's northern border "by engaging Hizballah, Syria, and Iran, as the principal agents of aggression in Lebanon."[11] Wurmser was, as Adam Shatz wrote in the *New York Review of Books* well before the second Lebanon war, "an open advocate of preemptive war against Syria and Hezbollah, a position favored by neoconservatives in and close to the Bush administration."[12] When Seymour Hersh reports, as quoted above, that Israel was interested in getting "the support of [Cheney's] office and the Middle East desk of the National Security Council," he is effectively saying that Olmert wanted the approval of Abrams and Wurmser, which he surely got. Beyond that basic fact, which is neither surprising nor controversial, little is known about the Bush administration's planning role in the months before the second Lebanon war.

Nothing in this account suggests that either Israel or the United States was conspiring to provoke a war in Lebanon. Given the simmering tensions along the border and Israel's legitimate concerns about Hezbollah's missiles and rockets, it made perfect sense for the IDF to formulate plans for addressing this threat. After all, every competent military leadership plans for contingencies that may never arise. It also made perfect sense for Israel to consult with its American patron about its plans, to make sure it was not preparing for a course of action that Washington might oppose.

"THE MIGHTY EDIFICE OF SUPPORT"[13]

Once the war began and Israel came in for severe criticism from all corners of the globe, the Bush administration provided Israel with extraordinary diplomatic protection. Its UN ambassador, John Bolton, whom Israel's UN ambassador once jokingly described as a sixth member of the Israeli delegation, vetoed a Security Council resolution that criticized Israel and worked assiduously for about a month to prevent the UN from imposing a cease-fire, so that Israel could try to finish the job with Hezbollah.[14] Secretary of State Condoleezza Rice downplayed the violence at a press conference, at one point dismissing it as the "birth pangs of a new Middle East."[15] Only when it became apparent that the IDF was not going to win a decisive victory did the Bush administration—and Israel—recognize the need for a cease-fire. During the ensuing negotiations that led to UN Resolution 1701, the United States went to great lengths to protect Israel's interests. In fact, as the resolution was being finalized, Israeli Prime Minister Ehud Olmert called President Bush on August 11 and thanked him for "safeguarding Israel's interests in the Security Council."[16]

The president frequently defended Israel's actions in public and never uttered a critical word. UN Ambassador Bolton told the Security Council that Hezbollah's goal was "to deliberately target innocent civilians, to desire their death," while the disproportionate numbers of Lebanese civilians killed by Israel were "the sad and highly unfortunate consequences of self-defense."[17] In addition to this diplomatic support, the administration provided Israel with military intelligence during the conflict, and when Israel started running low on precision-guided bombs, the president quickly agreed to send replacements.[18] During the height of the war, it successfully pressed Turkey and Iraq to deny permission to a plane loaded with missiles for Hezbollah to cross Turkish and Iraqi airspace on its way from Iran to Damascus.[19] As Shai Feldman, a well-connected Israeli scholar, noted during the latter stages of the war, "There is huge, huge appreciation here for the president."[20]

As we have seen in other contexts, Israel usually finds its strongest support in the U.S. Congress, and congressional behavior during the Lebanon conflict unequivocally confirmed this tendency. Democrats and Republicans competed to show that their party, not the rival one, was Israel's best friend. One Jewish activist said he thought that "it's a good thing to have members of Congress outdo their colleagues by showing that their pro-Israeli credentials are stronger than the next guy's."[21] In the end, there was virtually no daylight between the two parties regarding Israel's actions in Lebanon, which is remarkable when you think of the sharp differences between Democrats and Republicans on most other foreign policy issues, like Iraq, for example. Abraham Foxman, the head of the ADL, made this clear when he said, "The Democrats who are opposed to the president on 99 percent of things are closing ranks on Israel."[22]

Reflecting this bipartisan consensus, on July 20, 2006, the House of Representatives passed a strongly worded resolution condemning Hezbollah and supporting Israeli policy in Lebanon. The vote was 410–8. The Senate followed suit with a similar resolution, sponsored by sixty-two senators, including the leaders of both parties. A number of prominent Democrats, including the party's leaders in both the House and the Senate, tried to prevent Iraq's prime minister, Nuri al-Maliki, from addressing Congress, because he had criticized Israeli policy in Lebanon.[23] Howard Dean, the chairman of the Democratic party, who had been targeted by the lobby in the past, went so far as to call the Iraqi prime minister an anti-Semite.[24] Support in Congress for Israel was so overwhelming that it left Arab-American leaders stunned. Nick J. Rahall, a Democratic congressman of Lebanese descent, said that the House resolution made him "just sick in the stomach, to put it mildly." James Zogby, who heads the Arab American Institute, said, "This is so devastating. I thought that we'd come further than this."[25]

Potential presidential candidates for 2008—like Senators Hillary Clinton, John McCain, and Joe Biden (D-DE)—as well as former Speaker of the House Newt Gingrich, went to especially great lengths to convey their support for Israel.[26] The only exception was Senator Chuck Hagel (R-NE), who expressed mild reservations about Israel's response and America's support for it. Hagel's comments were largely ignored by his congressional colleagues as well as the lobby, although they undoubtedly did nothing to further his own presidential ambitions.[27]

The mainstream media also stood firmly behind Israel. *Editor & Publisher*, a distinguished journal that covers the newspaper industry, surveyed dozens of newspapers about a week after the war began and found that "almost none of them have condemned the Israeli attack on civilian areas and the infrastructure of Lebanon."[28] The twenty-four-hour cable news stations were filled with reports and commentary that portrayed the Jewish state as a beleaguered combatant that could do no wrong.

Israel did not fare as well on the front pages of newspapers and in the straight-out news coverage in the media. A Harvard study claims that "on the front pages of the *New York Times* and *Washington Post*, Israel was portrayed as the aggressor nearly twice as often in the headlines and exactly three times as often in the photos."[29] This news coverage was largely unavoidable, however, because Israel was causing much greater destruction in Lebanon than Hezbollah was causing in northern Israel. By the end of the fighting, Hezbollah had killed 43 Israeli civilians and damaged or destroyed about 300 buildings in Israel. The IDF, by contrast, had killed as many as 750 Lebanese civilians and damaged or destroyed roughly 16,000 Lebanese buildings.[30] Given those numbers, the camera quickly became Israel's enemy. Media coverage was also shaped by the fact that both Hezbollah and the Siniora government in Beirut favored a cease-fire almost as soon as the fighting started, while Israel wanted to prolong the war until its leaders realized that their war aims could not be achieved.

Editorial commentary remained relentlessly pro-Israel throughout the conflict, however, and it often crept into the news coverage, thus ensuring that the overall portrayal of Israel in the American media was very favorable. The situation in the mainstream media was nicely summed up in an article in the British newspaper the *Independent*: "There are two sides to every conflict—unless you rely on the US media for information about the battle in Lebanon. Viewers have been fed a diet of partisan coverage which treats Israel as the good guys and their Hezbollah enemy as the incarnation of evil . . . Not only is there next to no debate, but debate itself is considered unnecessary and suspect."[31]

What makes America's overwhelming support for Israel so remarkable is that the United States was the only country that enthusiastically supported Israel's actions in Lebanon. Almost every other country in the world, as well as the UN leadership, criticized Israel's reaction as well as Washington's unyielding support for it. These circumstances raise the obvious question: why was the United States so out of step with the rest of the world?

STRATEGIC FOLLY

One possible answer is that supporting Israel made eminently good strategic sense for the United States. But that is not the case. Israel's strategy for waging the war was guaranteed to fail because, as the Winograd Commission notes, "The assumptions and expectations of Israel's actions were not realistic." Israel's response reflected "weakness in strategic thinking," so the Bush administration was backing a losing strategy from the outset.[32]

Israel's main goal in the second Lebanon war was to deal a massive blow to Hezbollah's effectiveness as a fighting force. In particular, the Israelis were determined to eliminate the thousands of missiles and rockets that could strike northern Israel. Prime Minister Ehud Olmert drove this point home when he said, "The threat will not be what it was. Never will they be able to threaten this people they fired missiles at."[33] Similarly, the Israeli ambassador in Washington said, "We will not go part way and be held hostage again. We'll have to go for the kill—Hezbollah neutralization."[34] Writing in the *Wall Street Journal*, former Prime Minister Benjamin Netanyahu proclaimed that Israel's goal was straightforward: "Remove the missiles. Or destroy them."[35]

Israel had two different but complementary ways to try to neutralize Hezbollah's missiles and rockets. Israeli leaders were confident that they could use airpower to strike directly at those weapons and take almost all of them out.[36] They also had a more indirect approach for dealing with the problem. Specifically, they planned a classic punishment campaign, whereby the IDF would inflict massive pain on Lebanon's civilian population by destroying residences and infrastructure and forcing hundreds of thousands of people to flee their homes. Such a campaign would inevitably kill a significant number of civilians in the process. Olmert made this point clearly at a press conference right after the kidnapping, when he promised a "very painful and far-reaching" response.[37] The aim of the punishment campaign was to send a message to Lebanon's leadership that it was ultimately responsible for Hezbollah's actions, and therefore the country as a whole would pay a great price anytime Hezbollah attacked Israel. The prime minister was clear on this point as well: "The Lebanese government, of which Hezbollah is a member, is trying to undermine regional stability. Lebanon is responsible and Lebanon will bear the consequences of its actions."[38]

Both elements of this strategy were destined to fail from the start. Trying to disarm Hezbollah from the air was simply not feasible; even with an ample supply of smart bombs, there was no way the Israeli Air Force was going to eliminate Hezbollah's ten thousand to sixteen thousand rockets and missiles.[39] Most of those weapons were widely dispersed and located in caves, homes, mosques, and other hiding places. Moreover, even if the IDF managed to destroy a large portion of Hezbollah's inventory, Iran and Syria would have sent in replacements. Not surprisingly, it quickly became apparent that airpower was not having the advertised effect, as missiles and rockets continued to reach northern Israel daily. In fact, Hezbollah launched more missiles at Israel on August 13—one day before the cease-fire took effect—than on any other day of the war.[40]

In late July, the Olmert government decided to rectify the problem by sending large numbers of ground troops into Lebanon, claiming that Israel would need a few more weeks to defeat Hezbollah once and for all.[41] But this was another fool's errand. After all, the IDF had fought Hezbollah in Lebanon between 1982 and 2000, and Hezbollah had not only survived, it eventually forced Israel to withdraw in 2000. How was Israel now going to achieve in a few weeks what it could not accomplish in eighteen years? The ground offensive failed to produce decisive results and Israel had no choice but to accept a cease-fire on August 14.[42] Israel suffered its highest single day of casualties two days before the cease-fire went into effect.[43]

The second element of Israel's strategy—its attempt to punish Lebanon for allowing Hezbollah to operate freely—was also certain to backfire. A wealth of historical evidence and scholarly literature makes clear that inflicting pain on an adversary's civilian population rarely causes a rival government to throw up its hands and surrender to the attacker's demands.[44] On the contrary, the victims usually direct their anger at the attacker and, if anything, become more supportive of their own government. Indeed, Israel had twice before launched large-scale bombing campaigns against Lebanon—

Operation Accountability in 1993 and Operation Grapes of Wrath in 1996—and both failed to damage Hezbollah in any meaningful way or undermine its popular support.[45]

History repeated itself in 2006: in the wake of Israel's punishment campaign, Hezbollah's popularity surged in Lebanon (and across the Arab and Islamic world), and most Lebanese vented their rage at Israel and the United States rather than at Hezbollah or the government in Beirut.[46] But even if this case had turned out to be an anomaly and Israel's bombs had convinced Lebanon's leadership that it was now time to disarm Hezbollah, it did not have the capability to do that. Hezbollah was too powerful and the government was too weak.

After about two weeks of fighting, with Hezbollah still lobbing missiles and rockets at northern Israel and the punishment campaign backfiring, Israel began to define victory downward. Its leaders began emphasizing goals like eliminating Hezbollah's forward positions and deploying an international force to protect Israel against Hezbollah attacks.[47] Back in the United States, the *Forward* reported that "sources close to the White House and the Pentagon said [that] administration hawks have expressed disappointment and frustration about Israel's inability to deal a swift and decisive blow to Hezbollah." Some of Israel's more hawkish supporters began saying out loud that Israel was in danger of losing the war, and a few even questioned whether Israel was still a strategic asset for the United States. Charles Krauthammer wrote in the *Washington Post* on August 4 that the war gave Israel "an extraordinary opportunity" to make "a major contribution to America's war on terrorism." The United States, however, "has been disappointed" in Israel's performance, which "has jeopardized not just the Lebanon operation but America's confidence in Israel as well."[48]

When the war finally ended on August 14, both sides declared victory.[49] It was clear to most independent experts, however, that Hezbollah had come out ahead in the fight.[50] By virtually all accounts it performed well on the battlefield, and it was standing tall when the shooting stopped. It also retained thousands of missiles and rockets that threatened Israel, and its political position in Lebanon and the Islamic world was much improved by the war. Israel, on the other hand, failed to achieve its initial goals and the IDF had stumbled badly when it engaged Hezbollah. It has become manifestly clear with the passage of time—especially in Israel—that Hezbollah was the winner and Israel the loser. The Winograd Commission "was appointed due to a strong sense of a crisis and deep disappointment with the consequences of the campaign and the way it was conducted."[51] Its main findings are an unequivocal indictment of the three main architects of the war: Prime Minister Olmert, Defense Minister Amir Peretz, and General Dan Halutz, the IDF chief of staff.

DAMAGE TO U.S. INTERESTS

Leaving aside the issue of whether Israel or Hezbollah won the second Lebanon war, there is no question that U.S. interests suffered from its outright support for Israel's actions. As we have made clear, the United States currently faces three major problems in this region. The first problem is terrorism, which is mainly about vanquishing al Qaeda, although the United States also wants to neutralize Hamas and Hezbollah. The second concern is the remaining rogue states in the area, Iran and Syria. Both support terrorism, and Iran seems determined to master the full nuclear fuel cycle, which would put it a short step away from nuclear weapons. The third problem is the Iraq war, which the United States is in serious danger of losing. The Bush administration's unyielding support for Israel during the second Lebanon war has complicated Washington's ability to deal with each of these problems.

The conflict in Lebanon has complicated America's terrorism problem in two ways. It has reinforced anti-Americanism in the Arab and Islamic world, with Hezbollah leader Hassan Nasrallah describing Israel during the fighting as having been "armed with an American decision, with American weapons, and American missiles."[52] This perception surely will help al Qaeda and other terrorist organizations find new recruits who want to attack the United States or its allies. For example, in a poll taken in Lebanon in late August 2006, just after the fighting had ended, 69 percent of the respondents said that they considered America an "enemy of Lebanon." Less than a year earlier, in September 2005, the number was 26 percent.[53] In another poll taken in Lebanon in late August 2006, 64 percent of the respondents said that their opinion of the United States was worse after the fighting than before it. Nearly half of the respondents said that their opinion of America was "much worse" in the aftermath of the war.[54] A Zogby poll taken in the fall of 2006 in Saudi Arabia, Egypt, Morocco, Jordan, and Lebanon found that "in all five countries, attitudes towards the U.S. have worsened in the last year." U.S. policy in Lebanon contributed to that negative shift in attitudes, although the war in Iraq and Washington's policy toward the Palestinians were more important factors.[55] This increased hostility toward the United States will generate more public support for terrorists in the Middle East and elsewhere.

Furthermore, the conflict has increased Hezbollah's influence in Lebanon. This is partly due to its impressive performance against the IDF, which has normally defeated its Arab opponents decisively but failed to do so in this case. Israel's bombing campaign was also a major reason for Hezbollah's soaring popularity. When the war first began, many Lebanese were angry with Hezbollah for precipitating the conflict, especially because a "banner tourist season . . . was underway in Lebanon."[56] There was also much goodwill toward the United States among the Lebanese people at the beginning of the conflict, mainly because the Bush administration had played the key role in pushing Syria out of Lebanon in 2005. However, that goodwill toward the United States turned to outrage when Washington backed Israel's offensive; correspondingly, Hezbollah's standing in Lebanon rose dramatically.

One poll conducted in Lebanon after the war found that 79 percent of the respondents rated the performance of Hezbollah leader Nasrallah as either "good" or "great," while another poll found that 40 percent of Lebanese had a more positive attitude toward Hezbollah after the war, while just under 30 percent had a more negative view.[57] Although Hezbollah does not directly threaten the United States, it does threaten Israel and it is aiming to reverse the Cedar Revolution completely, which President Bush supported and which he extols as a successful case of democracy promotion. By the late fall of 2006, Hezbollah was throwing its increased weight around and threatening to bring down the pro-American government in Beirut headed by Fouad Siniora.[58] More worrisome is the real possibility that Hezbollah's actions will plunge Lebanon into another civil war. The United States has worked hard with its allies to prevent this outcome and has been successful so far. But in all likelihood the problem would not have arisen if Hezbollah had not been emboldened by its success and widespread support.

The conflict in Lebanon has also made it more difficult to deal with Iran and Syria. While there is no question that both countries support Hezbollah, the United States has a powerful interest in weakening or breaking those links, as well as the link between Damascus and Tehran.[59] Driving a wedge between Iran and Syria should not be difficult as they are not natural allies; Iran is theocratic and Persian, while Syria is secular and Arab. Instead, the Bush administration blindly supported Israel during the war and treated Hezbollah, Iran, and Syria as part of a seamless web of evil, pushing them closer together.[60]

On top of that, many neoconservatives called for Israel or the United States to attack Syria and Iran in the midst of the conflict.[61] Indeed, Meyrav Wurmser of the Hudson Institute said after the war that "many parts of the

American administration"—and almost certainly her husband, David Wurmser, and Elliott Abrams—were deeply upset with Israel for not having struck Syria as well as Hezbollah.[62] The result? This policy gave Iran even more reason to acquire nuclear weapons, so that it can deter an Israeli or U.S. attack on its homeland. And Iran and Syria have continued to arm and support Hezbollah, while helping to keep the United States bogged down in Iraq, so that it cannot attack either of them.[63]

The blowback had other consequences in Iraq: what happened in Lebanon also angered the Iraqis themselves, especially the Iraqi Shia, who feel a loose sense of allegiance to Hezbollah (which is also Shia). Indeed, the Shia rally for Hezbollah that took place in Baghdad on August 4 was reported to be the largest of its kind in the Middle East.[64] There have even been reports in the aftermath of the Lebanon war that Hezbollah is training the Iraqi militia of Moqtada al-Sadr, who is a bitter enemy of the United States.[65] The United States is in deep trouble in Iraq and cannot afford to further alienate the local population.

In order to confront these three issues—terrorism, rogue states, and Iraq—in the most effective way, Washington needs broad support from friendly regimes in the region like Egypt, Jordan, and Saudi Arabia. These regimes have no love for Hezbollah, and they might have supported the United States (and tacitly, Israel) had the American and Israeli response been more restrained. Indeed, in the first days of the conflict, the leaders of those countries were critical of Hezbollah for provoking it. But once Israel's disproportionate response was clear and the Bush administration firmly endorsed it, these leaders began to criticize Washington and to condemn Israel. The main reason that they turned against the United States and Israel was to protect themselves from their enraged publics.[66] American policy also angered allies in Europe as well as the Middle East, leaving the United States (and Israel) isolated and short of political clout, and raising doubts about whether President Bush is a reliable ally for dealing with the terrorist and proliferation threats.[67]

One might think that the sharp cleavage that developed between Arab leaders and their publics during the Lebanon war quickly dissipated when the shooting stopped and thus has had no serious long-term effects. But that would be wrong, as Arab public opinion remains deeply hostile to the United States, making it difficult for Arab regimes to help the Bush administration contain Iran's ambitions. The root of the problem is that the so-called Arab street fears the United States much more than it fears Iran. A Zogby poll released in February 2007 found that 72 percent of the respondents in six Arab countries identified the United States as their biggest threat, while only 11 percent identified Iran. Furthermore, 61 percent of the respondents said that Iran has the right to develop a nuclear capability, even though more than half of them think Iran is likely to go the next step and build nuclear weapons.[68]

It is also worth noting that the IDF's poor performance in Lebanon suggests that it will not be of great value to the United States in dealing with the threat environment that its actions helped create. As we argued in Chapter 2, Israel's policies nurture and inspire terrorist groups and complicate U.S. efforts to deal with rogue states like Syria and Iran, but Israel is not much of an asset for dealing with them.

Backing Israel's strategy in its war with Lebanon was not in America's strategic interest. It is hard to disagree with former State Department official Aaron Miller's observation in the middle of the conflict: "There is a danger in a policy in which there is no daylight whatsoever between the government of Israel and the government of the United States."[69]

BREAKING THE LAWS OF WAR

But what about the moral dimension? One might concede that U.S. support for Israel had significant strategic costs but argue that the United States has a moral obligation to back Israel's efforts to defend itself. Israel was attacked, so the argument runs, and it responded in a way that conformed to the laws of war. Indeed, some of Israel's supporters claim that its poor performance in Lebanon was due mainly to its strict adherence to these legal and moral principles. For example, Thomas Neumann, the executive director of the Jewish Institute for National Security Affairs, maintains that "it wasn't Hezbollah that tied Israel down as much as it was Israel's own sense of morality."[70]

On close inspection, however, this line of argument is not convincing. Israel clearly has the right to defend itself, and that right includes retaliating against Hezbollah with military force. Hardly anyone contests that basic point, and many of the governments and individuals who have criticized Israel's conduct never questioned its right to respond to Hezbollah's raid. But having the right to defend oneself does not mean that any and all measures are legally or morally permissible. The critical issue is whether Israel's actions in Lebanon during the summer of 2006 were consistent with the laws of war and with established standards of morality.

As discussed above, Israel's strategy explicitly and deliberately sought to inflict punishment on Lebanon's civilian population. One might easily get the impression that Israel initiated this punitive campaign in response to Hezbollah's own missile and rocket attacks against Israeli civilians, but that is not how the war actually evolved. It began on July 12, when Hezbollah fighters crossed into Israeli territory, killed three Israeli soldiers, and captured two more. As part of that operation, Hezbollah launched a few dozen rockets at some Israeli towns for the purpose of diverting the IDF's attention away from the abduction site. No Israeli civilians were killed in those diversionary attacks.[71] Nasrallah said immediately afterward at a news conference in Beirut, "We don't want an escalation in the south, not war."[72] Though unjustifiable, the Hezbollah raid was not an unusually provocative act, as both Israel and Hezbollah had been conducting violent—and sometimes lethal—incursions into each other's territory since Israel withdrew from southern Lebanon in May 2000.[73] Nasrallah had even made it clear months in advance that he was determined to kidnap some Israeli soldiers.[74]

Nevertheless, Israel responded to the abductions by launching a massive bombing campaign against Lebanon, which in turn led Hezbollah to follow suit and unleash its rockets and missiles at towns and cities across northern Israel. Specifically, the IDF struck Beirut International Airport among other targets on July 13, the day after Hezbollah struck across Israel's border. The IDF continued to pound Lebanon from the air on the 14th, striking at bridges and roads, as well as Nasrallah's office in Beirut. At this point, with more than fifty Lebanese civilians dead and damage to Lebanon's infrastructure mounting, Nasrallah promised "open war" against Israel, which meant extensive missile and rocket attacks.[75] Thus, although Hezbollah clearly precipitated the war by killing or capturing IDF soldiers on June 12, Israel initiated the large-scale attacks against civilians.

Israeli leaders emphasized from the start that all of Lebanon would pay a severe price in the war and this punishment would be the result of a deliberate Israeli policy, not merely "collateral damage." IDF Chief of Staff Halutz said at the beginning of the conflict that he intended to "turn back the clock in Lebanon by 20 years."[76] He also said at one point that "nothing is safe" in Lebanon.[77] He was true to his word. In a report issued in August 2006, just after the fighting ended, Amnesty International provided a detailed assessment of what the IDF wrought in Lebanon, which is worth quoting at length:

> During more than four weeks of ground and aerial bombardment of Lebanon by the Israeli armed forces, the country's infrastructure suffered destruction on a catastrophic scale. Israeli forces pounded

buildings into the ground, reducing entire neighborhoods to rubble and turning villages and towns into ghost towns, as their inhabitants fled the bombardments. Main roads, bridges and petrol stations were blown to bits. Entire families were killed in air strikes on their homes or in their vehicles while fleeing the aerial assaults on their villages. Scores lay buried beneath the rubble of their houses for weeks, as the Red Cross and other rescue workers were prevented from accessing the areas by continuing Israeli strikes. The hundreds of thousands of Lebanese who fled the bombardment now face the danger of unexploded munitions as they head home.

The Israeli Air Force launched more than 7,000 air attacks on about 7,000 targets in Lebanon between 12 July and 14 August, while the Navy conducted an additional 2,500 bombardments. The attacks, though widespread, particularly concentrated on certain areas. In addition to the human toll—an estimated 1,183 fatalities, about one third of whom have been children, 4,054 people injured and 970,000 Lebanese people displaced—the civilian infrastructure was severely damaged. The Lebanese government estimates that 31 "vital points" (such as airports, ports, water and sewage treatment plants, electrical facilities) have been completely or partially destroyed, as have around 80 bridges and 94 roads. More than 25 fuel stations and around 900 commercial enterprises were hit. The number of residential properties, offices and shops completely destroyed exceeds 30,000. Two government hospitals—in Bint Jbeil and in Meis al-Jebel—were completely destroyed in Israeli attacks and three others were seriously damaged.

In a country of fewer than four million inhabitants, more than 25 per cent of them took to the roads as displaced persons. An estimated 500,000 people sought shelter in Beirut alone, many of them in parks and public spaces, without water or washing facilities.

Amnesty International delegates in south Lebanon reported that in village after village the pattern was similar: the streets, especially main streets, were scarred with artillery craters along their length. In some cases cluster bomb impacts were identified. Houses were singled out for precision-guided missile attack and were destroyed, totally or partially, as a result. Business premises such as supermarkets or food stores and auto service stations and petrol stations were targeted, often with precision-guided munitions and artillery that started fires and destroyed their contents. With the electricity cut off and food and other supplies not coming into the villages, the destruction of super-markets and petrol stations played a crucial role in forcing local residents to leave. The lack of fuel also stopped residents from getting water, as water pumps require electricity or fuel-fed generators.[78]

Amnesty International is not alone in its assessment of the damage that the IDF inflicted in Lebanon. William Arkin, an American expert on military affairs and a self-proclaimed "fan of airpower," wrote in his *Washington Post* weblog that "in carrying out its punishment campaign, Israel has left behind a shocking level of destruction outside the direct battle zone. I hesitate to use the words 'laid to waste' and 'moonscape' in describing the conditions in urban Lebanon because the same kinds of words are thrown around so promiscuously in describing U.S. air strikes. But what Israel has wrought is far more ruinous than anything the U.S. military—specifically the U.S. Air Force—has undertaken in the era of precision warfare."[79]

One of the more devastating punitive tactics was Israel's use of cluster bombs, which spray large numbers of bomblets over a wide area. These bomblets are not only highly inaccurate; many of them do not explode, which effectively means that they become deadly land mines that continue to be a threat long after the end of hostilities. Given how lethal these weapons can be when used in civilian areas, the United States has always insisted that Israel use them against clearly defined military targets.[80] Indeed, as noted, the Reagan administration banned the sale of cluster bombs to Israel for six years during the 1980s, after it discovered that the IDF had used them against civilian areas in its 1982 invasion of Lebanon.[81]

In the last three days of the recent Lebanon war, when a cease-fire was known to be imminent, the IDF fired over one million bomblets into southern Lebanon, which has a population of 650,000.[82] The aim was to "saturate the area" with these small but deadly bombs. One Israeli soldier in an artillery battalion said, "In the last 72 hours we fired all the munitions we had, all at the same spot. We didn't even alter the direction of the gun. Friends of mine in the battalion told me they also fired everything in the last three days—ordinary shells, clusters, whatever they had."[83] Over the course of the entire war, the IDF is estimated to have fired roughly four million bomblets into Lebanon. When the fighting finally stopped in mid-August, UN officials estimated that there were about one million unexploded bomblets in the southern part of the country. Researchers from Human Rights Watch said that "the density of cluster bombs in southern Lebanon was higher than in any place they had seen."[84] One Israeli soldier who helped "flood" the area with cluster bombs said, "What we did was insane and monstrous, we covered entire towns in cluster bombs."[85] Jan Egeland, the UN's under-secretary-general for humanitarian affairs, labeled Israel's actions "shocking" and "completely immoral."[86] In the first eight months after the war, 29 Lebanese were killed by cluster bombs and another 215 were injured, 90 of them children.[87]

It seems intuitively clear that Israel's destructive campaign in Lebanon violated the laws of war. Still, that is not enough; it is important to understand what those laws are and exactly how Israel violated them.

The bedrock distinction that underpins the laws of war—as well as modern just war theory—is between civilian and military targets.[88] There is no question that states have the right to defend themselves by attacking each other's military assets. However, states are not supposed to attack civilian targets in another country unless they are transformed into military targets in the course of the war. If troops occupy a school or a church during a battle, for example, and use it as a base of operations, then it is permissible to attack them there. Furthermore, when attacking an adversary's military targets, states must make a determined effort to minimize collateral damage. This is where the well-known concept of proportionality comes into play. Specifically, states striking at military targets must make sure that there is not excessive collateral damage, given the particular value of those military targets. In short, states cannot attack enemy civilian targets on purpose or indiscriminately, and they must take great care to avoid collateral damage when striking at military targets.

Israel failed to observe both of these distinctions in the second Lebanon war. There is no question that Israel deliberately attacked a wide array of civilian targets in Lebanon, just as General Halutz said that they would. The description of the devastation in the Amnesty International report makes this clear. Remember, it concluded that Lebanon's "infrastructure suffered destruction on a catastrophic scale." That same report says at another point that Israel's bombing campaign resulted in "massive destruction of civilian infrastructure." Amnesty International issued another report in November 2006, which reinforced the findings in its August report. For example, it found that "in southern Lebanon, some 7,500 homes were destroyed and 20,000 damaged" and that in "the overwhelming majority of destroyed or damaged buildings it examined," there was "no evidence to indicate that the buildings were being used by Hizbullah fighters as hide-outs or to store weapons." Indeed, it "noted a pattern of destruction by Israeli attacks that indicated that Israeli forces had targeted objects that are indispensable to the survival of the civilian population."[89] In a separate study of Israel's offensive in Lebanon, Human Rights Watch (HRW) concluded that "Israel has violated one of the most fundamental tenets of the laws of war: the duty to carry out attacks on only military targets."[90]

It is also clear that Israel did not exercise sufficient care to avoid collateral damage when striking targets that it considered military in nature. HRW concluded that despite Israel's claims that it was "taking all possible measures to minimize civilian harm," there was, in fact, "a systematic failure by the IDF to distinguish between combatants and civilians."[91] Consider what happened in southern Lebanon, which the Israelis effectively turned into a "free-fire zone," where any person left in the area was considered a legitimate target. After warning the residents of that area to leave, Minister of Justice Haim Ramon— who had said that "we must reduce to dust the villages of the south"— announced on July 27 that "all those now in south Lebanon are terrorists who are related in some way to Hizbullah."[92] However, many residents had not left, and many of the people who remained were neither combatants nor members of Hezbollah. Amnesty International estimates that about 120,000 people remained throughout the conflict, many of them civilians. On August 7, the IDF spread leaflets over southern Lebanon warning that "any vehicle of any kind traveling south of the Litani River will be bombarded, on suspicion of transporting rockets, military equipment and terrorists."[93]

In light of these actions, Amnesty International concluded in its November report that "Israeli forces committed serious violations of international human rights and humanitarian law, including war crimes. In particular, Amnesty International has found that Israeli forces carried out indiscriminate and disproportionate attacks on a large scale."[94] Similarly, the HRW report finds that "the IDF consistently tolerated a high level of civilian casualties for questionable military gain."[95] At least one Israeli leader made no bones about the fact that Israel was violating the proportionality principle. Dan Gillerman, Israel's ambassador to the UN, said one week after the war started, "To those countries who claim that we are using disproportionate force, I have only this to say: You're damn right we are. Because if your cities were shelled the way ours were, if your citizens were terrorized the way ours are, you would use much more force than we are using."[96]

Gillerman's telling admission was an exception, however. Most Israelis and their American supporters respond to the charge that Israel engaged in disproportionate attacks by acknowledging that Israel may have killed a large number of innocent Lebanese, but they insist that it was because Hezbollah used them as human shields.[97] The evidence in Amnesty International's November report and in the HRW study contradicts that line of defense. One part of Israel's defense is the claim that Hezbollah prevented civilians from leaving southern Lebanon because it wanted to hide behind them. Amnesty International investigated this matter and found that the available evidence "does not substantiate the allegations that Hizbullah prevented civilians from fleeing, and in several cases points to the contrary."[98] Also, there is good reason to believe that Hezbollah fighters purposely avoided contact with civilians for fear that "they will sooner or later be betrayed by collaborators."[99]

But even more important, the available evidence, as the HRW study makes clear, does not support the claim that Israel ended up killing large numbers of civilians because Hezbollah used the civilians who remained in southern Lebanon as shields. To be clear, HRW does acknowledge that "Hezbollah occasionally did store weapons in or near civilian homes and fighters placed rocket launchers within populated areas or near U.N. observers," both of which "are serious violations of the laws of war."[100] In other words, there is some evidence that Hezbollah used civilians to protect its fighters and weapons. Nevertheless, those cases were clearly the exception, not the rule. "The vast majority killed," according to Kenneth Roth, HRW's executive director, "were civilians, with no Hezbollah military presence nearby."[101] Specifically, HRW examined twenty-four cases in detail, which included about one-third of the civilians killed in Lebanon at the time of the report.[102] It found no evidence in any of those cases that "Hezbollah deliberately used civilians as shields to protect them from retaliatory IDF attack."[103]

One could accept this finding and offer a different defense, claiming that although Hezbollah may not have deliberately used civilians as shields, it did fight from populated areas, especially when its fighters were defending their home village or town. In such cases, Hezbollah would not be violating the laws of war by "hiding behind civilians"; it would simply be defending its own territory. If this were the case, some may argue, Israel could not help but kill civilians in the process of targeting Hezbollah. Although Hezbollah often fought in and around towns and villages, this line of defense does not work either. In only one of the twenty-four cases researched by HRW "is there evidence to suggest that Hezbollah forces or weapons were in or near the area that the IDF targeted during or just prior to the attack."[104] In short, both Amnesty International's November report and the HRW study provide substantial evidence that contradicts Israel's claims about Hezbollah and its human shields.

Furthermore, the IDF clearly failed to distinguish between civilian and military targets when it saturated southern Lebanon with cluster bombs just before the cease-fire took effect. As one artilleryman put it, "We fired like madmen."[105] This particularly cruel action—which is hard not to see as an act of long-term vengeance—cannot be excused by either of the counter-arguments noted above. Nor can it be justified on the grounds that Hezbollah also committed war crimes when it fired missiles and rockets indiscriminately into northern Israel, killing Israeli civilians.

Given this overwhelming evidence, it is impossible to make the case that the United States supported Israel during the second Lebanon war because it was the morally correct policy choice. If morality were the issue, the Bush administration would have condemned both Israel's and Hezbollah's actions in Lebanon from the start.

THE LOBBY IN OVERDRIVE

AIPAC and other pro-Israel organizations worked overtime from the start to the finish of the war to make sure that America fully backed Israel. Four days after the war began, Nathan Guttman reported in the *Jerusalem Post* that "the American Jewish community has been demonstrating wall-to-wall support for Israel as it fights on two fronts."[106] The lobby raised money for the Jewish state, took out advertisements in newspapers, closely monitored the media, and sent its representatives to meet with legislators and staff in Congress, policy makers in the Bush administration, and influential media figures. Moreover, since the fighting ended, pro-Israel organizations have been hard at work dealing with the fallout from the war.

To see the lobby's impact, consider the following six incidents.

First, at the beginning of the war, there was a bipartisan effort to temper the House resolution supporting Israel by inserting language urging "all sides to protect civilian life and infrastructure." Congresswoman Nancy Pelosi (then House minority leader) and Senator John Warner (R-VA; then chairman of the Senate Armed Services Committee), among others, favored this change in the legislation, considering the moral issues at stake. One would think that such language would be unobjectionable, if not welcome. But AIPAC, which wrote the original resolution and was the main driving force behind it, strongly objected to this particular clause. John Boehner, the House majority leader, kept the proposed new language out of the resolution, which still passed 410–8.[107]

Second, Congressman Christopher Van Hollen (D-MD) wrote a letter to Secretary of State Condoleezza Rice on July 30, urging her "to call for an immediate cease-fire to be followed by the rapid deployment of an international force in southern Lebanon." He also wrote:

The Israeli response . . . has now gone beyond the destruction of Hezbollah's military assets. It has caused huge damage to Lebanon's civilian infrastructure, resulted in the large loss of civilian life, and produced over 750,000 refugees. Hezbollah is undeniably the culprit, but it is the Lebanese people—not Hezbollah—who are increasingly the victims of the violence. As a result, the Israeli bombing campaign, supported by the United States, has transformed Lebanese anger at Hezbollah into growing hostility toward Israel and the United States. The result has been a surge in the political strength and popularity of Hezbollah and its leader, Hasan Nasrallah, and the weakening of the already fragile Lebanese government . . . We have squandered an opportunity to isolate Hezbollah and strengthen our credibility and negotiating leverage in the region.[108]

Although Van Hollen's letter focused primarily on U.S. interests and supported Israel's right to defend itself, the lobby was furious with him for daring to criticize Israel and quickly moved to make it manifestly clear that he should have never written that letter.[109] Van Hollen met with various representatives from major Jewish organizations, including AIPAC, and the congressman immediately apologized, saying, "I am sorry if my strong criticism of the Bush Administration's failures has been interpreted as a criticism of Israel's conduct in the current crisis. That was certainly not my intention."[110] He emphasized that he would continue to be a strong advocate for Israel and shortly thereafter went on a five-day visit to Israel (sponsored by an AIPAC affiliate, the American Israel Education Foundation), accompanied by three pro-Israel activists from his district and a staffer from AIPAC itself.

Despite his apology, the leader of the Jewish Community Relations Council of Greater Washington told a reporter that Van Hollen "needs to continue to reach out to the Jewish community . . . to reassure the Jewish community he is going to be there" for Israel. The ADL's regional director for Washington said that as far as he was concerned, Van Hollen's response "doesn't undo the damage of the first letter."[111] The goal, of course, was not merely to chastise Van Hollen but also to remind other members of Congress of the costs of getting out of line on this issue.

Third, early in the war, President Bush gently encouraged Israel to be careful not to topple the democratically elected government in Lebanon, which he had helped put in power. "The concern," he said, "is that any activities by Israel to protect herself will weaken [the Lebanese] government, or topple that government."[112] Bush made it clear that he and his lieutenants had conveyed their views to Israeli leaders.

The lobby took issue with Bush and made it clear that his position was unacceptable. The *Forward* reported on July 14 that "the Bush administration is being criticized by some Israeli and Jewish communal officials for calling on Jerusalem not to undermine the democratically elected Lebanese government." Abraham Foxman of the ADL said, "The administration and Western countries want to shore up the Lebanese government but it is a misguided policy to do so and the same holds true for Abu Mazen . . . They feel it's better than a vacuum, but you should not support what's meaningless. And we knew from day one that Abu Mazen would go nowhere and that the Lebanese government would be ineffective."[113] In the wake of this criticism, Bush stopped warning Israel about the need to protect the American-backed government in Beirut.

Fourth, Tom Ricks, the well-known *Washington Post* journalist, said on CNN during the war that "some U.S. military analysts" had told him that "Israel purposefully has left pockets of Hezbollah rockets in Lebanon, because as long as they're being rocketed, they can continue to have a sort of moral equivalency in their operations in Lebanon."[114] In response, the Committee for Accuracy in Middle East Reporting in America condemned Ricks's remarks, and Ed Koch, the former mayor of New York City, wrote to Leonard Downie Jr., the executive editor of the *Post*, complaining about Ricks's comments. Koch said that they "are comparable to the age-old blood libel used by anti-Semites to incite pogroms in Europe." Downie wrote back to Koch, saying, "I have made clear to Tom Ricks that he should not have made those statements."[115] Why? Downie did not say. For his part, Ricks said, "The comments were accurate: that I said I had been told this by people. I wish I hadn't said them, and I intend from now on to keep my mouth shut about it."[116]

Fifth, pro-Israel groups conducted a large-scale campaign to smear Amnesty International and especially Human Rights Watch for their critical reports on Israel's bombing campaign. According to Alan Dershowitz, "Virtually every component of the organized Jewish community, from secular to religious, liberal to conservative, has condemned Human Rights Watch for its bias."[117] Both human rights organizations were unfairly accused of singling out Israel while largely ignoring Hezbollah and of misrepresenting important aspects of what was happening on the ground in Lebanon. At the same time, AIPAC sent out press releases designed to convey the message that the IDF was conducting surgical strikes against terrorists and avoiding civilians.[118]

Charges of anti-Semitism were quickly leveled at both human rights groups. Kenneth Roth, the executive director of HRW, took the brunt of those attacks, even though he is Jewish and his father was a refugee from Nazi Germany. The *Jerusalem Post*, for example, ran an op-ed by Gerald Steinberg titled "Ken Roth's Blood Libel." The *New York Sun* asserted in an editorial that Roth was partaking in the "de-legitimization of Judaism," because he criticized the IDF's strategy in Lebanon as an "eye for an eye—or more accurately in this case twenty eyes for an eye—[which] may have been the morality of some more primitive moment." Abraham Foxman reacted in a similar way to Roth's language, accusing him of employing "a classic anti-Semitic stereotype about Jews."[119]

Responding to such charges, the Georgetown law professor and columnist Rosa Brooks only slightly overstated the case when she wrote in the *Los Angeles Times* that "anyone familiar with Human Rights Watch—or with Roth—knows this to be lunacy. Human Rights Watch is non-partisan—it doesn't 'take sides' in conflicts. And the notion that Roth is anti-Semitic verges on the insane." Brooks went on to say, "But what's most troubling about the vitriol directed at Roth and his organization isn't that it's savage, unfounded and fantastical. What's most troubling is that it's typical. Typical, that is, of what *anyone* rash enough to criticize Israel can expect to encounter. In the United States today, it just isn't possible to have a civil debate about Israel, because any serious criticism of its policies is instantly countered with charges of anti-Semitism."[120]

Sixth, the lobby went to work to limit the damage from the cluster bomb controversy. On August 31, B'nai B'rith International sent a letter to Jan Egeland, the UN leader who had criticized Israel's use of cluster bombs, accusing him of acting "as an un-appointed moral arbiter with regard to disputed, unproven facts on the ground and the interpretation of international humanitarian law."[121] A week later, the Senate was debating legislation that would ban the use of cluster bombs in civilian areas and prohibit the transfer of those deadly weapons to countries that refused to accept that ban. AIPAC lobbied hard against the legislation, which went down to defeat by a vote of 70–30.[122]

Key organizations in the lobby have been open and candid in discussing their influence on U.S. policy in Lebanon. For example, AIPAC's president, Howard Friedman, wrote a letter to friends and supporters of his organization on July 30, which he began by saying, "Look what you've done!" He then wrote, "Only ONE nation in the world came out and flatly declared: Let Israel finish the job. That nation is the United States of America—and the reason it had such a clear, unambiguous view of the situation is YOU and the rest of American Jewry."[123] It is hardly surprising, therefore, that Israeli

Prime Minister Olmert said during the war, "Thank God we have AIPAC, the greatest supporter and friend we have in the whole world."[124]

Organizations like AIPAC and the ADL were not the only players in the lobby that were hard at work during the recent conflict. Journalists like Charles Krauthammer and William Kristol made the case, to use Kristol's words, that Israel's war is "our war, too."[125] Many Christian Zionists also rallied behind Israel. For example, the televangelist Pat Robertson made a three-day visit to Israel during the war "to offer," according to the *Jerusalem Post*, "his support for a country whose very existence he believes is threatened by Hizbullah." Robertson told the *Post*, "The Jews are God's chosen people. Israel is a special nation that has a special place in God's heart. He will defend this nation. So Evangelical Christians stand with Israel. That is one of the reasons I am here."[126] John Hagee's organization, Christians United for Israel, held a two-day Washington/Israel Summit in the capital in mid-July. It attracted thirty-five hundred people, and participants were encouraged to express their support for Israel to their senators and representatives.[127] The executive director of the Christian Friends of Israel offered a rather un-Christian insight: "This was certainly an unprovoked attack and Israel has every right to go in and pound them."[128]

Indeed, Israel did "go in and pound them" with the unconditional backing of the U.S. government and many in the lobby.

THE AMERICAN PUBLIC AND LEBANON

Was Washington's steadfast support for Israel's actions in Lebanon the result of the lobby's influence, or did it simply demonstrate that the American people are deeply committed to Israel? Perhaps Israel received unconditional support because U.S. public opinion demanded it. Jennifer Cannata, an AIPAC spokeswoman, made this familiar argument during the war. After denying that the lobby had any influence, she proclaimed that "the American people overwhelmingly support Israel's war on terrorism and understand that we must stand by our closest ally in this time of crisis."[129]

This line of argument is not convincing. What happened during the Lebanon war fits the pattern we have already seen: U.S. policy did not reflect the views of the American public. This point is clearly revealed in a wide array of survey results on six critical issues involving Lebanon. On the question of who is to blame for starting the conflict, an ABC News–*Washington Post* poll conducted August 3–6, 2006, found that 46 percent of the respondents said that Israel and Hezbollah were equally to blame.[130] Another 7 percent blamed Israel alone. A CBS News–*New York Times* poll conducted July 21–25, 2006, also found that 46 percent of the respondents blamed "both sides equally," while 5 percent blamed "mostly Israel."

Regarding the question of whether Israel had gone too far in its attacks, a *USA Today*–Gallup poll conducted July 21–23, 2006, found that 38 percent of the respondents said they "disapprove of the military action Israel has taken in Lebanon." In the ABC News–*Washington Post* poll, 32 percent of the respondents said they thought that Israel was using "too much force," while 48 percent said that Israel was "not justified in bombing Hezbollah targets located in areas where civilians may be killed or wounded." Fifty-four percent said that Israel "should do more" to avoid civilian casualties.

On whether the United States should support Israel or remain neutral in the conflict, the *USA Today*–Gallup poll found that 65 percent of the respondents said that the United States should take "neither side" in the conflict. In a Zogby poll taken August 11–15, 2006, 52 percent of the respondents said that the United States should remain neutral in the conflict.[131] In the CBS News–*New York Times* poll, 40 percent of the respondents said that the United States should not publicly support either Israel or Hezbollah and should "say or do nothing." Seven percent favored criticizing Israel, and 14 percent were unsure what to do. Thirty-nine percent favored supporting Israel. In an NBC News–*Wall Street Journal* poll taken July 21–24, 2006, 40 percent of the respondents opposed "U.S. military involvement in support of Israel" if the Lebanon war expanded to the point "where Israel is fighting several other nations in the region."

As to whether the United States and Israel should agree to an immediate cease-fire, a CNN poll conducted on July 19, 2006, found that 43 percent of the respondents thought that "Israel should agree to a cease-fire as soon as possible." In the ABC News–*Washington Post* poll, 35 percent of the respondents said that "Israel should agree to an immediate, unconditional cease-fire in Lebanon."

With respect to the consequences of the Lebanon war for America's terrorism problem, 44 percent of the respondents in the *USA Today*–Gallup poll said that they were "very concerned" that events in Lebanon "will increase the likelihood of terrorism against the United States." Thirty-one percent were "somewhat concerned" that the Lebanon war would worsen America's problem with terrorism. Finally, 35 percent of the respondents in the ABC News–*Washington Post* poll said that the Lebanon war would "hurt the situation for the United States in Iraq."

In short, there was a sizable gap between how Americans thought about Israel and the Lebanon war and how their leaders in Washington talked and behaved during that conflict. Mass opinion cannot explain why the Bush administration and Congress acted as they did in the summer of 2006.

DOING AMERICA'S BIDDING?

Another way to absolve the lobby of responsibility for American policy in Lebanon is to claim that the United States was the real driving force behind the war and that Israel was merely an obedient client state. Israel, in other words, was acting as a loyal ally and serving the Bush administration's interests in the Middle East. "The Second Lebanon War," the Israeli journalist Uri Avnery writes, "is considered by many as a 'War by Proxy.' That's to say: Hizbullah is the Dobermann of Iran, we are the Rottweiler of America. Hizbullah gets money, rockets and support from the Islamic Republic, we get money, cluster bombs and support from the United States of America."[132] Hezbollah leader Hassan Nasrallah apparently agrees, telling an Iranian television station that "the United States ordered the Zionist regime to invade Lebanon" and that Israel did so in order to "serve American ambitions in the Middle East."[133]

Although many U.S. officials regard Hezbollah as an enemy and were not sorry when Israel went after it, there are four good reasons to doubt the claim that Israel was simply doing Washington's bidding when it escalated the conflict with Hezbollah. If Israel were acting on America's behalf, its bombing campaign would have been confined to southern Lebanon and great care would have been taken to protect and strengthen the Lebanese government. After all, President Bush made it clear at the start of the crisis that he did not want to endanger the government in Beirut, which he had worked hard to install. More generally, the United States almost certainly would not have wanted to "turn the clock back in Lebanon by twenty years," as called for by the IDF's chief of staff.

There is also little evidence that the Bush administration planned the offensive and then pushed Israel to execute it. As discussed above, the available evidence about the planning process suggests that Israel had planned the Lebanon campaign in the months before the kidnapping on July 12, which it used as a pretext for launching it. Israel undoubtedly briefed the United States about the plan and got the administration's endorsement, but giving Israel the green light is not the same as using Israel as a client state and telling it what to do.

One sometimes hears the argument that the Bush administration encouraged Israel to bomb Lebanon because it would be an opportunity to test the weapons and strategy that the U.S. military might use in an air war against Iran's nuclear facilities. As one U.S. government consultant told Seymour Hersh, "Why oppose it? We'll be able to hunt down and bomb missiles, tunnels, and bunkers from the air. It would be a demo for Iran."[134] Aside from the fact that not opposing Israel's plan is different from pushing Israel to strike Hezbollah, the claim that American policy makers saw Lebanon as a dry run for Iran makes little sense, as the assigned tasks in these two scenarios have little in common. Attacking small groups of guerrillas armed with missiles and rockets who are hiding in the Lebanese countryside is a fundamentally different mission from bombing a handful of identifiable and firmly fixed nuclear installations in Iran. It is not clear what important lessons would be learned from an air war against Hezbollah that would help make a U.S. offensive war against Iran more effective.

Furthermore, there is evidence that in the spring of 2003, around the time of the fall of Saddam, Israel was urging the United States to attack Hezbollah, not the other way around. According to the *Forward*, the Israelis were warning American policy makers that "the militant Shiite organization threatens the stability of the Middle East and the security of the United States worldwide."[135] There is no evidence—at least in the public record—that the Bush administration was tempted to go after Hezbollah or that it encouraged Israel to handle that task itself.

Finally, Israel's history is at odds with this depiction of it as a tame client state for any country, the United States included. Israel has always been a tough-minded and self-interested actor on the international stage, which makes sense given the challenging regional environment it has faced since independence. Shabtai Shavit, the head of the Mossad from 1989 to 1996, made this point emphatically: "We do what we think is best for us, and if it happens to meet America's requirements, that's just part of a relationship between two friends." Regarding the Lebanon war, he added, "Hezbollah is armed to the teeth and trained in the most advanced technology of guerrilla warfare. It was just a matter of time. We had to address it."[136] These are not the words of a compliant proxy. Or as Moshe Dayan once remarked, "Our American friends offer us money, arms, and advice. We take the money, we take the arms, and we decline the advice."[137]

CONCLUSION

Ultimately, none of the alternative explanations can adequately account for American policy during the second Lebanon war. Nor can one find a compelling strategic or moral rationale that explains why the United States provided Israel with unyielding support while the rest of the world harshly criticized Israeli behavior. In fact, the lobby played the critical role in keeping the United States firmly aligned with Israel during the conflict, despite the strategic costs and dubious moral position this entailed.

The war in Lebanon has been a disaster for the Lebanese people, as well as a major setback for the United States and for Israel. The lobby enabled Israel's counterproductive response by discouraging the Bush administration from exercising independent judgment and influence either before or during the war. In this case, as in so many others, the lobby's influence has been harmful to U.S. as well as Israeli interests.

Until the lobby begins to favor a different approach, or until its influence is weakened, American policy in the region will continue to be hamstrung, to the detriment of all concerned. In the final chapter, we identify what U.S. policy ought to be, and we discuss how the lobby's negative impact might be mitigated or modified.

CONCLUSION:
WHAT IS TO BE DONE?

In Part I of this book, we argued that strategic and moral considerations could neither explain nor justify the current level of U.S. support for Israel. Nor could they account for the largely unconditional nature of that support, or for America's willingness to conduct its foreign policy in ways that are intended to safeguard Israel. The main explanation for this anomalous situation, we suggested, is the influence of the Israel lobby. Like other special interest groups, the individuals and organizations that make up the lobby engage in a number of legitimate political activities, in their case intended to push U.S. foreign policy in a pro-Israel direction. Some parts of the lobby also employ more objectionable tactics, such as attempting to silence or smear anyone who challenges the lobby's role or criticizes Israel's actions. Although the lobby does not get everything it wants, it has been remarkably successful in achieving its basic aims.

In Part II, we traced the lobby's impact on U.S. Middle East policy and argued that its influence has been unintentionally harmful to the United States and Israel alike. Washington's reflexive support for Israel has fueled anti-Americanism throughout the Arab and Islamic world and undermined the U.S. image in many other countries as well. The lobby has made it difficult for U.S. leaders to pressure Israel, thereby prolonging the Israeli-Palestinian conflict. This situation gives Islamic terrorists a powerful recruiting tool and contributes to the growth of Islamic radicalism. Turning a blind eye to Israel's nuclear programs and human rights abuses has made the United States look hypocritical when it criticizes other countries on these grounds, and it has undermined American efforts to encourage political reform throughout the Arab and Islamic world.

The lobby's influence helped lead the United States into a disastrous war in Iraq and has hamstrung efforts to deal with Syria and Iran. It also encouraged the United States to back Israel's ill-conceived assault on Lebanon, a campaign that strengthened Hezbollah, drove Syria and Iran closer together, and further tarnished America's global image. The lobby bears considerable, though not complete, responsibility for each of these developments, and none of them was good for the United States. The bottom line is hard to escape: although America's problems in the Middle East would not disappear if the lobby were less influential, U.S. leaders would find it easier to explore alternative approaches and be more likely to adopt policies more in line with American interests.

The lobby's influence has not helped Israel either, especially in recent years. U.S. aid has indirectly subsidized Israel's prolonged and costly effort to colonize the Occupied Territories, and the lobby has made it impossible for Washington to convince Israel to abandon this counterproductive policy. Its ability to persuade Washington to support this expansionist agenda has also discouraged Jerusalem from seizing opportunities—such as a peace treaty with Syria or full and prompt implementation of the Oslo Accords—that would have saved Israeli lives, divided Israel's adversaries, and shrunk the ranks of Palestinian extremists. Enabling Israel's refusal to recognize the Palestinians' legitimate aspirations has not made Israel safer. The long campaign to kill, imprison, or marginalize a generation of Palestinian leaders has helped bring groups like Hamas to power and reduced the number of Palestinian leaders who would welcome a negotiated settlement and be able to make it work. The U.S. invasion of Iraq—which Israel and the lobby both encouraged—turned out to be a major boon for Iran, the country many Israelis fear most. And by pressing U.S. officials to back Israel's assault on Lebanon, groups like the American Israel Public Affairs Committee, Christians United for Israel, the Anti-Defamation League, and the Conference of Presidents of Major American Jewish Organizations did further damage to the country they thought they were protecting. In all these cases, the lobby's actions were directly harmful to Israel.

What is to be done? To reverse the damage that recent U.S. policies have inflicted, a new strategy is clearly needed. But developing and implementing a different approach means finding ways to address the power of the lobby. Charting a fresh course will therefore require

- Identifying U.S. interests in the Middle East
- Outlining a strategy to protect those interests
- Developing a new relationship with Israel

- Ending the Israeli-Palestinian conflict through a two-state solution
- Transforming the lobby into a constructive force

Let us consider each of these steps.

WHAT ARE U.S. INTERESTS?

The overriding goal of U.S. foreign policy is to ensure the safety and prosperity of the American people. In pursuit of that end, the United States has always considered the security of the Western Hemisphere to be of paramount importance. In recent decades, policy makers have also considered three other regions of the world to contain strategic interests important enough to fight and die for: Europe, Northeast Asia, and the Persian Gulf.[1] These regions are important because they contain either concentrations of power or critical natural resources, and who controls them has profound effects on the global balance of power.

The United States has three distinct strategic interests in the Middle East. Because this region contains a large percentage of global energy supplies, the most important interest is maintaining access to the oil and natural gas located in the Persian Gulf. This objective does not require the United States to control the region itself; it merely needs to ensure that no other country is in a position to keep Middle East oil from reaching the world market. To do this, the United States has long sought to prevent any local power from establishing hegemony in the Gulf and to deter outside powers from establishing control of the region.

A second strategic interest is discouraging Middle Eastern states from acquiring weapons of mass destruction. As discussed in Chapter 2, the risk here is not the remote possibility of deliberate nuclear attack, nuclear blackmail, or a deliberate "nuclear handoff" to terrorists, because such threats are not credible in light of America's own nuclear deterrent. Rather, the United States opposes the spread of WMD in the region because it would make it more difficult to project power into the region and thus might complicate U.S. efforts to keep Middle East oil flowing. WMD proliferation also increases the dangers of accidental or unauthorized nuclear use. Given the potential for instability in some countries in the area, it also raises the risk that nuclear weapons or other WMD might fall into the wrong hands in the event of a coup or revolt, or be stolen by terrorists from poorly guarded facilities. For all these reasons, inhibiting the spread of WMD in the region is an important U.S. objective.

Third, the United States has an obvious interest in reducing anti-American terrorism. This goal requires dismantling existing terrorist networks that threaten the United States and preventing new terror groups from emerging. Both objectives are furthered by cooperating extensively and effectively with countries in the region, mostly in terms of intelligence sharing and other law enforcement activities. It is also imperative that the United States take all feasible steps to prevent groups like al Qaeda from gaining access to any form of WMD. Terrorists armed with WMD would be more difficult to deter than states with WMD, and they are likely to use them against America or its allies. Encouraging political reform and greater democratic participation can assist this goal as well—which in turn requires good relations with key regional powers—although the United States should be wary of rapid transformation and certainly should not try to spread democracy at the point of a gun.

Although we believe that America should support Israel's existence, Israel's security is ultimately not of critical strategic importance to the United States.[2] In the event that Israel was conquered—which is extremely unlikely given its considerable military power and its robust nuclear deterrent—neither America's territorial integrity, its military power, its economic prosperity, nor its core political values would be jeopardized. By contrast, if oil exports from the Persian Gulf oil were significantly reduced, the effects on America's well-being would be profound. The United States does not support Israel's existence because it makes Americans more secure, but rather because Americans recognize the long history of Jewish suffering and believe that it is desirable for the Jewish people to have their own state. As we have noted repeatedly, there is a strong moral case for supporting Israel's existence, and we believe the United States should remain committed to coming to Israel's aid if its survival were in jeopardy. But Americans should do this because they think it is morally appropriate, not because it is vital to their own security.

A DIFFERENT STRATEGY: THE CASE FOR "OFFSHORE BALANCING"

Since 9/11, the United States has pursued a policy of regional transformation in the Middle East. In pursuit of this remarkably ambitious strategy, the Bush administration has kept large numbers of American troops in the region, something the United States never did during the Cold War. This misguided policy has helped fuel America's terrorism problem and led to the ongoing debacle in Iraq. It has also done serious damage to the United States' reputation around the world, including its relationship with European and Arab allies.

America would be best served if it abandoned regional transformation and adopted a strategy of offshore balancing. This strategy would be less ambitious in scope but much more effective at protecting U.S. interests in the Middle East. In this strategy, the United States would deploy its military power—especially its ground forces—abroad only when there are direct threats to vital U.S. interests and only when local actors cannot handle these threats on their own.[3] Washington would remain diplomatically engaged under this approach, relying on air and naval power to signal its continued commitment to the region and to provide the capacity to respond quickly to unexpected threats. It would also maintain a robust intervention capability, along the lines of the original Rapid Deployment Force, whose units were stationed over the horizon or in the United States.

Offshore balancing is America's traditional grand strategy and was a key component of U.S. Middle East policy for much of the Cold War. The United States did not try to garrison the region and never attempted to transform it along democratic lines. Instead, it sought to maintain a regional balance of power by backing various local allies and by developing the capacity to intervene directly if the local balance of power broke down. The United States built the Rapid Deployment Force to deter or defeat a Soviet attempt to seize the oil-rich Persian Gulf, and Washington tilted toward Iraq in the 1980s to help contain revolutionary Iran. But when Iraq's conquest of Kuwait in 1990 threatened to tilt the local balance of power in Saddam's favor, the United States assembled a multinational coalition and sent a large army to smash Saddam's military machine and liberate Kuwait.

Offshore balancing is the right strategy for at least three reasons. First, it markedly reduces, but does not eliminate, the chances that the United States will get involved in bloody and costly wars like Iraq. Not only does this strategy categorically reject using military force to reshape the Middle East, it also recognizes that the United States does not need to control this vitally important region; it merely needs to ensure that no other country does. Toward that end, the strategy calls for husbanding U.S. resources and relying primarily on local allies to contain their dangerous neighbors. As an offshore balancer, the United States intervenes only as a matter of last resort. And when it does, it finishes the job as quickly as possible and then moves back offshore.

Second, offshore balancing will ameliorate America's terrorism problem.

One of the key lessons of the twentieth century is that nationalism and other forms of local identity remain intensely powerful political forces, and foreign occupiers invariably generate fierce resistance.[4] By keeping U.S. military forces over the horizon until they are needed, offshore balancing minimizes the resentment created when American troops are permanently stationed on Arab soil. This resentment often manifests itself in terrorism or even large-scale insurgencies directed at the United States.

Third, unlike regional transformation, offshore balancing gives states like Iran and Syria less reason to worry about an American attack and thus less reason to acquire WMD. The need to deter U.S. intervention is one reason Iran has sought a nuclear capability, and convincing Tehran to reverse course will require Washington to address Iran's legitimate security concerns and to refrain from issuing overt threats. The United States cannot afford to disengage completely from the Middle East, but a strategy of offshore balancing will make American involvement less threatening to states in the region and might even encourage some of our current adversaries to seek our help. Instead of lumping potential foes together in an "axis of evil" and encouraging them to join forces against us, offshore balancing facilitates a strategy of divide and conquer. Because U.S. interests are served so long as no hostile state or coalition is able to threaten a vital region such as the Persian Gulf, this basic approach makes good strategic sense.

In effect, a strategy of offshore balancing would reverse virtually all of America's current regional policies. Instead of continuing the fruitless effort to transform Iraq into a multiethnic and multisectarian democracy, the United States would withdraw as soon as possible and focus on containing the regional consequences of its foolhardy decision to invade. Instead of trying to topple the Assad regime in Syria, the United States would push Israel to give up the Golan Heights in exchange for a formal peace treaty. Not only would this bring Syria into the ranks of Arab countries that have formally accepted Israel's existence, but it would isolate Hezbollah in Lebanon, drive a wedge between Syria and Iran, and reduce Iran's ability to aid Hezbollah, Hamas, and Islamic Jihad. It would also encourage Damascus to help the United States deal with al Qaeda and other terrorist groups.

Finally, instead of threatening Iran with preventive war—an approach that fuels Iran's desire for WMD and allows President Ahmadinejad to use nationalist sentiment to deflect popular discontent—the United States would try to cut a deal on Iran's nuclear ambitions and put its hard-line leaders on the defensive. This approach would not eliminate all of the problems that the United States currently faces in the region, but it would be better for America and Israel than the policies endorsed by most groups in the lobby. We have tried their approach, and its failure is plain to see.

A NEW RELATIONSHIP: TREAT ISRAEL AS A NORMAL STATE

But what about Israel? What does offshore balancing say about U.S. relations with Israel, especially since it is of little strategic value for America?

The Jewish state is nearly sixty years old, and its existence is now recognized and accepted by almost all countries in the world. Its economy is developing rapidly and most Israelis are increasingly prosperous, even though its political system currently seems paralyzed by internal divisions, troubled by corruption, and rocked by repeated scandals. It is time for the United States to treat Israel not as a special case but as a normal state, and to deal with it much as it deals with any other country. In other words, the United States should support Israel's continued existence—just as it supports the existence of France, Thailand, or Mexico—and Washington should be prepared to intervene if Israel's survival were ever threatened.

Treating Israel as a normal state means no longer pretending that Israel's and America's interests are identical, or acting as if Israel deserves steadfast U.S. support no matter what it does. When Israel acts in ways that the United States deems desirable, it should have American backing. When it does not, Israel should expect to face U.S. opposition, just as other states do. It also implies that the United States should gradually wean Israel from the economic and military aid that it currently provides. Israel is now an advanced economy, and it will become even more so once it achieves full peace with its neighbors and reaches a final settlement with the Palestinians.

The United States would continue to trade with Israel, of course, and American and Israeli investors would undoubtedly continue to finance enterprises in each other's countries. Cultural, educational, and scientific exchanges would continue as they do today, and for the same reasons that the United States has extensive social connections with many other countries. The special personal and family connections between Israelis and Americans would remain intact as well. U.S. arms manufacturers would still be able to sell arms to Israel (as they do to other states in the region, subject to the relevant U.S. laws), and Washington and Jerusalem would undoubtedly share intelligence information and maintain other mutually beneficial forms of security cooperation. But there is little reason to continue the handouts that American taxpayers have provided since the early 1970s, especially when there are many countries that have greater needs. Ultimately, U.S. aid is indirectly subsidizing activities that are not in its national interest. Although the United States may have to offer some additional support in order to persuade Israel to grant the Palestinians a viable state, treating Israel as a normal country should eventually lead to a dramatic reduction in U.S. assistance.

ENDING THE ISRAELI-PALESTINIAN CONFLICT

Above all, the United States should use its considerable leverage to bring the Israeli-Palestinian conflict to an end. As the bipartisan Iraq Study Group noted in December 2006, "There must be a renewed and sustained commitment by the United States to a comprehensive Arab-Israeli peace on all fronts: Lebanon, Syria, and President Bush's June 2002 commitment to a two-state solution for Israel and Palestine . . . The United States does its ally Israel no favors in avoiding direct involvement to solve the Arab-Israeli conflict."[5]

U.S. leaders have been engaged in virtually every aspect of the peace process, but they have never used the full leverage at their disposal to push the process forward. While reaffirming its commitment to Israel's security within its pre-1967 borders, the United States should make it clear that it is dead set against Israel's expansionist settlements policy—including the land-grabbing "security fence"—and that it believes this policy is not in America's or Israel's long-term interests.

This approach means abandoning the Bush administration's moribund Road Map (which emphasized a timetable for negotiations) and instead laying out America's own vision for what a just peace would entail. In particular, the United States should make it clear that Israel must withdraw from almost all of the territories it occupied in June 1967 in exchange for full peace. Israel and the Palestinians will also have to reach agreement on the rights of displaced Palestinians to return to the lands they fled in 1948. Allowing this "right" to be exercised in full would threaten Israel's identity and is clearly infeasible. But the basic principle is both an essential issue of justice and an issue on which the Palestinians will not compromise save in the context of a final settlement. To resolve this dilemma, Israel will have to acknowledge a "right" of return—in effect acknowledging that Israel's creation involved the violation of Palestinian rights—and the Palestinians will have to agree to renounce this right in perpetuity in exchange for an appropriate level of compensation. The United States and the European Union could organize and finance a generous program of reconstruction aid to compensate the Palestinians, which would terminate all claims for their actual return into what is now and will forever remain Israeli territory.

It is sometimes said that Israel cannot make such concessions, because it is small and vulnerable and would be even more so were it to grant the Palestinians a viable state. But this familiar argument ignores how much Israel's strategic situation has changed since its early years (when, we should not forget, it still managed to defeat its various adversaries, and with little assistance from the United States). Israel is far more secure now than it was when it first occupied the West Bank and the Gaza Strip in June 1967. Israel's defense spending in that year was less than half the combined defense expenditures of Egypt, Iraq, Jordan, and Syria; today, Israel has signed peace treaties with Egypt and Jordan, Iraq is occupied by the United States and has little or no military power of its own, and Israel's defense budget is greater than Iran and Syria's combined. Israel's adversaries used to get substantial military aid from the Soviet Union; today, that superpower is gone and Israel's ties to the United States have grown. Israel had no usable nuclear weapons in 1967; today it has perhaps two hundred. Within the 1967 borders, in short, Israel is more secure than it has ever been, and it is its continued presence in the Occupied Territories—as well as the Golan Heights—that creates a serious security problem for Israel, primarily in the form of terrorist violence. Israel's supporters in the United States are doing it no favors by pressing Washington to continue subsidizing the occupation.

Some Israelis and Americans argue that the converse is true, that Israel's security situation is more perilous today than at any time since 1967. In particular, they argue that Islamic groups like Hamas and Hezbollah remain dedicated to Israel's destruction and are strongly backed by Syria and Iran, thereby creating a potentially lethal threat. There are two obvious responses to this line of argument. First, this view overstates the threat that terrorism poses to Israel—it is clearly a problem but not an existential threat—and, as discussed in Chapters 2 and 10, it also exaggerates the threat that Iranian WMD represent. Second, and more important, ending the occupation would also help divide and defuse the coalition of forces that doomsayers now see arrayed against Israel. Syria has made it clear it will make peace if it regains the Golan, and once it has its land back, it has promised to cut off support for Hezbollah and Hamas. Ending the occupation and helping create a viable Palestinian state will deprive Iran of local sympathizers and help turn groups like Hamas or Islamic Jihad from heroic defenders of a national cause into outdated obstacles to progress and prosperity.

The United States has ample justification for pressuring Israel to cut this deal: so long as it is bankrolling Israel, and jeopardizing its own security by doing so, it is entitled to say what it is willing to support and what it is going to oppose. The Clinton parameters laid out in December 2000 identify the basic outlines of a settlement and offer the best baseline for new negotiations, and President Bush and his successor should make it clear that this is our starting point. If a final status agreement can be reached, then the United States and the European Union should be willing to subsidize the new arrangements generously and help Israeli and Palestinian leaders deal with the rejectionists on both sides.

Ending the Israeli-Palestinian conflict would contribute to America's national interests in another way. Despite its military prowess and geographic location, Israel's strategic value to the United States is reduced by its own pariah status within the region. So long as the Palestinians are denied a state, Israel's isolation prevents it from participating whenever the United States is trying to assemble a "coalition of the willing." If the conflict were resolved and normal relations developed between Israel and the Arab world—as the current Arab League peace proposal envisions—then the United States would not pay a diplomatic price for backing Israel, and Israel would be able to join forces with the United States and its Arab allies when serious regional threats emerged. If the conflict were resolved, in short, Israel might become the sort of strategic asset that its supporters often claim it is.

If Israel remains unwilling to grant the Palestinians a viable state—or if it tries to impose an unjust solution unilaterally—then the United States should curtail its economic and military support. It should do so not because it bears Israel any ill will but because it recognizes that the occupation is bad for the United States and contrary to America's political values. Consistent with the strategy of offshore balancing, the United States would base its actions on its own self-interest rather than adhere to a blind allegiance to an uncooperative partner. In effect, the United States should give Israel a choice: end its self-defeating occupation of the West Bank and Gaza and remain a close U.S. ally, or remain a colonial power on its own.

This step is not as radical as it might sound: the United States would simply be dealing with Israel the same way that it has dealt with other colonial democracies in the past. For example, the United States pushed Britain and France to give up their colonial empires in the early years of the Cold War and forced them (and Israel) to withdraw from Egyptian territory following the 1956 Suez War. The United States has also played hardball with plenty of other countries—including close allies like Japan, Germany, and

South Korea—when it was in its interest do so. As discussed in Chapter 7, public opinion polls confirm that the American people would support a president who took a harder line toward Israel, if doing so were necessary to achieve a just and enduring peace.

This policy would undoubtedly be anathema to most—though perhaps not all—elements in the lobby and it would probably anger some other Americans as well. Moreover, present circumstances are hardly promising, given the violent divisions within the Palestinian community, the political weakness of Israel's current leaders, the Bush administration's abysmal track record in the region, and the eroding support for a two-state solution within Israel itself. Even some of the staunchest supporters of a negotiated two-state solution now lament that "the idea that negotiations conducted bilaterally between Israelis and Palestinians somehow can produce a final agreement is dead."[6]

But the question must be asked: What is the alternative? What vision of the future do hard-line defenders of Israel have to offer instead?

Given present circumstances, there are three possible alternatives to the two-state solution sketched above. First, Israel could expel the Palestinians from its pre-1967 lands and from the Occupied Territories, thereby preserving its Jewish character through an overt act of ethnic cleansing. Although a few Israeli hard-liners—including current Deputy Prime Minister Avigdor Lieberman—have advocated variants on this approach, to do so would be a crime against humanity and no genuine friend of Israel could support such a heinous course of action. If this is what opponents of a two-state solution are advocating, they should say so explicitly. This form of ethnic cleansing would not end the conflict, however; it would merely reinforce the Palestinians' desire for vengeance and strengthen those extremists who still reject Israel's right to exist.

Second, instead of separate Jewish and Palestinian states living side by side, Mandate Palestine could become a democratic binational state in which both peoples enjoyed equal political rights. This solution has been suggested by a handful of Jews and a growing number of Israeli Arabs.[7] The practical obstacles to this option are daunting, however, and binational states do not have an encouraging track record. This option also means abandoning the original Zionist vision of a Jewish state. There is little reason to think that Israel's Jewish citizens would voluntarily accept this solution, and one can also safely assume that individuals and groups in the lobby would have virtually no interest in this outcome. We do not believe it is a feasible or appropriate solution ourselves.

The final alternative is some form of apartheid, whereby Israel continues to increase its control over the Occupied Territories but allows the Palestinians to exercise limited autonomy in a set of disconnected and economically crippled statelets.[8] Israelis invariably bristle at the comparison to white rule in South Africa, but that is the future they face if they try to control all of Mandate Palestine while denying full political rights to an Arab population that will soon outnumber the Jewish population in the entirety of the land. In any case, the apartheid option is not a viable long-term solution either, because it is morally repugnant and because the Palestinians will continue to resist until they get a state of their own. This situation will force Israel to escalate the repressive policies that have already cost it significant blood and treasure, encouraged political corruption, and badly tarnished its global image.[9]

These possibilities are the only alternatives to a two-state solution, and no one who wishes Israel well should be enthusiastic about any of them. Given the harm that this conflict is inflicting on Israel, the United States, and especially the Palestinians, it is in everyone's interest to end this tragedy once and for all. Put differently, resolving this long and bitter conflict should not be seen as a desirable option at some point down the road, or as a good way for U.S. presidents to polish their legacies and garner Nobel Peace Prizes. Rather, ending the conflict should be seen as a national security priority for the United States. But this will not happen as long as the lobby makes it impossible for American leaders to use the leverage at their disposal to pressure Israel into ending the occupation and creating a viable Palestinian state.

The U.S. presidents who have made the greatest contribution to Middle East peace—Jimmy Carter and George H. W. Bush—were able to do so precisely because each was willing on occasion to chart a separate course from the lobby. As former Israeli foreign minister Shlomo Ben-Ami has written, "Carter had yet another vital advantage. A rare bird among politicians, and especially among residents of the White House, he was not especially sensitive or attentive to Jewish voices and lobbies . . . As it turned out, it was this kind of President—George [H. W.] Bush in the late 1980s is another case in point—who was ready to confront Israel head on and overlook the sensibilities of her friends in America that managed eventually to produce meaningful breakthroughs on the way to an Arab-Israeli peace."[10] Ben-Ami is correct, and his important insight underscores once again how the lobby's efforts have unwittingly undermined Israel's own interests.

The United States will have to put significant pressure on Israel to get it to accept the creation of a viable Palestinian state, which in practice means accepting a solution within the Clinton parameters. Although the Barak government accepted these parameters—albeit with significant reservations—in January 2001, broad support for the key elements of this solution is at present lacking. While a majority of Israelis—55 percent in 2007—support the establishment of a Palestinian state in principle, a recent survey reveals much less support for the main ingredients of the peace settlement described by President Clinton in December 2000. In particular, only 41 percent of Israelis support creating a Palestinian state on 95 percent of the West Bank and Gaza, even if Israel was allowed to keep its large settlement blocs. Just 37 percent would support transferring the Arab neighborhoods in East Jerusalem to the Palestinians, while only 22 percent favor transferring control of the Jordan River Valley to a Palestinian state in a few years. Finally, 27 percent support giving control of the Temple Mount to the Palestinians (with Israel retaining control of the Western Wall), and a mere 17 percent favor allowing a limited number of refugees to return to Israel.[11] In effect, there is widespread opposition in Israel to creating a viable Palestinian state, which means that any future president who hopes to settle this conflict will have to lean hard on Israel to change its thinking about how to achieve a two-state solution.

Israel's intransigence and the lobby's influence are not the only obstacles to a peaceful settlement, of course, and ending the conflict will require the United States (and others) to pressure the Palestinians as well. This will be much easier to do if the Palestinians and key Arab states see the United States as genuinely committed to a just peace and willing to act as an honest broker, instead of operating as "Israel's lawyer." A genuine effort to end the conflict—as opposed to the Bush administration's halfhearted commitment to the Road Map or Secretary of State Condoleezza Rice's meaningless regional visits—will force the Palestinians to make a real choice. As it stands now, there is little reason for the Palestinians not to support groups like Hamas, because the possibility of meaningful negotiations is remote and supporting the most radical groups costs little in the way of missed opportunities. But if the United States presses hard to help them gain a viable state, and Hamas is exposed as the main obstacle to that end, then the Palestinians would be more likely to turn against Hamas and seize the olive branch.

Israel's American backers need to recognize that denying the Palestinians their legitimate political rights has not made Israel safer, and those who have lobbied hardest for unconditional U.S. backing have ultimately nurtured Israeli and Palestinian extremism and inflicted unintended hardships on the very country that they seek to support. It is high time to abandon this bankrupt policy and pursue a different course.

The policies sketched here are no panacea, and they will not eliminate all the problems currently facing the United States in the Middle East. Achieving a final peace between Israel and the Palestinians will require all the parties to engage in difficult and probably violent confrontations with rejectionists on both sides. Israeli-Palestinian peace is not a wonder drug that will solve all the region's problems: it will by itself neither eliminate anti-Semitism in the region nor lead Arab elites to tackle the other problems that afflict their societies with new energy and commitment. But ending the conflict and adopting a more normal relationship with Israel will help the United States rebuild its image in the Arab and Islamic world and put it in a position where it can more credibly encourage the various reforms that are badly needed elsewhere in the region.

Some may argue that the problems the United States currently faces in the Middle East are an aberration, due primarily to the influence of one faction in the lobby—the neoconservatives. Once President Bush's second term is over and the neoconservatives are out of power, one might hope, U.S. foreign policy will revert to more sensible positions and America's regional position will quickly improve.

This hopeful forecast, alas, is too optimistic. Although a number of prominent neoconservatives no longer serve in government, they are still active in current policy debates. Some of them are advising 2008 presidential candidates and they remain a ubiquitous presence in the mainstream media. To date, few neoconservatives seem chastened by the havoc their policies have wrought, and even fewer have expressed any remorse about the human costs of their misguided advice. The think tanks that support them are still flourishing and influential inside the Beltway and will continue to influence American foreign policy after the next election.

Equally important, many of the major organizations in the lobby remain committed to the same policy agenda: steadfast support for an expansionist Israel at the expense of the Palestinians, confrontation with Israel's adversaries for the purpose of either fundamentally changing each country's foreign policy or toppling the regime, and maintaining a substantial American presence in the region over the longer term. As previously noted, none of the major presidential candidates has proposed a significant alteration in U.S. Middle East policy, and certainly nothing like the strategy we have outlined here. Thus, anyone who believes that the 2008 election will lead to markedly different policies is likely to be disappointed. This situation raises the obvious question: can anything be done to break the lobby's hold?

DEALING WITH THE LOBBY

In theory, there are four ways to mitigate the lobby's negative influence. First, one could try to *weaken* the lobby, either by reducing its resources or by removing some of its avenues of influence. Second, other groups could try to *counter* the lobby's influence over elected officials and the policy-making process, thereby shifting U.S. policy to a more evenhanded position. Third, academics and the media could *confront* the lobby's various arguments, in order to correct enduring myths and expose the weaknesses in the lobby's policy preferences. Finally, the lobby itself might *evolve* in a positive direction, retaining its current influence but advocating a different set of policies.

Weakening the Lobby?

The lobby would be less influential if it no longer enjoyed generous financial support, or if its ability to direct campaign contributions and to pressure media organizations declined. Neither of these developments is realistic, however, because it is not likely to lose wealthy and generous supporters anytime soon. Although the number of Americans who are unconditionally committed to Israel is declining, there will almost certainly be a sufficient number who feel strongly enough to give large sums to support the lobby's leading organizations. Banning such contributions is unlikely and would probably be illegal. Plus, trying to restrict support for pro-Israel groups would clearly be anti-Semitic, as all Americans are within their rights to contribute to any legitimate cause.

The obvious way to reduce the lobby's influence (along with other special interest groups) is campaign finance reform. Public financing of all elections would seriously weaken the link between the lobby and elected officials and make it easier for the latter to pressure Israel (or simply withdraw U.S. support) when doing so would be in America's interest. Such a step would not eliminate the lobby's influence, as politicians would still court Jewish and Christian Zionist voters, and groups and individuals within the lobby could still press their case with U.S. officials and work to shape public opinion. Campaign finance reform would almost certainly attenuate its influence, however, and would encourage more open deliberations within the corridors of power.

Unfortunately, the prospects for meaningful campaign finance reform are dim. Incumbents have too great a stake in the current system, and plenty of other special interest groups would join forces to resist any effort to revise the system that currently gives them disproportionate influence. It would probably take a bevy of Jack Abramoff–style scandals to convince Americans to purge private money from the electoral process. In the short term, trying to weaken the lobby directly is not going to work.

Countering the Lobby?

Creating a "counterlobby" to balance the Israel lobby is also likely to fail. As discussed in Chapter 4, Arab-American and Muslim groups are much weaker than the organizations in the Israel lobby, and the vaunted oil lobby exerts much less influence on foreign and national security policy than is commonly believed. Other countervailing organizations—such as the non-partisan Council for the National Interest or Americans for Middle East Understanding—are also significantly smaller and less well financed than the Israel lobby.

But even if these various groups were bigger and richer, they would still find it hard to overcome the collective action dynamics that lie at the heart of interest group politics. As noted earlier, pro-Israel groups succeed in part because their members place an especially high priority on backing Israel, which means that they tend to engage in single-issue politics—backing only candidates whose pro-Israel credentials are well established. Even if many Americans are aware that unconditional support for Israel is not in America's national interest, this issue is not the top priority for most of them, and there are significant differences among the various groups that are either skeptical of unconditional aid to Israel or strongly opposed to it. As a result, trying to balance the lobby's influence by pulling these disparate groups into a suffi-ciently cohesive coalition is not a promising strategy. We would also view at-tempts to form an explicitly "anti-Israel" lobby with grave misgivings, as this sort of group could easily foster a resurgence of genuine anti-Semitism.

Fostering More Open Discourse

The third option, which is much more promising than the first two, is to en-courage a more open debate about these issues, in order to correct existing myths about the Middle East and to force groups in the lobby to defend their positions in the face of a well-informed opposition. In particular, Amer-icans need to understand the real history of Israel's founding and the true story of its subsequent conduct. Instead of passively accepting the Leon Uris version of the Arab-Israeli conflict, Americans need to absorb and re-flect on the findings of Israel's "new historians," whose courageous scholar-ship has shed much-needed light on what the Zionists' campaign to build a

Jewish state in the midst of an indigenous Arab population entailed. Although the two situations are hardly identical, one cannot understand Zionism without understanding the long history of Christian anti-Semitism, and one cannot fathom contemporary Palestinian nationalism without being aware of the events surrounding the 1948 war, which Israelis call the War of Independence but Palestinians call *al-Nakba*, or "the Catastrophe."[12]

Because most Americans are only dimly aware of the crimes committed against the Palestinians, they see their continued resistance as an irrational desire for vengeance, or as evidence of unwarranted hatred of Jews akin to the anti-Semitism that was endemic in old Europe. Ignorance about the past also encourages Americans to reject the Palestinians' demands for compensation—especially the right of return—as utterly unjustified. Although we deplore the Palestinians' reliance on terrorism and are well aware of their own contribution to prolonging the conflict, we believe their grievances are genuine and must be addressed, even if, as noted above, some of their aspirations (such as the unrestricted right of return) will have to go unmet or be resolved in other ways. We also believe most Americans would support a different approach to the conflict if they had a more accurate understanding of past events and present conditions.

As the primary source of independent thinking in democratic societies, scholars and journalists should be encouraged to resist the lobby's efforts to shape public discourse and to encourage more open discussion of these important issues. The objective is not to single out Israel for criticism or to challenge the legitimacy of the Jewish state, but rather to help Americans gain a more accurate picture of how past behavior casts a giant shadow over the present. Israel will still have plenty of vocal defenders—as it should—but America would be better served if its citizens were exposed to the range of views about Israel common to most of the world's democracies, including Israel itself.

Journalists have a particular responsibility to ask hard questions during political campaigns. As noted at the beginning of this book, virtually all the major presidential candidates began the 2008 campaign by expressing a strong personal commitment to Israel and by making it clear that they favor unconditional U.S. support for the Jewish state and a confrontational approach toward its adversaries. Politicians should not get a free pass when they utter the usual pro-Israel platitudes. Reporters and commentators should insist that those who aspire to be president explain why they favor such strong support for Israel and ask if they support a two-state solution and will push hard for it once elected. The candidates should also be asked to consider whether a more conditional U.S. policy—for example, one that linked American military aid to genuine progress toward peace—might be good for the United States and Israel alike. And it should be fair game to ask those who aspire to the highest office in the land if their views have been influenced by campaign contributions from pro-Israel PACs or individuals, just as one might legitimately ask about the impact of contributions received from oil companies, labor unions, or drug manufacturers.

To foster a more open discussion, Americans of all backgrounds must reject the silencing tactics that some groups and individuals in the lobby continue to employ. Stifling debate and smearing opponents is inconsistent with the principles of vigorous and open dialogue on which democracy depends, and continued reliance on this undemocratic tactic runs the risk of generating a hostile backlash at some point in the future.

We condemn all attempts to silence legitimate forms of discussion and debate—including the occasional efforts to silence pro-Israel voices—and we hope that this book will contribute to a more open exchange of views on these difficult problems. Both the United States and Israel face vexing challenges in dealing with the many problems in the Middle East, and neither country will benefit by silencing those who support a new approach. This does not mean that critics are always right, of course, but their suggestions deserve at least as much consideration as the failed policies that key groups in the lobby have backed in recent years.

A New Israel Lobby?

Convincing groups within the lobby to support a different agenda would also advance the U.S. national interest. In practice, this development could involve strengthening more moderate forces that already exist—such as the Israel Policy Forum or Americans for Peace Now—or by creating new pro-Israel groups that support different policies. U.S. and Israeli interests would also be advanced by wresting power away from the hard-liners who now control AIPAC, the Zionist Organization of America, the Conference of Presidents, or the American Jewish Committee. Such efforts might also be strengthened by institutional reforms that would give the rank and file a greater voice in determining these organizations' policy positions.

Of course, this scenario requires both leaders and members of these organizations to recognize that the policies that many of them have backed in recent years have been in neither America's nor Israel's interest. They must also come to understand that clinging to these positions may condemn Israel to an even bleaker future. More sensible voices in the Jewish community will have to discard the taboo against public criticism of Israel and challenge

Israeli policies that are harmful to Israel and may even be harmful to Jews in the diaspora as well. We agree with Rabbi Ben-Zion Gold, director emeritus of Harvard University Hillel, who wrote in 2002 that "American Jews, who are the largest Diaspora community, have to discover their own focus . . . Those of us who criticize Israel do so because Israel is an important part of our identity, because criticism is an integral part of our traditional culture . . . We offer it as an expression of respect and love for the people of Israel."[13] Or as the *Economist* recently observed, "Helping Israel should no longer mean defending it uncritically . . . Diaspora institutions should . . . feel free to criticize Israeli politicians who preach racism and intolerance . . . [and] encourage lively debate about Israeli policies."[14]

Indeed, current conditions in the Middle East pose a serious dilemma for the more hard-line elements in the lobby. Instead of defending a weak state surrounded by enemies, created in the aftermath of a great historical tragedy, they are now forced to defend a powerful, modern, and prosperous state that is using its superior force to confiscate land from the Palestinians and to deny them full political rights, while dealing harshly with troubled neighbors such as Lebanon. When this behavior prompts criticism from sensible moderates, these groups are forced to try to smear and marginalize people who are obviously neither extremists nor anti-Semites. Condemning neo-Nazis or Holocaust deniers is a worthy enterprise, but smearing respected individuals such as Jimmy Carter, Richard Cohen, Tony Kushner, or Tony Judt, or attacking progressive groups like the Union of Concerned Zionists, is something very different and disturbing. The more the lobby's hard-liners attack any and all critics, the more they reveal themselves to be out of step with the broad American commitment to free speech and open discussion. And once virtually any criticism of Israel becomes equated with anti-Semitism, the charge itself threatens to become meaningless.

Convincing hard-line Christian Zionists to abandon their commitment to a greater Israel is less likely, given the central role that prophecies about the end-time play in dispensationalist theology, and given their apparent willingness to see the Middle East engulfed in a highly destructive "apocalyptic" war. Hope may be found in the tendency for evangelicals' agendas to shift in the perennial quest for new members and in the general tendency for these movements to fluctuate in strength over time. The next president is unlikely to be as sympathetic to these groups as George W. Bush has been, especially given the disastrous results that Bush's Middle East policies have produced. Jews in Israel and America may also realize that Christian Zionism is a dubious ally—especially when they consider the unappealing role they are expected to play in the end-time—and begin to distance themselves from the evangelicals' embrace.[15] For their part, Christian evangelicals should be encouraged to reflect on the human tragedy that Israel continues to inflict on the Palestinians and to consider whether their own commitment to a "greater Israel" is truly consistent with Christ's message of love and brotherhood.

Redirecting the lobby's agenda may seem far-fetched, but some of these organizations supported different policies in the past and there is no reason to assume that their current preferences are set in stone. Indeed, there are signs of growing disenchantment with the positions espoused by the major Jewish organizations and a renewed effort to cultivate Jewish voices that better reflect mainstream Jewish opinion. Groups like the Israel Policy Forum, Brit Tzedek v'Shalom, and Americans for Peace Now have become more visible and effective, and are reportedly pondering a merger designed to enhance their influence and encourage greater U.S. effort toward a two-state solution. A number of prominent American Jews have also considered founding a new lobbying group explicitly intended to provide a more reasonable alternative to AIPAC.[16]

Similar movements are occurring in other countries as well. In February 2007, a group of British Jews founded a new organization, Independent Jewish Voices (IJV), which favors the universal application of human rights law and a negotiated peace between Israelis and Palestinians. IJV condemns anti-Semitism, anti-Arabism, and Islamophobia, and was founded "in the belief that the broad spectrum of opinion among the Jewish population of this country is not reflected by those institutions which claim authority to represent the Jewish community as a whole." IJV's founding declaration also emphasized that "the battle against anti-Semitism is vital and is undermined whenever opposition to Israeli government policies is automatically branded as anti-Semitic."[17]

In Australia, Jews who are critical of Israeli policy and have found it difficult to voice their views have formed an organization called Independent Australian Jewish Voices. In November 2006, twenty-five peace researchers in Germany called for questioning the "special relationship" between Germany and Israel, because of Israel's actions against the Palestinians. A few months later, in March 2007, a heated controversy broke out within the German Jewish community when a small group of Jews issued "Berlin Declaration Shalom 5767," which, according to the *Forward*, criticized Israeli policy in the Occupied Territories and "the limits of open debate on matters in relation to the Middle East."[18] Initiatives like these remind us that the policy positions espoused by the most influential groups in the lobby do not represent the views of all (or even most) diaspora Jews, and they give reason to hope that many groups within the lobby might eventually bring their influence to bear in more constructive ways.

FINAL THOUGHTS

Israel's creation and subsequent development is a remarkable achievement. Had American Jews not organized on Israel's behalf and convinced important politicians to support their objectives, Israel might never have been established. U.S. and Israeli interests have never been identical, however, and Israel's current policies are at odds with America's own national interests and certain core U.S. values. Unfortunately, in recent years the lobby's political clout and public relations acumen have discouraged U.S. leaders from pursuing Middle East policies that would advance American interests and protect Israel from its worst mistakes. The lobby's influence, in short, has been bad for both countries.

There is, nonetheless, a silver lining in America's current plight. Because the costs of these failed policies are now so apparent, we have an opportunity for reflection and renewal. Although the lobby remains a powerful political force, its adverse impact is increasingly hard to overlook. A country as rich and powerful as the United States can sustain flawed policies for quite some time, but reality cannot be ignored forever.

What is needed, therefore, is a candid but civilized discussion of the lobby's influence and a more open debate about U.S. interests in this vital region. Israel's well-being is one of those interests—on moral grounds—but its continued presence in the Occupied Territories is not. Open debate and more wide-ranging media coverage will reveal the problems that the current "special relationship" creates and encourage the United States to pursue policies more in line with its own national interest, with the interests of other states in the region, and, we firmly believe, with Israel's interest as well.

NOTES

Unless otherwise noted, references to the following publications and news agencies are to their on-line versions: *American Prospect*, Associated Press, *Boston Globe*, *Chicago Sun-Times*, *Chicago Tribune*, *Christian Science Monitor*, *Daily Telegraph* (London), *Financial Times*, *Forward*, *Guardian*, *Ha'aretz*, *Independent*, *International Herald Tribune*, Inter Press Service, *Jerusalem Post*, *Jewish Week*, *Los Angeles Times*, *Nation*, *Newsweek*, *New York Review of Books*, *New York Sun*, *New York Times*, *Observer*, Reuters, *Sunday Telegraph* (London), *Sunday Times* (London), *Time*, *Times* (London), *USA Today*, *U.S. News & World Report*, *Wall Street Journal*, *Washington Monthly*, *Washington Post*, *Washington Times*, and *Weekly Standard*. We have also accessed some publications via the Lexis-Nexis, FACTIVA, or JSTOR digital archives.

INTRODUCTION

1. Joshua Mitnick, "Iran Threat Steals Show at Herzliya," *Jewish Week*, January 26, 2007. Also see Ron Kampeas, "As Candidates Enter 2008 Race, They Begin Courting Jewish Support," *JTA.org*, January 25, 2007; Ron Kampeas, "AIPAC Conference—The First Primary?" *JTA.org*, March 6, 2007; Joshua Mitnick, "Candidates Court Israel, Cite Iran Risks," *Washington Times*, January 24, 2007; and M. J. Rosenberg, "Pandering Not Required," Weekly Opinion Column, Issue #310, Israel Policy Forum, Washington, DC, February 9, 2007. Transcripts of the presentations by Edwards, Gingrich, McCain, and Romney can be found at www.herzliyaconference.org/Eng/_Articles/Article.asp?CategoryID=226&ArticleID=1599.
2. "Senator Clinton's Remarks to the American Israel Public Affairs Committee (AIPAC)," February 1, 2007, http://clinton.senate.gov/news/statements/details.cfm?id=268474. See Joshua Frank, "Hillary Clinton and the Israel Lobby," *Antiwar.com*, January 23, 2007; and E. J. Kessler, "Hillary the Favorite in Race for Jewish Donations," *Forward*, January 26, 2007.
3. Thomas Beaumont, "Up-Close Obama Urges Compassion in Mideast," *Des Moines Register* (online), March 12, 2007; James D. Besser, "Obama Set for Big Jewish Push," *Jewish Week*, February 16, 2007; Larry Cohler-Esses, "Obama Pivots Away from Dovish Past," *Jewish Week*, March 9, 2007; and Lynn Sweet, "Obama to Offer Pro-Israel Views at Chicago Gathering," *Chicago Sun-Times*, March 1, 2007.
4. For pro-Israel statements by McCain, Clinton, Obama, Romney, Richardson, and Brownback, see "The Road to the White House: Israel-US Ties," *Jerusalem Post*, May 24, 2007.
5. In his entertaining popular history *Power, Faith, and Fantasy: America in the Middle East 1776 to the Present* (New York: Norton, 2007), the Israeli-American author Michael B. Oren offers a number of vivid portraits of prior American involvement in the region. Implicit in his

argument, which he has made explicit in public presentations, is the idea that U.S. involvement in the Middle East long predates the creation of Israel and therefore current American support for the Jewish state has little to do with the activities of the Israel lobby. For a characteristic public statement to this effect, see Oren's address to the 2007 AIPAC Policy Conference, where he described AIPAC itself as "an expression of a nearly 400-year-long tradition in which the idea of a United States is virtually indivisible and inseparable from the idea of a re-created Jewish state. It is the embodiment of a conviction as old as this nation itself that belief in the Jewish state is tantamount to belief in these United States." This odd argument ignores how much the U.S. role in the Middle East has changed since 1776, and especially since 1948 and 1967. For the transcript, see www.aipac.org/Publications/Oren-PC-2007.pdf.

6. As the historian Peter L. Hahn puts it, "Prior to World War II, the United States took relatively little official interest in the Middle East. Although the European empires had long engaged in the so-called Eastern Question—a diplomatic rivalry for dominance in the Middle East (as well as South Asia)—the government in Washington identified no strategic or political interests in the area and thus avoided entanglement in the imperial rivalry there." See his *Crisis and Crossfire: The United States and the Middle East since 1945* (Washington, DC: Potomac Books, 2005), 1.

7. Macmillan also writes regarding the disposition of Palestine: "The United States, in contrast to what happened after the Second World War, played a minor role." See *Paris 1919: Six Months That Changed the World* (New York: Random House, 2001), 422–23.

8. On the origins of Saudi-American security cooperation, see Nadav Safran, *Saudi Arabia: The Ceaseless Quest for Security* (Cambridge, MA: Harvard University Press, 1985), 60–68; and Rachel Bronson, *Thicker than Oil: America's Uneasy Partnership with Saudi Arabia* (New York: Oxford University Press, 2006), chaps. 1–2. On the Baghdad Pact, see Stephen M. Walt, *The Origins of Alliances* (Ithaca: Cornell University Press, 1987), 58–59.

9. Wieseltier's comment appears in his review of the memoirs of Palestinian intellectual Sari Nusseibeh. See "Sympathy for the Other," *New York Times Book Review*, April 1, 2007, 13.

10. This charge was based on Carter's having written a brief note on a 1987 letter he had received from the daughter of a former Nazi prison guard who was protesting her father's deportation. Carter's one-sentence note expressed no sympathy for the former guard and did not recommend that any action be taken on his behalf but merely said he hoped the Office of Special Investigations (the U.S. agency responsible for prosecuting Nazi-era war crimes) would give "special consideration to affected families for humanitarian reasons." Yet this episode was used to smear Carter as somehow sympathetic to Nazism. See Daniel Freedman, "President Carter Interceded on Behalf of Former Nazi Guard," *New York Sun*, January 19, 2007.

11. Jodie T. Allen and Alec Tyson, "The U.S. Public's Pro-Israel History," Pew Research Center, July 19, 2006; and Pew Research Center for the People and the Press in association with the Council on Foreign Relations, "America's Place in the World 2005: An Investigation of the Attitudes of American Opinion Leaders and the American Public about International Affairs," November 2005, 11–12.

12. The poll was conducted by Zogby International between October 10 and October 12, 2006, on behalf of the Council for the National Interest. The results are available at www.cnionline.org/learn/polls/czandlobby/index2.htm.

13. Daniel Maliniak et al., "Inside the Ivory Tower," *Foreign Policy* 159 (March–April 2007): 66.

14. This is why Osama bin Laden originally wanted to attack the U.S. Capitol on September 11, 2001; he saw it as the leading bastion of support for Israel in the United States. "Outline of the 9/11 Plot," Staff Statement no. 16, National Commission on Terrorist Attacks Upon the United States, June 16, 2004, 4.

15. Michael Massing, "The Storm over the Israel Lobby," *New York Review of Books*, June 8, 2006; and Jeffrey Goldberg, "Real Insiders," *New Yorker*, July 4, 2005.

16. As Nadav Safran noted in his book on the U.S.-Israel alliance, "Jews are not the first ethnic

or religious group in America that has sought to influence American foreign policy in favor of kinsmen or co-religionists . . . Ethnoreligious politics, like the politics of interest groups in general, have been an inescapable consequence of the pluralism and multiplicity of interests in American life." *The United States and Israel* (Cambridge, MA: Harvard University Press, 1963), 276.

17. Useful works in this extensive literature include Tony Smith, *Foreign Attachments: The Power of Ethnic Groups in the Making of American Foreign Policy* (Cambridge, MA: Harvard University Press, 2000); *Ethnic Groups and U.S. Foreign Policy*, ed. M. E. Ahrari (Westport, CT: Greenwood Press, 1987); *Ethnicity and U.S. Foreign Policy*, 2nd ed., ed. A. A. Said (New York: Praeger, 1981); Charles McC. Mathias Jr., "Ethnic Groups and Foreign Policy," *Foreign Affairs* 59, no. 5 (Summer 1981); Alexander DeConde, *Ethnicity, Race and American Foreign Policy* (Boston: Northeastern University Press, 1992); Yossi Shain, "Ethnic Diasporas and U.S. Foreign Policy," *Political Science Quarterly* 109, no. 5 (1994–95); Paul Watanabe, *Ethnic Groups, Congress, and American Foreign Policy: The Politics of the Turkish Arms Embargo* (Westport, CT: Greenwood Press, 1984); Patrick J. Haney and Walt Vanderbush, "The Role of Ethnic Interest Groups in U.S. Foreign Policy: The Case of the Cuban-American National Foundation," *International Studies Quarterly* 43, no. 2 (June 1999); Max J. Castro, "Miami Vise," *Nation*, May 14, 2007; Gabriel Sheffer, *Diaspora Politics: At Home Abroad* (New York: Cambridge University Press, 2003); David King and Miles Pomper, "Congress and the Contingent Influence of Diaspora Lobbies: Lessons from U.S. Foreign Policy Toward Azerbaijan and Armenia," *Journal of Armenian Studies* 8, no. 1 (Summer 2004); and R. Hrair Dekmejian and Angelos Themelis, "Ethnic Lobbies in U.S. Foreign Policy: A Comparative Analysis of the Jewish, Greek, Armenian and Turkish Lobbies," Occasional Research Paper no. 13, Institute of International Relations, Panteion University of Social and Political Sciences, Athens, Greece, October 1997.

18. On the history of anti-Semitism, see James Carroll, *Constantine's Sword: The Church and the Jews; A History* (Boston: Houghton Mifflin, 2001); Edward H. Flannery, *The Anguish of the Jews: Twenty-Three Centuries of Antisemitism*, 2nd rev. ed. (New York: Paulist Press, 2004); Israel Pocket Library, *Anti-Semitism* (Jerusalem: Keter, 1974); and Marvin Perry and Frederick Schweitzer, *Anti-Semitism: Myth and Hate from Antiquity to the Present* (New York: Palgrave Macmillan, 2002). On the status and treatment of Jews in the Arab world, see Bernard Lewis, *Semites and Anti-Semites: An Inquiry into Conflict and Prejudice* (New York: Norton, 1986), chap. 5; and Charles D. Smith, *Palestine and the Arab-Israeli Conflict: A History with Documents*, 5th ed. (New York: St. Martin's Press, 2004), 8, 10–11.

19. Quoted in *The Middle East*, 5th ed. (Washington, DC: Congressional Quarterly, 1981), 68.

20. As an official Indian government committee noted in 2002, "Indo-Americans have effectively mobilized on issues ranging from the nuclear test in 1998 to Kargil, have played a crucial role in generating a favourable climate of opinion in the [U.S.] Congress . . . and lobbied effectively on other issues of concern . . . For the first time, India has a constituency in the United States with real influence and status. The Indian community in the United States constitutes an invaluable asset in strengthening India's relationship with the world's only superpower." *Report of the High Level Committee on the Indian Diaspora* (New Delhi: Government of India, January 2002), xx–xxi.

21. In addition to Gephardt's statement, quotations about AIPAC's influence by Bill Clinton, Newt Gingrich, and several other prominent figures were previously available at www.aipac .org/documents/whoweare.html#say (accessed January 14, 2005). AIPAC appears to have removed these statements from the current version of its website.

22. Alan M. Dershowitz, *Chutzpah* (Boston: Little, Brown, 1991), 16.

23. Quoted in Samuel G. Freedman, "Don't Blame Jews for This War," *USA Today*, April 2, 2003.

24. On the role of interest groups in American politics, see Frank R. Baumgartner and Beth L. Leech, *Basic Interests: The Importance of Groups in Politics and in Political Science* (Princeton: Princeton University Press, 1998); Richard L. Hall and Frank W. Wayman, "Buying Time: Moneyed Interests and the Mobilization of Bias in Congressional Committees,"

American Political Science Review 84, no. 3 (September 1990); Richard L. Hall and Alan V. Deardorff, "Lobbying as Legislative Subsidy," *American Political Science Review* 100, no. 1 (February 2006); John Mark Hansen, *Gaining Access: Congress and the Farm Lobby, 1919–1981* (Chicago: University of Chicago Press, 1991); Ken Kollman, *Outside Lobbying: Public Opinion and Interest Group Strategies* (Princeton: Princeton University Press, 1998); Richard A. Smith, "Interest Group Influence in the U. S. Congress," *Legislative Studies Quarterly* 20, no. 1 (February 1995); Raymond A. Bauer, Ithiel de Sola Pool, and Lewis Anthony Dexter, *American Business and Public Policy: The Politics of Foreign Trade* (Cambridge, MA: MIT Press, 1963); David B. Truman, *The Governmental Process: Political Interests and Public Opinion* (New York: Knopf, 1951); and James Q. Wilson, *Political Organizations* (New York: Basic Books, 1973).

25. See note 17 above.

26. George W. Ball and Douglas B. Ball, *The Passionate Attachment: America's Involvement with Israel, 1947 to the Present* (New York: Norton, 1992); Mitchell G. Bard, *The Water's Edge and Beyond: Defining the Limits to Domestic Influence on U.S. Middle East Policy* (New York: Transaction Books, 1991); Paul Findley, *They Dare to Speak Out: People and Institutions Confront Israel's Lobby* (Westport, CT: Lawrence Hill, 1985); J. J. Goldberg, *Jewish Power: Inside the American Jewish Establishment* (New York: Perseus Books, 1996); Anatol Lieven, *America Right or Wrong: An Anatomy of American Nationalism* (New York: Oxford University Press, 2004), chap. 6; Michael Lind, "The Israel Lobby," *Prospect* 73 (April 2002); Massing, "Storm over the Israel Lobby"; Michael Massing, "The Israel Lobby," *Nation*, June 10, 2002; Michael Massing, "Deal Breakers," *American Prospect*, March 11, 2002; Edward Tivnan, *The Lobby: Jewish Political Power and American Foreign Policy* (New York: Simon & Schuster, 1987); and James Petras, *The Power of Israel in the United States* (Atlanta, GA: Clarity Press, 2006). We do not agree with every assertion made in these works, but each contains useful information about the U.S.-Israeli relationship.

27. Steven L. Spiegel, *The Other Arab-Israeli Conflict: Making America's Middle East Policy from Truman to Reagan* (Chicago: University of Chicago Press, 1985); and Warren Bass, *Support Any Friend: Kennedy's Middle East and the Making of the U.S.-Israeli Alliance* (New York: Oxford University Press, 2003). Other useful works include Abraham Ben-Zvi, *The United States and Israel: Limits of the Special Relationship* (New York: Columbia University Press, 1993); Abraham Ben-Zvi, *Decade of Transition: Eisenhower, Kennedy and the Origins of the American-Israeli Relationship* (New York: Columbia University Press, 1998); Peter L. Hahn, *Caught in the Middle East: U.S. Policy Toward the Arab-Israeli Conflict, 1945–1961* (Chapel Hill: University of North Carolina Press, 2004); William B. Quandt, *Peace Process: American Diplomacy and the Arab-Israeli Conflict Since 1967*, 3rd ed. (Washington, DC: Brookings Institution Press, 2004); David Schoenbaum, *The United States and the State of Israel* (New York: Oxford University Press, 1993); and Peter Grose, *Israel in the Mind of America* (New York: Knopf, 1983).

28. Among the relevant works are Shlomo Ben-Ami, *Scars of War, Wounds of Peace: The Israeli-Arab Tragedy* (New York: Oxford University Press, 2006); Simha Flapan, *The Birth of Israel: Myths and Realities* (New York: Pantheon Books, 1987); Baruch Kimmerling, *Politicide: Ariel Sharon's War Against the Palestinians* (London: Verso, 2003); Benny Morris, *Righteous Victims: A History of the Zionist-Arab Conflict, 1881–1999* (New York: Knopf, 1999); Ilan Pappe, *The Ethnic Cleansing of Palestine* (Oxford, England: Oneworld Publications, 2006); Tom Segev, *One Palestine, Complete: Jews and Arabs Under the British Mandate*, trans. Haim Watzman (New York: Metropolitan Books, 2000); Tom Segev, *1967: Israel, the War, and the Year That Transformed the Middle East*, trans. Jessica Cohen (New York: Metropolitan Books, 2007); Avi Shlaim, *The Iron Wall: Israel and the Arab World* (New York: Norton, 2000); and Zeev Sternhell, *The Founding Myths of Israel: Nationalism, Socialism, and the Making of the Jewish State*, trans. David Maisel (Princeton: Princeton University Press, 1998).

29. See, for example, Nur Masalha, *Expulsion of the Palestinians: The Concept of "Transfer" in Zionist Political Thought, 1882–1948* (Washington, DC: Institute for Palestine Studies,

1992); Eugene L. Rogan and Avi Shlaim, eds., *The War for Palestine: Rewriting the History of 1948* (New York: Cambridge University Press, 2001); Norman G. Finkelstein, *Image and Reality of the Israel-Palestine Conflict* (London: Verso, 2001); and Rashid Khalidi, *The Iron Cage: The Story of the Palestinian Struggle for Statehood* (Boston: Beacon Press, 2006).

1: THE GREAT BENEFACTOR

1. "Address by PM Rabin to the U.S. Congress-26-Jul-94," Israel Ministry of Foreign Affairs, www.mfa.gov.il/MFA/Archive/Speeches; and Benjamin Netanyahu, "Speech to Joint Session of Congress, July 10, 1996," www.netanyahu.org/joinsesofusc.html.

2. According to the "Greenbook" of the U.S. Agency for International Development (USAID), which reports "overseas loans and grants," Israel received $153,894,700,000 (in constant 2005 dollars) from the United States through 2005. See http://qesdb.usaid.gov/gbk.

3. According to the Congressional Research Service, the United States did not provide Israel with any direct military assistance between 1949 and 1959. See Clyde Mark, "Israel: U.S. Foreign Assistance," *Issue Brief for Congress*, Congressional Research Service, April 26, 2005, 13–14, Table 3. The United States did sell Israel one hundred recoilless antitank rifles in 1958, partly as a reward for Israel's support during the 1958 Jordan crisis. See Warren Bass, *Support Any Friend: Kennedy's Middle East and the Making of the U.S.-Israeli Alliance* (New York: Oxford University Press, 2003), 151; and Douglas Little, "The Making of a Special Relationship: The United States and Israel, 1957–68," *International Journal of Middle East Studies* 25, no. 4 (November 1993): 566. William H. Mott IV reports that Israel obtained five hundred surplus U.S. half-tracks covertly during the War of Independence and also received some surplus tanks in 1951–52. Washington also helped subsidize Israel's purchase of French combat aircraft in 1954, "as part of U.S. military assistance to France for development of French military industry," and provided a similar subsidy for the purchase of French Mystere aircraft in 1955. Because France was the ostensible beneficiary of these subsidies, the amounts are not included in most descriptions of U.S. aid to Israel. Mott reports a total of $94.5 million in military assistance between 1946 and 1955 and an additional $189.1 million from 1956 to 1965. See William H. Mott IV, *United States Military Assistance: An Empirical Perspective* (Westport, CT: Greenwood Press, 2002), 176–77.

4. See Zach Levey, "Israel's Quest for a Security Guarantee from the United States, 1954–1956," *British Journal of Middle East Studies* 22, no. 1/2 (1995). Levey describes David Ben-Gurion as ambivalent about the virtues of a U.S. guarantee in this period; while recognizing the value of great-power protection, he also worried it might reduce Israel's autonomy. Levey also notes that some Israeli officials (most notably Moshe Sharett) saw a U.S. guarantee as a way to restrain the more aggressive policies favored by Ben-Gurion and others.

5. Michael Brecher, *Decisions in Israel's Foreign Policy* (New Haven: Yale University Press, 1975), 191–92, 220.

6. Avi Shlaim, *The Iron Wall: Israel and the Arab World* (New York: Norton, 2001), 172–73.

7. Ibid., 178–85; Benny Morris, *Righteous Victims: A History of the Zionist-Arab Conflict, 1881–2001* (New York: Vintage, 2001), 290, 297–300; Brecher, *Decisions in Israel's Foreign Policy*, 282–303; Steven L. Spiegel, *The Other Arab-Israeli Conflict: Making America's Middle East Policy from Truman to Reagan* (Chicago: University of Chicago Press, 1985), 74–82; and David Schoenbaum, *The United States and the State of Israel* (New York: Oxford University Press, 1993), 115–23.

8. According to Warren Bass, "The Kennedy Administration . . . constitutes the pivotal presidency in U.S.-Israel relations, the hinge that swung decisively away from the chilly association of the 1950s and toward the full-blown alliance we know today." *Support Any Friend*, 3. Abraham Ben-Zvi dates the beginning of the strategic partnership to the late 1950s, and especially to Israel's acceptance of the Eisenhower Doctrine (which pledged U.S. support for Middle Eastern countries threatened by "international communism") and to its support during various crises in Lebanon, Iraq, and Jordan. See *Decade of Transition: Eisenhower,*

Kennedy and the Origins of the American-Israeli Alliance (New York: Columbia University Press, 1998); and Little, "Making of a Special Relationship."

9. Kennedy was more circumspect in describing the U.S. commitment at a subsequent press conference. See Bass, *Support Any Friend*, 3, 183; and Spiegel, *Other Arab-Israeli Conflict*, 106–107.

10. Warren Bass correctly notes that the Israel lobby (which he describes as a "Washington powerhouse by the 1980s") was less powerful in the early 1960s and says that "there is virtually no documentary evidence that the Hawk sale was driven by domestic considerations." The absence of documentary evidence is not surprising, however, insofar as presidents and their advisers are unlikely to admit that important strategic choices are being shaped by domestic considerations. Bass also acknowledges that "while Israel's arguments [for the Hawk sale] were couched exclusively in strategic terms, the looming midterm elections—however hushed—could hardly have been a disincentive," observing further that "Kennedy was a political animal, and he knew that the Hawk sale could only help with pro-Israel voters and donors." Bass, *Support Any Friend*, 145–50. Also see Spiegel, *Other Arab-Israeli Conflict*, 106–10; and Mordechai Gazit, *President Kennedy's Policy Toward the Arab States and Israel* (Tel Aviv: Shiloah Center for Middle Eastern and African Studies, 1983), 30–55.

11. An agreement for the sale of A-4 Skyhawk fighter-bombers was also reached at this time, although the planes were not delivered until several years later. See Stockholm International Peace Research Institute (SIPRI), *The Arms Trade with the Third World* (New York: Humanities Press, 1971), 532, 535.

12. Mark, "Israel: U.S. Foreign Assistance," 6, 13.

13. Calculated from USAID, "Greenbook," at http://qesdb.cdie.org/gbk/index.html.

14. Ibid.; and *The Military Balance 2006* (London: International Institute for Strategic Studies, 2006).

15. Mark, "Israel: U.S. Foreign Assistance," 2, 10; and Matthew Berger, "Good News—and Bad—for U.S. Aid to Israel," *JTA.org*, March 28, 2003.

16. Edward T. Pound, "A Close Look at U.S. Aid to Israel Reveals Deals That Push Cost Above Publicly Quoted Figures," *Wall Street Journal*, September 19, 1991.

17. According to Clyde Mark of the Congressional Research Service's Foreign Affairs, Defense and Trade Division, Israel "receives favorable treatment and special benefits under U.S. assistance programs that may not be available to other countries." Mark, "Israel: U.S. Foreign Assistance," 8.

18. Jeremy M. Sharp, "U.S. Foreign Aid to Israel," *Report for Congress*, Congressional Research Service, January 5, 2006, 5–6.

19. Mark, "Israel: U.S. Foreign Assistance," 8–9.

20. "U.S. Assistance to Israel," http://telaviv.usembassy.gov/publish/mission/amb/assistance.html.

21. Duncan L. Clarke, Daniel B. O'Connor, and Jason D. Ellis, *Send Guns and Money: Security Assistance and U.S. Foreign Policy* (Westport, CT: Praeger, 1997), 24; Mark, "Israel: U.S. Foreign Assistance," 10; and Shirl McArthur, "A Conservative Estimate of Total Direct U.S. Aid to Israel: $108 Billion," *Washington Report on Middle East Affairs* (online), July 2006, 16–17.

22. Sharp, "U.S. Foreign Aid to Israel," 11.

23. The GAO also discovered that the Department of Defense had waived Israel's termination liability requirements (the amounts that buyers must hold in reserve to cover the costs of terminating a contract) but believes that "because of the likelihood of continued Israeli aid, the waiver represents a minimal risk." U.S. General Accounting Office, "Military Sales Cash Flow Financing," GAO/NSIAD-94-1024, Washington, DC, February 8, 1994, 3.

24. Mark, "Israel: U.S. Foreign Assistance," 8.

25. The contrast is vividly apparent when one compares the USAID country page for Israel (www.usaid.gov/policy/budget/cbj2007/ane/il.html) with the Web pages for other important U.S. aid recipients.

26. Mark, "Israel: U.S. Foreign Assistance," 7.

27. The CRS also reports that approximately 4 percent of the guaranteed amount is set aside in a treasury account as a reserve against default. For a loan of $10 billion, this appropriation amounts to approximately $400 million. See Mark, "Israel: U.S. Foreign Assistance," 3; Larry Nowels and Clyde Mark, "Israel's Request for U.S. Loan Guarantees," *Issue Brief for Congress*, Congressional Research Service, October 8, 1991; and Sheldon L. Richman, "The Economic Impact of the Israeli Loan Guarantees," *Journal of Palestine Studies* 21, no. 2 (Winter 1992).

28. According to the CRS's Mark, "It is estimated that Israel receives about $1 billion annually through philanthropy, an equal amount through short- and long-term commercial loans, and around $1 billion in Israel Bonds proceeds." See Mark, "Israel: U.S. Foreign Assistance," summary page. State of Israel Bonds are sold in the United States through the Development Corporation for Israel (DCI). These bonds are nonnegotiable and are seen by the government of Israel as a "stable source of overseas borrowing as well as an important mechanism for maintaining ties with Diaspora Jewry." Interest rates averaged about 4 percent from 1951 to 1989 (which meant a sharp "patriotic discount" as U.S. Treasury rates rose rapidly after 1980), but "the DCI bond offerings have had to move in recent years towards market pricing." Sales of Israel bonds reportedly reached $1.2 billion in 2006, and the cumulative total of funds raised through these bonds now exceeds $25 billion. See Suhas L. Ketkar, "Diaspora Bonds: Track Record and Potential," *World Bank Discussion Paper*, August 31, 2006; and Avi Krawitz, "Israel Bonds Raises $1.2 billion in 2006," *Jerusalem Post*, December 10, 2006.

29. Dale Russakoff, "Treasury Finds Bite in Israel Bonds; 1984 Law Places New Tax on Artificially Low Interest Rates," *Washington Post*, September 12, 1985; "Tax Report," *Wall Street Journal*, August 20, 1986; and Russell Mokhiber, "Bonds of Affection," *Multinational Monitor* (1988), http://multinationalmonitor.org/hyper/issues/1988/04/mm0488_10.html.

30. According to the IRS, to qualify for the deduction, a taxpayer's contribution "must be made to an organization created and recognized as a charitable organization under the laws of Israel. The deduction will be allowed in the amount that would be allowed if the organization was created under the laws of the United States, but is limited to 25% of [the taxpayer's] adjusted gross income from Israeli sources." "Charitable Contributions," Publication 526, U.S. Internal Revenue Service, 3, www.irs.gov/pub/irs-pdf/p526.pdf. Mexico and Canada appear to be the only other countries with similar provisions.

31. The clandestine effort to obtain arms for the Zionist military forces prior to independence is recounted in Leonard Slater, *The Pledge* (New York: Simon & Schuster, 1970).

32. Shimon Peres, *Battling for Peace: A Memoir* (New York: Random House, 1995), 119; Michael Karpin, *The Bomb in the Basement: How Israel Went Nuclear and What That Means for the World* (New York: Simon & Schuster, 2005), 135–37; and Avner Cohen, *Israel and the Bomb* (New York: Columbia University Press, 1998), 67, 70.

33. Friends of the Israel Defense Forces, "Mission Statement," www.israelsoldiers.org; and Aimee Rhodes, "New York Dinner Raises $18m for IDF," *Jerusalem Post*, April 3, 2007.

34. As a Bank of Jerusalem guide for Israeli charities recently advised, "While laws governing American contributions to foreign charities have always existed, they were vague and consequently, rarely enforced. Contributions from individuals and American 501c(3) corporations to Israeli charities were unsupervised and their ultimate use was difficult to trace and determine." The guide warns that this situation has changed significantly since September 11, 2001. Bank of Jerusalem, "Help Them Help You: A Recommendation for the Israeli Charity," www.bankjerusalem.co.il/indexE.php?page=588 (accessed March 28, 2007).

35. Gershom Gorenberg, *The Accidental Empire: Israel and the Birth of the Settlements, 1967–1977* (New York: Times Books/Henry Holt, 2006), 218–19. Similarly, the Israeli political scientist David Newman has reportedly described the Jewish Agency and the WZO as operating "under one umbrella, with the same officials, departments and administrators overseeing the activities." See Amy Teibel and Ramit Plushnick-Masti, "As Israel Leaves Gaza, Bill for Its Settlement Ambitions Is Shrouded in Mystery," Associated Press, August 10, 2005.

36. Nathaniel Popper, "Jewish Officials Profess Shock over Report on Zionist Body," *Forward*, March 18, 2005; and "Summary of the Opinion Concerning Unauthorized Outposts" (the Sasson Report), www.fmep.org/documents/sassonreport.html.

37. "U.S. Tax-Exempt Charitable Contributions to Israel: Donations, Illegal Settlements, and Terror Attacks Against the US," *Middle East Foreign Policy Research Note*, October 5, 2005, www.irmep.org/tec.htm.

38. International Monetary Fund, "World Economic Outlook Database for September 2006," www.imf.org/external/pubs/ft/weo/2006/02/data/index.aspx.

39. *Human Development Report 2006* (New York: United Nations Development Programme, 2006), http://hdr.undp.org/hdr2006/statistics; and Economist Intelligence Unit, "2005 Quality of Life Rankings," www.economist.com/media/pdf/QUALITY_OF_LIFE.pdf.

40. Mitchell G. Bard and Daniel Pipes, "How Special Is the U.S.-Israel Relationship?" *Middle East Quarterly* 4, no. 2 (June 1997): 43.

41. Bishara A. Bahbah, "The United States and Israel's Energy Security," *Journal of Palestine Studies* 11, no. 2 (Winter 1982): 118–30. For the text of the original agreement, see "Israel–United States Memorandum of Understanding, September 1, 1975" and "Memorandum of Agreement between the Governments of the United States of America and Israel—Oil," www.jewishvirtuallibrary.org/jsource/Peace/mou1975.html and www.jewishvirtuallibrary.org/jsource/Peace/cdoilmou.html. Also see "Oil from Iraq: An Israeli Pipedream," *Jane's Middle East/Africa Report*, April 16, 2003, www.janes.com/regional_news/africa_middle_east/news/fr/fr030416_1_n.shtml.

42. William B. Quandt, *Camp David: Peacemaking and Politics* (Washington, DC: Brookings Institution Press, 1986), 313; Spiegel, *Other Arab-Israeli Conflict*, 371–72; Moshe Dayan, *Breakthrough: A Personal Account of the Egypt-Israeli Peace Negotiations* (New York: Knopf, 1981), 274–76; "Israel: Oil Supply Arrangement," Memoranda of Agreement, United States Treaties and Other International Acts Series 9533, 30 UST 5994 (Washington, DC, March 1979), 5989–96; Judith Miller, "Israel Pressing U.S. on Oil Sales Accord," *New York Times*, August 17, 1980; and Steven Rattner, "U.S. and Israel Reach Agreement on Oil," *New York Times*, October 16, 1980.

43. USAID, "Greenbook."

44. Alfred Prados, "Jordan: U.S. Relations and Bilateral Issues," *Issue Brief for Congress*, Congressional Research Service, January 9, 2002; and USAID, "Greenbook."

45. The 1975 Israel-U.S. Memorandum of Understanding committed Washington to "make every effort to be fully responsive . . . to Israel's military equipment and other defense requirements" and "to continue to maintain Israel's defensive strength through the supply of advanced types of equipment."

46. Sharp, "U.S. Foreign Aid to Israel," 1.

47. David Rogers and Edward T. Pound, "How Israel Spends $1.8 Billion a Year at Its Purchasing Mission in New York," *Wall Street Journal*, January 20, 1992.

48. The Defense Security Assistance Agency (DSAA) was renamed the Defense Security Cooperation Agency in 1998.

49. According to the GAO, "Whereas other countries primarily use the government-to-government process, Israel uses commercial contracts for about 99 percent of its purchases . . . By using the commercial process, Israel can avoid the Defense Department's 3-percent administrative charge for FMS sales." There are also looser governmental oversight and approval guidelines for commercial sales to Israel. "DSAA is not required to review contracts and purchase orders from $50,000 to $500,000 until after Israel receives the FMS funds" and "DSAA does not review contracts and purchase orders below $50,000." Moreover, "the unusual way DSAA administers the Israeli program and staffing limitations complicate full implementation of the agreement to report . . . sensitive items." U.S. General Accounting Office, "Security Assistance: Reporting of Program Content Changes," GAO/NSIAD-90-115, Washington, DC, May 1990, 8–9, 14.

50. Quoted in Steven Pearlstein, "U.S. Military Office Defends Israeli Aid; Closer Scrutiny of

Program Described as Unnecessary," *Washington Post*, July 30, 1992. Also see David Rogers and Edward Pound, "The Money Trail: U.S. Firms Are Linked to an Israeli General at the Heart of a Scandal," *Wall Street Journal*, January 20, 1992; Rogers and Pound, "How Israel Spends $1.8 Billion"; Joel Brinkley, "Israeli General Pleads Guilty in Bribery Case," *New York Times*, March 28, 1991; Hillel Kuttler, "U.S. Defense Procurement Faults Led to Dotan Affair," *Jerusalem Post*, August 12, 1993; and U.S. General Accounting Office, "Foreign Military Aid to Israel: Diversion of U.S. Funds and Circumvention of U.S. Program Restrictions," GAO/T-OSI-94-9, Washington, DC, October 1993.

51. As of 2004, expenditures on the Lavi, Merkava, Arrow, and other programs amounted to $2.68 billion. See "U.S. Assistance to Israel."

52. Dov S. Zakheim, *Flight of the Lavi: Inside a U.S.-Israeli Crisis* (Washington, DC: Brassey's, 1996). Zakheim was deputy undersecretary of defense in the Reagan administration and an experienced defense analyst. He was also an Orthodox Jew and a strong supporter of Israel, yet his determined efforts to assess the true costs of the Lavi project and eventually to cancel it earned him repeated attacks on his character. Indeed, he reports that Israeli defense minister Moshe Arens once called him a "traitor to the family." See xv, 256–57. Also see Duncan L. Clarke and Alan S. Cohen, "The United States, Israel and the Lavi Fighter," *Middle East Journal* 40, no. 1 (Winter 1986); and James P. DeLoughry, "The United States and the LAVI," *Airpower Journal* 4, no. 3 (Fall 1990).

53. Mark, "Israel: U.S. Foreign Assistance," 8; Carol Migdalovitz, "Israel: Background and Relations with the United States," *Report for Congress*, Congressional Research Service, August 31, 2006, 19; and Duncan L. Clarke, "The Arrow Missile: The United States, Israel, and Strategic Cooperation," *Middle East Journal* 48, no. 3 (Summer 1994).

54. "Memorandum of Understanding Between the Government of the United States and the Government of Israel on Strategic Cooperation," November 30, 1981, posted on the website of the Avalon Project at Yale Law School, www.yale.edu/lawweb/avalon/mideast/pal03.htm.

55. Congress established the designation "Major Non-NATO Ally" in 1988, as part of U.S. Code Title 10 (Armed Forces). See Subtitle A, Part IV, Chapter 138, Subchapter II, Section 2350a. On Israel's designation, see Migdalovitz, "Israel: Background and Relations," 19.

56. Yitzhak Benhorin, "US to Double Emergency Equipment Stored in Israel," *Ynetnews.com*, December 12, 2006.

57. Feldman also notes that it would be difficult and costly for the United States to transport this matériel from Israel to its most likely area of deployment, the Persian Gulf. See Shai Feldman, *The Future of U.S.-Israel Strategic Cooperation* (Washington, DC: Washington Institute for Near East Policy, 1996), 45–46. Also see Clarke et al., *Send Guns and Money*, 162–63.

58. Benhorin, "US to Double Emergency Equipment."

59. These developments are documented in Spiegel, *Other Arab-Israeli Conflict*, 410–11; Migdalovitz, "Israel: Background and Relations," 18–19; Bard and Pipes, "How Special Is the U.S.-Israel Relationship?"; Clyde Mark, "Israeli–United States Relations," *Issue Brief for Congress*, Congressional Research Service, November 9, 2004, 9–10; and Schoenbaum, *The United States and the State of Israel*, 280–81.

60. Jeffrey T. Richelson and Desmond Ball, *The Ties That Bind: Intelligence Cooperation Between the UKUSA Countries* (Boston: Unwin Hyman, 1990), 173, 304; Jeffrey T. Richelson, "The Calculus of Intelligence Cooperation," *International Journal of Intelligence and Counterintelligence* 4, no. 3 (Fall 1990): 314; and Benjamin Beit-Hallahmi, *The Israeli Connection: Who Israel Arms and Why* (New York: Pantheon Books, 1987), 40–41.

61. Jeffrey T. Richelson, *The U.S. Intelligence Community*, 2nd ed. (Cambridge, MA: Ballinger, 1989), 275–77; and Seymour Hersh, *The Samson Option: Israel's Nuclear Arsenal and American Foreign Policy* (New York: Random House, 1991), 3–8.

62. Ephraim Kahana, "Mossad-CIA Cooperation," *International Journal of Intelligence and Counterintelligence* 14, no. 3 (July 2001): 416.

63. Robert Norris et al., "Israeli Nuclear Forces, 2002," *Bulletin of the Atomic Scientists* 58, no.

5 (September/October 2002): 73–75; and "Israel Profile: Nuclear," *Nuclear Threat Initiative*, www.nti.org/e_research/profiles/Israel/Nuclear/index.html.

64. Bass, *Support Any Friend*, 198, 206.

65. Ibid., 216, 219, 222.

66. Quoted in Karpin, *Bomb in the Basement*, 237.

67. Cohen, *Israel and the Bomb*, 193. The White House aide Robert Komer later claimed that Kennedy's decision to provide U.S. arms to Israel in the 1960s was part of a deliberate effort to convince Jerusalem not to go nuclear, but if this was in fact the objective, it clearly failed. As Michael Karpin notes, "Israel wanted both the 'product' of Dimona [i.e., nuclear weapons] as well as offensive weaponry from the United States. And this, ultimately, is what it got." *Bomb in the Basement*, 238.

68. Bass, *Support Any Friend*, 252.

69. Hersh, *Samson Option*, 188–89. Bass describes Johnson's approach to Dimona as being "willing to settle for a mutually tolerable level of duplicity." *Support Any Friend*, 252.

70. Avner Cohen, "Israel and Chemical/Biological Weapons: History, Deterrence, and Arms Control," *Nonproliferation Review* 8, no. 3 (Fall–Winter 2001).

71. Total Soviet aid to Cuba may have been as large as U.S. aid to Israel in some years (roughly $3 billion per annum), but these estimates use the official dollar-peso exchange rate and thus overstate the total amount of Soviet support. Cuba's population is also roughly twice that of Israel's, so Soviet aid per capita was substantially smaller than U.S. aid to Israel, and the United States has backed Israel for a longer period than Moscow subsidized Havana. Castro was also a tamer client. As Jorge Dominguez noted, "Cuba does not oppose Soviet interests; it exercises its autonomy mindful of, and consistent with those interests. At crucial times, as with the Soviet invasion of Afghanistan, Cuba has adopted policies at great cost to its own interests . . . And even over domestic Soviet policies at odds with Cuba's own, Cuba is circumspect in its criticisms of Moscow. The tight Soviet hegemony thus places real and significant limits on Cuba's autonomy." *To Make a World Safe for Revolution: Cuba's Foreign Policy* (Cambridge, MA: Harvard University Press, 1989), 111 and Appendix B.

72. Quandt, *Peace Process*, 249. Some sources claim that Begin did not in fact break his promise, arguing that he had not initiated the discussion of AWACS but had merely expressed strong opposition to the sale when members of Congress asked him about it. It is clear from Reagan's memoirs that the former president did not find this explanation of Begin's conduct convincing. "I didn't like having representatives of a foreign country—*any* foreign country—trying to interfere in what I regarded as our domestic political process and the setting of our foreign policy . . . I felt he'd [Begin] broken his word and I was angry about it." Ronald Reagan, *An American Life* (New York: Simon & Schuster, 1990), 412, 414–16.

73. The English text of Resolution 242 is reprinted in *The Arab-Israeli Conflict: Readings and Documents*, ed. John Norton Moore (Princeton: Princeton University Press, 1977), 1083–84. Also see David Pollock, *The Politics of Pressure: American Arms and Israeli Policy Since the Six Day War* (Westport, CT: Greenwood Press, 1982), 74.

74. Despite the growing level of U.S. aid after 1968, U.S.-Israeli relations were frequently strained by disputes over the level of U.S. military support and Israeli reluctance to accept any of the peace proposals offered by the various mediators. U.S. efforts to force Israeli concessions by restricting arms generally failed, however, and concessions were won only through pledges of additional support. See William B. Quandt, *Decade of Decisions: American Policy Toward the Arab-Israeli Conflict, 1967–1976* (Berkeley: University of California Press, 1977), 97–98, 100–102; Pollock, *Politics of Pressure*, 74–77; Brecher, *Decisions in Israel's Foreign Policy*, 487–88, 493–96; and Spiegel, *Other Arab-Israeli Conflict*, 190–91.

75. Quoted in Brecher, *Decisions in Israel's Foreign Policy*, 493.

76. These amounts are in constant 2005 dollars. USAID, "Greenbook."

77. Shlaim, *Iron Wall*, 603–605.

78. Dennis Ross, *The Missing Peace: The Inside Story of the Fight for Middle East Peace* (New York: Farrar, Straus and Giroux, 2004), 478.

79. Ben-Zvi continues: "Strategic ties between Washington and Jerusalem continued to develop during 1996–1999 . . . These included the prepositioning in Israel of weapons and ammunition during wartime, and the development of anti-missile systems including the Arrow, Nautilus and the Boost Phase Intercept. The two countries met regularly in such panels as the Joint Political Military Planning Group, the Joint Security Assistance Planning Group and the Joint Economic Development Group . . . Indeed, the joint American-Israeli committee for strategic planning . . . convened as scheduled on February 21, 1999, despite Israel's decision to suspend the redeployment stipulated in the Wye accords." "The United States and Israel: The Netanyahu Era," *Strategic Assessment* (Jaffee Center for Strategic Studies, Tel Aviv University) 2, no. 2 (October 1999).

80. On the fate of Ford's reassessment, see Quandt, *Decade of Decisions*, 267–71; Edward Tivnan, *The Lobby: Jewish Political Power and American Foreign Policy* (New York: Simon & Schuster, 1987), 89; Charles McC. Mathias Jr., "Ethnic Groups and Foreign Policy," *Foreign Affairs* 59, no. 5 (Summer 1981): 992–93; and Spiegel, *Other Arab-Israeli Conflict*, 296.

81. Carter later recalled, "I think Begin deliberately sabotaged the whole thing with the damn settlements. He knows he lied. He hadn't left Camp David twelve hours before he was under tremendous [domestic] pressure . . . There was never any equivocation when we left Camp David about the fact that there would be no settlements during the interim period, during which we would be negotiating the final peace agreement. That was absolutely and totally understood." Quoted in Kenneth W. Stein, *Heroic Diplomacy: Sadat, Kissinger, Carter, Begin, and the Quest for Arab-Israeli Peace* (New York: Routledge, 1999), 256.

82. Clinton's outburst is quoted in Hussein Agha and Robert Malley, "Camp David: The Tragedy of Errors," *New York Review of Books*, August 9, 2001, 60.

83. William B. Quandt, *Camp David: Peacemaking and Politics* (Washington, DC: Brookings Institution Press, 1986), 103–104.

84. Sharp, "U.S. Foreign Aid," 4.

85. Itamar Rabinovich, *The War for Lebanon, 1970–1985*, rev. ed. (Ithaca: Cornell University Press, 1985), 138–43.

86. William B. Quandt, *Peace Process: American Diplomacy and the Arab-Israeli Conflict Since 1967*, 3rd ed. (Washington, DC: Brookings Institution Press, 2004), 307–10; and Glenn Frankel, *Beyond the Promised Land: Jews and Arabs on the Hard Road to a New Israel* (New York: Simon & Schuster, 1994), 301–304.

87. The population growth rates for Israel proper in 1991, 1993, and 1994 were 4.9 percent, 2.5 percent, and 2.7 percent, respectively. "Sources of Population Growth: Total Israeli Population and Settler Population, 1991–2003," Foundation for Middle East Peace, Washington, DC, www.fmep.org/settlement_info/stats_data/settler_population_growth/sources_population_growth_1991_2003.html.

88. The Soviet Union/Russia used its veto 119 times between 1946 and 1985, but only four times since then. The United States did not issue its first veto until 1970 but had used it 82 times as of March 2007. "Changing Patterns in the Use of the Veto in the Security Council," Global Policy Forum, www.globalpolicy.org/security/data/vetotab.htm.

89. This position became known as the "Negroponte Doctrine." See Michael J. Jordan, "Symbolic Fight for Israel at U.N.," *Christian Science Monitor*, December 8, 2003.

90. The United States voted in favor of Security Council resolutions condemning Israel's bloody assault on Qibya in 1953 and its attack on Iraq's Osirak reactor in 1981. It also voted in favor of Resolutions 672 and 681 in 1990, which criticized Israel's deportation of Palestinians from the Occupied Territories. The United States abstained on Resolution 573 in 1985, which condemned Israel's bombing of the PLO headquarters in Tunis, and voted in favor of Resolution 1073 in 1996, which expressed concern over Israel's construction of a tunnel in the vicinity of the al-Aqsa Mosque in Jerusalem.

91. UN voting records obtained from http://unbisnet.un.org:8080. For a list of General Assembly resolutions concerning Israel, along with partial voting records, see www.jewishvirtuallibrary.org/jsource/UN/gatoc.html.

92. Marc Perelman, "International Agency Eyes Israeli Nukes," *Forward*, September 5, 2003.

93. Michael B. Oren offers an extensively researched but decidedly pro-Israel account of the war in *Six Days of War: June 1967 and the Making of the Modern Middle East* (New York: Oxford University Press, 2002); a convincing corrective is Roland Popp, "Stumbling Decidedly into the Six Day War," *Middle East Journal* 60, no. 2 (Spring 2006). For a recent and more balanced treatment by another Israeli historian, see Tom Segev, *1967: Israel, the War, and the Year That Transformed the Middle East*, trans. Jessica Cohen (New York: Metropolitan Books, 2007).

94. Wheeler is quoted in Spiegel, *Other Arab-Israeli Conflict*, 141; Johnson's remark to Eban is from Popp, "Stumbling Decidedly into the Six Day War," 304. Popp also notes that "almost no one inside the U.S. administration was in any doubt that the Israeli warnings [of an impending Arab attack] were without foundation" (302), and William Quandt reports that the CIA and Pentagon told Israeli Foreign Minister Abba Eban they "were convinced that Israel would easily win if hostilities were to begin, no matter who struck first." *Decade of Decisions*, 50.

95. The Israeli government sent telegrams to Foreign Minister Eban and Ambassador Avraham Harman in Washington on May 25, claiming an Arab attack was imminent and asking them to seek an immediate American commitment to treat an attack on Israel as akin to an attack on the United States. But as Tom Segev points out, "The Israeli intelligence assessment of the same evening was fairly different from what had been wired to Washington . . . [Prime Minister] Eshkol was obviously trying to mislead Eban, and through him President Johnson, in order to ensure U.S. support. On a copy of the telegram to Harman, Eshkol added in his own handwriting: 'All to create an alibi.'" *1967*, 256–57.

96. Meeting with Eban on the evening of May 26, Johnson gave him an aide-mémoire that ended, "I must emphasize the necessity for Israel not to make itself responsible for the initiation of hostilities. Israel will not be alone unless it decides to do it alone. We cannot imagine Israel will make this decision." Quoted in Brecher, *Decisions in Israel's Foreign Policy*, 393. Johnson repeated a similar warning in a letter to Eshkol on May 28.

97. In the words of William Quandt, Johnson "had no reason to be surprised when he was awakened on the morning of June 5 with the news that war had begun. After all, he had taken steps to assure the Israelis that the 'red light' of May 26 had turned yellow . . . The 'yellow light' hinted at in his letter to [Israeli Prime Minister Levi] Eshkol on June 3, and reiterated in remarks from [Abe] Fortas and [Arthur] Goldberg, meant 'be careful,' and 'don't count on the United States if you get into trouble.' But, as for most motorists, the yellow light was tantamount to a green one." Quandt also notes that "Johnson had not quite given the Israelis a green light, but he had removed a veto on their actions." *Peace Process*, 38, 41–42; and Cheryl Rubenberg, *Israel and the American National Interest: A Critical Examination* (Urbana: University of Illinois Press, 1986), 120.

98. In a review of Oren's *Six Days of War*, Quandt notes that "Johnson [told] the Israelis not to act alone, and for a while he really seemed to mean it. By the end of May, he had apparently changed his mind. The Israelis were quick to sense the change, and it mattered to them as they decided on war. But we still do not know why Johnson initially was so hesitant, then why he took a tough line with Israel, or why he subsequently changed his mind." "Book Review: *Six Days of War*," *Journal of Cold War Studies* 6, no. 4 (Summer 2004): 147. On the other pressures exerted on Johnson, including the letter-writing campaign, see Segev, *1967*, 253–54, 264–65, 304.

99. Quandt, *Peace Process*, 43–44.

100. On June 8, 1967, while the Six-Day War was under way, Israeli aircraft and torpedo boats attacked the U.S. Navy intelligence ship USS *Liberty*, which was in international waters off the Sinai Peninsula. The attack killed thirty-four U.S. sailors and caused extensive damage to the ship. Israel has long claimed that the attack was an accident based on mistaken identification, and it apologized to the United States and paid some $13 million in compensation. Survivors of the attack, other U.S. naval officers, and a number of U.S. officials (including CIA Director Richard Helms and Secretary of State Dean Rusk) believed the at-

tack was deliberate, and proponents of this view also claim that the subsequent investigations were cursory and incomplete. Other commentators defend Israel's version of the incident and regard it as a regrettable mishap. For different accounts, see James Bamford, *Body of Secrets: Anatomy of the Ultra Secret National Security Agency* (New York: Random House, 2002); A. Jay Cristol, *The Liberty Incident: The 1967 Attack on the U.S. Navy Spy Ship* (Washington, DC: Potomac Books, 2002); James M. Ennes Jr., *Assault on the Liberty: The True Story of an Israeli Attack on an American Intelligence Ship* (Gaithersburg, MD: Reintree Press, 2003); Oren, *Six Days of War*, 263–71; and Segev, *1967*, 386.

101. The diplomacy of the War of Attrition is summarized in Lawrence Whetten, *The Canal War: Four-Power Conflict in the Middle East* (Cambridge, MA: MIT Press, 1974). Useful Israeli perspectives include Ya'acov Bar-Siman-Tov, *The Israeli-Egyptian War of Attrition, 1969–1970* (New York: Columbia University Press, 1980); and Jonathan Shimshoni, *Israel and Conventional Deterrence: Border Warfare from 1953 to 1970* (Ithaca: Cornell University Press, 1988), chap. 4.

102. Quandt, *Decade of Decisions*, 147. Also see Pollock, *Politics of Pressure*, 112–14, 124, 126–27; and Brecher, *Decisions in Israel's Foreign Policy*, 510.

103. Henry Kissinger, *Years of Upheaval* (Boston: Little, Brown, 1982), 468.

104. By helping Israel gain the upper hand on the battlefield, Nixon and Kissinger sought to convince Egypt and Syria to accept a cease-fire and to recognize the limits of Soviet support. See Quandt, *Peace Process*, 113–15, 118.

105. Stein, *Heroic Diplomacy*, 78–79.

106. Ibid., 86, 90; William Burr, ed., *The October War and U.S. Policy* (Washington, DC: National Security Archive, October 7, 2003); and Quandt, *Peace Process*, 118.

107. "Kissinger Gave Green Light for Israeli Offensive Violating 1973 Cease-Fire," National Security Archive press release, October 7, 2003; and Quandt, *Peace Process*, 120, 461nn62, 63. Kenneth Stein reports that "Kissinger told Israeli leaders that if it was their intention to starve out the Egyptian Third Army, the United States would 'disassociate itself from it.' But Kissinger did not tell the Israelis not to better their military field advantage. Dayan wanted another seventy-two hours, and Kissinger acquiesced." Stein also notes, "With impunity and Kissinger's sanction, of which Sadat was not aware, Israel violated the cease-fire resolution." *Heroic Diplomacy*, 92.

108. "U.S.-Israel Memorandum of Understanding, September 1, 1975." The congressional legislation (Section 535, P.L. 98-473, October 12, 1984) added the stipulation that the PLO "renounce terrorism." See Clyde Mark, "Palestinians and Middle East Peace: Issues for the United States," *Issue Brief for Congress*, Congressional Research Service, October 24, 2002, 2.

109. Shlaim, *Iron Wall*, 337–40. As Steven Spiegel notes, "Here too the United States promised a unified strategy with Israel, thereby restricting America's ability to speak independently with the PLO." *Other Arab-Israeli Conflict*, 302. On the congressional action in 1984, see Clyde Mark, "Israeli–United States Relations," *Issue Brief for Congress*, Congressional Research Service, April 28, 2005, 9.

110. The pretext for war was the attempted assassination of the Israeli ambassador in London. This act fell well short of Haig's criterion, insofar as it had nothing to do with the situation along the Israeli-Lebanese border and was not ordered by Yasser Arafat or Fatah but by a dissident Palestinian group led by Abu Nidal. As Shlomo Ben-Ami observes, Haig "should have known that Israeli politicians are not especially sensitive to nuances and understatements when he used unnecessarily ambiguous language in his conversation with Sharon." See Ben-Ami, *Scars of War*, 179; Quandt, *Peace Process*, 250–51; Ze'ev Schiff, "The Green Light," *Foreign Policy* 50 (Spring 1983); Ze'ev Schiff and Ehud Ya'ari, *Israel's Lebanon War*, trans. Ina Friedman (New York: Simon & Schuster, 1984), 71–73; Avner Yaniv, *Dilemmas of Security: Politics, Strategy, and the Israeli Experience in Lebanon* (New York: Oxford University Press, 1987), 102–103, 105; and James McCartney, "Officials Say Haig Let Israel Think U.S. Condoned Invasion of Lebanon," *Philadelphia Inquirer* (online), January 23, 1983.

111. Shlaim, *The Iron Wall*, 416.

112. By the time the cease-fire went into effect, notes the Israeli historian Itamar Rabinovich, "The IDF had succeeded both in defeating the Syrian army in Lebanon and limiting the scope of the encounter . . . Equally significant, Syria by seeking an early ceasefire left Israel free to focus on Beirut. In the days following the ceasefire, Israeli forces continued their advance toward southern and eastern Beirut and established a territorial link with the forces of the Lebanese Front." *War for Lebanon*, 138.

113. Rabinovich continues: "Yet it became increasingly difficult to maintain that policy against accumulating criticism, particularly in the murky situation in Beirut in the latter part of June. These difficulties . . . induced the administration to distance itself demonstrably from Israel, but did not change the essence of its policy." Ibid., 146.

114. George P. Shultz, *Turmoil and Triumph: My Years as Secretary of State* (New York: Scribner, 1993), 112.

115. Quandt, *Peace Process*, 258–59.

116. Quoted in Edward R. F. Sheehan, *The Arabs, Israelis and Kissinger: A Secret History of American Diplomacy in the Middle East* (Pleasantville, NY: Reader's Digest Press, 1976), 199.

117. In his account of the peace process, the U.S. negotiator Dennis Ross offers numerous examples of the Clinton administration accommodating Prime Minister Ehud Barak's preferred negotiating tactics, particularly regarding the unsuccessful effort to reach a peace treaty with Syria. See Ross, *Missing Peace*, 530–32, 539, 550–51, 578–80. And as Agha and Malley note in their discussion of Camp David, "In the end, though, and on almost all these questionable tactical judgments, the US either gave up or gave in, reluctantly acquiescing in the way Barak did things out of respect for the things he was trying to do." "Camp David: The Tragedy of Errors," 60.

118. Ron Pundak, "From Oslo to Taba: What Went Wrong?" *Survival* 43, no. 3 (Autumn 2001): 40–41.

119. Agha and Malley, "Camp David: The Tragedy of Errors," 62–63.

120. "Lessons of Arab-Israeli Negotiating: Four Negotiators Look Back and Ahead," transcript of panel discussion, Middle East Institute, April 25, 2005; Nathan Guttman, "U.S. Accused of Pro-Israel Bias at 2000 Camp David," *Ha'aretz*, April 29, 2005; and Aaron D. Miller, "Israel's Lawyer," *Washington Post*, May 23, 2005.

121. "A History of Foreign Leaders and Dignitaries Who Have Addressed the U.S. Congress," http://clerk.house.gov/art_history/art_artifacts/foreignleaders.html. The first Israeli leader to address a joint session of Congress was Yitzhak Rabin in 1976; other states whose leaders have addressed multiple sessions of Congress in the same period include India (four), Ireland (three), Italy (three), and South Korea (three). If one begins counting in 1948 (the year Israel was founded), Israel is tied at six with France and Italy.

122. Bard and Pipes, "How Special Is the U.S.-Israel Relationship?" 41.

123. The question asked, "What's your opinion of U.S. policies in the Middle East—would you say they are fair, or do they favor Israel too much, or do they favor the Palestinians too much?" See Pew Global Attitudes Project, *Views of a Changing World 2003* (Washington, DC: Pew Research Center for the People and the Press, 2003), 5; and Pew Global Attitudes Project, "Wave 2 Update Survey; 21 Publics Surveyed, Final Topline (2003)," T-151, http://pewglobal.org/reports/pdf/185topline.pdf.

2: ISRAEL: STRATEGIC ASSET OR LIABILITY?

1. A.F.K. Organski, *The $36 Billion Bargain: Strategy and Politics in U.S. Assistance to Israel* (New York: Columbia University Press, 1990); Steven L. Spiegel, "Israel as a Strategic Asset," *Commentary*, June 1983; Steven L. Spiegel, *The Other Arab-Israeli Conflict: Making America's Middle East Policy from Truman to Reagan* (Chicago: University of Chicago Press, 1985); and Steven L. Spiegel, "U.S.-Israel Relations after the Gulf War," *Jerusalem Letter/ Viewpoints 117*, Jerusalem Center for Public Affairs, July 15, 1991. Also see Steven Rosen,

"The Strategic Value of Israel," *AIPAC Papers on U.S.-Israel Relations* (Washington, DC: American Israel Public Affairs Committee, 1982).

2. Quoted in Ben Bradlee Jr., "Israel's Lobby," *Boston Globe*, April 29, 1984.

3. See http://aipac.org/Publications/AIPACAnalysesIssueBriefs/The_U.S.-Israel_Strategic_Part nership.pdf; and http://aipac.org/Publications/AIPACAnalysesIssueBriefs/The_U.S.Israel_ Relationship.pdf.

4. Project for the New American Century, "Letter to President Bush on the War on Terrorism," September 20, 2001, www.newamericancentury.org/Bushletter.htm; and "Mission State-ment," Jewish Institute for National Secuity Affairs, www.jinsa.org/about/agenda/agenda.html.

5. Martin Kramer, "The American Interest," *Azure* 5767, no. 26 (Fall 2006): 24–25.

6. Efraim Inbar, "Still a Strategic Asset for the US," *Jerusalem Post*, October 8, 2006.

7. Not surprisingly, scholars like Spiegel, Organski, and Kramer downplay or dismiss the im-pact of domestic politics or lobbying groups on U.S. support for Israel. Organski claims that "U.S. policy decisions with respect to Israel have, in the main, been made by presidents and foreign policy elites both by themselves and for reasons entirely their own." Kramer suggests that "if the institutions of the [Israel] lobby were to disappear tomorrow, it is quite likely that American and other Western support would continue unabated." Spiegel describes the be-lief that the pro-Israel lobby has "great leverage" as a "myth." Despite these assertions, Spiegel's study contains numerous examples of the lobby shaping the perceptions and be-havior of key decision makers. Kramer's own career suggests that he does not believe his own argument, as he has devoted considerable time and effort to defending U.S. support for Israel and attacking those who question it. See Organski, *$36 Billion Bargain*, 27; Spiegel, *Other Arab-Israeli Conflict*, 386, 388; and Kramer, "American Interest," 31.

8. Scholars have analyzed Truman's decisions extensively, reaching varied conclusions about the importance of domestic politics and his sensitivities to Jewish opinion. It was clearly not the only factor that influenced his conduct as he sought to navigate the complex situation in Palestine, but virtually all accounts agree that the political preferences of American Jewry (magnified by the upcoming 1948 election) played a nontrivial role in his calculations. See Spiegel, *Other Arab-Israeli Conflict*, 47–48; Kenneth Ray Bain, *The March to Zion: United States Policy and the Founding of Israel* (College Station: Texas A & M Press, 1979), 195–97, 202; Zvi Ganin, *Truman, American Jewry, and Israel, 1945–1948* (New York: Holmes & Meier, 1979); and Michael B. Oren, *Power, Faith and Fantasy: America in the Middle East 1776 to the Present* (New York: Norton, 2007), 484, 488–89, 499.

9. Quoted in Jerome Slater, "Ideology vs. the National Interest: Bush, Sharon, and U.S. Policy in the Israeli-Palestinian Conflict," *Security Studies* 12, no. 1 (Autumn 2002): 167.

10. Warren Bass, *Support Any Friend: Kennedy's Middle East and the Making of the U.S.-Israel Alliance* (New York: Oxford University Press, 2003), 148–49; and David Schoenbaum, *The United States and the State of Israel* (New York: Oxford University Press, 1993), 136–37.

11. The Nixon/Kissinger strategy is summarized in William B. Quandt, *Peace Process: American Diplomacy and the Arab-Israeli Conflict in 1967*, 3rd ed. (Washington, DC: Brookings Insti-tution Press, 2005), 69–70, 92–94; Henry Kissinger, *White House Years* (Boston: Little, Brown, 1979), 1279, 1289–91, chap. 10; and Henry Kissinger, *Years of Upheaval* (Boston: Little, Brown, 1982), 195–205.

12. Israel allowed Western aircraft to overfly Israeli territory during the 1958 Jordan crisis, and agreed to a U.S. request to intervene in support of King Hussein following Syrian interven-tion in the 1970 clash between Hussein and the PLO. In the end, Jordanian air units at-tacked the Syrians on their own and the Syrians withdrew without Israel having to respond. U.S. officials were grateful for Israeli support in both cases, but as Alan Dowty notes, Israel's contribution to resolving the 1970 crisis was "secondary at best." Nigel Ashton also suggests that Hussein regarded Israel as a potential threat during the crisis and that U.S. officials mistakenly "credited Israel with helping the United States to win a cold war victory in what was, in reality, an inter-Arab struggle." Alan Dowty, *Middle East Crisis: Decisionmaking in 1958, 1970, and 1973* (Berkeley: University of California Press, 1984), 177; Nigel J. Ash-

ton, "Pulling the Strings: King Hussein's Role During the Crisis of 1970 in Jordan," *International History Review* 28, no. 1 (March 2006): 109; and Quandt, *Peace Process*, 79–83.

13. Dan Raviv and Yossi Melman, *Friends in Deed: Inside the U.S.-Israel Alliance* (New York: Hyperion, 1994), 66–68, 114–15.

14. For a sympathetic but skeptical analysis of the "strategic asset" argument by the longtime head of the Military Assistance Branch of the Office of Management and Budget, see Harry Shaw, "Strategic Dissensus," *Foreign Policy* 61 (Winter 1985–86).

15. Reportedly a response to the killing of an Israel bicyclist by infiltrators from Egypt, the Gaza raid has also been interpreted as Ben-Gurion's way of boosting Israeli morale, dramatizing his return to power, and reducing Nasser's growing prestige. But as Shlomo Ben-Ami observes, "Rather than cutting short Egypt's commitment to a war strategy, [the Gaza operation] enhanced it." *Scars of War, Wounds of Peace: The Israeli-Arab Tragedy* (New York: Oxford University Press, 2006), 77; Avi Shlaim, *The Iron Wall: Israel and the Arab World* (New York: Norton, 2001), 123–29; Michael Brecher, *Decisions in Israel's Foreign Policy* (New Haven: Yale University Press, 1975), 254–55, esp. note 1; and E.L.M. Burns, *Between Arab and Israeli* (New York: Ivan Obolensky, 1963), 20. Syria had similar motives for seeking Soviet arms during this period, and its desire for aid was intensified by an especially strong Israeli raid in December 1955. Stephen M. Walt, *The Origins of Alliances* (Ithaca: Cornell University Press, 1987), 62, esp. note 36.

16. On the Soviet Union's turbulent relationship with its Arab allies, see Mohamed Heikal, *The Sphinx and the Commissar: The Rise and Fall of Soviet Influence in the Middle East* (New York: Harper, 1976); Alvin Z. Rubinstein, *Red Star on the Nile: The Soviet-Egyptian Influence Relationship Since the June War* (Princeton: Princeton University Press, 1977); and Ya'acov Roi, ed., *From Encroachment to Involvement: A Documentary Study of Soviet Foreign Policy in the Middle East, 1945–1973* (New Brunswick, NJ: Transaction Books, 1974).

17. For a persuasive argument to this effect, see Jerome Slater, "The Superpowers and an Arab-Israeli Political Settlement: The Cold War Years," *Political Science Quarterly* 105, no. 4 (Winter 1990–91).

18. "Kissinger Memorandum: 'To Isolate the Palestinians,'" MERIP Reports no. 96 (May 1981): 24. This article is a memorandum of a June 1975 conversation between Kissinger and the so-called Klutznick Group, a gathering of Jewish-American leaders organized by Philip Klutznick, a former president of B'nai B'rith International and former U.S. secretary of commerce. Also see Quandt, *Peace Process*, 103–104.

19. Ussama Makdisi, "'Anti-Americanism' in the Arab World: An Interpretation of a Brief History," *Journal of American History* 89, no. 2 (September 2002): 538–39. Alfred Prados of the Congressional Research Service agrees, noting, "The United States, a latecomer to the Middle East, enjoyed a more favorable image in the region than did its European counterparts in the 19th and early 20th centuries." "Middle East: Attitudes Toward the United States," *Report for Congress*, Congressional Research Service, December 31, 2001, 2.

20. Shibley Telhami, *The Stakes: America and the Middle East* (Boulder, CO: Westview, 2002), 50–59; and Makdisi, "'Anti-Americanism' in the Arab World," 548–50.

21. Shaw, "Strategic Dissensus," 137.

22. *Moshe Dayan: Story of My Life* (New York: William Morrow, 1976), 512–13.

23. The total cost inflicted by the "oil weapon" was almost certainly larger, as it had long-term effects on inflation, real income, and productivity growth, as well as indirect effects on investment, currency price volatility, and other factors, but there is considerable disagreement among economists regarding the magnitude of these effects. On petroleum imports, see Dominick Salvatore, "Petroleum Prices and Economic Performance in the G-7 Countries," in Siamack Shojai and Bernard S. Katz, eds., *The Oil Market in the 1980s: A Decade of Decline* (New York: Praeger, 1992), 94; and Mancur Olson, "The Productivity Slowdown, the Oil Shocks and the Real Cycle," *Journal of Economic Perspectives* 2, no. 4 (Fall 1988): 43–69. The cost to OECD countries was to push their net oil import bill from $35 billion in 1973 to more than $100 billion in 1974. See Robert J. Lieber, *The Oil Decade: Conflict and Co-*

operation in the West (New York: Praeger, 1983), 21. The GDP estimate is that of the Federal Energy Administration and of many economists. See Edward N. Krapels, *Oil Crisis Management: Strategic Stockpiling for International Security* (Baltimore: Johns Hopkins University Press, 1980), 34; and Fiona Venn, *The Oil Crisis* (London: Longman, 2002), 154–55. The calculation for 2000 dollars uses data from Louis D. Johnston and Samuel H. Williamson, "The Annual Real and Nominal GDP for the United States, 1790–Present," Economic History Services, October 2005.

24. Quoted in Jeffrey Richelson, *The U.S. Intelligence Community*, 2nd ed. (Cambridge, MA: Ballinger, 1989), 277.

25. Quoted in Roland Popp, "Stumbling Decidedly into the Six Day War," *Middle East Journal* 60, no. 2 (Spring 2006): 300. Tom Segev has confirmed that Rostow's appraisal was essentially correct. See his *1967: Israel, the War and the Year That Transformed the Middle East*, trans. Jessica Cohen (New York: Metropolitan Books, 2007), 256–58.

26. Shlomo Brom, "The War in Iraq: An Intelligence Failure," *Strategic Assessment* (Jaffee Center for Strategic Studies, Tel Aviv University) 6, no. 3 (November 2003); "Selections from the Media, 1998–2003," ibid., 17–19; Gideon Alon, "Report Slams Assessment of Dangers Posed by Libya, Iraq," *Ha'aretz*, March 28, 2004; Dan Baron, "Israeli Report Blasts Intelligence for Exaggerating the Iraqi Threat," *JTA.org*, March 28, 2004; Greg Myre, "Lawmakers Rebuke Israeli Intelligence Services over Iraq," *New York Times*, March 29, 2004; and James Risen, *State of War: The Secret History of the CIA and the Bush Administration* (New York: Simon & Schuster, 2006), 72–73.

27. Kramer, "American Interest," 24–25.

28. Shaw also notes that "all Israelis are acutely aware of the burden for a country of only 4 million people of lives lost in even short, successful wars. Israel simply lacks the personnel to sacrifice on costly military adventures beyond its immediate neighborhood." "Strategic Dissensus," 130.

29. Quoted in Duncan L. Clarke, Daniel B. O'Connor, and Jason D. Ellis, *Send Guns and Money: Security Assistance and U.S. Foreign Policy* (Westport, CT: Praeger, 1997), 173. Another DOD official noted that Israel's "proximity to the Gulf is not enough to be of real use as a base for fighting there, except on paper. We need to get much closer in the event of any actual military contingency, and that's why we're going for forward basing in Oman." Israel's contribution would be limited to maintenance and possibly hospital facilities. See Joe Stork, "Israel as a Strategic Asset," in MERIP Reports no. 105, *Reagan Targets the Middle East* (May 1982), 12.

30. Shaw, "Strategic Dissensus," 133.

31. See the discussion of Operation Earnest Will at www.globalsecurity.org/military/ops/earnest_will.htm; and Dilip Hiro, *The Longest War: The Iran-Iraq Military Conflict* (New York: Routledge, 1991), 129–32, 166, 186–91, 202–204.

32. "Kissinger Memorandum," 25.

33. During the 1980 campaign, Reagan told the American Jewish Press Association that "Israel is a strategic asset for the U.S., [and] I believe we must have policies which give concrete expression to that position." See Stork, "Israel as a Strategic Asset," 3; and Ronald Reagan, *An American Life* (New York: Simon & Schuster, 1990), 410.

34. With respect to the latter element, Feldman says "the clearest manifestation of this phenomenon is the unique role of the influential American Israel Public Affairs Committee (AIPAC)." See his *The Future of U.S.-Israel Strategic Cooperation* (Washington, DC: Washington Institute for Near East Policy, 1996), 5–6.

35. Bernard Lewis, "Rethinking the Middle East," *Foreign Affairs* 71, no. 4 (Fall 1992): 110–11; Bernard Reich, *Securing the Covenant: United States–Israeli Relations After the Cold War* (Westport, CT: Praeger, 1995), 123; and Robert J. Art, *A Grand Strategy for America* (Ithaca: Cornell University Press, 2003), 137.

36. Waldegrave is quoted in David Kimche, *The Last Option: After Nasser, Arafat, and Saddam Hussein, the Quest for Peace in the Middle East* (New York: Scribner, 1991), 236; Lewis, "Re-

thinking the Middle East," 110–11. History repeated itself during the second Gulf War in 2003. The United States needed to assemble a large coalition in order to make its preventive war look legitimate, and it therefore worked overtime to persuade an array of countries to contribute troops to the "coalition of the willing." But Israel was absent from this list, even though its leaders and people strongly supported the war. We address this issue at greater length in Chapter 8.

37. Based on data from the Memorial Institute for the Prevention of Terrorism database, www.tkb.org.

38. Daniel Benjamin and Steven Simon have shown that some members of the Clinton administration placed a high priority on counterterrorism, but they also document how difficult it was to implement that priority during the 1990s. In their words, "The work was difficult because a government that had never viewed terrorism as a first-tier threat had neither the organization nor the laws to deal with it that way. In many agencies offices handling counterterrorism issues were bureaucratic backwaters, their managers carrying none of the heft of colleagues who deal with geographic regions or high-profile issues such as arms control." It is also instructive that the Bush administration did not place a high priority on terrorism upon taking office. See Daniel Benjamin and Steven Simon, *The Age of Sacred Terror* (New York: Random House, 2002), 221, 327–29; and Richard A. Clarke, *Against All Enemies: Inside America's War on Terror* (New York: Free Press, 2004), 227–36.

39. Put differently, the U.S. defense budget was over half the size of the entire combined economies of these four states (measured on a purchasing parity basis). Figures from *The Military Balance 2000–2001* (London: International Institute for Strategic Studies, 2001); and Central Intelligence Agency, *World Factbook 2000* (online).

40. For an excellent analysis of U.S. policy toward Iraq and Iran, and toward rogue states more generally, see Robert Litwak, *Rogue States and U.S. Foreign Policy: Containment after the Cold War* (Washington, DC: Woodrow Wilson Center Press, 2000). Although the Republican-controlled Congress generally favored more aggressive policies toward Iran and Iraq and occasionally voted to support stiffer sanctions and various antiregime exiles, the Clinton administration never undertook a serious effort at regime change.

41. Bruce W. Jentleson and Christopher A. Whytock, "Who 'Won' Libya? The Force-Diplomacy Debate and Its Implications for Theory and Policy," *International Security* 30, no. 3 (Winter 2005–2006); Ronald Bruce St. John, "Libya Is Not Iraq: Preemptive Strikes, WMD, and Diplomacy," *Middle East Journal* 58, no. 3 (Summer 2004); and Flynt Leverett, "Why Libya Gave Up on the Bomb," *New York Times*, January 23, 2004.

42. Litwak, *Rogue States and U.S. Foreign Policy*, 168–69.

43. Sharon is quoted in William Safire, "Israel or Arafat," *New York Times*, December 3, 2001; the unnamed official is quoted in Robert G. Kaiser, "Bush and Sharon Nearly Identical on Mideast Policy," *Washington Post*, February 9, 2003. Also see Nathan Guttman, "A Marriage Cemented by Terror," *Salon.com*, January 24, 2006.

44. "Netanyahu Speech Before the U.S. Senate," April 10, 2002, www.netanyahu.org/netspeacinse.html; and Benjamin Netanyahu, "Three Principles Key to Defeat of Terrorism," *Chicago Sun-Times*, January 7, 2002.

45. Ehud Barak, "Democratic Unity Is the Only Answer to Terrorism," *Times* (London), September 13, 2001.

46. "Entire Text of Olmert Speech to Congress," *Jerusalem Post*, May 24, 2006.

47. Robert Satloff, "Israel's Not the Issue, Pass It On," *Los Angeles Times*, October 10, 2001.

48. "Peace Can Only Come Once the US Gives Israel the Green Light to Eliminate Hamas and the Hezbollah," press release, Office of Charles Schumer, U.S. Senate, December 3, 2001, www.senate.gov/~schumer/1-Senator%20Schumer%20Website%20Files/pressroom/press_releases/PR00766.html.

49. HR Res. 392 (May 2, 2002); and S Res. 247 (April 22, 2002).

50. According to one account, "Even as speakers singled out [Yasser] Arafat as a problem requiring immediate action, they also portrayed him as but one partner in a much wider 'coalition

of forces' that included Iran, Iraq, and Syria . . . With regard to neutralizing these threats, regime change was the preferred option." See Dana Hearn, "AIPAC Policy Conference, 21–23 April 2002," *Journal of Palestine Studies* 31, no. 4 (Summer 2002): 67–68.

51. "Letter to President Bush on Israel, Arafat, and the War on Terrorism," Project for the New American Century, April 3, 2002, www.newamericancentury.org/Bushletter-040302.htm. The principal author of the open letter, William Kristol, offered the same view during Israel's 2006 war in Lebanon, writing that "while Syria and Iran are enemies of Israel, they are also enemies of the United States" and concluding, "This is our war, too." William Kristol, "It's Our War," *Weekly Standard*, July 24, 2006.

52. Maoz and Seale are quoted in Susan Taylor Martin, "Experts Disagree on Dangers of Syria," *St. Petersburg Times* (online), November 3, 2002. Also see Benjamin and Simon, *Age of Sacred Terror*, 194.

53. See, among many other studies, Tanya Reinhart, *Israel/Palestine: How to End the War of 1948*, expanded 2nd ed. (New York: Seven Stories Press, 2005); and Tanya Reinhart, *The Road Map to Nowhere: Israel/Palestine Since 2003* (London: Verso, 2006).

54. As Robert Pape has convincingly shown, suicide terrorism is a tactic that a diverse array of political movements have adopted, usually when they were weak and trying to defeat a democratic adversary engaged in what the terrorists regard as illegitimate occupation. See Robert A. Pape, *Dying to Win: The Strategic Logic of Suicide Terrorism* (New York: Random House, 2005).

55. Satloff, "Israel's Not the Issue"; Kramer, "American Interest," 29; Norman Podhoretz, "Israel Isn't the Issue," *Wall Street Journal*, September 20, 2001; Norman Podhoretz, "World War IV: How It Started, What It Means, and Why We Have to Win," *Commentary*, September 2004; Andrea Levin, "Don't Scapegoat Israel," *Boston Globe*, October 6, 2001; and Dennis Ross, "Bin Laden's Terrorism Isn't About the Palestinians," *New York Times*, October 12, 2001. Others making this point in response to our original article include Alan Dershowitz, "Debunking the Newest—and Oldest—Jewish Conspiracy: A Reply to the Mearsheimer-Walt 'Working Paper,'" John F. Kennedy School of Government Faculty Research Working Paper, Harvard University, April 2006, 29; Marc Landy, "Zealous Realism: Comments on Mearsheimer and Walt," *Forum* (Berkeley Electronic Press) 4, issue 1, article 6 (2006); and Steven Simon, "Here's Where 'The Israel Lobby' Is Wrong," *Daily Star*, May 4, 2006.

56. Abdel Mahdi Abdallah, "Causes of Anti-Americanism in the Arab World: A Socio-Political Perspective," *Middle East Review of International Affairs* 7, no. 4 (December 2003).

57. Qutb formed his impressions of America during a visit here in 1948 and was later executed by the Egyptian government in 1966. See Yvonne Y. Haddad, "Sayyid Qutb: Ideologue of Islamic Revival," in *Voices of Resurgent Islam*, ed. John Esposito (New York: Oxford University Press, 1983), 67–98.

58. Quoted in Makdisi, "'Anti-Americanism' in the Arab World," 555.

59. Steve Coll, *Ghost Wars: The Secret History of the CIA, Afghanistan, and Bin Laden, from the Soviet Invasion to September 10, 2001* (New York: Penguin Press, 2004), 250–51, 273; and "Transcript: The Yasin Interview," *60 Minutes*, June 2, 2002, www.cbsnews.com/stories/2002/06/02/60minutes/printable510847.shtml.

60. Anonymous [Michael Scheuer], *Through Our Enemies' Eyes: Osama bin Laden, Radical Islam, and the Future of America* (Washington, DC: Brassey's, 2002), 87.

61. Quoted in Lawrence Wright, *The Looming Tower: Al Qaeda and the Road to 9/11* (New York: Knopf, 2006), 75–76.

62. *Messages to the World: The Statements of Osama bin Laden*, ed. Bruce Lawrence (London: Verso, 2005), 4.

63. Benjamin and Simon, *Age of Sacred Terror*, 140–41.

64. Osama bin Laden, "From Somalia to Afghanistan" (March 1997), in Lawrence, *Messages to the World*, 46. For additional pre-9/11 condemnations of the United States for its support of Israel, and for accusations that the United States was colluding with Israel, see the following selections from the same volume: "Declaration of Jihad" (August 23, 1996), 30; "The

World Islamic Front" (February 23, 1998), 60–61; and "A Muslim Bomb" (December 1998), 66–70. Also see "Jihad against Jews and Crusaders" and "New Osama bin Laden Video Contains Anti-Israel and Anti-American Statements," on the Anti-Defamation League website, www.adl.org/terrorism_america/bin_l_print.asp.

65. Max Rodenbeck, "Their Master's Voice," *New York Review of Books*, March 9, 2006, 8. The books under review were Peter L. Bergen, *The Osama bin Laden I Know: An Oral History of al Qaeda's Leader* (New York: Free Press, 2006), and Lawrence, *Messages to the World*.

66. "Outline of the 9/11 Plot," Staff Statement no. 16, National Commission on Terrorist Attacks Upon the United States, June 16, 2004, 18. Also see Nathan Guttman, "Al-Qaida Planned Attacks during PM's Visit to White House," *Ha'aretz*, June 17, 2004; and Marc Perelman, "Bin Laden Aimed to Link Plot to Israel," *Forward*, June 25, 2004.

67. "Outline of the 9/11 Plot," 18.

68. Ibid., 4.

69. *The 9/11 Commission Report: Final Report of the National Commission on Terrorist Attacks Upon the United States* (New York: Norton, 2004), 145, 147.

70. On the First Intifada, see Joost R. Hiltermann, *Behind the Intifada: Labor and Women's Movements in the Occupied Territories* (Princeton: Princeton University Press, 1991); *Intifada: The Palestinian Uprising Against Israeli Occupation*, ed. Zachary Lockman and Joel Beinin (Boston: South End Press, 1989); Benny Morris, *Righteous Victims: A History of the Zionist-Arab Conflict, 1881–2001* (New York: Vintage, 2001), chap. 12; and Ze'ev Schiff and Ehud Ya'ari, *Intifada: The Palestinian Uprising, Israel's Third Front*, ed. and trans. Ina Friedmann (New York: Simon & Schuster, 1991).

71. Quoted in Michael Slackman, "As Crowds Demand Change, Lebanese Premier Is Puzzled," *New York Times*, December 11, 2006.

72. Pew Global Attitudes Project, *A Year After Iraq War: Mistrust of America in Europe Even Higher, Muslim Anger Persists* (Washington, DC: Pew Research Center for the People and the Press, March 16, 2004), 21.

73. Pew Global Attitudes Project, *What the World Thinks in 2002* (Washington, DC: Pew Research Center for the People and the Press, December 2002), 54.

74. Shibley Telhami, *The Stakes: America and the Middle East* (Boulder, CO: Westview Press, 2002), 96. Also see Ami Eden, "9/11 Commission Finds Anger at Israel Fueling Islamic Terrorism Wave," *Forward*, July 30, 2004.

75. Makdisi continues: "No account of anti-Americanism in the Arab world that does not squarely address the Arab understanding of Israel can even begin to convey the nature, the depth, and the sheer intensity of Arab anger at the United States." "'Anti-Americanism' in the Arab World," 552.

76. "Impressions of America 2004: How Arabs View America, How Arabs Learn About America" (Washington, DC: Zogby International, June 2004), 3–5; "Five Nation Survey of the Middle East" (Washington, DC: Arab-American Institute/ Zogby International, December 2006), 4; and Prados, "Middle East: Attitudes Toward the United States," 8.

77. Quoted in Peter Ford, "Why Do They Hate Us?" *Christian Science Monitor*, September 27, 2001.

78. *Report of the Defense Science Board Task Force on Strategic Communication* (Washington, DC: Office of the Undersecretary of Defense for Acquisition, Technology, and Logistics, September 2004), 40; and *9/11 Commission Report*, 376.

79. "Impressions of America 2004: A Six Nation Survey" (Washington, DC: Zogby International, 2004); Shibley Telhami, "Arab Public Opinion: A Survey in Six Countries," *San Jose Mercury* (online), March 16, 2003; John Zogby, *The Ten Nation Impressions of America Poll* (Utica, NY: Zogby International, April 11, 2002); and Shibley Telhami, "Arab Attitudes Towards Political and Social Issues, Foreign Policy, and the Media," a public opinion poll by the Anwar Sadat Chair of Peace and Development, University of Maryland, and Zogby International, October 2005, www.bsos.umd.edu/sadat/pub/survey-2005.htm.

80. *Changing Minds, Winning Peace: A New Strategic Direction for U.S. Public Diplomacy in the*

Arab and Muslim World, Report of the Advisory Group on Public Diplomacy for the Arab and Muslim World, submitted to the Committee on Appropriations, U.S. House of Representatives, October 1, 2003, 18. Also see Pew Global Attitudes Project, *Views of a Changing World 2003: War with Iraq Further Divides Global Publics* (Washington, DC: Pew Research Center for the People and the Press, June 3, 2003).

81. Warren Hoge, "U.N. Distances Itself from an Envoy's Rebuke of Israel and the U.S.," *New York Times*, April 24, 2004; "Brahimi's Israel Comments Draw Annan, Israeli Fire," *Ha'aretz*, April 23, 2004; and "Egyptian Prez: Arabs Hate US," www.cbsnews.com/stories/2004/04/20/world/printable612831.shtml.

82. David Shelby, "Jordan's King Abdullah Stresses Urgency of Mideast Peace Process," March 7, 2007, www.usinfo.state.gov.

83. "President Discusses War on Terror and Operation Iraqi Freedom," Cleveland, Ohio (White House, Office of the Press Secretary, March 20, 2006).

84. Charles Krauthammer, "The Tehran Calculus," *Washington Post*, September 15, 2006. Also see Bernard Lewis, "August 22," *Wall Street Journal*, August 8, 2006. For a similar statement by two Israeli scholars, see Yossi Klein Halevi and Michael B. Oren, "Contra Iran," *New Republic*, February 5, 2007. For the argument that Saddam Hussein was also irrational and undeterrable, see Kenneth M. Pollack, *The Threatening Storm: The Case for Invading Iraq* (New York: Random House, 2002).

85. Mao Zedong did make some blasé remarks about nuclear war before China got the bomb, but these statements were almost certainly intended to discourage other nuclear powers from trying to put pressure on Beijing. See Alice Langly Hsieh, *Communist China's Strategy in the Nuclear Era* (Englewood Cliffs, NJ: Prentice-Hall, 1962). Rusk's statement is found in *The China Reader*, Vol. 3: *Communist China*, ed. Franz Schurmann and Orville Schell (New York: Vintage, 1967), 508. On the Soviet Union, a classic statement is Richard Pipes, "Why the Soviet Union Thinks It Can Fight and Win a Nuclear War," *Commentary*, July 1977.

86. For the British diplomats' letter, see "Doomed to Failure in the Middle East," *Guardian*, April 27, 2004. Also see Nicholas Blanford, "US Moves Inflame Arab Moderates," *Christian Science Monitor*, April 26, 2004; Rupert Cornwell, "Allies Warn Bush That Stability in Iraq Demands Arab-Israeli Deal," *Independent*, June 10, 2004; Glenn Kessler and Robin Wright, "Arabs and Europeans Question 'Greater Middle East' Plan," *Washington Post*, February 22, 2004; and Robin Wright and Glenn Kessler, "U.S. Goals for Middle East Falter," *Washington Post*, April 21, 2004. The American letter can be found at www.wrmea.com/letter_to_bush.html.

87. Ze'ev Schiff, "Fitting into America's Strategy," *Ha'aretz*, August 1, 2003.

88. Jay Solomon, "Religious Divide: To Contain Iran, U.S. Seeks Help from Arab Allies," *Wall Street Journal*, November 24, 2006.

89. James A. Baker III and Lee H. Hamilton, co-chairs, *The Iraq Study Group Report* (Washington, DC: U.S. Institute of Peace, December 2006), 39.

90. On the "Lavon affair," see Schoenbaum, *The United States and the State of Israel*, 107–108. On Israel's various dealings with Iran, see "Israel-Iran Oil Deal Disclosed and Tied to Captives," *New York Times*, December 20, 1989; Youssef M. Ibrahim, "Oil Sale Disclosure Upsets Israeli-Iranian Contacts," *New York Times*, December 21, 1989; Bishara Bahbah, "Arms Sales: Israel's Link to the Khomeini Regime," *Washington Report on Middle East Affairs* (online), January 1987; and Benjamin Beit-Hallahmi, *The Israeli Connection: Who Israel Arms and Why* (New York: Pantheon Books, 1987), 3–22, 108–75. The Reagan administration did supply arms to Iran as part of the notorious Iran-contra arms scandal, but this covert operation was largely intended to secure the release of U.S. hostages in Lebanon and was widely seen as contrary to broader U.S. interests once it was exposed.

91. Quoted in Duncan L. Clarke, "Israel's Unauthorized Arms Transfers," *Foreign Policy* 99 (Summer 1995): 94.

92. Richard C. Stiener, "Foreign Military Aid to Israel: Diversion of U.S. Funds and Circumvention of U.S. Program Restrictions," testimony before the Subcommittee on Oversight and

Investigations, Committee on Energy and Commerce, House of Representatives (Washington, DC: U.S. General Accounting Office, October 1993), 22. Also see Edward T. Pound, "Israel Is Impeding U.S. Dotan Probe, Documents Show," *Wall Street Journal*, July 29, 1992; and Edward T. Pound, "U.S. Says Israel Withheld Help in Dotan Probe," *Wall Street Journal*, July 25, 1992.

93. On this protracted dispute, see Aluf Benn and Amnon Barzilai, "Pentagon Official Wants Yaron Fired," *Ha'aretz*, December 16, 2004; Caroline B. Glick and Arieh O'Sullivan, "Pentagon Denies It Wants Yaron Dismissed," *Jerusalem Post*, December 16, 2004; Nina Gilbert, "Yaron Won't Give Info on Arms Sales to China," *Jerusalem Post*, December 30, 2004; "Israeli, U.S. Talks on Weapons Deals with China End Without Result," *Ha'aretz*, June 29, 2005; Marc Perelman, "Spat Over Sales of Weapons Chilling Ties Between Jerusalem and Beijing," *Forward*, December 24, 2004; Marc Perelman, "China Crisis Straining U.S.-Israel Ties," *Forward*, August 5, 2005; Marc Perelman, "Israel Miffed over Lingering China Flap," *Forward*, October 7, 2005; Ze'ev Schiff, "U.S.-Israel Crisis Deepens over Defense Exports to China," *Ha'aretz*, July 27, 2005; and Janine Zacharia, "'Something Wrong' in US-Israeli Military Ties as Split Deepens on China," *Jerusalem Post*, December 26, 2004.

94. Quoted in Zacharia, "US-Israeli Military Ties."

95. Quoted in Duncan L. Clarke, "Israel's Economic Espionage in the United States," *Journal of Palestine Studies* 27, no. 4 (Summer 1998): 21. Also see Bob Drogin and Greg Miller, "Israel Has Long Spied on U.S. Say Officials," *Los Angeles Times*, September 3, 2004; "FBI Says Israel a Major Player in Industrial Espionage," *Jewish Bulletin* (online), January 16, 1998; Mark, "Israeli–United States Relations," November 9, 2004, 14–15; and Joshua Mitnick, "U.S. Accuses Officials of Spying," *Washington Times*, December 16, 2004.

96. The journalist Seymour Hersh claims that Israel passed some of the stolen intelligence to the Soviet Union in order to gain exit visas for Soviet Jews. Others have challenged this assertion, but Hersh stands by his story. Seymour M. Hersh, *The Samson Option: Israel's Nuclear Arsenal and American Foreign Policy* (New York: Random House, 1991), 285–305; and Seymour M. Hersh, "Why Pollard Should Never Be Released," *New Yorker*, January 18, 1999.

97. On these incidents, see Edward T. Pound and David Rogers, "Inquiring Eyes: An Israeli Contract with a U.S. Company Leads to Espionage," *Wall Street Journal*, January 17, 1992.

98. For an overview of the Franklin affair, see Jeffrey Goldberg, "Real Insiders: A Pro-Israel Lobby and an F.B.I. Sting," *New Yorker*, July 4, 2005. Rosen and Weissman have denied the charges and the case is still pending.

3: A DWINDLING MORAL CASE

1. "President Speaks to the American Israel Public Affairs Committee," Washington Convention Center, Washington, DC (White House, Office of the Press Secretary, May 18, 2004).

2. Quoted in Mark Chmiel, "Elie Wiesel and the Question of Palestine," *Tikkun.org*, November/December 2002.

3. Paul Breines, *Tough Jews: Political Fantasies and the Moral Dilemma of American Jewry* (New York: Basic Books, 1990), 54–59; Michelle Mart, *Eye on Israel: How America Came to View Israel as an Ally* (Albany: State University of New York Press, 2006), 169–74; Melani McAlister, *Epic Encounters: Culture, Media, and U.S. Interests in the Middle East, 1945–2000* (Berkeley: University of California Press, 2001), 159–65; Edward Tivnan, *The Lobby: Jewish Political Power and American Foreign Policy* (New York: Simon & Schuster, 1987), 50–51; and David Twersky, "Novelist Leon Uris Taught Jewish Readers to Stand Tall," *Forward*, June 27, 2003.

4. The principal myths are laid out and refuted in Simha Flapan, *The Birth of Israel: Myths and Realities* (New York: Pantheon Books, 1987).

5. For a brief but excellent summary of the "new history," see Avi Shlaim, "The New History of 1948 and the Palestinian Nakba," *Miftah.org*, March 18, 2004.

6. Meron Rappaport, "IDF Commander: We Fired More Than a Million Cluster Bombs in

Lebanon," *Ha'aretz*, September 12, 2006; and "Shooting Without a Target," *Ha'aretz* editorial, September 14, 2006.

7. Benny Morris, *1948 and After: Israel and the Palestinians* (New York: Oxford University Press, 2003), 13. Also see Flapan, *Birth of Israel*, 187–99.

8. Morris, *1948 and After*, 14. Morris sharply criticized our original article, "The Israel Lobby," in a lengthy essay ("And Now for Some Facts: The Ignorance at the Heart of an Innuendo," *New Republic*, May 8, 2006), alleging that we had made numerous historical errors. In particular, he challenged our interpretation of the military balance in the 1948 War of Independence, as well as our interpretation of several other key episodes of Zionist and Israeli history. Morris's critique required him to contradict his own very important early scholarship (and the work of other respected historians) that has done so much to illuminate Israel's founding and relationship with its Arab neighbors and the Palestinians. We believe this scholarship backs up our account of Israel's military superiority and territorial ambitions, as well as its policies on refugees. We have addressed Morris's charges in John J. Mearsheimer and Stephen M. Walt, "Setting the Record Straight: A Response to Critics of 'The Israel Lobby,'" December 12, 2006, 26–46, available at www.israellobbybook.com.

9. On the military balance in the 1948 war, see Trevor N. Dupuy, *Elusive Victory: The Arab-Israeli Wars, 1947–1974* (New York: Harper, 1978), 3–19, 121–25; Rashid Khalidi, "The Palestinians and 1948: The Underlying Causes of Failure," in *The War for Palestine: Rewriting the History of 1948*, ed. Eugene L. Rogan and Avi Shlaim (New York: Cambridge University Press, 2001), 12–36; Rashid Khalidi, *The Iron Cage: The Story of the Palestinian Struggle for Statehood* (Boston: Beacon Press, 2006), chap. 4; Haim Levenberg, *Military Preparations of the Arab Community in Palestine, 1945–1948* (Portland, OR: Frank Cass, 1993); Benny Morris, *The Birth of the Palestinian Refugee Problem Revisited* (New York: Cambridge University Press, 2004), chaps. 1, 3; Benny Morris, *Righteous Victims: A History of the Zionist-Arab Conflict, 1881–1999* (New York: Knopf, 1999), 187–89, 191–96, 215–23, 235–36, 241–42; Morris, *1948 and After*, 13–16; and Martin Van Creveld, *The Sword and the Olive: A Critical History of the Israeli Defense Forces* (New York: Public Affairs, 1998), 77–82.

10. Ilan Pappe, *The Ethnic Cleansing of Palestine* (Oxford: Oneworld Publications, 2006), 45.

11. Quoted in ibid., 22. For evidence that the Zionists understood that their fighting forces had a decisive advantage over the Palestinians and that this situation allowed them to pursue aggressive policies against the Palestinians, see ibid., esp. 22–23, 26, 41, 44–46, 70, 79, 84.

12. Morris, *1948 and After*, 15.

13. Ibid.

14. Morris, *Righteous Victims*, 393.

15. On the military balances in the 1956, 1967, and 1973 wars, see Dupuy, *Elusive Victory*, 146–47, 212–14, 231–44, 333–40, 388–90, 597–605, 623–33; Morris, *Righteous Victims*, 286–91, 311–13, 393–95; and Van Creveld, *The Sword and the Olive*, 137–38, 179–82, 239–43.

16. Israel's economy suffered a downturn in 2001–02, after the start of the Second Intifada in October 2000. Most experts believe, however, that the global economic meltdown was largely responsible for that downturn. An article in *Forbes* in late May 2002 summarizes the conventional wisdom: "The Israeli government and private economists estimate that two-thirds of the savage tumble in Israel's GDP growth, from 6.4% in 2000 to a current rate of zero, was due not to terrorism but to the worldwide slump led by high-tech." David Simons, "Cold Calculation of Terror," *Forbes*, May 28, 2002. The economy rebounded in 2003–05, even though the Palestinian uprising continued. Also see Emma Clark, "Israel's Neglected Economy," *BBC News* (online), September 2, 2002; Nadav Morag, "The Economic and Social Effects of Intensive Terrorism: Israel, 2000–2004," *Middle East Review of International Affairs* 10, no. 3 (September 2006); Neal Sandler, "Israel's Economy: As if the Intifada Weren't Enough," *BusinessWeek*, June 18, 2001; and Linda Sharaby, "Israel's Economic Growth: Success Without Security," *Middle East Review of International Affairs* 6, no. 3 (September 2002).

17. Amos Harel, "Israel Maintains Its Strategic Advantage, Says Jaffee Center," *Ha'aretz*, November 23, 2005. Also see Uri Bar-Joseph, "The Paradox of Israeli Power," *Survival* 46, no. 4 (Winter 2004–05); and Martin Van Creveld, "Opportunity Beckons," *Jerusalem Post*, May 16, 2003. The Jaffee Center has now been incorporated into a new institution, the Institute for National Strategic Studies.

18. Alan Dershowitz, "Debunking the Newest—and Oldest—Jewish Conspiracy: A Reply to the Mearsheimer-Walt 'Working Paper,'" John F. Kennedy School of Government Faculty Research Working Paper, Harvard University, April 2006, 22; and Martin Peretz, "Killer Angels: Murdering Jews, Then and Now," *New Republic*, April 15, 2002, 17–18.

19. Morris, *1948 and After*, 11–12. The subsequent Morris quotation in this paragraph is from ibid., 13.

20. Shlomo Ben-Ami, *Scars of War, Wounds of Peace: The Israeli-Arab Tragedy* (New York: Oxford University Press, 2006), 35–36. Also see Flapan, *Birth of Israel*, 119–52.

21. This conventional wisdom is reflected in Michael B. Oren, "Did Israel Want the Six-Day War?" *Azure* 5759, no. 7 (Spring 1999); and Michael B. Oren, *Six Days of War: June 1967 and the Making of the Modern Middle East* (New York: Oxford University Press, 2002).

22. The best new works on the origins of the 1967 war include Ben-Ami, *Scars of War*, 96–114; Norman G. Finkelstein, "Abba Eban with Footnotes," *Journal of Palestine Studies* 32, no. 3 (Spring 2003); Roland Popp, "Stumbling Decidedly into the Six-Day War," *Middle East Journal* 60, no. 2 (Spring 2006); and Tom Segev, *1967: Israel, the War, and the Year That Transformed the Middle East*, trans. Jessica Cohen (New York: Metropolitan Books, 2007).

23. Avi Shlaim, *The Iron Wall: Israel and the Arab World* (New York: Norton, 2000), 237.

24. Ibid., 235. Also see Stephen S. Rosenfeld, "Israel and Syria: Correcting the Record," *Washington Post*, December 24, 1999.

25. Ben-Ami, *Scars of War*, 100.

26. Segev, *1967*, 202–12, 295–96.

27. Quoted in ibid., 300. Also see ibid., 387–88.

28. Quoted in Ben-Ami, *Scars of War*, 76–77.

29. Morris, *Righteous Victims*, 387. Also see John J. Mearsheimer, *Conventional Deterrence* (Ithaca: Cornell University Press, 1983), 155–62.

30. Quoted in Mearsheimer, *Conventional Deterrence*, 159.

31. Yoram Meital, *Peace in Tatters: Israel, Palestine, and the Middle East* (Boulder, CO: Lynne Rienner, 2006), 148–52; Charles A. Radin, "Arabs Offer to Accept Israel with Conditions," *Boston Globe*, March 29, 2002; and Howard Schneider, "Arab Countries Unanimously Endorse Saudi Peace Plan," *Washington Post*, March 29, 2002.

32. According to the Law of Return, a "Jew" is defined as "a person who was born of a Jewish mother or has become converted to Judaism and who is not a member of another religion." The actual law and the relevant amendments can be found at Israel's Ministry of Foreign Affairs website, www.mfa.gov.il/MFA/MFAArchive/1950_1959/Law%20of%20Return%205710-1950. There has recently been discussion in Israel about passing legislation to recognize as Jewish those individuals who have a Jewish father but not a Jewish mother. See Shahar Ilan, "Bill Would Recognize Judaism Through Father," *Ha'aretz*, March 12, 2006.

33. The Declaration of the Establishment of the State of Israel can be found in John Norton Moore, ed., *The Arab-Israeli Conflict: Readings and Documents* (Princeton: Princeton University Press, 1977), 934–37.

34. David Ben-Gurion, *Israel: A Personal History*, trans. Nechemia Meyers and Uzy Nystar (New York: Funk and Wagnalls, 1971), 839.

35. These numbers are based on Central Bureau of Statistics, *Statistical Abstract of Israel, 2006*, Table 2.1, www1.cbs.gov.il/reader/; and Palestinian Academic Society for the Study of International Affairs, *Palestine Facts and Info*, "Population," www.passia.org/palestine_facts/facts_and_figures/0_facts_and_figures.htm. There are about 300,000 individuals living in Israel who are defined as "others" by the CBS. Most of them are family members of Jewish immigrants or are individuals who have Jewish ancestors but not a Jewish mother, and are

therefore not categorized as Jewish by the Israeli government. If one categorizes them as Jewish, then the total number of Jews in Israel would be about 5.6 million, not 5.3 million, which is the number the CBS uses.

36. A public opinion survey of Israeli Jews taken in February–March 2007 concluded that "the demographic challenge is of growing urgency to most of the Jewish population and helps define the collective approach to national security issues." Yehuda Ben Meir and Dafna Shaked, "The People Speak: Israeli Public Opinion on National Security, 2005–2007," Memorandum no. 90 (Tel Aviv: Institute for National Security Studies, May 2007), 10, 64–65. Also see Aluf Benn, "Israel's Identity Crisis," *Salon.com*, May 16, 2005; Larry Derfner, "Sounding the Alarm About Israel's Demographic Crisis," *Forward*, January 9, 2004; Jon E. Dougherty, "Will Israel Become an Arab State?" *NewsMax.com*, January 12, 2004; Lily Galili, "A Jewish Demographic State," *Ha'aretz*, June 28, 2002; and Gideon Levy, "Wombs in the Service of the State," *Ha'aretz*, September 9, 2002.

37. Shulamit Aloni, "A Country for Some of Its Citizens?" *Ha'aretz*, February 24, 2007. The Basic Law on Human Dignity and Liberty can be found on the Knesset website, www .knesset.gov.il/laws/special/eng/basic3_eng.htm.

38. Jonathan Cook, *Blood and Religion: The Unmasking of the Jewish and Democratic State* (Ann Arbor, MI: Pluto Press, 2006), 17–18. Also see Adalah and the Arab Association for Human Rights, "Equal Rights and Minority Rights for the Palestinian Arab Minority in Israel," a report to the UN Human Rights Committee on Israel's Implementation of Articles 26 and 27 of the International Covenant on Civil and Political Rights, July 1998; As'ad Ghanem, Nadim Rouhana, and Oren Yiftachel, "Questioning 'Ethnic Democracy': A Response to Sammy Smooha," *Israel Studies* 3, no. 2 (Fall 1998); David B. Green, "The Other Israelis," *Boston Globe*, February 25, 2007; Human Rights Watch, *Second Class: Discrimination Against Palestinian Arab Children in Israel's Schools* (New York, September 2001), chap. 8; Frances Raday, "Religion, Multiculturalism and Equality: The Israeli Case," in *Israel Yearbook on Human Rights*, Vol. 25 (1995), ed. Yoram Dinstein (The Hague: Martinus Nijhoff, 1996), 193–241; Ahmad H. Sa'di, "Israel as Ethnic Democracy: What Are the Implications for the Palestinian Minority?" *Arab Studies Quarterly* 22, no. 1 (Winter 2000); and Sammy Smooha, "Ethnic Democracy: Israel as an Archetype," *Israel Studies* 2, no. 2 (Fall 1997).

39. "The Official Summation of the Or Commission Report," published in *Ha'aretz*, September 2, 2003. For evidence of how hostile many Israelis were to the report's findings and recommendations, see "No Avoiding the Commission Recommendations," *Ha'aretz* editorial, September 4, 2003; and Molly Moore, "Israelis Look Inward After Critical Report," *Washington Post*, September 3, 2003. Also see Bernard Avishai, "Saving Israel from Itself: A Secular Future for the Jewish State," *Harper's*, January 2005; Ian Lustick, *Arabs in the Jewish State: Israel's Control of a National Minority* (Austin: University of Texas Press, 1980); and Chris McGreal, "Worlds Apart," *Guardian*, February 6, 2006.

40. Roee Nahmias, "Marriage to an Arab Is National Treason," *Ynetnews.com*, March 27, 2007; and Yoav Stern, "Poll: 50% of Israeli Jews Support State-Backed Arab Emigration," *Ha'aretz*, March 27, 2007. For similar results in a 2006 survey, see Eli Ashkenazi and Jack Khoury, "Poll: 68% of Jews Would Refuse to Live in Same Building as an Arab," *Ha'aretz*, March 22, 2006; Chris McGreal, "41% of Israel's Jews Favor Segregation," *Guardian*, March 24, 2006; Sharon Roffe-Ofir, "Poll: Israeli Jews Shun Arabs," *Ynetnews.com*, March 22, 2006; and Kenneth J. Theisen, "Racism Alive and Well in Israel?" Pittsburgh Independent Media Center (online), June 1, 2006.

41. Israeli Democracy Institute, "The Democracy Index: Major Findings 2003." This summary of the report can be found at www.idi.org.il/english/article.asp?id=1466.

42. According to a 2007 public opinion survey, 63 percent of Israeli Jews oppose including an Arab minister in the cabinet. In 2004, 75 percent opposed the idea, while 60 percent opposed it in 2005 and 2006. Ben Meir and Shaked, "The People Speak," 80. Also see ibid., 22, 79–82; Orly Halpern, "Arab Cabinet Pick Stirs 'Zionism-Racism' Debate," *Forward*, January 19, 2007; Gil Hoffman, "'Majadleh Slot the End of Zionism,'" *Jerusalem Post*, January 10,

2007; Ronny Sofer, "Cabinet Approves First Arab Minister," *Ynetnews.com*, January 28, 2007; and Scott Wilson, "In First, Arab Muslim Joins Israeli Cabinet," *Washington Post*, January 29, 2007.

43. Quoted in Justin Huggler, "Israel Imposes 'Racist' Marriage Law," *Independent*, August 1, 2003. Also see James Bennet, "Israel Blocks Palestinians from Marrying into Residency," *New York Times*, July 31, 2003; "Racist Legislation," *Ha'aretz* editorial, July, 19, 2004; "Racist Legislation," *Ha'aretz* editorial, January 18, 2005; and Shahar Ilan, "Law Denying Family Unification to Israelis and Palestinians Extended," *Ha'aretz*, March 21, 2007. Even the Anti-Defamation League criticized the legislation, albeit mildly. Nathan Guttman, Yair Ettinger, and Sharon Sadeh, "ADL Criticizes Law Denying Citizenship to Palestinians Who Marry Israelis," *Ha'aretz*, August 5, 2003.

44. Quoted in Tovah Tzimuki, "Government Supports Revocation of Citizenship," *Ynetnews.com*, January 8, 2007. Also see Saed Bannoura, "Israeli Knesset Passes Law to Revoke Citizenship of 'Unpatriotic' Israelis," International Middle East Media Center (online), January 10, 2007; Sheera Claire Frenkel, "'Disloyalty' Bill Passes First Hurdle," *Jerusalem Post*, January 10, 2007; Tom Segev, "Conditional Citizenship," *Ha'aretz*, January 11, 2007; and Yuval Yoaz, "Government to Back Bill Allowing Court to Rescind Traitors' Citizenship," *Ha'aretz*, January 7, 2007.

45. Quoted in Larry Derfner, "Rattling the Cage: A Bigot Called Bibi," *Jerusalem Post*, January 3, 2007. Also see Aluf Benn and Gideon Alon, "Netanyahu: Israel's Arabs Are the Real Demographic Threat," *Ha'aretz*, December 18, 2003; Ron Dermer, "The Nerve of Bibi," *Jerusalem Post*, January 9, 2007; Karina's Kolumn (Karina Robinson), "Benjamin Netanyahu: Israel's Prime Minister in Waiting," *Banker* (online), July 1, 2004; and Neta Sela, "Netanyahu: Pensions Cut—Arabs' Birth Rate Declined," *Ynetnews.com*, January 3, 2007.

46. These statements are not isolated examples. In early 2004, for example, Deputy Defense Minister Ze'ev Boim suggested that Palestinian terrorism is due to a "genetic blemish." His views were supported by another member of the Knesset, who said that terrorism is "in their blood," which is why an Arab "will stab you in the back" if you "turn your back" on him. Even Benny Morris, the historian whose earlier scholarship has done so much to reveal Israel's true policies toward the Palestinians, has nonetheless referred to them as "barbarians" who should be treated like "serial killers." Begin's comment is from Amnon Kapeliuk, "Begin and the 'Beasts,'" *New Statesman*, June 25, 1982, 12. Eitan's comments are from David K. Shipler, "Most West Bank Arabs Blaming U.S. for Impasse," *New York Times*, April 14, 1983; and Uzi Benziman, *Sharon: An Israeli Caesar* (New York: Adama Books, 1985), 264. Ya'alon's comment is from Ari Shavit, "The Enemy Within," *Ha'aretz*, August 27, 2002. Boim's comment and his supporter's comments are from Yuval Yoaz, "AG: Ethics Committee to Probe Racist Comments Made by MKs," *Ha'aretz*, August 10, 2004. Morris's comment is from Ari Shavit, "Survival of the Fittest," *Ha'aretz*, January 9, 2004.

47. Larry Derfner, "Rattling the Cage: The Racism of Israeli Youth," *Jerusalem Post*, January 17, 2007. Also see Ahiya Raved, "Youth Believe Arabs Dirty, Uneducated," *Ynetnews.com*, January 9, 2007.

48. Quoted in Ben Lynfield, "The Rise of Avigdor Lieberman," *Nation*, December 14, 2006. Also see Uri Avnery, "The Lovable Man? Lieberman and the Decline of Israeli Democracy," *Antiwar.com*, November 3, 2006; Akiva Eldar, "Let's Hear It for the Haiders," *Ha'aretz*, October 30, 2006; Leonard Fein, "The Fantasies of Avigdor Lieberman," *Forward*, October 20, 2006; Gershom Gorenberg, "The Minister for National Fears," *Atlantic*, May 2007; and Henry Siegman, "Hurricane Carter," *Nation*, January 22, 2007. Effi Eitam, the former head of the National Religious party, and Rehavam Ze'evi, an Israeli general who founded the right-wing Moledet party, were the previous government ministers who spoke out in favor of transfer.

49. "The Democracy Index: Major Findings 2003"; Yulie Khromchenko, "Survey: Most Jewish Israelis Support Transfer of Arabs," *Ha'aretz*, June 22, 2004; Yoav Stern, "Poll: Most Israeli Jews Say Israeli Arabs Should Emigrate," *Ha'aretz*, April 4, 2005; McGreal, "41% of Israel's

Jews"; Amiram Barkat and Jack Khoury, "Poll: Gov't Should Help Arab Citizens Emigrate," *Ha'aretz*, May 10, 2006; and Roffe-Ofir, "Poll." Also see Uzi Arad, "Swap Meet: Trading Land for Peace," *New Republic*, November 28 and December 5, 2005; Amnon Barzilai, "More Israeli Jews Favor Transfer of Palestinians, Israeli Arabs—Poll Finds," *Ha'aretz*, October 10, 2005; Arik Carmon, "A Blot on Israeli Democracy," *Ha'aretz*, December 12, 2005; Evelyn Gordon, "No Longer the Political Fringe," *Jerusalem Post*, September 14, 2006; Ben Lynfield, "Israeli Expulsion Idea Gains Steam," *Christian Science Monitor*, February 6, 2002; Stern, "Poll: 50% of Israeli Jews"; Matthew Wagner, "New Proposal: Transfer-for-Cash Plan," *Jerusalem Post*, January 21, 2007; and Steven I. Weiss, "Israeli Rightist Calls for Transfer of Arabs," *Forward*, September 15, 2006.

50. B'Tselem, "The Scope of Israeli Control in the Gaza Strip," www.btselem.org/english/Gaza_Strip/Gaza_Status.asp; David Sharrock, "Israel's 'Invisible Hand' Still Controls Gaza, Says Report," *Times* (London), January 15, 2007; and Scott Wilson, "For Gaza, a Question of Responsibility," *Washington Post*, March 21, 2007.

51. Jan Egeland and Jan Eliasson, "La catastrophe humaine de Gaza est une bombe à retardement," *Figaro* (online), September 28, 2006. Also see Steven Erlanger, "As Parents Go Unpaid, Gaza Children Go Hungry," *New York Times*, September 14, 2006; Steven Erlanger, "Years of Strife and Lost Hope Scar Young Palestinians," *New York Times*, March 12, 2007; Donald Macintyre, "Gaza in Danger of Turning into a 'Giant Prison,' Says Mideast Envoy," *Independent*, November 14, 2005; Rory McCarthy, "Occupied Gaza Like Apartheid South Africa, Says UN Report," *Guardian*, February 23, 2007; Sara Roy, "The Economy of Gaza," *Znet* (online), October 9, 2006; Mohammed Samhouri, "Looking Beyond the Numbers: The Palestinian Socioeconomic Crisis of 2006," Middle East Brief no. 16, Crown Center for Middle East Studies, Brandeis University, February 2007; United Nations Office for the Coordination of Humanitarian Affairs (OCHA), "Statement on Gaza by United Nations Humanitarian Agencies Working in the Occupied Palestinian Territory," August 3, 2006; and OCHA, "The Humanitarian Monitor: Occupied Palestinian Territory," no. 10, February 2007.

52. "Making the Law a Laughingstock," *Ha'aretz* editorial, December 31, 2006.

53. Steven Erlanger, "West Bank Sites on Private Land, Data Shows," *New York Times*, March 14, 2007; Nadav Shragai, "Peace Now: 32% of Land Held for Settlements Is Private Property," *Ha'aretz*, March 14, 2007. Also see Greg Myre, "For West Bank, It's a Highway to Frustration," *New York Times*, November 18, 2006; and "Legitimization of Land Theft," *Ha'aretz* editorial, February 27, 2007.

54. The first wave of European Jews to come to Palestine is known as the First Aliyah, and it covers the years from 1882 to 1903. There were slightly more than fifteen thousand Jews in Palestine in 1882 according to the Ottoman census. Justin McCarthy, *The Population of Palestine: Population History and Statistics of the Late Ottoman Period and the Mandate* (New York: Columbia University Press, 1990), 10–13, has excellent data for the years from 1850 to 1915. However, McCarthy's numbers, which are based on Ottoman census figures, exclude "an unknown number of Jewish immigrants who had kept their original citizenship." He notes further that "there would have been relatively few non-citizen Jews at that early date" and estimates the number as "perhaps one to two thousand." Thus the upper bound is probably seventeen thousand Jews in Palestine in 1882. Also see Mark Tessler, *A History of the Israeli-Palestinian Conflict* (Bloomington: Indiana University Press, 1994), 124.

55. The total population of Palestine in 1893 was roughly 530,000, of whom about 19,000 (3.6 percent) were Jewish. Arabs comprised the vast majority of the remaining population. McCarthy, *Population of Palestine*, 10.

56. This issue was revisited in the mid-1980s when Joan Peters published *From Time Immemorial: The Origins of the Arab-Jewish Conflict over Palestine* (New York: Harper, 1984). She claimed that when the Jews began arriving in Palestine from Europe, there were far fewer Arabs there than the conventional wisdom maintained, and that the Arabs moved to Palestine in large numbers only after the Jews began to develop the land. Peters's book was en-

thusiastically endorsed by a large number of prominent American Jews. However, shortly after its publication, a number of scholars showed that not only was *From Time Immemorial* based on a "highly tendentious use—or neglect—of the available source material," but its core thesis was dead wrong. Yehoshua Porath, "Mrs. Peters's Palestine," *New York Review of Books*, January 16, 1986. In a conversation with the *New York Times*, Porath, a distinguished Israeli historian, said that Peters's book was "a sheer forgery" and that in Israel it "was almost universally dismissed as sheer rubbish except maybe as a propaganda weapon." Colin Campbell, "Dispute Flares over Book on Claims to Palestine," *New York Times*, November 28, 1985. Also see Norman G. Finkelstein, *Image and Reality of the Israel-Palestine Conflict* (London: Verso, 2001), chap. 2.

57. Laurence J. Silberstein, *The Postzionism Debates: Knowledge and Power in Israeli Culture* (New York: Routledge, 1999), 51.

58. Ben-Ami, *Scars of War*, 9.

59. There were about 1.2 million Palestinians in addition to the 650,000 Jews living in Palestine in 1948, which translates into a population that was 65 percent Palestinian and 35 percent Jewish. See Morris, *1948 and After*, 14. Flapan uses population figures in which the Jews are 33 percent of the population (*Birth of Israel*, 44), while Morris uses 37 percent in *Righteous Victims* (186).

60. Some believe that Ben-Gurion and his followers had less ambitious territorial goals than Revisionists like Vladimir Jabotinsky. But as Avi Shlaim makes clear, "The difference between [Ben-Gurion] and the Revisionists was not that he was a territorial minimalist while they were territorial maximalists, but rather that he pursued a gradualist strategy while they adhered to an all-or-nothing approach." Shlaim, *Iron Wall*, 21. The Zionists were careful not to say much in public about their ultimate goals in Palestine, for fear it would anger the Arabs and the British and undermine their enterprise. Nevertheless, Ben-Gurion laid out his vision of what the borders of Israel would look like in a coauthored book that was written in Yiddish and published in the United States in 1918. In addition to what is today Israel, Ben-Gurion's vision included the Occupied Territories, southern Lebanon up to the Litani River, part of southern Syria, a large part of Jordan, and the Sinai Peninsula. Morris, *Righteous Victims*, 75.

61. Flapan, *Birth of Israel*, 103–104; and Morris, *Birth Revisited*, 69.

62. These quotes are from Flapan, *Birth of Israel*, 22; and Shlaim, *Iron Wall*, 21. For a more detailed discussion of the early Zionists' thinking about partition, see Mearsheimer and Walt, "Setting the Record Straight," 33–37.

63. Uri Ben-Eliezer, *The Making of Israeli Militarism* (Bloomington: Indiana University Press, 1998), 150.

64. Avi Shlaim, *The Politics of Partition: King Abdullah, the Zionists, and Palestine, 1921–1951* (New York: Oxford University Press, 1998). Also see Morris, *1948 and After*, 10; Benny Morris, *The Road to Jerusalem: Glubb Pasha, Palestine and the Jews* (London: I. B. Tauris, 2002); Ilan Pappe, *Britain and the Arab-Israeli Conflict, 1948–1951* (New York: St. Martin's Press, 1988); and Mary C. Wilson, *King Abdullah, Britain and the Making of Jordan* (New York: Cambridge University Press, 1987).

65. Benny Morris, "Revisiting the Palestinian Exodus of 1948," in *The War for Palestine: Rewriting the History of 1948*, ed. Eugene L. Rogan and Avi Shlaim (New York: Cambridge University Press, 2001), 40. Also see Ben-Ami, *Scars of War*, 33–34; and Shlaim, *Iron Wall*, 25.

66. Nur Masalha, *Expulsion of the Palestinians: The Concept of "Transfer" in Zionist Political Thought, 1882–1948* (Washington, DC: Institute for Palestine Studies, 1992); Morris, *Birth Revisited*, chap. 2; and Morris, "Revisiting the Palestinian Exodus," 39–48.

67. Quoted in Masalha, *Expulsion of the Palestinians*, 128. Also see Morris, *Righteous Victims*, 140, 142, 168–69. Ben-Gurion's statement is from a memorandum he wrote prior to the Extraordinary Zionist Conference at New York's Biltmore Hotel in May 1942.

68. Quoted in Michael Bar-Zohar, *Facing a Cruel Mirror: Israel's Moment of Truth* (New York: Scribner, 1990), 16.

69. Quoted in Shavit, "Survival of the Fittest." Also see Benny Morris, "A New Exodus for the Middle East?" *Guardian*, October 3, 2002. Ben-Gurion told the Central Committee of the Histadrut on December 30, 1947: "In the area allocated to the Jewish state there are not more than 520,000 Jews and about 350,000 non-Jews, mostly Arabs. Together with the Jews of Jerusalem, the total population of the Jewish state at the time of its establishment, will be about a million, including almost 40 percent non-Jews. Such a [population] composition does not provide a stable basis for a Jewish state. This [demographic] fact must be viewed in all its clarity and acuteness. With such a [population] composition, there cannot even be absolute certainty that control will remain in the hands of the Jewish majority . . . There can be no stable and strong Jewish state so long as it has a Jewish majority of only 60 percent." Quoted in Masalha, *Expulsion of the Palestinians*, 176.

70. Quoted in Morris, *Righteous Victims*, 169.

71. Morris, "Revisiting the Palestinian Exodus," 43–44.

72. Morris's *Birth Revisited* and Pappe's *Ethnic Cleansing of Palestine* provide detailed accounts of this event. Also see Meron Benvenisti, *Sacred Landscape: The Buried History of the Holy Land Since 1948*, trans. Maxine Kaufman-Lacusta (Berkeley: University of California Press, 2000), chaps. 3–4; and Masalha, *Expulsion of the Palestinians*, chap. 5. Morris notes that "the haphazard thinking about transfer before 1937 and the virtual consensus in support of the notion from 1937 on contributed to what happened in 1948 in the sense that they conditioned the Zionist leadership, and below it, the officials and officers who managed the new state's civilian and military agencies, for the transfer that took place. To one degree or another, these men all arrived at 1948, in no small measure owing to the continuous anti-Zionist Arab violence which played out against the growing persecution of Diaspora Jewry in central and eastern Europe, with a mindset which was open to the idea and implementation of transfer and expulsion. And the transfer that occurred—which encountered almost no serious opposition from any part of the Yishuv—transpired smoothly in large measure because of this pre-conditioning." Morris, "Revisiting the Palestinian Exodus," 48.

73. Erskine Childers, "The Other Exodus," *Spectator*, May 12, 1961; Flapan, *Birth of Israel*, 81–118; Walid Khalidi, "Why Did the Palestinians Leave Revisited," *Journal of Palestine Studies* 34, no. 2 (Winter 2005); Walid Khalidi, "The Fall of Haifa," *Middle East Forum* 35, no. 10 (December, 1959); Morris, *Birth Revisited*; and Pappe, *Ethnic Cleansing of Palestine*, 131. To be sure, some Arab commanders did instruct Palestinian civilians to evacuate their homes during the fighting, either to make sure that they did not get caught in a firefight or to ensure that they were not killed by the Zionist forces engaged in ethnically cleansing Palestinians. Fear of death at the hands of the Jews was an especially powerful motive to evacuate villages after the infamous massacre at Deir Yassin, where about 100 to 110 Palestinians were murdered on April 9, 1948. Morris, *Righteous Victims*, 209. As Morris reports, "The IDF Intelligence Service called Deir Yassin 'a decisive accelerating factor' in the general Arab exodus." *Righteous Victims*, 209. Orders to evacuate of this kind are not related to the myth of a voluntary or elite-directed evacuation. See Ben-Ami, *Scars of War*, 43–44.

74. Quoted in Morris, *Birth Revisited*, 318. For more detail on the Zionists' opposition to allowing the Palestinian refugees to return to their homes, see ibid., chap. 5.

75. Baruch Kimmerling, *Zionism and Territory: The Socio-Territorial Dimensions of Zionist Politics* (Berkeley, CA: Institute of International Studies, 1983), 143.

76. Pappe, *Ethnic Cleansing of Palestine*, xiii. Also see Walid Khalidi, ed., *All That Remains: The Palestinian Villages Occupied and Depopulated by Israel in 1948* (Washington, DC: Institute for Palestine Studies, 1992), which identifies the number of villages destroyed as 418, not 531. The difference in the number is a result of varying definitions of what constituted a Palestinian village. Pappe and several other Palestinian historians include some smaller communities in their count of villages, while Khalidi excludes them. Correspondence between authors and Ilan Pappe, May 15, 2007.

77. Quoted in Khalidi, *All That Remains*, xxxi.

78. Quoted in Nahum Goldmann, *The Jewish Paradox*, trans. Steve Cox (New York: Grosset and Dunlap, 1978), 99.

79. Quoted in Ian Lustick, "To Build and to Be Built By: Israel and the Hidden Logic of the Iron Wall," *Israel Studies* 1, no. 1 (Spring 1996): 200.

80. Quoted in Ben-Ami, *Scars of War*, 12.

81. Geoffrey Aronson, *Israel, Palestinians, and the Intifada: Creating Facts on the West Bank* (London: Kegan Paul International, 1990); Amnon Barzilai, "A Brief History of the Missed Opportunity," *Ha'aretz*, June 5, 2002; Amnon Barzilai, "Some Saw the Refugees as the Key to Peace," *Ha'aretz*, June 11, 2002; Moshe Behar, "The Peace Process and Israeli Domestic Politics in the 1990s," *Socialism and Democracy* 16, no. 2 (Summer–Fall 2002); Jimmy Carter, *Palestine: Peace Not Apartheid* (New York: Simon & Schuster, 2006); Adam Hanieh and Catherine Cook, "A Road Map to the Oslo Cul-de-Sac," *Middle East Report Online*, May 15, 2003; "Israel's Interests Take Primacy: An Interview with Dore Gold," in *bitterlemons.org*, "What Constitutes a Viable Palestinian State?" March 15, 2004, edition 10; Baruch Kimmerling, *Politicide: The Real Legacy of Ariel Sharon* (London: Verso, 2003); Nur Masalha, *Imperial Israel and the Palestinians: The Politics of Expansion* (London: Pluto Press, 2000); Tanya Reinhart, *The Road Map to Nowhere: Israel/Palestine Since 2003* (London: Verso, 2006); Sara Roy, "Erasing the 'Optics' of Gaza," *Daily Star* (online), February 14, 2004; and "36 Years, and Still Counting," *Ha'aretz*, September 26, 2003.

82. Quoted in Rashid Khalidi, *Palestinian Identity: The Construction of Modern National Consciousness* (New York: Columbia University Press, 1997), 147. Meir also said, "It was not as though there was a Palestinian people in Palestine considering itself as a Palestinian people and we came and threw them out and took their country away from them. They did not exist." Quoted in Masalha, *Imperial Israel*, 47.

83. Dayan quoted in Benny Morris, *Israel's Border Wars, 1949–1956* (New York: Oxford University Press, 1997), 12. Regarding the views of other IDF generals, see ibid. On Ben-Gurion's thinking, see Morris, *Righteous Victims*, 261, 290.

84. Morris, *Israel's Border Wars*, 11.

85. Quoted in Hanieh and Cook, "Road Map." Also see Akiva Eldar, "On the Same Page, Ten Years On," *Ha'aretz*, November 5, 2005; David Grossman, "The Night Our Hope for Peace Died," *Guardian*, November 4, 2005; and Michael Jansen, "A Practice That 'Prevents the Emergence of a Palestinian State,'" *Jordan Times* (online), November 10, 2005. Shlomo Ben-Ami makes it clear that not only Rabin but also his immediate successor, Shimon Peres, was opposed to creating a Palestinian state. *Scars of War*, 220. Finally, a clear majority of Israelis were opposed to creating a Palestinian state during Rabin's tenure as prime minister (1992–95). It was not until 1997 that at least half of Israeli Jews supported the establishment of a Palestinian state. At the time of the 1993 Oslo Accords, 35 percent favored creating a Palestinian state. Ben Meir and Shaked, "The People Speak," 64–65.

86. Hillary Clinton quoted in Tom Rhodes and Christopher Walker, "Congress Tells Israel to Reject Clinton's Pullout Plan," *Times* (London), May 8, 1998. On the White House response, see James Bennet, "Aides Disavow Mrs. Clinton on Mideast," *New York Times*, May 8, 1998. Also see Robin Dorf, "News Analysis: What Motivated Hillary's Call for a Palestinian State?" *JTA.org*, May 15, 1998; "Hillary's Folly," *Jewish Week* editorial, May 15, 1998; and Brian Knowlton, "Mrs. Clinton Starts Storm by Backing 'Palestine,'" *International Herald Tribune*, May 8, 1998.

87. "Ex-PM Shamir Objects to Palestinian State, but Still Supports Sharon," *Ha'aretz*, November 26, 2002; Benjamin Netanyahu, "A Limited Palestinian State," *Washington Post*, June 20, 2003. In a 1998 interview, Shamir said that Israel's boundaries ran "from the border of the kingdom of Jordan to the Mediterranean Sea" and said the "greatest danger" facing Israel was "the establishment of a Palestinian state in Israel." See "Yitzhak Shamir: A Lifetime of Activism," *Middle East Quarterly* 6, no. 2 (June 1999).

88. In a speech in October 2005, President Ahmadinejad reportedly called for Israel to be "wiped off the map," a statement widely interpreted as threatening the physical destruction

of the Jewish state and its inhabitants. A more accurate translation of Ahmadinejad's statement is "the occupation regime over Jerusalem should vanish from the page of time" (or alternatively, "be eliminated from the pages of history"). Instead of calling for the physical destruction of Israel, Ahmadinejad was suggesting that Israel's control over Jerusalem and Palestine should be seen as a temporary condition that should be reversed, like Soviet control of Eastern Europe or the shah's regime in Iran. While still provocative and highly objectionable, calling for the political dismantlement of the Jewish state in Palestine is not the same as calling for the physical destruction of Israel or its population. See Ethan Bronner, "Just How Far Did They Go, Those Words Against Israel?" *New York Times*, June 11, 2006; Jonathan Steele, "Lost in Translation," *Guardian*, June 14, 2006; and "Iranian President at Tehran Conference: 'Very Soon, This Stain of Disgrace [i.e., Israel] Will Be Purged from the Center of the Islamic World—and This Is Attainable,'" Middle East Media Research Institute, Special Dispatch Series no. 1013, October 28, 2005.

89. "Bombs," *New Republic* editorial, August 27 & September 3, 2001; Martin Peretz, "Good Fight," *New Republic*, May 27, 2002; and Martin Peretz, "Blows to Israel Must Never Go Unanswered," *Los Angeles Times*, September 5, 2003. Regarding Dershowitz, his most relevant work is *The Case for Israel* (Hoboken, NJ: John Wiley, 2003). For an incisive critique of that book, see Norman G. Finkelstein, *Beyond Chutzpah: On the Misuse of Anti-Semitism and the Abuse of History* (Berkeley: University of California Press, 2005). Also see Michael Desch, "The Chutzpah of Alan Dershowitz," *American Conservative*, December 5, 2005; and "Dershowitz v. Desch," *American Conservative*, January 16, 2006.

90. Yaakov Katz, "'IDF the Most Moral Army in the World,'" *Jerusalem Post*, June 11, 2006; Leslie Susser, "Israelis Question Army Morality," *JewishJournal.com*, December 17, 2004; and "Cabinet Communique," Israeli Ministry of Foreign Affairs, December 12, 2004, www.mfa.gov.il/MFA/Government/Communiques/2004/Cabinet%20Communique%2012-Dec-2004. Also see Richard Cohen, "Truth Massacred," *Washington Post*, August 6, 2002; and Neve Gordon, "Israel's Slippery Moral Slope," *In These Times* (online), January 31, 2003.

91. Meron Benvenisti, "The Model of the Mythological Sabra," *Ha'aretz*, September 12, 2002.

92. Morris, *Righteous Victims*, chaps. 2–5.

93. Quoted in Shabtai Teveth, *Ben-Gurion: The Burning Ground, 1886–1948* (Boston: Houghton Mifflin, 1987), 544.

94. Morris, *Birth Revisited*. Many Israeli documents concerning the events of 1948 remain classified; Morris anticipates "that with respect to both expulsions and atrocities, we can expect additional revelations as the years pass and more Israeli records become available." Morris, "Revisiting the Palestinian Exodus," 49. In fact, he maintains that the reported cases of rape he knows about are "just the tip of the iceberg." See Shavit, "Survival of the Fittest."

95. Quoted in Pappe, *Ethnic Cleansing of Palestine*, 69. For background on Ben-Gurion's comment, see ibid., 61–72.

96. Morris, *Israel's Border Wars*, 432. Also see ibid., 126–53, 178–84.

97. Gabby Bron, "Egyptian POWs Ordered to Dig Graves, Then Shot by Israeli Army," *Yedioth Ahronoth*, August 17, 1995; Ronal Fisher, "Mass Murder in the 1956 Sinai War," *Ma'ariv*, August 8, 1995 (copies of these two pieces can be found in *Journal of Palestine Studies* 25, no. 3 [Spring 1996]: 148–55); Galal Bana, "Egypt: We Will Turn to the International War Crimes Tribunal in the Hague If Israel Will Not Compensate Murdered Prisoners of War," *Ha'aretz*, July 24, 2002; Zehavit Friedman, "Personal Reminiscence: Remembering Ami Kronfeld," in Jewish Voice for Peace, *Jewish Peace News* (online), September 25, 2005; Katherine M. Metres, "As Evidence Mounts, Toll of Israeli Prisoner of War Massacres Grows," *Washington Report on Middle East Affairs* (online), February/March 1996; Roee Nahmias, "Egypt May Petition Hague over 'Murder of POWs,'" *Ynetnews.com*, March 6, 2007; Roee Nahmias, "Former Meretz Leader Decries 1967 War Crimes," *Ynetnews.com*, March 3, 2007; Meron Rapoport, "Into the Valley of Death," *Ha'aretz*, February 13, 2007; and Segev, *1967*, 371–76.

98. Avnery, "Crying Wolf?" *CounterPunch.org*, March 15, 2003; Robert Blecher, "Living on the

Edge: The Threat of 'Transfer' in Israel and Palestine," MERIP, *Middle East Report Online* 225 (Winter 2002); Kimmerling, *Politicide*, 28. Also see Noam Chomsky, *Fateful Triangle: The United States, Israel and the Palestinians*, 2nd ed. (Cambridge, MA: South End Press, 1999), 97; Morris, *Righteous Victims*, 328–29; Tanya Reinhart, *Israel/Palestine: How to End the War of 1948* (New York: Seven Stories Press, 2002), 8; Tom Segev, "The Spirit of the King David Hotel," *Ha'aretz*, July 23, 2006; and Segev, *1967*, 400–12, 523–42. Morris reports that 120,000 Palestinians applied to return to their homes right after the 1967 war, but Israel allowed only about 17,000 to come back. *Righteous Victims*, 329.

99. Avnery, "Crying Wolf?"; Ami Kronfeld, "Avnery on Ethnic Cleansing and a Personal Note," in Jewish Voice for Peace, *Jewish Peace News* (online), March 17, 2003; and Metres, "As Evidence Mounts."

100. Danny Rubinstein, "Roads, Fences and Outposts Maintain Control in the Territories," *Ha'aretz*, August 12, 2003.

101. "Report of the Commission of Inquiry into the Events at the Refugee Camps in Beirut," February 7, 1983. The report is commonly called "the Kahan Commission Report" after its chairman, Yitzhak Kahan. Also see Morris, *Righteous Victims*, 542–49; and Shlaim, *Iron Wall*, 415–17. Israeli soldiers did not do the killing at Sabra and Shatila; it was done by a Lebanese Christian militia (Phalangists) allied with Israel. After the IDF encircled the two Palestinian refugee camps, Sharon "ordered the IDF to allow the Phalangists to enter the . . . camps." The Phalangists and the Palestinians were not only bitter enemies, but the Phalangists were bent on revenge because their leader had just been assassinated. They were almost certain to massacre the Palestinians, a point that Israeli leaders involved in the operation knew or should have known. Once the killing started, Israeli soldiers quickly became aware that a massacre was taking place "but did nothing to stop it." Shlaim, *Iron Wall*, 416. President Bush has hailed former prime minister Ariel Sharon as a "man of peace," but questions concerning violence against civilians have dogged him for years. For example, in 1953, he commanded a unit that attacked the Jordanian town of Qibya and killed sixty-nine civilians; two-thirds of them were women and children. According to Benny Morris, "Sharon and the IDF subsequently claimed the villagers had hidden in cellars and attics and the troops had been unaware of this when they blew up the buildings. But in truth the troops had moved from house to house, firing through windows and doorways, and Jordanian pathologists reported that most of the dead had been killed by bullets and shrapnel rather than by falling masonry or explosions. In any event, the operational orders, from CO Central Command to the units involved . . . had explicitly ordered 'destruction and maximum killing.'" *Righteous Victims*, 278. Also see ibid., 276–79, 294–95, 494–560; Benziman, *Sharon*; Uzi Benziman, "The Cock's Arrogance," *Ha'aretz*, June 15, 2003; Thomas L. Friedman, *From Beirut to Jerusalem* (New York: Anchor Books, 1990), chaps. 6–7; Kimmerling, *Politicide*; Ze'ev Schiff and Ehud Ya'ari, *Israel's Lebanon War*, trans. Ina Friedman (New York: Simon & Schuster, 1984), 250–85; and Shlaim, *Iron Wall*, 90–92, 149–50, 384–423.

102. Perry Anderson, "Scurrying Towards Bethlehem," *New Left Review* 10 (July–August 2001): 5.

103. Morris, *Righteous Victims*, 341. For a detailed account of how Israel treats the Palestinians in the Occupied Territories, see Amira Hass, *Reporting from Ramallah: An Israeli Journalist in an Occupied Land*, ed. and trans. Rachel Leah Jones (Los Angeles: Semiotext(e), 2003). On Israel's use of torture, see B'Tselem and Hamoked (Center for the Defense of the Individual), "Utterly Forbidden: The Torture and Ill-Treatment of Palestinian Detainees," draft report, Jerusalem, April 2007; Glenn Frankel, "Prison Tactics a Longtime Dilemma for Israel," *Washington Post*, June 16, 2004; Ron Kampeas, "State Report Claims Israel Tortures Palestinian Detainees," *JTA.org*, March 8, 2007; Public Committee Against Torture in Israel, "'Ticking Bombs': Testimonies of Torture Victims in Israel," draft report, Jerusalem, May 2007; William F. Schulz, "An Israeli Interrogator, and a Tale of Torture," letter to *New York Times*, December 27, 2004; and Aviram Zino, "Report: High Court Permits Torture of Palestinians," *Ynetnews.com*, May 30, 2007. Israel has also been accused by B'Tselem of using Palestinian children as human shields. See "Israeli Soldiers Use Palestinian Minors and

an Adult as Human Shields in the Operation in Nablus," B'Tselem news release, Jerusalem, March 8, 2007.

104. The data and the quotes in this paragraph and the next one are from Swedish Save the Children, "The Status of Palestinian Children During the Uprising in the Occupied Territories," Excerpted Summary Material, Jerusalem, January 1990, in *Journal of Palestine Studies* 19, no. 4 (Summer 1990): 136–46. Also see Joshua Brilliant, "Officer Tells Court Villagers Were Bound, Gagged and Beaten. 'Not Guilty' Plea at 'Break Bones' Trial," *Jerusalem Post*, March 30, 1990; Joshua Brilliant, "'Rabin Ordered Beatings,' Meir Tells Military Court," *Jerusalem Post*, June 22, 1990; Jackson Diehl, "Rights Group Accuses Israel of Violence Against Children in Palestinian Uprising," *Washington Post*, May 17, 1990; James A. Graff, "Crippling a People: Palestinian Children and Israeli State Violence," *Alif* 13 (1993); Morris, *Righteous Victims*, 586–95; and Ronald R. Stockton, "Intifada Deaths," *Journal of Palestine Studies* 19, no. 4 (Summer 1990).

105. "Unbridled Force," *Ha'aretz* editorial, March 16, 2003. For other evidence, see Jonathan Cook, "Impunity on Both Sides of the Green Line," MERIP, *Middle East Report Online*, November 23, 2005; "When Everything Is Permissible," *Ha'aretz* editorial, June 6, 2005; "It Can Happen Here," *Ha'aretz* editorial, November 22, 2004; Chris McGreal, "Snipers with Children in Their Sights," *Guardian*, June 28, 2005; Chris McGreal, "Israel Shocked by Image of Soldiers Forcing Violinist to Play at Roadblock," *Guardian*, November 29, 2004; Greg Myre, "Former Israeli Soldiers Tell of Harassment of Palestinians," *New York Times*, June 24, 2004; Reuven Pedatzur, "The Message to the Soldiers Was Clear," *Ha'aretz*, December 13, 2004; and Conal Urquhart, "Israeli Soldiers Tell of Indiscriminate Killings by Army and a Culture of Impunity," *Guardian*, September 6, 2005.

106. Reuvan Pedatzur, "More than a Million Bullets," *Ha'aretz*, June 29, 2004; and Clayton E. Swisher, *The Truth About Camp David: The Untold Story About the Collapse of the Middle East Peace Process* (New York: Nation Books, 2004), 387–88.

107. These figures cover the period between September 29, 2000, and December 31, 2005, and are taken from B'Tselem press release, January 4, 2006.

108. Nathan Guttman, "'It's a Terrible Thing, Living with the Knowledge That You Crushed Our Daughter,'" *Ha'aretz*, April 30, 2004; Joshua Hammer, "The Death of Rachel Corrie," *MotherJones.com*, September/October 2003; Adam Shapiro, "Remembering Rachel Corrie," *Nation*, March 18, 2004; and Tsahar Rotem, "British Peace Activist Shot by IDF Troops in Gaza Strip," *Ha'aretz*, April 11, 2003.

109. Amnesty International reports that since the Second Intifada began in the fall of 2000, "Israeli authorities have routinely failed to investigate allegations of unlawful killings and other abuses of Palestinians by Israeli forces and settlers . . . Israeli forces have killed thousands of Palestinians, many of them unlawfully, yet scarcely any such incidents have been investigated properly and fewer still have resulted in the perpetrator being brought to justice . . . In the very few cases in which the Israeli authorities have conducted serious investigations into killings of Palestinians, resulting prosecutions have generally been unsuccessful or have resulted in the imposition of sentences that were not commensurate with the gravity of the offense." Amnesty International, "Road to Nowhere," December 2006, 27–28.

110. For a detailed discussion of Israeli behavior toward the Palestinians that makes extensive use of reports from different human rights groups, see Finkelstein, *Beyond Chutzpah*, chaps. 4–9.

111. Quoted in Molly Moore, "Ex–Security Chiefs Turn on Sharon," *Washington Post*, November 15, 2003; "Ex–Shin Bet Heads Warn of 'Catastrophe' Without Peace Deal," *Ha'aretz*, November 15, 2003. These comments were based on an interview in the Israeli newspaper *Yedioth Ahronoth* on November 14, 2003. A copy of the interview, titled "We Are Seriously Concerned About the Fate of the State of Israel," can be found on the Global Policy Forum website, www.globalpolicy.org/security/issues/israel-palestine/2003/1118fate.htm.

112. For example, B'Tselem reported that "in July [2006], the Israeli military killed 163 Palestinians in the Gaza Strip, 78 of whom (48 percent) were not taking part in the hostilities when

they were killed. Thirty-six of the fatalities were minors, and 20 were women. In the West Bank, 15 Palestinians were killed by Israeli forces in July. The number of Palestinian fatalities in July was the highest in any month since April 2002." August 3, 2006, press release, www.btselem.org/english/Press_Releases/20060803.asp. Amnesty International reports that from June 27, 2006, the date the IDF moved back into Gaza, through the end of November 2006, Israeli forces "killed more than 400 Palestinians and injured more than 1500 others in the Gaza Strip, including many unarmed civilians. Some 80 of those killed were children and more than 300 children were injured. In the same period, two Israeli civilians were killed and some 20 were injured in the south of Israel by rockets fired by Palestinian armed groups from Gaza." "Road to Nowhere," 8–9.

113. Quoted in Rory McCarthy, "UN Condemns Massive Human Rights Abuses in Gaza Strip," *Guardian*, November 21, 2006. For descriptions of the pain that the IDF has inflicted on the Palestinians living in Gaza, see Amnesty International, "Road to Nowhere," 7–13; Gideon Levy, "Gaza's Darkness," *Ha'aretz*, September 3, 2006; and OCHA, "The Humanitarian Monitor."

114. Quoted in Bill Maxwell, "U.S. Should Reconsider Aid to Israel," *St. Petersburg Times* (online), December 16, 2001. Also see Ron Pundak, "From Oslo to Taba: What Went Wrong?" *Survival* 43, no. 3 (Autumn 2001): 37.

115. Indeed, had Israel lost the Six-Day War in 1967 and some Arab ruler kept its population subjugated in the same conditions that the Palestinians have endured, the Israelis would almost certainly have used terrorism against their oppressors, and some Jews in the diaspora almost certainly would have mobilized to aid them, just as Irish Americans and overseas Tamils have backed terrorist groups in their ancestral homelands.

116. Morris, *Righteous Victims*, 147, 201. Also see Lenni Brenner, *The Iron Wall: Zionist Revisionism from Jabotinsky to Shamir* (London: Zed Books, 1984), 100; and Yehoshua Porath, *The Palestinian Arab National Movement: From Riots to Rebellion*, Vol. 2, 1929–1939 (London: Frank Cass, 1977), 238. Morris notes that during the 1948 war, the main Jewish terrorist groups "knowingly planted bombs in bus stops with the aim of killing non-combatants, including women and children." *Birth Revisited*, 80.

117. J. Bowyer Bell, *Terror Out of Zion: The Fight for Israeli Independence 1929–1949* (New Brunswick, NJ: Transaction Publishers, 1996), 103–253; Johann Hari, "Israel Should Remember Its Own 'Terrorist' Origins," *Independent*, July 24, 2006; Joseph Heller, *The Stern Gang: Ideology, Politics and Terror, 1940–1949* (Portland, OR: Frank Cass, 1995); Bruce Hoffmann, *The Failure of British Military Strategy Within Palestine, 1939–1947* (Israel: Bar-Ilan University, 1983); Morris, *Righteous Victims*, 173–80; and Tom Segev, *One Palestine, Complete: Jews and Arabs Under the British Mandate*, trans. Haim Watzman (New York: Henry Holt, 2000), chap. 22. According to Haim Levenberg, 210 of the 429 casualties from Jewish terrorism in Palestine during 1946 were civilians. The other 219 were police and soldiers. See Levenberg, *Military Preparations*, 72.

118. Bell, *Terror Out of Zion*, 336–40.

119. Quoted in Chomsky, *Fateful Triangle*, 485–86; and Bell, *Terror Out of Zion*, 340. On Shamir, see Avishai Margalit, "The Violent Life of Yitzhak Shamir," *New York Review of Books*, May 14, 1992. Shamir also said that his "proudest achievement" was "when, thanks to our efforts, we were able to fully unite all the underground groups fighting for the liberation of Israel." See "Shamir: Lifetime of Activism."

120. Barzilai, "Brief History."

121. "Palestinian Authority," *New Republic* editorial, February 18, 2002, 7.

122. The most objective accounts of what happened at Camp David and in the subsequent six months include Charles Enderlin, *Shattered Dreams: The Failure of the Peace Process in the Middle East, 1995–2002*, trans. Susan Fairfield (New York: Other Press, 2003); Jeremy Pressman, "Visions in Collision: What Happened at Camp David and Taba?" *International Security* 28, no. 2 (Fall 2003); Pundak, "From Oslo to Taba"; Jerome Slater, "What Went

Wrong? The Collapse of the Israeli-Palestinian Peace Process," *Political Science Quarterly* 116, no. 2 (July 2001); Deborah Sontag, "Quest for Mideast Peace: How and Why It Failed," *New York Times*, July 26, 2001; and Swisher, *Truth About Camp David.*

123. The figures in this paragraph and the next one are drawn from Pressman, "Visions in Collision," 16–18. Barak's offer also included a 1 percent land swap outside the West Bank, so some commentators describe his offer as being 92 percent rather than 91 percent.

124. The original territory assigned to Britain in the treaties that ended World War I included the east and west banks of the Jordan River. But in 1922, Britain created Transjordan (which later became Jordan) on the east bank. Henceforth, the British Mandate in Palestine included the territory that today comprises Israel, the Gaza Strip, and the West Bank. When we refer to Mandate Palestine, we mean the post-1922 territories, of which Israel makes up 78 percent and the Occupied Territories 22 percent.

125. Describing a lengthy interview with Ehud Barak about what happened at Camp David, Benny Morris writes: "But in the West Bank, Barak says, the Palestinians were promised a continuous piece of sovereign territory except for a razor-thin Israeli wedge running from Jerusalem through from Maale Adumim to the Jordan River." Benny Morris, "Camp David and After: An Exchange (1. An Interview with Ehud Barak)," *New York Review of Books*, June 13, 2002, 44. Also see the map in Pundak, "From Oslo to Taba," 46. For the Palestinian version of what the map looked like, see Orient House (Jerusalem), "Israel's Concessions," *Le Monde Diplomatique*, December 2000; and the map titled "Palestinian Characterization of the Final Proposal at Camp David," in Dennis Ross, *The Missing Peace: The Inside Story of the Fight for Middle East Peace* (New York: Farrar, Straus and Giroux, 2004). Contrary to both Barak and the Palestinians, Ross claims that the final map at Camp David gave the Palestinians control over a continuous piece of territory in the West Bank. See "Map Reflecting Actual Proposal at Camp David," ibid. Ross's assertion is not plausible, however, as even Barak admits that an Israeli-controlled road connecting Jerusalem with the Jordan River Valley would have bisected the West Bank. As long as Israel controlled that strategically important valley, it would need to be able to reach it with at least one well-defended connector road. Whereas Barak envisioned one connector road running eastward from Jerusalem, the Palestinians apparently envisioned a second one running eastward from the Ariel settlement to the Jordan River Valley. One might argue that the Israelis would eventually abandon those connector roads when they surrendered the Jordan River Valley. As noted, however, there was no guarantee that the Israelis would ever leave that valley, and even if they did, there was no guarantee that they would abandon the connector roads. The main reason for this continuing confusion about what the final map at Camp David looked like is that no official map was ever drawn up and, "at Barak's insistence, no written records were kept." Jerome Slater, "The Missing Pieces in the Missing Peace," *Tikkun.org*, May/June 2005.

126. Pressman, "Visions in Collision," 18.

127. Enderlin, *Shattered Dreams*, 243–51; Slater, "What Went Wrong?"; and Sontag, "Quest for Mideast Peace."

128. Quoted in "Norman Finkelstein & Former Israeli Foreign Minister Shlomo Ben-Ami Debate: Complete Transcript," *Democracy Now!* radio and TV broadcast, February 14, 2006.

129. There is no evidence that Arafat started the First Intifada either. See Morris, *Righteous Victims*, 561. "The main energizing force of the Intifada," Morris writes, "was the frustration of the national aspirations of the 650,000 inhabitants of the Gaza Strip, 900,000 of the West Bank, and 130,000 of East Jerusalem, who wanted to live in a Palestinian state and not as stateless inhabitants under a brutal, foreign military occupation." Ibid., 562.

130. Enderlin, *Shattered Dreams*, 284–85.

131. Quoted in Jeremy Pressman, "The Second Intifada: Background and Causes of the Israeli-Palestinian Conflict," *Journal of Conflict Studies* 22, no. 2 (Fall 2003): 116. Also see Yezid Sayigh, "Arafat and the Anatomy of a Revolt," *Survival* 43, no. 3 (Autumn 2001); Henry Siegman, "Partners for War," *New York Review of Books*, January 16, 2003, 24; Henry Siegman,

"Sharon and the Future of Palestine," *New York Review of Books*, December 2, 2004, 12; and Slater, "Missing Pieces."

132. Sharm El-Sheikh Fact-Finding Committee, *Final Report*, April 30, 2001, 7.

133. Ibid., 5.

134. Ian S. Lustick, "Through Blood and Fire Shall Peace Arise," *Tikkun.org*, May/June 2002; Pressman, "The Second Intifada"; Mouin Rabbani, "A Smorgasbord of Failure: Oslo and the Al-Aqsa Intifada," in *The New Intifada: Resisting Israel's Apartheid*, ed. Roane Carey (London: Verso, 2001), 69–89; Sara Roy, "Why Peace Failed: An Oslo Autopsy," *Current History* 101, no. 651 (January 2002); and Sara Roy, "Ending the Palestinian Economy," *Middle East Policy* 9, no. 4 (December 2002).

135. Ben-Ami, *Scars of War*, 264.

136. Roy, "Why Peace Failed," 9.

137. Ron Dudai, "Trigger Happy: Unjustified Shooting and Violation of the Open-Fire Regulations During the al-Aqsa Intifada," B'Tselem draft report, March 2002.

138. Yasser Arafat, "The Palestinian Vision of Peace," *New York Times*, February 3, 2002; Yasser Arafat, text of press conference, Geneva, December 14, 1988, in *Journal of Palestine Studies* 18, no. 3 (Spring 1989): 180–81; "Palestinians Affirm Israel's Right to Exist," *CNN.com*, December 14, 1998; Pressman, "Visions in Collision," 24–27; Yezid Sayigh, *Armed Struggle and the Search for State: The Palestinian National Movement, 1949–1993* (New York: Oxford University Press, 1997); and Jerome M. Segal, *Creating the Palestinian State: A Strategy for Peace* (Chicago: Lawrence Hill Books, 1989), chap. 1. One might argue that Arafat's commitment to the right of return for the Palestinians reveals that he was still bent on destroying Israel. But Arafat surely recognized that Israeli leaders would never agree to a peace settlement that would allow large numbers of Palestinians to move back into Israel. At the same time, however, it made good sense for Arafat not to soften his position on right of return before the negotiations, so that he could use this issue as a bargaining chip. Not surprisingly, there is considerable evidence that Palestinian leaders (including Arafat before he died) recognize that they will have to make major concessions on this important issue to get a final agreement. See Akiva Eldar and David Landau, "Arafat: Israel Is Jewish; Won't Cite Figure on Refugees," *Ha'aretz*, June 18, 2004; Associated Press, "PA Minister Sha'ath: Palestinian Right of Return Is Negotiable," *Ha'aretz*, August 20, 2003; Pressman, "Visions in Collision," 28–33; and M. J. Rosenberg, "Intractable Issue?" Weekly Opinion Column, Issue #144, Israel Policy Forum, Washington, DC, July 18, 2003.

139. Akiva Eldar, "Popular Misconceptions," *Ha'aretz*, June 11, 2004; Akiva Eldar, "While They Were Sleeping," *Ha'aretz*, September 17, 2001; Danny Rubenstein, "The Stronger Side Creates Reality," *Ha'aretz*, June 16, 2004; and Emmanuel Sivan, "What the General Is Allowed," *Ha'aretz*, June 14, 2004.

140. Pressman, "Visions in Collision," 25.

141. "Official Palestinian Response to the Clinton Parameters (and letter to international community)," January 1, 2001, www.robat.scl.net/content/NAD/negotiations/clinton_parameters/param2.php.

142. "Excerpts: White House Spokesman on Clinton-Arafat Talks," issued by Press Section, U.S. embassy in Israel, January 3, 2001; Transcript of "Clinton Speech on Mideast Peace Parameters (January 7, 2001)," Office of the White House Press Secretary, January 8, 2001; and Enderlin, *Shattered Dreams*, 344. Also see Akiva Eldar, "The Battle for Public Opinion," *Ha'aretz*, June 24, 2002, and Pressman, "Visions in Collision," 20, both of which make clear that Israel also had serious reservations about the Clinton parameters.

143. Sontag, "Quest for Mideast Peace"; and Enderlin, *Shattered Dreams*, 349–50.

144. Jeff Jacoby, "America Takes Side of Israel," *Boston Globe*, March 26, 2006. Block is quoted in Tony Czuczka, "Under Fire, Israel Lobby Rallies US Backers," *EUX.TV: The Europe Channel* (online), March 10, 2007. Also see Mart, *Eye on Israel*; and Martin Peretz, "Oil and Vinegar: Surveying the Israel Lobby," *New Republic*, April 10, 2006.

145. According to the historian Michelle Mart, during the Cold War "Israelis became 'American-

ized,' " and this transformation was due in good part to a sense of "Judeo-Christian unity." "The Cultural Foundations of the US/Israel Alliance," *Tikkun.org*, November 11, 2006.

146. Jodie T. Allen and Alec Tyson, "The U.S. Public's Pro-Israel History," Pew Research Center, July 19, 2006; "Americans' Support for Israel Unchanged by Recent Hostilities," Pew Research Center press release, July 26, 2006; and Robert Ruby, "A Six-Day War: Its Aftermath in American Public Opinion," Pew Research Center, May 30, 2007.

147. Allen and Tyson, "The U.S. Public's Pro-Israel History"; Pew Research Center for the People and the Press in Association with the Council on Foreign Relations, "America's Place in the World 2005: An Investigation of the Attitudes of American Opinion Leaders and the American Public About International Affairs," November 2005, 11–12.

148. "Conspiracy Theories and Criticism of Israel in Aftermath of Sept. 11 Attacks," Anti-Defamation League press release, November 1, 2001.

149. Steven Kull (principal investigator), "Americans on the Middle East Road Map" (Program on International Policy Attitudes, University of Maryland, May 30, 2003), 9–11, 18–19.

150. "American Attitudes Toward Israel and the Middle East," survey conducted on March 18–25, 2005, and June 19–23, 2005, by the Marttila Communications Group for the Anti-Defamation League.

151. Andrew Kohut, "American Views of the Mideast Conflict," *New York Times*, May 14, 2002.

152. On Israeli responsibility for the second Lebanon war, see the ABC News–*Washington Post* poll conducted on August 3–6, 2006, and the CBS News–*New York Times* poll conducted on July 21–25, 2006, both of which can be found in "Israel, the Palestinians," *PollingReport.com*. Regarding the United States not taking sides, see the *USA Today*–Gallup poll, ibid.; and the Zogby poll taken August 11–15, 2006, the results of which are described in "Zogby Poll: U.S. Should Be Neutral in Lebanon War," Zogby International press release, August 17, 2006.

4: WHAT IS THE "ISRAEL LOBBY"?

1. Andrew C. Revkin, "Bush Aide Edited Climate Reports," *New York Times*, June 8, 2005; and Andrew C. Revkin and Matthew Wald, "Material Shows Weakening of Climate Reports in Hundreds of Instances," *New York Times*, March 20, 2007.

2. Important works on ethnic lobbies and their impact on foreign policy include Tony Smith, *Foreign Attachments: The Power of Ethnic Groups in the Making of American Foreign Policy* (Cambridge, MA: Harvard University Press, 2000); *Ethnicity and U.S. Foreign Policy*, 2nd ed., ed. A. A. Said (New York: Praeger, 1981); *Ethnic Groups and U.S. Foreign Policy*, ed. M. E. Ahrari (New York: Greenwood Press, 1987); Paul Watanabe, *Ethnic Groups, Congress, and American Foreign Policy: The Politics of the Turkish Arms Embargo* (Westport, CT: Greenwood Press, 1984); and R. Hrair Dekmejian and Angelos Themelis, "Ethnic Lobbies in U.S. Foreign Policy: A Comparative Analysis of the Jewish, Greek, Armenian and Turkish Lobbies," Occasional Research Paper no. 13, Institute of International Relations, Panteion University of Social and Political Sciences, Athens, Greece, October 1997.

3. This is a common problem in political analysis. For example, the concepts of "liberal" and "conservative" are well understood and uncontroversial, and it is easy to think of exemplars of each type (for instance, Senator Ted Kennedy for "liberal" and former Congressman Newt Gingrich for "conservative"). There are, however, individuals who are harder to classify, such as Senator Joseph Lieberman or the late Senator Henry "Scoop" Jackson, both of whom were liberal on domestic issues but conservative on foreign policy issues.

4. Melvin I. Urofsky, *American Zionism from Herzl to the Holocaust* (Garden City, NY: Anchor Press, 1975), 1; and Steven T. Rosenthal, "Long Distance Nationalism: American Jews, Zionism, and Israel," in *The Cambridge Companion to American Judaism*, ed. Dana Evan Kaplan (New York: Cambridge University Press, 2005), 209.

5. Robert H. Trice, "Domestic Interest Groups and the Arab-Israeli Conflict," in Said, *Ethnicity and U.S. Foreign Policy*, 121–22.

6. Steven M. Cohen, *The 2004 National Survey of American Jews*, sponsored by the Jewish

Agency for Israel's Department of Jewish-Zionist Education, February 24, 2005. Also see *2006 Annual Survey of American Jewish Opinion*, conducted September 25–October 16, 2006, American Jewish Committee, October 18, 2006; Steven M. Cohen, "Poll: Attachment of U.S. Jews to Israel Falls in Past 2 Years," *Forward*, March 4, 2005; and M. J. Rosenberg, "Letting Israel Sell Itself," Weekly Opinion Column, Issue #218, Israel Policy Forum, Washington, DC, March 18, 2005. A recent report prepared for the American Jewish Committee notes that "there is a consensus among several studies that Israel is not central to young people's Jewish identity." Jacob B. Ukeles et al., "Young Jewish Adults in the United States Today," American Jewish Committee, September 2006, 34. Also see Amiram Barkat, "Young American Jews Are More Ambivalent Toward Israel, Study Shows," *Ha'aretz*, March 7, 2005.

7. As the Joint Program Plan of the National Jewish Community Relations Advisory Council (NJCRAC), a major Jewish agency, put it in 1957, "The American public accepted the American Jewish concern about Israel . . . as a natural, normal manifestation of interest based on sympathies and emotional attachments of a sort that are common to many Americans." Quoted in Jack Wertheimer, "Jewish Organizational Life in the United States Since 1945," *American Jewish Yearbook 1995* (New York: American Jewish Committee, 1995), 13.

8. Rosenthal, "Long Distance Nationalism," 211; and Thomas A. Kolsky, *Jews Against Zionism: The American Council for Judaism, 1942–1948* (Philadelphia: Temple University Press, 1990).

9. The shift is nicely captured by the evolving position of the Central Conference of American Rabbis (CCAR), the rabbinical body of Reform Judaism. In 1897, CCAR declared that "we totally disapprove of any attempt for the establishment of a Jewish state. Such attempts show a misunderstanding of Israel's mission," and it did not endorse the Balfour Declaration in 1917. In 1967, by contrast, CCAR declared "its solidarity with the State and People of Israel. Their triumphs are our triumphs. Their ordeal is our ordeal. Their fate is our fate." Quoted in Chaim I. Waxman, "All in the Family: American Jewish Attachments to Israel," in *A New Jewry? America Since the Second World War*, Studies in Contemporary Jewry: An Annual, Vol. VIII, ed. Peter Y. Medding (New York: Oxford University Press for the Institute of Contemporary Jewry, Hebrew University, 1992), 140.

10. Rosenthal, "Long Distance Nationalism," 212.

11. Waxman, "All in the Family," 134. To note one example, the first item listed on the American Jewish Congress's statement of its core agenda is the "safety and security of Israel and the world Jewish community," www.ajcongress.org/site/PageServer?pagename=about. The situation is similar today; there are more than ninety separate groups identified as "Israel-related" in the 2005 edition of the yearbook.

12. "Who We Are" and "What We Do," Conference of Presidents website, www.conference ofpresidents.org/content.asp?id=52. The Conference of Presidents was created in 1954 in response to Assistant Secretary of State Henry Byroade's complaint that it was difficult for him to deal with the many separate Jewish organizations and it would be useful if they would speak with one voice. See Edward Tivnan, *The Lobby: Jewish Political Power and American Foreign Policy* (New York: Simon & Schuster, 1987), 40–41.

13. This figure omits personal contributions and thus understates the role of pro-Israel campaign contributions. See www.crp.org/pacs/industry.asp?txt=Q05&cycle=2006. On the general phenomenon of "stealth PACs," see Richard H. Curtiss, *Stealth PACs: Lobbying Congress for Control of U.S. Middle East Policy*, 4th ed. (Washington, DC: American Educational Trust, 1996).

14. Jeffrey H. Birnbaum, "Washington's Power 25," *Fortune*, December 8, 1997. AIPAC was ranked number four in a similar study conducted in 2001. See Jeffrey H. Birnbaum and Russell Newell, "Fat and Happy in D.C.," *Fortune*, May 28, 2001.

15. Richard E. Cohen and Peter Bell, "Congressional Insiders Poll," *National Journal*, March 5, 2005; and James D. Besser, "Most Muscle? It's NRA, Then AIPAC and AARP," *Chicago Jewish Star*, March 11–24, 2005.

16. Dymally is quoted in Robert Pear with Richard L. Berke, "Pro-Israel Group Exerts Quiet Might as It Rallies Supporters in Congress," *New York Times*, July 7, 1987; Hamilton is

quoted in George D. Moffett III, "Israeli Lobby Virtually Unmatched," *Christian Science Monitor*, June 28, 1991.

17. On the role played by Brandeis, Wise, and others, see Irvine Anderson, *Biblical Interpretation and Middle East Policy: The Promised Land, America and Israel, 1917–2002* (Gainesville: University Press of Florida, 2005), 61–62; and Peter Grose, *Israel in the Mind of America* (New York: Knopf, 1983), 67–71. Truman's former business partner Eddie Jacobson convinced him to meet with Chaim Weizmann in 1948, and pro-Zionist advisers such as David Niles and Clark Clifford helped convince Truman to support the 1947 partition plan and to recognize the new state in 1948. For different views on the various influences that shaped Truman's decisions, see Peter L. Hahn, *Caught in the Middle East: U.S. Policy Toward the Arab-Israeli Conflict, 1948–1961* (Chapel Hill: University of North Carolina Press, 2006), 26–31 and chaps. 2–3; Zvi Ganin, *Truman, American Jewry, and Israel, 1945–1948* (New York: Holmes and Meier, 1979); Steven L. Spiegel, *The Other Arab-Israel Conflict: Making America's Middle East Policy from Truman to Reagan* (Chicago: University of Chicago Press, 1985), chap. 2; Kenneth Ray Bain, *The March to Zion: United States Policy and the Founding of Israel* (College Station: Texas A & M Press, 1979); and Warren Bass, *Support Any Friend: Kennedy's Middle East and the Making of the U.S.-Israeli Alliance* (New York: Oxford University Press, 2003), 23–34.

18. Lloyd Grove, "The Men with Muscle: The AIPAC Leaders, Battling for Israel and Among Themselves," *Washington Post*, June 14, 1991.

19. J. J. Goldberg, *Jewish Power: Inside the American Jewish Establishment* (New York: Basic Books, 1996), 158.

20. Stuart Eizenstat, "Loving Israel, Warts and All," *Foreign Policy* 81 (Winter 1990–91): 92.

21. Ibid.; and Melvin I. Urofsky, *We Are One! American Jewry and Israel* (Garden City, NY: Doubleday, 1978).

22. As Jack Wertheimer puts it, "There is little doubt that the preoccupations and mood of the organized Jewish community underwent profound changes in the wake of the Six Day War . . . American Jewry fully identified with Israel, an identification that galvanized the community to unprecedented amounts of philanthropic giving and volunteering." See "Jewish Organizational Life," 32; and Menahem Kaufman, "Envisaging Israel: The Case of the United Jewish Appeal," in *Envisioning Israel: The Changing Ideals and Images of North American Jews*, ed. Allon Gal (Jerusalem: Magnes Press/Hebrew University, 1996), 232–34.

23. Wertheimer, "Jewish Organizational Life," 32–33.

24. Ibid., 55.

25. Quoted in Wolf Blitzer, "The AIPAC Formula," *Moment*, November 1981, 23.

26. AIPAC does not disclose its annual budget; the numbers reported here are from Blitzer, "AIPAC Formula," 23; Lloyd Grove, "On the March for Israel; The Lobbyists from AIPAC, Girding for Battle in the New World Order," *Washington Post*, June 13, 1991; Jeffrey H. Birnbaum, "Pro-Israel Lobby Holds Meeting Amid Worries," *Washington Post*, May 19, 2005; Thomas B. Edsall and Molly Moore, "Pro-Israel Lobby Has Strong Voice," *Washington Post*, September 5, 2004; and James Petras, "AIPAC on Trial," *CounterPunch.org*, January 7–8, 2006.

27. Quoted in Goldberg, *Jewish Power*, 223.

28. Bass, *Support Any Friend*, 147. Also see Goldberg, *Jewish Power*, 197–203.

29. Goldberg, "Old Friend, Shattered Dreams," *Forward*, December 24, 2004; Esther Kaplan, "The Jewish Divide on Israel," *Nation*, July 12, 2004; Michael Massing, "Conservative Jewish Groups Have Clout," *Los Angeles Times*, March 10, 2002; Eric Yoffie, "Reform the Conference," *Forward*, August 2, 2002; and William Fisher, "U.S. Jewish Groups Press Mideast Peace," *Antiwar.com*, November 25, 2004.

30. Daniel Levy, "Is It Good for the Jews?" *American Prospect*, July 5, 2006.

31. Quoted in Sharon Samber, "Congress Urged Not to Link Israel Aid to China Arms," *JTA.org*, June 13, 2000.

32. See, for example, Americans for Peace Now, "Briefing for the 110th Congress: Securing Israel's

Future Through Peace," 8, www.donteverstop.com/files/apn/upl/assets/APN110thBBook.pdf.

33. According to the IPF website, "Israel Policy Forum believes that through a two-state solution to the Israeli-Palestinian conflict, Israel and its Arab neighbors, as well as the region as a whole, will become more secure, prosperous and stable." See www.ipforum.org/display.cfm?id=1.

34. Jewish Voice for Peace, "U.S. Military Aid to Israel," www.jewishvoiceforpeace/org/publish/printer_17.shtml.

35. Quoted in Tivnan, *The Lobby*, 93.

36. Quoted in Goldberg, *Jewish Power*, 206.

37. Ori Nir, "FBI Probe: More Questions Than Answers," *Forward*, May 13, 2005; Bookbinder is quoted in Wolf Blitzer, *Between Washington and Jerusalem: A Reporter's Notebook* (New York: Oxford University Press, 1985), 148.

38. On these incidents, see Hahn, *Caught in the Middle East*, 39–42, 46–51, 57–59, 79–82.

39. These activities (and the quoted Israeli communications) are described in Tom Segev, *1967: Israel, the War, and the Year That Transformed the Middle East*, trans. Jessica Cohen (New York: Metropolitan Books, 2007), 254, 264–65, 304–305.

40. Quoted in David Landau, "The Battle for Washington," *Ha'aretz*, March 28, 2003.

41. Jonathan Marcus, "Discordant Voices: The U.S. Jewish Community and Israel During the 1980s," *International Affairs* 66, no. 3 (July 1990): 546. Also see Sarah Bronson, "Orthodox Leader: U.S. Jews Have No Right to Criticize Israel," *Ha'aretz*, August 2, 2004; and Daniel Ben Simon, "Storm Warnings," *Ha'aretz*, November 14, 2003.

42. Rosenthal, "Long Distance Nationalism," 214; Bookbinder is quoted in Blitzer, *Between Washington and Jerusalem*, 147–48. Writing in the 1980s, the historian David Biale observed, "The ideological hegemony that Zionism achieved in the organized Jewish community in the last two decades has had the effect of stilling debate about many of the specific policies of the Israeli government." *Power and Powerlessness in Jewish History* (New York: Schocken Books, 1986), 189.

43. *2004 Survey of American Jewish Opinion*, conducted August 18–September 1, 2004, American Jewish Committee, September 21, 2004, question 16. Earlier surveys produced nearly identical results.

44. This account of Breira's brief history is based on Michael E. Staub, *Torn at the Roots: The Crisis of Jewish Liberalism in Postwar America* (New York: Columbia University Press, 2002), chap. 8; Tivnan, *The Lobby*, 90–96; Wertheimer, "Jewish Organizational Life," 39–43; and Goldberg, *Jewish Power*, 207–208.

45. Goldberg, *Jewish Power*, 208.

46. Tivnan, *The Lobby*, 76. David Biale offered a similar view in 1986, writing, "For the organized Jewish community, lack of support for Israel is tantamount to treason . . . Israel is the one issue over which lack of belief is treated as heresy." *Power and Powerlessness*, 188.

47. American Jewish leaders were openly upset when Prime Minister Yitzhak Shamir briefly backed a proposal to amend the Law of Return to require conversions to Judaism be conducted by Orthodox rabbis according to halakha (rabbinical law). As Rabbi Eric Yoffie of the American Reform movement put it, "If Reform rabbis in Israel are not rabbis and their conversions are not conversions, that means our Judaism is not Judaism, and that we are second-class Jews." Quoted in Rosenthal, "Long Distance Nationalism," 218. Also see Goldberg, *Jewish Power*, 337–42.

48. Lawrence Grossman, "Jewish Communal Affairs," *American Jewish Yearbook 1998* (New York: American Jewish Committee, 1998), 110–11; Tom Tugend, "Talk by N.Y. Times' Friedman Spurs ADL-ZOA Political Fuss," *JTA.org*, December 6, 1996; and Tom Tugend, "N.Y. Times Columnist Applauds ADL for Not Caving in to ZOA," *JTA.org*, December 13, 1996.

49. Inigo Gilmore, "U.S. Jewish Leader Hit over Letter," *Sunday Telegraph* (London), August 12, 2003; and Isi Liebler, "An Open Letter to Edgar Bronfman," *Jerusalem Post*, August 6, 2003.

50. These quotations are from Isi Liebler, "When Seymour Met Condi," *Jerusalem Post*, November

24, 2005; Ori Nir, "O.U. Chief Decries American Pressure on Israel," *Forward*, December 2, 2005; Ori Nir, "Rice Trip Raises Concern over U.S. Pressure on Israel," *Forward*, November 18, 2005; and Seymour D. Reich, "Listen to America," *Jerusalem Post*, November 13, 2005.

51. The author of the Americans for a Safe Israel pamphlet attacking Breira, Rael Jean Isaac, wrote a similar polemic against New Jewish Agenda, and the head of the ZOA's Washington chapter denounced the same group as "pro-Arab rather than pro-Israel." Hampered by recurring budget deficits and other challenges, New Jewish Agenda folded in 1992, after twelve years of tenuous existence. See Jack Wertheimer, "Breaking the Taboo: Critics of Israel and the American Jewish Establishment," in Gal, *Envisioning Israel*, 410–11; and Emily Nepon, "New Jewish Agenda: The History of an Organization, 1980–1992" (B.A. thesis, Goddard College, 2006), available at www.newjewishagenda.org.

52. The material in this paragraph is based on Kaplan, "Jewish Divide on Israel." In two other similar incidents, the Hillel program directors at the University of California at Santa Cruz and Ithaca College reportedly resigned after being reprimanded for publishing articles supporting Israeli and Palestinian opposition to the occupation.

53. Ari Paul, "Zionist vs. Zionist," *American Prospect*, January 4, 2007; Rebecca Spence, "Campus Coalition Split over Progressive Union," *Forward*, January 19, 2007; Rebecca Spence, "Groups Flip Flop as Controversy over Liberal Zionists Continues," *Forward*, February 2, 2007; Ben Harris, "Group That Criticized Israel to Stay in Campus Coalition Despite Protests," *JTA.org*, January 24, 2007; "L.A. Israeli Consul General to Foreign Ministry: UPZ and Breaking the Silence Programs Harm Israel's Image and Must Be Stopped," Zionist Organization of America press release, January 31, 2007, www.zoa.org/2007/01/la_israeli_cons.htm.

54. When asked, "In the current situation, do you favor or oppose the establishment of a Palestinian state?" the percentage of American Jews responding "in favor" was 54 percent in 2006, 56 percent in 2005, and 57 percent in 2004. "Annual Survey of American Jewish Opinion," 2006, 2005, and 2004, available at www.ajc.org.

55. Goldberg, *Jewish Power*, 161.

56. Ibid., 217. Also see 159–62, 170–75, 216–23. Also see Eric Alterman, "AIPAC Runs Right," *Nation*, October 10, 2006; Goldberg, "Old Friends"; Massing, "Conservative Jewish Groups"; Rosenthal, "Long Distance Nationalism," 217; and Mark Seal, "Sitting on the Sidelines," *Ha'aretz*, December 24, 2004.

57. In particular, Hoenlein served for a number of years as chairman of an annual dinner to raise funds to support Bet El, a militant Israeli settlement near Ramallah. See Michael Massing, "Deal Breakers," *American Prospect*, March 11, 2002; and Michael Massing, "The Israel Lobby," *Nation*, June 10, 2002.

58. Massing, "Deal Breakers." J. J. Goldberg offers a similar analysis, writing that "under [Tom] Dine, the ruling executive committee tripled in size. Formerly, the committee had been controlled by the heads of the New York–based national Jewish organizations. Now the Jewish community leaders were a minority, outnumbered by AIPAC's own contributors. Swelling the executive committee . . . removed the lobby from the national Jewish communal structure, such as it was, and placed it firmly in the hands of a few big donors whose only loyalty was to AIPAC." *Jewish Power*, 201.

59. Michael Massing, "The Storm over the Israel Lobby," *New York Review of Books*, June 8, 2006; and Matthew Dorf, "After Barak Win, AIPAC Reverses Opposition to a Palestinian State," *JTA.org*, May 28, 1999.

60. This episode is recounted in Goldberg, *Jewish Power*, 54–57.

61. Massing, "Deal Breakers"; and Levy, "Is It Good for the Jews?"

62. Peter Beinart and Hanna Rosin, "AIPAC Unpacked," *New Republic*, September 20, 1993, 20–23; and Goldberg, *Jewish Power*, 225–26.

63. Waxman, "All in the Family," 143–44.

64. Jonathan Woocher, "The Geo-Politics of the American Jewish Community," *Jerusalem Letter/Viewpoints* (online), Jerusalem Center for Public Affairs, January 15, 1992, 3.

65. Thomas L. Friedman, "Foreign Affairs: Mischief Makers," *New York Times*, April 5, 1995.

66. As Massing points out, the Israel Policy Forum has "managed to forge close ties with many influential members of Congress, but lacking a formal membership and strong fundraising apparatus, it cannot match the influence of AIPAC and the Conference." Massing, "Deal Breakers."

67. Among the best works on neoconservatism are Gary Dorrien, *The Neoconservative Mind: Politics, Culture, and the War of Ideology* (Philadelphia: Temple University Press, 1993); Gary Dorrien, *Imperial Designs: Neoconservatism and the New Pax Americana* (New York: Routledge, 2004); John Ehrman, *The Rise of Neoconservatism: Intellectuals and Foreign Affairs, 1945–1994* (New Haven: Yale University Press, 2005); Murray Friedman, *The Neoconservative Revolution: Jewish Intellectuals and the Shaping of Public Policy* (New York: Cambridge University Press, 2005); Francis Fukuyama, *America at the Crossroads: Democracy, Power, and the Neoconservative Legacy* (New Haven: Yale University Press, 2006); Mark Gerson, *The Neoconservative Vision: From the Cold Wars to the Culture Wars* (Lanham, MD: Madison Books, 1996); Goldberg, *Jewish Power*, 159–61; Stefan Halper and Jonathan Clarke, *America Alone: The Neoconservatives and the Global Order* (New York: Cambridge University Press, 2004); and Irving Kristol, *Neoconservatism: The Autobiography of an Idea* (New York: Free Press, 1995).

68. For an overview of neoconservative thinking about U.S. foreign policy, see John J. Mearsheimer, "Hans Morgenthau and the Iraq War: Realism Versus Neo-Conservatism," posted May 19, 2005, opendemocracy.com. An illustrative collection of neoconservative writings on foreign policy is *Present Dangers: Crisis and Opportunity in American Foreign and Defense Policy*, ed. William Kristol and Robert Kagan (San Francisco: Encounter Books, 2000); a perceptive portrait of the neoconservatives and their views on foreign policy is Ian Lustick, *Trapped in the War on Terror* (Philadelphia: University of Pennsylvania Press, 2006), chap. 4.

69. For a typical neoconservative statement about multilateralism and institutions, see Charles Krauthammer, "Democratic Realism: An American Foreign Policy for a Unipolar World," 2004 Irving Kristol Lecture, American Enterprise Institute, Washington, DC, February 10, 2004, 3. The neoconservative view of Europe is exemplified by Robert Kagan, *Of Paradise and Power: America and Europe in the New World Order* (New York: Knopf, 2003).

70. For a discussion of bandwagoning, see Stephen M. Walt, *The Origins of Alliances* (Ithaca, NY: Cornell University Press, 1987).

71. Max Boot, "What the Heck Is a 'Neocon'?" *Wall Street Journal*, December 30, 2002; and Max Boot, "Think Again: Neocons," *Foreign Policy* 140 (January–February 2004), 22. Also see Don Atapattu, "Interview with Middle East Scholar Avi Shlaim," *Nation*, June 16, 2004; Halper and Clarke, *America Alone*, 41, 58–60, 82, 167–68; Irving Kristol, "The Political Dilemma of American Jews," *Commentary*, July 1984, 23–29; and Jim Lobe, "Energized Neocons Say Israel's Fight Is Washington's," *Antiwar.com*, July 18, 2006.

72. Benjamin Ginsberg, *The Fatal Embrace: Jews and the State* (Chicago: University of Chicago Press, 1993), 231.

73. "A Clean Break: A New Strategy for Securing the Realm," prepared by the Institute for Advanced Strategic and Political Studies, 1996, www.iasps.org/strat1.htm. The study group that produced this report was chaired by Richard Perle, and its other members were James Colbert, Charles Fairbanks Jr., Douglas Feith, Robert Loewenberg, Jonathan Torop, David Wurmser, and Meyrav Wurmser.

74. Quoted in Dorrien, *Neoconservative Mind*, 344. Also see ibid., 343–45; Ginsberg, *Fatal Embrace*, 231–36; and John B. Judis, "The Conservative Wars," *New Republic*, August 11 and 18, 1986.

75. Patrick J. Buchanan, "Whose War?" *American Conservative*, March 24, 2003; and Paul Craig Roberts, "Neocon Treason," *Antiwar.com*, August 24, 2004.

76. Friedman, *Neoconservative Revolution*, i. Gal Beckerman noted that "acknowledging the Jewishness of neoconservatism has always triggered the red, flashing lights of anti-Semitism . . . But there is some truth to the suspicion. If there is an intellectual movement in America to

whose invention Jews can lay sole claim, neoconservatism is it." See "The Neoconservative Persuasion," *Forward*, January 6, 2006.

77. Max Blumenthal, "Born-Agains for Sharon," *Salon.com*, October 30, 2004; Darrell L. Bock, "Some Christians See a 'Road Map' to End Times," *Los Angeles Times*, June 18, 2003; Nathan Guttman, "Wiping Out Terror, Bringing on Redemption," *Ha'aretz*, April 29, 2002; Tom Hamburger and Jim VandeHei, "Chosen People: How Israel Became a Favorite Cause of Christian Right," *Wall Street Journal*, May 23, 2002; and Paul Nussbaum, "Israel Finds an Ally in American Evangelicals," *Philadelphia Inquirer* (online), November 13, 2005.

78. On how Christian beliefs influenced Balfour, see Anderson, *Biblical Interpretation*, 60–62. Some writers suggest that Christian beliefs also influenced Wilson's endorsement of the Balfour Declaration and Truman's support for Israel's creation, although neither was a dispensationalist. Ibid., 87–89; and Grose, *Israel in the Mind of America*, 67–71.

79. Timothy P. Weber, *On the Road to Armageddon: How Evangelicals Became Israel's Best Friend* (Grand Rapids, MI: Baker Academic, 2004), 188–96.

80. Weber, *On the Road to Armageddon*, 184. As Colin Shindler notes, "The growth of the Christian Right during the 1970s thus paralleled the growth of the Israeli Right—and both phenomena had been catalyzed by the Six Day War." See "Likud and the Christian Dispensationalists: A Symbiotic Relationship," *Israel Studies* 5, no. 1 (Spring 2000): 163.

81. As L. Nelson Bell wrote in *Christianity Today*, "That for the first time in more than 2,000 years Jerusalem is now completely in the hands of the Jews gives a student of the Bible a thrill and a renewed faith in the accuracy and validity of the Bible." Quoted in Weber, *On the Road to Armageddon*, 184.

82. Quoted in Jane Lampman, "Mixing Prophecy and Politics," *Christian Science Monitor*, July 7, 2004.

83. Daniel Pipes, "[Christian Zionism]: Israel's Best Weapon," *New York Post* (online), July 15, 2003; and Michael Freund, "Christian Zionists Key to Continued U.S. Support for Israel," *Jewish Press* (online), December 27, 2006.

84. Hagee quoted in Bill Berkowitz, "Pastor John Hagee Spearheads Christians United for Israel," *Media Transparency*, March 19, 2006, www.mediatransparency.org/story.php?storyID=116.

85. The quoted statements are from the IFCJ website, www.ifcj.org.

86. "The Apple of HIS Eye: Why Christians SHOULD Support Israel," John Hagee Ministries website, www.jhm.org/print-Israel.asp; and Andrew Higgins, "A Texas Preacher Leads Campaign to Let Israel Fight," *Wall Street Journal*, July 27, 2006.

87. "Zion's Christian Soldiers," *60 Minutes*, June 8, 2003, www.cbsnews.com/stories/2002/10/03/60minutes/printable524268/shtml.

88. Quoted in Lampman, "Mixing Prophecy and Politics."

89. Weber, *On the Road to Armageddon*, 226–27; Brent Boyer, "Arvada Church Champions Israeli Cause," *Denver Post* (online), November 22, 2002; and Danielle Haas, "U.S. Christians Find Cause to Aid Israel; Evangelicals Financing Immigrants, Settlements," *San Francisco Chronicle* (online), July 10, 2002.

90. Donald Wagner, "For Zion's Sake," *Middle East Report Online* 223 (Summer 2002): 55.

91. Quoted in Shindler, "Likud and the Christian Dispensationalists," 175.

92. "Robertson: God Punished Sharon," *Ynetnews.com*, January 6, 2006; "Robertson Suggests Stroke Is Divine Rebuke," *New York Times*, January 6, 2006; and "Robertson Apologizes to Sharon Family," *New York Times*, January 13, 2006.

93. Quoted in Barbara Slavin, "Don't Give Up 1967 Lands, DeLay Tells Israel Lobby," *USA Today*, April 23, 2002.

94. Matthews asked Armey to confirm that this was his view and Armey said "yes." Armey later backed away from his statement after being criticized for favoring ethnic cleansing of the Palestinians in the West Bank. See Matthew Engel, "Senior Republican Calls on Israel to Expel West Bank Arabs," *Guardian*, May 4, 2002; and "Richard Armey Supports Ethnic Cleansing of Palestinians," *Media Monitors Network*, May 2, 2002, www.mediamonitors.net/amr115.html.

95. "Peace in the Middle East," floor statement of Senator Inhofe, March 4, 2002, http://inhofe.senate.gov/pressapp/record.cfm?id=183110.

96. Shindler, "Likud and the Christian Dispensationalists," 156.

97. Grace Halsell, *Prophecy and Politics: Militant Evangelists on the Road to Nuclear War* (Westport, CT: Lawrence Hill, 1986), 71–76.

98. "Pat Robertson Forms Alliance with Mayor of Jerusalem," *Baptist Standard* (online), November 11, 2002; and "Israel Welcomes Christian Support in Battle for Survival, Sharon Aid[e] Says," *Christian Examiner* (online), September 6, 2002.

99. Quoted in Weber, *On the Road to Armageddon*, 214–18.

100. Quoted in Norton Mezvinsky, "The Impact of Christian Zionism on the Arab-Israeli Conflict," *NthPosition.com*, March 2005.

101. Jerry Falwell, "On the Threshold of Armageddon," *WorldNetDaily.com*, July 22, 2006; and Sarah Posner, "Lobbying for Armageddon," *AlterNet.org*, August 3, 2006.

102. Hal Lindsey, "Mushrooms over the Middle East," *WorldNetDaily.com*, January 12, 2007; and John Hagee, *Jerusalem Countdown: A Warning to the World* (Lake Mary, FL: Frontline, 2006), 17. Based on his own interpretation of scattered biblical passages, Hagee says that a strike on Iran will provoke Russia to lead an Arab coalition to war against Israel, which will be abandoned by the United States. God will then intervene to destroy Israel's invaders, but the resulting vacuum will be filled by the Antichrist, "who will be the head of the European Union." Under his command, the armies of the West gather in Israel to wage the battle of Armageddon against the "king of the East" (China), at which point Christ reappears to strike down the Antichrist and restore God's kingdom. Hagee concludes, "The end of the world as we know it is rapidly approaching" (113–22).

103. Christians United for Israel, "CUFI Membership Weekly Update," December 11, 2006, www.cufima.com/id10.html.

104. Shindler, "Likud and the Dispensationalists," 165–66; and Kristol, "The Political Dilemma of American Jews."

105. Perlmutter is quoted in Weber, *On the Road to Armageddon*, 232; Foxman's remarks are from "Jews and Evangelicals: Support for Israel Isn't Everything," *Time*, January 16, 2007.

106. Quoted in Bill Broadway, "The Evangelical-Israeli Connection: Scripture Inspires Many Christians to Support Zionism Politically, Financially," *Washington Post*, March 27, 2004.

107. For Hagee's disturbing attitudes toward Jews, see *Jerusalem Countdown*, 56–57, 109. On his appearance at the AIPAC Policy Conference, see Gregory Levey, "Inside America's Powerful Israel Lobby," *Salon.com*, March 16, 2007; "Christians for Israel," *Jerusalem Post* editorial, March 14, 2007; and Sarah Posner, "The Goy Who Cried Wolf," *American Prospect*, March 12, 2007.

108. Quoted in James D. Besser, "Hardline Pastor Gets Prime AIPAC Spot," *Jewish Week*, March 9, 2007.

109. Naomi M. Cohen, "Dual Loyalties: Zionism and Liberalism," in Gal, *Envisioning Israel*, 326.

110. Jo-Ann Mort, "An Unholy Alliance in Support of Israel," *Los Angeles Times*, May 19, 2002. The Alpher and Gorenberg quotations are from "Zion's Christian Soldiers." Also see Gershom Gorenberg, *The End of Days: Fundamentalism and the Struggle for the Temple Mount* (New York: Free Press, 2000); and Weber, *On the Road to Armageddon*, 231.

111. Tourism declined after the outbreak of the Second Intifada and September 11 but has rebounded since then. The United Nations Statistical Division estimates that Israel received $2.8 billion in tourism receipts in 2004, and Israeli officials report that approximately 29 percent of these tourists were Christian. See United Nations, *World Tourism Organization Statistical Database and Yearbook 2005* (New York: United Nations, 2005); Eric Silver, "Return of the Tourist," *Jerusalem Report* (online), February 21, 2005; Laurie Copans, "Israel: Tourism Surges as Christian Pilgrims Walk in the Footsteps of Jesus," *USA Today*, December 13, 2004; and William A. Orme, "Fighting in Mideast Blocks Wave of Christian Tourism," *New York Times*, November 11, 2000.

112. Anderson, *Biblical Interpretation*, 103, 138. This is also a central theme of Michael B. Oren's *Power, Faith and Fantasy: America in the Middle East 1776 to the Present* (New York: Norton, 2007), though he overstates its impact on U.S. policy decisions.

113. Anderson, *Biblical Interpretation*, 111, 114–15; and Ruth W. Mouly, *The Religious Right and Israel: The Politics of Armageddon* (Cambridge, MA: Political Research Associates, 1985).

114. Zev Chafets, "The Rabbi Who Loved Evangelicals (and Vice Versa)," *New York Times Magazine*, July 24, 2005.

115. In August 2006, the Vatican's envoy in the Holy Land and the bishops of the Episcopal, Evangelical Lutheran, and Syrian Orthodox churches in Jerusalem signed a declaration rejecting the teachings of Christian Zionism and accusing the movement of encouraging "racial exclusivity and perpetual war." See Matthew Tostevin, "Holy Land Churches Attack Christian Zionism," Reuters, August 31, 2006. A number of other mainstream Protestant churches have been critical of Israeli policy and have seriously considered "selective divestiture" from companies operating in Israel. The lobby, however, has worked hard to thwart these efforts and has been largely successful. See James D. Besser, "Church Poised to Kill Divestment," *Jewish Week*, June 23, 2006; Alan Cooperman, "Israel Divestiture Spurs Clash," *Washington Post*, September 29, 2004; Michael Conlon, "US Presbyterians Consider Divesting over West Bank," *Washington Post*, February 17, 2005; Laurie Goodstein, "Presbyterians Revise Israel Investing Policy," *New York Times*, June 22, 2006; Nathan Guttman, "A Warning Signal from the Churches," *Ha'aretz*, November 26, 2004; Chris Moore, "Mainline Protestants Challenge Israel Lobby," *Antiwar.com*, December 7, 2004; Marc Perelman, "Effort Eyed to Combat Divestment," *Forward*, July 15, 2006; and Rachel Pomerance, "Episcopal View on Mideast Conflict an Improvement, Jewish Groups Say," *JTA.org*, November 9, 2004.

116. The limited financial role of Christian Zionism is illustrated by relative donations to Israel following the 2006 war in Lebanon. According to *Ha'aretz*, Christian groups donated nearly $20 million to reconstruction and resettlement efforts in Israel; by comparison, the United Jewish Communities collected more than $340 million. See Daphna Berman, "Christians' Wartime Donations of $20m Went Largely Unheralded," *Ha'aretz*, November 3, 2006.

117. On the role of interest groups in American politics, see Frank R. Baumgartner and Beth L. Leech, *Basic Interests: The Importance of Groups in Politics and in Political Science* (Princeton: Princeton University Press, 1998); Richard L. Hall and Frank W. Wayman, "Buying Time: Moneyed Interests and the Mobilization of Bias in Congressional Committees," *American Political Science Review* 84, no. 3 (September 1990); John Mark Hansen, *Gaining Access: Congress and the Farm Lobby, 1919–1981* (Chicago: University of Chicago Press, 1991); Ken Kollman, *Outside Lobbying: Public Opinion and Interest Group Strategies* (Princeton: Princeton University Press, 1998); Richard A. Smith, "Interest Group Influence in the U.S. Congress," *Legislative Studies Quarterly* 20, no. 1 (February, 1995); David B. Truman, *The Governmental Process: Political Interests and Public Opinion* (New York: Knopf, 1951); and James Q. Wilson, *Political Organizations* (New York: Basic Books, 1973).

118. Quoted in Mary A. Barberis, "The Arab-Israeli Battle on Capitol Hill," *Virginia Quarterly Review* 52, no. 2 (Spring 1976): 209.

119. Trice, "Domestic Interest Groups," 125–26.

120. Quoted in Ben Bradlee Jr., "Israel's Lobby," *Boston Globe*, April 29, 1984.

121. Shai Feldman, *The Future of U.S.-Israeli Strategic Cooperation* (Washington, DC: Washington Institute for Near East Policy, 1996), 5–6.

122. Quoted in Grove, "On the March for Israel."

123. The Bard and Truman quotations are from Mitchell Bard, "The Israeli and Arab Lobbies," www.jewishvirtuallibrary.org. Also see Mark N. Katz, "Where Is the Arab Lobby?" *Middle East Times* (online), July 3, 2006; Noam N. Levey, "In Politicians' Pro Israel Din, Arab Americans Go Unheard," *Los Angeles Times*, July 23, 2006; Ali A. Mazrui, "Between the Crescent and the Star-Spangled Banner: American Muslims and U.S. Foreign Policy," *International*

Affairs 72, no. 3 (July 1996); Nabeel A. Khoury, "The Arab Lobby: Problems and Prospects," *Middle East Journal* 41, no. 3 (Summer 1987); and Andrea Barron, "Jewish and Arab Diasporas in the United States and Their Impact on U.S. Middle East Policy," in *The Arab-Israeli Conflict: Two Decades of Change*, ed. Yehuda Lukacs and Abdalla M. Battah (Boulder, CO: Westview, 1988), 238–59. The weakness of the "Palestinian lobby" in particular is captured in Nora Boustany, "Palestinians' Lone Hand in Washington," *Washington Post*, April 19, 2002; and George Gedda, "PLO Loses D.C. Office Because of Unpaid Rent," *Chicago Tribune*, April 12, 2002.

124. Trice, "Domestic Interest Groups," 123.

125. For a typical example, see Harold Siddiqui, "'Oil Lobby Determined to Have Its War' in Iraq," *Toronto Star* (online), January 19, 2003, www.commondreams.org.

126. Stephen Zunes, "The Israel Lobby: How Powerful Is It Really?" *Foreign Policy in Focus Special Report*, May 16, 2006; Noam Chomsky, "The Israel Lobby," *Znet* (online), March 28, 2006; and Martin Peretz, "Oil and Vinegar," *New Republic*, March 30, 2006.

127. See especially Craig Unger, *House of Bush, House of Saud: The Secret Relationship Between the World's Two Most Powerful Dynasties* (New York: Scribner, 2004). This theme was also a key part of Michael Moore's controversial documentary *Fahrenheit 9/11*.

128. In 2006, roughly 40 percent of U.S. crude oil imports came from Canada, Mexico, and Venezuela; Saudi Arabia provided only 14 percent. U.S. Department of Energy, *Petroleum Supply Monthly* (Washington, DC, February 2007), 58.

129. Bernard Gwertzman, "U.S. Said to Drop Jordan Arms Sale," *New York Times*, March 21, 1984.

130. Quoted in Congressional Quarterly, *The Middle East*, 68.

131. Trice, "Domestic Interest Groups," 137–38.

132. See www.api.org/policy. Foregn policy discussions are equally scarce on the ExxonMobil and British Petroleum websites.

133. Quoted in Tivnan, *The Lobby*, 194.

134. Trice, "Domestic Interest Groups," 137; and William B. Quandt, "United States Policy in the Middle East: Constraints and Choices," in *Political Dynamics in the Middle East*, ed. Paul Hammond and Sidney Alexander (New York: Elsevier, 1972), 529–30.

135. Danny Fortson, Andrew Murray-Watson, and Tim Webb, "Future of Iraq: The Spoils of War," *Independent*, January 7, 2007.

136. "Cheney Pushed for More Trade with Iran," *FOXnews.com*, October 9, 2004, www.foxnews.com/story/0,2933,134836,00.html.

137. Trice, "Domestic Interest Groups," 137–38.

138. These quotations are from Roger Hilsman, *The Politics of Policy Making in Defense and Foreign Affairs* (New York: Harper, 1971), 149; Bard, "Israeli and Arab Lobbies"; and "Pro-Israel Lobby on Capitol Hill," *BBC Newsnight* (online), May 8, 2003, http://news.bbc.co.uk/1/hi/programmes/newsnight/3010371.stm.

139. "In liberal democratic regimes," writes Sheffer, "most notably the United States, Canada, Australia, Denmark, Holland, and Norway, the Jews were able to maintain open and intensive relationships with the Jewish community in Palestine and later with Israel . . . Certain segments in those communities . . . demonstrated total loyalty to their host societies and governments . . . Those who openly identified as supporters of the Zionist movement and of the Jewish community in Palestine (the Yishuv) and later of Israel developed dual loyalties. The most resolute Zionists and other supporters of Israel adopted the divided-loyalties stance; that is, in certain respects they were loyal to their host countries, and other respects to the homeland." *Diaspora Politics: At Home Abroad* (New York: Cambridge University Press, 2003), 232–33.

140. Malcolm Hoenlein, "Crossing the Line of the Acceptable," *Ha'aretz*, December 31, 2004.

141. Pew Global Attitudes Project, "Muslims in Europe: Economic Worries Top Concerns About Religious and Cultural Identity" (Washington, DC: Pew Research Center for the People and the Press, July 6, 2006), 3.

142. Quoted in David K. Shipler, "On Middle East Policy, a Major Influence," *New York Times*, July 6, 1987.
143. Quoted in Kurt Eichenwald, "U.S. Jews Split on Washington's Shift on Palestinian State," *New York Times*, October 5, 2001.
144. David S. Cloud and Helene Cooper, "Israel's Protests Are Said to Stall Gulf Arms Sale," *New York Times*, April 5, 2007.
145. Henry Kissinger, *Years of Upheaval* (Boston: Little, Brown, 1982), 203.
146. Both quotations are from Goldberg, *Jewish Power*, 232, 235.
147. Eric Alterman, "Can We Talk?" *Nation*, April 21, 2003.
148. Stephen Steinlight, "The Jewish Stake in America's Changing Demography: Reconsidering a Misguided Immigration Policy," Backgrounder, Center for Immigration Studies, Washington, DC, October 2001, 10–11. For an earlier and equally revealing expression of this view, see Nathan Glazer, "McGovern and the Jews: A Debate," *Commentary*, September 1972, 44.
149. Samuel P. Huntington, *Who Are We? The Challenges to American National Identity* (New York: Simon & Schuster, 2004), 276–91.
150. Quoted in Massing, "Deal Breakers."
151. Hagee, "The Apple of HIS Eye"; and Wagner, "For Zion's Sake," 56. Also see Lee Underwood, "Israel's Right to the Land," January 4, 2004, http://christianactionforisrael.org .right.html.
152. Information about Lenny Ben-David is from www.israelunitycoalition.org/sbureau/ lbendavid.php.

5: GUIDING THE POLICY PROCESS

1. Twenty years ago, a senior State Department official told David Shipler of the *New York Times* that the lobby "tends to skew the consideration of issues . . . People don't look very hard at some options." Another former Reagan White House official remarked that while AIPAC was "a factor," he knew of "no case where it was decisive, at least in the analytical phase." But this official acknowledged that, in Shipler's words, "The greater influence seemed to be at the political, decision-making level." See David K. Shipler, "On Middle East Policy, a Major Influence," *New York Times*, July 6, 1987.
2. M. J. Rosenberg, "Kangaroo Congressional Hearing," Weekly Opinion Column, Issue #311, Israel Policy Forum, Washington, DC, February 16, 2007. Also see Michael F. Brown, "Dems' Disdain for Palestine," *TomPaine.com*, February 20, 2007; and Daniel Levy, "Yikes— Warmonger Daniel Pipes Testifying to Congress—Do They Learn Nothing?" February 12, 2007, www.tpmcafe.com.
3. Armey quoted in Jake Tapper, "Questions for Dick Armey: Retiring, Not Shy," *New York Times Magazine*, September 1, 2002; Klein quoted in Ron Kampeas, "On Somber Day, DeLay's Spirits Raised by Pro-Israeli Group's Support," *JTA.org*, October 2, 2005; and DeLay quoted in James Bennet, "DeLay Says Palestinians Bear Burden for Achieving Peace," *New York Times*, July 30, 2003.
4. After the 2006 congressional elections, 13 out of 100 senators and 30 out of 435 representatives were Jewish, percentages that are significantly higher than the Jewish proportion of the U.S. population, which is under 3 percent. Amiram Barkat, "Number of Jewish Parliamentarians Worldwide Reaches Record High," *Ha'aretz*, November 9, 2006.
5. Joseph Lieberman, "Speech to the AIPAC National Policy Conference," March 2007, http://lieberman.senate.gov/newsroom/release.cfm?id=270526; Charles Schumer, "The Peace Process Has Been One-Sided" (interview), *Middle East Quarterly* 7, no. 4 (December 2000); Henry Waxman, "Israel Fights for Survival," *Beverly Hills Weekly* (online), April 19, 2002; and Robert Wexler, "Israel and the Middle East," http://wexler.house.gov/issues.php?ID=19.
6. Quoted in Matthew E. Berger, "US Vote May Alter Stance on Middle East," *Jerusalem Post*, November 7, 2006.

7. Quoted in Janine Zacharia, "Lantos's List," *Jerusalem Post*, April 13, 2001. Also see Jeffrey Blankfort, "A Tale of Two Members of Congress and the Capitol Hill Police," *CounterPunch.org*, April 17, 2006; and Mark Simon, "Middle East Hits Home in House Race," *San Francisco Chronicle* (online), May 16, 2002.

8. Quoted in Mitchell Bard, "Israeli Lobby Power," *Midstream* 33, no. 1 (January 1987): 8.

9. For a further analysis of AIPAC's structure and operations, which complements the arguments offered here, see Michael Massing, "The Storm over the Israel Lobby," *New York Review of Books*, June 8, 2006. Also see Paul Findley, *They Dare to Speak Out: People and Institutions Confront Israel's Lobby*, 3rd ed. (Chicago: Lawrence Hill, 2003); and Michael Lind, "The Israel Lobby," *Prospect* 73 (April 2002).

10. The Clinton, Gingrich, Reid, and *New York Times* quotations were accessed from the AIPAC website, www.aipac.org/documents/whoweare.html#say, on January 14, 2005. The *New York Times* quotation was still on the site in May 2007; the others have been removed. Jeffrey Goldberg, "Real Insiders," *New Yorker*, July 4, 2005. Gingrich's statement is also quoted in Michael Kinsley, "J'accuse, Sort of," *Slate.com*, March 12, 2003.

11. Michael Massing, "Deal Breakers," *American Prospect*, March 11, 2002; and Massing, "Storm over the Israel Lobby."

12. The same article also noted that one in every five AIPAC board members was a top fundraiser for 2004 presidential candidates John Kerry and George W. Bush. Thomas B. Edsall and Molly Moore, "Pro-Israel Lobby Has Strong Voice," *Washington Post*, September 5, 2004.

13. David Biale, *Power and Powerlessness in Jewish History* (New York: Schocken Books, 1986), 186–87.

14. Friedman's statement was contained in a letter to AIPAC's members, congratulating them on helping maintain U.S. support for Israel during the 2006 war in Lebanon. It is quoted in John Walsh, "AIPAC Congratulates Itself on the Slaughter in Lebanon," *CounterPunch.org*, August 16, 2006. This policy has been standard operating procedure for some time. In 1987, AIPAC head Tom Dine told supporters that "in the 1985–86 campaign, AIPAC lay leaders and staff met with every senator up for re-election except one, plus 49 Senate challengers and 205 House challengers, including every new freshman member." Quoted in Robert Pear and Richard L. Berke, "Pro-Israel Group Exerts Quiet Might as It Rallies Supporters in Congress," *New York Times*, July 7, 1987.

15. Hayden also says his willingness to defend Israel's invasion of Lebanon in 1982 was the "mistake of my political career." Tom Hayden, "Things Come 'Round in Mideast," *truthdig.com*, July 18, 2006.

16. Harry Lonsdale, personal correspondence with authors, May 16, 2006. Lonsdale also notes that "I was still outspent by Senator Hatfield, and I lost the election," which confirms the obvious point that AIPAC does not succeed in every election.

17. Evans is quoted in John J. Fialka, "Linked Donations? Political Contributions from Pro-Israel PACs Suggest Coordination," *Wall Street Journal*, June 24, 1987.

18. Goldberg, "Real Insiders."

19. Charles R. Babcock, "Papers Link Pro-Israel Lobby to Political Funding Efforts," *Washington Post*, November 14, 1988; and Fialka, "Political Contributions from Pro-Israel PACs."

20. On the FEC's ruling, see John J. Fialka, "Pro-Israel Lobbying Group Is Accused of Breaking U.S. Campaign-Funds Law," *Wall Street Journal*, January 13, 1989; and Charles R. Babcock, "FEC Rules Pro-Israel Lobby, PACs Are Not 'Affiliated,'" *Washington Post*, December 22, 1990.

21. David D. Newsom, *The Public Dimension of Foreign Policy* (Bloomington: Indiana University Press, 1996), 187.

22. "Pro-Israel Contributions to Federal Candidates, 2005–2006," www.opensecrets.org/pacs/industry.asp?txt=Q05&cycle=20006.

23. Lexington, "Taming Leviathan," *Economist*, March 15, 2007; see also Kelley Beaucar Vlahos, "Pro-Israel Lobby a Force to Be Reckoned With," *FOXnews.com*, May 28, 2002; Massing, "Deal Breakers"; and Massing, "Storm over the Israel Lobby."

24. Quoted in Vlahos, "Pro-Israel Lobby."

25. These figures include PAC contributions only, not contributions from individuals. Calculated from the Center for Responsive Politics website, www.opensecrets.org.

26. Ron Kampeas, "Pro-Israel Political Funds in U.S. Target Friendly Incumbents—and Challengers," *JTA.org*, October 3, 2006.

27. Janet McMahon, "Record Pro-Israel PAC Contributions Failed to Save Senate Minority Leader Tom Daschle's Seat," *Washington Report on Middle East Affairs* (online), July 2005.

28. Jonathan Allen, "McKinney Opponent Rakes in Pro-Israel Cash," *The Hill*, August 2, 2006, www.hillnews.com. According to the Center for Responsive Politics, McKinney spent roughly $365,000 on her primary campaign, while victor Hank Johnson spent roughly $800,000 on the primary and general election combined. Also see David Firestone, "A Nation Challenged: The Lawmaker; Call to Study U.S. Stance on Mideast Draws Anger," *New York Times*, October 18, 2001; Nathan Guttman, "Lobbying for the Pro-Israel Candidates," *Ha'aretz*, July 7, 2004; "Mideast Fuels 2 Democratic Primaries," *Washington Post*, June 6, 2002; and Jonathan Weisman, "House Incumbents McKinney, Schwarz Fall in Primaries," *Washington Post*, August 9, 2006.

29. Goldberg, "Real Insiders."

30. John J. Fialka, "Pro-Israel Politics: Jewish Groups Increase Campaign Donations, Target Them Precisely," *Wall Street Journal*, August 3, 1983; and Richard H. Curtiss, *Stealth PACs: How Israel's American Lobby Seeks to Control U.S. Middle East Policy*, 4th ed. (Washington, DC: American Educational Trust, 1996), 47.

31. Goldberg, "Real Insiders." Also see David M. Halbfinger, "Generational Battle Turns Nasty in Alabama Primary," *New York Times*, June 3, 2002; Tom Hamburger, "Mideast Haunts Alabama Race," *Wall Street Journal*, May 31, 2002; "Money from Supporters of Israel Played Role in Alabama Upset," *New York Times*, June 27, 2002; Juliet Eilperin, "Davis Ousts Rep. Hilliard in Alabama Runoff," *Washington Post*, June 26, 2002; and Benjamin Soskis, "Pro-Israel Lobby Backing Challenger in Alabama Race," *Forward*, May 10, 2002.

32. Quoted in Edward Walsh, "Jewish PACs Flex Muscle: On Hill, Being Viewed as Anti-Israel Can Be Risky," *Washington Post*, May 10, 1986; and Curtiss, *Stealth PACs*, 65–66. For additional details on these cases, see Findley, *They Dare to Speak Out*, chap. 3.

33. Adlai Stevenson III, "The Black Book," unpublished book manuscript, undated; and personal correspondence with authors, March 22, 2007.

34. "Californian Spent $1.1 Million on Illinois Race," *New York Times*, October 10, 1985; Richard L. Berke, "Cranston Backer Guilty in Campaign Finance Case," *New York Times*, May 8, 1990; and Tom Tugend, "Israel Financial Backer Convicted on U.S. Election Law Charges," *Jerusalem Post*, May 7, 1990.

35. Quoted in Edward Tivnan, *The Lobby: Jewish Political Power and American Foreign Policy* (New York: Simon & Schuster, 1987), 191. The details in this paragraph are from ibid., 189–91. Also see Charles R. Babcock, "Pro-Israel Political Activists Enforce 'Percy Factor,'" *Washington Post*, August 7, 1986.

36. Quoted in John Diamond and Brianna B. Piec, "Pro-Israel Groups Intensify Political Front in U.S.," *Chicago Tribune*, April 16, 2002.

37. Lucille Barnes, "Retiring Sen. Jesse Helms Caved to Pro-Israel Lobby Halfway Through His Career," *Washington Report on Middle East Affairs*, March 2002, 34; and Tom Hamburger and Jim VandeHei, "Chosen People: How Israel Became a Favorite Cause of Christian Right," *Wall Street Journal*, May 23, 2002.

38. Freedman is quoted in Patrick Healy, "Clinton Vows to Back Israel in Latest Mideast Conflict," *New York Times*, July 18, 2006. Also see Adam Dickter, "Hillary: 'I Had a Lot to Prove,'" *Jewish Week*, November 18, 2005; Joshua Frank, "Hillary Clinton and the Israel Lobby," *Antiwar.com*, January 23, 2007; Rachel Z. Friedman, "Senator Israel," *National Review Online*, May 25, 2005; Ron Kampeas, "Candidates for 2008 Courting Jewish Support," *Jerusalem Post*, January 24, 2007; E. J. Kessler, "Hillary the Favorite in Race for Jewish Do-

nations," *Forward*, January 26, 2007; and Kristen Lombardi, "Hillary Calls Israel a 'Beacon' of Democracy," *Village Voice* (online), December 11, 2005.

39. Kessler, "Hillary the Favorite in Race for Jewish Donations"; campaign finance data from the Center for Responsive Politics, www.opensecrets.org.

40. Sometimes AIPAC and other pro-Israel groups just encourage potential foes to keep silent, as they did with John Sununu during the 2002 New Hampshire Senate race. Sununu had two liabilities: he is of Palestinian and Lebanese descent and some groups in the lobby thought his voting record was less than stellar. The National Jewish Democratic Council issued a press release saying his record on Israel-related issues "stands out—in a most unflattering way," and AIPAC made it clear he was a prime target, dispatching former Israeli Prime Minister Benjamin Netanyahu to campaign for Sununu's primary opponent. According to the executive director of the Republican Jewish Coalition, Sununu responded with "an encouraging position paper" that emphasized his commitment to preserving Israel's military superiority. After winning the election, Sununu offered only muted criticisms of Israel's bombing campaign in Lebanon in the summer of 2006. See National Jewish Democratic Council, "John Sununu: A Singular Voting Record," press release, October 28, 2002; and Matthew E. Berger, "New Republican Congress Retains Pro-Israel Bent," *JTA.org*, November 8, 2002. For additional background, see Franklin Foer, "Foreign Aid: A Middle East Proxy War in New Hampshire," *New Republic*, November 26, 2001; Ralph Z. Hallow, "Pro-Israel Lobby Looks for Deal with Sununu," *Washington Times*, September 4, 2002; and Ori Nir, "Despite Hype, Israel Lobby Sits Out Tight New Hampshire Race," *Forward*, November 8, 2002.

41. "A Letter to AIPAC," *New York Review of Books*, June 8, 2006.

42. Quoted in George D. Moffett III, "Israeli Lobby Virtually Unmatched," *Christian Science Monitor*, June 28, 1991.

43. Amitay is quoted in Berger, "New Republican Congress"; Carter is quoted in Yitzhak Benhorin, "Balanced Stand on ME Is Political Suicide, Says Carter," *Ynetnews.com*, February 26, 2007.

44. Richard L. Hall and Alan V. Deardorff, "Lobbying as Legislative Subsidy," *American Political Science Review* 100, no. 1 (February 2006).

45. Quoted in Camille Mansour, *Beyond Alliance: Israel in U.S. Foreign Policy*, trans. James A. Cohen (New York: Columbia University Press, 1994), 242.

46. Jonathan Weisman and Jeffrey H. Birnbaum, "Senate Passes Ethics Package," *Washington Post*, January 19, 2007; Nathan Guttman, "Jewish Groups to Challenge Ethics Reform," *Forward*, December 1, 2006; Jim Abourezk, "The Hidden Cost of Free Congressional Trips to Israel," *Christian Science Monitor*, January 26, 2007; and the AIEF entry at the Center for Public Integrity, www.publicintegrity.org.

47. Stephen Isaacs, *Jews and American Politics* (New York: Doubleday, 1974), 255–57.

48. Quoted in Seth P. Tillman, *The United States in the Middle East: Interests and Obstacles* (Bloomington: Indiana University Press, 1982), 67.

49. The text of the letter to Rice is from www.aipac.org/Publications/SourceMaterials CongressionalAction/Nelson-Ensign_Letter_FINAL.pdf. Also see Nathan Guttmann, "AIPAC Urges U.S. to End Contacts with Palestinian Authority," *Forward*, March 14, 2007.

50. Quoted in Lloyd Grove, "On the March for Israel; The Lobbyists from AIPAC, Girding for Battle in the New World Order," *Washington Post*, June 13, 1991.

51. Although AIPAC has been able to use its political muscle to avoid having to register as a foreign agent for another government, it is especially concerned about that problem today because of the Larry Franklin spy scandal, and thus it is going to considerable lengths to emphasize its "American side." See Ron Kampeas, "New Ruling in AIPAC Case Raises Questions about 'Foreign Agents,'" *JTA.org*, August 23, 2006; Ori Nir, "Leaders Fear Probe Will Force Pro-Israel Lobby to File as 'Foreign Agent,'" *Forward*, December 31, 2004; and Ori Nir, "Leaders Stress American Side of AIPAC," *Forward*, May 27, 2005.

52. "Sen. Hollings Floor Statement Setting the Record Straight on His Mideast Newspaper

Column," May 20, 2004, originally posted on the former senator's website (now defunct) but still available at www.shalomctr.org/node/620.

53. Quoted in Grove, "On the March for Israel."

54. Sharon's remark was published in an AIPAC advertisement in the *Chicago Jewish Star*, August 29–September 11, 2003; Olmert's statement is quoted in "To Israel with Love," *Economist*, August 5, 2006.

55. Jordan wrote, "Out of 125 members of the Democratic National Finance Council, over 70 are Jewish; In 1976, over 60% of the large donors to the Democratic Party were Jewish; Over 60% of the monies raised by Nixon in 1972 was from Jewish contributors; Over 75% of the monies raised in Humphrey's 1968 campaign was from Jewish contributors; Over 90% of the monies raised by Scoop Jackson in the Democratic primaries was from Jewish contributors; In spite of the fact that you were a long shot and came from an area of the country where there is a smaller Jewish community, approximately 35% of our primary funds were from Jewish supporters." Hamilton Jordan, Confidential File, Box 34, File "Foreign Policy/Domestic Politics Memo, HJ Memo, 6/77," Atlanta, Carter Library, declassified June 12, 1990.

56. Thomas B. Edsall and Alan Cooperman, "GOP Uses Remarks to Court Jews," *Washington Post*, March 13, 2003. Also see James D. Besser, "Jews' Primary Role Expanding," *Jewish Week*, January 23, 2004; Alexander Bolton, "Jewish Defections Irk Democrats," *The Hill* (online), March 30, 2004; and E. J. Kessler, "Ancient Woes Resurfacing as Dean Eyes Top Dem Post," *Forward*, January 28, 2005.

57. Isaacs, *Jews and American Politics*, 115–39; Amy Keller, "Chasing Jewish Dollars: Can GOP Narrow Money Gap in 2004?" *Atlanta Jewish Times* (online), January 17, 2003; and Kessler, "Hillary the Favorite in Race for Jewish Donations."

58. Jeffrey S. Helmreich, "The Israel Swing Factor: How the American Jewish Vote Influences U.S. Elections," *Jerusalem Letter/Viewpoints* (online) 446 (January 15, 2001):1.

59. Kampeas, "Candidates for 2008."

60. E. J. Kessler, "Lieberman and Dean Spar over Israel," *Forward*, September 12, 2003; and Stephen Zunes, "Attacks on Dean Expose Democrats' Shift to the Right," *Tikkun.org*, November/December 2003.

61. Zunes, "Attacks on Dean"; and James D. Besser, "Dean's Jewish Problem," *Chicago Jewish Star*, December 19, 2003–January 8, 2004.

62. E. J. Kessler, "Dean Plans to Visit Israel, Political Baggage in Tow," *Forward*, July 8, 2005; and Zunes, "Attacks on Dean."

63. A transcript of the Steiner-Katz conversation is available at www.wrmea.com/backissues/1292/9212013.html. Also see Thomas L. Friedman, "Pro-Israel Lobbyist Quits over Audiotaped Boasts," *New York Times*, November 5, 1992; and "Israeli Lobby President Resigns over Promises; Bragged to Contributor About Lies to Clinton," *Washington Times*, November 4, 1992.

64. John Heilprin, "Ex-Deputy Pleads Guilty in Abramoff Case," *Boston Globe*, March 23, 2007; and Stacey Schultz, "Mr. Outside Moves Inside," *U.S. News & World Report*, March 16, 2003.

65. Laura Blumenfeld, "Three Peace Suits; For These Passionate American Diplomats, a Middle East Settlement Is the Goal of a Lifetime," *Washington Post*, February 24, 1997; and Clayton E. Swisher, *The Truth About Camp David: The Untold Story About the Collapse of the Middle East Peace Process* (New York: Nation Books, 2004), 35–38, 183–87. In a review of *The Missing Peace*, Ross's account of the failed Middle East peace process, the Israeli historian Avi Shlaim described the Clinton team as "one of the most ardently pro-Israel" administrations in U.S. history and said that "it is difficult to think of an American official who is more quintessentially Israel-first in his outlook than Dennis Ross." Avi Shlaim, "The Lost Steps," *Nation*, August 30, 2004. Also see Michael C. Desch, "The Peace That Failed," *American Conservative*, November 8, 2004; and Jerome Slater, "The Missing Pieces in *The Missing Peace*," *Tikkun.org*, May 2005.

66. Samuel Berger, President Clinton's national security adviser, reports that at one point dur-

ing the negotiations at Camp David (July 2000), Dennis Ross commented, "If Barak offers anything more, I'll be against this agreement." Unedited transcript of "Comments by Sandy Berger at the Launch of *How Israelis and Palestinians Negotiate* (USIP Press, 2005)," U.S. Institute of Peace, Washington, DC, June 7, 2005, www.usip.org/events/2005/0607_beberger.pdf.

67. Hussein Agha and Robert Malley, "The Tragedy of Errors," *New York Review of Books*, August 9, 2001. The Palestinian complaint is quoted in Blumenfeld, "Three Peace Suits."

68. David K. Shipler, "On Middle East Policy, a Major Influence," *New York Times*, July 6, 1987.

69. Douglas Brinkley, "The Lives They Lived; Out of the Loop," *New York Times Magazine*, December 29, 2002.

70. Marius, of course, was not an anti-Semite. He merely wrote in the relevant review: "[The book's] account of the brutality of the Shin Bet, the Israeli secret police, is eerily similar to the stories of the Gestapo, the Geheimstaatspolitzei in Nazi-occupied territories, in World War II." Lloyd Grove, "The Outspoken Speechwriter; Gore Reverses Hiring Decision After Review Critical of Israel," *Washington Post*, July 19, 1995; and Richard Marius, "Al Gore and Me, or How Marty Peretz Saved Me from Packing My Bags for Washington," *Journal of Palestine Studies* 25, no. 2 (Winter 1996): 54–59.

71. Lawrence Kaplan, "Torpedo Boat: How Bush Turned on Arafat," *New Republic*, February 18, 2002.

72. Elliott Abrams, *Faith or Fear: How Jews Can Survive in a Christian America* (New York: Simon & Schuster, 1997), 181.

73. Nathan Guttmann, "From Clemency to a Senior Post," *Ha'aretz*, December 16, 2002.

6: DOMINATING PUBLIC DISCOURSE

1. Robert H. Trice, "Interest Groups and the Foreign Policy Process: U.S. Policy in the Middle East," *Sage Professional Papers in International Studies*, ed. V. Davis and M. East (Beverly Hills, CA: Sage Publications, 1976), 63–65.

2. Eric Alterman, "Intractable Foes, Warring Narratives," *MSNBC.com*, March 28, 2002.

3. Cathy Young of *Reason* magazine protested her inclusion on Alterman's list of "reflexively" pro-Israel pundits and Alterman acknowledged the error.

4. Kristof began by observing there was "no serious political debate among either Democrats or Republicans about our policy toward Israelis and Palestinians" and suggested that this was bad for all parties involved, including Israel itself. This point should have been uncontroversial, but it earned a letter of protest from the Anti-Defamation League and his views were described as a "one-sided blame-Israel approach" by CAMERA, a pro-Israel media watchdog group. See his "Talking About Israel," *New York Times*, March 18, 2007; "Letter to the Editor," *New York Times*, March 19, 2007, www.adl.org/media_watch/newspapers/20070319_NYTimes.htm; and CAMERA, "Kristof's Blame-Israel Rant," March 21, 2007, www.camera.org/index.asp?x_context=2&x_outlet=139&x_article=1303.

5. Quoted in Bret Stephens, "Eye on the Media by Bret Stephens: Bartley's Journal," *Jerusalem Post*, November 22, 2002.

6. Jerome N. Slater, "Muting the Alarm: The *New York Times* and the Israeli-Palestinian Conflict, 2000–2006," *International Security* 32, no. 2 (Fall 2007); and Howard Friel and Richard Falk, *Israel-Palestine on Record: How the New York Times Misreports Conflict in the Middle East* (London: Verso, 2007).

7. Max Frankel, *The Times of My Life and My Life with The Times* (New York: Random House, 1999), 401–403.

8. Quoted in Robert I. Friedman, "Selling Israel to America: The *Hasbara* Project Targets the U.S. Media," *Mother Jones*, February–March 1987.

9. Peretz's remark about his love for Israel is quoted in Alexander Cockburn and Ken Silverstein, *Washington Babylon* (London: Verso Books, 1996), 6. His statement about the "party line" at the *New Republic* is quoted in J. J. Goldberg, *Jewish Power: Inside the American Jew-*

ish Establishment (Reading, MA: Addison-Wesley, 1996), 299. *Time* magazine once described the *New Republic* under Peretz's guidance as "inflexible in its support of Israel." See William A. Henry III, "Breaking the Liberal Pattern," *Time*, October 1, 1984.

10. Quoted in Michael Massing, "The Israel Lobby," *Nation*, June 10, 2002.

11. Felicity Barringer, "Some U.S. Backers of Israel Boycott Dailies over Mideast Coverage That They Deplore," *New York Times*, May 23, 2002; Michael Getler, "Caught in the Crossfire," *Washington Post*, May 5, 2002; Tim Jones, "Pro-Israel Groups Take Aim at U.S. News Media," *Chicago Tribune*, May 26, 2002; Massing, "Israel Lobby"; and David Shaw, "From Jewish Outlook, Media Are Another Enemy," *Los Angeles Times*, April 28, 2002.

12. Quoted in Massing, "Israel Lobby."

13. Quoted in Friedman, "Selling Israel to America."

14. Ifshin is quoted in Lloyd Grove, "On the March for Israel; The Lobbyists from AIPAC, Girding for Battle in the New World Order," *Washington Post*, June 13, 1991. Also see Daniel Eisenberg, "AIPAC Attack?" *Columbia Journalism Review*, January/February 1993; Robert I. Friedman, "The Israel Lobby's Blacklist," *Village Voice*, August 4, 1992; Robert I. Friedman, "A PAC with McCarthy," *Village Voice*, August 25, 1992; Robert I. Friedman, "The Wobbly Israeli Lobby," *Washington Post*, November 1, 1992; Thomas A. Dine and Mayer Mitchell, "The Truth About AIPAC," *Washington Post*, November 14, 1992; and Lawrence N. Cohler, "The AIPAC Flap," *Washington Post*, December 5, 1992.

15. See, for example, "Conflict of Interest Fits NPR Bias," www.camera.org/index.asp?x_context=4&x_outlet=28&x_article=100; and Joel Berkovsky, "NPR Responds to Claims of Bias with Weeklong Series on Mideast," *JTA.org*, October 4, 2002.

16. For the actual ad, see www.camera.org/images_user/advertisements/large/CAMERA_CarterAD.pdf.

17. This discussion of CAMERA and NPR is drawn from Barringer, "Some U.S. Backers"; James D. Besser, "NPR Radio Wars Putting Jewish Groups in a Bind," *Jewish Week*, May 20, 2005; Samuel Freedman, "From 'Balance' to Censorship: Bush's Cynical Plan for NPR," *Forward*, May 27, 2005; Nathan Guttman, "Enough Already from Those Pro-Israel Nudniks," *Ha'aretz*, February 1, 2005; Mark Jurkowitz, "Blaming the Messenger," *Boston Globe Magazine*, February 9, 2003; E. J. Kessler, "Hot Seat Expected for New Chair of Corporation for Public Broadcasting," *Forward*, October 28, 2005; Gaby Wenig, "NPR Israel Coverage Sparks Protests," *Jewish Journal of Greater Los Angeles* (online), May 9, 2003; and Gila Wertheimer, "NPR Dismisses Protest Rallies," *Chicago Jewish Star*, May 30–June 12, 2003.

18. Bret Stephens, "An Open Letter to Ian Buruma," *Jerusalem Post*, September 5, 2003. Buruma's original piece is "How to Talk About Israel," *New York Times Magazine*, August 31, 2003.

19. Judt revealed this incident in an interview in a 2007 documentary, *The Israel Lobby*, produced by VPRO International, the Dutch public broadcasting corporation, and in a debate on the Israel lobby sponsored by the *London Review of Books*, which was held at Cooper Union in New York City on September 28, 2006. Videos of the documentary and the debate are available at www.scribemedia.org/2006/10/11/israel-lobby/ and www.youtube.com/profile?user=VPROinternational, respectively.

20. James Traub, "Does Abe Foxman Have an Anti-Anti-Semite Problem?" *New York Times Magazine*, January 14, 2007.

21. www.conferenceofpresidents.org/content.asp?id=34 and www.americasvoices.net. In this case a key official at an American organization (the Conference of Presidents) is describing the initiative as part of *Israel's* public relations (*hasbara*) activities.

22. On the growing role and activities of think tanks, see Donald E. Abelson, *American Think-Tanks and Their Role in U.S. Foreign Policy* (New York: St. Martin's Press, 1996); Trudy Lieberman, *Slanting the Story: The Forces That Shape the News* (New York: New Press, 2000); David M. Ricci, *The Transformation of American Politics: The New Washington and the Rise of Think Tanks* (New Haven: Yale University Press, 1993); James Allen Smith, *The Idea Brokers: Think Tanks and the Rise of the New Policy Elite* (New York: Free Press, 1991);

and Diane Stone, *Capturing the Political Imagination: Think-Tanks and the Policy Process* (Portland, OR: Frank Cass, 1996).

23. Joel Beinin, "Money, Media and Policy Consensus: The Washington Institute for Near East Policy," *Middle East Report Online*, January–February 1993, 10–15; Goldberg, *Jewish Power*, 221–22; and Mark H. Milstein, "Washington Institute for Near East Policy: An AIPAC 'Image Problem,'" *Washington Report on Middle East Affairs* (online), July 1991.

24. Quoted in Milstein, "Washington Institute."

25. *Toward Peace in the Middle East: Report of a Study Group* (Washington, DC: Brookings Institution Press, 1975).

26. Andrew Ross Sorkin, "Schlepping to Moguldom," *New York Times*, September 5, 2004. Saban is also a major supporter of Hillary Clinton's presidential campaign. Jeffrey H. Birnbaum and Matthew Mosk, "Clinton Fundraising Goes Full Force," *Washington Post*, February 7, 2007.

27. Leverett worked at Brookings's Saban Center from May 2003 to June 2006, where he was initially a visiting fellow and later a senior fellow. He had significant disagreements with his boss, Martin Indyk, over U.S. policy toward Iran and Syria. Leverett maintained that it made little sense to threaten Iran with a military strike if it did not abandon its nuclear program and that it made more sense to pursue a grand bargain with Tehran. Indyk held the opposite view. Leverett also disagreed with Indyk's view that the assassination of Prime Minister Rafic Hariri of Lebanon provided an excellent opportunity to undermine Syrian President Bashar al-Assad. Leverett was forced out of Brookings, partly because of his disagreements with Indyk and partly because he criticized Saban Center Research Director Kenneth Pollack's advocacy of the Iraq war. Interview with authors, October 17, 2006; correspondence with authors, June 6, 2007, June 12, 2007.

28. The 2005 forum was held in Israel and did feature one session with Palestinian President Mahmoud Abbas, Finance Minister Salam Fayad, and Civil Affairs Minister Mohamed Dahlan.

29. Foxman is quoted in David E. Sanger, "Iran's Leader Relishes 2nd Chance to Make Waves," *New York Times*, September 21, 2006. Also see "Ahmadinejad Talks to U.S. Think Tank," *Washington Post*, September 21, 2006; and Eli Lake, "N.Y.'s Jewish Leaders Reject Offer to Meet Iran's Leader," *New York Sun*, September 18, 2006.

30. James D. Besser, "Turning Up Heat in Campus Wars," *Jewish Week*, July 25, 2003; Ronald S. Lauder and Jay Schottenstein, "Back to School for Israel Advocacy," *Forward*, November 14, 2003; and Rachel Pomerance, "Israel Forces Winning Campus Battle, Say Students Attending AIPAC Meeting," *JTA.org*, December 31, 2002.

31. Michal Lando, "Christians to Train in Israel Advocacy," *Jerusalem Post*, May 14, 2007.

32. Besser, "Turning Up Heat"; and Pomerance, "Israel Forces Winning." In the spring of 2005, AIPAC hosted one hundred student government presidents (eighty of whom were not Jewish) at its annual conference. Nathaniel Popper, "Pro-Israel Groups: Campuses Improving," *Forward*, June 24, 2005.

33. "Policy Conference Highlights," www.aipac.org/2841.htm.

34. Jonathan S. Kessler and Jeff Schwaber, *The AIPAC College Guide: Exposing the Anti-Israel Campaign on Campus*, special ed. for the Hillel Foundation (Washington, DC: AIPAC, 1984); and Kristine McNeil, "The War on Academic Freedom," *Nation*, November 11, 2002.

35. Michael Dobbs, "Middle East Studies Under Scrutiny in U.S.," *Washington Post*, January 13, 2004; Michele Goldberg, "Osama University?" *Salon.com*, November 6, 2003; Kristine McNeil, "The War on Academic Freedom," *Nation*, November 11, 2002; and Zachary Lockman, "Behind the Battle over US Middle East Policy," *Middle East Report Online*, January 2004.

36. Tanya Schevitz, "'Dossiers' Dropped from Web Blacklist; Mideast Center Says Denouncing Professors Was Counterproductive," *San Francisco Chronicle* (online), October 3, 2002.

37. "The International Studies in Higher Education Act (HR 3077)," text from www.govtrack.us/congress/billtext.xpd?bill=h108-3077.

38. Stanley Kurtz, "Anti-Americanism in the Classroom," *National Review Online*, May 16,

2002; Martin Kramer, *Ivory Towers on Sand: The Failure of Middle East Studies in America* (Washington, DC: Washington Institute for Near East Policy, 2001).

39. The text of the joint letter is posted on Martin Kramer's website, www.geocities.org/martinkramerorg/Documents/HR3077/jointletter.htm.

40. Goldberg, "Osama University?"; Ron Kampeas, "Campus Oversight Passes Senate as Review Effort Scores a Victory," *JTA.org*, November 22, 2005; Stanley Kurtz, "Reforming the Campus: Congress Targets Title VI," *National Review Online*, October 14, 2003; McNeil, "War on Academic Freedom"; Ori Nir, "Groups Back Bill to Monitor Universities," *Forward*, March 12, 2004; Sara Roy, "Short Cuts," *London Review of Books*, April 1, 2004; and Anders Strindberg, "The New Commissars," *American Conservative*, February 2, 2004.

41. HR 609 [109th Congress], "College Access and Opportunity Act of 2006," www.govtrack.us/congress/bill.xpd?bill=h109-609.

42. See Martin Kramer, "Title VI Verdict," http://sandbox.blog-city.com/title_vi_verdict.htm; and Stanley Kurtz, "Title Bout: Bipartisan Hope for Middle East Studies Reform," *National Review Online*, April 2, 2007. Also see Committee to Review the Title VI and Fulbright-Hays International Education Programs, "International Education and Foreign Languages: Keys to Securing America's Future" (Washington, DC: National Research Council, 2007), 3.

43. Quoted in Scott Jaschik, "New Approach to International Education," *Inside Higher Ed* (online), www.insidehighered.com/news/2007/03/28/intl. Also see Sierra Millman, "Education Department Should Have High-Ranking Official to Oversee Foreign Language Study," *Chronicle of Higher Education Daily Report*, March 28, 2007.

44. Draft legislation, "Title VI International Education Programs," April 19, 2007. The draft legislation would require applicants for federal funding to "describe how the applicant will handle disputes regarding whether activities funded under the application reflect diverse perspectives and a wide range of views." A subsequent clause states that "if a complaint regarding activities funded under this title is not resolved under the process outlined in the relevant grantee's application, such complaint shall be filed with the Department [of Education] and reviewed by the Secretary."

45. The number 130 comes from Mitchell G. Bard, "Tenured or Tenuous: Defining the Role of Faculty in Supporting Israel on Campus," report published by the Israel on Campus Coalition and the American-Israeli Cooperative Enterprise, May 2004, 11. Also see Nacha Cattan, "NYU Center: New Addition to Growing Academic Field," *Forward*, May 2, 2003; Samuel G. Freedman, "Separating the Political Myths from the Facts in Israel Studies," *New York Times*, February 16, 2005; Jennifer Jacobson, "The Politics of Israel Studies," *Chronicle of Higher Education*, June 24, 2005, 10–12; Michael C. Kotzin, "The Jewish Community and the Ivory Tower: An Urgent Need for Israel Studies," *Forward*, January 30, 2004; and Nathaniel Popper, "Israel Studies Gain on Campus as Disputes Grow," *Forward*, March 25, 2005.

46. Quoted in Cattan, "NYU Center."

47. Shmuel Rosner, "Donor May Fund Georgetown Jewish Center to Give U.S. Leaders Another Viewpoint," *Ha'aretz*, June 14, 2006; Shmuel Rosner, "Academic Lies About Israel," *Ha'aretz*, June 14, 2006; and Stephen Santulli, "Jewish Program May Get Major Gift," *Hoya* (online), September 1, 2006.

48. For the original complaint, see Chicago Friends of Israel, "Jewish and Pro-Israel Students at the University of Chicago Subject to Intimidation and Hate," July 24, 2002, on the *Campus Watch* website. Also see Ron Grossman, "Mideast Conflict Boosts Tensions at U.S. Colleges," *Chicago Tribune*, October 17, 2002; Dave Newbart, "Allegations of Anti-Semitism on Campus," *Chicago Sun-Times*, November 4, 2002; Joshua Steinman, "University Professors Labeled Anti-Israeli by Campus Watch Site," *Chicago Maroon* (online), October 29, 2002; "University Responds to Anti-Semitic Incidents," *University of Chicago Magazine*, October 2002; and Sean Wereley, "Students Debate Presence of Anti-Semitism on Campus," *Chicago Weekly News*, October 17, 2002.

49. Jonathan R. Cole, "The Patriot Act on Campus: Defending the University Post-9/11," *Boston Review*, Summer 2003; Chanakya Sethi, "Khalidi Candidacy for New Chair Draws

Fire," *Daily Princetonian* (online), April 22, 2005; Chanakya Sethi, "Debate Grows over Khalidi Candidacy," *Daily Princetonian* (online), April 28, 2005; and "Scholarship, Not Politics, Is the Measure of a Professor," *Daily Princetonian* editorial (online), April 27, 2005.

50. Cole, "The Patriot Act on Campus."

51. Robert Gaines, "The Battle at Columbia University," *Washington Report on Middle East Affairs* (online), April 2005; Caroline Glick, "Our World: The Columbia Disaster," *Jerusalem Post*, April 4, 2005; Joseph Massad, "Witch Hunt at Columbia: Targeting the University," *CounterPunch.org*, June 3, 2005; Nathaniel Popper, "Columbia Students Say Firestorm Blurs Campus Reality," *Forward*, February 11, 2005; Scott Sherman, "The Mideast Comes to Columbia," *Nation*, April 4, 2005; and Chanan Weissman, "Film on 'Bias' at Columbia U. Sparks Fury Among Israeli Alumni," *Jerusalem Post*, February 6, 2005.

52. "Columbia University Ad Hoc Grievance Committee, Final Report, New York, 28 March 2005 (excerpts)," *Journal of Palestine Studies* 34, no. 4 (Summer 2005): 90–100.

53. Scott Jaschik, "Blackballed at Yale," *Inside Higher Ed* (online), June 5, 2006; Liel Liebovitz, "Middle East Wars Flare Up at Yale," *Jewish Week*, June 2, 2006; Steve Lipman, "Opening the Ivy Doors," *Jewish Week*, December 22, 2006; Philip Weiss, "Burning Cole," *Nation*, July 3, 2006; and the symposium "Posting Mortem," *Chronicle of Higher Education*, July 28, 2006.

54. Paul Findley, *They Dare to Speak Out: People and Institutions Confront Israel's Lobby*, 3rd ed. (Chicago: Lawrence Hill, 2003), 50–58; and "Stanford Apologizes to Ex-Representative McCloskey," *Washington Post*, July 28, 1983.

55. Peter Dombrowski, a faculty member at the Naval War College, reported this story to us on June 13, 2006, and confirmed it in e-mail correspondence on April 5, 2007.

56. "UM Deserves to Hear Both Sides on Israel Lobby," letter, *Montana Kaimin*, September 7, 2006; Trevor Kilgore, "Profs Off-Base in Labeling Lecturer as Anti-Semitic," letter, *Montana Kaimin*, September 8, 2006; Brenna Moore, "U.S. Foreign Policy Mistakes, Consequences Discussed by International Relations Expert," *Montana Kaimin*, September 12, 2006; Rob Chaney, "Professor Questions U.S.-Israeli Relationship," *Missoulian*, September 12, 2006; "Anti-Semitic Lecturer Bad for UM," letter, *Montana Kaimin*, September 13, 2006; and "Presidential Lecturer Starts Debate, Not Hatred," letter, *Montana Kaimin*, September 12, 2006. In October, the same lecture series featured Joseph Joffe, a well-known European foreign policy expert and a harsh critic of our original article. His presence did not appease the critics of the invitation to Walt, who continued their ultimately unsuccessful campaign to oust the coordinator of the lecture series. Hannah Heimbuch, "Lecture Series Not Skirting Foreign Policy," *Montana Kaimin*, October 26, 2006.

57. Ralph Blumenthal, "Cries to Halt Publication of Holocaust Book," *New York Times*, January 10, 1998; and Norman G. Finkelstein, *Beyond Chutzpah: On the Misuse of Anti-Semitism and the Abuse of History* (Berkeley: University of California Press, 2005), 55–56.

58. Jon Weiner, "Giving Chutzpah New Meaning," *Nation*, July 11, 2005; and the subsequent correspondence ibid., August 29, 2005. Also see "Dershowitz, Prof Spar over Plagiarism," *New York Times*, July 14, 2005; Neve Gordon, "The Real Case for Israel," *In These Times* (online), October 12, 2005; Jennifer Howard, "Calif. Press Will Publish Controversial Book on Israel," *Chronicle of Higher Education* (online), July 22, 2005; and Jon Wiener, "Chutzpah and Free Speech," *Los Angeles Times*, July 11, 2005.

59. Andy Humm, "Academic Freedom, Intimidation, and Mayoral Politics: The Case of Rashid Khalidi," *Gotham Gazette* (online), April 7, 2005; Julia Levy, "Khalidi Is Tapped to Teach Teachers About Middle East," *New York Sun*, February 15, 2005; Julia Levy, "Education Dept. Drops Columbia Prof. from Teaching Program for Teachers," *New York Sun*, February 16, 2005; and Alisa Solomon, "When Academic Freedom Is Kicked Out of Class," *Forward*, March 4, 2005.

60. Yaniv Halili, "New Yorkers to Study About Israel," *Ynetnews.com*, September 8, 2006; and David Andreatta, "Schools Back Israeli Teacher Course," *New York Post* (online), September 28, 2006. Pressure can even be exerted on private high schools. In January 2007, protests from concerned parents and the Jewish Community Relations Council of Silicon Valley led to the

cancellation of a talk by the Stanford University Professor Joel Beinin at the Harker School, a private school in San Jose. Beinin is Jewish and an avowed Zionist, but because he is also a critic of Israeli policies toward the Palestinians, it was apparently unacceptable for him to speak to a high school group. Joel Beinin, "Silencing Critics Not Way to Middle East Peace," *San Francisco Chronicle* (online), February 4, 2007.

61. Max Gross, "Israel Advocacy Coalition Targeting High Schools," *Forward*, January 23, 2004; Rachel Pomerance, "With Israel Issue Hot on Campus, Groups Train High School Advocates," *JTA.org*, January 22, 2004; and "New Pro-Israel Campaign Targets High School Students," *JTA.org*, June 2, 2004.

62. Jonathan Kessler, "Pro-Israel Activism Makes Comeback on Campus," *Forward*, December 26, 2003; Popper, "Pro-Israel Groups: Campuses Improving"; Barry Silverman and Randall Kaplan, "Pro-Israel College Activists Quietly Successful on Campus," *JTA.org*, May 9, 2005; and Chanan Tigay, "As Students Return to Campus, Activists Prepare a New Approach," *JTA.org*, September 1, 2005. Nevertheless, there are limits to the lobby's effectiveness on campuses. See Joe Eskenazi, "Book: College Campuses Quiet, but Anti-Israel Feeling Is Growing," *JTA.org*, November 29, 2005; and Gary Rosenblatt, "U.S. Grad Students Seen Hostile to Israel," *Jewish Week*, June 17, 2005.

63. Harris and Polish Consul General Krzystof Kasprzyk are quoted in Michael Powell, "In N.Y., Sparks Fly over Israel Criticism," *Washington Post*, October 9, 2006. Also see J. J. Goldberg, "A 'Lobby' Prof Asks: Can We Talk?" *Forward*, October 13, 2006; Larry Cohler-Esses, "Off Limits? Talk by Israel Critic Canceled," *Jewish Week*, October 6, 2006; and Ira Stoll, "Poland Abruptly Cancels a Speech by Local Critic of the Jewish State," *New York Sun*, October 4, 2006. A copy of the open letter can be found in "The Case of Tony Judt: An Open Letter to the ADL," *New York Review of Books*, November 16, 2006. For the ADL's response and a follow-up response by the two main authors of the original letter, see "The ADL & Tony Judt: An Exchange," *New York Review of Books*, November 30, 2006.

64. Graham Bowley, "Lunch with the FT: Tony Judt," *Financial Times*, March 16, 2007.

65. Quoted in "French Embassy Cancels N.Y. Book Launch over Author's Israel Views," *Ha'aretz*, October 10, 2006. Also Ed Pilkington, "US Free Speech Row Grows as Author Says Jewish Complaints Stopped Party," *Guardian*, October 11, 2006; and Henry Porter, "The Enemies of Free Speech Are Everywhere," *Observer*, October 15, 2006. The relevant passage in Callil's book reads as follows: "The French forget Vichy, Australians forget the Aborigines, the English forget the Irish, Unionists forget the Catholics of Northern Ireland, the United States forgot Chile and forgets Guantánamo. Everyone forgets East Timor and Rwanda. As I wrote this book, people constantly asked me how I could bear to write about such a villain and about such terrible things. In fact, horrors from the past did not deter me. What caused me anguish . . . was to live so closely to the helpless terror of the Jews of France, and to see what the Jews of Israel were passing on to the Palestinian people. Like the rest of humanity, the Jews of Israel 'forget' the Palestinians. Everyone forgets; every nation forgets." Carmen Callil, *Bad Faith: A Forgotten History of Family, Fatherland, and Vichy France* (New York: Random House, 2006), 437.

66. Jesse McKinley, "Play About Demonstrator's Death Is Delayed," *New York Times*, February 28, 2006; and Katharine Viner, "A Message Crushed Again," *Los Angeles Times*, March 1, 2006. Also see Rachel Irwin, "Censoring Rachel's Words?" *Jerusalem Post*, March 20, 2006; Edward Rothstein, "Too Hot to Handle, Too Hot to Not Handle," *New York Times*, March 6, 2006; and Philip Weiss, "Too Hot for New York," *Nation*, April 3, 2006.

67. Richard Ouzounian, "'Corrie' Cancelled in Canada," *Variety* (online), December 22, 2006.

68. Christine Dolen, "Theater Won't Stage Controversial Drama," *Miami Herald* (online), April 3, 2007. Dolen also reports that a successful Seattle production of the play elicited protests from three Jewish groups, which handed out leaflets to those attending.

69. Foxman is quoted in Jim McGee, "Jewish Group's Tactics Investigated," *Washington Post*, October 19, 1993. On the ADL case, see Chip Berlet and Dennis King, "ADL-Gate," *Tikkun*, July/August 1993; Jeffrey Blankfort, Anne Poirier, and Steve Zeltser, "The ADL Spy-

ing Case Is Over, but the Struggle Continues," *CounterPunch.org*, February 25, 2002; Phil Bronstein, "Suspect in Cop Spy Case Tells His Story," *San Francisco Examiner*, January 22, 1993; Lynne Duke, "Anti-Defamation League Sued: Rights Violations Alleged in Spying," *Washington Post*, October 22, 1993; Bob Egelko, "Jewish Defense Group Settles S.F. Spying Suit," *San Francisco Chronicle* (online), February 23, 2002; Robert I. Friedman, "The Enemy Within," *Village Voice*, May 11, 1993; "Inquiry Is Dropped over Spy Charges," *New York Times*, November 17, 1993; and "The ADL Snoops," *CounterPunch.org*, November 11, 1998.

70. As discussed in Chapter 4, we regard the term "Jewish lobby" as both misleading and inappropriate, as it implies that all Jews support the lobby's positions and ignores the non-Jewish individuals and groups that are also part of this loose coalition.

71. Mortimer B. Zuckerman, "A Shameful Contagion of Anti-Semitism in Europe," *U.S. News & World Report*, October 7, 2002; and Jeff Jacoby, "The Cancer of Anti-Semitism in Europe," *Boston Globe*, March 21, 2004.

72. Quoted in Tony Judt, "Goodbye to All That?" *Nation*, January 3, 2005.

73. Anti-Defamation League, "Attitudes Toward Jews, Israel and the Palestinian-Israeli Conflict in Ten European Countries," April 2004; and Pew Global Attitudes Project, *A Year After Iraq War: Mistrust of America in Europe Even Higher, Muslim Anger Persists* (Washington, DC: Pew Research Center for the People and the Press, March 16, 2004), 4–5, 26. On the ADL survey, see "ADL Survey Finds Some Decrease in Anti-Semitic Attitudes in Ten European Countries," ADL press release, April 26, 2004; and Shlomo Shamir, "Poll Shows Decrease in Anti-Semitic Views in Europe," *Ha'aretz*, April 27, 2004. These findings had virtually no effect on pro-Israel pundits, who continued to argue that anti-Semitism was rampant in Europe. See, for example, Daniel J. Goldhagen, "Europe's Toothless Reply to Anti-Semitism: Conference Fails to Build Tools to Fight a Rising Sickness," *Los Angeles Times*, April 30, 2004; and Charles Krauthammer, "The Real Mideast 'Poison,'" *Washington Post*, April 30, 2004.

74. Martin Peretz, "Cambridge Diarist: Regrets," *New Republic*, April 22, 2002, 50.

75. The data in this paragraph are from "Anti-Semitism in Europe: Is It Really Rising?" *Economist*, May 4, 2002.

76. Quoted in Marc Perelman, "Community Head: France No More Antisemitic Than U.S.," *Forward*, August 1, 2003. Also see Francois Bujon de l'Estang, "A Slander on France," *Washington Post*, June 22, 2002; and "French President Accuses Israel of Conducting Anti-French Campaign," *Ha'aretz*, May 12, 2002.

77. "French Police: Anti-Semitism in France Sharply Decreased in 2005," *Ha'aretz*, January 19, 2006.

78. "French Protest for Murdered Jew," *BBC News* (online), February 26, 2006; and Michel Zlotowski, "Large Memorial Held for Parisian Jew," *Jerusalem Post*, February 23, 2006.

79. Avi Beker, "The Eternally Open Gate," *Ha'aretz*, January 11, 2005; Josef Joffe, "A Boom, if Not a Renaissance, in Modern-Day Germany," *Forward*, July 25, 2003; Nathaniel Popper, "Immigrant Policy Eyed as German Community Swells," *Forward*, July 25, 2003; and Eliahu Salpeter, "Jews from the CIS Prefer Germany to the Jewish State," *Ha'aretz*, May 28, 2003. Also, the *Times* of London reported in the spring of 2005 that "an estimated 100,000 Jews have returned to Russia in the past few years, sparking a dramatic renaissance of Jewish life in a country with a long history of anti-Semitism." Jeremy Page, "Once Desperate to Leave, Now Jews Are Returning to Russia, Land of Opportunity," *Times* (London), April 28, 2005. Also see Lev Krichevsky, "Poll: Russians Don't Dislike Jews, and More Are Against Anti-Semitism," *JTA.org*, February 2, 2006.

80. The chairman of the Education Department of the Jewish Agency for Israel has been described as saying that "present day violent anti-Semitism originates from two separate sources: radical Islamists in the Middle East and Western Europe as well as the neo-Nazi youth element in Eastern Europe and Latin America." Jonathan Schneider, "Anti-Semitism Still a World Problem," *Jerusalem Post*, January 26, 2006.

81. "Study: Anti-Semitic Attacks Hit Record Level in Britain in 2006," *Ha'aretz*, February 1, 2007; and Community Security Trust, "Antisemitic Incidents Report 2006," www.thecst .org.uk.

82. Specifically, the London police reported that anti-Semitic attacks had dropped 25 percent over five years and that "racist attacks on black, Asian, and Arab people in London are significantly higher." The Global Forum figures showed a slight (3 percent) decrease in anti-Semitic incidents from 2005 to 2006. Jonny Paul, "Sharp Rise in U.K. anti-Semitism? Numbers Don't Add Up for Everyone," *JTA.org*, February 22, 2007.

83. For examples of this argument, Phyllis Chesler, *The New Anti-Semitism: The Current Crisis and What We Must Do About It* (San Francisco: Jossey-Bass, 2003); Hillel Halkin, "The Return of Anti-Semitism: To Be Against Israel Is to Be Against the Jews," *Wall Street Journal*, February 5, 2002; Barry Kosmin and Paul Iganski, "Judeophobia—Not Your Parents' Anti-Semitism," *Ha'aretz*, June 3, 2003; Amnon Rubinstein, "Fighting the New Anti-Semitism," *Ha'aretz*, December 2, 2003; Gabriel Schoenfeld, *The Return of Anti-Semitism* (San Francisco: Encounter Books, 2003); Natan Sharansky, "Anti-Semitism Is Our Problem," *Ha'aretz*, August 10, 2003; Yair Sheleg, "A World Cleansed of the Jewish State," *Ha'aretz*, April 18, 2002; and Yair Sheleg, "Enemies, a Post-National Story," *Ha'aretz*, March 8, 2003. For criticism of this perspective, see Akiva Eldar, "Anti-Semitism Can Be Self-Serving," *Ha'aretz*, May 3, 2002; Brian Klug, "The Myth of the New Anti-Semitism," *Nation*, February 2, 2004; Ralph Nader, "Criticizing Israel Is Not Anti-Semitism," *CounterPunch.org*, October 16/17, 2004; *Reframing Anti-Semitism: Alternative Jewish Perspectives*, ed. Henri Picciotto and Mitchell Plitnick (Oakland, CA: Jewish Voice for Peace, 2004); and Finkelstein, *Beyond Chutzpah*, chaps. 1–3.

84. Helen Nugent, "Chief Rabbi Flays Church over Vote on Israel Assets," *Times* (London), February 17, 2006. Also see Bill Bowder, "Sacks Seeks Talks after Synod Vote on Disinvestment," *Church Times* (online), February 17, 2006; "Bulldozer Motion 'Based on Ignorance,'" *Church Times* (online), February 10, 2006; Ruth Gledhill, "Church Urged to Reconsider Investments with Israel," *Times* (London), May 28, 2005; and Irene Lancaster, "Anglicans Have Betrayed the Jews," Moriel Ministries (UK) website, www.moriel.org/articles/israel/anglicans_have_betrayed_the_jews.htm. Also "U.K. Chief Rabbi Attacks Anglicans over Israel Divestment Vote," *Ha'aretz*, February 17, 2006.

85. That the Church of England was merely criticizing Israeli policy and not engaging in anti-Semitism is clearly reflected in the February 10, 2006, letter from the archbishop of Canterbury, Dr. Rowan Williams, to the chief rabbi, Jonathan Sacks, explaining the church's decision on divestment. "Archbishop: Synod Call Was Expression of Concern," Church of England website, www.cofe.anglican.org/news/pr2006.html.

86. Arnold Forster and Benjamin R. Epstein, *The New Anti-Semitism* (New York: McGraw-Hill, 1974). In their words, the "heart of the new anti-Semitism" was "a large measure of indifference to the most profound apprehensions of the Jewish people, a blandness and apathy in dealing with anti-Jewish behavior, a widespread incapacity or unwillingness to comprehend the necessity of the existence of Israel to Jewish safety and survival throughout the world" (324).

87. According to the Perlmutters, "It was anti-Semitism's velvet glove that provided the points for the [Reagan] administration's victory [in the AWACS deal]." Nathan Perlmutter and Ruth Ann Perlmutter, *The Real Anti-Semitism in America* (New York: Arbor House, 1982), 236.

88. In the Perlmutters' words, "Today the interest of Jews are not so much threatened by their familiar nemesis, crude anti-Semitism, as by a-Semitic governmental policies, the proponents of which may be free of anti-Semitism." These policies include "thirst of Western economies for recycled petrodollars," neo-isolationism, and compensatory group rights (such as affirmative action), among others. And in their view, "Jews today face greater jeopardy from quarters which though innocent of bigotry, nonetheless pose us greater danger than do our long time, easily recognizable anti-Semitic nemeses. Unchallenged and unchecked, these issues in sur-

face appearance Semitically neutral, can hurt Jews and resisted as need be, can loose once again classical anti-Semitism." *Real Anti-Semitism*, 9, 231–32.

89. Quoted in Hillel Halkin, "The Return of Anti-Semitism," *Commentary*, February 2002, 30.

90. Natan Sharansky, "Anti-Semitism Is Our Problem," *Ha'aretz*, August 10, 2003. Also Zuckerman, "Shameful Contagion."

91. Peter Novick, *The Holocaust in American Life* (New York: Houghton Mifflin, 1999); Jack Wertheimer, "Jewish Organizational Life," in *American Jewish Yearbook 1995* (New York: American Jewish Committee, 1995), 70; and Frank Rich, "The Booing of Wolfowitz," *New York Times*, May 11, 2002.

92. Leon Wieseltier, "Hitler Is Dead: The Case Against Jewish Ethnic Panic," *New Republic*, May 27, 2002 (both Hentoff and Rosenbaum are quoted in this article). Former Undersecretary of State Stuart Eizenstat offered a similar caution in April 2007, writing that "while antisemitism has not been extinguished, the gravity of the Holocaust has been imbedded on world opinion. Levels of general antisemitic attitudes have declined sharply. There has been a successful decades-long Catholic-Jewish dialogue, with important statements by the Vatican that diminish religious-based anti-Semitism . . . Most Western European countries have Holocaust remembrance days, and several have Holocaust memorial museums . . . Virtually every major European nation provides police protection for Jewish synagogues and religious schools. Antisemitic actions are met with firm responses, as in France, albeit belatedly." Stuart Eizenstat, "The Dangers Are Great, but It Is Not 1938," *Forward*, April 20, 2007.

93. Yossi Beilin, "The Case for Carter," *Forward*, January 16, 2007.

94. Prominent Israelis who have used the term include former Attorney General Michael Ben Yair, deputy mayor of Jerusalem Meron Benvenisti, peace activist Uri Avnery, former Education Minister Shulamit Aloni, and a number of Israeli peace groups. See Joseph Lelyveld, "Jimmy Carter and Apartheid," *New York Review of Books*, March 29, 2007. On Tutu and Kasrils, see Desmond Tutu and Ian Urbina, "Against Israeli Apartheid," *Nation*, June 27, 2002; and Jonny Paul, "South African Jewish Minister Sends Support to 'Israel Apartheid Week' Organizers," *Jerusalem Post*, February 22, 2007.

95. As Shmuel Rosner notes, Carter's critics "are almost all Jews," but as the Yossi Beilin quotation in the previous paragraph makes clear, not all Jews were critical of the former president. "The Carter Trap," *Ha'aretz*, January 15, 2007. On the very different reaction to Carter among non-Jews, see M. J. Rosenberg, "Israel's Increased Isolation," Weekly Opinion Column, Issue #308, Israel Policy Forum, Washington, DC, January 19, 2007.

96. Foxman is quoted in James Besser, "Jewish Criticism of Carter Intensifies," *Jewish Week*, December 15, 2006; and Martin Peretz, "Carter's Legacy," *The Spine* (*New Republic* weblog), November 28, 2006.

97. Deborah Lipstadt, "Jimmy Carter's Jewish Problem," *Washington Post*, January 20, 2007.

98. "Carter Defends Book on Israel Conflict," *Jerusalem Post*, January 21, 2007.

99. Specifically, Krauthammer referred to Fukuyama's argument as a "novel way of Judaizing neoconservatism" and said that "his is not the crude kind [of argument], advanced by Pat Buchanan and Malaysia's Mahathir Mohamad, among others, that American neoconservatives (read: Jews) are simply doing Israel's bidding, hijacking American foreign policy in the service of Israel and the greater Jewish conspiracy. Fukuyama's take is more subtle and implicit." Despite the distinction, Krauthammer was clearly suggesting that Fukuyama was a "subtle" anti-Semite. For the exchange, see Francis Fukuyama, "The Neoconservative Moment," *National Interest* 76 (Summer 2004); Charles Krauthammer, "In Defense of Democratic Realism," *National Interest* 77 (Fall 2004); Francis Fukuyama, "Letter," *National Interest* 78 (Winter 2004/05); and Charles Krauthammer, "Letter," *National Interest* 79 (Spring 2005).

100. Eliot Cohen, "Yes, It's Anti-Semitic," *Washington Post*, April 5, 2006; and Eli Lake, "David Duke Claims to Be Vindicated by a Harvard Dean," *New York Sun*, March 20, 2006.

101. Anti-Defamation League, "Mearsheimer and Walt's Anti-Israel Screed: A Relentless Assault

in Scholarly Guise," *ADL Analysis* (online), March 24, 2006; Josef Joffe, "Common Denominator," *New Republic Online*, April 10, 2006; Benny Morris, "And Now for Some Facts: The Ignorance at the Heart of an Innuendo," *New Republic*, May 8, 2006; Michael B. Oren, "Quiet Riot: Tinfoil Hats in Harvard Yard," *New Republic*, April 10, 2006; and Martin Peretz, "Oil and Vinegar: Surveying the Israel Lobby," *New Republic*, April 10, 2006.

102. William Kristol, "Anti-Judaism," *Wall Street Journal*, September 8, 2006; Ruth R. Wisse, "Israel Lobby," *Wall Street Journal*, March 22, 2006; and Shmuel Rosner, "Is Carter an Anti-Semite?" *Ha'aretz*, December 21, 2006.

103. The quotes are from Alvin H. Rosenfeld, "'Progressive' Jewish Thought and the New Anti-Semitism," American Jewish Committee, December 2006, v, 9. Also see Patricia Cohen, "Essay Linking Liberal Jews and Anti-Semitism Sparks a Furor," *New York Times*, January 31, 2007; Larry Cohler-Esses, "Anger over Broadside Aimed at Jewish Leftists," *Jewish Week*, February 9, 2007; Ben Harris, "Suddenly, Little-Noticed Essay Is Focus of Debate on Israel Criticism," *JTA.org*, February 7, 2007; Alan Wolfe, "Free Speech, Israel, and Jewish Illiberalism," *Chronicle Review* (of the *Chronicle of Higher Education*), November 17, 2006; and Gaby Wood, "The New Jewish Question," *Observer*, February 11, 2007.

104. Michael Lerner, "There Is No New Anti-Semitism," *Baltimore Chronicle & Sentinel* (online), February 2, 2007.

105. Kristof, "Talking About Israel"; George Soros, "Of Israel, America, and AIPAC," *New York Review of Books*, April 12, 2007; and "Diaspora Blues," *Economist* editorial, January 13, 2007.

106. Kristol, "Anti-Judaism." Kristol's solution is instead to accuse critics of Israel—including us—of "bigotry" and being "anti-Jewish."

INTRODUCTION TO PART II

1. For a good example of the conventional wisdom, see Nathan Guttman, "A Marriage Cemented by Terror," *Salon.com*, January 24, 2006.

7: THE LOBBY VERSUS THE PALESTINIANS

1. Thomas Oliphant, "A Delicate Balance," *Boston Globe*, September 18, 2001; and Jane Perlez and Patrick E. Tyler, "Before Attacks, U.S. Was Ready to Say It Backed Palestinian State," *New York Times*, October 2, 2001.

2. Robert G. Kaiser, "Bush and Sharon Nearly Identical on Mideast Policy," *Washington Post*, February 9, 2003.

3. Jane Perlez and and Katharine Q. Seelye, "U.S. Strongly Rebukes Sharon for Criticism of Bush, Calling It 'Unacceptable,'" *New York Times*, October 6, 2001. Also John Donnelly, "Nation Set to Push Sharon on Agreement," *Boston Globe*, October 10, 2001; Lee Hockstader, "Sharon Apologetic over Row with U.S.," *Washington Post*, October 7, 2001; Lee Hockstader and Daniel Williams, "Israel Says It Won't 'Pay Price' of Coalition," *Washington Post*, September 18, 2001; "Israel's Opportunity," *Los Angeles Times* editorial, September 18, 2001; and Jonathan Karp, "Sharon Cancels Peace Talks in Rebuff to U.S. Concerns," *Wall Street Journal*, September 24, 2001.

4. Julian Borger, "US Backs State for Palestine," *Guardian*, October 3, 2001; Kurt Eichenwald, "U.S. Jews Split on Washington's Shift on Palestinian State," *New York Times*, October 5, 2001; and Glenn Kessler, "Talking Points Aside, Bush Stance on Palestinian State Is Not a First," *Washington Post*, October 5, 2001. At the same time, Prime Minister Tony Blair made "Britain's strongest endorsement yet of Palestinian statehood." Michael Dobbs, "Blair Backs Creation of Palestinian State," *Washington Post*, October 16, 2001.

5. Hockstader, "Sharon Apologetic."

6. James Bennet, "Sharon Invokes Munich in Warning U.S. on 'Appeasement,'" *New York Times*, October 5, 2001; Perlez and Seelye, "U.S. Strongly Rebukes Sharon"; and Alan

Sipress and Lee Hockstader, "Sharon Speech Riles U.S.," *Washington Post*, October 6, 2001. For evidence that other Israelis shared Sharon's fears, see Israel Harel, "Lessons from the Next War," *Ha'aretz*, October 6, 2001.

7. Sipress and Hockstader, "Sharon Speech."

8. Donnelly, "Nation Set to Push Sharon"; Perlez and Seelye, "U.S. Strongly Rebukes Sharon"; and Sipress and Hockstader, "Sharon Speech."

9. Hockstader, "Sharon Apologetic"; and Serge Schmemann, "Raising Munich, Sharon Reveals Israeli Qualms," *New York Times*, October 6, 2001.

10. Quoted in Tim Weiner, "Israel Rebuffs Demands to End West Bank Raids," *New York Times*, October 24, 2001.

11. Suzanne Goldenberg, "Sharon Defies US Demand to Retreat," *Guardian*, October 24, 2001. Also see Peter Beaumont, "Defiant Israelis Abandon Pull-out," *Observer*, October 28, 2001; Suzanne Goldenberg, "Israel Lays Down Tough New Conditions for Withdrawal," *Guardian*, October 27, 2001; Dana Milbank and Lee Hockstader, "Israeli Incursion Strains Relations," *Washington Post*, October 24, 2001; and Staff and Agencies, "US Criticizes Israeli Offensive," *Guardian*, October 22, 2001.

12. William Safire, "'Israel or Arafat,'" *New York Times*, December 3, 2001. Also see Aluf Benn, "Analysis: Clutching at Straws," *Ha'aretz*, September 18, 2001; and "Excerpts from Talk by Sharon," *New York Times*, December 4, 2001.

13. Shlomo Shamir, "U.S. Jews: Sharon Is 'Worried' by Terrorism Distinction," *Ha'aretz*, September 18, 2001.

14. This letter was published in the *Weekly Standard*, October 1, 2001.

15. Quoted in James D. Besser, "Terror Clouds Bush Plan to Back Palestinian State," *Jewish News Weekly* (online), October 5, 2001.

16. Quoted in Kurt Eichenwald, "U.S. Jews Split on Washington's Shift on Palestinian State," *New York Times*, October 5, 2001. Also see Michael J. Jordan, "Bush Backed—Finally," *Jewish Journal of Greater Los Angeles* (online), October 12, 2001.

17. ADL press release, "ADL 'Extremely Troubled' by Comments from State Department Official," October 23, 2001. Also see Milbank and Hockstader, "Israeli Incursion."

18. Quoted in Kenneth R. Bazinet, "Israel Rejects Call for Pullout; Bush, Powell Demand Troops Leave Six Towns," *New York Daily News* (online), October 24, 2001.

19. Elaine Sciolino, "Senators Urge Bush Not to Hamper Israel," *New York Times*, November 17, 2001.

20. Quoted in Dana Milbank, "Bush Spokesman Gentle on Israeli Assault," *Washington Post*, December 3, 2001; and David Sanger, "U.S. Walks a Tightrope on Terrorism in Israel," *New York Times*, December 4, 2001. Also see Safire, "'Israel or Arafat.'"

21. Articles that raise doubts about the link between the Palestinians and the *Karine A* include Charles D. Smith, "The 'Do More' Chorus in Washington," *Middle East Report Online*, April 15, 2002; Brian Whitaker, "Voyage of the Arms Ship," *Guardian*, January 14, 2002; and Brian Whitaker, "The Strange Affair of Karine A," *Guardian*, January 21, 2002.

22. James Bennet, "Skipper Ties Cargo to Arafat's Group," *New York Times*, January 8, 2002; Lawrence F. Kaplan, "Torpedo Boat," *New Republic*, February 18, 2002; Ion Mihai Pacepa, "The Arafat I Know," *Wall Street Journal*, January 10, 2002; Tom Rose, "Arafat's Naval Adventure: It's Time for Him to Go," *Weekly Standard*, January 21, 2002; Robert Satloff, "Karine-A: The Strategic Implications of Iranian-Palestinian Collusion," Policy Watch #593, Washington Institute for Near East Policy, January 15, 2002; and Gerald M. Steinberg, "The Demilitarization Scam," *Jerusalem Post*, January 11, 2002. Also see Robert Satloff, "The Peace Process at Sea: The *Karine-A* Affair and the War on Terrorism," *National Interest* 67 (Spring 2002).

23. Powell said one week after the *Karine A* was seized, "The information we are receiving . . . makes it clear that there are linkages to the Palestinian Authority. I have not seen any information that yet links it directly to Chairman Arafat." "Powell Comments on Arms Shipment Seized by Israel," January 10, 2002, *CNN.com./Transcripts*. Arafat, who was under pressure from the Bush administration to take responsibility for the incident, eventually did so, al-

though he denied that he had prior knowledge of it. "Arafat Takes Blame for Arms Shipment," *BBC News* (online), February 14, 2002; Lee Hockstader, "Arafat Arrests 3 in Arms Incident," *Washington Post*, January 12, 2002; and "Powell Says Arafat Takes Responsibility," *New York Times*, February 14, 2002.

24. "Remarks by President George Bush and Prime Minister Ariel Sharon in Photo Opportunity," White House, February 7, 2002, a copy of which can be found on the Israeli Foreign Ministry website, www.mfa.gov.il/.

25. Keith B. Richburg and Molly Moore, "Israel Rejects Demands to Withdraw Troops," *Washington Post*, April 11, 2002. All quotes in this paragraph are from Fareed Zakaria, "Colin Powell's Humiliation: Bush Should Clearly Support His Secretary of State—Otherwise He Should Get a New One," *Newsweek*, April 29, 2002. Also see Mike Allen and John Lancaster, "Defiant Sharon Losing Support in White House," *Washington Post*, April 11, 2002, which describes the Bush administration's anger with Sharon.

26. Karen DeYoung, *Soldier: The Life of Colin Powell* (New York: Knopf, 2006), 383.

27. William Kristol and Robert Kagan, "'Senior White House Aides': Speak Up!" *Weekly Standard*, April 11, 2002.

28. Transcript of "Shields and Brooks," *NewsHour with Jim Lehrer*, April 12, 2002, www.pbs .org/newshour/bb/political_wrap/jan-june02/sb_4-12.html.

29. Elaine Sciolino, "Netanyahu Says Powell Mission 'Won't Amount to Anything' and Urges Arafat's Exile," *New York Times*, April 11, 2002.

30. Bob Woodward, *Bush at War* (New York: Simon & Schuster, 2002), 323–26.

31. Quoted in DeYoung, *Soldier*, 383. Bush had told Powell before he left for the Middle East, "I know how hard it's going to be. It's going to be very bad. But you've got enough standing . . . you'll get burned, but you can handle it. There'll be enough of you left when it's over." Ibid., 379.

32. John Simpson, "Israeli Leader Has More Power in Washington than Powell," *Sunday Telegraph* (London), April 14, 2002.

33. James D. Besser, "No Tennessee Waltz," *Jewish Week*, December 27, 2002; and Romesh Ratnesar, "The Right's New Crusade," *Time*, May 6, 2002. Also see Mike Allen and Juliet Eilperin, "White House and DeLay at Odds," *Washington Post*, April 26, 2002; and Judith Eilperin and Helen Dewar, "Lawmakers Endorse Israel's Offensive," *Washington Post*, May 3, 2002. Bush was feeling intense pressure not just from lawmakers but also from Jewish leaders and Christian evangelicals. See Allen and Lancaster, "Defiant Sharon"; Dan Balz, "Bush Statement on Mideast Reflects Tension in GOP," *Washington Post*, April 7, 2002; Elisabeth Bumiller, "Seeking to Stem Growing Political Fury, Bush Sends Conservative to Pro-Israel Rally," *New York Times*, April 16, 2002; Bradley Burston, "Background: Can Bush Afford to Press Sharon for Peace?" *Ha'aretz*, May 6, 2002; Alison Mitchell, "U.S. Political Leaders Seek Unity on Mideast, for Now," *New York Times*, April 12, 2002; William Safire, "On Being an Ally," *New York Times*, April 11, 2002; Diana Jean Schemo, "Over 100,000 Rally in Washington to Support Israel," *New York Times*, April 16, 2002; Alan Sipress, "Policy Divide Thwarts Powell in Mideast Effort," *Washington Post*, April 26, 2002; and Alan Sipress and Karen DeYoung, "U.S. Presses Ahead with Peace Efforts," *Washington Post*, May 9, 2002.

34. Ratnesar, "The Right's New Crusade."

35. Randall Mikkelsen, "White House Calls Sharon 'Man of Peace,'" Reuters, April 11, 2002; and Bill Sammon, "White House Softens Tone with Israel," *Washington Times*, April 12, 2002. Bush later told Sharon that he "took immense crap" for calling him a "man of peace." Glenn Kessler, "Bush Sticks to the Broad Strokes," *Washington Post*, June 3, 2003.

36. David Sanger, "President Praises Effort by Powell in the Middle East," *New York Times*, April 19, 2002; and Peter Slevin and Mike Allen, "Bush: Sharon a 'Man of Peace,'" *Washington Post*, April 19, 2002. For a transcript of the press conference, see "President Bush, Secretary Powell Discuss Middle East," White House, Office of the Press Secretary, April 18, 2002.

37. All quotes in this paragraph are from Matthew E. Berger, "D.C. Rally Is Large and Loud— but Will Bush Listen?" *JTA.org*, April 19, 2002. Also see Sharon Samber and Matthew E.

Berger, "Speakers Stick to Consensus Theme at National Solidarity Rally for Israel," *JTA.org*, April 15, 2002.

38. John Diamond, "Netanyahu Tells U.S. That Arafat 'Has to Go,'" *Chicago Tribune*, April 11, 2002; and Nathan Guttman, "Ladies and Gentlemen, Benjamin Netanyahu," *Ha'aretz*, April 15, 2002. Also see Benjamin Netanyahu, "The Root Cause of Terrorism," *Wall Street Journal*, April 19, 2002.

39. Eilperin and Dewar, "Lawmakers Endorse Israel's Offensive"; Juliet Eilperin and Mike Allen, "Hill Leaders Plan Votes on Pro-Israel Resolutions," *Washington Post*, May 2, 2002; and Alison Mitchell, "House and Senate Support Israel in Strong Resolutions," *New York Times*, May 3, 2002. See "2 Resolutions 'Expressing Solidarity with Israel,'" *New York Times*, May 3, 2002; and Matthew E. Berger, "Bills in Congress Boost Israel, Treat Arafat as Terrorist," *Jewish Bulletin* (online), April 26, 2002.

40. Arieh O'Sullivan, "Visiting Congressmen Advise Israel to Resist Administration Pressure to Deal with Arafat," *Jerusalem Post*, May 6, 2002.

41. Eli Lake, "Israeli Lobby Wins $200 Million Fight," United Press International, May 11, 2002.

42. Both quotes in this paragraph are from Jefferson Morley, "Who's in Charge?" *Washington Post*, April 26, 2002. Akiva Eldar noted just before Sharon steamrolled Bush, "Sharon has a lot of experience sticking it to the Americans . . . Ultimately, whether it was Palestinian terror, Arafat's mistakes, or domestic politics, the Americans were sent to the peanut gallery." See "Words Are Not Enough," *Ha'aretz*, April 8, 2002.

43. "President Bush Calls for New Palestinian Leadership," transcript of June 24, 2002, speech, White House, Office of the Press Secretary.

44. Quoted in Tracy Wilkinson, "In Mideast, Sharon Looks Like a Winner After Speech," *Los Angeles Times*, June 25, 2002.

45. Uzi Benziman, "Right-hand Man," *Ha'aretz*, June 28, 2002.

46. Aluf Benn, "Analysis: Ariel Sharon Agrees to His Own Ideas," *Ha'aretz*, July 5, 2002. Also see Elisabeth Bumiller and David E. Sanger, "Bush Demands Arafat's Ouster Before U.S. Backs a New State; Israelis Welcome Tough Line," *New York Times*, June 25, 2002; Glenn Kessler, "Framework for Peace Tough on Palestinians," *Washington Post*, June 25, 2002; and Don Wycliff, "Sharon Dictates and Bush Follows," *Chicago Tribune*, June 27, 2002.

47. "An Uncertain Road Map," *Washington Post* editorial, June 25, 2002; "A Plan Without a Map," *New York Times* editorial, June 25, 2002; Richard Cohen, "Answers on an Empty Page," *Washington Post*, June 27, 2002; Jonathan Freedland, "George W's Bloody Folly," *Guardian*, June 26, 2002; Jim Hoagland, "Thorny Details to Come," *Washington Post*, June 26, 2002; Gideon Samet, "Another Step Toward Nowhere," *Ha'aretz*, June 26, 2002; and Patrick E. Tyler, "Clear Terms, Murky Future," *New York Times*, June 25, 2002.

48. James Bennet, "Arafat Wants No. 2 Man in the P.L.O. as the Premier," *New York Times*, March 7, 2003.

49. "A Performance-Based Roadmap to a Permanent Two-State Solution to the Israeli-Palestinian Conflict," press statement, U.S. Department of State, Office of the Spokesman, April 30, 2003.

50. Quoted in Ami Eden, "Bush's Maneuvers Bewilder Jerusalem and Activists," *Forward*, June 6, 2003. Also see Ronald Brownstein, "Push for Peace Poses Domestic Political Risk for Bush," *Los Angeles Times*, June 5, 2003; and David E. Sanger, "Middle East Mediator: Big New Test for Bush," *New York Times*, June 5, 2003.

51. "Mr. Sharon's Promise," *Washington Post* editorial, December 16, 2002. Also see Akiva Eldar, "Truth or Consequences," *Ha'aretz*, December 12, 2002.

52. Ori Nir, "U.S. Groups Seek to Cast Peace 'Map' as a Threat," *Forward*, May 2, 2003; and Chemi Shalev, "Sharon Government Scrambles as Bush Prepares 'Road Map,'" *Forward*, March 21, 2003.

53. Shalev, "Sharon Government." Also see Glenn Kessler and Molly Moore, "Sharon's Refusal to Accept Plan Vexes Powell Trip," *Washington Post*, May 13, 2003; and Gideon Samet, "From Determination to Wimpiness," *Ha'aretz*, May 14, 2003.

54. "No New Sharon," *Ha'aretz* editorial, April 14, 2003.

55. Quoted in Nir, "U.S. Groups."

56. All subsequent quotes and information in this paragraph are from Nathan Guttman, "American Jews Tread Softly on 'Road Map' During War in Iraq," *Ha'aretz*, March 26, 2003.

57. Nir, "U.S. Groups." Also see Nathan Guttman, "Senators, Congressmen Put Pro-Israel Stance in Writing," *Ha'aretz*, April 18, 2003.

58. Ori Nir, "Right Slams Plan, Center Remains Quiet," *Forward*, June 6, 2003.

59. Charles Krauthammer, "The Roadblock on the Road Map," *Washington Post*, May 9, 2003.

60. Nir, "Right Slams Plan."

61. Bradley Burston, "Background: Betting on Abu Mazen—to Lose," *Ha'aretz*, May 1, 2003. Also see Dan Izenberg, "Bush Statehood Call Doesn't Faze Israel," *Jerusalem Post*, March 16, 2003.

62. Aluf Benn, "Analysis: The U.S. Is Now Micro-managing the Process," *Ha'aretz*, June 22, 2003; Uzi Benziman, "Corridors of Power: On the Road to Nowhere," *Ha'aretz*, June 13, 2003; Burston, "Background: Betting"; and Ori Nir, "No Discussion of Settlements, Diplomats Say," *Forward*, May 9, 2003.

63. Guy Dinmore and Harvey Morris, "'Road Map' Drivers Reluctant to Embark on First Leg of Journey," *Financial Times*, May 9, 2003.

64. Bradley Burston, "Background: Has Sharon's Hamas Hitlist Converted Bush?" *Ha'aretz*, June 17, 2003.

65. Ze'ev Schiff, "Focus: Americans Fear Abu Mazen Is Further Weakened," *Ha'aretz*, June 12, 2003.

66. Arnon Regular, "Hamas Says It Will Consider Renewing Cease-fire Dialogue," *Ha'aretz*, June 10, 2003.

67. "Sad, but Not Surprising," *Forward* editorial, June 13, 2003.

68. Burston, "Background: Sharon's Hamas Hitlist." Also see Uzi Benziman, "The Cock's Arrogance," *Ha'aretz*, June 15, 2003.

69. The information and quotations in this paragraph are from Dana Milbank, "Bush's Shift on Israel Was Swift," *Washington Post*, June 21, 2003. Also see Ori Nir, "American-Israeli Relations Strained Following Attack," *Forward*, June 13, 2003; and Steven R. Weisman and James Dao, "Bush Under Fire in Congress for Criticizing Israel," *New York Times*, June 12, 2003.

70. Glenn Kessler, "White House Backs Latest Israeli Attacks," *Washington Post*, June 13, 2003. Also see Burston, "Background: Sharon's Hamas Hitlist."

71. Quoted in Kessler, "White House Backs Latest Israeli Attacks."

72. "U.S. Congress Backs Israel's Response to Terrorist Attacks," *Ha'aretz*, June 26, 2003.

73. Edward S. Walker, the head of the Middle East Institute and a former U.S. diplomat, noted at the time that Bush "makes a statement and it rolls off Sharon's back. He has a credibility problem." Quoted in Kessler, "White House Backs Latest Israeli Attacks."

74. For a detailed map showing the proposed route of the "separation barrier," see the website of the Israeli human rights group B'Tselem, www.btselem.org/Download/Separation_Barrier_Map_Eng.pdf.

75. "President Bush Welcomes Prime Minister Abbas to White House," transcript of remarks by President Bush and Prime Minister Abbas, White House, Office of the Press Secretary, July 25, 2003.

76. Rupert Cornwell, "Sharon Rejects Bush's Call to Take Down 'Security' Fence," *Independent*, July 30, 2003; Herb Keinon, "Israel-US Rift Emerges over Security Fence Issue," *Jerusalem Post*, June 30, 2003; "PM: We Will Build Fence; Bush: PA Must Dismantle Terror Groups," *Ha'aretz*, July 30, 2003; and David Stout, "Israel to Continue Building Security Fence Criticized by Bush," *New York Times*, July 29, 2003.

77. Israel would receive $3 billion annually for three years. Ze'ev Schiff, "U.S. Warns of Financial Sanctions over Security Fence," *Ha'aretz*, August 3, 2003; "U.S. Officials Confirm Aid to Israel May Be Cut over Fence," *Ha'aretz*, August 5, 2003; Steven R. Weisman, "U.S. May Reduce Aid to Get Israel to Halt Barrier," *New York Times*, August 5, 2003; and Robin

Wright, "U.S. May Punish Israel for Building Fence in W. Bank," *Los Angeles Times*, August 5, 2003.

78. Quoted in Ori Nir, "Bush Eases Pressure on Both Sides over Peace Plan," *Forward*, August 8, 2003. Also see Stewart Ain, "Bush Rapped for Mulling Sanctions over Fence," *Jewish Week*, August 8, 2003; and Eric Marx, "Dems Blast Bush over Threats to Israel," *Forward*, August 15, 2003.

79. Quoted in James Bennet, "Israel Reportedly Willing to Delay Portions of Barrier," *New York Times*, August 8, 2003.

80. Nathan Guttman, "U.S. Confirms Fence Prompted Loan Cuts," *Ha'aretz*, November 27, 2003. Also see Guy Dinmore, "US 'to Withhold Funds' over Israeli Actions," *Financial Times*, September 15, 2003; and Richard W. Stevenson, "U.S. Cutting Loan Guarantees to Oppose Israeli Settlements," *New York Times*, September 17, 2003.

81. Douglas Jehl, "U.S. Wary of Steps by Israelis on Arafat," *New York Times*, September 12, 2003; "Powell Says U.S. Opposes Expulsion of Arafat," *New York Times*, September 12, 2003; and Steven R. Weisman, "Bush Administration Warns Israel Not to Expel Arafat," *New York Times*, September 8, 2003.

82. Dov Weisglass, a key Sharon adviser, later recounted that "at the end of the summer of 2003, we reached the sad conclusion that there is no one to talk to, no one to negotiate with. Hence the disengagement plan. Because when you're playing solitaire, when there is no one sitting across from you at the table, you have no choice but to deal the cards yourself." Quoted in Avi Shavit, "The Big Freeze," *Ha'aretz*, October 8, 2004.

83. Aluf Benn, "Sharon Met Secretly with U.S. Emissary," *Ha'aretz*, November 24, 2003; and Peter Slevin, "Delicate Maneuvers Led to U.S.-Israeli Stance," *Washington Post*, April 16, 2004. Also see Chris McGreal, "U.S. to Endorse Israeli Plans for Gaza," *Guardian*, February 18, 2004.

84. Yossi Alpher, "Middle East: Beware of Ariel Sharon Bearing Gifts," *International Herald Tribune*, April 13, 2004; Aluf Benn, "Israel's Identity Crisis," *Salon.com*, May 16, 2005; Meron Benvenisti, "Sharon's Second 'Big Plan,'" *Ha'aretz*, January 12, 2006; and "Indyk: Sharon's Plan to Pull Out of Gaza and Part of West Bank Could Lead to Increased Violence," interview with Martin Indyk conducted by Bernard Gwertzman, March 19, 2004, Council on Foreign Relations, www.cfr.org/publication/6882/.

85. Quoted in Shavit, "Big Freeze." Also see John Ward Anderson, "Sharon Aide Says Goal of Gaza Plan Is to Halt Road Map," *Washington Post*, October 7, 2004; Aluf Benn, "Analysis: The Adviser That Roared," *Ha'aretz*, October 8, 2004; and Terence Neilan, "Israeli Causes Uproar over Status of Road Map," *New York Times*, October 6, 2004.

86. "Rice: Israel Must Fulfill Its Responsibilities for Peace," *Ha'aretz*, August 25, 2003.

87. "Bush Says World Owes Sharon a 'Thank You,'" *Ha'aretz*, April 21, 2004; and George W. Bush, "Our Nation Is Stronger and Safer with Israel as an Ally," speech to the AIPAC Annual Conference, May 18, 2004. Also see "President Bush Commends Israeli Prime Minister Sharon's Plan," transcript of remarks by President Bush and Prime Minister Sharon, White House, Office of the Press Secretary, April 14, 2004.

88. Regarding the views of previous presidents, see Clyde R. Mark, "Israeli–United States Relations," *Issue Brief for Congress*, Congressional Research Service, August 29, 2002, 7. For Bush's comments, see "Statement by the President Regarding Israel-Arab Peace Process," April 14, 2004; and "President Bush's Letter to Prime Minister Sharon," April 14, 2004, both available at www.jewishvirtuallibrary.org/. Also see Slevin, "Delicate Maneuvers."

89. On the Arab reaction, see "Bush Says World Owes Sharon." Regarding the consequences for Bush's reelection, see E. J. Kessler, "Hardliners Knock Bush for Endorsing Sharon Initiative," *Forward*, April 23, 2004; Dana Milbank and Mike Allen, "Move Could Help Bush Among Jewish Voters," *Washington Post*, April 15, 2004; and Maura Reynolds and Peter Wallsten, "Bush Gains in Efforts to Win Over Jewish Vote," *Los Angeles Times*, May 19, 2004.

90. Thomas L. Friedman, "A Rude Awakening," *New York Times*, February 5, 2004.

91. "A Performance-Based Roadmap." Regarding the ongoing differences between Israel and

the Bush administration over the settlements, the following articles are a sample of many that have been written on the subject: "Bush Condemns Settlement Policy; UN Adopts Road Map," *Ha'aretz*, November 20, 2003; "Israel Has Stepped Up the Pace of Settlement Building," *Guardian*, March 3, 2004; Donald Macintyre, "Sharon Vows to Defy Bush over Expansion of Israeli Settlements," *Independent*, April 22, 2005; Greg Myre and Steven R. Weisman, "Israel to Build 600 Homes in 3 Settlements; U.S. Officials Are Critical," *New York Times*, October 3, 2003; Ze'ev Schiff, "U.S.: Israel Shirking Its Promises on Settlement Boundaries," *Ha'aretz*, March 15, 2005; Peter Slevin, "Bush Won't Press End to Israeli Settlements," *Washington Post*, July 28, 2002; and Amy Teibel, "U.S. to Israel: Stop Expanding Settlements," *Washington Post*, June 26, 2005.

92. Quoted in Karen DeYoung, "U.S. Decries Israeli Missile Strike, Ponders Effect on Peace Bid," *Washington Post*, July 24, 2002. Also see John Ward Anderson and Molly Moore, "Palestinians Vow Revenge after Gaza Missile Strike," *Washington Post*, July 24, 2002; James Bennet and John Kifner, "Palestinian Cease-Fire Was in Works Before Israeli Strike," *New York Times*, July 25, 2002; and James Bennet, "Stalemate in Mideast After Deadly Bombing," *New York Times*, July 28, 2002.

93. Jim Hoagland, "Sharon and the Big Picture," *Washington Post*, March 25, 2004. Also see Roane Carey and Adam Shatz, "Israel Plays with Fire," *Nation*, April 12, 2004; H.D.S. Greenway, "Assassination Fallout Bodes Ill for US," *Boston Globe*, March 26, 2004; Tony Karon, "How Israel's Hamas Killing Affects the U.S.," *Time*, March 23, 2004; Bill Nichols, "U.S. Objectives at Risk in Anti-Israel Backlash," *USA Today*, March 22, 2004; David R. Sands, "Israel's Killing of Yassin Puts U.S. in Line of Fire," *Washington Times*, March 23, 2004; and Brian Whitaker, "Assassination Method: Surveillance Drone and a Hellfire Missile," *Guardian*, March 23, 2004.

94. John Ward Anderson, "Top Hamas Leader in Gaza City Killed," *Washington Post*, April 17, 2004.

95. Hussein Agha and Robert Malley, "The Last Palestinian," *New York Review of Books*, February 10, 2005; Steven Erlanger, "Abbas Declares War with Israel Effectively Over," *New York Times*, February 14, 2005; Donald Macintyre, "Abbas Pledges to Seek Peace with Israel," *Independent*, January 16, 2005; and Arnon Regular and Amos Harel, "Report: Abbas to Declare Not All Refugees to Return to Israel," *Ha'aretz*, March 15, 2005.

96. "No Time for Dithering," *Forward* editorial, October 22, 2004; Ori Nir, "Influential American Jewish Coalition Balks at Endorsing Sharon's Gaza Plan," *Forward*, October 22, 2004; and Shlomo Shamir, "U.S. Jewish Leaders Split over Public Support for Pullout," *Ha'aretz*, October 17, 2004. Also see James D. Besser, "The Real Coalition: U.S. and Israel," *Jewish News Weekly* (online), May 5, 2006; and James D. Besser, "Olmert Capitalizes on Uncertainties in Washington," *Jewish News Weekly* (online), June 2, 2006.

97. Bradley Burston, "Hamas 'R' Us," *Ha'aretz*, January 18, 2006. Also see Akiva Eldar, "Kadima to a New Middle East," *Ha'aretz*, December 19, 2005; Akiva Eldar, "Who Needs Abu Mazen?" *Ha'aretz*, November 7, 2005; Ran HaCohen, "Hamas and Israel: Rival Twins," *Antiwar.com*, February 6, 2006; M. J. Rosenberg, "No Partner—As Always," Weekly Opinion Column, Issue #260, Israel Policy Forum, Washington, DC, February 3, 2006; Danny Rubenstein, "All We Did Was Switch the Non-Partner," *Ha'aretz*, February 5, 2006; and "Disarray Among the Palestinians," *New York Times* editorial, January 17, 2006.

98. Peter Baker and Glenn Kessler, "Israel Has 'Bold Ideas,' Bush Says," *Washington Post*, May 24, 2006; and Aluf Benn, "Analysis: George Bush Wants the Convergence Plan Too," *Ha'aretz*, May 24, 2006.

99. Ian Fisher and Steven Erlanger, "Israel: Troops Move into Gaza," *New York Times*, June 28, 2006.

100. Quoted in Aluf Benn, "PM: Unilateralism Has Been a Failure," *Ha'aretz*, January 9, 2007. Also see Yehuda Ben Meir and Dafna Shaked, "The People Speak: Israeli Public Opinion on National Security, 2005–2007," Memorandum no. 90 (Tel Aviv: Institute for National Security Studies, May 2007), 10, 20, 59–63; Akiva Eldar, "A Post-Zionist Agenda," *Ha'aretz*, Oc-

tober 8, 2006; Yoav Peled, "Illusions of Unilateralism Dispelled in Israel," *Middle East Report Online*, October 11, 2006; and Jeremy Pressman, "Israeli Unilateralism and Israeli-Palestinian Relations, 2001–2006," *International Studies Perspective* 7, no. 4 (November 2006).

101. When Secretary of State Condoleezza Rice was trying to move the peace process forward in 2007, Martin Indyk of the Brookings Institution said that "there are others in the administration who want to 'Powellize' her." Those "others" were surely the neoconservatives, and he meant that they wanted to markedly reduce her influence on U.S. Middle East policy, as they had done with Powell when he was secretary of state before her. Indyk is quoted in Jim Lobe, "Rice Faces Formidable White House Foe," Inter Press Service, February 21, 2007.

102. Aluf Benn and Avi Issacharoff, "Jordan: US Must 'Actively Push' to Revive Mideast Peace Efforts," *Ha'aretz*, January 14, 2007; Glenn Kessler, "Abbas Rejects 'Temporary Borders' for Palestinian State," *Washington Post*, January 15, 2007; and Associated Press, "Rice Restates US Road Map Commitment," *Jerusalem Post*, January 14, 2007.

103. The 2002 and 2007 Arab league proposals can be found on the website of the Israeli Regional Peace Movement, www.rpm.org.il/initiative.html.

104. Helene Cooper, "After the Mecca Accord, Clouded Horizons," *New York Times*, February 21, 2007.

105. Olmert also said, "I'll never accept a solution that is based on their return to Israel, any number," and "I don't think we should accept any kind of responsibility for the creation of this problem. Full stop." Quoted in Steven Erlanger, "Olmert Rejects Right of Return for Palestinians," *New York Times*, March 31, 2007.

106. "A Welcome Summit in Riyadh," *Ha'aretz* editorial, March 29, 2007. Also see Yossi Alpher, "Respond to Riyadh by Convening 'Consultations,'" *Forward*, April 13, 2007; Alon Ben-Meir, "Israel Must Choose Peace, Not Occupation," *Jerusalem Post*, April 10, 2007; Akiva Eldar, "The Lost Five Years of the Peace Process," *Ha'aretz*, March 15, 2007; Jonathan Freedland, "Now Is the Time to Call the Bluff of the Land of Missed Opportunities," *Guardian*, March 28, 2007; M. J. Rosenberg, "Go for the Saudi Plan," Weekly Opinion Column, Issue #316, Israel Policy Forum, Washington, DC, March 30, 2007; Ze'ev Tsahor, "Our Leaders' Blindness," *Ynetnews.com*, April 1, 2007; and "U.S. Should Insist Israel Engages with Arab Peace Plan," *Financial Times* editorial, March 20, 2007.

107. Orly Halpern, "Foxman, Wiesel Upbraid Israel for Pace of Peace Effort," *Forward*, May 18, 2007; Aluf Benn, "PM: I'm Ready to Negotiate Saudi Peace Plan with Arab Leaders," *Ha'aretz*, May 15, 2006; "PM Invites Arab Leaders to Talk Peace," *Jerusalem Post*, May 15, 2007; Akiva Eldar, "Headlines Instead of Initiatives," *Ha'aretz*, April 5, 2007; and Herb Keinon, "Israel to Brand Arabs as Peace Spoilers," *Jerusalem Post*, March 23, 2007.

108. Adam Morrow and Khaled Moussa al-Omrani, "Egypt: Israel Seen as Fighting Peace," Inter Press Service, April 12, 2007.

109. Nathan Guttman, "Rice Briefs Jewish Groups as Palestinians Make Deal," *Forward*, February 9, 2007. There was little need for Jewish groups to worry, as Rice had given no indication in the previous month that she would put forward her own ideas on what a final settlement might look like or put pressure on Israel. See Anne Gearan, "Rice Has Loose Agenda for Mideast Talks," *Chicago Tribune*, January 18, 2007; Glenn Kessler, "Rice Highlights Opportunities After Setbacks on Mideast Trip," *Washington Post*, January 19, 2007; and Thom Shanker and Greg Myre, "Rice Backs Mideast Moderates, but Offers No Plan," *New York Times*, January 14, 2007.

110. "Charade in Jerusalem," *New York Times* editorial, February 21, 2007. Also see Glenn Kessler, "Rice's Mideast Talks Yield Little Except a Promise to Meet Again," *Washington Post*, February 20, 2007; and Glenn Kessler, "Rice Looks Back for a Way Forward on Mideast Peace," *Washington Post*, February 21, 2007.

111. Tim Butcher, "Israel Snubs Condoleezza Rice," *Daily Telegraph* (London), March 28, 2007. Also see Helene Cooper, "Mideast Leaders to Hold Talks Twice a Month," *New York Times*, March 28, 2007; Glenn Kessler, "On Mideast Trip, Rice to Try a New Formula," *Washing-

ton Post, March 23, 2007; and Donald Macintyre, "Israel Resists Rice Plan for Talks on Peace Settlement," *Independent*, March 27, 2007.

112. Associated Press, "Israel Breaks Settlement Promise to U.S.," *MSNBC.com*, December 26, 2006; Associated Press, "U.S. Challenges Israel on Settlement," *MSNBC.com*, December 27, 2006; Steven Erlanger, "First Settlement in 10 Years Fuels Mideast Tension," *New York Times*, December 27, 2006; Mark Lavie, "Israel Approves New Housing in West Bank," *San Diego Union-Tribune* (online), January 15, 2007.

113. Uri Avnery, "Next to Israel, Not in Place of It," *London Review of Books*, March 8, 2007; Glenn Kessler, "Rice Cautions Israel on Syria," *Washington Post*, May 30, 2007; and Gideon Levy, "Israel Doesn't Want Peace," *Ha'aretz*, April 8, 2007.

114. Khalil Shikaki, "With Hamas in Power: Impact of Palestinian Domestic Developments on Options for the Peace Process," Working Paper #1, Crown Center for Middle East Studies, Brandeis University, February 2007.

115. Lobe, "Rice Faces Formidable White House Foe."

116. Daniel Levy, "Time to Change the Tune," *Ha'aretz*, March 24, 2007.

117. Quoted in Lobe, "Rice Faces Formidable White House Foe."

118. Aluf Benn and Shmuel Rosner, "Olmert Reminds Rice: Bush Is Still Her Boss," *Ha'aretz*, April 2, 2007. The "eye-to-eye" quotation is in this article.

119. Philip Zelikow, "Strategies for the Multifront War Against Radical Islamists," keynote address to the Weinberg Founders Conference at the Washington Institute for Near East Policy, September 15, 2006. Also see Nathan Guttman, "US Sees Link Between Iran, Peace," *Jerusalem Post*, September 18, 2006; and Shmuel Rosner, "State Dept. Adviser: U.S. Tying Iran Policy to Palestinian Issue," *Ha'aretz*, September 18, 2006.

120. Helene Cooper and David Sanger, "Rice's Counselor Gives Advice Others May Not Want to Hear," *New York Times*, October 28, 2006. Also see Helene Cooper, "Senior Aide to Rice Resigns from Post," *New York Times*, November 28, 2006; Yochi J. Dreazen, Cam Simpson, and Mariam Fam, "Mideast Turmoil Pressures Bush to Revise Tactics," *Wall Street Journal*, November 30, 2006; and Glenn Kessler, "Close Advisor to Rice Plans to Resign," *Washington Post*, November 28, 2006.

121. Glenn Kessler, "Rice Names Critic of Iraq Policy to Counselor's Post," *Washington Post*, March 2, 2007; Eli Lake, "Trouble Looming for Rice," *New York Sun*, March 5, 2007; and Jim Lobe, "Rice Picks Neocon Champion of Iraq War as Counselor," *Antiwar.com*, March 3, 2007.

122. James D. Besser, "New Fight Brewing on PA Aid, Contacts," *Jewish Week*, April 6, 2007; Helene Cooper, "Splits Emerge Between U.S. and Europe over Aid for Palestinians," *New York Times*, February 22, 2007; Nathan Guttman, "U.S., Israel at Odds over Palestinian Coalition," *Forward*, March 23, 2007; and Eli Lake, "N.Y. Lawmaker Freezes $86M Meant for Abbas," *New York Sun*, February 14, 2007.

123. Nathan Guttman, "As Capitals Cautiously Greet Palestinian Deal, Israel's Allies in D.C. Push for Pressuring Hamas," *Forward*, February 16, 2007.

124. Quoted in Besser, "New Fight Brewing."

125. Guttman, "As Capitals Cautiously Greet Palestinian Deal."

126. Besser, "New Fight Brewing"; Nathan Guttman, "Lawmakers Sign Protest on Palestinian Aid," *Forward*, March 30, 2007; Guttman, "U.S., Israel at Odds"; Rosenberg, "Go for the Saudi Plan"; and Shmuel Rosner, "Battles Lost and Won," *Ha'aretz*, March 22, 2007.

127. "Lowey Will Not Place Hold on Revised PA Security Assistance Proposal," press release from the Office of Congresswoman Nita M. Lowey, March 30, 2007.

128. "Poll: Americans Support Cutting Aid to Israel," Reuters, April 12, 2002; and Jean-Michel Stoullig, "Americans Want Cutback in Aid to Israel, If It Refuses to Withdraw: Poll," Agence France Presse, April 13, 2002. Also see *Israel and the Palestinians* (Program on International Policy Attitudes, University of Maryland, last updated August 15, 2002).

129. Steven Kull (principal investigator), *Americans on the Middle East Road Map* (Program on International Policy Attitudes, University of Maryland, May 30, 2003), 9–11, 18–19. Also

see Steven Kull et al., *Americans on the Israeli-Palestinian Conflict* (Program on International Policy Attitudes, University of Maryland, May 6, 2002).

130. "American Attitudes Toward Israel and the Middle East," survey conducted on March 18–25, 2005, and June 19–23, 2005, by the Marttila Communications Group for the Anti-Defamation League.

131. "US Scowcroft Criticizes Bush Admin's Foreign Policy," *Financial Times*, October 13, 2004. Also see Glenn Kessler, "Scowcroft Is Critical of Bush," *Washington Post*, October 16, 2004.

8: IRAQ AND DREAMS OF TRANSFORMING THE MIDDLE EAST

1. George Packer, *The Assassins' Gate: America in Iraq* (New York: Farrar, Straus and Giroux, 2005), 46. Former CIA director George Tenet offers a similar view, writing in his memoirs that "one of the great mysteries to me is when the war in Iraq became inevitable." George Tenet with Bill Harlow, *At the Center of the Storm: My Years at the CIA* (New York: Harper, 2007), 301.

2. As the *New York Times* columnist Thomas L. Friedman reportedly observed in May 2003, "It is not only the neoconservatives who led us to the outskirts of Baghdad. What led us to the outskirts of Baghdad is a very American combination of anxiety and hubris." See Ari Shavit, "White Man's Burden," *Ha'aretz*, May 4, 2003.

3. Quoted in Emad Mekay, "Iraq Was Invaded 'to Protect Israel'—US Official," *Asia Times Online*, March 31, 2004. We used these quotations in our original article in the *London Review of Books*, and Zelikow challenged our interpretation of them. We based our discussion on a full and unimpeachable record of his remarks, and his challenge has no basis in fact. For a more detailed discussion of Zelikow's charge and our response, see "Letters," *London Review of Books*, May 25, 2006. Zelikow also served with Rice on the National Security Council during the first Bush administration and later coauthored a book with her on German reunification. He was one of the principal authors of the document that is probably the most comprehensive statement of the Bush Doctrine: *The National Security Strategy of the United States of America* (Washington, DC: White House, September 2002).

4. Quoted in "US Assumes UK Help in Iraq, Says General," *Guardian*, August 20, 2002.

5. Quoted in an interview with Sascha Lehnartz, "Dann helfen uns eben die Osteuropaer," *Frankfurter Allgemeine Sonntagszeitung*, January 26, 2003. On the influence of the Defense Policy Board in Donald Rumsfeld's Pentagon, see Stephen J. Hedges, "Iraq Hawks Have Bush's Ear," *Chicago Tribune*, August 18, 2002.

6. Joe Klein, "How Israel Is Wrapped Up in Iraq," *Time*, February 10, 2003.

7. Senator Ernest F. Hollings, "Bush's Failed Mideast Policy Is Creating More Terrorism," *Charleston Post and Courier* (online), May 6, 2004; and "Sen. Hollings Floor Statement Setting the Record Straight on His Mideast Newspaper Column," May 20, 2004, originally posted on the former senator's website (now defunct) but still available at www.shalomctr.org/node/620.

8. "ADL Urges Senator Hollings to Disavow Statements on Jews and the Iraq War," Anti-Defamation League press release, May 14, 2004.

9. Matthew E. Berger, "Not So Gentle Rhetoric from the Gentleman from South Carolina," *JTA.org*, May 23, 2004; "Sen. Hollings Floor Statement"; and "Senator Lautenberg's Floor Statement in Support of Senator Hollings," June 3, 2004, http://lautenberg.senate.gov/newsroom/video.cfm.

10. Aluf Benn, "Scapegoat for Israel," *Ha'aretz*, May 13, 2004; Matthew Berger, "Will Some Jews' Backing for War in Iraq Have Repercussions for All?" *JTA.org*, June 10, 2004; Patrick J. Buchanan, "Whose War?" *American Conservative*, March 24, 2003; Arnaud de Borchgrave, "A Bush-Sharon Doctrine?" *Washington Times*, February 14, 2003; Ami Eden, "Israel's Role: The 'Elephant' They're Talking About," *Forward*, February 28, 2003; "The Ground Shifts," *Forward*, May 28, 2004; Nathan Guttman, "Prominent U.S. Jews, Israel Blamed for Start of Iraq War," *Ha'aretz*, May 31, 2004; Spencer S. Hsu, "Moran Said Jews Are Pushing War," *Washington Post*, March 11, 2003; Lawrence F. Kaplan, "Toxic Talk on War," *Washington*

Post, February 18, 2003; E. J. Kessler, "Gary Hart Says 'Dual Loyalty' Barb Was Not Aimed at Jews," *Forward*, February 21, 2003; Ori Nir and Ami Eden, "Ex-Mideast Envoy Zinni Charges Neocons Pushed Iraq War to Benefit Israel," *Forward*, May 28, 2004; and Robert Novak, "Sharon's War?" *CNN.com*, December 26, 2002.

11. Quoted in Akiva Eldar, "Sharp Pen, Cruel Tongue," *Ha'aretz*, April 13, 2007.

12. Michael Kinsley, "What Bush Isn't Saying About Iraq," *Slate.com*, October 24, 2002. Also see Michael Kinsley, "J'Accuse, Sort Of," *Slate.com*, March 12, 2003.

13. Nathan Guttman, "Some Blame Israel for U.S. War in Iraq," *Ha'aretz*, March 5, 2003.

14. Bill Keller, "Is It Good for the Jews?" *New York Times*, March 8, 2003.

15. Ori Nir, "FBI Probe: More Questions Than Answers," *Forward*, May 13, 2005.

16. Shai Feldman, "The Bombing of Osiraq—Revisited," *International Security* 7, no. 2 (Autumn 1982); and Dan Reiter, "Preventive Attacks Against Nuclear Programs and the 'Success' at Osiraq," *Nonproliferation Review* 12, no. 2 (July 2005).

17. Joel Brinkley, "Confrontation in the Gulf: Israelis Worried by U.S. Restraint," *New York Times*, August 30, 1990; Joel Brinkley, "Top Israelis Warn of Deep Worry over Diplomatic Accord in Gulf," *New York Times*, December 4, 1990; Hugh Carnegy, "Pullout Not Enough, Says Israel," *Financial Times*, January 10, 1991; Sabra Chartrand, "Israel Warns Against a Gulf Retreat," *New York Times*, December 6, 1990; Jackson Diehl, "Israelis Fear Iraqi Threat Will Endure," *Washington Post*, August 29, 1990; Rowland Evans and Robert Novak, "Israel's Call for Action," *Washington Post*, August 24, 1990; Michael Massing, "The Way to War," *New York Review of Books*, March 28, 1991; Martin Merzer, "Israel Hopes Diplomacy Won't Let Iraqi Stay in Power," *Miami Herald*, August 29, 1990; and "Sharon to Americans: Blast Iraqis Immediately," *Jerusalem Post*, August 12, 1990.

18. Aluf Benn, "Sharon Shows Powell His Practical Side," *Ha'aretz*, February 26, 2001.

19. Seymour Hersh, "The Iran Game," *New Yorker*, December 3, 2001; Peter Hirschberg, "Background: Peres Raises Iranian Threat," *Ha'aretz*, February 5, 2002; David Hirst, "Israel Thrusts Iran in Line of US Fire," *Guardian*, February 2, 2002; "Israel Once Again Sees Iran as a Cause for Concern," *Ha'aretz*, May 7, 2001; and Alan Sipress, "Israel Emphasizes Iranian Threat," *Washington Post*, February 7, 2002.

20. Robert Novak, "Netanyahu's Nuke Warning," *Chicago Sun-Times*, April 14, 2002; Robert Novak, "War on Iraq Won't Be 'Cakewalk,'" *Chicago Sun-Times*, April 25, 2002; and William Raspberry, "To Solve the Crisis," *Washington Post*, April 15, 2002.

21. Elizabeth Sullivan, "Sharon Aide Expects United States to Attack Iraq; He Says Saddam Must Be Stopped from Making Nuclear Arms," *Cleveland Plain Dealer* (online), May 3, 2002.

22. Quoted in Joyce Howard Price, "Peres Encourages U.S. Action on Iraq," *Washington Times*, May 12, 2002.

23. Ehud Barak, "No Quick Fix," *Washington Post*, June 8, 2002.

24. Quoted in Gideon Alon, "Sharon to Panel: Iraq Is Our Biggest Danger," *Ha'aretz*, August 13, 2002. Also see Nina Gilbert, "Iraq Poses Greatest Threat," *Jerusalem Post*, August 13, 2002.

25. "Israel to US: Don't Delay Iraq Attack," *CBSNews.com*, August 16, 2002. The Sharon and Peres quotations are from Aluf Benn, "PM Urging U.S. Not to Delay Strike Against Iraq," *Ha'aretz*, August 16, 2002. The Gissen quotation is from Jason Keyser, "Israel Urges U.S. to Attack," *Washington Post*, August 16, 2002. The Shiry quotation is from Ben Lynfield, "Israel Sees Opportunity in Possible US Strike on Iraq," *Christian Science Monitor*, August 30, 2002. Also see Anton La Guardia, "Sharon Urges America to Bring Down Saddam," *Daily Telegraph* (London), August 17, 2002; Reuven Pedhatzur, "Israel's Interest in the War on Saddam," *Ha'aretz*, August 4, 2002; Jonathan Steele, "Israel Puts Pressure on US to Strike Iraq," *Guardian*, August 17, 2002; Walter Rodgers, "Rice and Peres Warn of Iraqi Threat," *CNN.com*, August 16, 2002; Tony Snow et al., interview with Ra'anan Gissen, "Fox Special Report with Brit Hume," August 16, 2002; and Ze'ev Schiff, "Into the Rough," *Ha'aretz*, August 16, 2002.

26. Benn, "PM Urging U.S." For additional evidence that "Israel and its supporters" were deeply concerned in 2002 "that critics would claim that the United States was going to war on

Israel's behalf—or even, as some have suggested, at Israel's behest," see Marc Perelman, "Iraqi Move Puts Israel in Lonely U.S. Corner," *Forward*, September 20, 2002.

27. On the lobby's concerns in the run-up to the 1991 Gulf War, see John B. Judis, "Jews and the Gulf: Fallout from the Six-Week War," *Tikkun*, May/June 1991; Allison Kaplan, "Saddam Splits Jewish Lobby," *Jerusalem Post*, January 14, 1991; and David Rogers, "Pro-Israel Lobbyists Quietly Backed Resolution Allowing Bush to Commit U.S. Troops to Combat," *Wall Street Journal*, January 28, 1991. On Israel's concerns at the same time, see Brinkley, "Top Israelis Warn of Deep Worry"; Carnegy, "Pullout Not Enough"; Chartrand, "Israel Warns"; Diehl, "Israelis Fear Iraqi Threat"; and Merzer, "Israel Hopes." The Buchanan quotation is from Chris Reidy, "The War Between the Columnists Gets Nasty," *Boston Globe*, September 22, 1990.

28. Benn, "PM Aide"; and Keyser, "Israel Urges U.S. to Attack."

29. Quoted in Rodgers, "Rice and Peres Warn."

30. Benn, "PM Aide."

31. Alon, "Sharon to Panel." At a White House press conference with President Bush on October 16, 2002, Sharon said, "I would like to thank you, Mr. President, for the friendship and cooperation. And as far as I remember, as we look back towards many years now, I think that we never had such relations with any President of the United States as we have with you, and we never had such cooperation in everything as we have with the current administration." "President Bush Welcomes Prime Minister Sharon to White House; Question and Answer Session with the Press," transcript of press conference, U.S. Department of State, October 16, 2002. Also see Robert G. Kaiser, "Bush and Sharon Nearly Identical on Mideast Policy," *Washington Post*, February 9, 2003.

32. Shlomo Brom, "An Intelligence Failure," *Strategic Assessment* (Jaffee Center for Strategic Studies, Tel Aviv University) 6, no. 3 (November 2003): 9. Also see "Intelligence Assessment: Selections from the Media, 1998–2003," ibid., 17–19; Gideon Alon, "Report Slams Assessment of Dangers Posed by Libya, Iraq," *Ha'aretz*, March 28, 2004; Dan Baron, "Israeli Report Blasts Intelligence for Exaggerating the Iraqi Threat," *JTA.org*, March 29, 2004; Molly Moore, "Israel Shares Blame on Iraq Intelligence, Report Says," *Washington Post*, December 5, 2003; Greg Myre, "Israeli Report Faults Intelligence on Iraq," *New York Times*, March 28, 2004; Ori Nir, "Senate Report on Iraq Intel Points to Role of Jerusalem," *Forward*, July 16, 2004; and James Risen, *State of War: The Secret History of the CIA and the Bush Administration* (New York: Simon & Schuster, 2006), 72–73.

33. On the general phenomenon of buck-passing, see John J. Mearsheimer, *The Tragedy of Great Power Politics* (New York: Norton, 2001), 157–62.

34. Quoted in Perelman, "Iraqi Move."

35. Herb Keinon, "Sharon to Putin: Too Late for Iraq Arms Inspection," *Jerusalem Post*, October 1, 2002.

36. "Peres Questions France Permanent Status on Security Council," *Ha'aretz*, February 20, 2003.

37. Perelman, "Iraqi Move."

38. Shlomo Avineri, "A Haunting Echo," *Los Angeles Times*, November 24, 2002. Also see Benjamin Netanyahu, "The Case for Toppling Saddam," *Wall Street Journal*, September 20, 2002; and Nathan Guttman, "Shimon Peres Warns Against Repeat of 1930s Appeasement," *Ha'aretz*, September 15, 2002.

39. For some representative editorials, see "Next Stop, Baghdad," *Jerusalem Post* editorial, November 15, 2001; "Don't Wait for Saddam," *Jerusalem Post* editorial, August 18, 2002; "Making the Case for War," *Jerusalem Post* editorial, September 9, 2002. For some representative op-eds, see Ron Dermer, "The March to Baghdad," *Jerusalem Post*, December 21, 2001; Efraim Inbar, "Ousting Saddam, Instilling Stability," *Jerusalem Post*, October 8, 2002; and Gerald M. Steinberg, "Imagining the Liberation of Iraq," *Jerusalem Post*, November 18, 2001.

40. "Don't Wait for Saddam."

41. Ehud Barak, "Taking Apart Iraq's Nuclear Threat," *New York Times*, September 4, 2002.

42. Netanyahu, "The Case for Toppling Saddam." Also see Benjamin Netanyahu, "U.S. Must Beat Saddam to the Punch," *Chicago Sun-Times*, September 17, 2002.

43. See, for example, "Benjamin Netanyahu Testifies About Iraq to Congress," CNN Live Event, *CNN.com*, September 12, 2002; Jim Lobe, "Hawks Justify Iraq Strike as War for Democracy," Inter Press Service, September 27, 2002; and Janine Zacharia, "Netanyahu: US Must Guarantee Israel's Safety from Iraqi Attack," *Jerusalem Post*, September 13, 2002.

44. Aluf Benn, "Background: Enthusiastic IDF Awaits War in Iraq," *Ha'aretz*, February 17, 2003; James Bennet, "Israel Says War on Iraq Would Benefit the Region," *New York Times*, February 27, 2003; and Chemi Shalev, "Jerusalem Frets as U.S. Battles Iraq War Delays," *Forward*, March 7, 2003.

45. Quoted in James Bennet, "Clinton Redux," *The Atlantic@Aspen* weblog, July 8, 2006.

46. Asher Arian, "Israeli Public Opinion on National Security 2002," Jaffee Center for Strategic Studies, Tel Aviv University, Memorandum no. 61, July 2002, 10, 34.

47. Ephraim Yaar and Tamar Hermann, "Peace Index: Most Israelis Support the Attack on Iraq," *Ha'aretz*, March 6, 2003. Regarding Kuwait, a public opinion poll released in March 2003 found that 89.6 percent of Kuwaitis favored the impending war against Iraq. James Morrison, "Kuwaitis Support War," *Washington Times*, March 18, 2003. In a poll taken in Israel in early May 2007, 59 percent of the respondents said that the U.S. decision to invade Iraq was correct. "Poll Shows That Israel Is a Staunch American Ally," Anti-Defamation League press release, May 18, 2007. By that time, most Americans had concluded that the war was a tragic mistake.

48. "America's Image Further Erodes, Europeans Want Weaker Ties: a Nine-Country Survey," Pew Research Center for the People and the Press, Washington, DC, March 18, 2003. Also see Alan Travis and Ian Black, "Blair's Popularity Plummets," *Guardian*, February 18, 2003.

49. Gideon Levy, "A Deafening Silence," *Ha'aretz*, October 6, 2002.

50. See Dan Izenberg, "Foreign Ministry Warns Israeli War Talk Fuels US Anti-Semitism," *Jerusalem Post*, March 10, 2003, which makes clear that "the Foreign Ministry has received reports from the US" telling Israelis to be more circumspect because the U.S. media is portraying Israel as "trying to goad the administration into war."

51. Quoted in Dana Milbank, "Group Urges Pro-Israel Leaders Silence on Iraq," *Washington Post*, November 27, 2002.

52. David Horovitz, "Sharon Warns Colleagues Not to Discuss Iraq Conflict," *Irish Times*, March 12, 2003. Also see James Bennet, "Threats and Responses: Israel's Role; Not Urging War, Sharon Says," *New York Times*, March 11, 2003; and Aluf Benn, "Sharon Says U.S. Should Also Disarm Iran, Libya and Syria," *Ha'aretz*, February 18, 2003.

53. The influence of the neoconservatives and their allies was widely reflected before the war and is clearly reflected in the following articles, all written before or just after the war began: Joel Beinin, "Pro-Israel Hawks and the Second Gulf War," *Middle East Report Online*, April 6, 2003; Elisabeth Bumiller and Eric Schmitt, "On the Job and at Home, Influential Hawks' 30-Year Friendship Evolves," *New York Times*, September 11, 2002; Kathleen and Bill Christison, "A Rose by Another Name: The Bush Administration's Dual Loyalties," *CounterPunch.org*, December 13, 2002; Robert Dreyfuss, "The Pentagon Muzzles the CIA," *American Prospect*, December 16, 2002; Michael Elliott and James Carney, "First Stop, Iraq," *Time*, March 31, 2003; Seymour Hersh, "The Iraq Hawks," *New Yorker*, December 24–31, 2001; Michael Hirsh, "Hawks, Doves and Dubya," *Newsweek*, September 2, 2002; Glenn Kessler, "U.S. Decision on Iraq Has Puzzling Past," *Washington Post*, January 12, 2003; Joshua M. Marshall, "Bomb Saddam?" *Washington Monthly*, June 2002; Dana Milbank, "White House Push for Iraqi Strike Is on Hold," *Washington Post*, August 18, 2002; Susan Page, "Showdown with Saddam: The Decision to Act," *USA Today*, September 11, 2002; Sam Tanenhaus, "Bush's Brain Trust," *Vanity Fair* (online), July 2003; Patrick E. Tyler and Elaine Sciolino, "Bush Advisers Split on Scope of Retaliation," *New York Times*, September 20, 2001; and Jason A. Vest, "The Men from JINSA and CSP," *Nation*, September 2/9, 2002.

54. Janine Zacharia, "All the President's Middle East Men," *Jerusalem Post*, January 19, 2001.

55. "Rally Unites Anguished Factions Under Flag of 'Stand with Israel,'" *Forward*, April 19, 2002; and "Forward 50," *Forward*, November 15, 2002.

56. John McCaslin, "Israeli-Trained Cops," *Washington Times*, November 5, 2002; Bret Stephens, "Man of the Year," *Jerusalem Post* (Rosh Hashana Supplement), September 26, 2003; and Janine Zacharia, "Invasive Treatment," ibid. Other useful pieces on Wolfowitz include Peter J. Boyer, "The Believer," *New Yorker*, November 1, 2004; Michael Dobbs, "For Wolfowitz, a Vision May Be Realized," *Washington Post*, April 7, 2003; James Fallows, "The Unilateralist," *Atlantic*, March 2002; Bill Keller, "The Sunshine Warrior," *New York Times Magazine*, September 22, 2002; and "Paul Wolfowitz, Velociraptor," *Economist*, February 7, 2002.

57. See, for example, Douglas J. Feith, "The Inner Logic of Israel's Negotiations: Withdrawal Process, Not Peace Process," *Middle East Quarterly* 3, no. 1 (March 1996); and Douglas Feith, "A Strategy for Israel," *Commentary*, September 1997. For useful discussions of Feith's views, see Jeffrey Goldberg, "A Little Learning: What Douglas Feith Knew and When He Knew It," *New Yorker*, May 9, 2005; Jim Lobe, "Losing Feith, or Is the Bush Team Shedding Its Sharper Edges?" *Daily Star* (online), January 31, 2005; James J. Zogby, "A Dangerous Appointment: Profile of Douglas Feith, Undersecretary of Defense Under Bush," Middle East Information Center, April 18, 2001; and "Israeli Settlements: Legitimate, Democratically Mandated, Vital to Israel's Security and, Therefore, in U.S. Interest," Center for Security Policy, Transition Brief no. 96-T 130, December 17, 1996. Note that the title of the latter piece, which was published by an organization in the lobby, says that what is in Israel's interest is in America's national interest. In "Losing Feith," Lobe writes, "In 2003, when Feith, who was standing in for Rumsfeld at an interagency 'Principals' Meeting' on the Middle East, concluded his remarks on behalf of the Pentagon, according to the Washington insider newsletter, *The Nelson Report*, [National Security Adviser Condoleezza] Rice said, 'Thanks Doug, but when we want the Israeli position we'll invite the ambassador.'"

58. "A Clean Break: A New Strategy for Securing the Realm" was prepared for the Institute for Advanced Strategic and Political Studies in Jerusalem and published in June 1996. A copy can be found at www.iasps.org/strat1.htm.

59. Akiva Eldar, "Perles of Wisdom for the Feithful," *Ha'aretz*, October 1, 2002.

60. Packer, *Assassins' Gate*, 32.

61. "Israel's UN Ambassador Slams Qatar, Praises U.S. Envoy Bolton," *Ha'aretz*, May 23, 2006. Also see "Bolton Is Israel's Secret Weapon, Says Gillerman," *BigNewsNetwork.com*, November 18, 2006; and Ori Nir, "Senate Probes Bolton's Pro-Israel Efforts," *Forward*, May 6, 2005.

62. Marc Perelman, "Siding with White House, Groups Back Bolton," *Forward*, November 17, 2006; and "Dear John," *Forward* editorial, December 8, 2006.

63. Ori Nir, "Libby Played Leading Role on Foreign Policy Decisions," *Forward*, November 4, 2005.

64. "He Tarries: Jewish Messianism and the Oslo Peace," Rennert Lecture for 2002. Krauthammer fiercely defends Israel at every turn in his columns.

65. Asla Aydintasbas, "The Midnight Ride of James Woolsey," *Salon.com*, December 20, 2001; Anne E. Kornblut and Bryan Bender, "Cheney Link of Iraq, 9/11 Dismissed," *Boston Globe*, September 16, 2003; David E. Sanger and Robin Toner, "Bush and Cheney Talk Strongly of Qaeda Links with Hussein," *New York Times*, June 18, 2004; and R. James Woolsey, "The Iraq Connection," *Wall Street Journal*, October 18, 2001.

66. Goldberg added that "among Jewish lobbyists in the Beltway, support for the impending war is almost taken for granted—several are puzzled by the very suggestion that any kind of strenuous opposition to an Iraq invasion might emerge." Michelle Goldberg, "Why American Jewish Groups Support War with Iraq," *Salon.com*, September 14, 2002.

67. "An Unseemly Silence," *Forward* editorial, May 7, 2004.

68. Nacha Cattan, "Resolutions on Invasion Divide Jewish Leadership," *Forward*, October 11, 2002; Laurie Goodstein, "Threats and Responses: American Jews; Divide Among Jews Leads to Silence on Iraq War," *New York Times*, March 15, 2003; and Milbank, "Group Urges."

69. Matthew E. Berger, "Jewish Groups Back U.S. Stand on Iraq," *Jewish Journal* (online), October 18, 2002; and Jewish Council for Public Affairs, "Statement on Iraq," adopted by the JCPA Board of Directors, October 2002.

70. Mortimer B. Zuckerman, "No Time for Equivocation," *U.S. News & World Report*, August 26/ September 2, 2002. Also see Mortimer B. Zuckerman, "No More Cat and Mouse," *U.S. News & World Report*, October 28, 2002; Mortimer B. Zuckerman, "Clear and Compelling Proof," *U.S. News & World Report*, February 10, 2003; and Mortimer B. Zuckerman, "The High Price of Waiting," *U.S. News & World Report*, March 10, 2003.

71. Both quotes are from Goldberg, "Why American Jewish Groups."

72. Gary Rosenblatt, "The Case for War Against Saddam," *Jewish Week*, December 13, 2002. Also see Gary Rosenblatt, "Hussein Asylum," *Jewish Week*, August 23, 2002.

73. Ron Kampeas, "Cheney: Iran, Iraq a Package Deal," *JTA.org*, March 13, 2007.

74. Nathan Guttman, "Background: AIPAC and the Iraqi Opposition," *Ha'aretz*, April 7, 2003. Also see Dana Milbank, "For Israel Lobby Group, War Is Topic A, Quietly," *Washington Post*, April 1, 2003.

75. David Twersky, "A Bittersweet Affair for AIPAC," *New York Sun*, January 23, 2003. On the ADL, see Cattan, "Resolutions on Invasion"; Nacha Cattan, "Jewish Groups Pressed to Line Up on Iraq," *Forward*, August 23, 2002; and Nathan Guttman, "Groups Mum on Iraq, Despite Antiwar Tide," *Forward*, March 2, 2007.

76. Jeffrey Goldberg, "Real Insiders: A Pro-Israel Lobby and an FBI Sting," *New Yorker*, July 4, 2005. *Near East Report (NER)*, AIPAC's biweekly publication dealing with Middle East issues, is filled with articles dealing with Iraq in the months before the war began. Although none explicitly calls for invading Iraq, they all portray Saddam as an especially dangerous threat, leaving the reader with little doubt that both Israel and the United States will be in serious trouble if he is not toppled from power. See, for example, "Saddam's Diversion," *NER*, October 7, 2002; interview with Ze'ev Schiff, *NER*, October 21, 2002; interview with Amatzia Baram, *NER*, February 25, 2002; interview with Amatzia Baram, *NER*, October 7, 2002; interview with Kenneth M. Pollack, *NER*, September 23, 2002; "Arming Iraq," *NER*, July 1, 2002; and "Backing Saddam," *NER*, February 3, 2003.

77. John Bresnahan, "GOP Turns to Israeli Lobby to Boost Iraq Support," *Roll Call* (online), October 6, 2003.

78. Matthew E. Berger, "Bush Makes Iraq Case in AIPAC Appearance," *Deep South Jewish Voice* (online), May 11, 2004.

79. David Horovitz, "Editor's Notes: Wading into the Great Debate," *Jerusalem Post*, March 15, 2007. According to Ron Kampeas, Cheney's "message was not received enthusiastically. Only about one-third to one-half of the audience . . . applauded politely." See "Cheney: Iran, Iraq a Package Deal." Similarly, Nathan Guttman wrote that Cheney's speech "received a lukewarm welcome." See "Cheney Links Action on Iran to Winning Iraq," *Forward*, March 16, 2007. However, writing in *Salon*, Gregory Levey noted that "Cheney got a warm reception and forceful applause." See "Inside America's Powerful Israel Lobby," *Salon.com*, March 16, 2007.

80. On the reception Boehner and Pelosi received, see Guttman, "Cheney Links Action"; Levey, "Inside"; and Ian Swanson, "Pelosi Hears Boos at AIPAC," *The Hill* (online), March 13, 2007.

81. Guttman, "Groups Mum on Iraq."

82. Ibid.; and Jeffrey M. Jones, "Among Religious Groups, Jewish Americans Most Strongly Oppose War," Gallup News Service, February 23, 2007.

83. Shortly before the United States invaded Iraq, Congressman James P. Moran created a stir when he said, "If it were not for the strong support of the Jewish community for this war with Iraq, we would not be doing this." Quoted in Hsu, "Moran Said." However, Moran misspoke, because there was not widespread support for the war in the Jewish community. He should have said, "If it were not for the strong support of the neoconservatives and the leadership of the Israel lobby for this war with Iraq, we would not be doing this."

84. Samuel G. Freedman, "Don't Blame Jews for This War," *USA Today*, April 2, 2003. Also see

James D. Besser, "Jews Souring on Iraq War," *Jewish Week*, September 24, 2004; Goodstein, "Threats and Responses"; and Ori Nir, "Poll Finds Jewish Political Gap," *Forward*, February 4, 2005. The same situation obtained before the 1991 Gulf War. By the time Congress voted to endorse the war on January 12, 1991, "the only significant Washington Jewish organization not on record in favor of the administration's position was American Friends of Peace Now, which favored the continuation of sanctions." Judis, "Jews and the Gulf," 13. Despite the lobby's efforts to make the 1991 war happen, however, a large portion of the American Jewish community opposed the war, as was the case in 2003. For example, Jewish members of the House of Representatives voted 17–16 against the resolution authorizing war, while Jewish senators voted 5–3 against it. Ibid., 14. This outcome reflects the fact that in contrast to what happened in 2002–03, there was a serious debate in 1990–91 about whether to go to war against Iraq, as well as the fact that the lobby sometimes takes positions that are at odds with a substantial portion of the American Jewish community.

85. The January 26, 1998, letter can be found on the website of the Project for the New American Century, www.newamericancentury.org/iraqclintonletter.htm; the February 19, 1998, letter can be found on the Iraq Watch website, www.iraqwatch.org/perspectives/rumsfeld-openletter.htm. For background on the Committee for Peace and Security in the Gulf, see Judis, "Jews and the Gulf," 12. Also see the May 29, 1998, letter to Speaker of the House Newt Gingrich and Senate Majority Leader Trent Lott written under the auspices of PNAC, www.newamericancentury.org/iraqletter1998.htm. The neoconservatives, it should be emphasized, advocated invading Iraq to topple Saddam. See "The End of Containment," *Weekly Standard*, December 1, 1997; Zalmay M. Khalilzad and Paul Wolfowitz, "Overthrow Him," ibid.; Frederick W. Kagan, "Not by Air Alone," ibid.; and Robert Kagan, "A Way to Oust Saddam," *Weekly Standard*, September 28, 1998.

86. A copy of the Iraq Liberation Act can be found at www.iraqwatch.org/government/US/Legislation/ILA.htm.

87. John Dizard, "How Ahmed Chalabi Conned the Neocons," *Salon.com*, May 4, 2004; "Iraqi Myths," *Jerusalem Post* editorial, October 7, 1998; Seth Gitell, "Neocons Meet Israeli to Gain U.S. Backing," *Forward*, July 31, 1998; Kagan, "Way to Oust Saddam"; Martin Kettle, "Pentagon Balks at 'Idiotic' Law Urging Bay of Pigs–type Invasion of Iraq," *Guardian*, October 21, 1998; and Vernon Loeb, "Congress Stokes Visions of War to Oust Saddam; White House Fears Fiasco in Aid to Rebels," *Washington Post*, October 20, 1998. On JINSA, see "Concrete Responses to Saddam," *jinsa.org*, Report no. 79, August 10, 1998; "To Overthrow Saddam," *jinsa.org*, Report no. 82, October 2, 1998; "Spring 1998 Board Resolution—Iraq," *jinsa.org*, March 22, 1998; and "Resolution in Support of the Iraqi Opposition," *jinsa.org*, October 19, 1998.

88. See Clinton's comments after he signed the Iraq Liberation Act of 1998. Statement by the President, White House Press Office, October 31, 1998. Also see Kettle, "Pentagon Balks"; and Loeb, "Congress Stokes."

89. Vernon Loeb, "Saddam's Iraqi Foes Heartened by Clinton," *Washington Post*, November 16, 1998; Nicholas Lemann, "The Iraq Factor: Will the New Bush Team's Old Memories Shape Its Foreign Policies?" *New Yorker*, January 22, 2001; and Robert Litwak, *Rogue States and U.S. Foreign Policy* (Washington, DC: Woodrow Wilson Center Press, 2000), chap. 4.

90. Packer, *Assassins' Gate*, 41.

91. Jane Perlez, "Capitol Hawks Seek Tougher Line on Iraq," *New York Times*, March 7, 2001; and "Have Hawks Become Doves?" *Washington Times* editorial, March 8, 2001. Also see Stefan Halper and Jonathan Clarke, *America Alone: The Neo-Conservatives and the Global Order* (New York: Cambridge University Press, 2004), 129–31.

92. Richard A. Clarke, *Against All Enemies: Inside America's War on Terror* (New York: Free Press, 2004); and Ron Suskind, *The Price of Loyalty: George W. Bush, the White House, and the Education of Paul O'Neill* (New York: Simon & Schuster, 2004).

93. Bob Woodward, *Plan of Attack* (New York: Simon & Schuster, 2004), 12. Also see Lemann,

"Iraq Factor"; and Eric Schmitt and Steven Lee Meyers, "Bush Administration Warns Iraq on Weapons Programs," *New York Times*, January 23, 2001.

94. She also noted that if Iraq did get WMD, the appropriate U.S. response would be a "clear and classical statement of deterrence—if they do acquire WMD, their weapons will be unusable because any attempt to use them will bring national obliteration." Condoleezza Rice, "Promoting the National Interest," *Foreign Affairs* 79, no. 1 (January/February 2000): 60–62.

95. Timothy Noah, "Dick Cheney, Dove," *Slate.com*, October 16, 2002; Adam Meyerson, "Calm After Desert Storm," interview with Dick Cheney, *Policy Review* 65 (Summer 1993).

96. Quoted in Kessler, "U.S. Decision on Iraq Has Puzzling Past." Elliott and Carney ("First Stop, Iraq") report that neoconservatives like William Kristol were upset when Cheney was chosen as Bush's running mate, because of Cheney's position on ending the first Gulf War. But after 9/11, says Kristol, "neoconservatives happily 'consider him a fellow-traveler.'"

97. Elliott and Carney, "First Stop, Iraq"; Glenn Kessler and Peter Slavin, "Cheney Is Fulcrum of Foreign Policy," *Washington Post*, October 13, 2002; Kessler, "U.S. Decision on Iraq Has Puzzling Past"; and "Vice President Dick Cheney Talks About Bush's Energy Plan," interview with Tim Russert on NBC's *Meet the Press*, May 20, 2001. Although Cheney's views on conquering Iraq fundamentally changed after 9/11, this apparently did not happen overnight. See "The Vice President Appears on Meet the Press with Tim Russert," Camp David, Maryland, Office of the White House Press Secretary, September 16, 2001. Cheney's response to specific questions about Iraq does not indicate that he had changed his thinking about the need to topple Saddam five days after the Twin Towers fell.

98. Both Kagan quotations are from Packer, *Assassins' Gate*, 38. Also see similar comments by Packer himself in ibid., 32.

99. Woodward, *Plan of Attack*, 25–26.

100. Page, "Showdown with Saddam."

101. Elliott and Carney, "First Stop, Iraq." Woodward describes Wolfowitz as "like a drum that would not stop." *Plan of Attack*, 22.

102. Woodward, *Plan of Attack*, 1–44.

103. Regarding the neoconservatives' influence on Cheney, see Elliott and Carney, "First Stop, Iraq"; Page, "Showdown with Saddam"; Michael Hirsh, "Bernard Lewis Revisited," *Washington Monthly*, November 2004; Frederick Kempe, "Lewis's 'Liberation' Doctrine for Mideast Faces New Tests," *Wall Street Journal*, December 13, 2005; and Carla Anne Robbins and Jeanne Cummings, "How Bush Decided That Hussein Must Be Ousted from Atop Iraq," *Wall Street Journal*, June 14, 2002. On Ajami in particular, see Adam Shatz, "The Native Informant," *Nation*, April 28, 2003.

104. Jacob Weisberg, "Are Neo-cons History?" *Financial Times*, March 14, 2007. This article makes clear that Cheney and Lewis have a close relationship.

105. Woodward succinctly describes Libby's influence in *Plan of Attack* (48–49): "Libby had three formal titles. He was chief of staff to Vice President Cheney; he was also national security adviser to the vice president; and he was finally an assistant to President Bush. It was a trifecta of positions probably never held before by a single person. Scooter was a power center unto himself . . . Libby was one of only two people who were not principals to attend the National Security Council meetings with the president and the separate principals meetings chaired by Rice." Also see ibid., 50–51, 288–92, 300–301, 409–10; Bumiller and Schmitt, "On the Job and at Home"; Karen Kwiatkowski, "The New Pentagon Papers," *Salon.com*, March 10, 2004; and Tyler and Sciolino, "Bush Advisers Split."

106. Tyler and Sciolino, "Bush Advisers Split." Also see Bumiller and Schmitt, "On the Job and at Home"; and William Safire, "Phony War II," *New York Times*, November 28, 2002.

107. On Cheney's significant influence in the Bush administration, see Jeanne Cummings and Greg Hitt, "In Iraq Drama, Cheney Emerges as President's War Counselor," *Wall Street Journal*, March 17, 2003; Mark Hosenball, Michael Isikoff, and Evan Thomas, "Cheney's Long Path to War," *Newsweek*, November 17, 2003; Kessler and Slavin, "Cheney Is Ful-

crum"; Barbara Slavin and Susan Page, "Cheney Rewrites Roles in Foreign Policy," *USA Today*, July 29, 2002; and Woodward, *Plan of Attack*, 27–30.

108. Kessler, "U.S. Decision on Iraq Has Puzzling Past"; and Woodward, *Plan of Attack*, 410. Also see ibid., 164–65, 409.

109. Quoted in Eric Schmitt, "Pentagon Contradicts General on Iraq Occupation Force's Size," *New York Times*, February 28, 2003.

110. "This Goes Beyond Bin Laden," *jinsa.org*, September 13, 2001. Also see Vest, "The Men from JINSA and CSP."

111. This letter was published in the *Weekly Standard*, October 1, 2001. Among the signatories were William Bennett, Eliot Cohen, Aaron Friedberg, Donald Kagan, Robert Kagan, Jeane Kirkpatrick, William Kristol, Charles Krauthammer, Richard Perle, Norman Podhoretz, Stephen Solarz, and Leon Wieseltier.

112. Charles Krauthammer, "The War: A Road Map," *Washington Post*, September 28, 2001; and Robert Kagan and William Kristol, "The Right War," *Weekly Standard*, October 1, 2001. Also see "War Aims," *Wall Street Journal* editorial, September 20, 2001.

113. Michael Barone, "War by Ultimatum," *U.S. News & World Report*, October 1, 2001. Also see Bill Gertz, "Iraq Suspected of Sponsoring Terrorist Attacks," *Washington Times*, September 21, 2001; "Drain the Ponds of Terror," *Jerusalem Post* editorial, September 25, 2001; William Safire, "The Ultimate Enemy," *New York Times*, September 24, 2001; and Mortimer B. Zuckerman, "A Question of Priorities," *U.S. News & World Report*, October 8, 2001.

114. The April 3, 2002, letter can be found at www.newamericancentury.org/Bushletter-040302.htm.

115. Daniel Byman, Kenneth M. Pollack, and Gideon Rose, "The Rollback Fantasy," *Foreign Affairs* 78, no. 1 (January/February 1999).

116. Kenneth M. Pollack, *The Threatening Storm: The Case for Invading Iraq* (New York: Random House, 2002); Kenneth M. Pollack, "Why Iraq Can't Be Deterred," *New York Times*, September 26, 2002; Kenneth M. Pollack, "A Last Chance to Stop Iraq," *New York Times*, February 21, 2003; Martin S. Indyk and Kenneth M. Pollack, "How Bush Can Avoid the Inspections Trap," *New York Times*, January 27, 2003; and Martin S. Indyk and Kenneth M. Pollack, "Lock and Load," *Los Angeles Times*, December 19, 2002.

117. William Kristol, "The Axis of Appeasement," *Weekly Standard*, August 26/September 2, 2002; Robert Bartley, "Thinking Things Over: What We Learned," *Wall Street Journal*, September 9, 2002; Michael Ledeen, "Scowcroft Strikes Out," *National Review Online*, August 6, 2002; George Melloan, "Who Really Doubts That Saddam's Got to Go," *Wall Street Journal*, September 10, 2002; John O'Sullivan, "Chamberlain Deserves an Apology: Scowcroft, Hagel, and Raines Are No Chamberlains," *National Review Online*, September 3, 2002; "This Is Opposition? There Is No Revolt in the GOP Against Bush's Iraq Policy," *Wall Street Journal* editorial, August 19, 2002; and "Who Is Brent Scowcroft?" *New York Sun* editorial, August 19, 2002. None of the targets of the neoconservatives' ire were advocating appeasement of Iraq but instead favored containment over war.

118. William Safire, "Our 'Relentless' Liberation," *New York Times*, October 8, 2001. Also see William Safire, "Saddam and Terror," *New York Times*, August 22, 2002; and William Safire, "Big Mo," *New York Times*, November 19, 2001.

119. Robert Kagan, "On to Phase II," *Washington Post*, November 27, 2001; Robert Kagan and William Kristol, "What to Do About Iraq," *Weekly Standard*, January 21, 2002; and Safire, "Saddam and Terror."

120. Robert Kagan and William Kristol, "The U.N. Trap?" *Weekly Standard*, November 18, 2002; Charles Krauthammer, "A Costly Charade at the U.N.," *Washington Post*, February 28, 2003; George F. Will, "Stuck to the U.N. Tar Baby," *Washington Post*, September 19, 2002; and William Safire, "The French Connection," *New York Times*, March 14, 2003.

121. Krauthammer, "Our First Move." Also see Reuel Marc Gerecht, "A Necessary War," *Weekly Standard*, October 21, 2002; and Charles Krauthammer, "Where Power Talks," *Washington Post*, January 4, 2002.

122. An excellent account of the administration's campaign to sell the war is Frank Rich, *The Greatest Story Ever Sold: The Decline and Fall of Truth from 9/11 to Katrina* (New York: Penguin Press, 2006).

123. James Bamford, *A Pretext for War: 9/11, Iraq, and the Abuse of America's Intelligence Agencies* (New York: Doubleday, 2004), chaps. 13–14; Karen DeYoung, *Soldier: The Life of Colin Powell* (New York: Knopf, 2006), 440–46; and Woodward, *Plan of Attack*, 288–92, 297–301. Also see ibid., 72, 163.

124. Woodward, *Plan of Attack*, 290.

125. "Powell Regrets UN Speech on Iraq WMDs," *ABC News Online*, September 9, 2005.

126. Bamford, *Pretext for War*, 287–91, 307–31; Julian Borger, "The Spies Who Pushed for War," *Guardian*, July 17, 2003; David S. Cloud, "Prewar Intelligence Inquiry Zeroes in on Pentagon Office," *Wall Street Journal*, March 11, 2004; Seymour M. Hersh, "Selective Intelligence," *New Yorker*, May 12, 2003; Kwiatkowski, "New Pentagon Papers"; W. Patrick Lang, "Drinking the Kool-Aid," *Middle East Policy* 11, no. 2 (Summer 2004); Jim Lobe, "Pentagon Office Home to Neo-Con Network," Inter Press Service, August 7, 2003; Greg Miller, "Spy Unit Skirted CIA on Iraq," *Los Angeles Times*, March 10, 2004; Paul R. Pillar, "Intelligence, Policy, and the War in Iraq," *Foreign Affairs* 85, no. 2 (March–April 2006); James Risen, "How Pair's Finding on Terror Led to Clash on Shaping Intelligence," *New York Times*, April 28, 2004; and Eric Schmitt and Thom Shanker, "Threats and Responses: A C.I.A. Rival; Pentagon Sets Up Intelligence Unit," *New York Times*, October 24, 2002.

127. Risen, *State of War*, 72–73.

128. Lobe, "Pentagon Office." On Makovsky, see Jack Herman, "A Whole New Ballgame Overseas," *St. Louis Post-Dispatch*, February 20, 1989. This article was written when Makovsky was about to leave the United States and move to Israel. "I have strong feelings about helping to build a Jewish state," he told Herman. He then added, "It's like returning to your roots."

129. Borger, "The Spies."

130. Inspector General, Department of Defense, "Review of the Pre–Iraqi War Activities of the Office of the Under Secretary of Defense for Policy," Report no. 07-INTEL-04, February 9, 2007.

131. Franklin Foer, "Founding Fakers," *New Republic*, August 18, 2003.

132. Robert Dreyfuss, "Tinker, Banker, NeoCon, Spy," *American Prospect*, November 18, 2002. Also see "Who Will Lead a Free Iraq?" *jinsa.org*, May 9, 2003; and "Creating a Post-Saddam Iraq," *jinsa.org*, Report no. 481, April 6, 2005.

133. Quoted in Dreyfuss, "Tinker, Banker." Also see Matthew E. Berger, "Iraqi Exiles and Jews Form Unlikely Alliance," *Jewish News Weekly* (online), October 18, 2002; Juan Cole, "All the Vice-President's Men," *Salon.com*, October 28, 2005; and Michelle Goldberg, "The War over the Peace," *Salon.com*, April 14, 2003.

134. Quoted in Robert Dreyfuss, "Chalabi and AEI: The Sequel," *TomPaine.com*, November 10, 2005. Also see Laurie Mylroie, "Unusually Effective," *New York Sun*, November 8, 2005; and Michael Rubin, "Iraq's Comeback Kid," *National Review Online*, December 5, 2005.

135. Bernard Lewis, "Put the Iraqis in Charge," *Wall Street Journal*, August 29, 2003. Also see Ian Buruma, "Lost in Translation," *New Yorker*, June 14, 2004; and Michael Hirsh, "Bernard Lewis Revisited," *Washington Monthly*, November 2004.

136. Dizard, "How Ahmed Chalabi Conned the Neocons." In mid-June 2003, Benjamin Netanyahu announced, "It won't be long when you will see Iraqi oil flowing to Haifa." Reuters, "Netanyahu Says Iraq-Israel Oil Line Not Pipe-Dream," *Ha'aretz*, June 20, 2003. Of course, this did not happen and it is unlikely to happen in the foreseeable future. Also see Douglas Davis, "Peace with Israel Said to Top New Iraq's Agenda," *Jerusalem Post*, April 21, 2003.

137. Matthew E. Berger, "New Chance to Build Israel-Iraq Ties," *Jewish Journal* (online), April 28, 2003. Also see Bamford, *Pretext to War*, 293; and Ed Blanche, "Securing Iraqi Oil for Israel: The Plot Thickens," *Lebanonwire.com*, April 25, 2003.

138. Nathan Guttman, "Mutual Wariness: AIPAC and the Iraqi Opposition," *Ha'aretz*, April 27, 2003.

139. Quoted in Packer, *Assassins' Gate*, 41.
140. Friedman qualifed this remark by adding, "In the final analysis, what fomented the war is America's over-reaction to September 11." We agree; it was a combination of the neoconservatives' active promotion of the war, the support from key groups in the lobby, and a particular set of international and domestic circumstances that led the United States into the Iraqi quagmire. See Shavit, "White Man's Burden."
141. Noam Chomsky, "The Israel Lobby?" *Znet* (online), March 28, 2006. Also see Stephen Zunes, "The Israel Lobby: How Powerful Is It Really?" *Znet* (online), May 25, 2006.
142. One pundit notes that the "preferred slogan" of the antiwar forces in the run-up to the Iraq war was "no blood for oil." John B. Judis, "Over a Barrel," *New Republic*, January 20, 2003, 20. Also see William R. Clark, *Petrodollar Warfare: Oil, Iraq and the Future of the Dollar* (Gabriola Island, Canada: New Society Publishers, 2005); Michael Elliott, "The Selling of the President's War: Bush Should Take Israel and Oil Out of the Iraq Equation," *Time*, November 18, 2002; Michael Meacher, "This War on Terrorism Is Bogus," *Guardian*, September 6, 2003; Kevin Phillips, "American Petrocacy," *American Conservative*, July 17, 2006; and Sandy Tolan, "Beyond Regime Change," *Los Angeles Times*, December 1, 2002.
143. Judis, "Jews and the Gulf," 16–17.
144. Stephen J. Hedges, "Allies Not Swayed on Iraq Strike," *Chicago Tribune*, August 28, 2002; "Saudi Arabia Says It Won't Join a War," *New York Times*, March 19, 2003; "Saudis Warn US over Iraq War," *BBC News* (online), February 17, 2003; Jon Sawyer, "Saudi Arabia Won't Back War on Iraq without U.N. Authority, Prince Warns," *St. Louis Post-Dispatch* (online), January 23, 2003; "Scorecard: For or Against Military Action," *New York Times*, August 27, 2002; and Brian Whitaker and John Hooper, "Saudis Will Not Aid US War Effort," *Guardian*, August 8, 2002.
145. Peter Beinart, "Crude," *New Republic*, October 7, 2002; Michael Moran and Alex Johnson, "The Rush for Iraq's Oil," *MSNBC.com*, November 7, 2002; Anthony Sampson, "Oilmen Don't Want Another Suez," *Observer*, December 22, 2002; John W. Schoen, "Iraqi Oil, American Bonanza?" *MSNBC.com*, November 11, 2002; and Daniel Yergin, "A Crude View of the Crisis in Iraq," *Washington Post*, December 8, 2002.
146. Remarks by the Vice President to the Veterans of Foreign Wars 103rd National Convention, Nashville, Tennessee (White House, Office of the Press Secretary, August 26, 2002). Also see Remarks by the Vice President to the Veterans of the Korean War, San Antonio, Texas (White House, Office of the Press Secretary, August 29, 2002).
147. For a copy of the speech, see "In the President's Words: 'Free People Will Keep the Peace of the World,'" *New York Times*, February 27, 2003. Also see Remarks by the President to the United Nations General Assembly, New York (White House, Office of the Press Secretary, September 12, 2002); Remarks by the President to the Graduating Class, West Point (White House, Office of the Press Secretary, June 1, 2002); President's Inaugural Speech, Washington, DC (White House, Office of the Press Secretary, January 20, 2005); and *National Security Strategy of the United States* (2002).
148. Robert S. Greenberger and Karby Leggett, "President's Dream: Changing Not Just Regime but a Region: A Pro-U.S., Democratic Area Is a Goal That Has Israeli and Neoconservative Roots," *Wall Street Journal*, March 21, 2003. Also see George Packer, "Dreaming of Democracy," *New York Times Magazine*, March 2, 2003; Paul Sperry, "Bush the Nation-Builder: So Much for Campaign Promises," *Antiwar.com*, October 6, 2006; and Wayne Washington, "Once Against Nation-Building, Bush Now Involved," *Boston Globe*, March 2, 2004.
149. Charles Krauthammer, "Peace Through Democracy," *Washington Post*, June 28, 2002.
150. Barak, "Taking Apart."
151. Quoted in Lynfield, "Israel Sees Opportunity in Possible U.S. Strike on Iraq."
152. Benn, "Background."
153. Bennet, "Israel Says."

154. Shalev, "Jerusalem Frets."

155. See, for example, *Rebuilding America's Defenses: Strategy, Forces and Resources for a New Century*, Report of the Project for the New American Century (Washington, DC, September 2000), 14, 17–18.

156. Martin Indyk, "The Clinton Administration's Approach to the Middle East," speech to Soref Symposium, Washington Institute for Near East Policy, May 18, 1993. Also see Anthony Lake, "Confronting Backlash States," *Foreign Affairs* 73, no. 2 (March/April 1994).

157. Kenneth M. Pollack, *The Persian Puzzle: The Conflict Between Iran and America* (New York: Random House, 2004), 261–65.

158. Robert Kagan and William Kristol, eds., *Present Dangers: Crisis and Opportunity in American Foreign and Defense Policy* (San Francisco: Encounter Books, 2000); Charles Krauthammer, "Universal Dominion: Toward a Unipolar World," *National Interest* 18 (Winter 1989/90); Michael A. Ledeen, *Freedom Betrayed: How America Led a Global Democratic Revolution, Won the Cold War, and Walked Away* (Washington, DC: AEI Press, 1996); Joshua Muravchik, *Exporting Democracy: Fulfilling America's Destiny* (Washington, DC: AEI Press, 1991); Marina Ottaway et al., "Democratic Mirage in the Middle East," Policy Brief 20 (Washington, DC: Carnegie Endowment for International Peace, October 2002); Norman Podhoretz, "Strange Bedfellows: A Guide to the New Foreign-Policy Debates," *Commentary*, December 1999; "Statement of Principles," Project for the New American Century, June 3, 1997; and Albert Wohlstetter, "A Vote in Cuba? Why Not in Iraq?" *Wall Street Journal*, May 24, 1991.

159. On the neoconservatives' thinking about regional transformation, see Robert Blecher, "Free People Will Set the Course of History," *Middle East Report Online*, March 2003; Jack Donnelly and Anthony Shadid, "Iraq War Hawks Have Plans to Reshape Entire Mideast," *Boston Globe*, September 10, 2002; Halper and Clarke, *America Alone*, 76–90; Nicholas Lemann, "After Iraq: The Plan to Remake the Middle East," *New Yorker*, February 17, 2003; and Klein, "How Israel."

160. Quoted in Roula Khalaf, "Rice 'New Middle East' Comments Fuel Arab Fury over US Policy," *Financial Times*, July 31, 2006.

161. Orly Halpern, "Israeli Experts Say Middle East Was Safer with Saddam in Iraq," *Forward*, January 5, 2007. Also see Leslie Susser, "Iraq War: Good or Bad for Israel? Saddam's Execution Revives Debate," *JTA.org*, January 2, 2007.

162. Quoted in Chris McGreal, "Israelis May Regret Saddam Ousting, Says Security Chief," *Guardian*, February 9, 2006.

163. James A. Baker III and Lee H. Hamilton, co-chairs, *The Iraq Study Group Report* (New York: Random House, 2006), xv, 28–29, 43–45, 50–58. Tony Blair, who repeatedly called for settling the Israeli-Palestinian conflict, and who favors negotiating with Iran and Syria, said that the Iraq Study Group "offers a strong way forward." Quoted in Sheryl Gay Stolberg and Kate Zernike, "Bush Expresses Caution on Key Points in Iraq Panel's Report," *New York Times*, December 7, 2006. Also see Kirk Semple, "Syrian Official, in Iraq, Offers Assistance," *New York Times*, November 19, 2006.

164. Akiva Eldar, "The Gewalt Agenda," *Ha'aretz*, November 20, 2006.

165. Michael Abramowitz and Glenn Kessler, "Hawks Bolster Skeptical President," *Washington Post*, December 10, 2006; Associated Press, "Israel Experts Doubt Focusing on Israel-Arab Conflict Will Help in Iraq," *International Herald Tribune*, December 6, 2006; "Gates's Shocking Thinking on Iran," *Jerusalem Post* editorial, December 6, 2006; Nathan Guttman, "Baker Group Advisers 'Surprised,' 'Upset' at Report's Israel-Iraq Link," *Forward*, January 30, 2007; Jeff Jacoby, "Fighting to Win in Iraq," *Boston Globe*, December 3, 2006; Robert Kagan and William Kristol, "A Perfect Failure," *Weekly Standard*, December 11, 2006; Ron Kampeas, "ISG Fallout Continues with Query: Is Israeli-Arab Peace the Linchpin?" *JTA.org*, December 10, 2006; Jim Lobe, "Neocons Move to Preempt Baker Report," *Antiwar.com*, December 6, 2006; Marc Perelman, "As Washington Studies Iraq Report, Jerusalem Frets over Tehran

Talk," *Forward*, December 15, 2006; Shmuel Rosner, "Baker's Brew," *Ha'aretz*, December 8, 2006; and "The Iraq Muddle Group," *Wall Street Journal* editorial, December 7, 2006.

166. Quoted in Shmuel Rosner, "FM Livni: U.S. Must Stand Firm on Iraq," *Ha'aretz*, March 13, 2007. Also see Shmuel Rosner, "Livni to AIPAC: U.S. Can't Show Weakness on Iraq, Iran," *Ha'aretz*, March 12, 2007.

167. The Olmert quotations are from Bradley Burston, "Israel Must Stay the Hell Out of U.S. Debate on Iraq," *Ha'aretz*, March 13, 2007; and Hilary L. Krieger, "PM's AIPAC Talk Surprises Delegates," *Jerusalem Post*, March 13, 2007.

168. Burston, "Israel Must Stay." Also see Krieger, "PM's AIPAC Talk"; and Shmuel Rosner, "No Easy Answers on Israel and the Iraq Debate," *Ha'aretz*, March 13, 2007.

169. "President Bush Welcomes Prime Minister Olmert of Israel to the White House," White House, Office of the Press Secretary, November 13, 2006.

170. Quoted in James D. Besser, "Olmert Support for Iraq War Stirs Anger," *Jewish Week*, November 17, 2006.

171. David Horovitz, "Editor's Notes: Wading into the Great Debate," *Jerusalem Post*, March 15, 2007.

172. Quoted in Glenn Frankel, "A Beautiful Friendship?" *Washington Post Sunday Magazine*, July 16, 2006.

173. Martin Kramer, "The American Interest," *Azure* 5767, no. 26 (Fall 2006): 29. Kramer also claims that "the assertion that the Iraq war is being waged on behalf of Israel is pure fiction," a remark at odds with Prime Minister Olmert's statement to the 2007 AIPAC Policy Conference, where he explicitly linked Israel's security to victory in Iraq. See note 167 above. Also see Yossi Alpher, "Sharon Warned Bush," *Forward*, January 12, 2007.

174. Alpher, "Sharon Warned Bush." Also see Herb Keinon, "Sharon Warned Bush of Saddam Threat," *Jerusalem Post*, January 11, 2007.

175. See notes 21 and 25 above.

9: TAKING AIM AT SYRIA

1. James A. Baker III and Lee H. Hamilton, co-chairs, *The Iraq Study Group Report* (New York: Random House, 2006), 50.

2. Ferry Biedermann and Roula Khalaf, "Western Politicians Take the Road to Damascus," *Financial Times*, December 22, 2006; Nathan Guttman, "Senators Visit Damascus, Push for Syrian Talks," *Forward*, December 29, 2006; Hassan M. Fattah and Graham Bowley, "Pelosi Meets with Syrian Leader," *New York Times*, April 4, 2007; and Anthony Shadid, "Pelosi Meets Syrian President," *Washington Post*, April 4, 2007. Another U.S. congressman, Darrell Issa (R-CA), visited Assad the day after Pelosi's visit. Yoav Stern, Amiram Barkat, and Barak Ravid, "U.S. Republican Meets Assad Day after Contentious Pelosi Visit," *Ha'aretz*, April 5, 2007.

3. Richard M. Bennett, a well-regarded military analyst, succinctly describes the Syrian threat to Israel: "While it is still largely true that the Syrian military remains one of the largest and best-trained forces in the Arab world, it has significantly lost every major conflict with Israel since 1948. Its combat strength has deteriorated dramatically over the past 15 years as its equipment has become increasingly obsolescent, poorly maintained and short of spare parts." "Syria's Military Flatters to Deceive," *Asia Times Online*, July 28, 2006. Similarly, Arieh O'Sullivan writes, "The Syrian army does not pose a significant tactical threat to Israel and has no viable tactical war option . . . To put it bluntly, the Syrian army has not just stood still for the past two decades, but has gone backwards." "How Big a Threat?" *Jerusalem Post*, October 10, 2003. Also see Arieh O'Sullivan, "Jaffee Center: Syrian Military Weakening," *Jerusalem Post*, November 23, 2005; Susan Taylor Martin, "Experts Disagree on Dangers of Syria," *St. Petersburg Times* (online), November 3, 2002; Martin Sieff, "Eye on Iraq: Enter the Saudis," United Press International, November 27, 2006; and Stephen Zunes, "Bush Has Clear Run at Syria," *Asia Times Online*, March 2, 2005. For a description of Syria's mil-

itary capabilities, and comparative defense budget figures, see *The Military Balance, 2007* (London: International Institute for Strategic Studies, January 2007), 243–45.

4. Karen DeYoung, "U.S. Toughens Warnings to Syria on Iraq, Other Issues," *Washington Post*, April 15, 2003; Flynt Leverett, *Inheriting Syria: Bashar's Trial by Fire* (Washington, DC: Brookings Institution Press, 2005), 13–14; and Alfred B. Prados, "Syria: U.S. Relations and Bilateral Issues," *Report for Congress*, Congressional Research Service, June 22, 2006, 11–12. For the details of Syria's WMD and ballistic missile capabilities, see the "Syria Profile" of the Nuclear Threat Initiative (NTI) at www.nti.org/e_research/profiles/Syria/index.html.

5. Mainstream thinking in Israel about Syria's chemical weapons is summarized by Reuven Pedatzur: "The IDF reckoned the Syrians would not dare launch ballistic missiles topped with chemical warheads at Israel because it was clear to them that the price they'd pay would be so high, with painful IDF attacks on the Syrian rear, that it would not justify the first strike at Israel." "Update the Gas Masks, There's a Syrian Threat," *Ha'aretz*, August 5, 2003.

6. Quoted in Martin, "Experts Disagree."

7. Seymour M. Hersh, "The Syrian Bet," *New Yorker*, July 28, 2003. Also see Richard Spring, "This Is Not Another Iran," *Guardian*, October 27, 2006.

8. The generally good relations that existed between Syria and the United States during the 1990s are reflected in the following memoirs of key figures in the Clinton administration: Madeleine Albright with Bill Woodward, *Madame Secretary: A Memoir* (New York: Miramax Books, 2003); Bill Clinton, *My Life* (New York: Vintage Books, 2004); Warren Christopher, *Chances of a Lifetime: A Memoir* (New York: Scribner, 2001); and Dennis Ross, *The Missing Peace: The Inside Story of the Fight for Middle East Peace* (New York: Farrar, Straus and Giroux, 2004). Also see Helena Cobban, *The Israeli-Syrian Peace Talks: 1991–96 and Beyond* (Washington, DC: U.S. Institute of Peace Press, 1999), which provides a detailed account of the negotiations among Israel, Syria, and the United States during the years Rabin and Peres were prime minister; and Itamar Rabinovich, *The Brink of Peace: The Israeli-Syrian Negotiations* (Princeton: Princeton University Press, 1998).

9. Quoted in Douglas Jehl, "Clinton in the Middle East: The Overview; Clinton Reports Progress in Talks in Syrian Capital," *New York Times*, October 28, 1994. Also see "Clinton in the Middle East; Assad and Clinton Speak: Shared Quest for Peace," *New York Times*, October 28, 1994.

10. Henry Kissinger, *Years of Renewal* (New York: Simon & Schuster, 1999), chap. 33; and William B. Quandt, *Peace Process: American Diplomacy and the Arab-Israeli Conflict Since 1967* (Washington, DC: Brookings Institution Press, 1993), 250–54.

11. Leverett, *Inheriting Syria*, 134. Also see Jim Lobe, "The Damascus Dance," *Antiwar.com*, October 28, 2006; "Syrian Ambassador Calls for Comprehensive Peace Settlement in the Middle East," Imad Moustapha address at Burkle Center, UCLA, June 2, 2005, www.international.ucla.edu/bcir/article.asp?parentid=25567; and Volker Perthes, "The Syrian Solution," *Foreign Affairs* 85, no. 6 (November/December 2006).

12. Hersh, "Syrian Bet."

13. Flynt Leverett notes that "U.S. policy toward Syria . . . has fluctuated between efforts to facilitate Israeli-Syrian agreements and attempts to isolate and pressure Damascus to change its terms and tactics for achieving a peaceful settlement" (*Inheriting Syria*, 7). While Leverett is certainly correct, he never explains what accounts for that fluctuation, although his book provides much evidence that Israel and the lobby are the main forces behind those policy shifts.

14. The Golan Heights Law was passed by the Israeli Knesset in December 1981 and extended Israeli law to the territory of the Golan. It does not contain the word "annexation," however, or refer to Israeli "sovereignty" over the heights. During the Knesset debate on the legislation, Prime Minister Menachem Begin responded to a critic by saying, "You use the word annexation, but I am not using it." Ian S. Lustick, "Has Israel Annexed East Jerusalem?" *Middle East Policy* 5, no. 1 (January 1997); and "The Golan Heights Law," www.mfa.gov.il/MFA/Peace+Process/Guide+to+the+Peace+Process/Golan+Heights+Law.htm.

15. "Golan Statistics," www.jewishvirtuallibrary.org/jsource/Peace/golanstats.html; "Settlements in the Golan Heights," Foundation for Middle East Peace, Settlement Report 17, no. 1 (January–February 2007); and "Regions and Territories: The Golan Heights," *BBC News* (online), April 26, 2007.

16. Clinton, *My Life*, 883–84; Cobban, *Israeli-Syrian Peace Talks*, chap. 3; Leverett, *Inheriting Syria*, 47; and Ross, *Missing Peace*, 111. The "Rabin deposit" is sometimes referred to as the "pocket commitment" or the "Rabin pocket."

17. Although Netanyahu has denied that he was willing to return to the June 4, 1967, Syria-Israel border ("I Never Agreed to Full Golan Withdrawal," *IsraelNationalNews.com*, June 23, 2004), there is considerable evidence that he did agree to that position when he was prime minister (1996–99). See Akiva Eldar, "Ex-MI Chief: 'Netanyahu Was Ready to Give up All of the Golan,'" *Ha'aretz*, June 24, 2004; Clinton, *My Life*, 883; Ross, *Missing Peace*, 527–28, 577; and Daniel Pipes, "The Road to Damascus: What Netanyahu Almost Gave Away," *New Republic*, July 5, 1999. On Barak, see Clinton, *My Life*, 883–88, 903; Leverett, *Inheriting Syria*, 47–48; and Ross, *Missing Peace*, chaps. 20–22. Ross notes that "Barak's position on peace with Syria was less forthcoming than Netanyahu's." Ibid., 528.

18. Clyde Haberman, "Israelis Look to Clinton Trip for Progress with Syrians," *New York Times*, October 25, 1994.

19. Ross, *Missing Peace*, 589.

20. Clinton, *My Life*, 883–88, 903. According to Ofer Shelah, "Most of the top brass [in Israel] agrees with the view put forward by Bill Clinton in his book, 'My Life': that Barak got cold feet because of opinion polls showing the Israeli public opposed the territorial price demanded by the Syrians." See "The Situation: Syrian Offer of Talks Throws a Wrench into Sharon's Plans," *Forward*, September 17, 2004. Also see Jerome Slater, "Lost Opportunities for Peace in the Arab-Israeli Conflict: Israel and Syria, 1948–2001," *International Security* 27, no. 1 (Summer 2002): esp. 97–100; and Akiva Eldar, "Between Katzrin and Nahariya," *Ha'aretz*, July 24, 2006. Barak, however, denied Clinton's charge. See Yifat Zohar, "Barak Rejects Clinton's Charges of Missed Syria Deal," *Maariv International* (online), June 29, 2004.

21. Quoted in "Sharon Suggests Future Attacks on Syria," *New York Times*, October 17, 2003. Also see Aluf Benn, "U.S. Officials Eyeing Possible Assad Successors," *Ha'aretz*, October 3, 2005; Ori Nir, "Bush Seeks to Pressure Iran, Syria on Weapons," *Forward*, January 2, 2004; and Ofer Shelah, "Pressured, Assad Offers Charm Campaign," *Forward*, January 9, 2004.

22. Quoted in Harry de Quetteville, "Syria Threat over Golan Puts Israel on War Alert," *Daily Telegraph* (London), September 30, 2006. Also see Larry Derfner, "Why Israel Must Talk to Syria," *Jerusalem Post*, November 9, 2006; Tovah Lazaroff, "Peretz Open to Syrian Talks," *Jerusalem Post*, September 27, 2006; and Gideon Samet, "O.K. from a Declining America?" *Ha'aretz*, December 20, 2006.

23. Quoted in Amnon Meranda, "'Israel Will Never Return Golan Heights,'" *Ynetnews.com*, March 14, 2007. Also see "EU Backs Syria's Aim to Regain Golan Heights—Solana," *Ynetnews .com*, March 14, 2007.

24. Yoav Stern and Aluf Benn, "PM Associates: Syria Will Support Terror, Even with Golan," *Ha'aretz*, December 17, 2006.

25. "Israeli Opinion Regarding Peace with Syria and Lebanon," www.jewishvirtuallibrary.org/ jsource/Politics/golanpo.html.

26. Shelah, "The Situation." Also see Aluf Benn, "United States Leaving Syrian Track to Israel's Discretion," *Ha'aretz*, January 9, 2004; Aluf Benn and Amos Harel, "IDF Presses Sharon for Talks with Syria," *Ha'aretz*, January 8, 2004; Shlomo Brom, "Israel-Syria Negotiations: A Real Possibility?" *Strategic Assessment* (Jaffee Center for Strategic Studies, Tel Aviv University) 7, no. 1 (May 2004); "Israel 'Can Give Up Golan to Syria,'" *Straits Times*, August 14, 2006; "Jerusalem's Rejectionists," *Ha'aretz* editorial, January 9, 2004; Ilan Marciano, "Foreign Ministry Official: Syria Ready to Negotiate," *Ynetnews.com*, December 26, 2006; and Ori Nir, "As Israel Debates Syrian Overture, Washington Presses to Stop Talks," *Forward*, December 17, 2004.

27. Yaakov Lappin, "New Forum Pushes for Syria Talks," *Ynetnews.com*, January 28, 2007; and Roi Mandel, "Former Shin Bet Chief Calls for Dialogue with Syria," *Ynetnews.com*, January 29, 2007.

28. "Don't Turn Syria Away," *Ha'aretz* editorial, December 18, 2006; and "Respond to Assad, Convince Bush," *Ha'aretz* editorial, December 21, 2006. On Peretz, see Gideon Alon, Aluf Benn, and Yoav Stern, "Olmert: Now Is Not Time to Start Talks with Syria, Bush Opposed," *Ha'aretz*, December 17, 2006; and Gideon Alon, "Olmert, Peretz Spar over Syrian Overtures," *Ha'aretz*, December 18, 2006.

29. Moshe Maoz put the point well: "Regardless of what the administration's position is, Sharon doesn't want to negotiate because he doesn't want to give up the Golan Heights." Quoted in Nir, "As Israel Debates."

30. Quoted in Ori Nir, "U.S. Advice to Israelis: Don't Start Syria Talks," *Forward*, January 23, 2004.

31. "A Serious Proposal," *Ha'aretz* editorial, December 30, 2003; Aluf Benn, "UN Envoy Urges Israel to Exploit Syrian Peace Moves," *Ha'aretz*, January 9, 2004; de Quetteville, "Syria Threat"; and Marc Perelman, "Syria Makes Overture over Negotiations," *Forward*, July 11, 2003.

32. Ze'ev Schiff, "The Peace Threat from Damascus," *Ha'aretz*, December 8, 2003. In the late summer of 2004, after Syria made another peace offer, an article in the *Forward* began with the following playful paragraph: "As if he didn't have enough problems, what with the mounting right-wing opposition to his disengagement plan, Palestinian terrorism stirring anew and his governing coalition in turmoil, Prime Minister Sharon now has trouble on his northern front. Syria, Israel's most intractable foe, is offering to make peace." Shelah, "The Situation."

33. Quoted in Stern and Benn, "PM Associates."

34. Ibid.; and "Syria Expert: Assad's Overtures Serious," *Jerusalem Post*, December 31, 2006. Also see "You Can't Bring Peace to Iraq Without Working with Syria," interview with Syria's deputy prime minister, *Spiegel Online*, February 21, 2007.

35. Alon, Benn, and Stern, "Olmert: Now Is Not Time"; Aluf Benn, "Bush vs. Olmert," *Ha'aretz*, February 8, 2007; Akiva Eldar, "Closed-Door Policy," *Ha'aretz*, February 26, 2007; Akiva Eldar, Mazal Mualem, Shmuel Rosner, and Yoav Stern, "PM: Conditions Not Ripe for Talks with Syria," *Ha'aretz*, December 8, 2006; "Israel, Syria and Bush's Veto," *Forward* editorial, December 22, 2006; Shmuel Rosner, Akiva Eldar, and Yoav Stern, "Olmert Rejects Talks with Syria, Says Conditions Are 'Not Ripe,'" *Ha'aretz*, December 7, 2006; Samet, "O.K. from a Declining America"; and Ze'ev Schiff, Amos Harel, and Yoav Stern, "U.S. Takes Harder Line on Talks Between Jerusalem, Damascus," *Ha'aretz*, February 24, 2007.

36. Aluf Benn, "Israel, U.S. Sources Say Views on Israel-Syria Talks Unchanged," *Ha'aretz*, May 25, 2007; Akiva Eldar, "U.S. Ambassador: We Won't Stop Israel from Talking to Syria," *Ha'aretz*, March 14, 2007; and Ze'ev Schiff, "U.S. Envoy Denies Pressure on Israel Not to Engage in Talks with Syria," *Ha'aretz*, May 23, 2007. Also see Hilary Leila Krieger, "'No New Overture to Syria in the Works,'" *Jerusalem Post*, March 7, 2007.

37. Benn, "Israel, U.S. Sources Say."

38. Peretz quoted in Alon, Benn, and Stern, "Olmert: Now Is Not Time"; Samet, "O.K. from a Declining America?" Also see Uzi Benziman, "Help, They Want Peace," *Ha'aretz*, January 17, 2007.

39. Akiva Eldar, "Secret Understandings Reached Between Representatives from Israel and Syria," *Ha'aretz*, January 16, 2007. The next two quotations in this paragraph are from ibid. Also see Akiva Eldar, "Exclusive: Full Text of Document Drafted During Secret Talks," *Ha'aretz*, January 16, 2007; Akiva Eldar, "Background: From Turkey, Via Europe, to Damascus," *Ha'aretz*, January 16, 2007; "Olmert: No Government Officials Involved in Secret Syria Talks," *Ha'aretz*, January 17, 2007; and M. J. Rosenberg, "When Uncritical Support Leads to Disaster," Weekly Opinion Column, Issue #307, Israel Policy Forum, Washington, DC, January 19, 2007.

40. Quoted in Fattah and Bowley, "Pelosi Meets with Syrian Leader." Also see Hassan M. Fattah, "Pelosi, Warmly Greeted in Syria, Is Criticized by White House," *New York Times*, April 4, 2007; and Shadid, "Pelosi Meets Syrian President."

41. Quoted in Fattah and Bowley, "Pelosi Meets with Syrian Leader." Also see Ron Kampeas, "Rhetorical Battle over Pelosi Trip," *JTA.org*, April 8, 2007; and Yoav Stern and Amiram Barkat, "PMO: Pelosi Did Not Carry Any Message from Israel to Assad," *Ha'aretz*, April 5, 2007.

42. "Olmert to Assad: Israel Willing to Withdraw from Golan Heights," *Ynetnews.com*, June 8, 2007; Aluf Benn and Yoav Stem, "MK Orlev: PM Willing to Sell Golan Heights in Order to Stay in Power," *Ha'aretz*, June 8, 2007; and Aluf Benn and Yoav Stern, "Peres Downplays Chances of New Syria Talks, Says Damascus Not Ready," *Ha'aretz*, June 10, 2007. According to these reports, Bush was consulted and "said the United States would not stand in Israel's way." See "Olmert to Assad." Also see Sever Plocker, "Suddenly Syria," *Ynetnews.com*, June 10, 2007, which explains why Olmert's call for talks is an "empty political gesture."

43. See, for example, "Sharon Wants U.S. Action Against Syria," *NewsMax.com*, April 16, 2001.

44. Hersh, "Syrian Bet"; Molly Moore, "Sharon Asks U.S. to Pressure Syria on Militants," *Washington Post*, April 17, 2003; Ori Nir, "Jerusalem Urges Bush: Next Target Hezbollah," *Forward*, April 11, 2003; Ori Nir, "Sharon Aide Makes the Case for U.S. Action Against Syria," *Forward*, April 18, 2003; Marc Perelman, "Behind Warnings to Damascus: Reassessment of Younger Assad," *Forward*, April 18, 2003; and Daniel Sobelman and Nathan Guttman, "PM Urges U.S. to Keep Heat on Syria, Calls Assad 'Dangerous,'" *Ha'aretz*, April 15, 2003.

45. The Sharon quotations and his list of demands are from Sobelman and Guttman, "PM Urges U.S. to Keep Heat on Syria." Also see Moore, "Sharon Asks U.S."

46. Herb Keinon, "Sharon Criticized for Public Statements on Syria-US Tension," *Jerusalem Post*, April 16, 2003.

47. Quoted in Nir, "Sharon Aide Makes the Case." Also see DeYoung, "U.S. Toughens Warnings"; and Moore, "Sharon Asks U.S."

48. Nir, "Sharon Aide Makes the Case." Also see DeYoung, "U.S. Toughens Warnings"; and Perelman, "Behind Warnings."

49. Ephraim Halevy, "The Post-Saddam Middle East: A View from Israel," address at the Soref Symposium 2003, Washington Institute for Near East Policy, www.washingtoninstitute.org/templateC07.php?CID=147.

50. Moore, "Sharon Asks U.S." The Alpher quotation is from ibid. Also see Marc Perelman, "Syria Makes Overture over Negotiations," *Forward*, July 11, 2003.

51. Perelman, "Behind Warnings"; Laurie Copans, "Israeli Military Boss Claims Iraq Had Chemical Weapons," Associated Press, April 26, 2004; Dany Shoham, "An Antithesis on the Fate of Iraq's Chemical and Biological Weapons," *International Journal of Intelligence and CounterIntelligence* 19, no. 1 (Spring 2006); Ira Stoll, "Saddam's WMD Moved to Syria, an Israeli Says," *New York Sun*, December 15, 2005; and Ira Stoll, "Iraq's WMD Secreted in Syria, Sada Says," *New York Sun*, January 26, 2006.

52. Michael Casey, "Israeli Ambassador Believes Truck Used in Bombing of UN Headquarters Came from Syria," Associated Press, August 21, 2003; and "Israeli Envoy Links Syria to UN Blast, Stirs Flap," Reuters, August 21, 2003.

53. Hersh, "Syrian Bet." Rabinovich also made it clear to Hersh that "Israel has urged Washington not to open the back channel to Assad." Instead, Israel wanted the United States to play hardball with the Syrian leader.

54. *Ending Syria's Occupation of Lebanon: The U.S. Role*, report of the Middle East Study Group (Philadelphia: Middle East Forum, May 2000).

55. Jordan Green, "Neocons Dream of Lebanon," *ZNet* (online), July 23, 2003; David R. Sands, "Hawks Recycle Arguments for Iraq War Against Syria," *Washington Times*, April 16, 2003; and United States Committee for a Free Lebanon home page, www.freelebanon.org.

56. Matthew E. Berger, "AIPAC Mounts New Offensive to Display Support of Congress," *JTA.org*, April 22, 2002. The full title of the proposed legislation was the Syria Accountability and Lebanese Sovereignty Restoration Act.

57. Regarding the proposed legislation, see Zvi Bar'el, "Deciphering the Syrians," *Ha'aretz*, July 9, 2003; "The Return of the Syria Accountability Act," *NewsMax.com*, April 19, 2003; and

Claude Salhani, "The Syria Accountability Act: Taking the Wrong Road to Damascus," *Policy Analysis* 512 (Washington, DC: Cato Institute, March 18, 2004).

58. Ron Kampeas, "Bush, Once Reluctant on Sanctions, Prepares to Take Tough Line with Syria," *JTA.org*, March 16, 2004.

59. Wolfowitz quoted in Nathan Guttman, "Some Senior U.S. Figures Say Syria Has Crossed the Red Line," *Ha'aretz*, April 14, 2004; Perle quoted in Michael Flynn, "The War Hawks: The Right Flexes Muscle with New U.S. Agenda," *Chicago Tribune*, April 13, 2003. On Wolfowitz, also see Leverett, *Inheriting Syria*, 151–52.

60. Perelman, "Behind Warnings." James Woolsey, a prominent hawk on the Defense Policy Board, was arguing right after Baghdad fell that the United States was involved in World War IV and its main adversaries included "fascists" in states like Syria. Barbara Slavin, "Some See Victory Extending Beyond Iraq," *USA Today*, April 11, 2003.

61. Flynn, "The Right Flexes Muscle." Also see John R. Bolton, "Beyond the Axis of Evil: Additional Threats from Weapons of Mass Destruction," remarks to the Heritage Foundation, Office of the Press Secretary, U.S. Department of State, May 6, 2002.

62. Douglas Jehl, "New Warning Was Put Off on Weapons Syria Plans," *New York Times*, July 18, 2003; Marc Perelman, "State Department Hawk Under Fire in Intelligence Flap over Syria," *Forward*, July 25, 2003; and Warren P. Strobel and Jonathan S. Landay, "Intelligence Data on Syria Now Disputed," *Philadelphia Inquirer* (online), July 17, 2003.

63. Nathan Guttman, "US: Syria Supporting Terror Groups Developing WMD," *Ha'aretz*, September 16, 2003.

64. Quoted in Robin Wright, "U.S. Insists Syria Alter Its Course," *Los Angeles Times*, April 14, 2003. Also see Martin Indyk's and Dennis Ross's tough-minded rhetoric about Syria in Hersh, "Syrian Bet."

65. Frank Gaffney Jr., "Who's Next in Line?" *Washington Times*, April 15, 2003.

66. Lawrence F. Kaplan, "White Lie," *New Republic*, April 21 & 28, 2003. Also see William Kristol and Lawrence F. Kaplan, *The War over Iraq: Saddam's Tyranny and America's Mission* (San Francisco: Encounter Books, 2003).

67. Jed Babbin, "Regime Change, Again," *National Review Online*, November 12, 2003.

68. Marc Ginsberg, "Bashing Bashar," *Weekly Standard*, April 28, 2003.

69. Quoted in Robert Fisk, "Western 'Intelligence' Services," *Independent*, September 29, 2003. Also see Babbin, "Regime Change"; and Prados, "Syria," 10.

70. DeYoung, "U.S. Toughens Warnings"; and Melissa Radler, "Bill to Impose Sanctions on Syria Brought to Congress," *Jerusalem Post*, April 13, 2003.

71. Sands, "Hawks Recycle Arguments."

72. "Engel Meets with Sharon in Jerusalem," press release from Office of Congressman Eliot Engel, August 18, 2003; "NY Congressman Says Will Push Bill to Pressure Syria," *Ha'aretz*, August 19, 2003; and Janine Zacharia and Arieh O'Sullivan, "Sharon Tells Congressmen US Must Pressure Assad More," *Jerusalem Post*, August 19, 2003.

73. Bar'el, "Deciphering the Syrians." Also see Matthew E. Berger, "Struggle over Syria Looms," *Jewish News of Greater Phoenix* (online), September 27, 2002; Barbara Slavin, "White House Stops Blocking Syria Bill," *USA Today*, October 8, 2003; and Janine Zacharia, "US Probes Syria Policy," *Jerusalem Post*, September 18, 2002.

74. Salhani, "Syria Accountability Act," 5.

75. Hersh, "Syrian Bet"; and Salhani, "Syria Accountability Act," 6. Also see Leverett, *Inheriting Syria*, which reveals much evidence of the deep split within the Bush administration over how to deal with Syria.

76. Kampeas, "Bush, Once Reluctant."

77. "Statement by the President on H.R. 1828," White House, Office of the Press Secretary, December 12, 2003; and Janine Zacharia, "Bush Signs Syria Accountability Act," *Jerusalem Post*, December 14, 2003.

78. Hersh, "Syrian Bet." Other pieces discussing the advantages for the United States of coop-

erating with Syria include Clifford Krauss, "U.S. Welcomes Thaw in Relations with 'Pragmatic' Syria," *New York Times*, January 2, 2003; Martin, "Experts Disagree"; James Risen and Tim Weiner, "C.I.A. Is Said to Have Sought Help from Syria," *New York Times*, October 30, 2001; Salhani, "The Syria Accountability Act"; and Zunes, "Bush Has Clear Run."

79. Leverett, *Inheriting Syria*, 142.

80. Hersh, "Syrian Bet"; and Perelman, "Syria Makes Overture."

81. Leverett, *Inheriting Syria*, 142. Also see Hersh, "Syrian Bet."

82. Julian Borger, "Bush Vetoes Syria War Plan," *Guardian*, April 15, 2003. Also see Hersh, "Syrian Bet"; and Warren P. Strobel and John Walcott, "Bush Advisers Debating Syria's Role in Terrorism," *Miami Herald* (online), January 11, 2004.

83. Robin Wright and Glenn Kessler, "Some on the Hill Seek to Punish Syria for Broken Promises on Iraq," *Washington Post*, April 30, 2004. Also see Glenn Kessler, "President Imposes Sanctions on Syria," *Washington Post*, May 12, 2004; Marc Perelman, "Israel Blames Attacks on Syria-Iran Axis," *Forward*, July 14, 2006; Barbara Slavin, "U.S. Warns Syria; Next Steps Uncertain," *USA Today*, September 17, 2003; and Janine Zacharia, "U.S. May Postpone Syria Sanctions," *Jerusalem Post*, March 19, 2004.

84. Schiff, "The Peace Threat."

85. Benn, "United States Leaving Syrian Track."

86. Nir, "As Israel Debates"; and Nir, "U.S. Advice."

87. After Baghdad fell in 2003, two articles published in the *Forward* hinted at how Israel and the lobby have influenced U.S. policy toward Syria. In a piece from mid-April, the author wrote: "A sudden flurry of U.S. warnings to Syria in recent days indicates that Washington has undertaken what Israel and its supporters here have been urging for months: a comprehensive reassessment of Syrian ruler Bashar Assad." Perelman, "Behind Warnings." A few months later, in mid-July, the same author wrote: "During the past several months, top Israeli officials have warned their American counterparts and audiences about Assad's unreliability. American officials have echoed the stance, and press reports have speculated about possible American military intervention in Syria." Perelman, "Syria Makes Overture."

88. Jim Lobe, "Are They Serious About Syria?" *Antiwar.com*, December 17, 2004; Eric S. Margolis, "Syria in the Sights?" *American Conservative*, March 28, 2005; and "Serious About Syria?" *Wall Street Journal* editorial, December 15, 2004.

89. Quoted in Yitzhak Benhorin, "Neocons: We Expected Israel to Attack Syria," *Ynetnews.com*, December 16, 2006.

90. Richard Boucher, Daily Press Briefing, U.S. State Department, May 24, 2005; Douglas Jehl and Thom Shanker, "Syria Stops Cooperating with U.S. Forces and C.I.A.," *New York Times*, May 24, 2005; Michael Hirsh and Kevin Peraino, "Dangers in Damascus," *Newsweek*, October 17, 2005; and "Syria Halts Cooperation with U.S.," *CNN.com*, May 24, 2005.

91. Leverett, *Inheriting Syria*, 134–42; and Prados, "Syria," 8–11.

92. Jim Lobe, "Bush Under Growing Pressure to Engage Syria," Inter Press Service, October 27, 2006. Also see Jim Lobe, "Damascus Now Seen as Pivotal in Mideast Crisis," Inter Press Service, July 25, 2006.

93. There have been scattered reports in the media that Israeli leaders might have lost their enthusiasm for regime change in Syria, given what has happened in Iraq since Saddam was toppled from power. See Stewart Ain, "Israel Getting Dragged into Syrian Mess," *Jewish Week*, October 28, 2005; and Ori Nir, "America, Israel Bracing for Violence from Syria," *Forward*, December 2, 2005. While this may be true, Israel remains deeply committed to making sure that Washington pursues a confrontational policy toward Damascus.

10: IRAN IN THE CROSSHAIRS

1. For details of Iran's WMD and ballistic missile capabilities, see the "Iran Profile" of the Nuclear Threat Initiative at www.nti.org/e_research/profiles/Iran/index.html; International Institute for Strategic Studies, *Iran's Strategic Weapons Programmes: A Net Assessment* (New

York: Routledge, 2005); and Uzi Rubin, "The Global Reach of Iran's Ballistic Missiles," Memorandum no. 86 (Tel Aviv: Institute for National Security Studies, November 2006).

2. "Iranian President at Tehran Conference: 'Very Soon, This Stain of Disgrace [i.e., Israel] Will Be Purged from the Center of the Islamic World—and This Is Attainable.'" Middle East Media Research Institute, Special Dispatch Series no. 1013, October 28, 2005. For a more detailed discussion of the translation of Ahmadinejad's speech, see note 88 in Chapter 3.

3. The two best indicators of potential military power are population size and wealth, though a country's actual military capability depends on how efficiently it translates these assets into skilled and well-equipped military forces. Iran has a substantially larger population and considerably more wealth than Iraq, its nearest competitor in the Persian Gulf region. For example, Iran had about a 3:1 advantage in population over Iraq in 1989 (54.5 versus 17.6 million), and about a 2.4:1 advantage in 2006 (65 versus 26.8 million). U.S. Census Bureau, "International Data Base," Updated August 24, 2006. Using GDP as an indicator of wealth, Iran had a 4:1 advantage in 1985 (179.8 versus US$44.2 billion) and a 3.9:1 advantage in 2000 (101 versus US$25.9 billion). World Bank, "Country at a Glance" (Iran and Iraq), August 13, 2006; and World Bank Group, "World Development Indicators Database," Iran Data Profile and Iraq Data Profile, April 2006.

4. This is the title of an article by Alissa J. Rubin in the *Los Angeles Times*, December 10, 2006. Also see Geoffrey Kemp, "Iran and Iraq: The Shia Connection, Soft Power, and the Nuclear Factor," Special Report 156 (Washington, DC: U.S. Institute of Peace, November 2005); "Iran Grows Strong, the World Yawns," *Ha'aretz* editorial, December 13, 2006; Liz Sly, "Iranian Influence Soaring in Iraq," *Chicago Tribune*, March 8, 2007; Megan K. Stack and Borzou Daragahi, "Iran Was on Edge; Now It's on Top," *Los Angeles Times*, February 18, 2006; and Edward Wong, "Iran Is in Strong Position to Steer Iraq's Political Future," *New York Times*, July 3, 2004.

5. Quoted in Trita Parsi, "Israeli-Iranian Relations 1970–2001: Ideological Calculus or Strategic Rivalry?" (PhD diss., Johns Hopkins University, April 2006), 413, also 159–62, 262–63, 275–76, 300–301, 392–93, 406–11. Also see Trita Parsi, "Israel and the Origins of Iran's Arab Option: Dissection of a Strategy Misunderstood," *Middle East Journal* 60, no. 3 (Summer 2006); and Trita Parsi, "The Geo-Strategic Roots of the Israeli-Iranian Enmity," *Heartland-Eurasian Review of Geopolitics* 4 (Summer 2005).

6. Bernard Lewis, "August 22: Does Iran Have Something in Store?" *Wall Street Journal*, August 8, 2006.

7. For a careful and convincing analysis that deterrence would work against a nuclear Iran, see Barry R. Posen, "A Nuclear Armed Iran: A Difficult but Not Impossible Policy Problem" (Washington, DC: Century Foundation, 2006); and Barry R. Posen, "We Can Live with a Nuclear Iran," *New York Times*, February 27, 2006. French President Jacques Chirac made this point in January 2007 but had to quickly retract his remarks because it is politically incorrect in the West to say that a nuclear Iran could be deterred. See Elaine Sciolino and Katrin Bennhold, "Chirac Strays from Assailing a Nuclear Iran," *New York Times*, February 1, 2007.

8. Ray Takeyh, "Iran's Nuclear Calculations," *World Policy Journal* 20, no. 2 (Summer 2003).

9. After all, this is what Iraq did after the Israelis eliminated its nascent nuclear capability in 1981. See Dan Reiter, "Preventive Attacks Against Nuclear Programs and the 'Success' at Osiraq," *Nonproliferation Review* 12, no. 2 (July 2005).

10. Zbigniew Brzezinski, "Do Not Attack Iran," *International Herald Tribune*, April 26, 2006; James Fallows, "Will Iran Be Next?" *Atlantic*, December 2004; and Michael J. Mazarr, "Strike Out: Attacking Iran Is a Bad Idea," *New Republic*, August 15, 2005.

11. Michael Smith and Sarah Baxter, "US Generals 'Will Quit' if Bush Orders Iran Attack," *Sunday Times* (London), February 25, 2007.

12. Parsi, "Israel-Iranian Relations," 285–97, 354–61, 400–401; and Gary Sick, "The Clouded Mirror: The United States and Iran, 1979–1999," in ed. John L. Esposito and R. K. Ramazani, *Iran at the Crossroads* (New York: Palgrave, 2001), 204.

13. David Hoffman, "Israel Seeking to Convince U.S. That West Is Threatened by Iran," *Washington Post*, March 13, 1993.

14. Parsi, "Israeli-Iranian Relations," 402. For elaboration on Israel's influence on the formulation of dual containment, see ibid., 297–99; and Kenneth M. Pollack, *The Persian Puzzle: The Conflict Between Iran and America* (New York: Random House, 2004), 261–65.

15. Pollack, *Persian Puzzle*, 269.

16. For the official line on dual containment, see Martin Indyk, "The Clinton Administration's Approach to the Middle East," speech to Soref Symposium, Washington Institute for Near East Policy, May 18, 1993. Also see Sick, "Clouded Mirror," 198–99, 209n13.

17. Regarding Rafsanjani's efforts to reach out to the United States, see Ali M. Ansari, *Confronting Iran: The Failure of American Foreign Policy and the Next Great Crisis in the Middle East* (New York: Perseus Books, 2006), 115–46; Parsi, "Israeli-Iranian Relations," 257–66; Pollack, *Persian Puzzle*, chaps. 9–10; and R. K. Ramazani, "Reflections on Iran's Foreign Policy: Defining the 'National Interests,'" in Esposito and Ramazani, *Iran at the Crossroads*, 217–22.

18. Parsi, "Israeli-Iranian Relations," 298–99. Useful critiques of dual containment include F. Gregory Gause III, "The Illogic of Dual Containment," *Foreign Affairs* 73, no. 2 (March/April 1994); and Barbara Conry, "America's Misguided Policy of Dual Containment in the Persian Gulf," Foreign Policy Briefing no. 33 (Washington, DC: Cato Institute, November 10, 1994).

19. Zbigniew Brzezinski and Brent Scowcroft, *Differentiated Containment: U.S. Policy Toward Iran and Iraq*, report of an Independent Study Group on Gulf Stability and Security (New York: Council on Foreign Relations, 1997), 5–32; and Gary Sick, "Rethinking Dual Containment," *Survival* 40, no. 1 (Spring 1998).

20. Parsi, "Israeli-Iranian Relations," 304–305; and Pollack, *Persian Puzzle*, 269–70.

21. Parsi, "Israeli-Iranian Relations," 305.

22. Pollack quoted in ibid., 308. Pollack reportedly added that the Clinton administration "only saw Iran through the prism of Tehran's attitude towards the Israeli-Palestinian conflict." Quoted in ibid., 309.

23. AIPAC, "Comprehensive U.S. Sanctions Against Iran: A Plan for Action," Washington, DC, April 2, 1995.

24. Pollack, *Persian Puzzle*, 270–71.

25. The following discussion of the Conoco case and the various sanctions imposed on Iran by the Clinton administration is based on Sasan Fayazmanesh, "The Politics of the U.S. Economic Sanctions Against Iran," *Review of Radical Political Economics* 35, no. 3 (Summer 2003); Herman Franssen and Elaine Morton, "A Review of US Unilateral Sanctions Against Iran," *Middle East Economic Survey* 45, no. 34 (August 26, 2002); Dilip Hiro, *Neighbors Not Friends: Iraq and Iran After the Gulf Wars* (New York: Routledge, 2001), chap. 9; Kenneth Katzman, "The Iran-Libya Sanctions Act (ILSA)," *CRS Report for Congress*, Congressional Research Service, October 11, 2006; Laurie Lande, "Second Thoughts," *International Economy* 11, no. 3 (May/June 1997); Pollack, *Persian Puzzle*, chaps. 9–10; and Sick, "Clouded Mirror,"198–207.

26. "Remarks at the World Jewish Congress Dinner in New York City—President Bill Clinton Speech—Transcript," April 30, 1995, www.findarticles.com/p/articles/mi_m2889/is_n18_v31/ai_17157196. Also see Agis Salpukas, "Conoco's Deal in Iran Faces Board Hurdle," *New York Times*, March 14, 1995; and Daniel Southerland and Ann Devroy, "Clinton Bars U.S. Oil Pacts with Iran," *Washington Post*, March 15, 1995.

27. Parsi, "Israeli-Iranian Relations," 310.

28. Executive Order 12959, White House, Office of the Press Secretary, May 8, 1995.

29. Todd Purdum, "Clinton to Order a Trade Embargo Against Tehran," *New York Times*, May 1, 1995; and "Remarks at the World Jewish Congress."

30. Pollack, *Persian Puzzle*, 273.

31. Parsi, "Israeli-Iranian Relations," 308, 311, 329–30.

32. A. M. Rosenthal, "Plugging the Leak," *New York Times*, March 14, 1995.

33. Parsi, "Israeli-Iranian Relations," 312. An AIPAC official, according to another source, claimed that Congress wrote the legislation "with us sentence by sentence." Franssen and Morton, "Review of US Unilateral Sanctions." Also see George Moffett, "Push to Widen Libya Sanctions Riles US Allies," *Christian Science Monitor*, January 24, 1996.

34. Pollack, *Persian Puzzle*, 287.

35. Quoted in Brzezinski and Scowcroft, *Differentiated Containment*, 6.

36. James Schlesinger, "Fragmentation and Hubris: A Shaky Basis for American Leadership," *National Interest* 49 (Fall 1997): 5.

37. Fayazmanesh, "Politics of the U.S. Economic Sanctions," 231–35.

38. Reuters, "Call for 'Détente' as Tehran Swears in a Moderate President," *Australian*, August 5, 1997; Douglas Jehl, "Iranian President Calls for Opening Dialogue with U.S.," *New York Times*, December 15, 1997; and "Transcript of Interview with Iranian President Mohammad Khatami," *CNN.com*, January 7, 1998.

39. "Interview with Khatami"; and Parsi, "Israeli-Iranian Relations," 330–36.

40. On the Clinton administration checking with the Israelis, see Pollack, *Persian Puzzle*, 319. For a more general discussion of the steps the Clinton administration took in response to Khatami's overtures, see Hiro, *Neighbors*, chap. 10; Parsi, "Israeli-Iranian Relations," 331–45; Pollack, *Persian Puzzle*, 319–42; and Sick, "Clouded Mirror," 200–206.

41. Quoted in Parsi, "Israeli-Iranian Relations," 329.

42. Ansari, *Confronting Iran*, chap. 5; Hiro, *Neighbors*, 235–40; Pollack, *Persian Puzzle*, 325–42; and Ray Takeyh, *Hidden Iran: Paradox and Power in the Islamic Republic* (New York: Henry Holt, 2006), 44–54, 110–16.

43. Yerah Tal, "U.S., Iran in Secret Talks," *Ha'aretz*, December 15, 1997.

44. Sick, "Clouded Mirror," 210n32.

45. Eli Lake, "Israel, U.S. Jewish Lobby Disagree on Iran Sanctions," United Press International, September 23, 2000.

46. Quoted in Parsi, "Israeli-Iranian Relations," 298.

47. Quoted in ibid., 403. During the early 1990s, Sneh played a key role in making the case that Iran was a deadly threat to Israel. See ibid., 286.

48. Quoted in Alan Sipress, "Israel Emphasizes Iranian Threat," *Washington Post*, February 7, 2002. This article, which was written as Sharon was arriving in Washington, makes clear that Jerusalem was "redoubling efforts to warn the Bush administration that Iran poses a greater threat than the Iraqi regime of Saddam Hussein." Also see Seymour M. Hersh, "The Iran Game," *New Yorker*, December 3, 2001; Peter Hirschberg, "Background: Peres Raises Iranian Threat," *Ha'aretz*, February 5, 2002; David Hirst, "Israel Thrusts Iran in Line of US Fire," *Guardian*, February 2, 2002; "Israel Once Again Sees Iran as a Cause for Concern," *Ha'aretz*, May 7, 2001; Dana Priest, "Iran's Emerging Nuclear Plant Poses Test for U.S.," *Washington Post*, July 29, 2002; and Ze'ev Schiff, "Iran: Clear and Present Danger," *Ha'aretz*, May 31, 2002.

49. Stephen Farrell, Robert Thomson, and Danielle Haas, "Attack Iran the Day Iraq War Ends, Demands Israel," *Times* (London), November 5, 2002; and Stephen Farrell and Robert Thomson, "The Times Interview with Ariel Sharon," ibid.

50. Quoted in "Ambassador to U.S. Calls for 'Regime Change' in Iran, Syria," *Ha'aretz*, April 28, 2003.

51. Steven R. Weisman, "New U.S. Concerns on Iran's Pursuit of Nuclear Arms," *New York Times*, May 8, 2003.

52. Shimon Peres, "We Must Unite to Prevent an Ayatollah Nuke," *Wall Street Journal*, June 25, 2003.

53. Jim Lobe, "US Neo-Cons Move Quickly on Iran," Inter Press Service, May 27, 2003.

54. Marc Perelman, "Pentagon Team on Iran Comes Under Fire," *Forward*, June 6, 2003. Also see Marc Perelman, "White House Is Aiming to Raise Iranian Nukes at U.N. Security Council," *Forward*, May 9, 2003; and Marc Perelman, "New Front Sets Sights on Toppling Iran Regime," *Forward*, May 16, 2003.

55. William Kristol, "The End of the Beginning," *Weekly Standard*, May 12, 2003.
56. Michael Ledeen, "The Others," *National Review Online*, April 4, 2003. Ledeen also wrote in mid-April 2003 that "it is impossible to win the war on terrorism so long as the regimes in Syria and Iran remain in power." He went on to say that "the good news is that both are vulnerable to political attack." Quoted in Ronald Brownstein, "Those Who Sought War Are Now Pushing Peace," *Los Angeles Times*, April 17, 2003. Also see Alex Koppelman, "Iranian Regime Change: 'Faster, Please!'" *Salon.com*, January 15, 2007.
57. Daniel Pipes and Patrick Clawson, "Turn Up the Pressure on Iran," *Jerusalem Post*, May 21, 2003; and Lawrence Kaplan, "Iranamok," *New Republic*, June 9, 2003.
58. A copy of the flyer advertising the conference, which was titled "The Future of Iran: Mullahcracy, Democracy, and the War on Terror," can be found at www.aei.org/events/eventID .300/event_detail.asp. Also see Jordan Green, "Neocons Dream of Lebanon," *ZNet* (online), July 23, 2003; and Lobe, "Neo-Cons Move Quickly."
59. Connie Bruck, "Exiles: How Iran's Expatriates Are Gaming the Nuclear Threat," *New Yorker*, March 6, 2006; Lobe, "Neo-Cons Move Quickly"; Ron Perelman, "New Front Sets Sights on Toppling Iran Regime," *Forward*, May 17, 2003; and "Shah of Iran's Heir Plans Overthrow of Regime," *Human Events* (online), May 1, 2006.
60. All information is from "Senator Brownback Announces Iran Democracy Act with Iranian Exiles," press release from the National Iranian American Council, May 20, 2003; and "Iran Democracy Act Passed, but No Money to Opposition and Satellite TV's," press release from the National Iranian American Council, July 24, 2003.
61. Lobe, "Neo-Cons Move Quickly."
62. Michael Ledeen, "The Iranian Hand," *Wall Street Journal*, April 16, 2004.
63. "President Discusses War on Terror and Operation Iraqi Freedom," talk in Cleveland, Ohio (White House, Office of the Press Secretary, March 20, 2006).
64. Quoted in Ori Nir, "Groups to Bush: Drop Iran-Israel Linkage," *Forward*, May 12, 2006.
65. Associated Press, "John McCain Jokes About Bombing Iran at U.S. Campaign Stop," *International Herald Tribune*, April 19, 2007.
66. "The Road to the White House: Israel-U.S. Ties," *Jerusalem Post*, May 24, 2007.
67. Nir, "Groups to Bush." Also see James D. Besser and Larry Cohler-Esses, "Iran-Israel Linkage by Bush Seen as Threat," *Jewish Week*, April 21, 2006; James D. Besser, "JCPA Delegates Spurn Israel Demands," *Jewish Week*, March 2, 2007; "Groups Fear Public Backlash over Iran," *Forward*, February 2, 2007; Ron Kampeas, "As Jewish Groups Huddle, Quagmire in Iraq Undermines Resolve on Iran," *JTA.org*, February 28, 2007; and Jim Lobe, "Jewish Community Worried About Iran Backlash," Inter Press Service, May 10, 2006.
68. Quoted in Besser and Cohler-Esses, "Iran-Israel Linkage."
69. Quoted in Ori Nir, "Bush Overture to Iran Splits Israel, Neocons," *Forward*, June 9, 2006.
70. Gareth Porter, "Strategy Paper Reveals Bush Won't Attack Iran," Inter Press Service, June 20, 2006.
71. James Bamford, "Iran: The Next War," *Rolling Stone*, July 24, 2006; Seymour M. Hersh, "The Coming Wars," *New Yorker*, January 24/31, 2005; Seymour M. Hersh, "The Iran Plans," *New Yorker*, April 17, 2006; Seymour M. Hersh, "Last Stand," *New Yorker*, July 10, 2006; Seymour M. Hersh, "The Redirection," *New Yorker*, March 5, 2007; and "Iran: The Next Strategic Target," Seymour Hersh interview with Amy Goodman of Democracy Now!, *AlterNet.org*, January 19, 2005. Also see Peter Baker, Dafna Linzer, and Thomas E. Ricks, "U.S. Is Studying Military Strike Options on Iran," *Washington Post*, April 9, 2006; Perelman, "Pentagon Team on Iran"; and Craig Unger, "From the Wonderful Folks Who Brought You Iraq," *Vanity Fair* (online), March 2007. All of the quotations in this paragraph are from Hersh, "Coming Wars."
72. The information in this paragraph is drawn from Helene Cooper and Mark Mazzetti, "To Counter Iran's Role in Iraq, Bush Moves Beyond Diplomacy," *New York Times*, January 11, 2007; Tony Karon, "The Problem with Confronting Iran," *Time*, January 16, 2007; Eli Lake, "GIs Raid Iranian Building in Irbil," *New York Sun*, January 12, 2007; David E. Sanger,

"Opening a New Front in the War, against Iranians in Iraq," *New York Times*, January 15, 2007; David E. Sanger and Michael R. Gordon, "Rice Says Bush Authorized Iranians' Arrest in Iraq," *New York Times*, January 13, 2007; and Trita Parsi, "Bush's Iraq Plan: Goading Iran into War," Inter Press Service, January 17, 2007.

73. Helene Cooper, "U.S. Not Pushing for Attack on Iran, Rice Says," *New York Times*, June 1, 2007. Also see Arnaud de Borchgrave, "Guns of August?" United Press International, June 4, 2007; Steven C. Clemons, "Cheney Attempting to Constrain Bush's Choices on Iran Conflict: Staff Engaged in Insubordination Against President Bush," *Washington Note* weblog, May 24, 2007, www.thewashingtonnote.com/archives/002145.php; Michael Hirsh and Mark Hosenball, "Cheney vs. Rice: A Foreign-Policy Showdown," *MSNBC.com*, June 11, 2007; and Glenn Kessler, "Cheney Backs Diplomacy on Iran Program, Rice Affirms," *Washington Post*, June 2, 2007.

74. These quotations are from the "Agreed Statement" of October 21, 2003, a copy of which can be found in International Institute for Strategic Studies, *Iran's Strategic Weapons Programmes*, 19. For the details of the negotiations between Iran and the EU-3, see ibid., chap. 1; International Institute for Strategic Studies, *Strategic Survey, 2004/5* (New York: Routledge, May 2005), 196–200; and International Institute for Strategic Studies, *Strategic Survey, 2006* (New York: Routledge, 2006), 210–22.

75. Kaveh L. Afrasiabi, "The Myth of the EU Olive Branch," *Asia Times Online*, August 13, 2005; Ansari, *Confronting Iran*, chap. 7; British American Security Information Council, "EU3 Negotiations with the Islamic Republic of Iran: Not Out of the Woods Yet and Time Is Short, Very Short," BASIC Notes: Occasional Paper on International Security Policy, July 2005; and Hersh, "Last Stand."

76. Elissa Gootman, "Security Council Approves Sanctions Against Iran over Nuclear Program," *New York Times*, December 24, 2006; Colum Lynch, "Sanctions on Iran Approved by U.N.," *Washington Post*, December 24, 2006. Also see Nazila Fathi, "Iran Is Defiant, Vowing to U.N. It Will Continue Nuclear Efforts," *New York Times*, December 25, 2006; Ron Kampeas, "The Iran Sanctions Package: Some Assembly Required, Teeth Not Included," *JTA.org*, December 25, 2006; Nasser Karimi, "Iran Rebuffs U.N., Vows to Speed Up Uranium Enrichment," *Washington Post*, December 25, 2006; and Neil King, "U.S. Bid to Limit Iran Gets Wary Response," *Wall Street Journal*, December 29, 2006.

77. Daniel Bilefsky, "Europe Approves More Sanctions Against Iran," *New York Times*, April 24, 2007; Daniel Dombey and Gareth Smyth, "New EU Sanctions Raise Pressure on Iran," *Financial Times*, April 23, 2007; Warren Hoge, "U.N. Council Gets New Draft Decree on Iran Nuclear Sanctions," *New York Times*, March 16, 2007; Colum Lynch, "U.N. Backs Broader Sanctions on Tehran," *Washington Post*, March 26, 2007; Colum Lynch, "U.S., Allies Agree to Drop Proposed Iran Travel Ban," *Washington Post*, March 10, 2007; and Thom Shanker, "Security Council Votes to Tighten Iran Sanctions," *New York Times*, March 25, 2007.

78. Hersh, "The Redirection."

79. Nathan Guttman, "Activists Set to Push New Sanctions against Iran," *Forward*, March 9, 2007. Also see Eli Lake, "AIPAC Will Press for Hard Line on Iran Regime," *New York Sun*, March 7, 2007; Ian Swanson, "Chairmen Try to Tighten Screws on Iran," *The Hill* (online), March 14, 2007; and Steven R. Weisman, "U.S. Tightens Financial Squeeze on Iran," *International Herald Tribune*, March 20, 2007.

80. Richard Beeston and James Bone, "Hostage Fears over Troops Seized by Iran," *Times* (London), March 24, 2007; Sarah Lyall, "Iran Seizes 15 Britons on Patrol in Persian Gulf," *New York Times*, March 24, 2007; Vali Nasr and Ray Takeyh, "What We Can Learn from Britain About Iran," *New York Times*, April 5, 2007; and Kevin Sullivan, "15 Britons Taken to Tehran as Iran Dispute Intensifies," *Washington Post*, March 25, 2007.

81. Guttman, "Activists Set to Push"; Lake, "AIPAC Will Press"; and Weisman, "U.S. Tightens Financial Squeeze." On Europe's reluctance to reduce its economic dealings with Iran, see Steven R. Weisman, "Europe Resists U.S. Push to Curb Iran Ties," *New York Times*, January 30, 2007.

82. All of the quotations in this paragraph are from Hassan M. Fattah, "Saudi King Condemns U.S. Occupation of Iraq," *New York Times*, March 28, 2007. Also see William J. Broad and David E. Sanger, "With Eye on Iran, Rivals Also Want Nuclear Power," *New York Times*, April 15, 2007; Rachel Bronson, "Good Neighbors: What Saudi Arabia Wants," *New Republic Online*, April 3, 2007; Helene Cooper, "U.S. Feels Sting of Winning Saudi Help with Other Arabs," *New York Times*, March 30, 2007; Helene Cooper and Jim Rutenberg, "A Saudi Prince Tied to Bush Is Sounding Off-Key," *New York Times*, April 29, 2007; Hassan M. Fattah, "Bickering Saudis Struggle for an Answer to Iran's Rising Influence in Middle East," *New York Times*, December 22, 2006; and Jonathan Steele, "As US Power Fades, It Can't Find Friends to Take on Iran," *Guardian*, February 2, 2007.

83. "Israeli PM Olmert Addresses Congress," *Washington Post*, May 24, 2006. Olmert also visited the White House and made his views on Iran clear to President Bush. See "President Bush and Prime Minister Ehud Olmert of Israel Participate in Joint Press Availability," White House, Office of the Press Secretary, May 23, 2006. The Israeli scholar Benny Morris has also laid out an apocalyptic vision of what will happen to Israel if Iran acquires nuclear weapons. See Benny Morris, "Essay: This Holocaust Will Be Different," *Jerusalem Post*, January 18, 2007; and Benny Morris, "The Second Holocaust Is Looming," *israelinsider.com*, January 15, 2007.

84. Lally Weymouth, "Israel's P.M. on Iran, Lebanon, Palestinian State," *Newsweek* interview, *MSNBC.com*, November 11, 2006. Also see Uzi Benziman, "Trigger-Happy (On the Button)," *Ha'aretz*, December 17, 2006; "Iran Complains to UN Security Council over Sneh Comments," *Ha'aretz*, November 11, 2006; and Ronny Sofer, "IDF: Only US Operation Can Stop Iran," *Ynetnews.com*, October 12, 2006.

85. Quoted in Gil Yaron, "Missile Raid Would Hit Iran Nuclear Plants—Olmert," *Ynetnews.com*, April 28, 2007.

86. Oded Tira, "What to Do with Iran?" *Ynetnews.com*, December 30, 2006.

87. The Sharon quotation is from Uzi Mahnaimi and Sarah Baxter, "Israel Readies Forces for Strikes on Nuclear Iran," *Sunday Times* (London), December 11, 2005. The more recent report (and the Israel denial) is from Uzi Mahnaimi and Sarah Baxter, "Revealed: Israel Plans Nuclear Strike on Iran," *Sunday Times*, January 7, 2007; and Uzi Mahnaimi and Sarah Baxter, "Israel Denies Planning Iran Nuke Attack," Associated Press, January 7, 2007. Also see Richard Boudreaux, "Israel Sounds Alarm on Iran's Nuclear Efforts," *Los Angeles Times*, February 7, 2007; and Ilene Prusher, "Israel Buzzes over Notion of Attacking Iran," *Christian Science Monitor*, January 16, 2007.

88. "'Israel May Have to Act Alone,'" *Spiegel* interview with Avigdor Lieberman, *Spiegel Online*, February 12, 2007.

89. For a sample of the voluminous literature on this matter, see Stewart Ain, "Israel Urging U.S. to Stop Iran Nukes," *Jewish Week*, October 7, 2005; Martin S. Indyk, "Iran's Bluster Isn't a Bluff," *Los Angeles Times*, November 1, 2005; Ron Kampeas, "With Time Short on Iran Nukes, AIPAC Criticizes Bush Approach," *JTA.org*, December 2, 2005; Yossi Klein Halevi and Michael B. Oren, "Israel's Worst Nightmare: Contra Iran," *New Republic*, February 5, 2007; Frederick Kempe, "Elie Wiesel Sounds the Alarm Regarding Iran," *Wall Street Journal*, June 20, 2006; Dafna Linzer, "Pro-Israel Group Criticizes White House Policy on Iran," *Washington Post*, December 25, 2005; Ori Nir, "Israeli Aides Warn U.S. Not to Drop Ball on Iran," *Forward*, December 9, 2005; Ori Nir, "Jewish Groups Press for Iran Sanctions," *Forward*, September 23, 2005; Ori Nir, "Groups Push for Sanctions, Fear U.S. Will Falter on Iran," *Forward*, September 1, 2006; Marc Perelman, "Groups Head to Emirates, as Worries Grow over Iran," *Forward*, January 19, 2007; and Brad Sherman, "The Unmet Threat of a Nuclear Iran," *Forward*, October 27, 2006.

90. Joshua Muravchik, "Operation Comeback," *Foreign Policy* 157 (November/December 2006): 68.

91. Quoted in Yossi Melman, "To Attack or Not to Attack?" *Ha'aretz*, January 24, 2007.

92. Shmuel Rosner, "AIPAC Conference Focuses on Hamas and Iran," *Ha'aretz*, March 7, 2006; and

Guttman, "Activists Set to Push." Also see "Iran's Pursuit of Nuclear Weapons," www.aipac.org/Publications/AIPACAnalysesIssueBriefs/Irans_Pursuit_of_Nuclear_Weapons(1).pdf.

93. Quoted in James D. Besser, "Hardline Pastor Gets Prime AIPAC Spot," *Jewish Week*, March 9, 2007.

94. Quoted in "Christians for Israel," *Jerusalem Post* editorial, March 14, 2007.

95. Maggie Haberman, "Israel Fans Groan over Hill Speech," *New York Post* (online), February 2, 2007.

96. Jonathan Allen, "Iran Language Draws Opposition as Democrats Near Agreement on Supplemental," *CQ Today*, March 8, 2007; "Dems Abandon War Authority Provision," Associated Press, March 13, 2007; Eli Lake, "Democrats Retreat on War Funds," *New York Sun*, March 14, 2007; "Engel's Finest Hour," *New York Sun* editorial, March 14, 2007; and John Walsh, "Why Is the Peace Movement Silent About AIPAC?" *CounterPunch.org*, April 17, 2007.

97. Capuano is quoted in Walsh, "Peace Movement Silent," which also discusses Kucinich's response.

98. Leon Hadar, "Osirak Redux?" *American Conservative*, January 15, 2007; Gideon Rachman, "Talk of Another Preventive War in the Middle East Is Folly," *Financial Times*, November 21, 2006; and Scott Ritter, *Target Iran: The Truth About the White House's Plans for Regime Change* (New York: Nation Books, 2006), 203–206.

99. Quoted in Jim Lobe, "Pressure Grows on Bush to Engage Iran Directly," *Antiwar.com*, May 26, 2006.

100. The survey was conducted by Bar-Ilan University and the Anti-Defamation League, and found that "fully 71 percent of Israelis believe that the United States should launch a military attack on Iran if diplomatic efforts fail to halt Tehran's nuclear program." See Aluf Benn, "Poll: 71% of Israelis Want U.S. to Strike Iran if Talks Fail," *Ha'aretz*, May 18, 2007.

101. The original Clark quote was in "The Huffington Post" on January 4, 2007, www.huffingtonpost.com/arianna-huffington/dc-notes-wes-clark-is-_b_37837.html. The Yglesias quote is from Matthew Yglesias, "Smears for Fears," *American Prospect* (online), January 23, 2007. Also see James D. Besser, "Gen. Clark's Controversy," *Jewish Week*, January 12, 2007; Nathan Guttman, "Top Dem Wesley Clark Says 'N.Y. Money People' Pushing War with Iran," *Forward*, January 12, 2007; and Shmuel Rosner, "The General and the 'Money People,'" *Ha'aretz*, January 9, 2007. An article in the *Forward* discussing fears in the American Jewish community of being blamed for an American war against Iran nevertheless conceded that "Jewish groups are indeed playing a lead role in pressing for a hard line on Iran." The article also noted that "many advocacy efforts, even when not linked to Israel, carry indelibly Jewish fingerprints." See "Groups Fear Public Backlash."

102. Ritter, *Target Iran*, 211.

103. For an excellent discussion of what a grand bargain with Iran would look like, see Flynt Leverett, *Dealing with Tehran: Assessing U.S. Diplomatic Options Toward Iran* (New York: Century Foundation, 2006), 19–25.

104. The following discussion of Iran's failed attempts to reach out to the Bush administration is based on Gregory Beals, "A Missed Opportunity with Iran," *Newsday* (online), February 19, 2006; Bruck, "Exiles"; Leverett, *Dealing with Tehran*, 11–16; Flynt Leverett and Hillary Mann, "What We Wanted to Tell You About Iran," *New York Times*, December 22, 2006; Glenn Kessler, "In 2003, U.S. Spurned Iran's Offer of Dialogue," *Washington Post*, June 18, 2006; Nicholas D. Kristof, "Diplomacy at Its Worst," *New York Times*, April 29, 2007; Jim Lobe, "Bush Administration Divided over Road to Tehran," *Foreign Policy in Focus*, August 11, 2003; Jim Lobe, "Bush Administration Paralyzed over Iran," *Asia Times Online*, August 9, 2003; Gareth Porter, "How Neocons Sabotaged Iran's Help on al-Qaeda," *Antiwar.com*, February 23, 2006; Gareth Porter, "Burnt Offering," *American Prospect*, June 6, 2006; Gareth Porter, "Neocons Blocked 2003 Nuclear Talks with Iran," *Antiwar.com*, March 29, 2006; and Gareth Porter, "Iran Proposal to US Offered Peace with Israel," *Antiwar.com*, May 25, 2006.

105. The 2003 proposal described in this paragraph was spelled out in an Iranian document that

was transmitted to the State Department and the White House. A copy can be found on the *New York Times* columnist Nicholas D. Kristof's website, http://kristof.blogs.nytimes.com/.

106. James A. Baker III and Lee H. Hamilton, co-chairs, *The Iraq Study Group Report* (New York: Vintage Books, 2006), 50–52.

107. On Afghanistan, see David Rohde, "Iran Is Seeking More Influence in Afghanistan," *New York Times*, December 27, 2006.

108. Jim Lobe, "Pressure Grows on Bush," *Antiwar.com*, May 26, 2006; and Steven R. Weisman, "U.S. Is Debating Talks with Iran on Nuclear Issue," *New York Times*, May 27, 2006. It is also worth noting that support among American Jews for a U.S. attack against Iran has sharply declined. In the fall of 2005, 49 percent supported military action; only 38 percent supported it in the fall of 2006. "Poll: U.S. Jews Back Strike against Iran—by Israel," *Forward*, October 27, 2006.

109. Steven Kull, "Americans Assess US International Strategy," WorldPublicOpinion.org poll, conducted by the Program on International Policy Attitudes, December 7, 2006. Also see "Baker-Hamilton Redux: The U.S. Public Remains Enthusiastic About the Bipartisan Proposals," Pew Research Center, May 29, 2007.

110. Thomas L. Friedman, "Not-So-Strange Bedfellow," *New York Times*, January 31, 2007.

111. Marc Perelman, "As Washington Studies Iraq Report, Jerusalem Frets over Tehran Talk," *Forward*, December 15, 2006. Also see Nathan Guttman, "Groups Mute Criticism of Iraq Report," *Forward*, December 15, 2006.

11: THE LOBBY AND THE SECOND LEBANON WAR

1. Human Rights Watch estimates that 1,125 Lebanese were killed in the war, about 300 to 350 of whom were combatants. Personal correspondence with HRW, May 24 and 30, 2007. The one-third figure for children is from Amnesty International, "Israel/Lebanon: Deliberate Destruction or 'Collateral Damage'? Israeli Attacks on Civilian Infrastructure," Report MDE 18/007/2006, August 23, 2006. Regarding the damage to infrastructure, see ibid.; Amnesty International, "Israel/Lebanon: Out of All Proportion—Civilians Bear the Brunt of the War," Report MDE 02/033/2006, November 21, 2006; and "Middle East Crisis: Facts and Figures," *BBC News* (online), August 31, 2006.

2. On the Winograd Commission's mandate, see *Ha'aretz* Staff, "The Main Findings of the Winograd Partial Report on the Second Lebanon War," *Ha'aretz*, May 1, 2007.

3. Quoted in Matthew Kalman, "Israel Set War Plan More than a Year Ago: Strategy Was Put in Motion as Hezbollah Began Increasing Its Military Strength," *San Francisco Chronicle* (online), July 21, 2006. Also see Martin Fletcher's comments to Tim Russert on *Meet the Press* shortly after the war began, "Transcript for July 16," *MSNBC.com*, July 16, 2006; Bernard Gwertzman, "Steinberg: Israel Hoping Attacks on Hezbollah Serve as a Warning to Iran," interview with Gerald M. Steinberg, Council on Foreign Relations, August 1, 2006; Yagil Levy, "A Voluntary 'Putsch,'" *Ha'aretz*, July 24, 2006; Andrea Mitchell, "U.S. Stands Alone in Defending Israel," *MSNBC.com*, July 13, 2006; Robert Novak, "No Political Upside in Criticizing Israel," *Chicago Sun-Times*, August 7, 2006; and Tanya Reinhart, "Israel's 'New Middle East,'" *CounterPunch.org*, July 27, 2006.

4. Seymour M. Hersh, "Watching Lebanon," *New Yorker*, August 21, 2006. Similarly, Matthew Kalman writes, "In the years since Israel ended its military occupation of southern Lebanon, it watched warily as Hezbollah built up its military presence in the region. When Hezbollah militants kidnapped two Israeli soldiers last week, the Israeli military was ready to react almost instantly." Kalman, "Israel Set War Plan."

5. See "Main Findings of the Winograd Partial Report." Olmert's testimony to the Winograd Commission is reported in Aluf Benn, "PM Says Decided on Response to Abductions Months Before War," *Ha'aretz*, March 8, 2007. Also see Aluf Benn, "Report: Interim Findings of War Won't Deal with Personal Failures," *Ha'aretz*, March 8, 2007; Josef Federman, "Reports: Israel Ready Before Lebanon War," *Washington Post*, March 9, 2007; Amos Harel,

Nir Hasson, Mazal Mualem, and Aluf Benn, "Officers Slam PM for Planning War but Not Preparing IDF," *Ha'aretz*, March 9, 2007; and Nir Hasson, "Senior IDF Officer to Haaretz: PM Did Not Order Us to Prepare for War," *Ha'aretz*, March 12, 2007.

6. Hersh, "Watching Lebanon"; and Kalman, "Israel Set War Plan." Also see "Israel: Did Blair Know All Along?" *Daily Mail* (online), August 14, 2006.

7. Hersh, "Watching Lebanon."

8. The Project for the New American Century sent an open letter signed by a host of prominent neoconservatives to President Bush on September 20, 2001, which said that "any war against terrorism must target Hezbollah." This letter was published in the *Weekly Standard*, October 1, 2001.

9. Helene Cooper, "Rice's Hurdles on Middle East Begin at Home," *New York Times*, August 10, 2006. Also see Sidney Blumenthal, "The Neocons' Next War," *Salon.com*, August 3, 2006; Hersh, "Watching Lebanon"; and Shmuel Rosner and Aluf Benn, "How to Win Friends and Influence Governments," *Ha'aretz*, July 28, 2006.

10. Marc Perelman, "Cheney Taps Syria Hawk as Adviser on Mideast," *Forward*, October 31, 2003. Also see Jim Lobe, "New Cheney Adviser Sets Syria in His Sights," Inter Press Service, October 20, 2003. John Hannah is another important neoconservative who was on Cheney's staff before and during the Lebanon conflict. Robert Dreyfuss, "Vice Squad," *American Prospect*, May 2006; and Janine Zacharia, "Bush Appoints Mideast Advisers," *Jerusalem Post*, February 7, 2001.

11. "A Clean Break: A New Strategy for Securing the Realm" was prepared for the Institute for Advanced Strategic and Political Studies in Jerusalem and published in June 1996. A copy can be found on the institute's website, www.iasps.org/strat1.htm.

12. Adam Shatz, "In Search of Hezbollah," *New York Review of Books*, April 29, 2004. Also see Mark Hosenball and Michael Isikoff, "Secret Proposals," *Newsweek*, August 9, 2004.

13. These are the words the *Economist* used to describe U.S. support for Israel during the Lebanon war. See "To Israel with Love," *Economist*, August 5, 2006.

14. Speaking before the war, Israeli ambassador Dan Gillerman told a B'nai B'rith meeting in New York, "Today the secret is out. We really are not just five diplomats [at Israel's UN mission]. We are at least six including John Bolton." Quoted in Irwin Arieff, "Israel's UN Ambassador Slams Qatar, Praises Bolton," Reuters, May 22, 2006. On Bolton's actions, see Associated Press, "Bolton: US Wanted Hizbullah Eliminated," *Jerusalem Post*, March 22, 2007; "Bolton Admits Lebanon Truce Block," *BBC News* (online), March 22, 2007; Robin Wright, "Strikes Are Called Part of Broad Strategy," *Washington Post*, July 16, 2006; and "U.S. Vetoes Criticism of Israel, *New York Times*, July 13, 2006.

15. Transcript of "Special Briefing on Travel to the Middle East and Europe," July 21, 2006, www.state.gov/secretary/rm/2006/69331.htm; and Roula Khalaf, "Rice 'New Middle East' Comments Fuel Arab Fury over U.S. Policy," *Financial Times*, July 31, 2006.

16. Quoted in Warren Hoge and Steven Erlanger, "U.N. Council Backs Measure to Halt War in Lebanon," *New York Times*, August 12, 2006.

17. "Remarks by Ambassador John R. Bolton, U.S. Representative to the United Nations, on the Situation in the Middle East, at the Security Council Stakeout, July 17, 2006," USUN Press Release #174 (06). Bolton's unyielding defense of Israel prompted the Union of Orthodox Jewish Congregations of America to break with its tradition of "not getting involved in personnel appointments" and ask the Senate to make him the permanent ambassador to the UN. Rosner and Benn, "How to Win Friends."

18. Blumenthal, "Neocons' Next War"; and David S. Cloud and Helene Cooper, "U.S. Speeds Up Bomb Delivery for the Israelis," *New York Times*, July 22, 2006.

19. John Diamond, "Officials: U.S. Blocked Missiles to Hezbollah," *USA Today*, August 18, 2006.

20. Quoted in Sheryl Gay Stolberg, "Bush's Embrace of Israel Shows Gap with Father," *New York Times*, August 2, 2006.

21. Quoted in David J. Silverman, "Politicking over Israel: Jewish State Becomes Fodder in

Congressional War," *JTA.org*, August 15, 2006. Also see Jim VandeHei, "Congress Is Giving Israel Vote of Confidence," *Washington Post*, July 19, 2006.

22. Quoted in Silverman, "Politicking over Israel." At a rally supporting Israel's actions in the war, the *New York Times* reported that "the fervor was at such a pitch that President Bush, who has defended Israel's actions, received praise from a lineup of politicians that was almost 100 percent Democratic." Clyde Haberman, "At Israel Rally, a Word Fails," *New York Times*, July 18, 2006.

23. James D. Besser, "Scoring Points with the Israel Issue," *Jewish Week*, July 28, 2006; and "To Israel with Love."

24. Brian Skoloff, "Dean Calls Iraqi PM an 'Anti-Semite,'" *Seattle Post-Intelligencer* (online), July 26, 2006.

25. Rahall quoted in Anne Plummer Flaherty, "House Overwhelmingly Backs Israel in Vote," *Guardian*, July 20, 2006; Zogby quoted in Noam N. Levey, "In Politicians' Pro-Israel Din, Arab Americans Go Unheard," *Los Angeles Times*, July 23, 2006.

26. On Clinton, see Gal Beckerman, "New York Jews Rally in Support of Israel," *Jerusalem Post*, July 18, 2006. On McCain, see Christopher Grimes, "European Criticism of Israel 'Amazes' Senator," *Financial Times*, July 18, 2006. On Biden and Gingrich, see their comments on *Meet the Press* with Tim Russert on July 16, 2006. Also see Michael Abramowitz, "Conservative Anger Grows over Bush's Foreign Policy," *Washington Post*, July 19, 2006.

27. Novak, "No Political Upside."

28. "Editorials Continue to Back Wide Air War Against Lebanon," *Editor & Publisher*, July 20, 2006. Also see Greg Mitchell, "Few Editorials Find Fault with the Bombing of Beirut," *Editor & Publisher*, July 18, 2006. One important exception to this general pattern was Nicholas D. Kristof, "In Lebanon, Echoes of Iraq?" *New York Times*, July 25, 2006.

29. Quoted in Marvin Kalb and Carol Saivetz, "The Israeli-Hezbollah War of 2006: The Media as a Weapon in Asymmetrical Conflict," Faculty Research Working Paper RWP07-012, John F. Kennedy School of Government, Harvard University, February 2007, 15. The Kalb and Saivetz study, which is written from a pro-Israel perspective, argues that Israel was treated unfairly by the media because it is an "open society" and Hezbollah is a "closed society." Because the study focuses on news coverage of the conflict and largely ignores editorials and commentary, it is able to argue that Israel tended to be portrayed in a more negative light than Hezbollah. The claim that Israel was at a disadvantage in the media because of its relative openness is unconvincing, because journalists could clearly see what was happening in both Israel and Lebanon.

30. The number of civilians killed is based on the figures from Human Rights Watch described in note 1 above. The number of buildings damaged or destroyed is from "Middle East Crisis: Facts and Figures."

31. Andrew Gumbel, "America's One-Eyed View of War: Stars, Stripes, and the Star of David," *Independent*, August 15, 2006. Also see "Is America Watching a Different War? American, Lebanese and Israeli Panel on How the US Media Is Covering the Invasion of Lebanon," *DemocracyNow.org*, August 3, 2006.

32. "Main Findings of the Winograd Partial Report." The report also says that "the ability to achieve military gains having significant political-international weight was limited" and that "some of the declared goals of the war were . . . in part not achievable by the authorized modes of military action."

33. Quoted in Larry Cohler-Esses, "Israel Seeks to Redefine Victory," *Jewish Week*, August 4, 2006. Also see Jack Khoury, "Top IDF Officer: We Knew War Would Not Get Our Soldiers Back," *Ha'aretz*, April 26, 2007; and Ori Nir, "Israel Seeks to Eliminate Iran's Hezbollah Option," *Forward*, July 14, 2006.

34. Quoted in Wright, "Strikes Are Called."

35. Benjamin Netanyahu, "No Ceasefire in the War on Terror," *Wall Street Journal*, July 22, 2006.

36. A senior Israeli commander told the *New York Times*, "The army was planning on 15 days of

air war before any ground forces were considered . . . We didn't want to do any ground assault and thought we could create the conditions for a cease-fire without a major ground assault." Quoted in Steven Erlanger, "Israeli Officer Says Army Aims to Kill Nasrallah," *New York Times*, August 20, 2006.

37. Both Olmert quotations in this paragraph are from "PM Olmert: Lebanon Is Responsible and Will Bear the Consequences," transcript of press conference, Israeli Ministry of Foreign Affairs, July 12, 2006.

38. This basic strategy has a long tradition in Israeli military policy. During the 1950s, for example, Israeli reprisals against Jordanian army and police units were partly intended to convince the Jordanian government to crack down on Palestinian groups that were conducting cross-border raids into Israel. See Jonathan Shimshoni, *Israel and Conventional Deterrence: Border Warfare from 1953 to 1970* (Ithaca: Cornell University Press, 1988), chap. 2.

39. Noam Ophir, "Look Not to the Skies: The IAF vs. Surface-to-Surface Rocket Launchers," *Strategic Assessment* (Jaffee Center for Strategic Studies, Tel Aviv University) 9, no. 3 (November 2006).

40. Uzi Rubin, "Hezbollah's Rocket Campaign Against Northern Israel: A Preliminary Report," Jerusalem Issue Brief (Jerusalem Center for Public Affairs) 6, no. 10 (August 31, 2006).

41. Jonathan Finer and Edward Cody, "No Cease-Fire Soon, Israeli Leader Says," *Washington Post*, August 1, 2006; and Yochi J. Dreazen and Marc Champion, "U.S., Israel Start to Diverge as Casualties Mount," *Wall Street Journal*, August 1, 2006.

42. Amos Harel, "Analysis: Hezbollah Is Still Showing No Signs of Breaking," *Ha'aretz*, July 20, 2006; John Kifner, "Israel Is Powerful, Yes. But Not So Invincible," *New York Times*, July 30, 2006; Ze'ev Schiff, "A Strategic Mistake," *Ha'aretz*, July 20, 2006; Ari Shavit, "An Aerial War," *Ha'aretz*, July 20, 2006; "What About the Missiles?" *Ha'aretz* editorial, August 3, 2006; and Martin Van Creveld, "In This War, Too, Victory Is Unlikely," *International Herald Tribune*, August 2, 2006.

43. John Kifner and Greg Myre, "After U.N. Accord, Israel Expands Push in Lebanon," *New York Times*, August 13, 2006.

44. The seminal work on this subject is Robert A. Pape, *Bombing to Win: Air Power and Coercion in War* (Ithaca: Cornell University Press, 1996). Also see John J. Mearsheimer, *The Tragedy of Great Power Politics* (New York: Norton, 2001), 85–110.

45. Amnesty International, "Unlawful Killings During Operation 'Grapes of Wrath,'" July 1996; Warren Christopher, "A Time to Act," *Washington Post*, July 28, 2006; Human Rights Watch, "Operation Grapes of Wrath: The Civilian Victims," September 1997; Ze'ev Schiff, "Strategic Mistake"; and Avi Shlaim, "Israel's Error, Then and Now," *International Herald Tribune*, August 4, 2006.

46. Beirut Center for Research and Information, "Poll Finds Support for Hezbollah's Retaliation: Opinions Diverge on Sectarian Lines—But Not Completely," July 29, 2006; Dahr Jamail, "Hezbollah Rides a New Popularity," *Antiwar.com*, August 8, 2006; Nadim Ladki, "US Policy Alienates All the Lebanese," *Gulf Times* (online), August 1, 2006; Neil MacFarquhar, "Tide of Arab Opinion Turns to Support for Hezbollah," *New York Times*, July 28, 2006; and Shibley Telhami, "Hezbollah's Popularity Exposes al-Qaeda's Failure to Win the Hearts," *San Jose Mercury News* (online), July 30, 2006.

47. Cohler-Esses, "Israel Seeks to Redefine Victory"; Steve Erlanger, "Israel Seeks Hint of Victory," *New York Times*, August 13, 2006; Anshel Pfeffer, "Analysis: The IDF's New Definition of Victory," *Jerusalem Post*, July 26, 2006; and Zeev Sternhell, "The Most Unsuccessful War," *Ha'aretz*, August 2, 2006.

48. Charles Krauthammer, "Israel's Lost Moment," *Washington Post*, August 4, 2006; and Ori Nir, "Conservatives Slam Israeli War Strategy," *Forward*, August 11, 2006. Also see Bret Stephens, "Israel Is Losing This War," *Wall Street Journal*, August 1, 2006; and "Olmert and Bush," *Wall Street Journal* editorial, August 1, 2006. The IDF's performance in Lebanon did not improve between the time these pieces were written and the war ended on August 14, 2006.

49. For claims that Israel won, or at least did not lose, the war, see Nahum Barnea, "Think Again: Israel vs. Hezbollah," *Foreign Policy* 157 (November–December 2006); Cameron S. Brown, "Iran's Investment Just Went Down the Tubes," *Ha'aretz*, September 10, 2006; Shai Feldman, "The Hezbollah-Israel War: A Preliminary Assessment," Middle East Brief no. 10 (Crown Center for Middle East Studies, Brandeis University, September 2006); Michael A. Fletcher, "Hezbollah the Loser in Battle, Bush Says," *Washington Post*, August 15, 2006; Efraim Halevy, "Blind Date," *New Republic*, August 14 & 21, 2006; Shmuel Rosner, "U.S. Diplomats Begin Viewing Lebanon War as Success," *Ha'aretz*, September 15, 2006; and Asher Susser, "Lebanon: A Reassessment," *Jerusalem Post*, September 13, 2006. It was imperative for Israel and the lobby to spin the war as an Israeli victory, even if only barely, so that Americans would continue to view Israel as a reliable ally. Leon Hadar makes that case in "Neocons amid Lebanon's Rubble: A Challenge to Krauthammer's Israel-as-Strategic-Asset Argument," *National Interest* (online), September 14, 2006. In this regard, it is worth noting that Charles Krauthammer, who saw Israel losing the war on August 4 ("Israel's Lost Moment"), wrote a column on September 1 ("Hezbollah's 'Victory,'" *Washington Post*) proclaiming that "Hezbollah may have won the propaganda war, but on the ground it lost. Badly." Nevertheless, most Israeli officers thought otherwise. See Amos Harel, "Chief Education Officer: We Lost Lebanon War," *Ha'aretz*, September 22, 2006; and Hanan Greenberg, "Officers Slam IDF War Conference," *Ynetnews.com*, January 2, 2007. Also, the *New York Times* reported that a poll taken for *Ha'aretz* just before the war ended found that only 20 percent of Israelis thought Israel was winning, 30 percent thought Israel was losing, and 43 percent thought that neither side was winning. See Hoge and Erlanger, "U.N. Council Backs Measure." Most Israelis concurred with this assessment after the war, as a poll taken in early 2007 found that 51 percent of the respondents believed that neither side had won the war, while 26 percent said that Hezbollah had won and 23 percent said that Israel had won. Ben Meir and Shaked, "The People Speak," 9, 20–21. Furthermore, a poll taken shortly after the war ended found that 63 percent of the respondents believed that Prime Minister Olmert should resign; 74 percent thought that Defense Minister Amir Peretz should resign; and 54 percent believed that General Dan Halutz, the IDF chief of staff, should resign. "Poll: Majority Wants Olmert Out," *Ynetnews.com*, August 25, 2006.

50. For an excellent assessment of the conflict, which argues that Hezbollah ultimately was the winner, see the three-part series in *Asia Times Online* by Alastair Crooke and Mark Perry: "Winning the Intelligence War," October 12, 2006; "Winning the Ground War," October 13, 2006; and "The Political War," October 14, 2006. Also see Anthony H. Cordesman, "Preliminary 'Lessons' of the Israeli-Hezbollah War," Center for Strategic and International Studies, Washington, DC, August 17, 2006; Ron Tira, "Breaking the Amoeba's Bones," *Strategic Assessment* (Jaffee Center for Strategic Studies, Tel Aviv University) 9, no. 3 (November 2006); and Amir Kulick, "Hizbollah vs. the IDF: The Operational Dimension," in ibid.

51. "Main Findings of the Winograd Partial Report." Also see Gregory Levey, "Israel's Surge of Despair," *Salon.com*, February 15, 2007.

52. "Hizbullah Secretary-General Hassan Nasrallah Calls upon Arab Leaders to Promote Cease-Fire in Meetings with the Americans," Middle East Media Research Institute, TV Monitor Project, Clip no. 1219, August 3, 2006, www.memritv.org/Transcript.asp?P1=1219 on May 17, 2007.

53. See the Information International Poll, August 22–27, 2006, in Gary C. Gambill, ed., "Lebanese Public Opinion," *Mideast Monitor* 1, no. 3 (September–October 2006).

54. "Poll: 64% of Lebanese Say Opinion of U.S. Worsened After War," *Ha'aretz*, November 14, 2006. Also see Jim Lobe, "Backing for Israel Stymies Larger U.S. Aims in the Region," *Antiwar.com*, July 22, 2006; Jim Lobe, "Losing Arab Allies' Hearts and Minds," Inter Press Service, December 14, 2006; Shmuel Rosner, "They Know You Know They're Winning," *Slate.com*, December 4, 2006; and Shibley Telhami, "Annual Arab Public Opinion Survey" (with Zogby International), results from Lebanon poll taken November 11–16, 2006.

55. Zogby International, "Five Nation Survey of the Middle East," poll conducted for Arab

American Institute, December 2006. Also see Zogby International, "AAI Poll: Continuing Conflict in Iraq and Palestine Deepens U.S.-Arab Rift with Growing Costs to Both Sides," December 14, 2006.

56. Thanassis Cambanis, "Travel Industry Suffers Another Blow in Lebanon," *Boston Globe*, September 4, 2006.

57. Information International Poll, August 22–27, 2006; and Telhami, "Annual Arab Public Opinion Survey." It is also worth noting that most Lebanese apparently do not blame Hezbollah for starting the war, as one poll found that 84 percent of the respondents "agree that the Israel-Lebanon war was a consequence of a joint Israel-US attempt to impose a Middle East order." See the Center for Strategic Studies poll published in Gambill, "Lebanese Public Opinion."

58. "Another Killing in Lebanon," *New York Times* editorial, November 23, 2006; "Beirut Rally Attracts Huge Crowd," *BBC News* (online), December 10, 2006; Akiva Eldar, "Israel Fears Siniora Government May Fall," *Ha'aretz*, December 3, 2006; "Fleeting Gains from Lebanon War?" *Jewish Week*, December 8, 2006; Michael Slackman, "Anti-Syrian Minister Is Assassinated in Lebanon," *New York Times*, November 21, 2006; "Lebanon on the Brink," *Chicago Tribune* editorial, November 23, 2006; Tim McGirk, "Losing Lebanon," *Time*, December 3, 2006; Jim Quilty, "Winter of Lebanon's Discontent," *Middle East Report Online*, January 26, 2007; and Anthony Shadid, "As Crises Build, Lebanese Fearful of a Failed State," *Washington Post*, June 5, 2007.

59. Michael Slackman, "Iran's Strong Ties with Syria Complicate U.S. Overtures," *New York Times*, December 28, 2006.

60. Rafael D. Frankel, "Israel Troubled That War in Lebanon Drove Its Enemies Closer," *Christian Science Monitor*, September 22, 2006.

61. Blumenthal, "Neocons' Next War"; Max Boot, "Israel Should Hit Syria First," *Los Angeles Times*, August 23, 2006; Daniel J. Goldhagen, "Israel's Way Out," *Los Angeles Times*, August 8, 2006; William Kristol, "It's Our War," *Weekly Standard*, July 24, 2006; Michael Ledeen, "The Thirties All Over Again?" *National Review Online*, July 31, 2006; Ori Nir, "U.S. Ripped for Inaction on Israeli, Syrian Front," *Forward*, August 4, 2006; Michael B. Oren, "Necessary Steps for Israel," *Washington Post*, July 14, 2006; Michael B. Oren, "Why Israel Should Bomb Syria: Attack Add," *New Republic Online*, July 17, 2006; Tom Regan, "US Neocons Hoped Israel Would Attack Syria," *Christian Science Monitor*, August 9, 2006; and George F. Will, "Transformation's Toll," *Washington Post*, July 18, 2006.

62. Yitzhak Benhorin, "Neocons: We Expected Israel to Attack Syria," *Ynetnews.com*, December 16, 2006. Also see Jim Lobe, "Neo-Cons Wanted Israel to Attack Syria," Inter Press Service, December 18, 2006.

63. Robin Hughes, "Iran Replenishes Hizbullah's Arms Inventory," *Jane's Defence Weekly*, January 3, 2007; Yaakov Katz, "Syria Resupplying Hizbullah with Long-Range Missiles," *Jerusalem Post*, December 4, 2006; David R. Sands, "Iran, Syria Rebuild Hezbollah," *Washington Times*, October 25, 2006; Elaine Shannon and Tim McGirk, "Iran and Syria Helping Hizballah Rearm," *Time*, November 24, 2006; and Ronny Sofer, "Ashkenazi: Hizbullah Trying to Move South of Litani," *Ynetnews.com*, April 29, 2007.

64. Damien Cave, "Protestors in Baghdad Denounce U.S. and Israel," *New York Times*, August 4, 2006; Andy Mosher, "In Baghdad, Shiites Rally for Hezbollah," *Washington Post*, August 5, 2006; and "Tens of Thousands Rally in Baghdad to Show Support for Hezbollah," *USA Today*, August 4, 2006.

65. Michael R. Gordon and Dexter Filkins, "Hezbollah Said to Help Shiite Army in Iraq," *New York Times*, November 28, 2006.

66. MacFarquhar, "Tide of Arab Opinion." Also see Scott MacLeod, "Egypt's Mubarak: 'No Light at the End of the Tunnel,'" *Time*, July 27, 2006; "Saudi Arabia Harshly Criticizes Hezbollah for Escalating Mideast Crisis," Associated Press, July 14, 2006; and Andy Mosher, "From Arab Leaders, Sympathy for Civilians but Not Hezbollah," *Washington Post*, July 18, 2006.

67. Philip Gordon and Jeremy Shapiro, "US Has Emerged as a Loser in the Middle East," *Financial Times*, August 20, 2006; Richard Holbrooke, "The Guns of August," *Washington Post*, August 10, 2006; Howard LaFranchi, "Why Europe, US Differ on Mideast," *Christian Science Monitor*, August 4, 2006; Neil MacFarquhar, "Anti-U.S. Feeling Leaves Arab Reformers Isolated," *New York Times*, August 9, 2006; Tyler Marshall, "On Cease-Fire, U.S. Diplomacy Again Takes a Go-It-Alone Path," *Los Angeles Times*, August 1, 2006; Tyler Marshall and Alissa J. Rubin, "U.S. Clout a Missing Ingredient in Mideast," *Los Angeles Times*, August 8, 2006; Mark Perry and Alastair Crooke, "The Loser in Lebanon: The Atlantic Alliance," *Asia Times Online*, August 8, 2006; "The US and Israel Stand Alone," interview with Jimmy Carter, *Spiegel Online*, August 15, 2006; and Robin Wright and Colum Lynch, "US at Odds with Allies on Mideast Conflict," *Washington Post*, July 20, 2006.

68. Peter Kiernan, "Middle East Opinion: Iran Fears Aren't Hitting the Arab Street," *WorldPoliticsWatch.com*, March 1, 2007. Also see Jim Lobe, "Arabs Less Worried About Iran," Inter Press Service, February 8, 2007.

69. Quoted in Stolberg, "Bush's Embrace." Also see John B. Judis, "Bush's Failed Israel Strategy: Apocalypse Now," *New Republic Online*, August 2, 2006.

70. Quoted in Nir, "Conservatives Slam Israeli War Strategy." Also see Eliot Cohen, "Nasrallah's War: Observations upon Returning from Israel," *Berlin Journal* 13 (Fall 2006): 23–25.

71. Three IDF soldiers died in the initial Hezbollah raid, and five more perished in the IDF's initial attempt to rescue the captured personnel. Helena Cobban, "The 33-Day War," *Boston Review*, November/December 2006; Amos Harel, "Hezbollah Kills 8 Soldiers, Kidnaps Two in Offensive on Northern Border," *Ha'aretz*, July 13, 2006; "Hezbollah Warns Israel over Raids," *BBC News* (online), July 12, 2006; Greg Myre and Steven Erlanger, "Clashes Spread to Lebanon as Hezbollah Raids Israel," *New York Times*, July 13, 2006; and Anthony Shadid and Scott Wilson, "Hezbollah Raid Opens 2nd Front for Israel," *Washington Post*, July 13, 2006.

72. Quoted in Shadid and Wilson, "Hezbollah Raid." Nasrallah made it clear again after the war that he was not interested in a war with Israel when he said that he would not have ordered the raid had he known that it would lead to war. Zvi Bar'el, "Analysis: Nasrallah Is Still in Charge," *Ha'aretz*, August 28, 2006; and Rory McCarthy, "Hizbullah Leader: We Regret the Two Kidnappings That Led to War with Israel," *Guardian*, August 28, 2006.

73. Shlomo Brom, "The Confrontation with Hezbollah," Tel-Aviv Note no. 177, Jaffee Center for Strategic Studies, July 13, 2006; Margot Dudkevitch, "UN-Brokered Cease-Fire Holds after Hizbullah Shells Mount Dov," *Jerusalem Post*, February 3, 2006; "Israeli Army Targets Hezbollah," *Los Angeles Times*, February 4, 2006; Herb Keinon, "Security Council Condemns Hizbullah," *Jerusalem Post*, November 24, 2005; Greg Myre, "Israel Strikes Northern Gaza and Lebanon with Planes," *New York Times*, December 28, 2005; Anders Strindberg, "Hizbullah's Attacks Stem from Israeli Incursions into Lebanon," *Christian Science Monitor*, August 1, 2006; Scott Wilson, "Hezbollah Shelling Kills 1; Ends Calm on Israeli Border," *Washington Post*, June 30, 2005; Scott Wilson, "Hezbollah, Israeli Forces Clash on Lebanese Border," *Washington Post*, November 22, 2005; and Scott Wilson, "Violence Flares Across Israel-Lebanon Border," *Washington Post*, May 29, 2006.

74. Margot Dudkevitch, "Nasrallah Vows More Kidnapping Attempts," *Jerusalem Post*, November 27, 2005.

75. "Day-by-Day: Lebanon Crisis—Week One," *BBC News* (online), July 19, 2006.

76. Quoted in Chris McGreal, "Capture of Soldiers Was 'Act of War' Says Israel," *Guardian*, July 13, 2006. Former Prime Minister Ehud Barak told CNN just before the war ended, "It's time to do all we can to destroy as much as we can of the infrastructure in the next 12 to 13 hours, and then we'll see what is next." Quoted in Cobban, "The 33-Day War."

77. Quoted in Hassan M. Fattah and Steven Erlanger, "Israel Blockades Lebanon; Wide Strikes by Hezbollah," *New York Times*, July 14, 2006.

78. Amnesty International, "Israel/Lebanon: Deliberate Destruction."

79. William M. Arkin, "Israel's Failed Strategy of Spite," August 15, 2006, http://blog.washingtonpost.com/earlywarning/2006/08/did_israel_win.html.

80. David S. Cloud, "Inquiry Opened into Israeli Use of U.S. Bombs," *New York Times*, August 25, 2006; and Richard Moyes and Thomas Nash, *Cluster Munitions in Lebanon* (London: Landmine Action, November 2005), 7–12.

81. Richard Ben Cramer, "Israel Criticized for Use of Indiscriminate Bombs," *Washington Post*, June 30, 1982; Kevin Danaher, "Israel's Use of Cluster Bombs in Lebanon," *Journal of Palestine Studies* 11–12, nos. 4, 1 (Summer–Autumn 1982); Judith Miller, "U.S. Bars Cluster Shells for Israel Indefinitely," *New York Times*, July 28, 1982; and "U.S. Removes Ban on Bombs to Israel," *Washington Post*, December 7, 1988.

82. Cloud, "Inquiry Opened into Israeli Use of U.S. Bombs"; Human Rights Watch, "Israeli Cluster Munitions Hit Civilians in Lebanon," press release, July 24, 2006; Greg Myre, "Israel Orders Investigation of Bomb Use in Lebanon," *New York Times*, November 21, 2006; Meron Rappaport, "IDF Commander: We Fired More Than a Million Cluster Bombs in Lebanon," *Ha'aretz*, September 12, 2006; "Shooting Without a Target," *Ha'aretz* editorial, September 14, 2006; and Michael Slackman, "Israeli Bomblets Plague Lebanon," *New York Times*, October 6, 2006.

83. Quoted in Meron Rappaport, "What Lies Beneath," *Ha'aretz*, September 8, 2006.

84. Quoted in "U.N. Official Denounces Israel Cluster Bomb Use," *MSNBC.com*, August 30, 2006.

85. Quoted in Rappaport, "IDF Commander."

86. "U.N. Official Denounces Israel Cluster Bomb Use."

87. Associated Press, "UN Envoy: Israel Broke Int'l Law in War," *Jerusalem Post*, April 13, 2007. Also see Thomas Nash, *Foreseeable Harm: The Use and Impact of Cluster Munitions in Lebanon, 2006* (London: Landmine Action, October 2006).

88. The key work on the subject is Michael Walzer, *Just and Unjust Wars: A Moral Argument with Historical Illustrations*, 4th ed. (New York: Basic Books, 2006).

89. Amnesty International, "Israel/Lebanon: Out of All Proportion," 26, 28, 45.

90. Human Rights Watch, "Fatal Strikes: Israel's Indiscriminate Attacks Against Civilians in Lebanon," hrw.org, vol. 18, no. 3 (August 2006): 3.

91. Ibid. Also see Peter Bouckaert, "For Israel, Innocent Civilians Are Fair Game," *International Herald Tribune*, August 3, 2006; Peter Bouckaert, "White Flags, Not a Legitimate Target," *Guardian*, July 31, 2006; and Kenneth Roth, "Fog of War Is No Cover for Causing Civilian Deaths," *Forward*, August 4, 2006.

92. The Ramon quotations are in Mark Levine, "Qana Rules," *CommonDreams.org*, July 31, 2006; and Amnesty International, "Israel/Lebanon: Out of All Proportion," 21. Also see Gideon Levy, "Days of Darkness," *Ha'aretz*, July 30, 2006.

93. Amnesty International, "Israel/Lebanon: Out of All Proportion," 21–22, 28–30.

94. Ibid., 64.

95. Human Rights Watch, "Fatal Strikes," 5.

96. Quoted in Shimon Golding, "New Yorkers Rally for Israel," *Jewish Press* (online), July 19, 2006.

97. Steven Erlanger, "With Israeli Use of Force, Debate over Proportion," *New York Times*, July 19, 2006; and Lt. Col. Reuven Erlich, "Hezbollah's Use of Lebanese Civilians as Human Shields," Intelligence and Terrorism Information Center, Center for Special Studies, Israel, November 2006. This study was supported by the IDF and the Israeli Ministry of Foreign Affairs. For a brief critique, see Kenneth Roth, "Violation of Rules of War in Israel's Lebanon Attacks," letter to the editor, *Wall Street Journal*, December 19, 2006.

98. Amnesty International, "Israel/Lebanon: Out of All Proportion," 63–64.

99. Mitch Prothero, "The 'Hiding Among Civilians' Myth," *Salon.com*, July 28, 2006.

100. Human Rights Watch, "Fatal Strikes," 3.

101. Roth, "Violation of Rules of War."

102. Sarah Leah Whitson, "Armchair Sleuths," letter to the editor, *Jerusalem Post*, September 7, 2006.

103. Human Rights Watch, "Fatal Strikes," 3. Also see Amnesty International, "Israel/Lebanon: Out of All Proportion," 59–64, which reaches the same conclusion.

104. The "Fatal Strikes" report (3, 5) notes that HRW researchers found no evidence of military activity around any of the twenty-four areas targeted by the IDF. However, after doing further research, it turned up evidence of military activity at one of the areas. Personal correspondence from HRW to authors, May 30, 2007.

105. Quoted in Amnesty International, "Israel/Lebanon: Out of All Proportion," 26.

106. Nathan Guttman, "American Jews Mobilize for Israel," *Jerusalem Post*, July 16, 2006. Also see Jacob Berkman, "Emergency Drive Tops $320 Million; Shifts Toward Rebuilding Israel's North," *JTA.org*, October 10, 2006; Laurie Goodstein, "As Mideast Churns, U.S. Jews and Arabs Alike Swing into Action," *New York Times*, July 28, 2006; Avi Krawitz, "Israel Bonds Raises $1.2 Billion in 2006," *Jerusalem Post*, December 10, 2006; Ori Nir, "Bush Urged to Give Israel More Time for Attacks," *Forward*, July 21, 2006; and Shmuel Rosner, "Despite Criticism, War Raises Genuine Concern for Israel to the Fore," *Ha'aretz*, August 20, 2006.

107. Ari Berman, "AIPAC's Hold," *Nation*, July 29, 2006; and Silverman, "Politicking over Israel."

108. Letter from Congressman Chris Van Hollen to Secretary of State Condoleezza Rice, July 30, 2006, www.buzzflash.com/articles/releases/6.

109. Shmuel Rosner reported on August 9 that "Congressman Chris Van Hollen (D-MD) enraged some pro-Israel lobby groups when he sent a letter to Secretary of State Condoleezza Rice, urging her 'to call for an immediate ceasefire' in Lebanon. He'll have a meeting with AIPAC representatives as early as today in which he will hear that this was an unacceptable move." See "Rosner's Mid-Term Diary: On the Mid-Terms, the Mideast, the Jewish Voters and Israel," *Ha'aretz*, August 10, 2006.

110. Quoted in Eric Fingerhut, "Van Hollen Issues Clarification; Some Critics Still Question Commitment to Israel," *Washington Jewish Week* (online), August 16, 2006. Also see Eric Fingerhut, "Van Hollen 'Advice' Draws Critics," *Washington Jewish Week* (online), August 10, 2006; and Eric Fingerhut, "At Odds," *Washington Jewish Week* (online), August 30, 2006.

111. Both quotations are from Fingerhut, "Van Hollen Issues Clarification."

112. Quoted in Elise Labott, "U.S. Worried Israeli Operations Could Weaken Lebanese Government," *CNN.com*, July 14, 2006. Also see Peter Baker, "U.S. Urges Restraint by Israel," *Washington Post*, July 14, 2006; Fattah and Erlanger, "Israel Blockades Lebanon"; and Wright, "Strikes Are Called Part of Broad Strategy."

113. Quoted in "Bush Criticized over Concern for Lebanese Regime," *Forward*, July 14, 2006.

114. Transcript of "Coverage of War in the Middle East," on CNN's *Reliable Sources*, August 6, 2006.

115. For the correspondence between Downie and Koch, see Kathryn J. Lopez, "Ed Koch and Len Downie," in "The Corner," *National Review Online*, August 17, 2006; and Alex Safian, "Updated: *Post*'s Thomas Ricks Charges Israel Intentionally Leaving Hezbollah Rockets Intact," www.camera.org/index.asp?x_context=2&x_outlet=38&x_article=1174.

116. Quoted in Leora Folk, "Washington Post Editor Rebukes His Reporter for Television Comments on Israel," *New York Sun*, August 18, 2006.

117. Alan Dershowitz, "What Is 'Human Rights Watch' Watching?" *Jerusalem Post*, August 25, 2006. Also see Alan Dershowitz, "Amnesty International Redefines 'War Crimes,'" *Jerusalem Post*, August 31, 2006. The attacks on Amnesty International and Human Rights Watch have continued in the war's aftermath. See Gerald Steinberg, "Scrutinize Amnesty International," *New York Sun*, May 23, 2007; and Marc Stern, "The Media Was Misled by Amnesty's Legal Advocacy," *Forward*, March 30, 2007.

118. Ken Silverstein, "AIPAC Points to Legion of Doom in Bekaa Valley," *Harper's* (online), August 10, 2006; "Israel Taking Significant Steps to Prevent Casualties as Hizballah Hides Behind Civilians," AIPAC memo, August 1, 2006; and "Israel's Defensive Actions in Lebanon and Gaza," AIPAC FAQ, July 24, 2006.

119. Gerald M. Steinberg, "Ken Roth's Blood Libel," *Jerusalem Post*, August 27, 2006; "Roth's Supersessionism," *New York Sun* editorial, July 31, 2006; and Abraham Foxman, "No Accident," *New York Sun*, August 2, 2006. Also see Avi Bell, "Getting It Straight," *New York Sun*, July 25, 2006; Joshua Muravchik, "Human Rights Watch vs. Human Rights," *Weekly Stan-*

dard, September 11, 2006; Rabbi Aryeh Spero, "Why Liberals Refuse to Admit the Reality of Islamic Fascism," *Human Events* (online), August 16, 2006; "Roth's False God," *New York Sun* editorial, August 8, 2006; and "Sharansky Speaks," *New York Sun* editorial, September 12, 2006.

120. Rosa Brooks, "Criticize Israel? You're an Anti-Semite!" *Los Angeles Times*, September 1, 2006. For excellent discussions of the smearing of Human Rights Watch, see Aryeh Neier, "The Attack on Human Rights Watch," *New York Review of Books*, November 2, 2006, 41–44; and Philip Weiss, "Israel Lobby Watch," *Nation*, September 18, 2006. Also see Kathleen Peratis, "Diversionary Strike on a Rights Group," *Washington Post*, August 30, 2006; and Ian Seiderman, "Right of Reply: Biased Against Israel?" *Jerusalem Post*, September 11, 2006.

121. Quoted in Nathan Guttman and Yaakov Katz, "Israel Condemned for Cluster Bomb Use," *Jerusalem Post*, September 7, 2006.

122. Nathan Guttman, "US Senate Rejects Bid to Curb Use of Cluster Bombs," *Jerusalem Post*, September 8, 2006. This account of AIPAC's role in defeating the legislation is based on information from Human Rights Watch. Personal correspondence from HRW to authors, September 13, 2006; September 14, 2006; May 30, 2007.

123. Quoted in John Walsh, "AIPAC Congratulates Itself on the Slaughter in Lebanon," *CounterPunch.org*, August 16, 2006.

124. Quoted in "To Israel with Love."

125. William Kristol, "It's Our War: Bush Should Go to Jerusalem—and the U.S. Should Confront Iran," *Weekly Standard*, July 24, 2006. Also see Jim Lobe, "Energized Neocons Say Israel's Fight Is Washington's," *Antiwar.com*, July 18, 2006; Krauthammer, "Israel's Lost Moment"; and Charles Krauthammer, "Lebanon: The Only Exit Strategy," *Washington Post*, July 19, 2006.

126. Quoted in Tovah Lazaroff, "'Evangelicals the World Over Are Praying Fervently for Israel,'" *Jerusalem Post*, August 9, 2006. Also see George Conger, "US Support for Israel Soars After Hizbullah War," *Jerusalem Post*, August 27, 2006.

127. "To Israel with Love."

128. Quoted in Daphna Berman, "U.S. Jewish, Christian Groups Back Lebanon Operation," *Ha'aretz*, July 14, 2006. Also see Zev Chafets, "I Want Falwell in My Foxhole," *Los Angeles Times*, July 23, 2006.

129. Quoted in Flaherty, "House Overwhelmingly Backs Israel." This line of argument is also reflected in "To Israel with Love."

130. Unless otherwise noted, all of the survey data in this section are from "Israel, the Palestinians," *PollingReport.com*.

131. "Zogby Poll: U.S. Should Be Neutral in Lebanon War," Zogby International press release, August 17, 2006.

132. Uri Avnery, "America's Rottweiler," *Gush-Shalom.org*, August 26, 2006. Also see Yossi Ben-Ari, "America's Honey Trap," *Ynetnews.com*, July 24, 2006; Lawrence F. Kaplan, "America's Proxy War: Other Means," *New Republic*, July 31, 2006; and Shmuel Rosner, "America's Deadly Messenger," *Ha'aretz*, July 19, 2006.

133. Ali Waked, "Nasrallah: U.S. Pressured Israel into War," *Ynetnews.com*, May 7, 2007.

134. Quoted in Hersh, "Watching Lebanon." Also see Cobban, "The 33-Day War."

135. Ori Nir, "Jerusalem Urges Bush: Next Target Hezbollah," *Forward*, April 11, 2003. Also see Daniel Sobelman and Nathan Guttman, "PM Urges U.S. to Keep Heat on Syria, Calls Assad 'Dangerous,'" *Ha'aretz*, April 15, 2003.

136. Quoted in Hersh, "Watching Lebanon."

137. Quoted in Avi Shlaim, *The Iron Wall: Israel and the Arab World* (New York: Norton, 2001), 316.

CONCLUSION: WHAT IS TO BE DONE?

1. On this point, see Robert J. Art, *A Grand Strategy for America* (Ithaca: Cornell University Press, 2004), 45–46.

2. This statement may seem surprising, given the tendency for Americans simply to assume that Israel's security is vital to our own. In 2000, for example, a self-appointed commission of prominent foreign policy experts reported that preserving Israel as a free state was a "vital" U.S. interest, but the commission never explained why this was so or how Israel's fate would affect U.S. security or well-being. More sensibly, Robert Art asserts that "Israel has little strategic value to the United States and is in many ways a strategic liability. Nonetheless, America's ties with Israel run deep, the U.S. affinity with another democracy is strong, and the moral commitment to its preservation is clear." See Commission on America's National Interests, *America's National Interests* (Cambridge, MA: Belfer Center for Science and International Affairs, 2000); and Art, *Grand Strategy for America*, 137.

3. The elements of offshore balancing are spelled out in Christopher Layne, "From Preponderance to Offshore Balancing: America's Future Grand Strategy," *International Security* 22, no. 1 (Summer 1997); John J. Mearsheimer, *The Tragedy of Great Power Politics* (New York: Norton, 2001), chap. 7; and Stephen M. Walt, *Taming American Power: The Global Response to U.S. Primacy* (New York: Norton, 2005), 222–23, 235–36.

4. On this point, see Robert A. Pape, *Dying to Win: The Strategic Logic of Suicide Terrorism* (New York: Random House, 2005).

5. James A. Baker III and Lee H. Hamilton, co-chairs, *The Iraq Study Group Report* (Washington, DC: U.S. Institute of Peace, 2006), 39.

6. Hussein Agha and Robert Malley, "The Road from Mecca," *New York Review of Books*, May 10, 2007, 43. Agha and Malley also write, "Nor is there much ideological enthusiasm remaining for a two-state solution. Israelis accept it and most believe it is inevitable, but gone is the passion or zeal" (44).

7. See, for example, Ali Abunimah, *One Country: A Bold Proposal to End the Israeli-Palestinian Impasse* (New York: Metropolitan Books, 2006); Josef Asevar, "Mideast Solution: A Confederation," *Jewish Journal* (online), November 3, 2003; Meron Benvenisti, "What Kind of Binational State?" *Ha'aretz*, November 20, 2003; Richard Boudreaux, "Arabs Say Israel Is Not Just for Jews," *Los Angeles Times*, February 22, 2007; Tony Judt, "Israel: The Alternative," *New York Review of Books*, October 23, 2003; Isabel Kershner, "Noted Arab Citizens Call on Israel to Shed Jewish Identity," *New York Times*, February 8, 2007; and Yaakov Lappin, "Academic: Israeli-Arabs Want End of Jewish State," *Ynetnews.com*, January 22, 2007.

8. A May 2007 World Bank report sharply criticized Israel's system of internal controls and checkpoints in the Occupied Territories, arguing that these impediments "have fragmented the territory into ever smaller and more disconnected cantons" and that "sustainable economic recovery will remain elusive if large areas of the West Bank remain inaccessible for economic purposes and restricted movement remains the norm for the vast majority of Palestinians and expatriate Palestinian investors." See World Bank Technical Team, "Movement and Access Restrictions in the West Bank: Uncertainty and Inefficiency in the Palestinian Economy," May 9, 2007, 1–2, http://siteresources.worldbank.org/INTWESTBANKGAZA/Resources/WestBankrestrictions9Mayfinal.pdf.

9. In 2007, a BBC World Service poll of twenty-eight thousand people in twenty-seven countries found that Israel had the worst image of the dozen countries listed, with 56 percent of respondents reporting it was a "negative" influence in the world and only 17 percent saying its influence was "positive." Iran's image was second worst: 54 percent negative and 18 percent positive. See Bradley Burston, "The BBC Poll: Israel as Satan's Bastard Child," *Ha'aretz*, March 6, 2007; and "Israel, Iran Top 'Negative List,'" *BBC News* (online), March 6, 2007. On the occupation's corrupting effects, see Dror Wahrman, "Is Israel Falling Apart?" *History News Network*, March 5, 2007, www.hnn.us/articles/35958.html.

10. Shlomo Ben-Ami, *Scars of War, Wounds of Peace: The Israeli-Arab Tragedy* (New York: Oxford University Press, 2006), 167.

11. Yehuda Ben Meir and Dafna Shaked, "The People Speak: Israeli Public Opinion on National Security, 2005–2007," Memorandum no. 90 (Tel Aviv: Institute for National Security Studies, May 2007), 65–67.

12. See the references in notes 28 and 29 in the Introduction.

13. Rabbi Gold also quoted former Prime Minister Yitzhak Shamir's warning to American Jews that "we cannot afford the luxury of public disagreement, or public criticism that plays right into the hands of our enemies," and responded by saying, "I fail to understand how a prime minister of a democratic nation with an active political opposition would attempt to silence Jewish criticism abroad . . . Wherein the danger of American Jewish criticism? Is it the criticism that is harmful or the policies and actions that are criticized?" Rabbi Ben-Zion Gold, "The Diaspora and the Intifada: The Responsibility of American Jews," *Boston Review*, October/November 2002.

14. "Diaspora Blues," *Economist* editorial, January 13, 2007, 14–15. Also see "Second Thoughts About the Promised Land," ibid., 53–56.

15. On this issue, see the recent column by Rabbi Eric Yoffie, president of the Union for Reform Judaism, "When We Let John Hagee Speak for Us," *Forward*, May 18, 2007.

16. Nathan Guttmann, "Dovish Groups Mull Mega-Merger in Bid to Build Peace Powerhouse," *Forward*, May 30, 2007; Amiram Barkat, "New Pro-Israel Lobby as Alternative to AIPAC," *Ha'aretz*, November 12, 2006; Bernd Debusmann, "Soros Adds Voice to Debate over Israel Lobby," *Washington Post*, April 15, 2007; Guy Dinmore, "Jewish Lobby for Peace with Palestinians Gathers Pace in US," *Financial Times*, October 24, 2006; Gary Kamiya, "Can American Jews Unplug the Israel Lobby?" *Salon.com*, March 20, 2007; Gregory Levey, "The Other Israel Lobby," *Salon.com*, December 19, 2006; and Gidon D. Remba, "Wanted: A Moderate Pro-Israel Lobby," *Ha'aretz*, November 17, 2006.

17. As of April 2007, the IJV declaration had garnered more than four hundred signatures. For the declaration and list of signatories, see the Independent Jewish Voices website, www.ijv.org.uk. Also see Martin Hodgson, "British Jews Break Away from 'Pro-Israeli' Board of Deputies," *Independent*, February 5, 2007; and Ned Temko, "Furor over Jewish Critics' Challenge to State of Israel," *Observer*, February 4, 2007.

18. Ben Weinthal, "German Jews Feud over Criticizing Israel," *Forward*, March 9, 2007. Also see Jason Frenkel, "Dissidents Set for Australia-Wide Media Campaign," *Australian Jewish News* (online), March 1, 2007; Antony Loewenstein, *My Israel Question* (Carlton, Australia: Melbourne University Press, 2007); and "Why the 'Special Relationship' Between Germany and Israel Has to Be Reconsidered," Manifesto of 25 German Peace Researchers, November 15, 2006, www.tlaxcala.es/pp.asp?lg=en&reference=1569.

ACKNOWLEDGMENTS

Authors rarely work alone, and we are certainly no exception. We are deeply grateful for the help that others gave us, and it is a pleasure to acknowledge their assistance.

This book began life as an article in the *London Review of Books*, and as recounted in the preface, that article might never have been published were it not for the courage and vision of the *LRB*'s editor, Mary-Kay Wilmers. This book would not exist without her. After our original article was published, Moises Naim, the editor of *Foreign Policy*, organized a symposium on the "Israel lobby" in the July/August 2006 issue of that journal. That debate helped turn the discussion away from ad hominem attacks directed at our article and us and toward a more serious consideration of these issues, and we appreciate the fair-minded way in which he managed the exchange.

We have discussed our ideas about the lobby in presentations at Columbia University, Congregation Kam Isaiah Israel, Cornell University, the Council on Foreign Relations, Emerson College, Georgetown University, the Empire Salon, the National Press Club, the Nieman Fellows program at Harvard University, and the University of Montana, Missoula. These sessions helped us refine our arguments further, and we are grateful to the organizers of these events—Richard Betts, Rabbi Arnold Wolf, Jae-Jung Suh, Nigel Gibson, Rania Kiblawi, John Henry, Mohamed Nimer, Callie Crossley, and Richard Drake—and to the various participants who attended and offered us criticism and advice.

The following individuals gave us valuable comments on some or all of the manuscript: Kirk J. Beattie, Harvey Cox, Michael Desch, John C. Green, Ian Lustick, Steven E. Miller, Trita Parsi, Jeremy Pressman, William

Quandt, Eugene Rogan, Jerome Slater, Stephen Van Evera, Martin Walt IV, and Sarah Leah Whitson. We offer a special note of thanks to Peter Novick, who provided insightful and very detailed suggestions in near-record time, and sanded many rough edges in our prose. The views expressed in this book are our own, of course, and we are responsible for any errors that remain.

Our efforts were aided by research assistance from Vaidyanatha Gundlupet in Chicago and Paul MacDonald in Cambridge, and our other assistants—David Wright at Harvard and Souvik De at the University of Chicago—were, as usual, indispensable. David Enders and especially Max Fraser fact-checked the manuscript with care and dispatch, and we thank them for their efforts and their ability to meet a tight deadline.

Our agent, Bill Clegg, was an energetic and wise supporter from the beginning; his enthusiasm and his able guidance are greatly appreciated. And we are doubly glad that he got us to Farrar, Straus and Giroux. Working with FSG has been a delightful experience, and we are grateful to its publisher, Jonathan Galassi, and the rest of the staff for their good spirits and unfailing professionalism. Our editor, Eric Chinski, deserves a special word of appreciation: his perceptiveness, sensitivity to nuance, and consistently high standards drove us to produce a much better book. Cynthia Merman did a superb job of copyediting, and Gena Hamshaw handled logistics smoothly and cheerfully.

Lastly, writing a lengthy book inevitably imposes a toll on an author's family and friends. Neither of us could have written this book alone, or without the love and support from our wives, children, and a number of wonderful friends and colleagues. We apologize for those moments of detachment, distraction, and irritability that we undoubtedly exhibited over the past year, and we thank you all for your patience. We owe you.

INDEX